DENNIS CHRISTOPHER Jo

ex libris:
dennis christopher jovenetti

Twentieth

Century

Russia

★

SECOND EDITION

TWENTIETH

CENTURY RUSSIA

DONALD W. TREADGOLD

University of Washington

★
★
★
★
★
★
★
★
★
★

RAND MCNALLY & COMPANY · *Chicago*

RAND McNALLY HISTORY SERIES
Fred Harvey Harrington, *Advisory Editor*

PRINTED IN THE U.S.A. BY RAND McNALLY & COMPANY
LIBRARY OF CONGRESS CATALOG CARD NUMBER 64:14118
Sixth Printing, 1970

For

WARREN

In the hope
that his generation
will be better equipped
than mine
to understand
Russia and Communism

Author's Note

This book is an attempt to summarize what is known about the main lines of development of Russia and the Soviet Union since 1900, and to establish a sound framework for further investigation and study. In the West and the free countries of Asia and Africa, where the search for the truth is regarded as valuable in itself, continual efforts are needed to examine and re-examine the available evidence and, perhaps equally important, to consider what basic questions must be asked—whether or not they are as yet soluble—about the USSR.

The book is organized around the chief threads of political change, but considerable space is devoted also to the transformation that occurred in the economy, literature and the other arts, and religion, and mention is made of the major developments in the non-Russian borderlands. Attention is given to the growth of Russian Marxism and Marxist organization, to the role of Marxism-Leninism as the official ideology of the Soviet state, and to the Kremlin's use of foreign Communist parties in its efforts at expansion; in cases where such efforts had significant effects, I have provided a minimum of general information about the domestic political scene in the countries in question. I have briefly sketched the main lines of policy and practice of Communist parties which have come to power outside the USSR, with or without Soviet military support, particularly with the purpose of comparing them with Soviet policy and practice.

I have endeavored to serve the needs of the student and general reader, who are concerned with fundamental issues but lack an extensive factual knowledge of Russian affairs, and also of the scholar, who must necessarily be constantly engaged in a re-examination and re-evaluation of his own general views and specific judgments and so may benefit from a systematic treatment of the subject whether or not he agrees with it fully. In writing the book I have used the results of recent research and thought, especially those produced by the last generation of Western scholars, and I have attempted to acknowledge such use in the appropriate places. However, I assume full responsibility for the point of view taken throughout and for all judgments made in the book.

I am indebted for suggestions in improving the manuscript to Professors John A. Armstrong of the University of Wisconsin, Richard Pipes of Harvard University, and Franz Michael, John S. Reshetar, Jr., and Udo Posch of the University of Washington. Professor George E. Taylor, Director of the Far Eastern and Russian Institute, gave me constant moral and material support, for which I am most grateful. Miss Gladys Greenwood, Associate Editor of Far Eastern and Russian Institute publications at the University of Washington, gave me indispensable assistance through her unfailing good sense and firm standards of precision. My obligations to my wife and my mother, who assisted me in many ways, cannot be set forth here.

I acknowledge my intellectual debt to Professors Georges Florovsky and Michael Karpovich of Harvard University and Professor Karl A. Wittfogel of the University of Washington. For better or worse, they have profoundly stimulated my thinking about the problems with which the book deals. None of the three has read the manuscript, and none is likely to agree with everything I have said. However, if I had not known them I should have been less likely to associate the ideals of wisdom with the ideals of scholarship, and I should be less aware than I am of the defects of the work I have done and will do.

The system of transliteration from Russian used is that of the Library of Congress except that final ий and ый are rendered "y," all soft and hard signs are omitted in transcription, and initial Ю and Я are rendered "Yu" and "Ya" respectively. Technical terms and last names are transliterated in this manner; first names are given in their English equivalents unless they are better known in the Russian: for example, "Fëdor Dostoevsky" and "Andrei Zhdanov" rather than "Theodore Dostoevsky" and "Andrew Zhdanov." Anyone who has faced such problems knows that they are seldom solved to the satisfaction of everyone. Dates are given in New Style (Gregorian calendar) throughout, except when otherwise indicated in the text.

DONALD W. TREADGOLD

UNIVERSITY OF WASHINGTON
MARCH 31, 1958

CONTENTS

MAPS: BY WILLIS R. HEATH

The illustrations are grouped in a separate section following page 258.

Part ONE

New Currents in Old Russia

From

Absolutism to

Totalitarianism

INTRODUCTION

THE PEOPLES AND THE LAND

Slightly more than half the people who inhabit what the West calls "Russia"—that is, the Union of Soviet Socialist Republics—are Russians, or Great Russians. The Russian language which they speak is closely related to Belorussian and Ukrainian, and the three languages together make up the Eastern Slavic subdivision of the Slavic branch of the Indo-European family.[1] The three peoples who speak them number about 150 million, or three-quarters of the 200 million inhabitants of the USSR.

The first Slavic state on what later became Russian soil was organized in the ninth century in the region of Kiev. The Kievan state of "Rus" had disintegrated into small independent principalities by about 1240, when the territory was attacked and conquered by the Mongols. An important effect of the Mongol conquest was the devastation of the vicinity of Kiev and the consequent separation of the Eastern Slavs into two sections, to the west and northeast of the ruined city. The western section fell under the control of the large Lithuanian state (which was later

• [1] The two other subdivisions are the Western Slavic (Polish, Czech, and Slovak) and Southern Slavic (Serbo-Croatian, Slovene, and Bulgarian).

absorbed by Poland) and became differentiated into two groups, the Belorussians and the Ukrainians. The remainder of the Eastern Slavs, to the northeast of Kiev, came to be ruled by the Grand Prince of Moscow, who in effect assumed the position of viceroy for the Mongols. This group was known as Great Russians.

The principate of Muscovy threw off its dependence on the Mongols about 1450, consolidated its control over the Great Russians, and expanded into the Belorussian and Ukrainian regions held by Poland-Lithuania. About 1700, under Peter the Great, Muscovy was renamed the Russian Empire. During the next two centuries the rest of the Eastern Slavic peoples (except for some Ukrainians in Austria-Hungary) were brought under imperial rule.

By this time many non-Slavic nationalities were ruled from St. Petersburg, which Peter the Great had made the capital of the new Empire. A small Jewish community had appeared in seventeenth-century Muscovy, and a few years before 1800 Catherine the Great established a Jewish "pale" of settlement in the western territories newly annexed from Poland. Finnic peoples had lived intermingled with Russians for centuries, and Finland proper was taken from Sweden during the Napoleonic Wars. At the same time a truncated Polish state was added to the Empire, although sizable Polish territories went to Prussia and Austria. On the Baltic Sea lived the Estonians, whose language was akin to the Uralic tongue of the Finns, and the Latvians and Lithuanians, whose languages belonged to the Indo-European family. Indo-European languages were also spoken by the Moldavians in Bessarabia, the Armenians in the Caucasus, and the Tadzhiks on the Afghan border. Turkic peoples were scattered from the Crimea through the Ural region into Siberia and Central Asia, the chief ones being known today as Kazakhs, Uzbeks, Turkmens, Kirghiz, Azerbaijani, and Yakuts. Their linguistic relatives of the Altaic family, the Mongols and the Tungus, were found here and there from the Caspian to the Pacific. Finally there were the Georgians and other peoples in the Caucasus, whose languages defy tidy classification.

Several of the minority peoples, such as the Georgians and Armenians, had a history of civilization and independence which long antedated their attachment to the Russian Empire. As the new ideology of nationalism spread throughout nineteenth-century Europe, peoples which in modern times had never known independent national existence, such as the Ukrainians, developed nationalist aspirations. Frequently, nationalist or autonomist currents were associated with socialist or other socially revolutionary views in the thought and writing of the intellectuals among the national minorities. These were often severely repressed by the au-

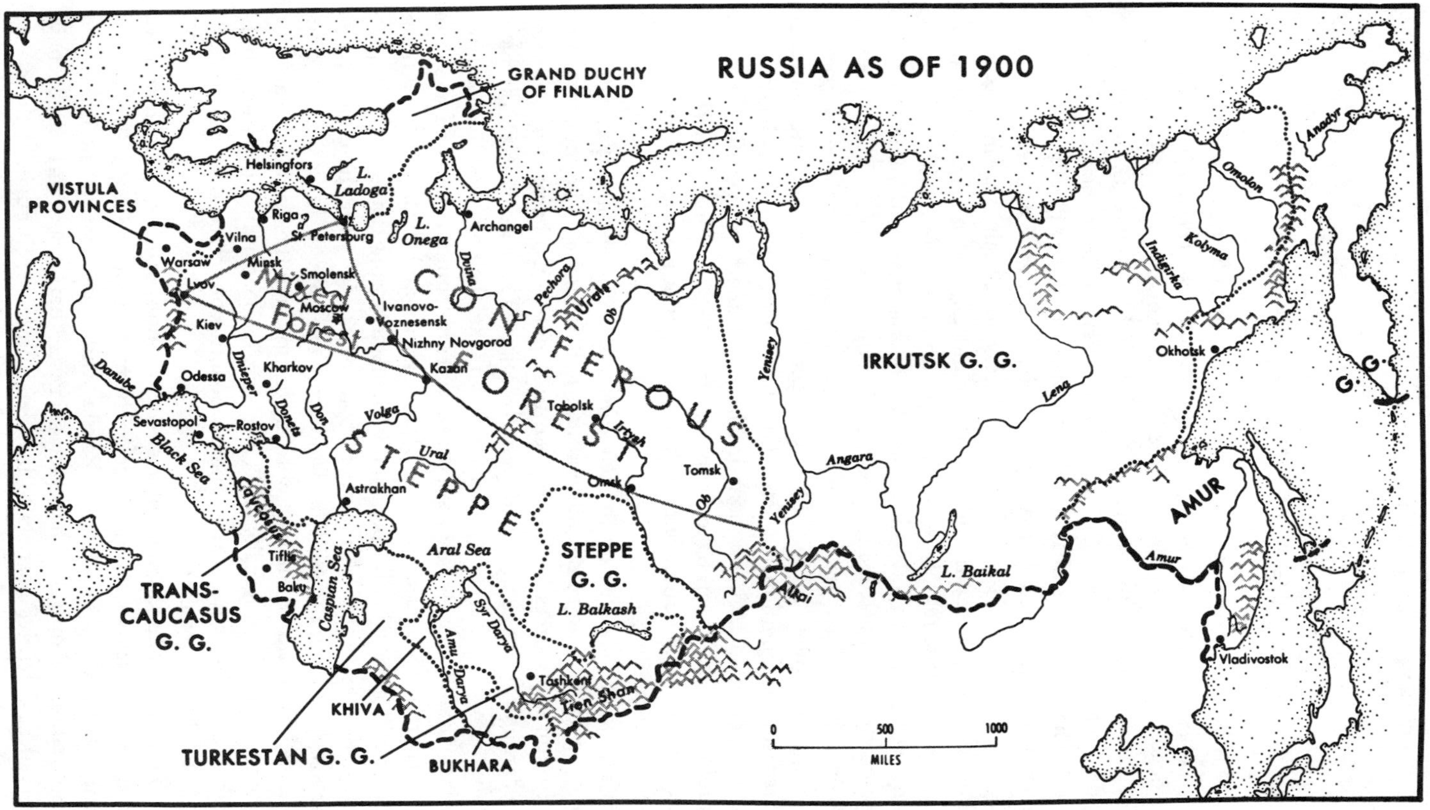
RUSSIA AS OF 1900
GRAND DUCHY OF FINLAND
VISTULA PROVINCES
Helsingfors
L. Ladoga
Riga
St. Petersburg
L. Onega
Archangel
Vilna
Warsaw
Minsk
Smolensk
Lvov
Mixed Forest
Moscow
Ivanovo-Voznesensk
Nizhny Novgorod
Kiev
Kazan
CONIFEROUS FOREST
Dvina
Pechora
Urals
Ob
Dnieper
Kharkov
Odessa
Danube
Donets
Don
Sevastopol
Rostov
Black Sea
Volga
Tobolsk
Irtysh
Tomsk
Yenisey
STEPPE
Ural
Astrakhan
Omsk
Caucasus
Tiflis
Baku
Caspian Sea
Aral Sea
TRANS-CAUCASUS G. G.
STEPPE G. G.
L. Balkash
Syr Darya
Amu Darya
Tashkent
Tien Shan
KHIVA
TURKESTAN G. G.
BUKHARA
Altai
IRKUTSK G. G.
Angara
Lena
L. Baikal
Okhotsk
Indigirka
Kolyma
Omolon
Anadyr
G. G.
AMUR
Amur
Vladivostok
0
500
1000
MILES

thorities of St. Petersburg, but only after the middle of the nineteenth century were active measures of "Russification" carried out, as a conscious Russian nationalism was formulated in influential circles.

The very name "Russian Empire" (*Rossiiskaia Imperiia*) implied the official preference in fact given the Russian language and those who spoke it, and to the Russian Orthodox Church and its adherents, over minority peoples and religions. The name "Ukrainian" was unknown to imperial law. The Jews were treated as a separate group, but chiefly for purposes of religious discrimination and disabilities which were applied to them by law and custom. However, the picture had certain shadings. Russian Poland (at least for a time) and Finland enjoyed a type of autonomy within the Empire. There was little effort to interfere with the religion and customs of the Moslem peoples or the Lamaistic Buddhists and pagans of Asiatic Russia; in fact schismatic or sectarian Russian Christians suffered far more from governmental pressures than non-Christians (except the Jews). Individual foreigners, especially Germans, but also Frenchmen, Englishmen, Scots, and others, often received privileged treatment and held high positions in the government, universities, and the professions. In general the Emperors treated a multinational state as if it were a single nation but refrained from pressing such a policy to its logical conclusion.

The land inhabited by the Russians and national minorities is for the most part flat and cold, and less than half is tillable. The immense store of natural resources has never been fully put to use because of the great geographical impediments to transportation. The vast network of rivers, most of which rise near Moscow and make their way to the Caspian, Black, Baltic, and White seas, was for a millennium the chief mode of transport in European Russia. Roads were—and even today in many areas still are—few and poor, and when the spring thaws came, impassable. Railroads are still unable to compensate fully for the deficiency in roads. The rivers of Siberia, wide and long, are of little use for commerce. They run from the south to empty into the Arctic Ocean, and though Cossacks originally crossed Siberia by boat, using the rivers' tributaries and portages between them, modern commerce does not lend itself to the same methods.

The mountains do not interfere with transportation. The Urals—by American or Swiss standards scarcely more than rolling hills—are the only range of consequence in Russia which does not lie along or near international borders. That fact suggests that mountains might have served as defensive barriers to invaders; however, throughout the course of Russian history, they have proved useless from a military standpoint.

The ranges between Central Asia and China open conveniently in northern Sinkiang, which permitted nomadic conquerors to travel westward through the Ili gap, while the easily passable Urals give way to flat plain several hundred miles from the Caspian Sea, allowing the nomads to proceed without hindrance to plunder whatever section of Europe attracted them.

Russia is protected on the south from Iran and India, where defense has not been needed, but it is completely exposed on the west whence invaders have marched repeatedly, from the Teutonic Knights in the thirteenth century to the armies of Hitler in the twentieth. The Soviets have pushed their borders westward to the Carpathians, where they never were before; but the Carpathians do not separate the Soviets from enemies, and in the era of nuclear warfare mountains are no longer much protection to anyone. Moreover, the mountains do nothing to lessen the rigors of the climate. They are high in the south, cutting off warmth, but there are none in the north of a size to prevent the Siberian Arctic winds from sweeping south and westward.

Most of the land of Russia consists of plains. The black-earth (*chernozëm*) strip which runs broadly across the south of European Russia, narrowing and disappearing in central Siberia, contains very rich soil. South of this strip in Central Asia lies a great desert (although there are sizable irrigated areas in the valleys southeast of the Aral Sea), and north of it a vast wooded expanse extends from the Baltic Sea to the Pacific Ocean. Much of the central Russian forest has long since been cleared for agriculture, but most of the woodland has never been able to support a large population because of cold temperatures and poor soil. Except for the inhospitable Central Asian desert, a Mediterranean-type or warmer climate is found only along a tiny strip of the southern Crimea and the eastern Black Sea coast, which today are dotted with Soviet state sanatoriums.

THE CHARACTER OF RUSSIAN ABSOLUTISM

By the nineteenth century Russian state and society had assumed a despotically regulated pattern which had been imprinted on the borderlands to a considerable extent. That pattern, whose chief characteristics were correctly identified by the early revolutionaries as autocracy and serfdom, had not taken shape in Russia until modern times. In the period of the Kievan state and its succession principalities under the Mongol yoke, medieval Russia had enjoyed a more fluid type of political and social organization. Trading city-states in the north, such as Novgorod and Pskov, which maintained close ties with Western Europe, had a large, free farmer class and a turbulent form of self-government in which the urban masses took part. The Kievan and other princes were restrained from arbitrary deeds by the popular assembly (*veche*), and although there were slaves, there was also a very numerous class of agriculturists whose relationship with their landlords was a contractually circumscribed one.

When the Muscovite princes threw off the Mongol yoke, they began to claim despotic prerogatives, partly in conscious or unconscious imitation of their former Mongol overlords and of their Byzantine coreligionists, whose primacy in the Orthodox world they claimed to have inherited when the Turks captured Constantinople in 1453. The Tsars (as they now styled themselves) of Muscovy subjugated the northern trading city-states, dispersed the old assemblies, and although they summoned an assembly representative of the estates (*Zemsky Sobor,* or Assembly of the Land), it never acquired any power to limit the will of the monarch. In order to crush the old independent aristocracy (the boyars, who served any given prince at will), the Tsars built up a new noble serving class (the *dvoriane* or gentry). In return for the support of the gentry, the state allowed them to reduce to serfdom the peasants who lived on their newly-granted lands. The old village institution of peasant self-government, the commune (*mir* or *obshchina,* though the terms mean slightly different things at different times), was partially converted into an organ subservient to both the gentry landlords and the state, and was used to enforce the increasing weight of fiscal and other obligations which the peasants owed to both.

The last Tsar and first Emperor, Peter the Great, virtually completed the long process of fixing the population into a small number of social classes with legally defined obligations and rights. Chiefly these were the gentry (into which the remnants of the boyars passed), the merchant groups, the state peasants (who lived on state lands and had no gentry landlords), and the private serfs—the last two groups constituting the great mass of the people of Russia. The remaining few slaves passed into serfdom.

In later Muscovite theory, the task of the peasants was to produce food, pay taxes, and (for a selected number of them) to serve as common soldiers in the army, while their gentry lords were bound to serve the state all their lives as civil officials or military officers. During the eighteenth century the obligations of the gentry were reduced and finally abolished, while their powers over their serfs became virtually those of slaveowners. However, they never attained the prerogatives of the earlier

Western feudal lords, or even those of the contemporary nobles of the Germanic countries, and remained excluded from political power.

The imperial authority was vested in the Emperor alone. His will was not limited by law or any regularly constituted political body. The agency of his will was the imperial bureaucracy, whose powers reached far down into local affairs. In practice the Emperors did not press their powers to their theoretical limits. The opinions of their advisers and their judgment of the state of mind of the various social classes (chiefly of the legally-favored gentry), the laws (especially after they were codified in the early nineteenth century), and their public allegiance to the precepts of the Christian religion, all had varying but substantial effects in restraining the monarchs from the extremes of arbitrariness. The Emperors did not attempt to exact positive commitments to an official ideology from creative artists and writers. Penalties were applied to revolutionary agitation by the secret police and the courts, but in a form and degree mild and irregular in comparison with twentieth-century totalitarianism.

The old pattern of autocracy and serfdom was greatly modified under Alexander II (1855–1881). Through the Emancipation edict and accompanying legislation serfdom was abolished. Other "Great Reforms" gave the freed peasant a share in a newly-created system of provincial and county self-government (the zemstvo), set up elective city councils for urban administration, and vastly improved the administration of justice and the method of recruitment of soldiers, from both of which the old principle of class preferment was eliminated. Nevertheless, the institution of autocracy remained intact, despite certain measures envisaging its limitation considered by Alexander II in his last days, which were laid aside only after he was assassinated by revolutionaries.

Through the efforts of officials responsive to gentry demands for restoration of their pre-Reform privileges, the Great Reforms were to some degree abridged in letter and spirit during subsequent decades. Mass discontent and the political demands of the intelligentsia combined to produce a ferment which erupted in the Revolution of 1905. As a result an Imperial Duma, or legislative assembly, was established as part of a new semiconstitutional system comparable to that of Prussia. The old absolutism was substantially modified, and in the later years of Nicholas II's reign (1894–1917) showed signs of breakdown. Meanwhile the peasantry was making progress in the direction of economic independence, and the old class lines were crossed ever more frequently. Russian culture was developing new variety, refinement, and also breadth. The growth of industry was very rapid. The final breakdown of Tsarist absolutism in the midst of the domestic strains produced by the First World War seemed to foreshadow the establishment of some type of "open society" in Russia.

THE COMING OF TOTALITARIANISM

The revolutions of 1905 and 1917 were mass upheavals not planned by anyone and anticipated by few; however, the revolutionary leadership devolved upon the few members of the intelligentsia who had worked out an a priori analysis of events and a program which they wished to put into effect. The revolutionary intelligentsia were unanimous in desiring the end of autocracy and the creation of a democratic government, and most of them supported some kind of plan for a socialist society. The masses generally believed themselves to be fighting for freedom and political rights and economic independence—or, as the slogan of the old peasant uprisings and two of the early revolutionary societies had it, "land and liberty."

The shape of the revolution depended not merely on programs, however, but on leadership. A new regime might draw on the experience of the old bureaucracy, or "public men" who had worked in the zemstvos, city councils, or the Duma, or on the fervor and dedication of the inexperienced intelligentsia. After Lenin and the Bolsheviks seized power in the October Revolution, that section of the intelligentsia who were Bolshevik or pro-Bolshevik, along with many Bolshevik workers and a few peasants, undertook to construct a new type of government—even though Lenin for a time used prerevolutionary bureaucrats, army officers, and the like where needed.

When the Communists (as the Bolsheviks renamed themselves in 1918) had defeated their antagonists in the Civil War, their regime was still in the process of changing. Almost immediately after the seizure of power a new secret police and Red Army were organized, under the leadership and control of the expanding Communist Party. Although Lenin made concessions to the peasants and small businessmen and traders through the New Economic Policy (inaugurated in 1921), the Communist Party retained its monopoly of political power. Intra-Party debates about how far the policy of economic concessions should be pursued became intertwined with personal and factional rivalries. From the Party struggles of the twenties Stalin emerged as dictator over both the Party and the country.

After 1928 Stalin unleashed the apparatus of terror (directed against the mass of the population) and purge (directed against Communist Party members) in order to revolutionize the economy and social system and to consolidate his own power. Great numbers of arrests were carried out by the secret police, thereby intimidating the whole population and filling the concentration camps with a large labor force whose use on public works was economically significant. By the late thirties Stalin had built up a totalitarian dictatorship resting on three institutional pillars: the Party organization, the secret police, and the army.

Soviet totalitarianism was designed to achieve several ends: to preserve and strengthen Communist (and Stalin's personal) power and to stifle overt political opposition; to plan and operate accordingly the entire economic system and to root out the remnants of individual enterprise; to stamp out local nationalist or autonomist feeling in the borderlands and to subject them to Moscow's fiat; to prevent or punish any academic or creative work which ran counter to the currently applied ideological line in the arts, social sciences, and even to a considerable extent in the sciences, and to force intellectuals to render overt and active support to that line; to crush organized religion, and when that proved difficult, to confine its scope of activity, and wherever possible to use the religious hierarchies for Soviet propaganda purposes; to create an all-pervading atmosphere of fear and coercion in which the potential nonconformist hesitated, in full awareness of the penalties which might be visited upon him at any moment, even to speak freely to members of his own family; and, finally, to prepare the way for an extension of Soviet power wherever the opportunity might arise, eventually to cover the entire globe.

Although the whole structure of dictatorship seemed on the verge of crumbling under the initial shock of Hitler's invasion in 1941, Stalin managed to mount a successful counterattack, retain power, and strengthen the system following the Nazi defeat. After a sustained effort at retrenchment, accompanied by the sharpest ideological repression of any period of Soviet history to date, Stalin died, yielding power to a group of his chief assistants. First Malenkov and Beria, then Khrushchëv and Bulganin, with their henchmen, sought to reach a new equilibrium of power, retaining the totalitarian structure while using its instruments much more sparingly than Stalin did. Obvious debate and hesitation at the summit of power served as a signal for expressions of individual criticism and mass discontent. Some of the criticism was countenanced or even encouraged by Stalin's successors, but in other cases anti-Soviet violence and (in the case of Hungary) full-scale revolution resulted.

Recently scholars have speculated as to whether totalitarianism might be peacefully transformed into some kind of semi-open society, or whether, in the words of Merle Fainsod, "the totalitarian regime does not shed its police-state characteristics; it dies when power is wrenched from its hands."[2] The future of Soviet totalitarianism will at least in part depend upon the actions and wills of individuals and groups among both rulers and ruled. Because men are not always predictable, the future of political and social systems is not always foreseeable. Since, however, men must act on the scene which historical development has prepared for them, and since their wishes may therefore not fully determine what they can achieve, the peoples outside the Soviet orbit may be better prepared to understand whatever the future may bring, and to act intelligently, by careful study of the Russian past.

It is argued by some that the Russians (or this or that minority people) have never known freedom and therefore could not want it, or could not attain it unassisted; by others, that the Russians have always been freedom-loving, only with difficulty amenable to authority, turbulent and rebellious, that they showed their true face in the independent Cossack bands and in perpetual flight from their oppressors into the wilderness or abroad, and will some day spontaneously rise and destroy their present tyrants. It is true that in modern times Russia has lain under a despotism, then, after a fleeting interval, under a totalitarian dictatorship. It is also true that many men and women thought, wrote, fought, and died to try to create something different. He who studies the history of twentieth-century Russia, so laden with unspeakable suffering and disappointed hopes for her peoples, may be led to echo Virgil: *O passi graviora, dabit deus his quoque finem!* But the historian must not confuse hope with foresight.

• [2] *How Russia is Ruled* (Cambridge: Harvard University Press, 1954), p. 500.

The Russian People

★
★
★
★
★
★
★
★
★
★

CHAPTER 1

MOSCOW AND ST. PETERSBURG

If one could revisit Russia as it was in the year 1900, the most profitable way to use a few days might be to concentrate on Moscow and St. Petersburg (which would be renamed Petrograd in 1914 and Leningrad in 1924). Such a visit would reveal signs of the inner tensions between different cultural currents and epochs which were central to the development of modern Russia. During the last five centuries in particular, one of the most important of such tensions was between influences stemming from Eastern as against Western Europe—that is, between the heritage of the Greek and Orthodox Empire and succession states of Byzantium on the one hand, and currents originating in Latin and Catholic states and, later, in part from Protestant and Germanic nations on the other.

The boundary between the areas in which the two influences were paramount begins at the southern shore of the Barents Sea, follows the eastern borders of Finland, the Baltic states, and Poland, then roughly those between the old Austro-Hungarian Empire and the Balkan countries, ending in the Adriatic Sea. Russia lies entirely east of that line, yet for much of her history Byzantine and Western influences competed for ascendancy in the theory and practice of her government and church and in her secular thought.

About 1450 Russia was emerging from over two centuries of Mongol and Moslem domination,[1] at the same historical moment when the Moslem Turks were conquering the last remnants of the Byzantine Empire and occupying its capital, Constantinople, the chief city of Eastern Orthodoxy. As B. H. Sumner writes, "Byzantium brought to Russia five gifts: her religion, her law, her view of the world, her art and writing."[2] They had been transmitted to the Kievan state beginning in the tenth century, before any real cultural barriers had been erected between Eastern and Western Europe.

The first serious challenge to Byzantine ideas in Russia came in the fifteenth century. Not long after the fall of Constantinople to the Turks, Ivan III (the first Muscovite prince to take the title "Tsar") married Sophia, niece of the last Byzantine emperor. However, Sophia had been reared in Rome, not Constantinople, and she brought a retinue of Italians with her to Moscow. Thus began a flow of Latin and Catholic political and religious influences which grew stronger during the sixteenth and seventeenth centuries, until the head of the Russian church, Patriarch Nikon, formulated a clearly papal theory of ecclesiastical supremacy which was narrowly defeated, not by other clergymen who held fast to the Byzantine tradition of "symphony" between church and state, but by the Tsar Alexis in the name of state authority.

Around 1700 Peter the Great inaugurated a new cultural revolution. Swiftly and often brutally the Catholic influences were pushed aside in favor of ideas and institutions borrowed from the Protestant and Germanic north. Although Latin became the language of the schools of the eighteenth century, the prevailing ideas were not those of Rome. They mirrored the Lutheran and Anglican church establishment, Atlantic mercantilism, and Swedish and German state administration. It has been said that Peter broke through "a window into Europe," but European contacts were far older. The old windows looking south toward Byzantium and then Rome were shuttered up; Peter's new one looked westward toward Stockholm, Amsterdam, and London. Its physical embodiment was the city of St. Petersburg, built on a marsh with the same prodigal brutality which Peter showed in changing the Russian state and church and the manner of life of the nobility.

The mass of the Russian people were little affected by either the Italian attendants of Sophia Paleologus or the German and Dutch advisers of

• [1] The Mongols were pagan, but the state of the Golden Horde, which ruled Russia, became heavily Turkicized and accepted the Moslem faith.

• [2] *Survey of Russian History* (2nd rev. ed.; London: Duckworth, 1947), p. 178.

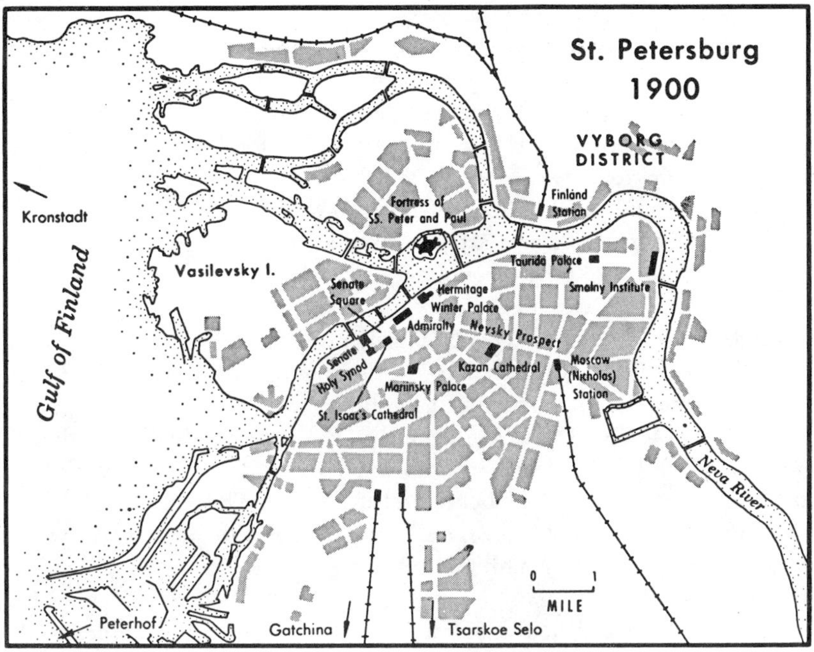
St. Petersburg
1900
VYBORG
DISTRICT
Kronstadt
Gulf of Finland
Vasilevsky I.
Fortress of
SS. Peter and Paul
Finland
Station
Taurida Palace
Smolny Institute
Senate
Square
Hermitage
Winter Palace
Admiralty
Nevsky Prospect
Senate
Holy Synod
Kazan Cathedral
Moscow
(Nicholas)
Station
Mariinsky Palace
St. Isaac's Cathedral
Neva River
0
1
MILE
Peterhof
Gatchina
Tsarskoe Selo

Moscow—1900
SOKOLNIKI
St. Petersburg
Yaroslavl
Station
Nicholas Station
Kazan Station
Yauza River
Kursk
Station
Bell Tower
of Ivan III
PRESNIA
DISTRICT
KREMLIN
Red Square
Cathedrals of the Assumption
Archangel
Annunciation
St. Basil's
Cathedral
Ordynka
Moskva River
ZAMOSKVORECHE
0
1
MILE

Peter the Great. They remained Orthodox, although not Greek in any direct sense, since from the time of the conversion of Russia to Christianity the liturgy had been in a language (Church Slavonic) akin to their own. Like most simple peoples, they were distrustful of foreign innovations. The center of their world was Moscow, which had been affected by European architectural and other influences but was still a city which had grown spontaneously, without any attempt at planning or reconstruction, and was older than the Mongol conquest.

Moscow was the capital from the time that its Grand Prince declared his independence of the Mongols, shortly after 1450, until just after 1700 when it was officially displaced by St. Petersburg. Even then it remained a sort of second capital, so that the phrase "the two capitals" refers to both cities. Moscow lay at the center of European Russia's magnificent system of rivers, with near access to the Western and Northern Dvinas, the Dnieper, the Don, the Donets, and the Volga. The city took its name from the smaller river Moskva, and grew in the shape of a wheel whose hub was the *Kreml* or Kremlin, a fortified enclosure on the north bank of the river.

Moscow is steeped in the oldest Russian traditions and memories. In the center of Moscow's Kremlin are three ancient cathedrals where old Russia's pomp and pageantry had unfolded. In the Cathedral of the Archangel, all the Tsars before Peter the Great are buried. In the Annunciation, the Tsars were baptized and married. In the Assumption, the Emperors were crowned. Close by the cathedrals is the Bell Tower of Ivan the Great (Ivan III, Sophia's husband), from whose height the city of Moscow was viewed at different times by Joseph II of Austria, Napoleon, and the celebrated Madame de Stael. The Kremlin forms a rough triangle, along whose hypotenuse to the east lies Red Square, whose name was convenient for, but not conferred by, the Bolsheviks.[3] At the south end of the Square stands the fantastically ornamented Cathedral of St. Basil the Blessed, which was pillaged by the Poles in 1611, used as a stable for French horses in 1812, and today serves as an inappropriate background for Communist parades. From the Kremlin, radial streets extend in all directions, including the *Ordynka,* a reminder that Moscow princes once took that route to carry tribute to the Mongols in the southeast, who were known as the Golden Horde (*Orda*).

If Moscow was a part and even the center of the life of old Russia, St. Petersburg was an intrusive symbol of foreign innovation. The Slavophiles used the slogan "back to Moscow," signifying abandonment of

• [3] The name originally meant "beautiful"; the etymology is suggested by the relation between the modern Russian *prekrasnyi* (beautiful) and *krasnyi* (red).

St. Petersburg in favor of the pre-Petrine past; the Westernizers regarded the city as a visible sign of the progress which they thought could come and had come only from the West. St. Petersburg was built near the Gulf of Finland on the Neva River, near which Prince Alexander Nevsky earned his sobriquet by virtue of a victory against the Swedes five centuries before Peter the Great.

The heart of St. Petersburg was the south bank within the loop of the Neva, a district cut through by the straight artery called the *Nevsky Prospekt,* which leads from the Moscow Station down to the Admiralty on the edge of the river. Just east of the Admiralty is the Winter Palace, residence of the Tsar when he came to the city from the palaces of Tsarskoe Selo (today Pushkin) or Peterhof (today Petrodvorets) a few miles away. The Winter Palace was designed by the Italian architect Rastrelli; an appendage to it was the Hermitage, Russia's finest art museum (which today has taken over the entire Palace), housing collections of Rembrandt and the Spanish and French painters which are among the world's best. Not far from the Palace is the famous equestrian statue of Peter the Great which inspired Pushkin's poem *The Bronze Horseman.* Between St. Isaac's and Kazan cathedrals (the latter is today an antireligious museum) nearby is the Mariinsky Palace, the former seat of the Imperial Council. This body, created by Alexander I in 1809, had the task of preparing and considering legislation for the Emperor's approval. After the Revolution of 1905 it was made partially elective and was transformed into the upper house of Russia's new parliament.

Just west of the Admiralty are the buildings of the Senate and the Holy Synod, now museums. Peter the Great founded the Senate, which ruled in his stead during his journeys, but under his successors became transformed into the country's supreme judicial authority. In the adjoining Senate Square occurred the events of the Decembrist uprising of 1825, Russia's first attempted revolution in the modern style. The Holy Synod was the body created by Peter the Great to provide state control over the Russian Orthodox Church, on the model of the Protestant "established churches" he had seen in England and the German states.

Walking east along the Neva, one would see on the north bank the Fortress of St. Peter and St. Paul, where many distinguished revolutionaries were held for a time. It had been the first building in St. Petersburg and had become the symbolic prison of the old regime. At first, defense against the Swedes had been concentrated here, but it was later moved westward to Kronstadt, the island base whose garrison was to figure prominently in the revolutions of 1905 and 1917. Further east, one would be opposite the Finland Station, the place of Lenin's triumphant arrival in 1917. Beyond is the Taurida Palace, built by Catherine the Great for the most capable of her many favorites, Prince Potëmkin of Taurida (the Crimea). In 1906 this Palace became the seat of the newly-created legislative assembly, the Imperial Duma, and in 1917 of the Provisional Government. Around the bend of the Neva is the Smolny Institute, Catherine the Great's school for young ladies, which became Bolshevik headquarters in 1917.

St. Petersburg was the monument not only of its great builder but also of the whole Imperial period, from the time when Peter took the title of "Emperor" until the last ruler, Nicholas II, was induced to abdicate. The Empire was an attempt to remake the nation on the foundation of the West European Reformation and Enlightenment and the Germanic bureaucratic principles of the Hohenzollern and Hapsburg monarchies—whose empires, like that of the Romanovs, perished in World War I. In 1918 the Bolsheviks moved the capital back to Moscow. They did so in part for strategic reasons, but they also had in mind a repudiation of the Empire for which St. Petersburg stood. This repudiation was indeed in certain respects superficial. Since the Bolsheviks based their doctrines on those of Karl Marx, who owed much to the Enlightenment tradition, and in their practice borrowed heavily from German bureaucracy, they could scarcely claim to reject *in toto* Peter's heritage to Russia, and as time went on they in fact emphasized their links with him—even to an unwarranted extent. Still less could the Bolsheviks claim ties with the religious and patriarchal Russia of old Moscow.

In any case, by 1918 the city of Moscow could no longer serve as a valid symbol of the truly "old" in Russia, the Byzantine tradition. The "old" was defended only by a few (and not necessarily influential) clergymen; and, in a way, by the Russian people, although their voice had never directly counted for much in the life of their nation.

THE EXPANSION OF RUSSIAN SETTLEMENT

The Eastern Slavs became agricultural settlers first in the mixed-forest zone within the triangle bounded by the three cities (built later) of St. Petersburg, Kazan, and Lvov (or Ukrainian, Lviv; or Polish, Lwów; or German, Lemberg). It was on the southern edge of that area that the Kievan state of Rus developed. It collapsed in the twelfth century, just before the Mongols rode in to establish overlordship over both the mixed-forest zone and the largely empty steppe to the south. Under Mongol rule the Russians organized a new center of state power farther east in that triangle, around Moscow. At the same time traders and explorers from the city-state of Novgorod penetrated the vast coniferous forests which border on the mixed-forest triangle, and even crossed the Ural Mountains into a tiny corner of what was to be called Siberia.

In the view of Sir John Maynard, the Russian is "a sort of land-sailor."[4] It is a shrewd observation, comparable to the perception by Windwagon Smith, the character in American frontier legend, that if the landlubbers would simply treat the Western prairie like an ocean, many of their problems would diminish. The Russians moved southeast from the mixed-forest into the rich, unforested steppe and east into the forests of Siberia as if they were sailing to new lands, during the same centuries of the early modern era in which West Europeans were experiencing their "Age of Discovery." Sometimes Russians (or Cossacks, as the roving, chiefly Slavic freebooters of the steppe came to be called) moved in the rear of the conquering armies of the Muscovite Tsar, sometimes ahead of them.

Moscow officially threw off the Mongol yoke in 1480, and one hundred years later crushed the succession states of the defunct Mongol Empire which lay along Moscow's southeastern borders from Astrakhan to western Siberia. Only the Crimea, whose Moslem ruler had found a new protector in Ottoman Turkey when the Golden Horde disintegrated, managed to survive until Turkey was sufficiently weakened for the Russians to annex its Crimean dependency just before 1800. When Moscow seized the small Tatar khanate in western Siberia, it found that it had broken through the thin Mongol crust and that all of northeastern Asia lay open. The conquest of this vast area, explored by Cossacks actually traveling in boats (see map, p. 5), took only a little over fifty years. To the south of Siberia the Russians encountered the Chinese Empire, and in 1689 made their peace with it. They then turned northward and penetrated up to the Bering Strait, finally crossing to Alaska, from which they withdrew only in the latter part of the nineteenth century.

Into the territories freed from the Mongols north of the Black and Caspian seas and opened for settlement in north Asia, there moved a steady stream of Russian peasants, seeking freedom from serfdom and onerous state obligations, and a chance to build a new life for themselves. Private landlords did not follow them to Siberia, which never knew serfdom. At first no landlords followed them into the south either, and there grew up free and self-governing Cossack bands whose only bond was Orthodox Christianity and whose only master was themselves.

However, the southern steppes were the target not only of the conquering armies of (or fugitive peasants from) Muscovy, but of Poland-Lithuania and Turkey as well. Until the end of the eighteenth century

• [4] *Russia in Flux* (New York: Macmillan, 1948), p. 14.

these two nations, along with Sweden, kept Russian armies fighting continually in the north and west, while on the south the Tatars[5] from the Crimea continued their raids far into Russia. The Tatar danger required yearly mobilization along the line of fortified outposts on Moscow's southern frontier. Poland was neutralized by 1667, Sweden by 1721, Turkey by 1774. Shortly after the western borders had been thereby secured, Russian domination moved to the Black Sea and into the Crimea, and the Tatar raids ceased.

By 1800 the territory inhabited by Eastern Slavs was almost wholly under the control of the Russian Empire. When the south fell under Imperial rule, serfdom soon followed. Imperial decrees of Catherine the Great and others turned over to servitude thousands upon thousands of Ukrainians. By the time of the Emancipation of the serfs in 1861, there remained in the south few free peasants and not much free land. In Siberia the peasants were freer and there were vast expanses of good land to be had for the taking; however, migration was severely restricted by law (which was often evaded) until the latter part of the nineteenth century.

During the Napoleonic Wars the Empire annexed Poland, Finland, Bessarabia, and much of the Caucasus. Though much of this territory was tillable, it was already fully inhabited. The expansion of the Russian peoples thereafter had to take place within the confines of the Russian state. The only later acquisitions of significance, the Far Eastern provinces including Vladivostok (1858–1860) and Central Asia (1868–1885), could not support many immigrants. During the nineteenth and early twentieth centuries, millions of people moved south and east to outlying regions of the Empire, while West and South Europeans were crossing the Atlantic in even greater numbers to the New World.

The colonization of the steppe has been interpreted by several major historians of Russia as the central thread in her whole development. Vasily Kliuchevsky, perhaps the greatest of the Russians who wrote the story, asserted, "Russia's history, throughout, is the history of a country undergoing colonization. . . . Migration, colonization constituted the basic factor of our history, to which all other factors were more or less directly related."[6] B. H. Sumner, perhaps the ablest foreigner to study

• [5] Less correctly, "Tartars." Note that while the words "Mongol" and "Tartar" or "Tatar" are often used interchangeably for the Golden Horde in Russia, the Mongols and the Turkic "Tatars" were and are different peoples, speaking different languages. The substantial Turkicization of the Golden Horde which occurred after the Mongol conquest accounts for the confusion of terms.

• [6] *Kurs russkoi istorii* (Moscow, 1937; reprint, Ann Arbor, 1948), Vol. I, pp. 20–21.

Russia, declared, "throughout Russian history one dominating theme has been the frontier; the theme of the struggle for the mastering of the natural resources of an untamed country, expanded into a continent by the ever-shifting movement of the Russian people."[7]

Although the Russian might be a natural "land-sailor," he was not necessarily a born nomad. There was much in the political and social institutions of old Russia to provoke men to attempt an escape to freedom. Part of the migration was also prompted by the phenomenal growth of the population during the nineteenth century. In Peter the Great's time there were only 13 million people in the Empire, less than in France. By the end of the Napoleonic Wars a century later, the population had tripled and Russia was the most populous country in Europe. Probably around 1880 the total passed 100 million, and reached 170 million in 1914.

All these people had to live somewhere. In the less fertile mixed-forest zone congestion on the land was growing serious, and in the steppe to the south population density was highest of all. The additional population might choose to leave the land, and throughout the nineteenth century and later many peasants streamed into the cities to find work in new industrial plants, although they frequently kept alive their membership in their old village communes (see p. 106) and other ties with the village. If they wished to remain on the land, they could try to solve their problems either by migrating to areas where there was room to employ the old farming methods, or by changing the ancient and wasteful three-course open-field strip system.

During the last century of Tsarism millions of peasants migrated, illegally or legally, to the southern and eastern frontier. At the same time the old farming methods, which were closely linked with the functions of the village commune, began to be gradually replaced by new ones. As migration opened up new opportunities for many in the east, the old system was slowly breaking down in the west. As long as the commune continued to carry out periodical redistribution of land—a function encouraged by the state to assure the payment of taxes and the furnishing of recruits on an equitable and reliable basis—there could be little incentive either to improve the land which a family occupied or to limit the increase of that family. However, despite Alexander III's (1881–1894) efforts to keep the commune alive, redistribution was coming to an end. Moreover, in the northwestern provinces, spontaneous enclosure of the common land into individual peasant farms was taking place in imitation of German and other western neighbors. In Siberia the commune never

• [7] Sumner, *op. cit.*, p. 9.

had much more than a shadowy existence. During the early decades of the twentieth century, in many localities of both west and east the communal system was giving way to individual, intensive, diversified farming coupled with the raising of livestock, the development of craft industry, the growth of agricultural co-operatives, and altogether the tracing of a new path for much of Russian agriculture to follow.

Logically, migration might have been expected to defer the time of the necessary readjustments in Russian agriculture by draining off population from areas of worst congestion and thus making change less urgent. Certain reactionaries advocated large-scale migration for that very reason, as certain revolutionaries deprecated any such movement in the hope that not readjustment but revolution would result. In fact migration may, by relieving some overcrowding, have smoothed the adoption of new methods here and there; but more important, the migrants themselves were accepting agricultural innovation, and showing by example what could be done by an individual farmer. The commune was the object of a frontal attack by Prime Minister Stolypin's agrarian legislation during the last years of Tsarism. Millions of peasants were trying their luck as farmers in the new east, other millions were leaving the communes to enclose new farms in the west. All of them were in search of a better life through economic improvements and a new vision of moral self-sufficiency.

PEASANTS AND OTHER RUSSIANS

In 1900 eighty to ninety per cent of the Russian people were peasants, and an even larger percentage were Christians, as they had been since the time of the Kievan state. The Russian peasants had had a good deal of freedom in the early centuries, but in the early modern period had been pressed into serfdom, just as the serfs of medieval Western Europe were winning freedom. They had been emancipated in 1861, after the Germanic empires had already freed their serfs. At that time the Russian peasants were liberated either from private landlords, to whom about half of them had been in virtual personal bondage, or from the state, which had controlled the other half. However, they did not then become free farmers; they remained bound to the village commune.

The village commune was not peculiar to Russia. There were similar institutions in ancient Germany and modern India, but the Russian commune had been given distinctive shape by action of the state. Before 1861 the needs of the government included taxes and recruits; after 1861 there was added the collection of the redemption payments, which the peasant owed the state as purchase price for the land received at Emancipation. Many officials felt that the commune should also replace the landlord as an agency of authority and a channel of loyalty. Efforts toward that end, however, were not very successful.

The peasants' age-old devotion to the land was expressed in the old Russian proverb, "We are yours [addressing the landlords], but the land is ours." Toward the beginning of the twentieth century it was rapidly becoming theirs by rental or purchase, as the portion left to the landlords at Emancipation passed out of their increasingly inefficient or impoverished hands. Simultaneously the commune was withering in fact and in law, and its lien of ownership on peasant fields was disappearing as its fiscal and other political powers over the peasant came to an end. Their ancient thirst for "land and liberty" was much nearer to being satisfied than ever before; they were legally free men, on the way to becoming owners of their own farms, and although their political rights and privileges were still circumscribed and not always fully understood or even exercised, they had a vote for the Duma and a growing consciousness of the hitherto mysterious realm of politics. They kept their diet of cabbage soup and bread and vodka, their wrapped stockings enclosed in boots, their squatting dances and fur caps, and the rest of their traditions. Yet new staples, clothes, and customs might also find acceptance, as the peasants became free farmers and obtained a range of choices denied them before. Their fundamental aspirations were very old, yet the realization of some of them was new.

A small percentage of Russians had by 1900 become industrial workers. Many retained their ties with the village, and during the economic collapse of the Civil War period Lenin was to be alarmed by what appeared to be the evaporation of the Russian proletariat, as peasant-workers returned to the land in search of food and security. Nevertheless, a few years or decades of city life had left their imprint. The miserable living conditions, so common in the early stages of industrialization in other countries, generated a willingness in many factory laborers to listen to revolutionary agitators and to try to puzzle out their "little books" of propaganda. Peasant unrest had been chronic in Russia for centuries, but even the great peasant revolts (the last was that of Pugachëv in the 1770's) had had virtually no chance of success because, originating in the borderlands, they were smashed as they approached the centers of state power. However, worker unrest developed in the centers themselves, shook the government in 1905, and toppled it in 1917.

It is difficult to determine how much of the traditional peasant outlook had been altered by the relatively brief sojourn in urban industrial life. Although Lenin worried about the danger that the workers would "stop" at "trade-union consciousness," the reformist trade-union principle never obtained much of a foothold among them. "Socialism"—no doubt understood in various senses and often very imperfectly—was offered as a dramatic solution to their widespread and searing miseries and accepted by large numbers of them in that spirit. Even if it was only a small minority which espoused socialism, it was a noisy and active minority. Socialist views tended to go along with militant atheism, as the two were directly linked in Marxist doctrine, although among the Russian workers, as elsewhere, there were religious socialists and nonsocialist atheists. In general the urban workers found themselves in a setting so different from the village that religious practices could not have the same role in their lives as before, but some of them entered urban congregations, and many others retained their faith even if not their habits of church attendance and religious observances.

As a whole the Russian people remained Christian, as they had been for a thousand years. For them, as for so many peasant peoples, the Church was the fount of their ideology, the reminder and sanction of their morals, the symbolic commemorator of their birth, baptism, marriage, and death, and the center of their social and community life. The high clergy of the two capitals were often wealthy and influential, but the village priests shared the poverty and even the outlook of the peasants among whom they lived and worked. If the peasant had a grievance against his village clergyman, it was more likely to be personal than institutional.

The official church was the Russian branch of the Eastern Orthodox Church, whose superior dignitary was the Patriarch of Constantinople. The Russian Church had acquired autocephalous status (that is, autonomy under its own patriarch) before 1600. Its emancipation from the headship of Constantinople, never more than a shadowy type of final appellate court in ecclesiastical matters, was followed in only a century by the very real subjection to the Russian state, which was effected by Peter the Great and lasted until 1917.

In the late seventeenth century the Russian Orthodox Church experienced its only schism of importance, when the so-called Old Believers rejected the official hierarchy, some maintaining their own clergy and others recognizing no clergy at all. Since then the Old Believers had suffered varying degrees of oppression by the state. They made up tightly-knit, hard-working, puritanical communities, scattered over European and Asiatic Russia.

Besides the schismatics, there were several sects composed of Christians who claimed no continuity with the official church (the Old Believers did), such as the *Dukhobors* ("spirit-fighters"), the *Molokane* ("milk-drinkers"), the orgiastic *Khlysty,* and the sexually mutilated *Skoptsy.* Protestantism had made negligible headway among the common people, except in the Lutheran Baltic states where there was an upper class of German origin. Among the Russians, the Baptists were the only Protestant denomination with a sizable following, and even they were few. Roman Catholicism, which was popularly identified with Polish-Lithuanian oppression of the Orthodox Eastern Slavs, had no Great Russian converts worth mentioning. The western Ukrainians, who had been Orthodox before 1596, were forcibly incorporated into the Roman obedience by Poland through the establishment in that year of a Slavonic-rite "Uniat" church. For over a century Ukrainian resistance to the Unia continued. However, the Uniat church acquired a hold on many Ukrainians which was not entirely broken when Poland was partitioned in the late eighteenth century and the Tsars ordered the reabsorption of its dioceses into Orthodoxy.[8]

Until 1907, when restrictions were relaxed somewhat, the five million Jews of the Russian Empire were required to live in certain areas, but they were always permitted by the state to practice their religion, though they suffered from periodic anti-Jewish pogroms, which certain local authorities did little to prevent or punish. Islam had a larger representation, mainly among the Tatar and Turkic peoples who made up the bulk of the population of Central Asia and were scattered here and there in the east and south of European Russia. Although it was identified with the Golden Horde and the Ottoman Turks, Islam tended to excite condescension in the Russians rather than the fear and hatred felt for the Roman Catholics. The Tatars who practiced Islam were mostly poor and backward. Moreover, some Russians knew that the Mongols had made no attempt to interfere with Christianity once the conquest was over, and that even the Turks permitted Orthodoxy to be practiced freely in the Ottoman Empire. Finally, the Kalmyks near the Caspian and the Buriat Mongols near Lake Baikal practiced Buddhism or shamanism without serious interference from the Russian authorities. Except for the Jews, the Empire was always gentler with its non-Christians than with Christian heretics.

To the peasant of 1900 Christianity did not mean anything very different from what it meant to his ancestors. That was no defect in Chris-

• [8] The last Uniat diocese in the Russian Empire was absorbed only in 1875; however, the church continued to exist among the Ukrainians of the Austrian Empire, who came under the Polish and Czechoslovak governments in 1919. After the annexation of their lands by the USSR, the Uniat church was suppressed there as well in 1946.

tian eyes. Although Christianity may be compatible with a theory of progress, it does not imply one; it seeks to minister to the universal qualities of man regardless of time and place. There were "modernist" movements within the high clergy, whose members were discussing whether Christianity could or should be reconciled with science, socialism, and other innovations in thought. The lower clergy to some extent took part in the new political agitation, and numerous priests appeared in the Imperial Duma after the 1905 Revolution, which had started with a procession of workmen, led by a priest, on which the authorities had fired ("Bloody Sunday"). But baptisms, weddings, and masses were the same as before, and there is no evidence that the religious faith of the Russian people had weakened substantially in the years when the revolutionary movement was growing strong.

The Russian peasant always had ardent admirers, including a host of foreign travelers from Mackenzie Wallace to John Maynard and Bernard Pares. He also had his critics, and often the educated men in Russia and in the West who sympathized with him and pitied him still despised him and justified the whip laid on his back by the Soviets, if not the Tsars. In the peasant's make-up could be found many seeming contradictions. He was almost always hospitable to strangers and outsiders, including beggars and criminals, for whom there was traditional and widespread sympathy. At the same time he might be distrustful or hostile to foreigners who were thought to be influential in the central or local government or economy. He was respectful of learning and had often managed to acquire a smattering of it; numerous foreign travelers were dumfounded at the books they encountered in isolated peasant homes. Yet he was often illiterate and ignorant, and some responded to the shattering events of 1917 by telling one another that there was a new Tsar named *"Revoliutsiia."* The peasant was generally devoted to his family, and yet frequently would drink up the last kopek, insensible to the suffering which resulted. He was an assiduous and often shrewd farmer, yet commonly damaged his own soil by ruinous methods. He was a soldier whose powers of endurance and tenacity and sense of discipline were fabulous; nevertheless, in 1917 peasant soldiers ran away from the front by the thousands. He was humbly law-abiding, yet might cheat the government's agents regularly and on occasion rise up against them in blood. He revered the Tsar as his "Little Father," though he seems to have been little moved by the demise of the monarchy in 1917. He was a fervent Christian, who practiced extensively the virtues of forgiveness and brotherly love, but still might keep here and there a pagan remembrance or custom, and at times could be guilty of bestial cruelty. He was a contradictory person indeed, but possibly no more so than any other human being.

The peasant was preoccupied with the fate and fortune of himself and of his own family. He always had, in addition, a strong sense of community; but even in the village he neither held goods nor tilled the soil in common with his neighbors. Generations of intellectuals tried in vain to find socialism in him. The Communists did realize he was no socialist, but they did not learn how fiercely he would resist socialism until they undertook to introduce it in the countryside. His aspirations were modest: he sought security based on the enterprise of his family and the respect and freedom to which a human being is entitled—or, as the old leaders of the serf revolts had put it, "land and liberty."

In the past the Russian peasants had revolted against authority many times. There were four great peasant uprisings in modern Russian history, the first just after 1600, the second in the 1670's, the third just after 1700, the fourth in the 1770's. Each began as a movement among the Cossacks of the southern frontier, rolled up like a cyclone toward Moscow, and was put down by regular army troops. Their unlettered chiefs, Bolotnikov, Razin, Bulavin, and Pugachëv, were possessed of a peasant cleverness, but had no clear idea what they wanted or how to get it. Many peasants followed them; there was no one else to follow. Actually such revolts were mainly aimed at the officialdom, whom the people tended to blame for their miseries. It was thought that if somehow they could get through to the Tsar he would listen to their troubles and help them as a father would. The rebel leaders thus appealed to the principles of the traditional monarchy, and Pugachëv even pretended to be the rightful Tsar himself.

The same confidence in the "Little Father" permeated the workers of St. Petersburg who marched to his palace on "Bloody Sunday" in 1905, but the bullets fired that day virtually killed that confidence forever. The peasant riots later that year and the next also cast doubt on village loyalty. Nicholas II had more sympathy for the peasants than understanding of their plight. When he stumbled onto ministers who had a program for relieving it, he was still unable to use the success of agrarian reform as a means for reviving peasant trust in the monarchy. The gentry were too preoccupied with their own grave economic problems to be of much help. Communication between the peasants and the upper classes was faint and interrupted. It was as if one tried to shout from St. Petersburg to Moscow.

The State and the Intelligentsia

CHAPTER 2

THE CENTRAL GOVERNMENT

In 1900 the government of the Russian Empire was an absolute monarchy, as it had always been and as the Tsardom of Muscovy had been before it. Like most "absolute rulers," the monarch had legally unlimited powers, but in actual fact he was guided to a considerable extent by the opinions of his closest advisers, as well as their and his own estimates of what actions were desirable, necessary, or possible.

Since the reign of Alexander I (1801–1825), an Imperial Council had existed to consider legislation and issue it, given the approval of the Emperor. The Council had no legal powers independent of the sovereign's will, but in practice it had great influence on the course of legislation. About the same time a Committee of Ministers was established, in order to co-ordinate the work of the individual ministries which Alexander I created to replace the inefficient "colleges" (*collegia*) of Peter the Great as agencies of central administration. Although certain ministries worked well, the Committee achieved little co-ordination among them. There was no prime minister until 1905, although the Minister of Interior usually had in fact more power than any other single minister and tended to make what unitary domestic policy there was. The Governing Senate, which had acted as a sort of collective viceroy in the days of its creator, Peter the Great, was by 1900 mainly a judicial body, the highest court of appeal in the Empire.

The whole structure was bureaucratic. As Michael Karpovich writes, "It was now a Grand Monarchy of the same type which had arisen in Western Europe during the first centuries of the modern period. It stood in particularly close relationship to the German monarchies of the Hapsburgs and the Hohenzollerns. Its psychology was practically the same as that in Berlin and in Vienna. Its ideal was a 'regulated state'—an essentially western conception—and it liked to attribute to itself a civilizing mission within the boundaries of the Empire."[1]

It is disputed whether any Russian group, in particular the gentry, attained the degree of power within or against the despotic state which the Germanic landowners possessed, but it is certainly true that the Tsarist government was strongly influenced by the German monarchies, and not merely by imitation. There were many men of German origin in high places and had been since the time of Peter the Great, as the Slavophiles noted with chagrin. The extent of the German influence in the nineteenth century is illustrated by the general who, on being asked by Nicholas I what favor he could confer in recognition of services, replied, "Your Majesty, make me a German!"

The Russian bureaucracy was patterned on the Germanic bureaucracies in its titles and its method of operation and was not substantially inferior to them in efficiency or quality of personnel. There were well-trained and enlightened government servants like Michael Speransky, originator of Alexander I's state reforms, Paul Kiselëv, author of Nicholas I's reforms relating to the state peasants, and Nicholas Miliutin, one of the important figures guiding the Great Reforms of Alexander II. There also were incapable or reactionary figures who reached positions of authority, like Dmitry Sipiagin and Viacheslav von Plehve, successive interior ministers under Nicholas II, whom even the ultraconservative old counsellor, Pobedonostsev, stigmatized as "fool" and "scoundrel," respectively.

LOCAL GOVERNMENT

Whether officials were wise or foolish, there was no check on their power either at the central or local level except the will of the Emperor. The imperially-appointed governors of the fifty-odd provinces which had been established as administrative units by Catherine the Great,

• [1] *Imperial Russia, 1801–1917* (New York: Henry Holt, 1946), p. 8.

were responsible to the Ministry of Interior in St. Petersburg, but there was no limitation on their authority from within their provinces. In 1864 elective boards and assemblies (the zemstvos) had been set up within each province (*guberniia*) and county (*uezd*), and since that time there had been a division of function rather than of legal powers between the governor and the local zemstvos. The zemstvo boards came to be made up mainly of the more liberal local gentry; the more conservative landlords tended to forfeit their potential influence through lack of interest or participation, while the other classes were underrepresented on the elective boards partly because of lack of education.

There were Imperial officials at the county, and from 1889 onward, at the township (*volost*) level. The township usually comprised several villages. At both the township and village levels, self-government had existed since 1861 (and the village assembly had existed for centuries before), in the form of assemblies in which the male householders elected elders (of the village, *starosta,* singular; of the township, *starshina*). The township assembly also elected an executive board and a court which dealt with minor civil and criminal cases in which only peasants were concerned. The village assembly was charged with the collective responsibility of all householders for payment of taxes and provision of recruits to the armed forces, as well as for the "redemption payments" for land acquired at the time of the Emancipation in 1861. These functions were either being abolished or falling into disuse during the last years of Tsarism. Recruitment was made universal, instead of a special peasant obligation, in 1874. The "soul tax" (introduced by Peter the Great, which taxed the individual "soul," not the amount of land he worked), for which the commune had been collectively responsible, was abolished in 1885. Joint responsibility for the redemption payments was ended in 1903, and the remaining payments due were cancelled in 1906. Beginning in that year Prime Minister Stolypin undertook to break up the commune entirely (see p. 106).

INTELLECTUALS—CLERICAL AND SECULAR

At each level the imperial government worked through its own officials, the bureaucracy. In early Muscovite times it was recruited from the boyars (the old hereditary nobility) and later from the gentry; after Peter the Great it contained a generous admixture of non-Russians (especially Germans) and Russians who were sons of the lower clergy and other "lower ranks." By the nineteenth century the bureaucracy had developed its own ethos and a consciousness of its own interests, intertwined with its dynastic (rather than national) loyalty, but apart from and often in conflict with the interests of the gentry, its original parent group. During the first half of the nineteenth century another group of sons of gentry, the intelligentsia (see p. 33), broke with its class of origin and the government to which the gentry remained loyal, and dedicated itself to the destruction of privilege and the whole system of autocracy.

During the Middle Ages (the period of the Kievan state and the Mongol yoke) as well as early modern times (the Muscovite period), the intellectuals were almost all clergymen, in Russia as elsewhere in medieval Europe. The heads of the church, metropolitans (before 1589) and patriarchs, were among the Tsar's most influential advisers, and the clergy served as an important channel through which new theological and other ideas entered Russia. It was the desire of Peter the Great to educate the gentry in a manner designed to make possible increasing secularization of the state, and thus to take ideological leadership out of the hands of the clergy. He was also willing to reach far outside the circle of the privileged classes to find advisers and assistants. In the eighteenth century many influential thinkers were nonclerics, from Pososhkov, a peasant-born writer on mercantilism, to Lomonosov, "Russia's Benjamin Franklin." The clergy still had its intellectuals, but they were no longer the official ideologists, and they never regained that position. Often they continued to resist the theological or other innovations which Peter the Great and his successors borrowed from the West, and some of them battled with the lay procurators of the Holy Synod whom Peter placed in charge of the church and who tended to reflect Western influences of various kinds. However, their primacy in the field of ideas passed to others.

THE IMPACT OF WESTERN SECULARISM

The gentry became increasingly Westernized in language (French or German came to be used more often than Russian in their households), manner of life, and outlook during the eighteenth century. A small but growing group of them studied and espoused West European ideas. In particular they wrestled with the implications of the intellectual revolution produced by the eighteenth-century Enlightenment.

The Enlightenment, although prepared by earlier thinkers, emerged full-blown in France in the generation of the 1760's to the 1780's. Its adepts enthroned "reason" and "nature" in place of God. Voltaire's objective was to "destroy the infamous thing," by which he meant not so much Christianity *in toto* as the institutional and political ascendancy of the church and the clergy, as well as the primacy of Christian ideas. The men of the Enlightenment gained a wide hearing and an influential following immediately, but they still had to contend for a long period with the clergy and Christian-oriented laymen. Jews, practicing or apostate, played an important part in the rise of secular intellectuals everywhere in Europe, but the former Christians were perhaps more decisive.

The French Revolution gave the early generations of secular thinkers their first great opportunity. The faith in reason which inspired Condorcet, while in prison, to write an optimistic essay on human progress, led other men to justify the shedding of blood for the sake of a more rational order of government and society. However, as there followed a political reaction to the French Revolution, so there ensued an intellectual reaction against "reason," in the form of the Romantic movement. Especially in Germany and England the Romantics, led by Hegel and Schelling, looked for reality beyond the immediately given and observed, and sought truth beyond the tangible. If the French Rationalists were the first wayward sons of the Christians, the German Romanticists were the grandsons who to a degree played the part of returning prodigals. Feuerbach perceived this quality in them when he, with partial justice, attacked Hegelian concepts as harboring "the deceased spirit of theology."

The Romantics were followed by a generation which made a fuller and seemingly final rejection of religion. They were the Darwinian-minded "social scientists," who followed what they conceived to be the lead of the new biology, which made God dispensable. Darwinism itself did more. It postulated a theory of evolutionary change which the intellectuals eagerly embraced and applied not merely to the human species, as Darwin suggested, but also to human society and the state. Evolutionary doctrines did not begin with Darwin, but Darwinism in Western Europe and America gave them wide popularity. It was sometimes used, by such men as Herbert Spencer, to justify certain existing institutions, but more often it was employed to attack them as obsolete. Nicholas Danilevsky and a few others turned Darwinism to conservative purposes, but in Russia Reform Darwinists were the rule.

Russia had representatives of each of the generations of intellectuals mentioned. She had her Rationalists, like Alexander Radishchev, who wrote in a Jeffersonian vein, "Man is born into the world the equal of any other." She had Romantics, including Alexis Khomiakov and the other Slavophiles, who dreamed of a moral union between Tsar and people which would repudiate German bureaucratic principles and revive the true Russian spirit. Her Reform Darwinists, such as Dmitry Pisarev, advocated a vigorous critique of all existing institutions, believing that what was good and adapted to the needs of the day would survive.

Each group was trying to work out its own relationship to the universe, using the philosophical tools fashionable throughout Europe at the moment. Later Russians and Westerners alike were sometimes misled into interpreting these men and their thought as uniquely Russian phenomena. Radishchev seemed to be concerned mainly with the problem of serfdom in Russia. The Slavophiles were regarded as apologists for Tsarist absolutism, instead of the dedicated champions of sweeping moral regeneration they were in their youth, or the moderate reformers some of them lived to become. Young firebrands like Pisarev were dubbed "nihilists," or apostles of destruction in the peculiar Russian style, whereas *nihil* (Latin for "nothing") was only an abbreviation for their axiom that nothing should merit belief which perished in the test of rigorous scientific investigation.

THE INTELLIGENTSIA

In the early nineteenth century there was taking shape a group of men and women (often boys and girls in chronological age) which called itself and was called by others the Russian intelligentsia. The word *intelligentsia* is a Russian one borrowed from Latin. A Western name was appropriate, because the distinctive feature of the group was a series of shared assumptions which it took from the West. The Russian intelligentsia was bound together not by class origin or wealth or economic function but by commitment to certain ideas, upon which it acted with varying degrees of success at different times. The group may be defined as the politically-oriented portion of the educated class—that portion which was preoccupied with ideas concerning what state and society were like and what they ought to be like, in Russia as well as in the rest of the world. A painter or composer who cared only for his art would not qualify; an industrial worker or businessman or landlord who had a smattering of political theory might. The intelligentsia cut across class lines. Princes and the sons of village clergymen found themselves concerned with the same problems, writing for the same magazines, even members of the same underground political organizations.

An air of dedication—which, carried to its logical extreme, would prompt Lenin to declare that he would not listen to Beethoven because it made him feel soft and weak—and a sense of risk pervaded the Russian intelligentsia. Men could be found in most European countries who also were willing to stake their freedom and their lives on their politics, but in the West other groups which were political, but took their politics less seriously, were stronger than in Russia. The Russian intelligentsia developed a fervor and often a fanaticism of their own, but applied them to the advancement of a stock of ideas which were largely imported from England, France, and Germany.

ATTEMPTS AT POLITICAL ACTION

The first generation of secularized intellectuals in the West had been neither political democrats nor social radicals. They had thus been able to gain the favor of monarchs who were themselves attracted by Enlightenment thought and accordingly became known as the "enlightened despots." Their ideological mentors were seldom fully satisfied with the monarchs' performance; Voltaire broke with Prussia's Frederick the Great and Diderot was disappointed in Catherine the Great of Russia. Beginning in the 1780's, radicals and revolutionaries, adhering to many of the same Enlightenment tenets as their predecessors, impatiently dethroned rulers, and after the Napoleonic Wars the politically-minded intellectuals found themselves barred from access to European courts.

The Russian generation of young gentry-officers who reached France with the armies of Alexander I in 1814 still trusted their monarch. He himself had been educated in the new French ideas and before the war with Napoleon had seemed to be moving in the direction of the liberal and constitutional regime and the radical social reforms which certain of his advisers urged. After the war the young officers lost hope that Alexander would lead the reform movement, and began to form secret societies. When Alexander I died in 1825, confusion over who should succeed him gave the veterans their opportunity, and they were named "Decembrists" after the abortive coup which they attempted in the last month of the same year.

For the next twenty years the intelligentsia abstained from overt political action while they debated Russia's place in the world and what her future should be. By the middle of the century most of them had become philosophically secularized and politically revolutionary. Until 1917 they remained bent on root-and-branch transformation of Russia, by violence if necessary. It was tacitly assumed, naturally enough, that the intelligentsia, or some of them, would emerge from the coming revolution in the seats of power. The interest in power for its own sake was never openly expressed; moreover, it was not the conscious motivation of the revolutionaries. Their objective was the power to do what needed to be done for the Russian people, even though there was ample disagreement about what that was.

It was hoped that power could be torn from the hands of autocratic

Tsarism and placed in the hands of the people by means of a popularly elected Constituent Assembly—as Alexander Herzen expressed it after his experience with the French revolutionary movement. That assembly should determine the type of government and society which Russia should have; it was widely assumed that the government would be republican and socialist. Each revolutionary group, however, had its own complex view of what would or should be the lineaments of the new Russia. In order for the electorate-to-be to grasp the necessity of adopting a particular party program, its millions had to be properly educated. Therefore propaganda and agitation were essential, not to bring about the revolution, which was regarded as inevitable, but to complete it in a way which would conform to the demands and expectations of the group in question.

THE REVOLUTIONARY MOVEMENT

The memory of the Decembrists was kept alive by young men and women who believed, in the words of Pushkin, that "from the spark [of 1825] shall come the flame" of revolution. They were restrained from further attempts to overthrow the regime not by any lack of will, but by the police system of Nicholas I and by their own belief that it was necessary to learn from the mistakes of the Decembrists and to prepare carefully for the next move.

The revolutionary movement which led directly to the uprising of 1917 was begun with Alexander Herzen, who emigrated to Paris and London to study and prepare for the great upheaval which he expected would come to Russia one day. Up to 1847, when Herzen left Russia, the intelligentsia had been made up of scions of the gentry, and he himself belonged to that group. Shortly afterward, however, the character of the revolutionary youth began to change substantially. Side by side with the gentry, there appeared the *raznochintsy* or "mixed-rank" intelligentsia, consisting of sons of the middle class, professional men, and sons of the village clergy. One of the priests' sons was Nicholas Chernyshevsky, whose quarrels with Herzen can be traced to their different social origins as well as to their divergent political views.

At the same moment, among intellectuals all over Europe there was spreading a new "hardness," and artistic and political "realism," partly produced by the failure of hopes in what has been called the "revolution of the intellectuals" in 1848. Herzen himself experienced disillusionment while witnessing the shooting of workers in Paris by government troops and sharing the gloom which followed the partial restoration of the pre-1848 regimes in so many European capitals. The lone echo of the revolutions of 1848 in Russia was the arrest and imprisonment of the Utopian-socialist Petrashevsky circle, including Fëdor Dostoevsky, who later became one of Russia's and the world's greatest novelists. The Russian intelligentsia did not react to the destruction of the Petrashevsky circle so much as to the continent-wide change in temper. The new zest for action and scorn of sentiment found ready enthusiasts among the *raznochintsy* of Chernyshevsky's generation. During the 1860's revolutionary manifestoes and societies began to appear, and they multiplied almost decade by decade thereafter.

The Great Reforms of Alexander II (1855–1881) (see p. 9) did not succeed in dampening the fervor of the young revolutionaries. Herzen had a moment of panic in which he repeated Julian the Apostate's murmur, "Thou hast conquered, O Galilean!"—but it must be recalled that the original was a cry of despair and a verbal surrender to an enemy, not an avowal of conversion. Those revolutionaries who were disheartened by the prospect that Imperial reform might succeed did not renounce their opposition to autocracy. The Emperor had ended serfdom, but he remained an autocrat. The radical youth wanted as before to overthrow his government.

If in the first half of the nineteenth century the intelligentsia had produced more thought than action, the emphasis was thereafter reversed. That is not to say that ideas came to be regarded as superfluous, but rather that the revolutionaries demanded a philosophy with activist political implications. Often their philosophy was positivist, following the Frenchman Auguste Comte, who limited the source of knowledge to sensory data and (at least verbally) rejected metaphysics as a valid branch of knowledge. Some of the young positivists, like Pisarev, had little concern with politics, but most of the politically-minded were positivist, or naturalist, and believed in applying the methods of Darwinian biology to questions earlier considered the province of the humanities rather than of science.

As the century drew near its close, a new challenger appeared in the field of philosophy. The young Russians discovered Marx. Marxism, like positivism, was naturalist in its epistemology, but in its ontology denied the existence of an unknowable. In other words, they used the same methods as the positivists to reach conclusions before which the positivists shrank back. If positivism did not necessarily demand action, Marxism (at least in its orthodox form) did. It actually became in Russia a philosophical force which had an impact far broader than its political adherents, and it was soon an imperious and uncompromising competitor among organized revolutionary circles.

POPULISM

During the 1860's the foremost current in revolutionary politics was that of populism (*narodnichestvo*). Populism had only a vaguely outlined political philosophy, and therefore it is sometimes very difficult to determine who was a "populist" and who was not. Its psychology combined an articulation of the bad conscience which afflicted the gentry intelligentsia with a rationalization of the *raznochintsy* drive for a new type of state and society, as well as for power for enlightened men like themselves.

The "conscience-stricken nobleman," as the contemporary phrase went, was one who felt he owed a crushing debt to the whole body of serfs, whose toil had yielded his ancestors and himself the opportunity for wealth, leisure, and education. The type was allied to the "superfluous man" of Russian literature, as exemplified by Pushkin's Eugene Onegin, Lermontov's Pechorin, and Turgenev's Rudin. Such characters sought meaning for their gilded lives and either failed to find any or turned to a life of self-effacing, even purposeless, action. By the 1860's the "conscience-stricken nobleman" might seek to expiate his feelings of guilt in either of two ways. Like the father of organized populism, Peter Lavrov, he could embrace preparation for revolution, or he could, like the zemstvo liberals, devote himself to piecemeal, local improvement work as a means of creating the prerequisites for constitutional government for Russia as a whole. The populists generally despised efforts to improve a structure which they regarded as beyond repair and which they wished to destroy.

The first active political venture of populism was a remarkable and spontaneous attempt by thousands of revolutionary youths to discharge their debt to the peasantry. Abroad, especially in Zurich, many of them had imbibed populist doctrines. When the Russian government took fright at reports of the influences to which they were being subjected and summoned them to return home, they went eagerly. Fired by Herzen's injunction, "Go to the people!" they moved into the country districts to preach the new gospel in the villages. Peasant reactions varied from polite mystification to outright hostility. The sole success of the "going to the people" movement came in its later stages as the result of a trick, when a few students provoked a minor uprising in Chigirin by persuading the peasants that the Emperor wanted them to attack the nobles who were frustrating his intention to grant them more land.

After their failure to arouse the peasantry in 1873–1874, the populists organized a society called *Land and Liberty (Zemlia i Volia)*. When used as the slogan of the old serf revolts and afterward, this phrase had been understood by the peasants to mean that they should receive land as their own possession and liberty from the obligations imposed by the state and their landlords, from the interference of officialdom in their own affairs, and perhaps something more. The populists were less interested in what the peasants understood by "land and liberty" than in what, in their view, it ought to mean. They had little patience with the peasants' religious outlook or their desire for property.

The men of *Land and Liberty* shared a positivist epistemology, a naturalist metaphysics, and devotion to the Western ideal of socialism. Like the Western socialists, they found repellent the realities of contemporary Western society. They disliked Victorian delicacy, industrial slums and factory miseries, and bourgeois parliamentarism. They had enough of their Western contemporaries' "realism" to appreciate that socialist Utopias are not to be had for the asking. The inexorable processes of history, they felt, were on their side, although they clung to the belief that the "critically-thinking individual" could channel and utilize these processes in order to create a good society. The revolutionary should be able to discern the germ of future development within the institutions given by the past.

The populists placed their hopes in the peasant commune. The Slavophiles had believed it to be a survival of the ancient and virtuous Russian feeling of "corporateness" (*sobornost'*) in a Christian sense, but the populists saw in it the nucleus of the future socialist order. In the "going to the people" movement, they had striven to bring what they regarded as the true nature of the commune into the consciousness of the peasants. Since they had failed completely, what should they attempt to do next?

Some fiery, impatient spirits believed they could frighten the government into making concessions by murdering a few high officials—preferably personally reprehensible ones, but not necessarily. The terrorists registered a number of notorious successes, but other populists recoiled from assassination, regarding it either as evil or historically useless. In 1879 *Land and Liberty* split in two over the issue. The terrorists formed a group known as *The People's Will (Narodnaia Volia)*, the antiterrorists another called *The Black Partition (Chërnyi Peredel)*.[2] Agents of *The People's Will* embarked on a series of fantastic adventures, even penetrating the Winter Palace and blowing up the Imperial dining room in a vain attempt to kill Alexander II. In 1881 they succeeded in assassinating him, but the police caught the culprits and tracked down their associates. There have been few more grotesque tragedies than that of the execution or imprisonment of the deeply moral and humanitarian boys and girls

• [2] The name referred to the distribution of gentry or state lands to the peasantry for which the peasants hoped.

who had in their zeal murdered the ruler who perhaps had done more to improve the lot of the Russian people than any other single person in their history.

Following the assassination of Alexander II, a "dead period" set in for the revolutionary movement. For a decade there were no further serious attempts at party organization or political action of any kind. Many populists turned to literary work and economic and historical writing. The zemstvo liberals, who had failed to persuade Alexander II to grant a constitution to Russia, had no hope that Alexander III (1881–1894) would do so. They watched glumly and impotently as his most influential advisers attempted to reverse the policy of the Great Reforms of his murdered predecessor. By 1883 the liberal assistants of Alexander II had been thrust aside. The question was less whether domestic improvement could be achieved, either through further reform or by revolution, than whether the inroads of reaction could be held within bounds.

In 1883 there occurred in far-off Switzerland a political conversion whose significance lies solely in much later events, yet one which began a series of developments fateful for Russia and the world. George Plekhanov, a follower of *The Black Partition,* abandoned populism and embraced Marxism.

At that moment the Russian intelligentsia was apparently farther away than ever from state power. The Decembrists had been friends and associates of Alexander I; Herzen, although not on good terms with Nicholas I, knew him personally. Since then the gulf of ideas between the throne and the intelligentsia had become unbridgeable, while the gulf of social origin had grown so wide that mutual understanding even on the level of feelings was virtually impossible. The battle between the regime and the revolutionaries was irrevocably joined. It was to be fought in two phases. The first began in the 1890's and ended in the abortive Revolution of 1905; the second commenced shortly afterward and led to the successful uprising of 1917. The question whose importance was long misconceived by both antagonists was: What role would be played by the giant, silent bystander in this struggle, the Russian people?

Marxism Comes to Russia

★
★
★
★
★
★
★
★
★
★

CHAPTER 3

THE RUSSIAN RECEPTION OF MARX

The failures of the revolutionary movement in the 1870's led Plekhanov and others to reject the central teachings of populism. The moral obligation to serve the common people was discarded in favor of the morally neutral doctrine of historical inevitability; faith in the peasant as the vehicle of revolution yielded to a reliance on the industrial worker; the attempt to build a new society from the foundations upward, starting with the commune, was abandoned, and it was decided that the central government must be taken over if social change was to be effective. In summary, the revolutionaries should prepare for the inevitable march of the proletariat toward state power, and this was precisely the teaching of Karl Marx.

No man was ever such a failure in his lifetime and such a success afterward as Marx. That he should require substantial treatment in a work devoted to twentieth-century Russia is only a part of the evidence supporting this fact. Although his principles were modified in theory and practice by his followers in various ways, probably no single individual outside the great religions has ever preached doctrines which have had a greater impact on humanity than his. To be sure, Marx himself never intended to "preach a doctrine," least of all one universally applicable without modification or extension. He believed he was merely discovering the meaning of history; when men understood that meaning, they would be able to act with an understanding and a foresight denied to all previous generations.

Marx's philosophy came to Russia not as a surprise or sudden importation, but after the Western thinkers whom he acknowledged as his predecessors had already become known in Russia in their own right. If British political economy, French Utopian socialism, and German idealist philosophy were the forerunners of Marxism in the West, so were they in Russia. Adam Smith and David Ricardo were read and discussed in the early nineteenth century; Saint-Simon and Fourier were popular in the Petrashevsky circle, whose members attempted to establish a Fourierian phalanstery in the 1840's. In the same decade differences of view about Hegel had led to the end of personal friendships within the circle of Herzen and his friends. Russians had been at least as interested in Hegel as Germans had been, as interested in Saint-Simon as Frenchmen. The men whose thought formed the raw material of Marx's ideas were well known to Russians before he actually put his system on paper.

THE DEVELOPMENT OF MARX'S THOUGHT

Karl Marx was born in the German Rhineland in 1818, the son of a Jew who had become a Protestant. By the age of twenty he had entered the University of Berlin and joined a circle of young Hegelians there. What appealed to Marx in Hegel's thought was his conception of the universe as a single whole, in which every bit and piece was related to every other one, in contrast to the older British empiricism, which tended to look at the bits and pieces carefully and separately. Hegel saw mankind as one organism, living and evolving, and he glorified man's reason, which would make the world itself reasonable as man came to understand the reason which resided in things. Thus for Hegelians there was no sharp division between the realms of thinking and being; or, as Hegel himself put it, "The real is the rational, and the rational is the real."

However, Hegel was not so naive as to think that gradual and smooth progress had been the law of history. He interpreted history as a series of sharp, sometimes ugly, stabs and jerks forward and backward, as the net result of which a civilization or mankind as a whole moved forward. This type of motion was conceived to resemble the rhythm of an intelligent dialogue, as Socrates had talked to his pupils, and Hegel therefore termed this motion "dialectical." A made an assertion, B denied it, C denied the denial—or "negated the negation"—and in so doing stated the truth more accurately than either A or B had done. The idea of ancient Oriental civilization had been that one (the despot) is free; of classical civilization, that some (the citizens) are free; Germanic civilization affirmed that every man is free. He is, and ought to be free—to Hegel what was desirable was also necessary, and so it remained to Marx.

So far Marx followed Hegel. Leaving Berlin, he returned home and then made his way to Paris. There he read the works of Ludwig Feuerbach, who examined Hegel's views on religion and concluded that his idealism embodied "the deceased spirit of theology." "Idealism" meant not that Hegel was addicted to high-flown or impossible standards or aims, but that he believed that the fundamental stuff of reality was "idea" with a capital "I," and that external objects and institutions were important only as representing ideas—as for example the state was seen as the embodiment of divine purpose, "the march of God on earth." Like Feuerbach, Marx could find no place for God in his philosophy. While he was pondering this obstacle, he met Friedrich Engels, who was two years younger than he. Engels was the son of a well-to-do manufacturer; he himself remained an affluent and pleasure-loving bourgeois while he fought, and helped and financed Marx to fight, the capitalist order.

In their attempt to cleanse Hegel of error, Marx and Engels found the thought of Saint-Simon and also Proudhon useful. What was most significant about society, the French thinkers contended, was the play of economic forces and social classes. Marx's account of his solution was that he abruptly realized that Hegel's thought was standing on its head, and what was needed was simply for it to be set upright. That is, the dialectic was the correct method of analyzing reality, but it was not mind, but matter, which constituted reality. Some sympathetic critics of Marx, like G. D. H. Cole, have suggested that what Marx really meant was that not matter but the economic process underlay human history. It is certainly true that Marx's writing dealt not with natural science but with either economic history or political history interpreted as the reflection of economic developments. Engels made a few excursions into the field of science, but they were weak at best. Nevertheless, Marx and Engels called their system dialectical materialism, in order to emphasize its difference from Hegelianism, with its smuggled-in God. One may take them at their word.

THE COMMUNIST MANIFESTO

By the middle 1840's Marxism was nearing the dimensions of a system. In the *Communist Manifesto* of 1847 Marx and Engels popularized it for the use of the Communist League, a small and unimpressive association of West European radicals. The *Manifesto* was a short pamphlet in which historical materialism (Marxian philosophy applied to human affairs) is expounded as a guide to and a prediction of action. The way goods are produced—the "mode of production"—and the structure of social classes defined in terms of how each fits into the productive process, are made the basis for all history. The classes behave in an antithetical, a dialectical manner; that is, they struggle. The battle for ownership of the means of production and for the political power which such ownership confers is incessant. Thus all history is said to be the history of class struggle between the exploiter and exploited class of the given moment. In the past there were four modes of production, the Asiatic (as found in China or India), slavery (as in Greece and Rome), feudalism (the Western Middle Ages), and capitalism (nineteenth-century England).

Part I of the *Communist Manifesto* is an application of historical materialism to the situation at the time of writing. The rise of the bourgeoisie and its positive contributions and features are traced, as well as the emergence of its negative characteristics, preparing the way for its destruction. Part II adds to the historical exposition a doctrine of politics. Marx wrote elsewhere that "because the living conditions of the proletariat represent the focal point of all inhuman conditions in contemporary society, because the human being is lost in the proletariat, but has won a theoretical consciousness of loss and is compelled by unavoidable and absolutely compulsory need—the practical expression of necessity—to revolt against this humanity, the proletariat can and must emancipate itself." In the *Manifesto* he declared that the "Communist Party"—at that time no such organization, properly speaking, existed—was the most progressive and resolute section of the working class of all countries, and that its one objective was to destroy all bourgeois governments and carry the proletariat to political power in all countries.

Part III of the *Manifesto* consists of an attack on all other socialist factions, each of which is interpreted as an expression of the interests of some class other than the proletariat and therefore dangerous to the cause of Communism. Part IV deals with other left-wing political parties, indicating the usefulness of short-term alliances with certain of them to achieve the overthrow of "feudal" regimes or to weaken existing "bourgeois" governments. Special mention is made of Germany, "because that country is on the eve of a bourgeois revolution that is bound to be carried out under more advanced conditions of European civilization and with a much more developed proletariat than that of England" or France at the time of their "bourgeois revolutions." Here was a text of particular interest to Russian Marxists. Russia presumably could benefit from the same factors which applied to Germany and thus might win a speedy victory in crossing over the barriers from feudalism to capitalism to socialism.

MARX AND RUSSIA

Unfortunately the *Manifesto,* as E. H. Carr points out, was deficient in two respects which were to cause Lenin difficulty in applying Marxism to Russia.[1] The problems of nationalism and the peasantry were passed over briefly. The proletariat was said to "have no country." Consequently the orthodox Marxists of Russian Poland, for example, taking Marx at his word, refused to consider any plan for a Polish nation; as a result they remained insignificant in strength, while another group which called itself the Polish Socialist Party (P.P.S.), but was openly nationalist, attracted wide support. For the same reason the intellectuals of such borderlands as Armenia, Georgia, and the Baltic states gravitated to populism more often than to Marxism. Lenin's tortuous attempts to solve the "national question," in which efforts he found Stalin useful, were for a long time fruitless if measured by the growth of Bolshevism among the national minorities of the Empire. Marx's treatment of the peasants was an even more serious problem for the Marxists in Russia. He noted the service of capitalism to mankind in rescuing people from the "idiocy of rural life" and lumped peasants with small shopkeepers and the like as "petty bourgeoisie." Lenin made heroic efforts to compensate for such cavalier treatment of the group which made up the overwhelming majority of the whole population of the country, but Marx was no help to him.

Of course Marx did not have Russia particularly in mind in writing the *Manifesto.* He did make several later comments, especially in the preface written jointly with Engels to a Russian edition of the *Manifesto.* "Today," they declared, "Russia forms the vanguard of revolutionary action in Europe"; and they ended with the conditional but optimistic prophecy, "If the Russian Revolution becomes the signal for a proletarian revolution in the West, so that both complement each other, the present Russian common ownership of land may serve as the starting point for a communist development." Here Marx suggested an even more prodigious leap in history than the one he hoped for in Germany: from a mode of

• [1] Edward Hallett Carr, *Studies in Revolution* (London: Macmillan, 1950), pp. 25–37.

production at least partly primitive-communist, over slavery, feudalism, and capitalism to communism.

In fact the Russian Marxists paid little attention to the allusion to primitive communism and most often spoke as if Russia were basically "feudal," though rapidly developing a capitalist sector in its economy. It was tidier to do so, and also less embarrassing, for their ideological adversaries, the populists, had long said that the Russian peasant commune could develop directly into rural socialism. The fact that Marx himself said the very same thing, and repeated it in a letter to a populist leader, could be forgiven only because Marx died in the same year that Russian Marxism was born.

MARX'S LATER YEARS

The *Communist Manifesto* predicted revolution, and revolution actually followed in a matter of weeks. In 1848 almost every great capital of Europe was shaken by turmoil, but within a year the republican or radical forces had been routed. Communism also seemed to be a lost cause, not that its "specter" to which Marx referred in the *Manifesto* had materialized in 1848; among the revolutionaries had appeared certain of the radical groupings which he criticized, but no "Communists" had been visible. Nevertheless for Marx, as for orthodox Marxists ever since, failure was regarded as temporary and hopes were simply deferred.

In 1853 Marx withdrew from overt political activity to spend his days in the British Museum in London reading and writing. For a decade he was occupied with a work on political economy. From Manchester Engels helped him through more than one crisis in the family finances; Marx declared wryly, "I don't suppose anyone has ever written about 'money' and suffered such a lack of it himself." But he managed to publish the first volume of *Capital* in 1867, and for the rest of his life he worked on the remaining two volumes, which were published by Engels after his death. The whole work included both a theoretical exposition of the nature of the "capitalist" economic system and a history of modern capitalism.

During Marx's later years he witnessed the formation of the First International Workingmen's Association in 1864, the war of the Paris Commune in 1871, and the consequent collapse of the International as a result of dashed hopes and government repression. In writing about the Commune, Engels hailed its "shattering of the former State power and its replacement by a new and really democratic State." At the same time he warned against the retention of the state in any form, and traced the "superstitious reverence" for the state to the conception that the state is "the Kingdom of God on earth"; in other words, to Hegel. Lenin was to expand these comments on what the proletariat ought to do with the state in his pamphlet of 1917, *The State and Revolution.*

At the last Marx was puzzled and pleased to note that *Capital* was translated into Russian before any other foreign language, in 1872, by a populist named Danielson ("Nikolai-on" was his pen name), and that like some earlier works, it sold well in Russia. He was hopeful that the Russo-Turkish War of 1877–1878 might lead to Russian defeat and thereby bring the Russian revolution closer. In 1883 he died.

THE TEACHINGS OF MARXISM

According to Vilfredo Pareto, Marxism is like a bat: some see in it a mouse, others a bird. Our concern here is less with what Marx's followers made of his ideas than with which of them he himself believed to be fundamental. As a matter of fact, Marx was probably understood by posterity as well as any theorist who advocated doctrines of comparable complexity. It is a tribute to his intelligibility that even revisionist Marxists knew quite well which of his teachings they were discarding and which they were accepting. Even if they wanted a mouse, they knew they had to extract it from a bat.

Briefly and simply, Marxism begins with two basic propositions. First, matter exists and nothing else does. Second, matter changes constantly in accordance with the "laws" of the dialectic; that is, it changes by the interpenetration of opposites, through which quantitative change becomes qualitative and the antithesis of a given thesis is itself denied to form a new synthesis, and so on over and over again. The two propositions combine to form the philosophy of dialectical materialism. That aspect of it which undertakes to explain history is known as historical materialism. The body of this doctrine can be stated in Marx's own words:

> In the social production of their means of existence men enter into definite, necessary relations which are independent of their will, productive relationships which correspond to a definite stage of development of their material productive forces. The aggregate of these productive relationships constitutes the economic structure of society, the real basis on which a juridical and political superstructure arises, and to which definite forms of social consciousness correspond. The mode of production of the material means of existence conditions the whole process of social, political and intellectual life. It is not the consciousness of men that determines

their existence, but, on the contrary, it is their social existence that determines their consciousness. At a certain stage of development the material productive forces of society come into contradiction with the existing productive relationships, or, what is but a legal expression for these, with the property relationships within which they had moved before. From forms of development of the productive forces these relationships are transformed into their fetters. Then an epoch of social revolution opens. With the change in the economic foundation the whole vast superstructure is more or less rapidly transformed. In considering such revolutions it is necessary always to distinguish between the material revolution in the economic conditions of production, which can be determined with scientific accuracy, and the juridical, political, religious, aesthetic or philosophic—in a word, ideological forms wherein men become conscious of this conflict and fight it out. Just as we cannot judge an individual on the basis of his own opinion of himself, so such a revolutionary epoch cannot be judged from its own consciousness; but on the contrary this consciousness must be explained from the contradictions of material life, from the existing conflict between social productive forces and productive relationships. A social system never perishes before all the productive forces have developed for which it is wide enough; and new, higher productive relationships never come into being before the material conditions for their existence have been brought to maturity within the womb of the old society itself. Therefore, mankind always sets itself only such problems as it can solve; for when we look closer we will always find that the problem itself only arises when the material conditions for its solution are already present or at least in process of coming into being. In broad outline, the Asiatic, the ancient, the feudal and the modern bourgeois modes of production can be indicated as progressive epochs in the economic system of society. Bourgeois productive relationships are the last antagonistic form of the social process of production—antagonistic in the sense not of individual antagonism, but of an antagonism arising out of the conditions of the social life of individuals; but the productive forces developing within the womb of bourgeois society at the same time create the material conditions for the solution of this antagonism. With this social system, therefore, the prehistory of human society comes to a close. . . .[2]

• [2] Karl Marx, Author's Preface to *A Contribution to the Critique of Political Economy*, 1859, in Emile Burns, *A Handbook of Marxism* (New York: International Publishers, 1935), pp. 371–373.

To restate the doctrine of historical materialism, the "material productive forces" determine the "productive relationships" which are the basis of history, the social classes and the interaction between them, which has always had the character of antagonism. In other words, what is crucial to the Marxian theory of history is the concept of class struggle. A class, in Marx's view, is a function of the mode of production; it is composed of individuals whose relationship to the productive process is similar, whatever their external or conscious differences. History is the history of class struggles, but when capitalism ends it will enter a new phase. This conviction leads Marx to term all previous history "prehistory" to distinguish it from the epoch ahead, when reason and consciousness will determine mankind's actions and society will no longer be dependent on the organization of production. Until that time ideas will be derived from the economic process, and all questions about human society can be answered, as Lenin put it, by tracing them to "who exploits whom" in a given situation; in other words, who owns the means of production and who does not.

Neither in Hegel nor in Marx was there any clear distinction between the descriptive and the normative. The "is" and "ought" of history merged closely into each other. As Marx put it in his *Theses on Feuerbach,* "The philosophers have only *interpreted* the world in various ways; the point however is to *change* it." Therefore a history implied a politics; theory and practice were inseparable, and right theory and right practice were dependent one upon the other. History showed that the proletariat would win, and the self-destructive tendencies of capitalism would help bring this to pass. However, with the emergence of the "rational" to the level of the "real," the action of individuals or groups of intellectuals could be important or decisive in hastening the ultimately inevitable denouement of "prehistory." Then it would come about that, in Marcuse's phrase, "reason, when determined by rational social conditions, is determined by itself."[3] The role of human intelligence and of intellectuals was thus clearly set forth. It was the task of the scholar to forsake history as a Muse and take it up as a political and military plan of campaign.

THE POLITICS OF MARXISM

Marx did not consider himself responsible for the way in which Communist political action would have to be worked out. In reference to the Paris Commune, he suggested that the proletariat would have to seize and

• [3] Herbert Marcuse, *Reason and Revolution* (2nd ed.; New York: The Humanities Press, 1954), p. 319.

"to each according to his ability,
to each according to his need."

destroy the old state machinery, substituting simpler forms (but still state machinery) of its own as long as remnants of antagonistic classes remained to be dealt with. The new "dictatorship of the proletariat" would thereupon undertake to build a new type of economic order. In his *Critique of the Gotha Program* (of the newborn German Marxist party), Marx distinguished between two phases through which the new order would develop, "socialism" and "communism." Under both man would work according to his ability; under socialism he would be remunerated according to the amount of his work, under communism according to the extent of his need. There were a few other hints and suggestions, but no plans for organization of a Communist political party or for the state which that party would establish on the ruins of the old capitalist one. If Communism was a specter, Marx did little to make it materialize.

The transformation of Marxism into a political force was the work of others. The First International Workingmen's Association, founded in 1864, was not led by Marx, who like Engels thought congresses and meetings to be of little value. His opposition to the rather disorderly views and activities of the Russian anarchist, Michael Bakunin, led to the disruption of the International—whose members were in any case suffering from the aftermath of the Paris Commune—but he did little to organize or lead it toward positive action. The First International was, in any event, not so much an association of Communist parties as a loose federation of labor groups.

It was only in the later 1870's that Marxist parties began to be formed. In order to escape the onus of the Paris Commune they called themselves "Social Democratic" rather than "Communist." (Lenin was to negate this negation by reviving the label "Communist" during the First World War.) The first Social Democratic party, which remained the senior and strongest until the Bolshevik Revolution, was the German one. It was formed out of a merger of the followers of Ferdinand Lassalle, whose Hegelian devotion to the state had only a superficially Marxian gloss, and the German Marxists led by August Bebel and Wilhelm Liebknecht. The merger, carried through at a congress in Gotha in 1875, provoked objections from Marx which went unheeded. The German party remained an amalgam of narrow-construction Marxists with deviationists and innovators, even after it adopted a more orthodox Marxist program in 1891.

The first prominent Revisionist, Edward Bernstein, approved the development of German Social Democracy along rather empirical and reformist lines. Moreover, he attempted to provide theoretical justification for such moderation by pointing out that current economic changes disproved Marx's prophecies of the progressive impoverishment of the proletariat and the increasing concentration of capital in fewer and fewer hands. Bernstein concluded that there would be and should be no sudden cataclysmic revolution, that the proletariat was in the process of acquiring fatherlands in Western Europe, and that to assist not revolution but evolution was the proper task of the Social Democrat. Meanwhile Georg von Vollmar and other party members from the agricultural south of Germany pointed to Marx's sins of omission and commission on the agrarian problem and rejected the proposed expropriation of peasant property. Vollmar's views impressed the German party less than those of Bernstein. All orthodox Marxists regarded the elimination of peasant smallholding as essential, and in consequence a delegate to the Halle Congress of 1890 noted sadly and correctly, "We have not got as yet a single Social Democratic peasant." However, the German Marxists were sufficiently flexible to acquire a large following of industrial workers, though not enough support to reach the opportunities and dangers of national power.

The parties which were organized in the 1880's in France, Italy, Austria, Holland, Belgium, the Scandinavian countries, and England were either very weak in numbers or very broad in their Marxism. In France the orthodox Marxists under Jules Guesde remained for years a small group, and in England the followers of H. M. Hyndman never did succeed in creating a large orthodox Marxist party. Marx and Engels criticized and squabbled with Social Democratic leaders in several countries. After Marx's death, a Second International was formed in 1889, containing some groups the orthodoxy of whose Marxism was highly dubious, but purporting to be an association of Marxist political parties.

It was in 1883 that George Plekhanov became a Marxist. A Russian Marxist party was not even nominally established until 1898, and a permanent party organization came into being only in 1903. By 1883 Marx was dead; Engels lived until 1895. At Marx's graveside Engels declared, "Just as Darwin discovered the law of evolution in organic nature, so Marx discovered the law of evolution in human history. . . ." Whatever the merit of this contention, it was true that Marx's contribution to Communism was its history. Its politics remained to be worked out successfully. In the countries where the Second International was represented, the Social Democratic parties seemed to prosper to the extent that they abandoned or ignored Marxist theory. Russia was to prove no exception, but Lenin was to provide an innovation: he would ignore Marxist theory when it suited him, without abandoning belief in or the intention of realizing any fundamental part of Marx's vision.

Lenin's and other Opposition Parties

CHAPTER 4

RUSSIAN LIBERALS ORGANIZE

The conversion of Plekhanov to Marxism in 1883 marks the end of one period and the beginning of another in the growth of the revolutionary movement, but for about a decade thereafter political activity languished. The few Marxists remained in Western Europe, writing pamphlets but little else. The populists glumly contemplated the ruins of their organizations, and dispersed after the assassination of Alexander II. The liberals continued to work in the zemstvos. In 1882 one of the more radical liberals, Ivan Petrunkevich, spoke out rejecting the idea of any kind of constitution granted from "above" and echoed Herzen's demand for a Constituent Assembly. As moderates yielded to reactionaries in the entourage of Alexander III, however, the zemstvo liberals fell silent.

The accession of Nicholas II in 1894 roused modest hopes once more. A zemstvo delegation suggested in indirect language that it would be a good idea for the Tsar to grant a constitution to the Russians, as his grandfather had already been instrumental in doing for the Bulgars. However, this petition was interpreted as merely a plea that zemstvo representatives be granted legislative powers—a not wholly unreasonable interpretation—and Nicholas II promptly branded the proposal as "senseless dreams." Little more was heard from the zemstvo men for several years.

At the end of the decade the liberals took their first steps in the direction of organization. A sort of structured liberal salon, called simply *The Conversation* (*Beseda*), and an association of zemstvo liberals, the Zemstvo Union, made their appearance. In both groups could be found prominent representatives of the three liberal factions which crystallized a few years later. There were Left-liberals who followed the uncompromising stand of Ivan Petrunkevich, which brought them close to the immediate demands of the revolutionary parties; the able historian, Paul Miliukov, soon came to be their leader. They were regarded as too radical and too rationalistic by the Right-liberals, such as the lawyer Basil Maklakov, who took a more empirical and legally-oriented view. A third group consisted of the successors of the earlier Slavophiles, headed by Dmitry Shipov.

The Slavophiles of the turn of the century, like their predecessors of fifty years before, relied on the hope of establishing a new moral and emotional climate, wherein Tsar and people would through mutual confidence somehow participate together in the governing of the country without necessarily erecting any legal limitations on the power of the monarch. Shipov and his friends distrusted any attempt to solve the nation's problems by creating new institutions or passing new laws. Cut off by their ideology from any possibility of an understanding with other opposition groups of the time, they failed also to win any kind of sympathetic hearing among court circles or the bureaucracy. After the October Manifesto of 1905, which granted a kind of constitution, they became, as they themselves put it, "constitutionalists by imperial decree," and disappeared as an independent political force.

The Left- and Right-liberals were the factions from which the liberal political parties sprang. They agreed with each other that fundamental political and social reforms were essential and that some kind of constitutional regime was a prerequisite to successful reform. Miliukov and the Left-liberals were aggressive proponents of thoroughgoing change, often dragging along behind them Maklakov and others who said "but" and "wait" whenever their more impatient fellows would listen. The Left-liberals coalesced around a newspaper published abroad (as the revolutionary press was, to avoid censorship) named *Liberation* (*Osvobozhdenie*), and so became known as Liberationists. They held congresses in Western Europe and kept contact with their sympathizers inside Russia. In October 1904 in Paris they joined with certain revolutionary parties in a common manifesto calling for an end to the Tsarist regime. In fact, their fundamental strategy was to make common cause with the revolutionaries until the traditional civil liberties and a constitutional regime were wrested from the Tsar, which they expected would require some kind of demonstration of force. Once that moment came, the Left-liberals anticipated a separation of interests and a severance of friendly political relations between themselves and the extreme Left.

The Left-liberals of Russia were not addicted to the doctrines of laissez faire, the Manchester school, or the early English liberals. They favored a government in which the people would rule by universal, secret, direct, and equal suffrage—the formula of the "Four Tails," which all the leftist parties championed. They favored an executive responsible to the legislature—that is, a parliamentary system like that of Western European countries, whether or not the monarch would remain as a figurehead. As the liberal writer Kizevetter put it, they "ascribed great significance to state interference in economic relations in the interest of social justice."[1] In other words, they believed in sweeping legislation designed to improve peasant agriculture, industrial working conditions, education, and the like. Much of the improvement was intended to come through government ownership; the Left-liberals had little enthusiasm for either private enterprise in industry or independent peasant smallholding in agriculture.

The Right-liberals, such as Maklakov, were skeptical of the efficacy of wholesale reform through legislation, and thought the passage of any single measure less necessary than the establishment of the rule of law in general. They were alarmed by the willingness of Miliukov and his fellows to make common cause with the revolutionaries and to accept the slogan, "No enemy on the Left." However, their voice was largely drowned out in the radical enthusiasm which pervaded the intelligentsia of the period just preceding and during the Revolution of 1905.

Miliukov and the Liberationists concentrated their political efforts on the professional men and, more broadly, on the intelligentsia who were to the right of orthodox Marxism. They exerted a strong influence on the Group of Zemstvo-Constitutionalists which was formed in 1903, and tried to use the Group as a lever of attraction on the larger and more inclusive Zemstvo Union, which had been meeting irregularly since 1896. The Liberationists staked a good deal on their attempt to support and dominate the "professional unions"[2] established just before 1905, including

• [1] A. A. Kizevetter, *Na rubezhe dvukh stoletii* (*Vospominaniia 1881–1914*) (Prague, 1929), p. 89.

• [2] The prestige of these organizations was high, as indicated by the fact that the Russian abbreviation for them, "*profsoiuzy*," came to mean trade unions in general, and retains that meaning in contemporary Soviet usage.

unions of academicians, lawyers, agronomists, physicians, veterinarians, pharmacists, railway employees, writers, engineers and technicians, teachers, accountants, and "unions" for the Equality of Women and the Equality of Jews. The Group of Zemstvo-Constitutionalists joined the thirteen mentioned to form a Union of Unions in 1905.

However, just as the Zemstvo Union proved not radical enough for the Liberationists, the Union of Unions proved too radical for their liking. As a result, while the Revolution of 1905 was in full course, Liberationists and Zemstvo-Constitutionalists joined to form a Constitutional Democratic Party (known as "Kadets" from the Russian initials, "ka" and "de"). Into this party went the Left-liberals en masse, and also a few of the Right-liberals, like Maklakov, who still hoped that their zealous colleagues could be brought to substitute a policy of seeking all possible improvements for an all-or-nothing wager on a revolutionary upheaval. However, the majority of Right-liberals broke with the rest of the intelligentsia to form a frankly compromising party, the Union of October 17, or "Octobrist" party.[3] While the suffrage was broad, the Kadets could muster a great deal more popular support than the Octobrists, but it was soon to be limited.

THE POPULISTS REARM THEMSELVES

The populists were slow in recovering from the catastrophe of 1881, when the greatest success of terrorism—the assassination of the Emperor—had led to the destruction of their organizations. The new populist journalists, such as Nicholas Mikhailovsky and V. P. Vorontsov, attacked Western-style capitalism and asserted that it either could not or should not come to Russia. Others took steps to seek a new kind of political footing. A few, led by Mark Natanson, founded in 1893 an abortive Party of People's Right, whose aim was to bring about an alliance between populist intellectuals and liberals. However, most populists remained hostile to the liberals, contemptuously ascribing to them an attitude of *meshchanstvo* (roughly, "bourgeois-ness"), or a quasi-Victorian attachment to law, order, and orderliness.

In the early 1890's there appeared a new current in populism which was soon to become dominant. Young populists undertook propaganda work among the new factory workers of St. Petersburg, Moscow, and the provincial cities, and started to call themselves Socialist Revolutionaries (S.R.'s). Outtalked and overshadowed by the Marxists of the two capitals,

• [3] October 17 (Old Style; October 30, New Style), 1905, was the date of the issuance of the October Manifesto; see p. 77.

the new S.R.'s did win a following in the provinces: in Minsk, Saratov, Tambov, and elsewhere. Establishing contact with a parallel current among populist *émigrés* in Western Europe, they attempted to found a political party in 1898, but the police moved in and action was postponed.

Even after the Marxists began their activities in Russia, the police continued to regard the populists as the most dangerous revolutionary group. They had spawned one terrorist organization and presumably might soon produce another, while the Marxists opposed terrorism (like the populists of the *Black Partition,* they considered it historically useless) and seemed to be most interested in talking and writing. The police's fear of a renewal of violence was well founded. Beginning at the turn of the century, a new generation of would-be political assassins appeared in the ranks of the S.R. movement. The S.R. leaders were not enthusiastic about terrorism, but they did not oppose it in principle, nor did they want the new populism to be split, as its predecessor had been in 1879, by a debate over the value of terrorist tactics.

The problem was solved by setting up a "Battle Organization" within the party. In effect the group was urged to go off and do its dirty work without unduly bothering the rest of the S.R.'s. Though its numbers were small, it included some of the most prominent party members, such as Gregory Gershuni, a capable and dynamic leader, and Evno Azef, a puzzling figure who for years served simultaneously as a vigorous and creative S.R. theorist and terrorist and as an apparently loyal agent of the Tsarist secret police.

The Battle Organization managed to assassinate a number of key officials; they killed two successive ministers of interior, Sipiagin in 1902 and Plehve in 1904, Grand Duke Sergei, governor-general of Moscow, in 1905, and many lesser officials. The effect of these murders without malice was not only to attract attention to the S.R.'s, but also to mobilize public sympathy for the apprehended assassins rather than for the murdered men. For example, Kaliaev, who killed Sergei, aroused widespread approval by his apology to the widowed grand duchess, but little thought seemed to be given to her late husband. The main concern of the S.R. leaders was that such activity should not claim a disproportionate share of the party's energies, and they concentrated on the less melodramatic objectives of mass agitation and propaganda.

The new populism found its chief theorist in Victor Chernov, who came from Tambov. During the 1890's the attention of the whole intelligentsia was fixed on the debates between the Marxists and the populists. The controversy shook the youth as nothing else had done since the Westernizer-Slavophile polemics of the 1840's. At the start the issue seemed to be, should, or would, capitalism come to Russia? The Marxists refused to discuss "should," but declared that capitalism not merely would come, but had arrived. The populists cried that it should not, but they became increasingly touchy about the facts as urban industry grew rapidly and visibly. The Marxists spoke from the strong ground of a sophisticated and complex doctrine and never lacked an answer even if it did not entirely conform to the facts. The doctrinal foundations of populism had never been overly firm, and the populists of the nineties were often a trifle vague on the subject of first principles. Chernov listened to a debate at which an elderly populist, baited by the Marxists into stating his "program," shouted, "I'll tell you! It is propaganda, agitation, terror!" When prodded to explain what ends these instruments were intended to reach, the old man was only reduced to mute rage. Chernov concluded that he had to do better than that.

His point of departure was a recognition of the arrival of capitalism in Russia. Therefore the new populism had to orient itself toward the factory as well as the village and include the industrial proletariat within the "people" from whom the populists had taken their name. Marxist historical teachings about the course of industrial capitalism he accepted with few reservations, but he found what Marx had to say about the effects of capitalism on agriculture unsatisfactory. In fact, in his better-known writings Marx devoted very little space to that subject and never displayed great concern for the welfare of the peasantry. In accepting the cause of the urban workers as his own, Chernov did not forget or minimize the old populist devotion to their peasantry—or to their image of it. Chernov pointed to the text from Marx's own preface to the Russian edition of the *Communist Manifesto,* suggesting that in Russia socialism might build directly on the village commune. He admitted that the proletariat would be the vanguard of the coming revolution, but he insisted that the peasantry would play the role of "the fundamental, main army"; he thought that the socialized enterprise in the city would find its counterpart in a reorganized commune as the unit for rural production.

Much of Marxism was uncongenial to Chernov. Like his populist forebears, he emphasized the role of the will, of passion, of creativity as against the doctrine of determinism. He deprecated "the intellectual seductions of Marxism, corrupting in its symmetry." But he wanted to make common cause with the Marxists, as he was willing to accept liberal collaboration for what be believed it was worth, in order to overthrow Tsarism and launch a revolutionary regime aiming at socialism. He still was suspicious of liberal *meshchanstvo,* as he scented hidden leanings in that direction among the Marxists. In the S.R. view, the Marxists harbored too much fondness for capitalism and all its fruits. Later the S.R.'s acquired the reputation for being "moderate" socialists, but this can be more easily explained by the size and heterogeneity of the party in 1917 than by its official doctrines. In the early 1900's, there was no doubt in the minds of the S.R.'s that it was they, not the Marxists, who stood on the far Left.

Following the lead of Chernov, the S.R.'s managed to start an underground newspaper called *Revolutionary Russia,* and from among its contributors and sympathizers to form a "party" at a conference held in Kharkov in 1900. Within a year or two several other like-minded Russian and *émigré* groups became affiliated with the new party. First came the newspaper and then the organization; the same sequence of events applied to the Liberationists and the Marxists as well. The fiery heat generated by the polemics of Russian revolutionary journalism, the denunciations and charges provoked by a phrase here or an article there, the great impact of all this on organizational activity—these things were natural concomitants of a situation in which the revolutionaries operated at great distances from one another and often from their homeland, subject to police surveillance abroad and the constant danger of arrest of persons and confiscation of presses within Russia.

From the new S.R. organization came a steady flow of pamphlets to workers and peasants, who called them "the little books," and seldom understood them very well. There sprang up an S.R. Peasant Union[4] and a whole network of local party committees, some of which leaned toward close liaison with Marxist groups, provoking horror in the Marxist leaders and deep uneasiness among the S.R.'s in the national organization. The S.R.'s established working relations with certain small autonomist, liberal, or socialist groups among the intelligentsia of the Caucasus, the Baltic states, and other borderlands. The S.R.'s and their minor allies dominated a conference of opposition parties held in Paris in October 1904. The Liberationists attended the meeting, but the Marxists, after first suggesting that they might come, not only absented themselves but denounced the whole affair as "bourgeois" in character.

THE RISE OF RUSSIAN MARXISM

From the beginning Russian Marxists confronted a dilemma which did not trouble Western Marxists. Russia, they declared, was in a feudal or semifeudal stage. Their more careful theorists discussed complications

• [4] Not to be confused with the All-Russian Peasant Unions of 1905 and later, which had no official party affiliation.

caused either by the commune, which might be a survival of primitive communism, or by the fact that prior to the Great Reforms half the Russian peasantry lived on state land, which suggested Asiatic society. However, practical politics left little room for qualification, and the basic assumption of the Russian Marxists was that the "ruling class" in Russia was the gentry, or a mixture of the gentry and the rising industrial bourgeoisie. Capitalism was the next stage, and as a mode of production was already rapidly spreading in Russia. The next political development was thus bound to be a bourgeois revolution, through which the capitalists would take over the state and settle down for a period of full and unrestrained development of capitalism.

This was the first and most logical conclusion drawn from elementary Marxism, and it did not please the Russian Marxists at all. They thereupon introduced more palatable complications. They pondered Marx's suggestion in the *Communist Manifesto* that in the Germany of 1848, owing to the presence of a highly developed proletariat within Germany and the proximity of a ripened capitalism in England and France, the Marxists might lead the way from "feudalism" very rapidly through, or skip over, capitalism into the socialist era. Then they looked again at Russia and pointed gleefully to a high concentration of industry in a few localities, an industry characterized by a high proportion of very large plants employing many workers; they looked hopefully westward, to see capitalism in full bloom in Germany, France, England, and the United States; and they concluded that a world proletarian revolution, in which Russia could take part, was already on the horizon.

So far the Russian Marxists moved more or less in step with one another. Having vanquished their populist foes in the debates of the 1890's, sending them either scurrying to the cover of a semi-Marxism or silencing them altogether, they proceeded to examine one another and detect a disturbing variety of deviations from Marxist orthodoxy. They had been zealous about proving that capitalism was inevitable and imminent for the Russian economy; they now had to take note of a few writers who were going on to say that it was a good thing, too. Such men, including Peter Struve and others, were dubbed "legal Marxists."[5] Their doctrine was actually a Russian variant of German Revisionism, which, following Edward Bernstein, held that Marx had failed to foresee that capitalism would not bring about either its own violent destruction or

• [5] This was a slightly misleading term, since such orthodox Marxist writers as Plekhanov had also managed to get books past Tsarist censors and thus published in the legal press, but most Marxists who published legally were not orthodox.

the impoverishment of the proletarian masses. The Revisionists therefore advised efforts directed toward reform rather than revolution. By the mid-1890's the Russian Revisionists had not been silenced, but it was made clear to them that they were not wanted in Marxist ranks—not that many of them wanted to stay.

The theoretical heresy of "legal Marxism" was almost at once replaced by the practical heresy of "Economism." Russia's new industries experienced their first great strikes in 1895–1897. One result was that the government was forced into legislating a limitation (see pp. 70 and 100) on the working day. The Marxist leaders who had agitated among the workers felt they deserved the credit for this, and having achieved one such success ought to work for more like it. The group of St. Petersburg Marxists who published the newspaper *Workers' Cause* advocated further struggle for improved hours, wages, and working conditions—that is, emphasis on "economic" activity. Lenin (who was himself arrested at the time of the St. Petersburg strikes), Plekhanov, and others denounced this group. It was charged with abdicating the leadership of the *political* struggle, always the Marxists' first order of business, and thus allowing the liberals to move into the breach.

When Lenin, the future Bolshevik leader, and Julius Martov, the future Menshevik leader, emerged from Siberian exile in 1900, they were at one with all the veteran theorists of Russian Marxism—Plekhanov, Axelrod, Zasulich, and others—in setting as their first task the destruction of "Economism." To this end, and to provide a theoretical center around which a party could be organized, they founded a newspaper. It was called *The Spark* (*Iskra*) in allusion to Pushkin's remark about the Decembrists, "From the spark will come the flame." *The Spark* began to appear in 1900. Lenin attacked the Economists in a long pamphlet entitled *What is to be Done?* in 1902. By 1903 the orthodox leaders who had been publishing *The Spark* thought their job was done, and a party congress was summoned in Brussels (it moved to London in a few days). At this meeting the Economist heresy was given formal burial. The *Spark* group celebrated victory, and then abruptly split irretrievably in two.

BOLSHEVIKS AND MENSHEVIKS

Like the S.R.'s, the Marxists had attempted to found a party in 1898 but had been dispersed by the police. At the II Congress in 1903 (the number "I" was assigned to the hapless 1898 Congress), there was established a Russian Social Democratic Labor Party, on the basis of adherence to orthodox Marxism. In fact, however, what the congress founded was not one party but two. During the sessions there took shape two opposed factions, Bolsheviks and Mensheviks. The names mean "majority men" and "minority men" respectively, referring originally to the two sides on a vote taken in the congress about the make-up of a new editorial board for *The Spark*. Prior to this vote Lenin's faction was outnumbered, and he acquired a scant majority only after a good deal of complicated maneuvering took place. He then promptly labeled his faction the Majority, which proved as shrewd of him as it was fatuous of Martov to accept the permanent designation of the Minority.

At the congress, the issue between Bolsheviks and Mensheviks seemed to be whether a rigid or a broad criterion was to be used for selection of a party member. In *What is to be Done?* Lenin had already contended that the party leadership should consist of a small group of "professional revolutionaries," rather than the sort of more or less accidental leadership which might take over at any moment in a mass party. However, close attention had not been paid to the reason Lenin wanted a tightly controlled party direction. It has been said that in a mass party, there was danger that the Tsar's detectives might penetrate the ranks. But in 1902 neither Azef, Malinovsky, nor any of the other double agents had suffered the exposure which later embarrassed the revolutionary parties. Lenin's argument was that a tight leadership was needed for self-defense, not so much against Tsarism as against the bourgeoisie, against the liberals who would always try to take over the workers' movement and introduce "mere trade-unionist" ideas in place of revolutionary political objectives. What Lenin feared was an effort to "convert Social Democracy into a democratic reformist party . . . to introduce bourgeois ideas and bourgeois elements into socialism."[6] In order to prevent the liberals from infiltrating Marxism with their men and their ideas, he deemed it essential to choose party members with the utmost care.

Lenin believed that the Economist camp was already so infiltrated, and that the Mensheviks were willing to open the way to such infiltration. Yet while he charged the Economists with neglecting the political struggle, the Mensheviks agreed with their fellows in the *Spark* group (indeed the majority of the *Spark* writers became Mensheviks) in emphasizing political work as the paramount necessity. Wherein then did the difference between Bolsheviks and Mensheviks really lie?

All the orthodox Marxists of *The Spark* thought that Russia, under conditions of developed European capitalism, could pass rapidly from feudalism of sorts through capitalism to socialism or, putting the matter

• [6] From *What is to be Done? The Essentials of Lenin* (2 vols.; London: Lawrence & Wishart, 1947), Vol. I, p. 154.

in political terms, could bring about a socialist revolution not long after a bourgeois revolution occurred. Lenin, building on the work of J. A. Hobson and others, was later to explain that capitalism had been able to prolong its life in Europe through exploitation of overseas areas, and further to argue that it had become even more international in character since Marx's time. Therefore a decisive blow at one part of the capitalist system would certainly involve the whole of the system. Lenin applied his theory of imperialism, "the highest stage of capitalism," to Russia by contending that Russia was part of the exploiting imperialist network, insofar as it had its own capitalist class and exploited its own "backward" eastern areas, and at the same time was partly a victim of the machinations of French, German, and other West European capitalists through large investments and loans. Lenin hoped that the Western proletariat, especially through the strong German Social Democratic party, would be able to contribute mightily to the general overthrow of capitalism, but he intended that the Russian party should also take a prominent role and perhaps even initiate the whole upheaval.

At this point the divergencies between Bolsheviks and Mensheviks emerge. The Mensheviks believed that, while it was true that a proletarian revolution might break out all over Europe in a crisis, the Russian Marxists could not speculate on such an event. Their task was first to help bring about a bourgeois revolution in Russia which could involve the vigorous and even leading participation of the proletariat, although it was bound to promote the interests of the bourgeoisie. The Marxists might push the bourgeois liberals into a degree of radicalism not native or congenial to them, but the Marxists could not take the government into their hands themselves without setting themselves socialist tasks—tasks which at that historical stage they could not possibly fulfill. Therefore there was no other way for Marxists to take part in the political events they believed imminent without allying themselves with liberal elements. As Plekhanov wrote, "a significant interval" must separate bourgeois and proletarian revolutions, and any attempt by Marxists to seize and hold power during that interval would inevitably discredit Russian Social Democracy, since the proletariat would demand socialist measures which were not in the power of the socialists to give at that time.

Lenin and the Bolsheviks repudiated this view. They agreed that at the outset the revolution must be "bourgeois." However, the bourgeois liberals were contemptible beyond any hope of redemption and useless as political allies. Therefore the correct method of participating in the bourgeois revolution was through alliance with the most numerous of that element in Russia, namely the peasantry. Since the peasantry as a whole was being drawn more and more into agricultural capitalist relations and strove to free its property from precapitalist fetters, the peasant masses could bring about the bourgeois revolution under proper leadership—that is, under the guidance of the proletariat and its Marxist spokesmen. When the revolution was victorious, there would be set up a "revolutionary democratic dictatorship of proletariat and peasantry," without the participation of any bourgeois liberals. The unfolding of the revolution in the West might open the way to the second stage, that of proletarian revolution; or, if this did not occur immediately, the Russian proletariat, no longer together with all the peasantry, but still with the poorest, semiproletarian peasant elements, could pass on to socialist revolution and the construction of a socialist order.

The Mensheviks counted on what could be done by a loosely organized, mass party of workers. They had little fear of bourgeois liberal infiltration; they had little trust in or hope for what the peasantry might do. The Bolsheviks feared the liberals would successfully subvert a loose party, and so favored a tightly-knit and exclusive one; they expected a great peasant revolt which, lacking any conscious leadership of its own, would follow the lead of the Social Democrats. These were the clashing views of the two wings of Russian Marxism as expressed in analysis and tactics. The emotional roots of the clash can be traced to Lenin's deep-seated fear and hatred of the liberals and of everything "bourgeois," which disrupted the united front of the editors of *The Spark* at the II Congress and from then on provoked taunts and suspicions of "Jacobinism," "Blanquism," "dictatorial tendencies," and the like.

One gifted Marxist who was present at the II Congress never became an adherent of either the Menshevik or the Bolshevik view as just outlined, nor did he become a wholehearted and loyal member of either faction, although he was a Menshevik for a time and later on joined the Bolsheviks. He was Leon Trotsky, born Bronstein, son of a Jewish farmer of the Ukraine. Trotsky was troubled by the split in the party mainly because he thought it had occurred over the wrong issue. Like the Mensheviks, he placed no hope in the peasantry; like the Bolsheviks, he hated the bourgeois liberals. Precisely because he found no trustworthy allies for the proletariat within Russia, he emphasized most strongly the need to find them outside, in the industrial workers of Western Europe. Russia would pass directly from the bourgeois to the proletarian stage—through what he called "uninterrupted" or "permanent" revolution—with the help of the workers of Germany and other nations of the West. Trotsky was to devote his best efforts to patching up party differences—in vain—from 1903 to 1917, when he became convinced that Lenin had adopted the views he had long espoused, and he was then belatedly received into Bolshevik ranks.

Following the II Congress, Russian Social Democrats found themselves divided in two. The Bolsheviks had the party Central Committee, but no newspaper, for the Mensheviks gained control of *The Spark* and then, a few months later, the Central Committee as well. Lenin was not daunted. Both Marxist factions organized workers' groups and party committees in widely scattered areas of Russia; at the local level the differences between Bolsheviks and Mensheviks were seldom as clearly stated or understood, or produced such antagonisms, as among the top leaders. When big strikes erupted in the south of Russia in 1903 and the war with Japan began in 1904, there was ample opportunity for revolutionary agitation, and for the time being factional differences yielded the spotlight to the exigencies of mass action and street fighting.

For ten years prior to the Revolution of 1905 and during the decade which followed, the intelligentsia devoted much of their energies to underground propaganda, agitation, and debates over the future of the revolutionary movement. In part the devouring passions of the revolutionaries can be explained by their lack of opportunity for free expression and free participation in politics and government under the Tsarist regime. Such liberals as Miliukov, who understood this, expected that once free institutions and representative government came to Russia, their hotheaded socialist and revolutionary friends would calm down and acquire the qualities of moderation and reasonableness which characterized many Western Social Democrats. Miliukov did not foresee that Lenin's variety of socialism would cause any special problems, for the good reason that during the early years of the century the groups which would be called "moderate" socialists in 1917 were still behaving much like the Bolsheviks. The outlines of "Leninism" were still blurred.

LENIN AND LENINISM

Vladimir Ilich Ulianov, better known as Lenin, was born in Simbirsk in 1870. He was the son of the provincial school inspector, who had been raised to the ranks of nobility through promotion in government service, hence the legend that Lenin was a "nobleman." Probably his first contact with the events of the revolutionary movement was the arrest and execution of his eldest brother, Alexander, in 1887, for leading an unsuccessful attempt to assassinate Alexander III under the auspices of *The People's Will.*

Young Vladimir went from the Simbirsk secondary school to the University of Kazan, but was expelled after a few months for taking part in a student demonstration. It was then that he began to read Marx, and he organized a Marxist circle in Samara, where his family had moved. In 1891 he took and passed the law examinations of St. Petersburg University as an extern (that is, he never attended classes there). Returning to Samara, he neglected law practice for his Marxist circle, and in 1893 he moved on to St. Petersburg and full-time revolutionary activity for good. At the age of twenty-three he earned himself the nickname of "The Old Man" for his ability and intensity; he laughed, not at jokes, but when he solved a knotty theoretical problem.

After his arrest in 1895 he was soon exiled to Siberia, where he was joined by Nadezhda Krupskaia, who became his wife and lifelong co-worker. Under the lenient conditions imposed on exiles in Tsarist Russia (and generally the same leniency was enjoyed by Soviet exiles during the 1920's, after which all privileges were removed), Lenin was able to have books and paper, and wrote his first major work, *The Development of Capitalism in Russia,* while he was in Siberia. The book's very title, as well as its substance, was directed against the populists. Like virtually every other book or article he ever wrote, it coupled immediate polemical purpose with exposition of general principles. Most of his later important books and pamphlets were aimed, not at adversary or competitor groups or parties, nor at the Tsarist government, whose turpitude and historical obsolescence he took for granted, but rather at other Social Democrats and even Bolsheviks. His sole philosophical work, *Materialism and Empirio-Criticism* (written in 1908), was largely an attack on fellow Bolsheviks; his two most important interpretations and extension of Marxist historical and political theory, *Imperialism, the Highest Stage of Capitalism* (1916) (see p. 112), and *The State and Revolution* (1917), assailed foreign and other Russian Social Democrats. In the sense that for him thinking and acting (indeed, fighting) could never be separated, he was a better Marxist than most. His personal life was always subordinated to his political objectives. He refused to listen to Beethoven because it made him feel weak. The story is told that he decided against pursuing one liaison because, as he told the lady, she was "not a Social Democrat," to which she amicably but accurately replied that he was "only a Social Democrat." However, being a Social Democrat, or rather a Bolshevik, meant to him, in all aspects of life, obligations of which he never lost sight during his waking hours and scarcely in his dreams.

Lenin nowhere attempts to set forth an integrated doctrine of "Leninism," partly because he was too busy with the polemical or practical needs of the moment, partly because he regarded himself as a Marxist and not the author of some new doctrine. That estimate of himself is defensible on both empirical and logical grounds: many Marxists became Leninists without consciously changing their position, and ground for Lenin's central contentions may be found in Marx. It is likewise clear that Leninism is not the only possible or existing latter-day variety of Marxism, although it is true that persons who accept Marxism fully but reject Leninism seem neither numerous nor prominent. The Trotskyites, who reject Stalin's doctrines and practices, regard themselves as both good Marxists and good Leninists. It is at any rate true that Marx did not pretend to be the author of an analysis valid for the future, but regarded future change, whose nature he did not claim to be able to predict, as certain. Lenin undertook to analyze developments subsequent to Marx's time, an undertaking of which Marx would no doubt have approved, but more important, one which the terms of Marxism itself suggested.

In extending Marxist historical analysis, Lenin sought to explain why European capitalism had prolonged its life and disappointed Marx's hope of imminent proletarian revolution (see p. 45). The Leninist analysis of imperialism was widely accepted, and is influential today in Asia and Africa even among those who are not consciously or fully Marxists or Leninists. The aspects of Lenin's doctrine which have troubled many admirers of Marx and which seem most at variance with the emphasis of Marx's chief works constitute Lenin's politics. To be sure, his argument that "professional revolutionaries" were needed to lead the proletarian party was conditioned by his view of Tsarism and his belief that bourgeois infiltration was more dangerous in the Russia of his time than elsewhere. However, he himself undertook to establish a Communist International composed of parties modeled on that of Russia, and sanctioned a tradition which has formed all Communist parties in the partly illegal and underground mold he set for the Russian party, even though its leaders may not be barred from part-time practice of another profession than revolutionism.

Lenin's prescriptions for party organization were closely linked with his strong revolutionary activism. As Alfred G. Meyer points out, "in the long range of historical perspective [Lenin] looked at the world through the eyes of Marx and subscribed to everything the latter had said about the inevitable breakdown of capitalism and the dawn of socialism. In that sense Lenin was an orthodox Marxist, and he joined other orthodox believers within the Second International in their fight against revisionism. At the same time Lenin's short-range analysis . . . tended to yield different results. In place of the fighting optimism typical of Marx, he substituted a fighting pessimism, based on the realization that things were not developing in as smooth and rapid a fashion as the Marxist algebra of revolution had foretold."[7] Out of fear that he might, at least for the time being, fail, and the perspective of revolution might fade, Lenin advocated and practiced a type of active leadership which was governed not by morality but merely by expediency, and he claimed that such leadership was not only capable of directing the cause of the whole proletariat, but moreover was indispensable to the success of that cause. Without the proper leadership of the intellectuals, proletarian class-consciousness could not develop beyond what he scornfully termed "trade-union consciousness," that is, reformist demands, and the revolution would not occur soon. Strictly speaking, it is hard to see how Lenin could ever expect it to occur at all.

In his insistence on the role of a revolutionary elite, Lenin was sharply criticized by the Mensheviks and other Social Democrats in Russia and abroad for being a follower of the Jacobins, or Blanqui, or their Russian admirers such as Tkachëv, or other populists who emphasized the importance of the "critically-thinking individual" in history. Lenin's elitist activism perhaps owed inspiration to all these sources and more, but he saw himself as involved with the problem as Marx posed it: against the background of the historical inevitability of socialism, to change the world which philosophers had so far only interpreted.

However, Lenin's teachings on party organization led him into the further problem of how the party should behave when it had attained power. There is no doubt that he took Marx's slogan, "dictatorship of the proletariat," seriously and literally. However, if the party shall lead the proletariat to power, it must certainly secure and maintain that power, and it must be ruthlessly employed against all who would undermine or weaken it, intentionally or otherwise, regardless of the class origin of the individuals concerned. Trotsky correctly foresaw that Leninism implied a situation wherein "the organization of the Party takes the place of the Party itself; the Central Committee takes the place of the organization; and finally the dictator takes the place of the Central Committee. . . ." The fact that he himself, over a decade later, shared in the dictatorship when it already lay in fewer hands than those of the Central Committee, only bears out the accuracy of his prophecy. Lenin wrote many times of the genuine democracy which would come after the revolution, but it could only be realized if the masses understood the truth of history, which was in the custody of the party elite. Lenin assumed that they would or

• [7] Reprinted by permission of the publishers from Alfred G. Meyer, *Leninism* (Cambridge, Mass.: Harvard University Press, Copyright 1957, by The President and Fellows of Harvard College), p. 84.

could come to understand and failed to ask himself what would have to be done if they did not. The unsolved practical problem he left as a legacy to his successors, including Stalin.

On the eve of the Revolution of 1905, however, such perspectives were not being weighed seriously, even by Trotsky. For a decade the Marxists, liberals, and S.R.'s had discussed and quarreled over their views of history, their expectations, their programs, within their own ranks and with rival groups. However, they were apparently united in having faith that a Russian revolution was imminent and would first bring conditions of "bourgeois" freedom and a freely chosen government. After that, it was tacitly agreed, some would confine themselves to social reform and some would go on to fight for socialism. But the "old regime" would have been destroyed root and branch: the Tsar would be stripped of his powers or his position, the Orthodox Church would be disestablished or destroyed, the peasantry would be fully enfranchised and freed from any economic or political influence of their former landlords, and Russia would become a "modern" state. None of them doubted that absolutism would soon lie behind, and democracy lie ahead. Few of them suspected what Lenin understood by "democracy," but still fewer thought that Lenin would hold in his hands the future of Russia.

The Russo-Japanese War and the Revolution of 1905

CHAPTER 5

THE REGIME OF NICHOLAS II

Nicholas II (1894–1917) was very poorly equipped by nature and nurture to cope with the new economic and political currents at work around his throne. His stern and strong-willed father, Alexander III (1881–1894), gave him a principled conservative, Constantine Pobedonostsev, as tutor, and bequeathed to him unlimited power as monarch. But his father could not give him either the strength of character or breadth of understanding which were required to deal with the endless crises of his reign.

The last Tsar lived an exemplary and tender family life. His chief moral defect lay in the duplicity he repeatedly exhibited toward his ministers. He was often gruff and curt with those in favor, expansive and warm toward those he was about to dismiss. Less than a month after his accession, he married the former Princess Alix of Hesse-Darmstadt—like every Russian consort since the time of Peter the Great (with the single exception of Nicholas's own mother), a German. It was a marriage of love, and Nicholas's affections extended to no one else but his children, four daughters and the boy Alexis, born in 1904, the joy of his parents' life. It was soon learned that Alexis suffered from hemophilia, inherited from his mother, and the desperate family's efforts to save the boy's life later led to the incredible episode of Rasputin. The deeper cause of Rasputin's influence, as well as of many of Nicholas's troubles, lay in the Tsar's refusal to concern himself with political questions and his interpretation of his duty as one confined to maintaining the autocracy as his father had passed it on to him.

From the beginning of Nicholas's reign he made this unmistakably clear. A few months after his accession he rejected the constitutionalist hints of a zemstvo delegation with the words, "Let every one know that I . . . shall safeguard the principles of autocracy as firmly and unwaveringly as did my . . . father." (see p. 51). Certain liberal elements, saddened by such intransigence, continued to hope for the co-operation of the throne in inaugurating moderate political reforms. Other liberals expected and even welcomed the gauntlet thrown down by the Emperor; if it was to be all or nothing, revolution was the only answer. The socialists had long been of this opinion and remained so.

The ingredient lacking to make a revolution had not been the will of the revolutionary intelligentsia, nor an autocrat striking an uncompromising pose—Alexander III was a quite unequivocal absolutist. What had been wanting was expression of mass dissatisfaction with the regime. The villages had long known chronic discontent, but before 1902 there were many years without peasant riots, and jacqueries had been proverbially unsuccessful in bringing about political changes anyway. However, the new urban working class, together with school and university student bodies widely permeated with revolutionary ideas, provided a tinder which the radical parties were rapidly learning to set aflame. Mass demonstrations and violence became endemic during the reign of Nicholas II, provoked by imperial or bureaucratic ineptitude, or by conditions for which the regime was not responsible but with which it failed to deal effectively. The failures of the government to meet the crises which developed during the Russo-Japanese War, and later during World War I, were decisive in encompassing its own downfall.

REACTION AND OPPRESSION

Nicholas II carried on his father's nationalism, curtailment of the rights of the minority nationalities, and restrictions on non-Orthodox religious groups. Nicholas applied to Finland the measures prepared by Alexander III which were designed to limit Finnish autonomy, respected by Russian monarchs since 1809. By a manifesto of February 1899 he in effect abrogated the Finnish constitution and placed the function of making laws for Finland under the Russian Imperial Council. Both the Finns and the

Russian opposition groups reacted with sharp protests. In such borderlands as the Baltic and the Caucasus, political organizations demanding cultural autonomy or more made their appearance, especially among the Latvians, Georgians, and Armenians. Ukrainian intellectuals, who were permitted a degree of cultural freedom in neighboring Austrian Galicia, demanded similar or wider privileges from the Russian Tsar.

Although certain of Alexander III's advisers, such as Count Pahlen (who chaired a committee which recommended removal of all disabilities on the Jews), tried to restrain him, he pursued a strongly anti-Semitic policy. Jews could enroll in higher schools only under quota limits and were excluded from law practice and the zemstvos and city councils. The most influential bureaucrats feared the prominence of Jews in both the revolutionary movement and in business. St. Petersburg was sensitive to Western condemnation of anti-Semitism, however, and the government managed to keep down pogroms to a large extent up to the time of the 1903 outbreak in Kishinëv, which received world-wide publicity. By then Jewish political organizations had been formed, motivated less by any new anti-Semitic measures of Nicholas II than by his inconsistency of policy toward the Jews. In 1897 Zionism appeared with its contention that Jews must build their own exclusive nation, since everyone else insisted on building his own. A Jewish Marxist Bund was organized among the industrial workers of Poland and the Belorussian provinces.

Partly inspired by the zeal of Pobedonostsev, Christian dissenters also were persecuted. In 1894 the Stundists, a Russian variant of the Baptists, were prohibited from holding services. The pacifist Dukhobors, who had been made subject to military service like everyone else by the army reform of 1874, had migrated to Cyprus and in 1899 moved on to Canada. Their arrival there served to deepen foreign hostility to Tsarism. The fifteen per cent of the Empire's population who in 1897 were dissenters from Russian Orthodoxy had no love for the regime of Nicholas II.

Among the Orthodox Russian population, the mass movement which most encouraged the revolutionaries was the mounting wave of strikes. The industrial boom of the early 1890's led to Russia's first significant strike movement in 1895–1897. The chief official supporter of industrialization, Minister of Finance Sergei Witte, asserted bluntly that the strikes had been provoked by mismanagement, and in 1897 the government passed a law limiting working hours to eleven and a half per day, but still rounded up and punished those strike leaders whom it could find.

Certain officials, recognizing the justice of the workers' economic grievances, thought it advisable to lend them support, also hoping thereby to steal the thunder of the revolutionary agitators. S. V. Zubatov, an ex-revolutionary who had become an agent of the security police, was allowed to form workers' associations whose members were encouraged to read the books of the German Revisionist, Bernstein, and demand improvements in working conditions. This remarkable movement, which has been called "police socialism," spread rapidly in 1901–1902. In 1903, after widespread strikes had occurred in the south, the government became alarmed and tried to bring the risky experiment to an end. However, it was to be a police socialist leader, Father George Gapon, who was to organize the revolutionary demonstration of "Bloody Sunday," inaugurating the Revolution of 1905.

The university students had also begun to organize demonstrations and strikes. In 1899 a clash with the authorities of St. Petersburg University led to what was in effect a general strike in Russian higher education, and a number of student strikers were drafted into the army as punishment. In 1901 a former student (he was a Socialist Revolutionary, but was not a member of the party's Battle Organization) (see p. 55) assassinated the minister of education, Bogolepov. In vain Nicholas II tried both leniency and harshness as ways of quieting student unrest.

The S.R. Battle Organization unleashed its terrorist campaign with a series of political murders or attempted murders of provincial governors and other officials, climaxed by the killing of two successive ministers of interior, Sipiagin and Plehve, in 1902 and 1904. The zemstvo organizations, while not countenancing violence, began in 1901, after a period of inactivity, to meet for political discussion and publish liberal demands which contributed to the growth of public opposition to the regime. Finally the most dangerous form of mass action, in the view of many officials, reappeared with the peasant riots of 1902 in the Ukraine.

If Plehve, minister of interior when the Russo-Japanese War broke out, did not (as alleged) hope that a "small, victorious war" would drown the flames of unrest in a wave of patriotic fervor, he might well have done so. The revolutionary movement was growing swiftly. The rebellious intelligentsia were reaching ever-widening circles of the politically unsophisticated and providing slogans and leaders for the expression of their grievances. The government had neither the monarch, the ministers, nor the policy required to deal with the situation.

IMPERIALISM IN THE FAR EAST

In form, the foreign policy of Nicholas II was comparable to and patterned after that of the other East European monarchies, Germany and Austria-Hungary, and was not so different from that of the West European democracies, France and Great Britain. The main effort of all the great powers was not so much to win control over new territories as to preserve the European status quo. However, mutual distrust and the suspicion of a given power that another sought to change the status quo at its expense often provoked crises. Since in the last quarter of the nineteenth century most of the great powers of Europe were extending their influence and possessions in Asia and Africa, there was much friction in the latter areas and also concern as to whether imperialist gains, losses, or transfers abroad might upset the balance of interests in Europe itself.

While the Western powers operated in overseas areas, Russian imperialism was concerned with contiguous territory. Along Russia's southern borders, there lay a politically spongy and malleable band of states extending thousands of miles, from Ottoman Turkey to Manchu China, from which the Russians were excluded by British power. On the far eastern end of that band of states, however, Britain was a less important contestant than Japan, a newcomer to imperialist competition. A number of Russian officials thought Japan might safely be challenged and bested in Manchuria and Korea.

Japan's military mettle had been tested only once since her emergence from seclusion and her dramatic Westernization. In the war of 1894–1895 with the weak and crumbling Chinese Empire, Japan had won the victory. However, Russia had promptly organized diplomatic intervention of the great powers to bring about modification of the peace terms in China's favor. Russia's reward was a concession to build a railway across northern Manchuria from Chita to Vladivostok. This Chinese Eastern Railway connected with the unfinished Trans-Siberian route, which would otherwise have had to follow a much longer and more difficult course on Russian soil to the north to reach Vladivostok.

In 1898, following a renewed imperialist scramble for Chinese concessions, Russia obtained the further right to build a railway spur from Harbin on the new Chinese Eastern to Port Arthur on the Liaotung Peninsula, and a lease of the peninsula itself. There was some debate within the Russian government as to how much risk it was wise to court in pressing a forward policy in the Far East. The chief advocate of a cautious line, Minister of Finance Witte, was overruled by the enthusiastic imperialists, one of whom was Foreign Minister Muraviëv. Even when Muraviëv died and was replaced by the cautious Lamsdorf in 1900, the imperialists kept the ear of the Emperor. During the Boxer Rebellion rebels attacked the Chinese Eastern, and Russia retaliated by military occupation of the whole of Manchuria. An adventurer named Bezobrazov persuaded Nicholas II to finance a timber concession on the Yalu River on the northern border of Korea, in which country Russian influence had become decisive. Plehve, who became interior minister in 1902, was identified with the more aggressive policy, and when the following year Witte was dismissed from the finance ministry, advocates of restraint were virtually silenced.

Anticipating trouble, the Japanese attempted overtures to St. Petersburg. When a viceroy was appointed by the Tsar to administer both the Liaotung Peninsula and the Amur region, thus closing a political vise on Manchuria from north and south, Tokyo concluded that the Bezobrazov clique had won out. In January 1904 the Japanese attacked the Russian fleet at Port Arthur without bothering to declare war.

THE WAR WITH JAPAN

The course of the Russo-Japanese War was marked by an uninterrupted series of Russian defeats on land and sea. Russia suffered from severe handicaps from the outset. The Trans-Siberian Railway remained an inadequate supply route, since it was not yet finished in the area of Lake Baikal; from the beginning Russian land forces in the Far East were outnumbered; the British and American governments and public opinion tended to support the Japanese out of both financial interest and sentiment. However, the war was lost by mismanagement in the field. Japanese troops proceeded to assault Russian positions in two directions, north toward Mukden and south toward Port Arthur. Port Arthur was besieged almost at once and surrendered in December 1904. In August and September the Russians lost two battles, at Liaoyang and the Sha River, and in February 1905 the battle of Mukden ended in another defeat which narrowly missed becoming a rout. Nevertheless the Russian armies remained in being, and the *coup de grâce* was administered not by land but by sea.

The capable Admiral Makarov took over the damaged Port Arthur squadron in February 1904, but in April he went down with his ship when it was struck by a mine. In August the fleet tried to break out of besieged Port Arthur to reach Vladivostok, but it was intercepted and destroyed. There ensued a fantastic episode in which the Russians tried to replace their Far Eastern fleet with their Baltic squadron. In October 1904 Admiral Rozhdestvensky sailed from the Gulf of Finland, shooting at several English fishing smacks on the way in the belief that they were Japanese torpedo boats. In May 1905 he finally reached the Tsushima Strait off Korea, where he was met by the Japanese and his fleet promptly sunk.

There was now virtually no alternative for the Russians except to make peace. Witte was retrieved from the bureaucratic discard and sent to Portsmouth, New Hampshire, where he negotiated the peace treaty on September 5, 1905. Russia conceded Japanese hegemony in Korea, the annexation of southern Sakhalin, and the lease of the Liaotung Peninsula and the South Manchurian Railway, but the Empire was extricated from the war, and the cost seemed not excessive in view of the grave crisis which the government was then facing at home.

THE REVOLUTION OF 1905

The Tsar and his officials expected the outbreak of war to rally patriotic support to the side of the regime, but the effect was mainly the opposite. One section of the Liberationists wavered briefly, but the other wing shouted them down with expressions of unequivocal defeatism; one radical wrote, "Let the idol of Autocracy be overthrown in the waters of the Yellow Sea." The whole revolutionary camp took the same position. A variety of professional and semipublic bodies seized the occasion of the war to meet in order to discuss the "crisis," denounce the government, and demand reform.

Only a few months after the war broke out, the S.R.'s assassinated Minister of Interior Plehve. He was replaced by Prince Peter Sviatopolk-Mirsky, who announced a "new course" in which he would endeavor to inspire the trust of enlightened public opinion. In November 1904 the zemstvo men met in national congress, demanded that the Tsar grant a legislative assembly, and summoned local bodies to discuss their demands. The resulting "banquet campaign" (as it was labeled with France's 1848 Revolution in mind) drew in a variety of urban groups, including the municipal councils. The Mensheviks advocated efforts to include worker participation in these discussions, but very little of the plan was realized. Mirsky persuaded Nicholas II to promise to adopt some of the zemstvo men's demands in the hope of calming the gathering revolutionary storm. However, the Tsar balked at a legislative assembly, and in consequence Mirsky resigned and was replaced by A. G. Bulygin.

The first violence came on the heels of the fall of Port Arthur. A puzzling quasi-political priest, George Gapon, leader of a workers' group which had arisen as a "police socialist" union (see p. 71), was the instigator. He persuaded himself that it was his duty to lead a procession to the Winter Palace in order to claim redress of grievances from the Emperor personally and used revolutionary language in his appeals. The procession was fired upon by order of one of the grand dukes (Nicholas II was absent from the Palace). The event was termed "Bloody Sunday" and may be considered the beginning of the Revolution of 1905.

In 1905, for the first time in the history of modern Russia, millions of people in the cities as well as villages took part in a genuine mass movement, although they were far from unanimous in their goals. The political slogan of the hour was that of the opposition parties, whose platforms were substantially in harmony on immediate objectives; it demanded a "Four-Tail Constituent Assembly," that is, a body to be elected on the basis of universal, secret, equal, and direct suffrage to decide the future form of government. Other widespread demands were for enactment of full civil liberties, especially freedom of speech, press, and assembly, and prescription of an eight-hour maximum working day. For the socialist parties, the demands amounted to realization of a bourgeois regime, under which they could fight for the final goal of socialism; for the liberals, they would inaugurate democracy, under which all other political and social problems could be dealt with in time. Any public attempt to express some more modest demand was usually shouted down.

The evidence does not suggest that either the industrial workers or the peasants were chiefly interested in political changes, although the spokesmen of their organizations formed during 1905 repeated the demands which had been voiced by the zemstvos and municipal councils. The officials would not and the uneducated masses could not think up any slogans which could compete successfully with those of the intelligentsia. After Bloody Sunday, Mirsky could only wring his hands and, reportedly, lament, "Everything has failed. Let us build jails." The initiative seemed to lie in the hands of the revolutionaries. Strikes, demonstrations, and public meetings grew in number and boldness, and in February the S.R.'s killed the Grand Duke Sergei.

The Tsar issued a series of contradictory edicts, coupling threats with promises. Two weeks after the assassination of Sergei, Nicholas hurled an imperial anathema at the opposition but simultaneously signed a rescript to Minister of Interior Bulygin promising a consultative assembly and a ukase to the Senate confirming the right of every subject "to be heard directly by the monarch." The promise of a "Bulygin Duma" was ignored by the opposition, and such a body never met. However, the ukase to the Senate was interpreted by many as blanket permission to carry on political agitation—not that the revolutionary leaders were waiting for permission. In May the Union of Unions, including in its make-up fourteen "professional unions," was founded under strong Liberationist influence. In July a Peasant Union came into being, under the urging of S.R.'s and other revolutionaries. The zemstvo representatives were holding frequent sessions. At length they sent a deputation to the Emperor which had no visible effect on his actions, but the July zemstvo congress, angry at being snubbed, reacted by open demands for a Constituent Assembly. The radical Petrunkevich declared, "Now we must go to the people, and not to the Tsar."

On August 19 the government issued the promised law for a "Bulygin" or consultative Duma, but it made no impression on the opposition leaders. The conclusion of peace with Japan in the same month earned no plaudits; the opposition denounced the treaty terms and declared they revealed the incompetence of the government. The strike movement, which had been mounting almost from month to month, now became the spearhead of political action. Real trade-unions were practically non-existent, and during the autumn the strikers seldom presented employers with any demands for better working conditions or wages. In fact, many employers, sympathizing with the political movement, continued to pay their workers while on strike.

In late September and early October the movement swelled toward a dramatic climax. A railway strike on October 20 spread rapidly throughout all communications, and then to most industries. The first successful general strike in modern history became a reality without any over-all planning. On October 26 there was organized in St. Petersburg a Council (*sovet* or Soviet) of Workers' Deputies, beginning with thirty or forty delegates from a single district of the city and rapidly rising above the five hundred mark, theoretically on the basis of a deputy for every five hundred workers in the factories.

The St. Petersburg Soviet was later evaluated by one of its leaders, Leon Trotsky, as a "general staff of the revolution." It might be more accurate to describe it as the device by which the revolutionary intellectuals rallied the urban workers to the support of the political program they advocated. In the Soviet the Mensheviks, Socialist Revolutionaries, and Bolsheviks worked together, maintaining harmony not through the orders of a leader, but rather through a common analysis of the "historical tasks" in prospect. There was no room for the views of those who regarded strikes as a method of improving living and working conditions for industrial laborers, or in any event those who considered any major improvement possible aside from a successful revolution. In October 1905 the striking workers followed the lead of the revolutionary intellectuals in the political struggle which the Marxists had long advocated and predicted; few of them were Marxists, but that too had been expected. The result of the struggle was paralysis throughout the economy and panic among the leaders of the government.

THE OCTOBER MANIFESTO

A few weeks earlier Witte had returned from making peace at Portsmouth to find the country rent by strikes, demonstrations, and even mutinies in the armed forces. When the general strike of October occurred, Witte advised the Emperor to decide between a constitutional regime and a military dictatorship, but declared he would take part only in the former. Nicholas II finally yielded. On October 30 the Emperor issued the "October Manifesto," drafted by Witte, and simultaneously appointed him Russia's first prime minister.

After declaring that the revolutionary disturbances filled his "heart with great and deep grief," Nicholas declared that he had "found it necessary to unite the activities of the Supreme Government, so as to insure the successful carrying out of the general measures laid down by US for the peaceful life of the state." He continued, "We lay upon the Government the execution of OUR unchangeable will:

"1. To grant to the population the inviolable right of free citizenship, based on the principles of the freedom of person, conscience, speech, assembly, and union.

"2. Without postponing the intended elections for the State Duma and in so far as possible, in view of the short time that remains before the assembling of that body, to include in the participation of the work of the Duma those classes of the population that have been until now entirely deprived of the right to vote, and to extend in the future, by the newly created legislative way, the principles of the general right of election.

"3. To establish as an unbreakable rule that no law shall go into force without its confirmation by the State Duma and that the persons elected by the people shall have the opportunity for actual participation in supervising the legality of the acts of authorities appointed by US." The Tsar ended with an appeal to "all the true sons of Russia" to help reestablish order in the country.[1]

The Manifesto was too much for the conservatives, much too little for the opposition. Only the Union of October 17 or "Octobrist" party, which took its name from the date of the Manifesto and organized in its defense against both Left and Right, professed satisfaction. There was widespread rejoicing among ordinary people who, although unable to subject the document to legal exegesis, understood that Russia was freer than before. The ranks of the opposition, led by the St. Petersburg Soviet, were thrown into confusion. The country hung poised in a new but uneasy balance,

• [1] Quoted portions of translation of Emanuel Aronsberg in Frank A. Golder, ed., *Documents of Russian History, 1914–1917* (New York: The Century Co., 1927), pp. 627–628.

and the Soviet, faced by impending collapse of its strike, called it off hastily. The public watched to see "whether Khrustalëv[2] would arrest Witte, or Witte would arrest Khrustalëv." The government waited for its opportunity, which came with an unsuccessful attempt at a second general strike in November. Witte arrested Khrustalëv, and a few days later his successor as chairman, Trotsky, and the whole Soviet.

By this time the Soviet form of organization had spread far beyond St. Petersburg; in fact, the first Soviet had been organized as early as June in the textile center of Ivanovo-Voznesensk. With the collapse of the Soviet in the capital, the initiative passed to Moscow. The Moscow Soviet launched a third general strike in December which soon became an armed uprising in the Presnia district of the city. However, Moscow's population did not rise as hoped, and government troops from the capital crushed the revolt.

The repression of the Moscow uprising marked the virtual end of the Revolution of 1905 in the cities, but a revolt of a different sort, beginning later but lasting longer, took place in the countryside. Especially in the overcrowded provinces lying near the fiftieth parallel and in the Baltic, village riots mounted in the autumn and continued into the spring of 1906. In ten provinces alone almost thirty million rubles' worth of damage was done. The intelligentsia endeavored to mobilize peasant opinion and action behind their political program through the Peasant Union and other organizations, but the attempt was a failure. Neither the intelligentsia nor the government seemed to understand very clearly what had happened in the countryside. The first returns from the elections for the new assembly, held in March, led Witte to exclaim, "Thank God, the Duma will be peasant." Indeed the First Duma was to a large extent peasant in its composition, but the deputies came neither to profess their loyalty to the regime nor to follow the revolutionaries' lead, but for purposes of their own most easily summed up in the old phrase, "land and liberty."

THE FIRST DUMA

Russia emerged from the Revolution of 1905 with several important reforms, some of them promulgated during the period of struggle and almost ignored at the time. In April religious toleration had been granted, in August university autonomy restored, in October Finnish autonomy partly restored, in November the redemption payments for Emancipation

[2] The shadowy, nonparty figure who was the first chairman of the St. Petersburg Soviet.

lands canceled. The October Manifesto had ⑤granted civil liberties—which were subsequently abridged at times in law or in fact, but never abolished ⑥—and a legislative assembly.

What the new assembly would be like remained to be seen. In February the new Duma was declared to be merely the lower house of a two-chambered legislative body. The old Imperial Council became the new upper house, half of its members (instead of all, as before) being appointees of the crown, half being elected by the zemstvos, nobles, commerce and industry, the clergy, the universities, and the Finnish diet. Laws were to require the approval of both houses and the Emperor, and though the Duma had control over much of the budget, it could not question military and certain other types of expenditure. Since the ministry was to remain appointive and, like that of Germany, responsible only to the Emperor, the Duma's powers were far short of those of the British House of Commons, which was the standard of much liberal judgment. These and other constitutional changes were codified by the Fundamental Laws issued on May 6, 1906, on the eve of the opening of the Duma.

The franchise for election of deputies to the Duma was unequal and indirect, but it was close to universal, partly because the government still believed in the loyalty of the peasantry when the law was issued, on December 24, 1905. At first all the revolutionary parties decided to boycott the election. Only when they realized that the country took it seriously did they try to repair the consequences of their blunder. The Mensheviks entered the lists in the Caucasus and emerged with several seats in the Duma; the S.R.'s set to work to try to influence the large number of nonparty peasant deputies; only the Bolsheviks found themselves uneasy bystanders, deprived of influence over the Duma.

The Kadets went into the elections at full tilt. They emerged the single most powerful party in number of deputies, and although they lacked a majority, they became the leaders of the Duma. Their participation in the assembly was not a sign of reconciliation with the regime; on the contrary, they intended to utilize it for revolutionary purposes, as the French States General had been used in 1789. The second largest group of deputies was to begin with not a party fraction at all; it was a caucus of men calling themselves the *Trudoviki* (Toilers), who were the closest thing to direct spokesmen the peasantry had. The real conservatives were entirely absent, and the Octobrists, the only group which supported the institutions in which they undertook to participate, were but a handful.

The course of the First Duma was short and stormy. The Tsar's speech from the throne was immediately answered by a unanimous manifesto demanding a full-fledged representative democracy and land expropria-

Duma was extremely weak in most regards.

tion on behalf of the peasants immediately. An appearance by Prime Minister Goremykin, a lazy but wily bureaucrat who had been substituted for Witte just before the Duma opened, provoked a prompt vote of censure. A land bill which had no chance of Imperial acceptance was moved along parliamentary channels toward passage, but the First Duma was dissolved before a vote could be taken, after a turbulent existence of only two months. The Kadet leaders made for Finland, where in the "Vyborg Manifesto" they called for passive resistance from the public as a protest against the Duma's dissolution, but response was negligible. Neither the socialists' tactics in the strikes nor the liberals' tactics in the Duma had succeeded in bringing about "bourgeois" democracy. The major figures in the struggle were left to try to decide what had happened.

The government had ridden out the urban storm in some alarm, but with a deep conviction that the countryside was "healthy." However, as peasant riots grew serious, and especially after the *Trudoviki* followed the Kadet lead in legislating land expropriation, the bureaucrats were compelled to recognize that the "loyalty" of the peasantry was a mirage. Having confidently felt that victory was near during the general strikes, the revolutionary leadership had counted on the support of the peasantry, but this calculation also proved unwarranted. If the peasantry had gone anywhere, it had gone to the parliamentary institutions which the revolutionaries scorned and assumed to be a matter of indifference to the peasants. Nevertheless, they had failed to obtain from the Duma what was apparently their first concern, a land reform. Plainly the peasantry remained a powerful potential which the right leadership could presumably exploit. The eleven years from 1906 to 1917 were marked by redoubled efforts by both government and revolutionaries to win over rural Russia.

The "Silver Age" of the Arts

★
★
★
★
★
★
★
★
★
★

CHAPTER 6

CENSORSHIP FROM LEFT AND RIGHT

Under the oppressive regime of Nicholas I (1825–1855) and the milder reign of Alexander II (1855–1881), Russia experienced a "Golden Age" of literature. Under the intermittently severe censorship and repression of Nicholas II (1894–1917), Russia enjoyed a "Silver Age" in literature as well as in other arts. Artists and writers were plagued by officials who scented radicalism; they were also subjected to strong pressures of a quite different kind from the revolutionary-minded intelligentsia. Under neither Nicholas did the regime exact positive conformity to a set of governmentally prescribed ideological principles. The official censorship confined itself to suppressing or threatening to suppress offensive material, chiefly in the field of journalism. The unofficial "censorship of the Left," however, demanded positive conformity in several of the arts. It asked that creative artists serve revolutionary political ends and applied a variety of sanctions against artists who balked. This kind of censor could not seize a newspaper or book, nor exile an artist, but it could make it difficult for him to get a public hearing and could even sometimes hound him into bewildered silence. Despite these very different kinds of pressures, the artists and writers of the reign of Nicholas II managed to attain high creative levels and to spread appreciation of the arts among a broader public than ever before in Russia.

The "temporary" censorship rules of 1882 remained in force up to the Revolution of 1905. By their provisions newspapers and magazines which had been officially warned three times could be subjected to preliminary censorship. There were other laws which were intended chiefly for use as a political counter-weapon against the revolutionary intelligentsia. In 1905–1906 preliminary censorship of periodicals and books was abolished, but published material alleged to violate the law still could be and was seized from time to time as long as Tsarism lasted.

The "censorship of the Left" operated in a subtler but not necessarily less effective manner. Since the time of the capable but rather single-minded critic Vissarion Belinsky (1811–1848), the intelligentsia had deemed any theory or practice of the independence of the arts, such as use of the slogan, "art for art's sake," to be treasonable to the revolutionary cause. The so-called "social command" of the radical critics was that art should serve as an instrument of social improvement. Since most of the radicals thought that no effective reforms could be enacted without a complete overturn of the existing system, the "social command" tended to insist that art should exist only for the sake of the coming revolution. Works of art and literature which did not portray the wickedness of the government, the miseries of the common people, or the virtues of the revolutionary intelligentsia, were often ignored, scorned, or savagely attacked, as Belinsky had macerated Gogol's *Correspondence with Friends.* Nonpolitical activity by the younger generation might be equated with reactionary politics or be subject to invasion by revolutionary youth who considered their own aims more important than any others. For example, at the University of Moscow in the 1890's the students were left with only one extracurricular organization which enjoyed official recognition, the student orchestra and choir. Certain young radicals, including the future S.R. leader Victor Chernov, systematically set about to capture this organization for purposes of revolutionary propaganda. They succeeded, and the result was that the government disbanded the orchestra and choir.

Against such pressure from two directions, the nonpolitically-minded were placed in a difficult position indeed. The government seldom directly interfered with them. The chief obstacle to their charting their own course was the power of the "social command," for the radicals maintained ascendancy over the literary and to some extent the whole intellectual world throughout the reign of Alexander III. The radical domination was successfully challenged, however, in the 1890's, and the "Silver

Age" followed. Although the "social command" remained influential, the defenders of the independence of the artist won a hearing. When, a quarter-century later in 1915, Maxim Gorky protested against the staging of Dostoevsky's *The Possessed* (a novel critical of the revolutionaries) at the Moscow Art Theater, the protest was widely regarded as a last gasp of the "censorship of the Left" (a censorship by no means limited to those who, like Gorky, were Bolsheviks).

At that time artists and critics of many different persuasions were indeed able to reach the public. It was not a reversal of trend in the world of the arts but the political events of the Revolution and Civil War which changed the picture drastically. Those events raised Gorky himself to the position of dean of Communist letters and led to the artistic and personal ruin of his opponents—many of whom, it should be said to his personal credit, he tried to help and save. In the end Gorky himself fell victim to the "censorship of the Left," which had become transmuted into a weapon of the Soviet power and was applied with a rigor unmatched by any of the pre-totalitarian censorships.[1]

NEW CURRENTS IN LITERATURE

It was in the field of literature that the Russian arts had first attained world renown by producing works of genius in European genres. In the 1820's and 1830's Alexander Pushkin and Michael Lermontov had written great poetry, and Nicholas Gogol great prose. During the 1860's and 1870's Fëdor Dostoevsky, Leo Tolstoy, and Ivan Turgenev had produced great novels. However, Dostoevsky's *The Brothers Karamazov* (which, along with Tolstoy's *War and Peace,* marks the high point of genius in the Russian novel), written in 1880, was the last of the great novels. During the Silver Age, as Wladimir Weidlé writes, "Russian literature produced no genius comparable to Tolstoy or Dostoevski or Pushkin or Gogol, but in all branches of letters the number of talented writers had never been so great, their public so large or the general level of its culture so high."[2]

Since Belinsky's time poetry as a genre had been rather unpopular, except for the "civic poetry" of such writers as Nicholas Nekrasov (author of *Who Can be Happy and Free in Russia?*). Novels had been approved

• [1] The fate of Gorky is the subject of an interesting novel partly based on what is known of the facts: Igor Gouzenko, *The Fall of a Titan* (London: Cassell, 1954).

• [2] Wladimir Weidlé, *Russia: Absent and Present,* trans. A. Gordon Smith (New York: John Day, 1952), p. 88.

by the radical critics if they had an intentional "social emphasis." If such emphasis was lacking, the critics often provided it for the puzzled author. The radicals reigned supreme in the field of literary criticism, and from that stronghold they exerted great influence on the arts in general. In the words of D. S. Mirsky, "only a small minority of thinking people—but among them perhaps the most independent, original, and sincere minds of the day—showed a critical attitude towards the dogma of agnosticism and democracy, and strove towards a creative revival of Christian and national ideals."[3] The minority did not by any means consist entirely of Christians or Russian nationalists. Its diversity of outlook was considerable, but it was united in its resentment of the "censorship of the Left."

The challenge to the ascendancy of the radical critics began in the early years of the reign of Alexander III. In 1884 two articles appeared in a Kiev newspaper questioning the validity of the "social command." A few years later A. L. Volynsky (pseudonym of Flekser) began to do the same in the pages of the St. Petersburg magazine *Northern Messenger*. The journal's circulation rose from a few hundred to several thousand before it was wrecked by the censor, for personal rather than ideological reasons. In 1892 Dmitry Merezhkovsky produced a book called *Symbols,* which showed the influence of the poetic conceptions of Baudelaire and Edgar Allan Poe. The following year he wrote *On the Present Condition of Russian Literature and the Causes of its Decline*. The work served as a sort of manifesto on behalf of the younger artists in search of new directions who were beginning to appear.

In 1894 Valery Briusov, a twenty-year-old student at Moscow University, published three short books whose intent was clearly *épater les bourgeois*. His poem of a single line: "O cover thy pale legs!" produced a sensation. But he was more than an *enfant terrible,* and soon he and his friends became recognized as a new school of poets, the "symbolists." Sometimes they were bitterly attacked, sometimes gently satirized, as by the philosopher Vladimir Soloviëv (which flattered and delighted Briusov). Briusov was joined first by the exuberant Constantine Balmont: "Who is equal to me in the power of song? No one!" A few years later there appeared the troubled but original Andrew Bely, and finally perhaps the most gifted of the symbolists, Alexander Blok. A number of other talented poets, as well as literary critics and hangers-on, grouped themselves around either Briusov's *Scorpio* publishing house in Moscow or the circle which met Wednesday evenings (usually until early morning) at the St. Petersburg apartment, known as "the Tower," of Viacheslav Ivanov.

• [3] D. S. Mirsky, *A History of Russian Literature,* ed. Francis J. Whitfield (New York: Knopf, 1949), pp. 324–325.

The name "symbolism" was taken from the French contemporary school which included Rimbaud and Mallarmé, but the Russians were far from simple imitators. They combined a crusading spirit of innovation with an effort at re-evaluation of the whole Russian literary past. The symbolists shared with certain of their rival and successor schools the aims of rejecting the "social command" for art and of developing appropriate techniques and forms for expressing their own individuality, philosophical convictions and mystical insights, and anticipations of the future.

By 1911 Nicholas Gumilëv, Anna Akhmatova, and Osip Mandelshtam were rebelling against symbolism, and they adopted the title "Acmeists." They declared, "We want to admire a rose because it is beautiful, not because it is a symbol of mystical purity." The Acmeists wanted to deepen the poetic sense of immediacy, but they were in accord with the symbolists in seeking to refine the craft of poetry. Gumilëv's *A Prayer* is illustrative:

Fearful sun, menacing sun,
Like the mad face
Of God going through space,

Burn the present, oh! sun,
That the future may last,
But protect the past.[4]

At the same time that the Acmeists were starting to work, the Futurists (taking their name at least from Italian futurism) were experimenting in rowdy and startling fashion with the uses of the sounds of words rather than or aside from their meaning. One of them, Vladimir Mayakovsky, became the declamatory poet of the Bolshevik Revolution but later proclaimed by his suicide his failure to adapt himself to the Soviet order.

Poetry rose from a position of neglect to impose "its own laws on fiction and drama," and on other prose as well. The distinctive work of Basil Rozanov, with its partly Christian, partly naturalistic religion of the family and procreation, and the searchings of Leo Shestov for God beyond logic and reason, are permeated with poetic feeling. The stories and plays of Anton Chekhov, which became so well known in the West, the novellas of Ivan Bunin, such as *The Gentleman from San Francisco,* much of the work of Leonid Andreyev, who seemed to be an old-style "realist," and particularly the writing of the prose symbolist Alexis Remi-

• [4] Translation reprinted by permission of the publishers from Leonid Strakhovsky, *Craftsmen of the Word* (Cambridge, Mass.: Harvard University Press, Copyright 1949, by The President and Fellows of Harvard College), p. 5.

zov, reflect the impact of the new poetic currents of the time. The new aesthetic and individualist ideas were debated and discussed in such places as Ivanov's "Tower" apartment. There were many other such gathering points; some of the futurists preferred the cafes. For the leading lights of the Silver Age, it was a period of passionate though often transitory love affairs and marriages, stormy and broken friendships, and slightly aberrant ideological quests, but it was an exciting time to be alive.

A type of writing very different in spirit from the modernists was developed by Maxim Gorky, to some extent by Leonid Andreyev, and several others. Gorky rose rapidly from a provincial proletarian background to national renown; by 1900 he became the most popular writer in Russia. He was a Social Democrat and, when the party split, became a Bolshevik. In a few years, however, as Mirsky indicates, Gorky sank to the level of Bolshevik "party pet." Before the Revolution of 1905 Andreyev displaced him in public favor, but his vogue was transitory. If any single fad succeeded that of Andreyev, it was the brief cult of Artsybashev, whose artistically crude, straightforwardly sexual novel, *Sanin,* experienced a *succès fou* and was read for a time by all the students, waitresses, and clerks, no doubt often with undesirable moral consequences. *Sanin* was, however, only a somewhat unpleasant bubble on the surface of the great churning and boiling pot of the Russian literary renaissance. The politically single-minded and artistically unimaginative atmosphere of the 1880's had yielded to a whole spectrum of diverse creative currents, developing side by side.

MUSIC AND PAINTING

The death of Dostoevsky in 1881 and that of Turgenev in 1883 mark the passing of the great age of the Russian novel;[5] in somewhat similar fashion the passing of Mussorgsky in 1881 and that of Tchaikovsky[6] in 1893 bring to an end the age of solitary giants and inaugurate a period of gifted individual diversity in music. Serious professional training in music had begun in Russia only in the 1860's, owing largely to the schools established in the two capitals by the brothers Anton and Nicholas Rubinstein.

The influence of the rather conventional and Westernized schools was challenged in the same decade by a group of talented amateurs, led by

[5] Tolstoy lived until 1910, but the religious experience he underwent in 1880 separated his later works somewhat from those of the other great novelists.

[6] By all standard systems of transliteration the name should begin in English with "Ch," but the "T" has long since passed into accepted usage.

Mily Balakirev, who became known as the "Mighty Band" (*Moguchaia Kuchka*). The group aggressively espoused "Russian" music, reflecting the same nationalism which was expressed, although rather less attractively, in the policy of Alexander III. Modest Mussorgsky represented, especially with his two great operas *Boris Godunov* and *Khovanshchina*, the highest achievements of this circle. A survivor of the Mighty Band, Nicholas Rimsky-Korsakov, arranged both of Mussorgsky's masterpieces and also Alexander Borodin's *Prince Igor*, unfinished at his death in 1887. Rimsky-Korsakov lived until 1908, writing distinguished music, but by the time of his death new currents had invaded the musical scene. Sergei Rachmaninov[7] attempted to continue the lyric tradition of Tchaikovsky, but the change in fashions left him more popular abroad than in Russia.

In the 1890's, as Miliukov puts it, "we approach the moment when, like painting, Russian music became cosmopolitan without, however, losing its national character."[8] The pioneer of the new movement was Alexander Skriabin, fragile, iconoclastic, and addicted to such odd ideas as that of a "Mystery," wherein all would join the performance and there would be no audience. He spent much time in the West. Western composers like Debussy and Ravel were beginning to discover Russian music and were considerably influenced by Mussorgsky fifteen years after his death. Western acclaim and the changing public mood in Russia combined to revive Mussorgsky's operas, with leading roles sung by the glorious voice of Fëdor Shaliapin.[9] Following the Revolution of 1905 *Boris Godunov* and *Khovanshchina* were triumphantly performed both in Russia and the West.

The new currents in music were linked with innovations in literature and the visual arts in the *World of Art* (*Mir Iskusstva*) group, formed in 1898 by Sergei Diagilev and others, which published a magazine of the same name until 1902. They included the impressionism of Vladimir Rebikov, who set poems of the symbolists Balmont and Briusov to music, and the expressionism of Igor Stravinsky, as shown in *The Fire Bird*, which he composed for the Ballet Russe in 1910, and his subsequent *Petrushka* and *The Rite of Spring*. In this period Stravinsky was justifiably compared with the German Schoenberg. Stravinsky's music contained exotic and also "Russian" elements, but the music and the composer himself were soon to be absorbed into Europe, and later America.

• [7] The transliteration by standard systems should be "Rakhmaninov."

• [8] Paul Miliukov, *Outlines of Russian Culture: Part III: Architecture, Painting, and Music*, ed. Michael Karpovich, trans. V. Ughet and E. Davis (Philadelphia: University of Pennsylvania Press, 1943), p. 121.

• [9] The spelling "Chaliapin" was often used in the West.

Sergei Prokofiev, in such early works as his *Classical Symphony,* returned to more conventional forms but with a far from antiquarian spirit. Stravinsky soon did much the same thing, but the two differed both as musicians and men; Prokofiev became a Soviet composer, whereas Stravinsky in an important sense ceased to be Russian at all. Especially after Diagilev's Festival of Russian Music in Paris in 1907, the last years of the Tsarist period witnessed a fruitful and congenial interchange and appreciation between musicians and publics of Russia and the West.

In painting as in music a change of line occurred in the 1890's. Academic training in painting was older than in music, dating back to the organization of the Academy of Arts in St. Petersburg under Catherine II (its founding date was even earlier, 1758). In the 1850's a rebellion against the academism of St. Petersburg was organized by Moscow painters at about the same time that a new art school was founded there. The rebels, who called themselves the Itinerants, were strongly civic-minded, realist, and nationalist in a way which invites comparison with the Mighty Band in music. Their outstanding painter, Ilia Repin, produced works of social message such as the famed "Volga Boatmen," as well as of historical realism, like the hair-raising "Ivan the Terrible Embracing the Body of His Son," at which knots of people gaze in horror in Moscow's Tretiakov Gallery to this day.

As Alexander Benois[10] wrote in 1902, "in the seventies and even in the eighties there was no connection between [the Russian painters] and the truly creative art in the West. . . . But during the last ten years conditions have changed very rapidly. Thanks to frequent exhibitions of the works of Western artists in St. Petersburg and Moscow, the greater accessibility of foreign travel, and wide circulation of illustrated art publications, we were brought nearer to the West. . . . We saw our own art from a different point of view."[11] The young artistic revolutionaries, banding together in *The World of Art* group, repudiated both traditional academism and Itinerant realism. However, Repin, who was by that time both dean of the Academy and the foremost Itinerant, belonged to their group for a time, which illustrates their lack of insistence on a single artistic line.

The young men of *The World of Art* sought inspiration in the modern West and in the Orient. They also looked to Russia's own artistic heritage, especially its medieval iconography. Igor Grabar and other members of the group were instrumental in rediscovering these forgotten masterpieces and in establishing the study and restoration of them on a scientific

• [10] Standard transliteration should be "Benua."

• [11] Quoted in Miliukov, *op. cit.*, p. 63.

footing. Victor Surikov, who painted a memorable canvas of Yermak's successful assault on the Tatar khanate of Sibir and a striking picture of the *"Boyarynia Morozova,"* was known for his historical subjects but praised by *The World of Art* group for his artistic sense. The French impressionist influence was displayed by Arkhip Kuindzhi, the colors of whose paintings have unfortunately darkened, and the less derivative Isaac Levitan and Valentine Serov. Michael Vrubel used subjects drawn from folklore but applied to them an inner vision, comparable to that of William Blake, shown in such paintings as "The Demon." The outstanding painters of *The World of Art* group itself, as distinguished from those influenced by or admired by it, include Alexander Benois and Nicholas Roerich.

THE CULTURAL SCENE

The formation of *The World of Art* group, whose influence owed most to Sergei Diagilev, a young man who was an artist but even more an impresario, and the foundation a little later of the Moscow Art Theater by Stanislavsky and Nemirovich-Danchenko, gave great impetus to the new movements in the arts. Diagilev was instrumental in the rapid development of a superb ballet which, fusing the arts of scenery painting, choreography, and music, assumed first place in the world and kept it. The Ballet Russe, founded in 1909, developed such peerless dancers as Nijinsky and Pavlova. The first puzzling, then popular, plays of Chekhov, wherein characters were made "equal" in prominence for purposes of portrayal by the Art Theater company, also illustrated the new threads which were linking the individual arts to each other. The Russian cultural scene became known in the West. In 1900 the paintings of Russian artists were shown at the Paris Exposition; in 1906 an Exhibition of Russian Art was held in Paris; in 1909 the Ballet Russe began its Western seasons. *The World of Art* group's rediscovery of the Russian artistic past, especially the icon, was shared with Europe and America.

Simultaneously the Russian public gained increased familiarity with the great historic figures and productions of West European culture. Merezhkovsky began the work of popularization with such books as *The Romance of Leonardo da Vinci,* and it was continued by others with the result that many more Russians read *Faust* and the *Divine Comedy,* Molière and Shakespeare, Balzac and Dickens, than ever before. The literate public was more than ever conscious of the distinction which Russia had attained within European culture without sacrificing Russian individuality. After Dostoevsky and Tolstoy, Russia no longer needed to prove that she could produce artistic geniuses of the first magnitude. For the moment there were no more giants in Russia, nor in the West either. The difference between the cultural level of Eastern and Western Europe was no longer such as to make Slavophiles glorify it or Westernizers deprecate it. The cultural base of the Silver Age was solider and broader by far than that of the Golden Age.

The artistic renaissance was accompanied by new philosophical searchings of diverse kinds. Following the unsuccessful Revolution of 1905, such intellectual re-evaluation was carried still further. The impression has gained currency that Russia's intellectuals, disillusioned with politics as a result of the miscarried revolution, fled their social responsibilities into the sexualism of *Sanin* or into "religious mysticism." This impression distorts reality. The nonpolitical currents of thought were forming rapidly as early as the 1890's and cannot be equated simply with the disappointments of frustrated revolutionaries. Indeed, in large part the pre-1905 nonpoliticals remained so, as did the pre-1905 revolutionaries, but the new generation saw its goals in different terms. In the 1890's, Mirsky suggests, "between atheism and progress, on the one hand, and religion and political reaction, on the other, the alliance was complete. To dissolve these alliances, and to *undermine the supremacy of political over cultural and individual values,* was the task of the generation of intellectuals who came of age in the last decade of the nineteenth century" (italics mine).[12]

To assert the independence of cultural and individual values meant different things to different people. To Chekhov, it meant explaining to "those who read between the lines trying to find a definite trend of thought" that "I am neither liberal nor conservative, nor gradualist, nor ascetic, nor indifferentist. I should like to be an independent artist—and that is all. . . . Any trade mark or label to me means a prejudice." Chekhov had no religious faith nor any interest in philosophy pursued as an independent discipline; his outlook was profoundly influenced by his medical and scientific training. To Ivanov-Razumnik and Alexander Blok, independence meant not avoiding politics but viewing political developments from the standpoint of a transcendent socialist messianism, and they later welcomed the Bolshevik Revolution as a means of realizing the mission of the "Scythians" (Blok wrote a poem with that title) to change the world. To such men as Nicholas Berdiaev, Sergei Bulgakov, and others who wrote a symposium called *Signposts* (*Vekhi*) in 1909, independence meant an attempt to apply religious insights to the post-1905 situation.

• [12] Mirsky, *op. cit.*, p. 407.

The old civic morality of the radical, socialist, and atheist intelligentsia was being undermined by the new civic morality of the Christian liberals of *Signposts,* by the scientific individualism of Chekhov, and by other philosophical currents. The result was a creative and fruitful colloquy among diverse viewpoints, which gave the artist and thinker the opportunity to choose the concept of obligation he preferred, to join a group or not, to subordinate his art to his politics (if he had any) or not, to adopt his own view of his or Russia's place in the world and the future.

ART APPRECIATION AND EDUCATION

The over-all effect of the Silver Age was simultaneously to extend the base and raise the level of cultural activity. According to Weidlé,

> Even during the war, on the very outbreak of the revolution, the reading of a new poem by Alexander Blok or Anna Akhmatova was for many an important personal event, a joy or an anguish, an intimate communion with reality. When Scriabin was at the piano, his music evoked an emotion that was very much more than mere aesthetic pleasure. To hear Shaliapin or Sobinov, to see a Meyerhold production or one at the Art Theatre, to be transported once more by that strange voice of the great Komissarjevskaia, young students of both sexes would queue at the box-offices in their hundreds [*sic*] all night. New writers and artists seemed to be born every day; universities and picture-galleries, every institution devoted to the arts or sciences or letters, were being transformed or modernised under one's very eyes; the country's past was being studied with more love than ever, and with more objectivity. Ikons, the most beautiful painting that Russia had ever produced, were being discovered once more after being forgotten for centuries. Privately, too, there were fine collections being made of pictures and drawings, books, engravings and all works of art; exhibitions, both of ancient and modern art, could always be sure of attracting crowds. Ancient churches throughout the country, ancient towns and dwelling-houses, were now for the first time being gazed on with wonder not only by artists but by ordinary travellers.[13]

What Weidlé is pointing out is that the art of the Silver Age evoked a wide public response—in fact, one wider than ever before. Only a

[13] Weidlé, *op. cit.,* pp. 90–91.

relatively few people could be invited to Ivanov's apartment on Wednesday evenings, but multitudes could be induced to look again at the monuments of their country's rich past with the "shock of recognition." Even the rural folk could be persuaded to keep alive their traditional or even half-forgotten arts, such as the lacquer-painting of Palekh or the singing of ancient poems in the Lake Onega district, their dances and costume-making, when the educated urbanites showed interest through visits and questions or even a merely financial demand for such things.

Mass education may not necessarily produce mass interest in the fine arts, but it is essential if public awareness of creative effort is to be extensive. And education was moving in the direction of mass instruction. In 1887 Minister of Education Delianov had ordered the schools to get rid of the children of "coachmen, valets, cooks, washerwomen, small shop-keepers, and other people whose children it would be wrong to draw away from the environment to which they belong." Delianov correctly observed the influx of lower-class children into Russian schools, but he was unable to check it.

Whereas in 1888 the classical secondary schools had 62.9% students from gentry and official families, 26.9% of townsmen, and only 6.2% of peasants; in 1910 the gentry children had decreased to 37.3%, the townsmen had risen to 39%, the peasants to 18.4%. In the nonclassical schools, in 1888 the percentages were 53.9% gentry and officials, 31.1% townsmen, and 11.4% peasants; in 1910 they had altered to 25.6% gentry, 42.8% townsmen, and 28.1% peasants. Of young people who reached school age in 1914, 918 per 1000 in the towns and 710 per 1000 in the country could read and write. In contrast, of those who reached school age in 1920, 347 per 1000 in towns and 171 per 1000 in the rural areas were literate. Universities and higher schools multiplied; one estimate is that in 1914 there were over a hundred, in which some 150,000 students were enrolled.

In 1908 the Third Duma passed a bill providing for free and compulsory public instruction for all children aged eight to eleven. The plan, which required a great expansion of school building and teacher training, was scheduled for realization in 1922. In 1911 a much more ambitious bill was passed by the Duma but was rejected by the Imperial Council (see p. 108). Count P. N. Ignatiev, who was appointed minister of education in 1915, had still more sweeping plans for expansion and reorganization of public education, but there was no time for their consideration before the Revolution.

The intellectuals who produced the Silver Age and the enlarged audience for the arts which popular education was building provide impressive evidence of the fact that in the early twentieth century Russia was finding a new cultural footing for herself. Diagilev and Stanislavsky, Nijinsky and Pavlova, Rimsky-Korsakov and Stravinsky, Tolstoy and Chekhov, Gorky and Blok became European and world figures in their lifetime, and there were many innovators of real merit who deserved wider recognition outside Russia than could be gained before the Revolution. In the realm of culture, Russia was more nearly at one with Europe than she had been at any time since the days of the Kievan state.

Growth of the Russian Economy

CHAPTER 7

SERF AGRICULTURE AND INDUSTRY

In medieval times Russia had a mixed economy, in which the work was done by peasants and craftsmen ranging in status from slavery through a variety of types of temporary bondage to freedom. Under the Muscovite Tsardom the mass of the people was reduced to serfdom. Until the seventeenth century the peasants who were settled on boyar or gentry estates had the traditional right of settling up with their landlords (if they wished or were able to do so) and leaving on a certain day in the autumn of each year. Many departed without making a settlement; the landlords could secure their forcible return, but if the fugitives could escape detection for a certain period, a statute of limitations protected them. In order to safeguard the gentry's capacity to render state service, the Muscovite state intervened to halt the movement of peasants from one estate to another, to state lands, or into the lands beyond state borders in the south and east. By the time of the 1649 Code of the Tsar Alexis, both the right of departure and the statute of limitations had been terminated. The flight of the peasants became unconditionally illegal (although it certainly did not end), and the earlier contractual relationship between peasant and landlord was replaced by statutory peasant servitude. Thus serfdom came to Russia (as it did also to Austria and Prussia) at a time when it was disappearing in Western Europe.

At first serfdom was mainly confined to agriculture. Most production was in fact agricultural. The output of the estate handicraftsman (*kustar'*) satisfied peasant needs for finished goods and part of the urban demand until around the middle of the eighteenth century. However, some industry existed in Muscovy. In the two centuries before Peter the Great there grew up iron works near Tula and Moscow, plants for the processing of salt and potash in the Kama and upper Volga valleys, and some leather, rope, linen, glass, and soap factories. Part of this industrial development took place through state enterprise, part of it through the activity of wealthy boyars. But after the Muscovite Tsardom destroyed the independence of Novgorod and Pskov, Russia did not experience the sort of autonomous and economically active urban development seen in Western Europe and, owing to the borrowing from Germany of the "Magdeburg Law," which granted self-government and other privileges, in the towns of Poland-Lithuania.

The economic reforms of Peter the Great were in great part motivated by ideas borrowed from contemporary economic theories of the West, especially mercantilism. Mercantilism preached state initiative in economic development; however, such a policy had a rather different effect in Eastern Europe, particularly in Russia, than in the West whence mercantilist theories sprang. In Russia, where private traders were closely dependent on the state, and the mass of the people was either enserfed to private landlords or directly tributary to the state, industry and commerce could not be developed very far by governmental encouragement or support of private entrepreneurs, by means of which the West achieved such striking results. State power and financial resources had to be employed directly. Peter brought about a marked increase in state industrial efforts, and he also gave over large numbers of peasants into the new class of "possessional" serfs, who were ascribed to new privately-owned factories rather than to landlords. The result of Peter's economic labors was to extend the initiative of the government, already so powerful in Russia, into the economy in a manner which made the state stronger than ever and left little room for private ownership or enterprise to develop independently.

To be sure, manufacturing grew considerably though irregularly during the seventeenth and eighteenth centuries, and by no means entirely as a result of state initiative. Certain foreigners, like Tames in linen, Vinius and Akem in iron, and Marcelis in armaments, took an active part. In the mid-eighteenth century the government transferred into private hands many of the factories it had operated under Peter. However, it kept many plants, controlled all production in the "possessional" factories, though they were owned by private persons, and regulated the whole economy in many ways.

By the time of Catherine the Great the emphasis on "freedom" of industry and trade advocated by the classical economists of the West made its mark on Russian governmental policy. In 1753 the Empress Elizabeth had already abolished internal customs duties. Catherine assisted the gentry to enter the field of manufacturing, which Peter had tended to restrict to the state and the merchant class. During the eighteenth century new industrial centers began to develop; for example, a new iron and copper center appeared in the Urals, using better techniques than the old Tula works.

EMANCIPATION AND THE INDUSTRIAL REVOLUTION

By the early 1800's new machinery and new technology imported or copied from the West made their appearance in Russian factories. The older Ural iron, linen, and woolen industries were gradually surpassed by new types of manufacturing and new industrial centers. As in England, the Industrial Revolution in Russia owed much to the growth of cotton manufacturing, beginning in Ivanovo-Voznesensk and spreading into the Vladimir and Moscow provinces. A German named Knoop, who had been a clerk in England, equipped and built a number of factories in the middle of the century. A popular couplet of the 1840's ran: "No church without a *pop* [priest], No mill without a Knoop." By that time the new cotton industry's employees consisted almost entirely of hired rather than serf laborers. Whereas Russia up till 1800 produced more pig iron than England, it fell far behind in the subsequent decades, partly because of the lower output of the serf workers used in the Ural plants. However, a new iron center was being developed in the Ukraine, pioneered by an Englishman, J. Hughes, who gave his name to Yuzovka (today Stalino).

The inferior productivity of serf labor in industry was one factor in bringing about the freeing of the serfs, but probably more important was the mounting number of peasant revolts during the reign of Nicholas I. The precipitating factor for all the Great Reforms of Alexander II, including Emancipation, was the Crimean War, which exposed the economic and other weaknesses of Russian society in glaring fashion. Emancipation was favored by many revolutionaries who thought chiefly in terms of the eventual coming of socialism, and by officials, including

Alexander II himself, who thought in terms of order and justice. Probably few gentry or merchants clearly anticipated the profits which agriculture or industry based on free labor might bring, and in fact many were unable to make the transition to capitalism and were ultimately ruined by the Emancipation.

Others managed to become agricultural or industrial entrepreneurs. To do so they required not only free labor, but also capital. Already there were sizable private fortunes in Russia, derived originally from such diverse sources as war booty, military contracts, gifts of the ruling house, private banking, leases, monopolies, and the like. In addition former serf-owners received government bonds (for whose value the ex-serfs had to reimburse the state) in payment of the land taken from them and given the peasants at Emancipation. In the post-Great Reform era, the entrepreneurs were drawn partly from the previously wealthy class, but also it was easier for men from the lower ranks of society to rise in status and to accumulate capital. By the end of the nineteenth century a new industrialist class, including such families as the Morozovs and the Guchkovs, was becoming both powerful and socially acceptable. Meanwhile there emerged a new proletariat, recruited from the former household serfs (who were freed without land) and also from former state and private serfs who sought a livelihood in the growing industries.

Within a generation after Emancipation the Industrial Revolution had begun to make its mark upon Russia, but old habits lingered. The Western, or at least British, traditions of enterprise, risk, and self-help did not thrive in Russia, partly because state control had been so extensive for so long. Western technology began to be borrowed early but was extended slowly. Not until the 1890's did mechanical weaving take over the cotton industry, open-hearth methods the steel industry; rotary and turbine methods of oil-drilling were not tested until 1911. Railway construction began in 1836, but an extensive network built and run by Russians did not make headway until the 1890's. As a result of the technical lag in Russia, sometimes remarkable inventions appeared, such as Ladygin's incandescent lamp and Popov's wireless telegraph, which never became widely known because there was no place to use them under the technological conditions prevailing in Russia.

The gentry who continued to try to live on their land by using the hired labor of their former serfs or other peasants did less well than the new industrialists. There was ample demand in the West for Russian agricultural products, especially bread grains, and much was shipped out through Odessa and other ports. During the early seventies it was profitable to export, but after 1875 world grain prices began to turn downward, and by 1894 Russian wheat and rye export prices had declined by approximately a third. The crop failure and subsequent famine of 1891–1892, coming on the heels of the fall in prices, brought disaster to many producers. Few of the gentry had had reason to develop habits of thrift and financial foresight, and their burden of debts, in many cases already heavy before Emancipation, now became almost insupportable. Neither the efforts of Alexander III's ministers nor their own exertions were able to arrest the decline of the gentry, which continued generally down to the Revolution.

During the seventies and eighties the growth of industry was steady but not yet spectacular. Foreigners continued to play a prominent role, witness the Swedish Nobel brothers' oil operations in Baku. Nevertheless, Russians furnished most of the capital for the more than three hundred joint-stock companies which were founded in the sixties and seventies. Most of these were banks, railroads, and steamship companies, but some capital also went into factory enterprise. The new private banks were supplemented by a reorganized State Bank.

Industrial and commercial expansion was checked somewhat by a depression in 1873–1875 and another in 1881–1882. The plight of the workers, who toiled fourteen hours a day or more for low wages and under inadequate conditions of sanitation and safety, became still worse. The new enterprises did not recover immediately from the slump, and it was only around 1890 that a pronounced upturn in business activity occurred.

THE PROSPERITY OF THE 1890'S

The upturn, however, soon became a boom. During the 1890's the number of enterprises increased by over a quarter, the number of workers by almost sixty per cent, and the value of production more than doubled. Such data indicate that industry was becoming increasingly concentrated in plants with a large labor force. Concentration tended to be geographical as well, rapid growth taking place in a small number of industrial regions. The coal industry almost tripled its output in the 1890's, the Donets Basin coming to produce almost 70% of the total in 1900. The oil industry also increased its production by nearly three times; in 1900 Baku furnished 95% of it. Iron ore output was more than tripled; over half in 1900 came from Krivoi Rog and the surrounding region of the Ukraine, while the old Ural iron industry faded into insignificance. Cotton and other industries also underwent increasing concentration. It has been computed that almost half of all industrial workers in Russia in 1902 were employed by plants with a labor force numbering one thousand or more.

One of the most striking aspects of the boom of the 1890's was railway construction. Russia's vast land area still suffered severely from poor communications. In the first half of the seventies five thousand miles of rail lines were laid, but thereafter progress lagged for fifteen years. This figure was nearly reached again in the first half of the nineties, and in the second half over ten thousand miles of line were built. This was the period of greatest construction before the Revolution, but Russia was still left with a far less adequate rail network than the advanced industrial powers of Western Europe. About half of the capital used for the building of railways came from the central government, which also guaranteed a portion of the private loans employed. A large share of these state funds came from indirect taxation, especially from the vodka monopoly. One is tempted to say that even if Russia's communications were landbound, they had an extensive liquid foundation.

Of the capital invested in Russia's railroads in 1900, some 70% came from the government, which had expended nearly half of its share during the 1890's alone. Only about 7% came from foreign investment. Nevertheless the outside funds which had gone into railways were significant, for they formed the first sizable Western investment in the Russian economy. Once foreign capital invaded the Russian rail network, it spread rapidly into Russian industries as well. Sergei Witte, minister of finance from 1892 to 1903, who did his best to stimulate industrial development generally, worked hard to attract Western capital in order to hasten the process. Whereas investment from other countries accounted for over a third of all corporation capital in 1890, it approached one-half of the total in 1900. In mining, for example, its share reached 70%, though it was only 42% in metallurgy, and in textiles it was negligible.

In 1900 the nation holding the largest share of foreign investment was Belgium, with almost 300 million rubles; next came France and Germany with around 220 million rubles each; Britain's share was about 135 million, and America's only 8 million. France had been first in 1890, and by 1914 she was first again, with about one-third of all nongovernmental foreign investments, while next in order came Britain, Germany, and Belgium. The French investors went heavily into mining and metallurgy, the British into mining, especially in the Urals and eastward, the Germans into a number of industries particularly in the western regions, the Belgians into the metallurgy of the Ukraine.

Witte was also instrumental in the floating of large government loans, much of the proceeds of which were expended by the Russian government in railway and industrial development. In 1914 nearly half of the national debt was held abroad, and of this figure France held a preponderant 80%. Although it was German loans that helped carry through the Russo-Japanese War, both public and private French money had a greater influence on Russian foreign policy and was one important consideration in Russia's alignment with the Entente powers. It also enabled the government to ride out the Revolution of 1905 and the uncertain period of the First Duma. Witte supported the protectionist tariff which had been enacted in 1891, following a policy then fashionable in the West. However, it led to two tariff wars with Germany over grain prices, at the beginning and end of his ministry, which embittered Russo-German relations and further tightened the connection with the French.

Toward the middle of the nineties, the growing industrial proletariat had begun to voice protests at the abominable working conditions prevailing in the new factories. There was a swiftly increasing demand for labor, which was partly met by a new outpouring of peasants into industry on the heels of the disastrous famine of 1891–1892. However, the demand remained unsatisfied, and the workers felt themselves in a strong position to insist that they benefit from the boom of the nineties. Beginning in 1894 a wave of strikes gained momentum in and near St. Petersburg up to the time of the textile strike in the summer of 1896 and spread into the Moscow region. The government responded by enacting the first important piece of Tsarist labor legislation, in June 1897 (see p. 59). The law limited the workday to eleven and a half hours and prohibited labor on Sundays and holidays in plants employing more than twenty workers; it also provided for inspection and enforcement. Actually inspection was unevenly carried out, but the fact remained that strikes had brought about significant government intervention on the workers' side. It is a paradox that by stepping in, the government strengthened the hand of those revolutionaries who told the workers that strikes should be political rather than economic. There were no large labor unions before 1905, and up to 1917 they remained weak; in both revolutionary years the intelligentsia assumed leadership of the workers virtually by default.

Witte's policy of industrialization continued to bear fruit after his effort to solve the labor crisis through the 1897 law. In the field of government finance he achieved his greatest success by introducing the gold standard in 1897. Russia had nominally possessed silver convertibility for a few years following 1840, but that system had collapsed before it was officially abandoned in 1858. Although the landowners profited from the existence of an unstable paper currency, which produced in effect a financial premium for exporters, Witte was not greatly concerned about them. His introduction of a gold currency was designed to increase the industrialists' ability to attract foreign capital, as well as to stabilize the financial side of domestic trade. A painful effort to build up gold reserves succeeded in raising them above the value of the notes in circulation by 1897, at which time the new system was enacted into law.

Russian industry grew rapidly in the nineties; in fact, more rapidly than the industry of the other major powers. From 1880 to 1900 Russia moved from seventh to fourth place in the smelting of pig iron, and the percentage increase in output of iron, coal, and cotton textiles was greater than in any other country including the United States. Such rapid industrial growth incidentally settled the argument which raged between the populists and the Marxists during the 1890's as to whether Russia could somehow escape "capitalism."

In the Empire's borderlands there was considerable industrial development. Poland's industry, especially in textiles, grew rapidly and spawned a more literate and impatient proletariat than that of Russia. Baku in Transcaucasia was Russia's greatest oil center, and Georgia produced important quantities of manganese, coal, etc. Tashkent and other cities of Turkestan developed cotton-ginning and other mills. Although during this period the chief feature of the Siberian economy was the development of peasant agriculture by millions of new immigrants, Siberia also came to produce butter, forest products, and other goods which were sold in quantity west of the Urals and abroad.

BUST AND BOOM

As the decade of the 1890's ended, Russia's prosperity faltered and halted. By 1899 a business crisis common to all of Europe was being felt in Russia. Prices of finished goods began to fall rapidly, and industrial output slackened. Although a number of workers were discharged, and the bargaining position of labor was weakened, a new strike movement made its appearance in 1902–1903. This time the Marxist agitators had a puzzling competitor for the leadership of organized workers, the government itself. The experiment in "police socialism," authored by Zubatov, chief of the Moscow secret police, was somewhat too successful, and after the strikes of the summer of 1903 it was largely abandoned (see p. 71). The workers had genuine grievances and were determined to air them, but only the revolutionary leaders were prepared to furnish direction.

An industrial revival began in 1903, but the strike movement continued. The labor scene remained turbulent until the great political strikes which occurred during the Revolution of 1905. The year 1904 saw a new peak in industrial production, but partly owing to the disturbance in the economy which accompanied the revolutionary events, there followed four years of leveling off or slight decrease in output.

In 1909 a new upsurge began. The major trends continued much as before. Industrial production became even further concentrated in plants which had a large labor force. The newer regions, for example the Donets Basin, improved their position vis-à-vis the older ones, such as the Urals. In general Russian capitalism went on expanding rapidly, although the rate of growth seems to have leveled off somewhat. According to Molotov, per capita production in Russia was one-eighth of that of the United States in 1900, but dropped to one-eleventh in 1913; it was one-sixth of Germany's in 1900, one-eighth in 1913.[1] However, Russia had permanently become one of the world's major industrial producer nations.

An important feature of the two decades following 1900 was the formation of syndicates and concentration of ownership in Russia's industrial structure. In 1902 a great metallurgical syndicate (*Prodamet*) was formed to sell the metal produced by plants whose output was almost three-quarters of all metal sales, and an agreement was soon reached to regulate and apportion production, prices, and market territory. However, the plants at Yuzovka in the Ukraine and the Polish mills stayed out of this arrangement. Syndicates were also formed for the sale of iron pipes, special-alloy pig iron and mined ore, coming to include the greater part of the mining and metallurgy of the south. The Ural region established other and weaker syndicates. Farm machinery and railway car construction industries followed suit. About three-quarters of all coal production was syndicated in the combination called *Produgol*. Such associations were less conspicuous in light industry; they made some headway in maritime shipping enterprise. In general, the type of amalgamation taking place was not the formation of unified trusts, but syndicates based on sales agreements. No important trusts appeared in Tsarist Russia; that remained for the Soviets to bring about under state ownership and control.

• [1] Cited by Peter I. Lyashchenko, *History of the National Economy of Russia to the 1917 Revolution*, trans. L. M. Herman (New York: Macmillan, 1949), p. 674.

From 1909 to 1913 production was again climbing rapidly. Pig iron output rose from 175 to 283 million poods; iron and steel, from 163 to 246; coal, from 1,591 to 2,214.[2] Oil lagged, and did not reach the 1905 level again before the Revolution, largely because of the damage done to the Baku oilfields during the Revolution of 1905. Farm machinery, cotton and linen output increased, and sugar production mounted swiftly. Under the conditions of economic prosperity and greater political freedom (resulting from the October Manifesto) in the final years of Tsarism, labor unions made some progress, although not enough to produce a leadership capable of competing effectively with the revolutionaries. One union complained that "the membership . . . resembles rather a crowd of wandering gypsies than a properly organized body." It is true that stable organization and solidarity among members tended to be only gradually realized in other industrial countries, but Russia's union movement did not exist long enough to permit any estimate of how it might have developed.

In the period between revolutions agriculture underwent some of the most dramatic changes in the whole Russian economy. Certain of these changes, such as the attempted destruction of the ancient village commune and the enclosure of individual land under the Stolypin laws, had social and political as well as economic causes and results. The appearance of large numbers of peasants who had full legal title to the land they worked, and the spread of enclosed farms (of one contiguous plot as contrasted with the scattered-strip system characteristic of the communal farms), placed small independent agriculture on a much more solid footing than before (see p. 107). Although the large landowners continued to decline and even disappear from the economic scene, it appears that the peasantry was able not only to fill the gap thereby created in the export market but also to increase the volume of agricultural products sent abroad. The value of cereal products exported increased 133% between 1901–1905 and 1911–1913; the value of animal products 241%. Much of the produce of the independent peasant farms was for home consumption; it improved diet and health without appearing in trade statistics.

At the outbreak of the war, the economic structure of Russia presented a mixed picture of strength and weakness, rapid and slow development, foreign and domestic control, profit and loss, governmental fiat and private initiative. During World War I Russia failed to utilize its wealth and resources to the maximum. In part the failure must be laid

• [2] A pood equals 36 pounds.

to the economy: the backwardness of technique, the inefficiency of business methods, the inadequate transportation system, and other structural weaknesses. However, even more important, and probably decisive, was the misdirection or lack of direction of industrial effort on the part of the government, which in 1914 lay in the hands of the least capable officials on the scene for a generation, perhaps for a century or more.

The

Last Years

of Tsarism

CHAPTER 8

STOLYPIN AS PRIME MINISTER

At the time the First Duma was dissolved, Peter Stolypin was appointed prime minister, replacing Goremykin. Stolypin was the most capable and clear-sighted official to serve Nicholas II and the best government servant since Michael Speransky, a century earlier. His policy was twofold: to restore order and to institute reform. That is, he attempted to break up the revolutionary groups and also to undermine their popular support by carrying through necessary social and political changes. He was a monarchist, but he was also a constitutionalist, and he desired to work harmoniously with the new Duma in the passage of reform legislation.

In his social and economic policy Stolypin staked virtually everything on turning the peasant into a small proprietor. By satisfying the peasant's immediate needs and establishing the legal and economic bases for his further self-improvement, Stolypin hoped to recapture for the regime the loyalty of the villages, which he well knew it had lost. His peasant policy had begun to germinate in his mind some years earlier. He was a landowner from Kovno who had, at home and as governor in the adjoining province of Grodno, observed a striking and puzzling phenomenon. Spontaneously, by force of example of German neighbors who practiced farming on small plots, peasants here and there were dissolving their village communes and consolidating the scattered strips into farmsteads. A Danish economist named Carl Koefoed, who was employed in the vicinity, noticed the same phenomenon with equal surprise but observed it with greater care. When Stolypin was appointed prime minister he profited from Koefoed's observations.

The village commune had legal, political, economic, and social functions and powers. Legally it owned the land (the *nadely,* or "allotments") given the peasants to use at Emancipation, and to it was entrusted the joint liability of the peasantry for the provision of recruits for the armed forces, and for the payment of the "soul tax" (levied on the individual, not the land he tilled) and of the "redemption payments" to the state for allotment land. Collective responsibility for all three had been legally terminated by 1906, but the ownership of allotment lands remained formally in the hands of the commune, whether it was of the hereditary-tenure type common in the Belorussian and Ukrainian regions, or the repartitional-tenure type prevalent in the Great Russian areas. The commune, through the village assembly, acted as an agency of self-government and determined matters affecting diverse aspects of social life. It made certain economic decisions affecting the time and manner of performing agricultural operations; the most important one was the periodic redistribution of strips of land, which was carried out by the repartitional-tenure type of commune.

By the beginning of the twentieth century, the practice of repartition had increasingly fallen into disuse, and Stolypin assumed that it would and should disappear entirely. He believed that therefore there was no further justification for the system of holding scattered strips of land, by which a rough equality had been secured to all households—each family having about the same amount of desirable and undesirable land, measured by whether it was more or less hilly, fertile, or distant from the village. In order for the strips to be replaced by enclosed contiguous plots, the commune must cease to have legal title to the land. Therefore, beginning in late 1906, Stolypin introduced laws which permitted the peasant to become a Western-style farmer in two stages: first he could obtain title as full owner of the scattered strips currently allotted for his use, then he could consolidate them into a single plot. The first step consisted simply of drawing up legal papers, but the second entailed the actual reshuffling of holdings, which required an incredibly complex surveying operation, overshadowing in difficulty the Emancipation itself.

The results were soon such as to confound the skeptics—of whom there were many, including all of the opposition parties. As the movement of enclosure gained momentum, Stolypin exulted, "You cannot stop it with cannon." The scorn of the revolutionaries changed to alarm, and Lenin grumbled, "The homesteads are helping out a handful of the rich. But the masses continue to starve as heretofore." Nevertheless he clearly recognized that if Stolypin's program continued it would make revolution immeasurably more difficult to bring about. By 1917 some two-thirds of the peasant households of the country had completed the first step, that of obtaining title. One-tenth had finished the immeasurably more complex step of enclosure and had become independent farmers. Whether or not, as Geroid T. Robinson has suggested,[1] the success of the Stolypin program was accounted for in large part by governmental pressure, there is no contesting its remarkable results. In the view of other authorities, the program succeeded because it was compatible with one of the most deep-seated aspirations of the Russian peasantry, the desire to own and manage their own land.

Stolypin's relations with the Dumas were less successful than his land program. When a Second Duma was elected, he found it to be different from its Kadet-dominated predecessor but no more disposed to discharge parliamentary functions. Since the revolutionaries had abandoned their boycott as useless, a sizable extreme Leftist contingent had been elected; and correspondingly greater activity by reactionary forces, who viewed the October Manifesto as a pernicious innovation, produced a large Rightist delegation as well. The "Union of October 17," or Octobrist party, which based its policy on acceptance of the Manifesto, had an uneasy centrist position to maintain. Alexander Guchkov, their leader, was willing to co-operate with Stolypin. However, the centrists were helpless before the two extremist groups which hated each other but shared the objective of preventing the Duma from functioning. Stolypin concluded that no assembly chosen under the existing suffrage law could work. After the Second Duma had sat for two months, Stolypin persuaded the Tsar to dissolve it, as he had the First Duma. There followed immediately the promulgation of a new electoral law on June 16, 1907, which drastically curtailed the suffrage. The edict was contrary to the Fundamental Laws of 1906, and the Left vigorously denounced Stolypin. In the Third Duma, which met in the closing months of 1907 and lasted out its term of five years, the revolutionaries were reduced to a handful. Stolypin now encountered his most active opposition from the Right, but the centrist forces were strong enough to carry through a legislative program in harmony with the existing government.

• [1] Geroid Tanquary Robinson, *Rural Russia Under the Old Regime* (New York: Macmillan, 1949), p. 264.

Meanwhile he was carrying out his program of "pacification," that is, repression of the revolutionary groups. A renewal of terrorism by the Socialist Revolutionaries was countered by widespread arrests. In 1908 the accidental exposure of the amazing case of the double agent Evno Azef, who had served both the Tsarist police and the S.R. party, apparently with a degree of loyalty to both, nearly wrecked the party. The Social Democrats were also hunted down systematically, and by 1908 the chief leaders were either driven abroad (like Lenin and Trotsky) or exiled to Siberia (like Stalin). While the violence lasted, Stolypin used field courts-martial against the revolutionaries, and the phrase "Stolypin's neckties" was used to describe the hangman's nooses which dispatched many offenders.

Both the legality and the political wisdom of Stolypin's antirevolutionary measures were widely criticised, even by some who generally sympathized with his aims. However, it is fair to point out that the government was not seeking merely to punish the leaders of the 1905 Revolution or to intimidate those doctrinally committed to destroy it, but also had to deal with continuing violence. In 1906–1907 the revolutionaries murdered more than four thousand officials and carried out many bank robberies in order to replenish party coffers. Stolypin himself narrowly missed assassination in August 1906 by revolutionaries who maimed his son and daughter.

In the Third Duma the Octobrists, led by Guchkov, were the largest single group. They were willing to co-operate with Stolypin in his land program, which was vigorously opposed by all parties of the Left (including the liberal Kadets) as well as by the Right, which feared for the fate of the gentry. Guchkov and Stolypin finally quarreled, and toward the end of his ministry Stolypin was leaning less on the Octobrists than on his own new party, the Nationalists.

Nevertheless, the Third Duma in general devoted itself to serious legislative action in a manner which discouraged both the extreme Left and the extreme Right and encouraged constitutionalists among the officialdom and in the Duma itself. It passed several measures relating to improvement of the peasants' condition west of the Urals and facilitating migration to Asiatic Russia. It enacted laws for accident insurance and sickness benefits which established active participation by labor representatives in their administration. In 1908 it provided for the step-by-step establishment of a compulsory free school system for all children aged eight to eleven (a four-year curriculum), and three years later a proposal to speed up the realization of this goal was passed by the Duma but was rejected by the Imperial Council. However, even by the timetable of the 1908 law, all Russia's children would have been in school by 1922. The plan of the 1911 draft was revived by the government in 1915, but the war crisis was then overshadowing all else and no action was taken.

Stolypin's Rightist opponents, who killed the 1911 school bill, were strongly entrenched in the Imperial Council. His conflict with the Right came to a head over a bill to introduce the zemstvo into the western provinces, favoring Belorussian and Ukrainian peasants at the expense of the Polish gentry. Stolypin chose the moment when the Imperial Council threw out the bill, previously passed by the Duma, to force the issue. Both houses were prorogued for three days. During this time he enacted the zemstvo bill into law in accordance with Article 87 of the Fundamental Laws, which authorized emergency decrees by the government when the legislative bodies were not sitting. (Although such decrees were to remain in force only on condition that they were subsequently approved by the Duma within a certain period, sometimes this stipulation was simply ignored.) Stolypin forced the Emperor to this step under threat of resignation. Public opinion condemned the move, even though there was widespread sympathy for the zemstvo bill which thereby became law. Nicholas II did not like ministers who forced his hand—as Witte had done with the October Manifesto—and probably Stolypin would have been dismissed if he had not been murdered in September 1911. His assassin was a double agent of the Azef stripe, whose motives remain cloudy to this day.

Under Stolypin's ministry, the Tsarist government made its last best effort. The major officials understood both the nature of peasant aspirations and the magnitude of the revolutionary threat to all they held dear. Stolypin's able assistant, A. V. Krivoshein, survived him in life but not for long in power. V. N. Kokovtsev, competent but unimaginative, became the nominal chief of government. In January 1914 the prime ministry passed to I. L. Goremykin, who for generations had been getting feebler and lazier in government service and at the age of seventy-five managed to appear and act decades older.

THE ASCENDANCY OF RASPUTIN

The real power tended to pass, not to Stolypin's successors, but to the court. Ministers were ever more frequently named on the basis of their acquaintanceship with Gregory Rasputin (whose real name was Novykh). This figure, truly unparalleled in history, was a *starets* or "holy man"—not, as has often been said, a member of the clergy—from the Tobolsk region. He owed his ascendancy in political affairs to his personal influence over the Imperial family, especially the Empress. The heir to the throne, the boy Alexis, had inherited hemophilia from his mother and stood in constant danger of death from any slight injury. More than once the intervention of Rasputin coincided with the cessation of bleeding, and the Empress regarded him as a "man sent by God" to preserve her son and the dynasty from destruction. Rasputin's personal behavior was continually provoking scandals, some of which involved ladies of St. Petersburg's highest society. The Empress received police reports about all this and dismissed them with the remark, "Read the Apostles: they kissed as a sign of greeting." If Rasputin was responsible for the survival of her boy, surely he could be trusted in the tedious realm of politics.

Rasputin had been introduced to the Imperial family in 1905, but as long as Stolypin lived he was able to prevent the "holy man's" influence from penetrating the government to any extent. However, after Stolypin's assassination Rasputin's political importance grew rapidly. The Left found in him a convenient symbol of corruption and decay in the regime; but it was the centrists and reactionaries who attacked him sharply in the Duma, for they recognized in him a formidable threat to any kind of possibility of efficient government. His political views were not a major issue; his influence was exerted, not necessarily on behalf of conservative or reactionary policies, but to advance to posts of authority his friends and confidants, many of whom proved incompetent and weak-minded. This psychopathic tragicomedy was played up to the time when any serious Russian participation in World War I came to an end. In December 1916 Rasputin was assassinated by a cabal of courtiers and conservatives.

In 1912 the domestic situation, deprived of Stolypin's strong hand, was swiftly deteriorating. In that year the massacre of strikers in the Lena goldfields led to widespread public outcry and turmoil in the Duma. Russia's industrial prosperity was opening the way to another strike movement which mounted in 1913 and the early months of 1914. The progress of rural reform in European Russia and the building of a new and prosperous peasant society in Siberia continued despite Stolypin's removal, but they had little direct effect on the unstable condition of the cities and none on the paralysis which was creeping over the central government. Under such circumstances Russia entered the World War.

THE COMING OF THE WAR

The war was the result of the foreign policy of all major European powers in an age of secret diplomacy and political and economic competition outside Europe. It was not "imperialism," in the sense Lenin used the word, which brought war. It was not competition for overseas investment targets or markets, nor rivalry between the governments of nations which had surplus capital to dispose of, which precipitated the conflagration (see p. 112). Perhaps the most important underlying cause was nationalism, in particular the unsatisfied nationalist aspirations of the Serbs and the nationalist pride of Austro-Hungarian and Russian public opinion on the most influential levels. The powder keg had been readied for the nationalist spark by the formation of the alliance between Austria-Hungary and Germany (and Italy, which, however, refused later to implement the alliance and eventually fought on the opposite side) on the one hand and the entente between Great Britain, France, and Russia on the other.

Russia found herself in unwonted company. Britain had been her chief diplomatic bugbear of recent times, the power which had frustrated Russian objectives in regard to Turkey, clashed with Russian influence in the Middle East, and supported Japan in restraining Russian expansion in the Pacific. France was Russia's ancient enemy, the ally of her formerly most dangerous neighbors (Turkey and Poland), and since the French Revolution ideological hostility had been added to the historic antagonism between governments. In contrast, Germany had been Russia's closest friend, as she had been England's, too, up to the last decades of the century. Until the middle of the century, Austria had also been friendly toward Russia. In 1849 Nicholas I had crushed the revolution in Hungary and handed the country back to the Hapsburgs, asking nothing in return; however, Austria adopted a hostile attitude during the Crimean War, and since then relations between the two powers had become increasingly embittered. Bismarck's attempt to mediate foundered on Austro-Russian rivalry for influence over the emerging independent states of the Balkans.

There were many diplomatic crises near the turn of the century, but those which led to the war were in the Balkans. Traditionally the Serbs, even more than other Slavs outside Russia, looked to St. Petersburg for sympathy, which Pan-Slav circles willingly gave, and support, which the government was often reluctant to give if the risk seemed great. In 1908 Austria flouted Serbian nationalism by annexing Bosnia-Herzegovina; in 1913 it succeeded in setting up an independent Albania, barring Serbia from the Adriatic; in June 1914 Serbian nationalists assassinated the heir to the Austrian throne in Sarajevo, and Vienna retaliated by an ultimatum to Serbia, followed by a declaration of war on July 28. Russia had the choice of permitting Austria once again to humiliate and possibly destroy Serbia, or to come to its aid. The first alternative would have been a confession of national weakness and moral abasement in the eyes of public opinion within Russia and abroad. After hesitating between partial mobilization (intended as a threat to Austria but a reassurance to Germany) and general mobilization, on July 30 the Russian government decided on the latter. The result was general war.

Within Russia there were immediate and strong manifestations of patriotism. To an assembly of dignitaries in the Winter Palace the Tsar solemnly repeated the oath taken by Alexander I in 1812, vowing not to make peace while a single enemy remained on Russian soil. He then stepped onto the balcony, while the multitude below fell on their knees and sang "God Save the Tsar" as it had not been sung in Russia for many years. The Duma met and voted war credits. The pattern of the West European socialists' behavior in the face of the war waged by their "capitalist" governments was approximated in the Duma, where Alexander Kerensky, leader of the Trudovik party, led the revolutionaries in abstaining from the vote on war credits but in offering help in defending the country.

In Lenin's eyes the war was nothing but an "imperialist" war—that is, a war into which the development of capitalism in its highest stage had unavoidably thrown the governments of the European powers, which were struggling for a new redivision of the world's colonies and spheres of influence. He took for granted that the "capitalist" governments would behave as they did; his chief animus was directed against the parties and men of the Second International who either in theory or in practice supported or condoned to any degree whatsoever the war efforts of their respective governments. In effect the Second International ceased to function at the outbreak of war. The majority of the German, Austrian, French, English, and Belgian socialists accepted a "class truce." However, socialists of Russia, Italy (which declared war on Austria-Hungary in May 1915 but not on Germany until August 1916), the neutral nations, and dissidents from other belligerent powers tried to restore the International on the basis of rejecting the "truce." At Zimmerwald in September 1915 and Kienthal in April 1916 they met for that purpose, but they were themselves divided, since Lenin wished not to go back to the prewar organization but to launch a new Third International devoted to active revolutionary preparations. The meetings failed, but Lenin's leadership of the "Zimmerwald Left" foreshadowed the direction in which he led the Bolsheviks when he returned to Russia in 1917. Before that time, however, few Russians knew or cared who he was or what he thought about the war or anything else.

THE WAR ON THE EASTERN FRONT

The government of Russia was unprepared for war, but so were the British and, later, the United States governments. What was decisive was that the government was incapable of carrying out preparations and was unable or unwilling to utilize the patriotic enthusiasm of the people and public bodies toward effective prosecution of the war. The gigantic enterprise of mobilization took place successfully, with little effort by recruits to evade service and much evidence of willingness to fight, but many were neither trained nor supplied properly. The Duma set to work to organize Red Cross assistance and the zemstvos and municipalities to improve supply services, but the government received their offers of support coolly and lackadaisically.

The whole economy was greatly strained by the war. Although the mobilization did not severely damage peasant farming (since women and boys could fill the breach, and much produce was consumed rather than sold), it did great harm to the large estates (which depended on hired labor, and produced chiefly for market). The inroads of war in the west, by cutting down the cultivated area available to Russia, further diminished the food supply. The railway network, insufficient even for peacetime needs, was not adequately maintained or furnished with rolling stock, owing to the stringent economies carried out by the communications ministry from 1909 right up to 1915. Instead of taking measures to increase production, the government initially told manufacturers to anticipate a decrease in demand because of the shrinkage of international trade, and the warning led many to slash their output.

Civilian rule in areas adjacent to the front was at once replaced by military control. The commander-in-chief was the Grand Duke Nicholas, the Emperor's uncle, who was popular among the soldiers but none too competent in his post. His military government in the western provinces provoked innumerable complaints, which consumed a good deal of the time of the central authorities without leading to any significant result. The army's officer corps ranged from good to indifferent in quality, and the majority of the recruits lacked proper training and equipment. This force was hurled into a battle in which the vastnesses of distance, numbers of men, and quantities of supplies were greater than in any previous military campaigns.

The Russian plan was to strike through Austrian Galicia, in order to save Serbia, prevent an attempt to seize Russian Poland from the right flank, and to annex "Russian" (Ukrainian) territory held by Austria-Hungary. However, the crisis which immediately developed on the

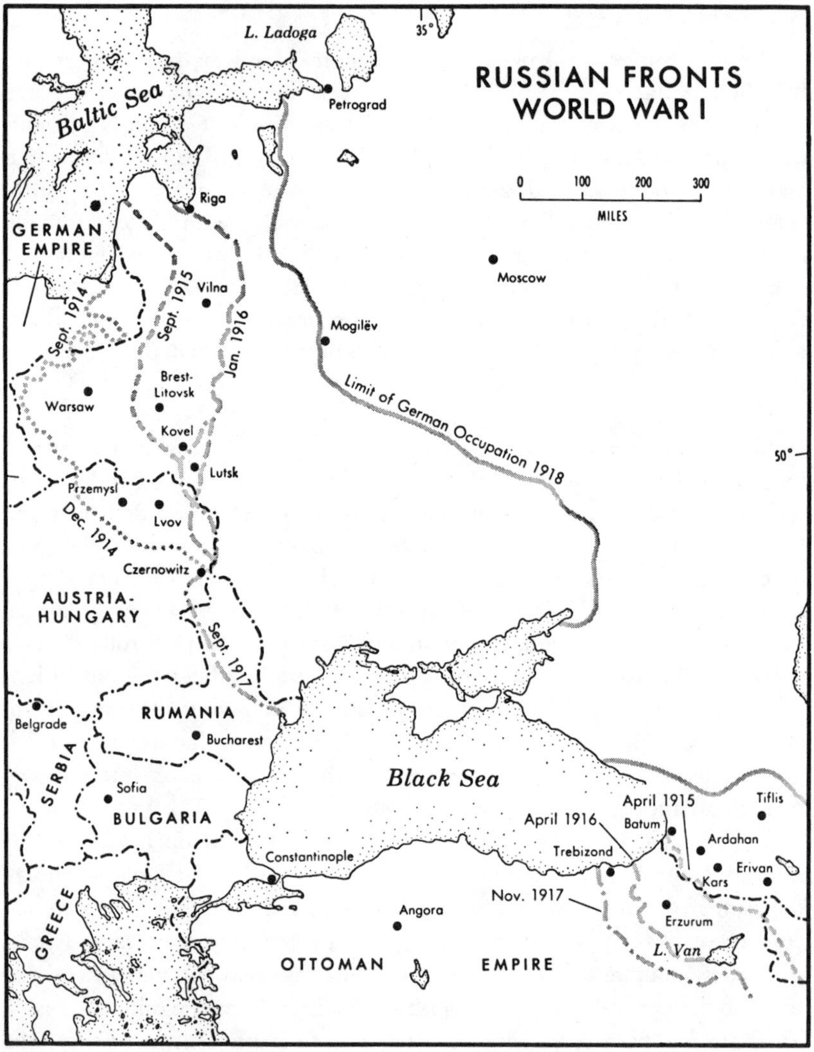

Western front because of the German dash for Paris led the Russian command to mount a hasty offensive against the Germans in East Prussia. Their armies were shattered by Hindenburg and Ludendorff in battles in which the Russians lost some three hundred thousand men. Nevertheless the simultaneous Russian offensive in Galicia, using twice the number of troops which were deployed on the German front, hurt the Austrians even more than the Germans had hurt them. Russian troops captured Lvov, and by the middle of September 1914 they were nearing Przemysl. The Germans had diverted troops from the Marne battlefront to meet the danger in East Prussia; the diversion slowed down their offensive and thus helped to bring about the stalemate in the West which continued for almost the whole duration of the war. In the fall campaign the Russian armies had helped to save France, damaged Austria severely, and although defeated in East Prussia had repulsed a German thrust toward Warsaw.

At the beginning of hostilities St. Petersburg had announced as Russian war aims the reunification of Poland as an autonomous state of the Russian Empire and the annexation of the Austro-Hungarian territories inhabited by Ukrainians (although the word "Ukrainian" was not used). A few weeks later Foreign Minister Sergei Sazonov announced a program of "Twelve Points," which Woodrow Wilson's Fourteen were to resemble in many details. They even included affirmation of the "principle of nationalities" as determining future territorial changes. The main objective of "the three allies" was said to be "to strike at German power and its pretensions to military and political domination"; Austria-Hungary was to become a triple monarchy (Bohemia was to take its place beside the two existing divisions), but would not be dismembered.[2] Sazonov's policy of close harmony with Britain and France and genuine autonomy for Poland aroused little enthusiasm on the Rightist side. However, when Turkey was drawn into the war in November 1914 through the guidance of the pro-German war minister, Enver Pasha, and the question of the Straits entered diplomatic and public discussion, the Right warmed to the cause of the war.

Sazonov was not primarily interested in the Straits, but when the British prepared to seize the Dardanelles at the beginning of 1915 he became suspicious that they intended either to annex Constantinople themselves or to turn it over to Greece. Both conservatives and liberals in the Duma supported Sazonov in seeking Allied acceptance of Russian control of the Straits. In March 1915, with certain reservations and accompanying compensation for Britain in Persia and France in Syria, the Western Allies conceded the point in the secret Straits Agreement. The collapse of Turkey was widely anticipated at the time of the British landing at Gallipoli in April; this expectation finally led Italy to enter the war on the conditions outlined in the secret Treaty of London the same

• [2] The text of the Twelve Points is given in C. Jay Smith, Jr., *The Russian Struggle for Power, 1914–1917* (New York: Philosophical Library, 1956), pp. 46–48.

month. By the treaty Russia consented to Italian annexation of a part of the South Slav coast; Serbs and other South Slavs protested, but they had only rumors to tell them what had been done.

THE CRISIS OF 1915

The spring campaign of 1915 opened with the Russian capture of Przemysl in Galicia in March. The Russian armies pressed on toward Hungary, and the very existence of the Dual Monarchy seemed in danger. However, on May 2 the Germans and Austrians began a full-scale offensive, and the tide turned very rapidly, wiping out the Russian gains of the previous fall and early spring. On July 1 a new combined Austro-German offensive began, closing a gigantic pincers on Poland. By early August the Austrians had advanced to Lutsk; the Germans captured Warsaw and continued on to take Brest-Litovsk and, in September, Vilna. By October the Eastern front ran roughly from Riga south to Czernowitz.

It is surprising that the Russian armies were extricated from the disaster at all. It was not that troops could nor would not fight, but because of the faulty replacement system, front-line units were short of manpower, and the deficiency in munitions was grave. There were staggering casualties—two million in 1915 alone. The civilian population retreated with the armies voluntarily, or, more often, because they were ordered to do so. Well over three million refugees were hurled into the interior, despite the protests of the civilian authorities at the policy of the high command responsible for the human flood.

The shock of defeat did produce a temporary improvement in the domestic situation. A new effort at "mobilization of industry" sharply reversed the previous passive economic policy of the government. In the summer of 1915 "special councils" were established for national defense, transportation, fuel, food, and refugees by initiative of the Duma; war industries committees were set up at the urging of business circles; and the Unions of Zemstvos and Towns *(Zemgor)* took an increasingly active role in the supply crisis.

The liberals took heart when four of the most reactionary ministers were removed from the government. The occasion for their fall was the continuing debate about treatment of Poland. In February 1915 the Poles were given a new and sympathetic governor-general, Prince Engalychev, and even the reactionary military governor of Galicia was persuaded to take a more pro-Polish view by Professor Stanislaw Grabski of the University of Lvov. The Emperor was prevailed upon by the Sazonov camp to order an end to restrictions on the Roman Catholics of Poland and to promise the Poles zemstvo institutions. Minister of Interior N. A. Maklakov and others sharply opposed the concessions to Poland but committed political suicide by linking their opposition with support of immediate peace with Germany, and in June the Emperor dismissed them. The majority of the Duma was alarmed by the military debacle and hoped that the Emperor could be persuaded to adopt a political line of national unity. In September the formation was announced of a Progressive Bloc of parties ranging from the Kadets to the Progressive Nationalists, demanding a "united government consisting of persons who enjoy the confidence of the country and are in agreement with the legislative chambers . . .," the end of religious and ethnic discrimination, restrictions on trade-unions, extension of the Great Reforms, and an amnesty for religious and political offenders. Many public groups echoed the manifesto, some flatly demanding a ministry responsible to the Duma.

Although the majority of the ministers was willing to accept the program of the Progressive Bloc, Prime Minister Goremykin was not. He ran to the Empress, who was by now nearly all-powerful, and obtained the proroguing of the Duma. Two days later, on September 18, Nicholas II dismissed his uncle and himself assumed the command at the front. The military consequences of this Imperial gesture were fortunately not serious, since his chief of staff, General Alexeev, was capable and had good judgment, and there was also a new and energetic war minister, General Polivanov. However, the effect on the domestic situation was much worse; the direction of government was left in the hands of the Empress and Rasputin. Public opinion was aghast, and in spite of Goremykin's efforts, ten ministers begged the Emperor to reconsider his fateful decision to assume the command—quite in vain. Several were soon dismissed for their courage, and in February 1916 even Goremykin was replaced by Boris Stürmer. Stürmer's mental endowments were still more modest than those of his predecessor; his chief asset was that he was the choice of Rasputin. In the Duma one reactionary deputy, begging consent to his violation of the ban on the use of the "enemy language," German, uttered two words: "Oberhofmeister [the official title of a court post which the man held] Stürmer."

At the beginning of 1916 the military situation looked bleak. In the closing months of 1915, on the heels of the Russian defeat, Bulgaria had been drawn in on the side of the Central Powers, both Serbia and Montenegro had been completely overrun, and the British assault on the Dardanelles had been abandoned. Nevertheless the picture was not wholly dark. Russia had suffered a grievous blow, but the army could still fight, and no one publicly discussed any other aim than victory;

moreover, it was realized that the Central Powers were also war-weary. Owing to the initiative taken by private and semipublic bodies, the munitions and supply situation had been considerably improved. On the Caucasian front, Russian troops pushed into Turkish Armenia, reaching Trebizond in April 1916.

On the Eastern front, Russia could still mount an offensive. After several changes of plan, Alexeev decided to concentrate on the Austrians. Under General Brusilov, a large-scale attack began in June and made swift progress. Brusilov's forces recaptured Lutsk, and neared the railway junction of Kovel; the number of Austrian prisoners approached half a million. Rumania, which had engaged in hard bargaining with the Allies for many months, finally entered the war in August. The German chief of the general staff, General von Falkenhayn, who had been preoccupied with the West and the siege of Verdun, was promptly relieved by Hindenburg, who had consistently advocated a decision in the East. Austria, caught by surprise, was compelled to ease its pressure on Italy.

However, the Russians had suffered a third of a million casualties even while the offensive was making progress. German forces were rushed from the Western front; Brusilov continued to attack, and the total of Russian casualties for the year approached a million, but nothing was gained, and his forces were nearly demoralized. The entry of the Rumanians, though it alarmed the enemy, proved disastrous for the Allies. In a swift campaign the Central Powers crushed Rumania, entering the capital, Bucharest, on December 6, 1916.

In the spring of 1916, partly because of French pressure but in line with Sazonov's policy, the Russian government prepared a new declaration about Poland, promising a separate Polish Council of Ministers and a two-house legislature. Especially in view of Brusilov's success on the front in Poland in the summer, Alexeev gave Sazonov strong support. The Emperor was won over to the declaration, but Rasputin opposed it. In July Stürmer and the Empress visited the Tsar at Supreme Headquarters at Mogilëv, and obtained Sazonov's dismissal, even though the decision for Polish autonomy (for the time being secret) was to stand.

THE FALL OF THE MONARCHY

The final crisis of the regime began in the fall of 1916. In the capital an atmosphere of intrigue and suspicion poisoned serious efforts to continue the war. In September the appointment as minister of interior of A. D. Protopopov, a Duma deputy and a moderate liberal, had an effect opposite to that intended. It was revealed that he was Rasputin's choice, and at least as serious was the exposure of his mental deterioration to the verge of insanity. In November the Duma reconvened. Poor Stürmer, who understood little of what was happening but was blamed by all shades of public opinion for the military debacle, was scheduled to announce to the Duma both the secret agreement on the Straits and the decision on Polish autonomy. However, he could not bring himself to go through with the plan. The sensational speech of the session was made not by Stürmer but by the Kadet leader, Paul Miliukov. He angrily enumerated the failures of governmental policy, mentioning the Empress and Stürmer by name, and ending each indictment with the question, "Is this stupidity or treason?" In the ensuing uproar Nicholas could either have dismissed Stürmer or have chastised his critics into silence. On Alexeev's urging, he dismissed Stürmer but did nothing further to quell rising dissatisfaction with the government.

The reactionary deputy, Purishkevich, now attacked Rasputin openly in the Duma. Schemes for a palace coup were being bruited around the court with little effort at secrecy. In the last days of December a conspiracy of Purishkevich, the Emperor's nephew, and one of his cousins by marriage planned and executed the murder of Rasputin. This puzzling figure, who combined a personally scandalous and corrupt manner of life with a peasant's naive and ignorant love for his country, had to be poisoned, shot, and drowned before he would die, in an evening of horror and suspense. An episode unprecedented in the modern annals of a great country thus reached an appropriately melodramatic denouement. The Empress was deeply shocked but helpless to suggest anything further. The Emperor could only appoint as prime minister a friend of the Empress's, Prince N. D. Golitsyn, who was utterly unprepared for office. In fact he said that he took the post to have one more memory for his old age, which indeed was already upon him.

In the beginning of February 1917 the country was full of rumors of coming change, peaceful or violent. However, an inter-Allied military conference was held in Petrograd to plan the campaigns for the year, and the Emperor went off to Supreme Headquarters at Mogilëv, leaving behind him a capital in which everything appeared on the surface to be normal and calm. On March 8 demonstrations were held celebrating International Women's Day, which merged with crowds in rioting in protest at the shortage of bread in Petrograd. The garrison commander wired reports to the Emperor at the front, who merely ordered that the disturbances be halted. The day before he had written to the Empress, "I greatly miss my half-hourly game of patience every evening. I shall take up dominoes again in my spare time."

As the riots continued, the Emperor could think of nothing but to prorogue the Duma, which he did on March 11. The next day the Duma met in defiance of the order and elected a provisional committee composed of members of the Progressive Bloc (see p. 117) and two representatives of parties to the left of it, Alexander Kerensky (Trudovik) and N. S. Chkheidze (Menshevik). The committee had the vague mission "to restore order and to deal with institutions and individuals." The garrison was still patrolling the streets. "But a junior French diplomat," writes Sir John Maynard, "took note of a trifling incident. He saw a Cossack wink to the rioters."[3] By evening the garrison had broken discipline and was no longer at the disposal of its commander. On the same day, March 12 (February 27, O.S.),[4] the Taurida Palace was invaded by men who, entering rooms not occupied by the Duma, founded a Petrograd Soviet of Workers' Deputies, modeling itself on the institutions prominent in the 1905 events. (On March 15, taking note of the attitude of the soldiers in the capital and at the front, it was to rename itself the Soviet of Workers' and Soldiers' Deputies.)

By the night of March 13 most of the old ministry was under arrest. The same night the Emperor tried to reach Petrograd, but his train was halted and sent on to Pskov. There General Alexeev, other high officers, and two Progressive Bloc leaders, V. V. Shulgin (Progressive Nationalist) and Alexander Guchkov (Octobrist), talked with the Emperor, begging him to abdicate. He decided first to turn over the throne to his son but then changed his mind, and on March 15 he abdicated in favor of his brother, Grand Duke Michael. A delegation from the provisional committee of the Duma (by now renamed the Provisional Government) waited on the Grand Duke, who found it prudent to refuse. The monarchy thus perished without a murmur from either the dynasty or its supporters.

Although his family had ruled Russia over three centuries, and although he had previously accepted demands for reform only rarely and under great pressure, Nicholas II renounced power calmly. On his train the next day he wrote in his diary, "I had a long and sound sleep. Woke up beyond Dvinsk. Sunshine and frost. . . . I read much of Julius Caesar." He and the whole imperial family were detained in ambiguous circumstances in the palace at Tsarskoe Selo outside of Petrograd. It was planned that they would be sent to England, but the plans never bore fruit. During the succeeding months Nicholas developed a certain enthusiasm for the man who most nearly became his successor in power, Ker-

• [3] *Russia in Flux*, p. 177.

• [4] The conventional date of the February Revolution, so called from the old calendar in use in Russia until February 1/14, 1918.

ensky. In July he wrote in his diary that Kerensky "was the right man in the right place. The more power he gets, the better." In the summer of 1917 the Romanovs were moved to Siberia, and in July 1918 they were all murdered by the Communists.

Nicholas II was a man who wished the best for his country and his people, and he sometimes recognized and tried to correct the abuses others pointed out to him. But he also made a series of stupid mistakes, and failed to understand the grave problems which Russia faced. Perhaps the least competent of his dynasty for a century, he was weak, and so were many of the high officials he appointed and trusted, but he also found able advisers, such as Stolypin, Witte, and Krivoshein. However, even if they were strong and competent, the officials had to operate within the framework of an oppressive bureaucratic system. Although its nominally all-embracing power had fortunately long been tempered by inefficiency, and some of its former functions had latterly been entrusted to the zemstvos, city councils, and the Duma, nevertheless the structure of Tsarism remained strong enough to discourage or override any political initiative which came from outside it, as shown in the period of Russia's participation in World War I.

Russia's government proved itself unequal to the strain of conducting twentieth-century warfare, in which the front depended heavily on the morale and political and economic vitality of the rear. As the political bankruptcy of the regime became increasingly clear, many expected that it would crumble and in so doing open the way to a continuation and acceleration of the enormous changes in Russian society during the past half-century. In Russia and its borderlands, the years of Nicholas II's reign witnessed a speedy industrial growth; a sweeping transformation of the peasantry into small proprietors; the rapid spread of education; new, diverse, and original cultural developments; the schooling of a generation in political experience through the zemstvos, municipalities, the Duma, and the courts; and an amazing growth of Siberia. Nicholas II and the government favored most of these changes, although they were not originated or even steadily supported by the regime.

When the Communists came to power, however, they either reversed these currents, so full of promise for Russia's future, or (as in the case of education and industrialization) brought them under the control of the Soviet state and used them to serve their own purposes. The old dynastic absolutism left behind it much that was healthy and promising which the new totalitarianism stifled or corrupted. Russia's tragedy lay in the fact that although many of those who led or supported the Revolution did so in the hope of giving free rein to the currents of modernization, nevertheless the new regime which emerged was ultimately committed not to creative economic, social, political, and cultural diversity but to monolithic unity of all aspects of life. While Nicholas II and his government no doubt stunted Russian political growth, they left many other realms of life alone to develop as they might. The men of the February Revolution desired more state control of society, not less, but by making the government responsive to the people's wishes they intended that change should depend on initiative from below. The Communists aimed at total control and initiative from above, and in the generations which followed the extent to which they achieved their aims was impressive indeed.

Part TWO

The Communists Take Power

The February Revolution

★
★
★
★
★
★
★
★
★
★

CHAPTER 9

PROSPECTS FOR DEMOCRACY

According to Alexander Kerensky, the February Revolution "marked the end of a long and painful trail from pure absolutism to absolute democracy. That which only the day before appeared as a distant dream came true so suddenly and so very completely. . . . The people themselves were in power, the people themselves were the owners of Russia." In contrast to the earlier English, American, and French revolutions, the Russian Revolution proclaimed the theory of democratic government as a settled principle at the moment the monarch fell from power. Even the most conservative of the principal White leaders in the Civil War, General Wrangel, angered his fellow monarchists by declaring that the question of the monarchy was one which only the people could decide. There were virtually no theorists of royal absolutism left the day after the Romanov dynasty yielded its power. The real questions were, what sort of democratic government should there be, and what should it do? Could the people of Russia find institutions and leaders through which their wishes could be expressed? This was the problem of democracy in Russia, as it may one day be again, as it is in many other countries today, since in the modern state there is no way for "the people" to exercise power directly.

From the beginning there was some doubt as to where the real power lay. On March 12 two authoritative bodies had been organized in the Taurida Palace, the provisional committee of the Duma and the Petrograd Soviet of Workers' Deputies. On March 15 they were renamed; the former assumed the title of Provisional Government, the latter of Petrograd Soviet of Workers' and Soldiers' Deputies. As he abdicated, Nicholas II appointed Prince George Lvov prime minister, in order that power should be legally transferred to his successor. Led by Wilson's America, the Allies were soon to recognize the Provisional Government as the legitimate one. However, it actually existed only by sufferance of the Soviet.

The Provisional Government consisted of representatives of the major parties of the Duma Left and Center—the parties of the Right very nearly evaporated overnight. The Kadets furnished the prime minister, Lvov, a figure who owed his prominence more to his war work in *Zemgor* than to his party regularity, and the foreign minister, Paul Miliukov, gifted historian and the real party leader, who was also the most influential man in the cabinet. The Octobrists contributed their leader, Alexander Guchkov, as war and navy minister. The prominent Ukrainian businessman, M. I. Tereshchenko, became minister of finance. There was only one representative of the revolutionary parties, Alexander Kerensky, who was minister of justice. The former leader of the Trudoviks, he became a "March S.R.," as did many others who had belonged to one of the small parties or to no party prior to the Revolution. Both Lvov and Kerensky exhibited an intoxication with history, rather than a clear appraisal or a firm policy. Kerensky repeated over and over, "I am sent by the revolution," and similar phrases; in fact, he seemed an inexhaustible font of speeches, orders, and activities of all sorts, and constantly managed to appear to be in several places at the same time.

Kerensky was the only revolutionary in the cabinet, but even he was not there because his party, or the Soviet in which his party shared control with the Mensheviks, wanted him to be. The Soviet decided to stand aside from the Provisional Government, and he violated the decision, telling the Soviet what he had done and then departing abruptly before it could remonstrate with him. The Petrograd Soviet began with a seemingly spontaneous meeting of revolutionary leaders on the afternoon of March 12. They established an Executive Committee for the Soviet, which did not convene until evening. The Soviet was supposed to represent the workers of the Petrograd factories, but it is difficult to determine how accurately it did so. Almost three weeks elapsed before it was decided to have one deputy for each two thousand workers (or soldiers), and even this rule was not always followed.

The Taurida Palace soon became something like a madhouse, filled with milling deputies, ministers, petitioners, onlookers, etc., and the Soviet moved its headquarters elsewhere. Business was done by a handful of men within the Executive Committee of the Petrograd Soviet, who continued to make the important decisions even after soviets had spread all over the country and, in June, a national Central Executive Committee had been elected by the I Congress of Soviets. The first act of the Petrograd Executive Committee was to issue the famed Order No. 1, which provided for the setting up in every army unit of elective committees and announced that military orders of the Provisional Government should be obeyed only if they did not conflict with Soviet orders. The actual effect of this order was to initiate election of officers and open the way to a breakdown of the discipline and morale of the army on the widest scale.

Although Order No. 1 was nothing if not a governmental act, it was not followed by any other such acts of significance. The policy of the Petrograd Executive Committee was to abstain from exercising the authority which it in fact possessed, and upon which the Provisional Government depended. The reason for this puzzling behavior must be sought in revolutionary political theory—specifically the view of the Mensheviks, who dominated their partnership with the S.R.'s in controlling the Soviets (until September). In Menshevik eyes, the February Revolution was a "bourgeois revolution"; history determined that power must be held by bourgeois liberals; it was the task of the workers' party to refrain from compromising itself in the workers' eyes by taking power and undertaking historical tasks which were bound to be premature and could only discredit the party (see p. 61). The Menshevik leaders of the Executive Committee, Chairman Chkheidze, M. I. Skobelev, N. N. Sukhanov, and others, took this theory very seriously. The Socialist Revolutionaries, never as sure of themselves about doctrine as their Marxist colleagues, went along with it despite some grumbling. Sukhanov recounts how he chatted with Miliukov, the Kadet leader and presumably the foremost "bourgeois liberal." Identifying himself ironically as "your worst enemy," Sukhanov proceeded to tempt Miliukov with what he regarded as historically inevitable: "Do you propose, now that we are in an atmosphere of revolution, to take state power into your own hands?" and was much annoyed that he received only an equivocal and puzzled answer.[1]

• [1] N. N. Sukhanov, *The Russian Revolution, 1917*, ed., abridged, and trans. Joel Carmichael (London: Oxford University Press, 1955), p. 56.

The theory of obligatory abstention from power was compromised from the start by Kerensky's participation in the Provisional Government, as well as by Order No. 1, and was soon to be stretched still further. Nevertheless, it was not discarded. As a result the Provisional Government limped along, dependent on the Soviet, in a situation which was characterized by Trotsky in the phrase, "dual power." Dual power, wherein one agency would not and the other could not rule, prevented any possibility of effective government.

FIRST CRISIS OF THE PROVISIONAL GOVERNMENT

On March 16 the Provisional Government, in agreement with the Executive Committee of the Petrograd Soviet, announced its objectives. They included the convening of a Constituent Assembly (for which generations of revolutionaries had waited), immediate granting of unqualified civil liberties, democratization of local government, and an amnesty to political prisoners. The amnesty had largely taken effect already. On April 2 equal rights were granted to all irrespective of race or religion. Democratic self-government was not achieved, although a proliferation of committees and officials occurred which made local authority in fact supreme in large areas of the country, and a little later many of the self-constituted local bodies submitted to free elections. However, the Constituent Assembly was continually postponed. Since the government and the major parties insisted that all major decisions, including the determination of the new constitutional structure, the ending of the war, and the distribution of land, must await the assembly, the delay was of fundamental importance. Everything the government did was bound to be temporary and conditional. The leaders of the Soviets declared that they could not take power; the Provisional Government explained that it could not use its power until the Constituent Assembly was convened. The result was mounting public impatience and a growing breakdown of reliance on law and government.

In March the political spectrum was distributed as follows: the Kadets and Octobrists dominated the Provisional Government, the Mensheviks and Socialist Revolutionaries controlled the Soviets and thereby wielded the actual power in the cities but refused to assume a share of responsibility in the government. The Bolsheviks were only a small minority in the Petrograd Soviet. At the outset they wavered between the old Leninist hostility to the Mensheviks, their new Soviet, and the government it supported on the one hand, and on the other an enthusiasm for whatever was being done in the name of the "revolution," willingness to reconcile themselves with their old Menshevik comrades, and a sense of obligation to maintain "working class" unity.

The Kadets and the Octobrists were the first to go. The occasion was a dispute about whether to continue the war. Addressing the Western Allies, who had just recognized the Provisional Government, Miliukov explained that the Revolution had been a protest against the bungling of the war effort and that Russia would now fight better than ever. In a newspaper interview on April 5 he spelled out the war aims which Guchkov as war minister and he as foreign minister were pursuing; he mentioned among other things the annexation of Constantinople as an "immemorial" national objective. (The Straits Agreement was still unknown to the public.) Miliukov's statement provoked a flurry of denunciation and further explanation between the Soviet leaders and himself. The attitude of the Soviet toward the war was far from clear. On March 27 it had issued a "Manifesto to the Peoples of the World" which tried to harmonize the views of those who favored going on with the war and those who wanted to bring it to an end, without knowing quite how it might safely be done. The formula "peace without annexations and indemnities" was widely used, and the newspaper *Izvestiia* (*News;* the organ of the Soviet) proposed the slogan, "war for freedom." On May 1 another note of Miliukov to the Allies, employing the phrase "war to decisive victory," served as a signal for demonstrations in front of the new seat of government, the Mariinsky Palace. Miliukov could find no effective support for his policy, and as a result, Guchkov resigned on May 13 and Miliukov followed two days later.

LENIN'S "APRIL THESES"

By this time the exiled revolutionary leaders were returning to Petrograd: the Menshevik Heracles Tsereteli, and the Socialist Revolutionary Victor Chernov, who assumed the leading role in their parties; the Bolsheviks Joseph Stalin and Leo Kamenev from Siberia; then Trotsky and Lenin from abroad. Lenin arrived at the Finland Station in Petrograd on April 16, after his journey in the famous "sealed train" which the German authorities had allowed to go through in the hope that its cargo would weaken Russia's war effort. For three years Lenin had raged impotently against the Western Social Democrats' "betrayal" of the Marxist cause by their refusal to oppose the war (see p. 112). His first utterances on his return to Russia restated these views and announced a startling program of action on the war and other issues.

He offered his program to a slightly dazed Bolshevik party in the "April

Theses." In retrospect what they did not contain appears quite as important as what they did. They did *not* demand "peace and land," which was the Bolshevik slogan in the fall. First of all, said Lenin, it was necessary to understand that the war from the start had been imperialist and would remain so until the bourgeoisie, which ruled all European countries including Russia (after the February Revolution), was overthrown. "The fundamental question is," declared Lenin, "which class is waging the war? . . . When the masses declare they want no conquests, I believe them. When Guchkov and Lvov say they want no conquests, they lie." Here he applied the doctrine of *Imperialism, the Highest Stage of Capitalism,* to the current moment, using the rule of thumb which he crudely but effectively phrased, "who exploits whom?"

As he later explained it, the bourgeois revolution was being completed, but not as he had hoped. In 1905 he had envisaged two possible outcomes of the first revolutionary stage, either a simple "bourgeois dictatorship" or his own prescription, a "revolutionary democratic dictatorship of proletariat and peasantry." In 1917, however, *both* alternatives (represented respectively by the Provisional Government and the Soviets) had been realized simultaneously, and the first had spoiled the second; the tail was wagging the dog. Therefore—the logic is Lenin's—the Bolsheviks had to push on to the second stage, that of rule by proletariat and *poor* peasantry, that is, to the socialist revolution. The way to do so was to convert imperialist war into civil war.

Secondly, Lenin demanded that the Bolsheviks oppose the Provisional Government and uphold the slogan, "All Power to the Soviets." The Soviets, even though unfortunately still dominated by the Mensheviks and S.R.'s, must be prodded into taking power and then as soon as possible must be transformed into correctly class-conscious (that is, Bolshevik) bodies. Their next move should be "not the introduction of socialism as an immediate task," but merely the placing of social production under Soviet control. As for the land, all of it should be nationalized in principle, but most important was the conversion of the remaining estates into socialist farms. The Bolsheviks "must make it clear that small peasant farming under a commodity production system *offers no escape* for mankind from the poverty and oppression of the masses" (italics original). Finally, the party should break with the Second International, change its own name from Social Democratic (written with the word Bolshevik in parentheses following) to "Communist," and establish a new International of like-minded parties.

The other Bolshevik leaders reacted to the April Theses with groans and protests and only after a time accepted them, with misgivings. The

Mensheviks found confirmation of their suspicion that the Leninists had all along been opportunists cloaking themselves in Marxist doctrines. Trotsky, who had avoided identification with either Social Democratic faction, triumphantly declared that in the April Theses Lenin had accepted *his* doctrine, and that in approving them the Bolshevik party had "rearmed itself." He himself, along with a number of his followers, was admitted to the party not long afterwards.

The effect of the Theses was to popularize the slogan, "All Power to the Soviets" and to weaken further the prestige of the Provisional Government in the eyes of the politically-minded semi-intellectuals and workmen of Petrograd, many other cities, and at the front. Its appeal was strong because it struck directly at the anomaly of the doctrinally-based refusal of the Soviet leaders to assume the reins of government as they could have done. For that very reason the Theses had little effect in increasing the support of the Bolsheviks; Lenin did not appear to advance his own party as a claimant to power. The Bolsheviks continued to grow, but for the time being other parties grew as fast or faster.

THE FIRST COALITION

With the resignations of Guchkov and Miliukov, the liberal parties lost their last chance to maintain an independent lead in the government. On May 18 a new cabinet was formed in which Lvov remained prime minister and minister of interior, Kerensky succeeded Guchkov as war minister, and Tereshchenko replaced Miliukov as foreign minister. There were ten non-socialist ministers, but there were also six socialists. They entered the cabinet, not in defiance of the Soviet's views as Kerensky had done, but with the approval of their respective party leaderships and acknowledged their responsibility to their party organizations. The two most important new socialist ministers were the effective leaders of the main socialist parties. Victor Chernov, leader and chief theoretician of the S.R.'s from the beginning, became minister of agriculture. Heracles Tsereteli, who was not only the Mensheviks' strongest man but also the most influential single leader of the Petrograd Soviet, became minister of posts and telegraphs.

The cabinet of May 18 became known as the First Coalition and signified a partial reversal of the Menshevik stand against taking power. The socialists still refused to take all power or all responsibility for governing but agreed to accept a minor share of both. The main figure in the First Coalition cabinet was not Lvov but Kerensky. Although Kerensky was nominally an S.R., he depended for his undoubted popularity not on the support of his party, but on the adulation of people who were intoxicated with "revolution" in much the same way that Kerensky himself was. The S.R. leaders, in fact, were more embarrassed than pleased by his prominence, finding the prestige he gave the party insufficient compensation for the indifference he displayed toward party decisions.

Kerensky was conscious that the issue of the war had wrecked the first cabinet, and he was determined to resolve it. He planned an offensive which would place Russia in a position to make an effective peace through proving the army's continuing capacity to fight. As "persuader-in-chief" he ranged up and down the front addressing the soldiers and using flamboyant phrases: "I summon you forward, to the struggle for freedom, not to a feast, but to death. We, revolutionaries, have the right to death." The morale of the army had been severely undermined by the socialist-sponsored Order No. 1 and the activities of party agitators among the soldiers. It had been further shaken by the Bolshevik propaganda against the war—the nuances of Lenin's "first revolution then peace" position escaped not only the soldiers but also many Bolshevik propagandists. However, Kerensky managed to kindle what fighting spirit yet remained. The Allies urged him on, and the Soviet grudgingly consented to a large-scale operation.

On July 1 an offensive was launched against the Austrians, toward Lvov in Galicia. Initially it made progress, but the enemy did not surrender in large numbers or stop fighting, and the question of whether further advance was compatible with the concept of a "defensive war" was debated by army committees at the front. The solution was provided by the soldiers themselves; one does not risk his life willingly when his fellows are openly debating the wisdom of doing so. By July 14 the offensive had come to a halt. A few days later the Austrians and Germans struck back and the Russian front first sagged, then collapsed. Troops fled in disorder, and some continued in the direction of home. From then on desertion increased from month to month. There could be no question of resuming the offensive while the restoration of discipline was opposed by the Soviet, which had contributed so largely to its destruction in the first place.

Kerensky now had to face popular demonstrations directed against his government. The Bolsheviks had planned one for June 23, but the Mensheviks and S.R.'s denounced the idea and called instead for a united-front manifestation of support for the government on July 1. The Soviet leaders miscalculated; the demonstration contained more banners bearing Bolshevik slogans than those supporting the government. The slogan, "All Power to the Soviets," gained increasing support. The pent-up impatience of the Petrograd mob was spurred by the failure of the Galician offensive. On July 16 and 17, which became known as the July Days, disorder and violence erupted.

Apparently the July Days began spontaneously among military units in Petrograd which supported the Bolsheviks, and after some hesitation Lenin and the other party leaders decided to take part. Huge crowds of people, many armed, roamed the streets, and a mob besieged the Taurida Palace with the demand that the Menshevik-S.R. leaders of the Soviet Executive Committee take power. The confusion surrounding the "All Power to the Soviets" slogan was well illustrated by the howls of the crowd against Tsereteli and the actual seizure of Chernov. A nameless hoodlum who waved his fist in Chernov's face and shouted, "Take the power, you son of a bitch, when they offer it to you!" expressed the widespread puzzlement of the urban masses with the intricacies of revolutionary theory. If Trotsky had not rushed up to deliver a timely short oration, Chernov might have been lynched; yet presumably he and Tsereteli would have become the main figures in the sort of government for which the mob was demonstrating.

The Bolsheviks, having assumed the leadership of the demonstrators, seem not to have taken any decision as to what to do if the Soviet leaders refused—as they did—to take power. When the S.R. minister of justice, Pereverzev, passed out to certain military units material purporting to prove that Lenin was a paid agent of the Germans, there was a definite reaction in favor of the government. On July 18 loyal forces raided *Pravda* and the Bolshevik headquarters, and there was an effort to arrest the Bolshevik leaders which netted only Anatole Lunacharsky, the mildest of them, and Trotsky.

THE SECOND COALITION

Despite the government's tardy show of firmness, it was in the throes of collapse. Prince Lvov resigned on July 21, chiefly in protest at the policy of Minister of Agriculture Chernov. Chernov had refused to enact the S.R. land program, following the Menshevik lead in observing the presumed laws of history, but he did want to push through the stoppage of all land sales except by official permission and did so four days after Lvov resigned. Kerensky replaced Lvov as prime minister, but over two weeks elapsed before he could put together a new cabinet. Whereas the First Coalition had had a socialist minority, in the Second Coalition there were eleven socialists out of eighteen. Nevertheless, the cabinet was less radical than the previous one. The majority of its members consisted of new appointees who had not personally experienced the responsibilities of a minister, but the July Days had had a sobering effect on them and on the parties they represented.

The Bolsheviks evaluated the effect of the July Days in their VI Congress (the first since that held in London in 1907), which met in Petrograd in mid-August, maintaining security precautions. It was reported that the party membership had risen from eighty thousand in April to two hundred thousand, of whom almost half were in and around Petrograd and Moscow. The Trotskyites were welcomed into membership. The principal decision which the Congress adopted was to renounce the slogan "All Power to the Soviets." The July demonstrations had failed, and the charge that Lenin was a German agent had palpably damaged Bolshevik prestige. As a result Lenin declared, "The substance of the matter is that it is already now impossible to take power peacefully. . . ." The Menshevik-S.R. Soviets had proved impervious to Bolshevik manipulation, and the party would therefore concentrate on the factory committees, in which it already had the upper hand. Actually Lenin gave up hope in the Soviets too soon, for only a few weeks later they started to go over to the Bolsheviks. The important point is that he regarded the Soviets, like any body other than the Bolshevik party, as purely instrumental to the task of seizing power in the name of the "proletariat and poor peasantry."

The new prime minister, Kerensky, was alarmed by the Bolshevik threat to his government, and also was forcefully reminded by the July Days that he ruled by grace of the Soviets, who could take power at any time even if they thus far had refused to do so. Accordingly he attempted to find institutional support and backing elsewhere. The Provisional Committee of the Duma was still functioning, and on May 10 the surviving members of all four Dumas met informally to discuss the situation; however, the socialists watched such bodies suspiciously, scenting in them a danger of "counterrevolution," and Kerensky had little enthusiasm for them anyway. He sought to create his own forums of public opinion. On August 25 he summoned a Moscow State Conference, including all former Duma deputies along with representatives of Soviets, unions, local governments, and many other associations. Chief among the speakers who addressed this unwieldy gathering of nearly twenty-five hundred persons were General Lavr Kornilov and Kerensky himself. On July 31 Kerensky had appointed Kornilov commander-in-chief, replacing General Brusilov (who two months earlier had succeeded General Alexeev, who had taken command when the monarchy fell). Kornilov, the son of a peasant family, had gained renown by successfully escaping from the Austrians after his capture in 1915 and was popular with the troops. In his speech he referred to an anticipated German offensive toward Riga, and he warned that "we must not allow that order in the rear should be the result of the loss of Riga."

The Left interpreted Kornilov's warning as a threat to surrender Riga to the Germans in order to find an excuse for establishing a military dictatorship; others thought that Kornilov might be a suitable person to restore law and order. Of course Kerensky was not in favor of chaos; when the Second Coalition had been formed, he had spoken of the need for "iron rule," but he meant his own, not someone else's. His own speech at the Conference, however, did not suggest firmness: "Let my heart become stone, let all the springs of faith in man perish, let all the flowers and wreaths of man dry up—I shall throw far away the keys of my heart, which loves men, I will think only about the state." (Woman's voice: "You cannot do that, your heart will not permit it.") Flamboyance is a matter of taste, but Kerensky's weakness was that oratory became a substitute for action.

THE KORNILOV AFFAIR

Kornilov's forcefulness had justified Kerensky's faith in him as a commander. He had done what seemed impossible by stabilizing the front after the collapse of the Galician offensive, and he had restored some measure of discipline in the army. However, he was unable to hold Riga when the expected German offensive materialized, and the city fell on September 3. The military crisis led certain ministers to attempt to implement Kornilov's call for "order in the rear" by restoring the death penalty behind the lines, as it had been restored at the front—by Kerensky's order, before Kornilov had been appointed commander.

On September 5 Boris Savinkov, former terrorist but now acting minister of war, requested Kornilov to send a cavalry corps to Petrograd to be ready if a Bolshevik uprising should occur. However, Kornilov had already decided to send a force to the capital to effect a reconstruction of the cabinet, with Kerensky participating. V. N. Lvov,[2] who had been procurator of the Holy Synod earlier under the Provisional Government, undertook a strange task of mediation between Kerensky and Kornilov in which, because of his ineptness, each thought Lvov was the representative of the other. On September 8, through Lvov's efforts, an agreement was reached for the "legal and peaceful" replacement of Kerensky by Kornilov, although Kerensky was to remain in the cabinet. More accurately, Lvov thought agreement had been reached, but Kerensky, treating its

• [2] Not to be confused with Prince George Lvov, the former prime minister.

text as an ultimatum, arrested Lvov and dismissed Kornilov. The commander-in-chief refused to acknowledge the order of dismissal and denounced the Provisional Government, asserting that "under the pressure of the Bolshevik majority of the Soviets," it acted "in full agreement with the plans of the German general staff. . . ."

Did Kornilov attempt to overthrow the Provisional Government? Early on September 10 Kerensky, under pressure from both his cabinet colleagues and other army officers, tried to stop publication of charges to that effect—too late The cavalry corps was on its way to Petrograd. Whatever the intentions of its commander, General Krymov, the soldiers were certainly in no mood to carry out a seizure of power. In fact Krymov was arrested before he reached Petrograd and after an interview with Kerensky committed suicide. On September 14 Kornilov surrendered to arrest at Mogilëv. Kerensky himself assumed the title of commander-in-chief, while at length General N. N. Dukhonin became his chief of staff.

It seems plain that Kornilov was seeking to establish a "strong government," and had violated an order of duly constituted authority. However, it was his intention to strengthen the Provisional Government, not to overthrow it or to restore the monarchy, whatever effect his actions had or might have had. As Trotsky wrote, if this was Bonaparte, it was but a pale shadow of him. The only ones to profit from the imbroglio were the Bolsheviks, who wrenched from the Soviet an official authorization to form a Red Guard. The Bolsheviks maintained that they would not fight for Kerensky but would fight against Kornilov. It was their good fortune that no occasion arose in which they were required to translate this dialectical slogan into action.

The Kornilov affair brought about the collapse of the Second Coalition. On September 14 Kerensky, dismissing a number of S.R. ministers, formed a ministerial "directory" of five. Reconstructing another coalition cabinet proved difficult. The Executive Committee of the Soviet regarded the Kadets, as well as the whole "bourgeoisie," as compromised by their support of, or ambivalence toward, Kornilov's alleged "counterrevolutionary plot." On September 27 the Executive Committee summoned a Democratic Conference, made up chiefly of the Left membership of the Moscow State Conference, but no firm decisions could be reached. Not until October 8 was Kerensky able to form a Third Coalition cabinet, including ten socialists (a majority, as before) and six non-socialists.

In order to pacify the Left, Kerensky had been trying to free himself from any taint of the Kornilov affair. He proclaimed Russia a republic, punished the officers involved or suspected of involvement with Kornilov's cause, arrested such moderate politicians as Guchkov, and, in the end most important of all, he freed Trotsky and other Bolshevik prisoners. He reiterated orders for the observance of strict discipline in the army, but nevertheless a number of officers were lynched by their troops as suspected supporters of Kornilov.

REVOLUTION FROM BELOW

By this time discipline in the ranks had broken down almost completely. An effort to create "shock" battalions, approved by Brusilov while he was commander-in-chief, had negligible results. The application of the decree restoring the death penalty, issued in July, had never been seriously attempted. Deserters streamed eastward from the front, especially after the disappearance of Kornilov, who proved to be the last commander determined to maintain the army as a fighting force. By October, according to one official report, the army was "a huge crowd of tired, poorly clad, poorly fed, embittered men united by common longing for peace and general disillusionment." During 1917 the Russian units that had been sent to France and Macedonia also disintegrated.

The soldiers were, as Lenin said, "peasants in uniform." If their government did not want them to be soldiers, as they finally decided must be the case, then they had business enough waiting for them at home. Once discipline had collapsed, the revolutionary cry of "land and liberty," older even than the fallen dynasty, took priority in the soldiers' minds over any manifestoes or appeals from new governments, Soviets, or committees. In mounting numbers, they simply went home to get the land.

Already in March agrarian "disorders" had begun, and they increased rapidly in the fall. The repeated warnings by successive cabinets that the land question must await the Constituent Assembly were ignored. Illegal encroachments took place everywhere. The peasants pastured their cattle on gentry meadows, or cut gentry wood, or refused to pay rent, or cultivated gentry land without asking leave, or took gentry supplies or belongings without payment, and finally demanded the houses and estates. More often than not there was no violence; the landlords were persuaded to get out for their own good, and often enough of the old patriarchal relationship between lord and serf survived so that partings were amicable or even tearful. If peasants sometimes murdered landlords, often they also "lynched, apparently with the best of conscience, some army deserter or tramp who had been caught stealing horses. In short the peasants' complete contempt for the property rights of the landlords was accompanied by a keen attachment to their own. . . ."[3] Far from throwing all rights of ownership into question, the peasants tended to follow a simple rule: The estates belonged not just to anyone but to those peasants whose families had before 1861 been owned by, worked for, or rented land from the particular landlord involved.

The Socialist Revolutionaries were the party which had most influence in the countryside in 1917, but this does not prove that the peasants were S.R.'s at heart any more than the 1906 elections prove that they were really Kadets (see p. 79). No party stood for what they wanted, namely, increase of their own private holdings through seizure of the land of the gentry, state, and church. In vain did the S.R.'s declare, quite accurately, that "socialization [their complicated land program] of the land cannot be confused with arbitrary seizure of it for personal advantage." Not only the peasants, but also many nominal S.R.'s in the "peasant committees" or in the local peasant Soviets, were happily guilty of such confusion. The upper echelons of the party seemed even farther removed from the peasants they claimed to "represent" than the urban revolutionary cabals from the workers.

Already in March Soviets of Peasant Deputies had begun to spring up alongside the Soviets of Workers' and Soldiers' Deputies. In May the Peasant Soviets held a national congress which was dominated by the S.R.'s and in which the Bolsheviks had only a handful of deputies. The Congress called for enactment of the S.R. program of "socialization" of land (which demanded the abolition of private ownership and the establishment of a "labor norm" for land to be occupied by the peasant family without payment—that is, a family was to occupy no more land than it could cultivate itself). The Congress reiterated, however, again in accordance with S.R. doctrine, that the land problem must await solution at the meeting of the Constituent Assembly. Minister of Agriculture Chernov defended this position before the assemblage. For the rest the Congress echoed the line of the Menshevik-S.R. leadership of the Workers' and Soldiers' Soviets: support of the Provisional Government, continuation of a defensive war, and so forth.

The peasantry as a whole neither knew nor cared about the Menshevik theory of revolution or the S.R. formulations on the land question. Neither Lvov, Kerensky, Chernov, nor anyone else succeeded in making any dent in the peasants' determination to divide the land among those who were deemed to have rights over it, and no one seriously tried to prevent them from carrying out their intentions. Exhortations against

• [3] William Henry Chamberlin, *The Russian Revolution, 1917–1921* (2 vols.; New York: Macmillan, 1952), Vol. I, pp. 254–255.

violence may have sounded paradoxical coming from the S.R.'s, who had assassinated more people before the Revolution than the peasants killed while it was in progress. The peasants had neither the knowledge nor the time for paradoxes; they simply divided the property at hand.

While the peasants were carrying out a revolution which was quite independent of party debates and government orders, the workers were scarcely in a position to act on their own. The peasantry numbered well over a hundred million, scattered over a vast area, while the industrial workers (including those in transportation) made up only about four million excluding families. They were concentrated in and around relatively few cities, each of which in 1917 resounded with organized political activity. The trade-unions had remained weak up to the time of the Revolution, but during 1917 their organizations grew very rapidly. By the end of the year they had a membership of more than two and a quarter million. Two of the strongest groups in the unions were the metal workers of Petrograd and the textile workers of Moscow.

However, the unions had competitors as spokesmen for the proletariat. A few days after the February Revolution factory committees (*fabrichno-zavodskie komitety*) began to appear. The demand, already popular in 1905, for the introduction of an eight-hour day was advanced by both unions and factory committees. This time the Petrograd employers accepted the demand at once; those of Moscow followed grudgingly, and others fell into line. In a reaction to the harsh factory discipline which had prevailed under the Tsar, the workers sometimes gave the foremen rough handling. In general they celebrated their new freedom by taking off for a political meeting at the smallest provocation. This habit, coupled with the widespread substitution of payment by time for payment by piece, served to reduce industrial output. Some employers closed down factories because of supply shortages. There were both lockouts and strikes; prices rose faster than wages, and no one seemed to know how to check inflation. The industrial crisis embittered the rivalry between the Bolshevik-led factory committees and the trade-unions, influenced by the Mensheviks and S.R.'s. The factory committees sought to gain acceptance for Lenin's proposal of "workers' control"—which meant the dominant participation of workers' committees within each plant in factory administration—while the trade-unions were cool to the idea.

By fall the position of the workers, especially the less skilled, was growing desperate. More and more employers were either closing the doors of their plants or trying to turn them over to the government. Prices climbed higher as the supply of food and consumers' goods dwindled. The government fulminated against illegal acts and anarchy but took no decisive steps to restore industrial stability. Since the Mensheviks and S.R.'s participated in the government, they got much of the blame, and this was an important factor in the passage of the Soviets of Workers' Deputies into Bolshevik hands beginning in early September. The Mensheviks had always worried lest they discredit themselves in the workers' eyes, since they could not introduce socialism if they should take power prematurely. The Soviets which they led were indeed being discredited, not because they failed to introduce socialism, but because they spent their time debating political questions while the economic crisis disrupted urban life and drove the workers close to despair. While the peasants depended mainly on their own resources, the workers were forced to rely on others to keep in operation the factories on which their livelihood depended. The Soviets apparently would not act to do so, and the employers were no longer able to. It seemed that the Bolsheviks alone promised a way out of the crisis.

REVOLUTION IN THE BORDERLANDS

While the Russian-inhabited areas of the Empire were in turmoil, the borderlands had a chance for autonomist or independence movements to make headway. The end of the war witnessed a new nationalist upsurge among the peoples of eastern Europe, Asia, and elsewhere. The submerged national groups of the empires of Austria-Hungary and Turkey were shortly to tear them into pieces. As Russia virtually ended her part in the war a year and a half earlier than the other powers, the Russian minorities began to assert themselves first.

Out of the multitude of minorities within the Russian Empire, only the Poles and Finns had enjoyed some degree of autonomy during the nineteenth century. The deepest national antagonism within the Empire was probably that between the Russians and the Poles. The Poles were proud of the past achievements of their country and regarded Russians generally as less civilized than they, while the Russians and Ukrainians remembered Polish domination of their lands and invasions of the heart of Russia and hated the Poles' Roman Catholic religion. Nevertheless, the question of Poland offered the least difficulty, for the Polish-inhabited territories were occupied by the Germans and Austrians. On March 29 the Provisional Government promised Poland independence, although the only practical consequence of this act was the formation of some Polish units in the Russian army—units which maintained discipline in the face of the Russian military collapse until disarmed by the Germans.

Finland's status under the Empire was by far the best of any of the national minorities, but the last two Emperors had sought to limit its autonomy. In March the Provisional Government made a number of concessions to the Finns, but the Finnish Social Democrats demanded independence, an issue which the Russians declared was something the Constituent Assembly must decide. In July the Finnish S.D.'s finally prevailed upon the Finnish Diet—a body which had existed under the Empire—to proclaim what amounted to independence. The Provisional Government retorted by dissolving the Diet and calling new elections resulting in a majority for the non-socialists under Pehr Svinhufud. Negotiations were continuing between the new Diet and the Provisional Government when the Bolsheviks seized power.

The Tsars had recognized no such entity as the Ukraine. During the nineteenth century Ukrainian intellectuals had gathered to work for the cause of their new nationalism in Lemberg (Lvov) in Austro-Hungarian territory, where the Austrians permitted and even encouraged their activities, since they threatened Russia far more than the Dual Monarchy. The movement had adepts also in Kiev and among intellectuals in other parts of the Russian Ukraine. Whether or not Ukrainian nationalism was, as Florinsky asserts, "a weak and artificial growth,"[4] the intellectuals who espoused it assumed the direction of political events in the Ukraine soon after the February Revolution. The first effort of the Ukrainian leaders, through the self-constituted Central Rada (Council), was to obtain autonomy by agreement with the Provisional Government of Kerensky, who had from Duma days the reputation of sympathy for the Ukraine. Meanwhile, however, the Rada endeavored to govern the Ukraine as a separate administrative unit.

In June a kind of ministry, known as the General Secretariat, was established by the Rada under the chairmanship of the novelist Volodimir Vinnichenko. He was a member of the Ukrainian Social Democratic party (which, to the chagrin of the Russian S.D.'s in the Ukraine, fellow-traveled with the Ukrainian nationalists). A few days later a delegation from the Provisional Government came to Kiev to confer with the General Secretariat. After long discussion an agreement was reached whereby Ukrainian autonomy was recognized *de facto*. Though not broad enough to satisfy the extreme Ukrainian nationalists, the agreement conceded more than most of the Kadet ministers of the Provisional Government were willing to accept. They resigned in protest, but the Ukrainian issue

• [4] Michael T. Florinsky, *Russia: a History and an Interpretation* (2 vols.; New York: Macmillan, 1953), Vol. II, p. 1424.

was shunted aside by the prolonged crisis provoked by the July Days in Petrograd. There was little further Russian discussion of the Ukrainian issue before the Bolshevik coup.

However, the Rada itself had to face wide discontent within the Ukraine. The Ukrainian peasants, like those of Russia, were increasingly impatient with delays on the "land problem." Although Ukrainian army units were formed and the sailors of the Black Sea Fleet ran up the Ukrainian flag, they did not want to continue fighting any more than Russian soldiers and sailors did. The Bolsheviks in the Ukraine played a double game; they criticized the Rada, and especially the Ukrainian S.D.'s, for nationalist tendencies, while at the same time they courted popularity in the Ukraine by supporting the Rada's side in negotiations with the Provisional Government, thereby also multiplying difficulties for the authorities in Petrograd whom they opposed. As the Bolshevik coup approached, the Ukrainian nationalists virtually made common cause with the Bolsheviks.

In Belorussia there occurred a pale reflection of events in the Ukraine. One recent scholar doubts that in 1917 the Belorussian masses had "any consciousness of ethnic separateness"[5] at all, and certainly Belorussian political parties were almost nonexistent. A Belorussian Rada was established in July, but the Russian Bolsheviks and S.R.'s were the only parties to gain any considerable strength in the region before the October Revolution.

Estonia, Latvia, and Lithuania had developed native nationalist movements, and autonomist aspirations spread rapidly there in 1917. In Transcaucasia the Menshevik- and S.R.-dominated Soviets of Tiflis and Baku were the focal points of political discussion. Georgia was a stronghold of Menshevism and had given Russia some of its most prominent Menshevik leaders, such as Chkheidze and Tsereteli. In contrast, Azerbaijan and Armenia had produced their own nationalist parties, the Mussavat and Dashnaktsutiun respectively. The Armenian Dashnaktsutiun actively supported the Allied war effort, provoking the Turks to conduct a stupendous massacre of one million Armenians in Turkish territory in 1915. Fear and hatred of the Turks led the Armenians to give fervent support to the Provisional Government. In 1917 Georgia and Armenia thus held the Caucasus to relative tranquillity, and friction with Petrograd was at a minimum.

In Central Asia there had also been violence during the World War, although on a much smaller scale than in Armenia. Although the Kazakhs

• [5] Richard Pipes, *The Formation of the Soviet Union* (Cambridge: Harvard University Press, 1954), p. 73.

(then called Kirghiz) had enjoyed considerable autonomy and exemption from military service, in 1916 the Tsarist government decided to draft some of them for rear-area duty. The order came at a time of increasing friction between Kazakhs and Russian settlers over the steppe lands and was interpreted as an act of further Russian encroachment on native rights. The Kazakhs retaliated by attacking Russian settlers, especially in Semirechensk province, and killing thousands of them. The rebellion was put down, and some three hundred thousand natives were driven off their lands, many of them into Chinese Sinkiang.

In 1917 Central Asian leaders concerned themselves with both religious and political demands. Kazakh congresses met in Orenburg, seeking to create a "Greater Kirghizia," and founded a nationalist party called the Alash-Orda. On the initiative of the Moslem deputies of the Duma, a nationwide Moslem Congress met in Moscow in May, proclaimed the emancipation of Moslem women, and established a religious administration independent of state control for all Russian Moslems, somewhat as the Russian Orthodox Church did in 1917. The Congress also made plans for a federal solution for the problem of autonomy for the Moslem peoples. Such peoples included the Bashkirs, Crimean Tatars, and others in addition to the Central Asian groups. By the summer of 1917 Kazakhs were trickling back across the Chinese border to their former homes in Russian territory. Russian settlers in the areas from which the natives had been evicted, either to defend their new homes or from motives of revenge, attacked the returning Kazakhs brutally and killed over eighty thousand. The October coup found the Central Asian steppes in a state of conflict and disorder, with relations between the Russians and natives far more bitter than they had been for generations.

Farther south, in Turkestan, the native leaders formed a Turkestan Moslem Central Council, dominated by liberal Moslems, although there was also a weaker conservative faction. However, the chief city of Turkestan, Tashkent, was dominated by the local Soviet, led by Mensheviks and S.R.'s. The Soviet was striving to keep the Russian minority from being swamped by the Moslems in the event that universal suffrage and effective regional autonomy were introduced. The Provisional Government failed to harmonize these conflicting interests and to establish its own authority. In September the Tashkent Soviet, swinging in a Bolshevik direction, attempted a coup and arrested the agents of Petrograd, but a military expedition was dispatched and order was temporarily restored.

Thus the control of the Provisional Government over the borderlands was almost universally tenuous and nominal. Everywhere local nationalists demanded autonomy, pro-Menshevik-S.R. groups temporized, and Bolsheviks exploited the confusion as best they could. Throughout the borderlands the Bolsheviks, although they started 1917 with negligible strength or none at all, built up a following and gained prestige by playing upon whatever grievances and antagonisms existed, never hesitating to push toward intransigence groups or parties which they intended to destroy as soon as they could.

If the Provisional Government had taken measures to establish some kind of federation, it might have held the borderlands. However, the dogmas prevailing in Petrograd blocked decisive action of any kind. Part of the reason for inaction was the Provisional Government's adherence to the principle that no solution was possible prior to the Constituent Assembly. At least as important, however, was the Menshevik-S.R. insistence that those who had such power as there was should not rule, while those who were trying to rule should not be given real power. If there had been no disciplined and organized force, such as the Bolsheviks, ready to turn the situation to its own advantage, the period of turmoil might well have been lived through somehow. But the Bolsheviks were present and visible to those who, more or less unwittingly, prepared the ground on which Bolshevik tactics could succeed.

The end of the Provisional Government came less than a month after the Third Coalition was formed on October 8. During the Kornilov episode Kerensky had appealed to the Bolshevik party for aid and had released the arrested Bolshevik leaders, who were untroubled by any feelings of gratitude to the man whose overthrow they proceeded to organize. The Central Executive Committee of the Soviets had summoned a Democratic Conference, making plain its dissatisfaction with the Moscow State Conference where some approval of Kornilov had been demonstrated. Kerensky refused to recognize the Democratic Conference as an official body, but he wished to summon a new forum which could provide some semblance of representative support for the government. The statute for the Constituent Assembly was published at last, and elections were fixed for late November.

At length Kerensky and the Soviets reached a compromise whereby a new body recognized by both was summoned. It was called the Provisional Council of the Republic, or "Pre-Parliament," and met on October 20. It was dominated by the socialists, and there were only 150 non-socialists out of a membership of 550. The Bolsheviks walked out of its first meeting, and Kerensky knew very well what they had gone to do, but he declared, "I have more strength than I need. They will be finally smashed."

It was by now plain to the Mensheviks and S.R.'s not only that a Bolshevik coup was in prospect but also that it might have a good chance of success unless the government acted speedily. On the afternoon of November 6, the orthodox leaders of the two parties forced through the Council of the Republic a resolution demanding immediate action on the questions of peace and land. Fëdor Dan, a prominent Menshevik, and Abram Gots, an S.R., went to Kerensky and insisted that poster and telegraph immediately carry the word to the country that this was the aim of the Provisional Government. At this ultimatum Kerensky threatened to resign, but the Bolsheviks were already beginning to take over the city of Petrograd.

The October Revolution

★
★
★
★
★
★
★
★
★
★

CHAPTER 10

BOLSHEVIK GAINS BEFORE THE COUP

By autumn the Bolsheviks had gained markedly both in membership and popular support. On the Russian political scene those were two different things, particularly in the case of the Bolsheviks, whose closely-knit and disciplined organization always more nearly approximated a military unit than a political party in the sense hitherto familiar in the West. In strength the party had increased to over two hundred thousand members. In popularity the gains had been manifold and striking. In the spring the Bolsheviks had controlled the factory committees, but the much larger trade-unions distrusted them, and in no sense could such control be equated with leadership of the industrial proletariat. At the I Congress of Soviets which opened in Petrograd on June 16, the Bolsheviks had 105 deputies, the S.R.'s 285, the Mensheviks 248; Lenin's party was outnumbered more than five to one by the socialist coalition. The Bolsheviks had labored mightily among the soldiers to make their Military Organization influential, but progress was slow. As for the peasantry, even in November the Bolsheviks' "independent power in the countryside was still negligible," writes E. H. Carr, who is by no means inclined to minimize Bolshevik achievements.[1]

However, even at the time of the I Congress of Soviets the balance had begun to shift in favor of the Bolsheviks. On June 14 the Workers' Section of the Petrograd Soviet had voted by a narrow margin to support the Bolshevik slogan, "All Power to the Soviets." The Soldiers' Section at that time was still dominated by the Menshevik-S.R. coalition. The Kornilov affair, during which the Bolsheviks had been authorized to form Red Guards openly, swung the Soldiers' Section over. On September 13 both sections of the Petrograd Soviet adopted a Bolshevik resolution, and a more decisive vote occurred on September 21. Meanwhile, on September 18, the Moscow Soviet had also passed to the Bolsheviks; in Krasnoiarsk, Ekaterinburg, and many other cities of the south and east the same thing took place. The October elections to the Moscow ward councils, held under universal suffrage, indicated that a major shift of opinion was under way. Comparing the October results with those of elections held in July, one observes a sharp decline in the aggregate vote, but the Bolsheviks increased their percentage from 11% to 51%, while the Kadet vote held steady numerically (and thus leaped proportionately, from 17% to 26%), and the S.R. and Menshevik support disintegrated. The last two parties named polled 70% in July, but only 18% in October. These data may furnish a fair index of what happened in the autumn in the large cities: the Bolsheviks drove home to the active political elements their claim to stand firmly for the broad revolutionary slogans of peace and land and thus won many supporters away from the two moderate socialist parties.

The Bolsheviks were immensely successful in exploiting to their own advantage the failure of the Galician offensive, the Kornilov episode, and other events. The fact that Prime Minister Kerensky was nominally an S.R. but would not follow the decisions of his own party, although he demanded its loyalty, hampered the socialist leaders in meeting the competition of Lenin, who was able to count on the generally unswerving support of his party. Such opportunities, nevertheless, could not have been utilized as they were if it had not been for the theoretically-grounded insistence of Tsereteli and the Mensheviks that history did not permit them to exercise the power which was in fact theirs. The socialist ambivalence about power opened a gap in the ranks of the supporters of the February Revolution through which the Bolsheviks were ultimately able to drive with an ease which surprised even themselves.

• [1] Edward Hallett Carr, *The Bolshevik Revolution, 1917–1923* (3 vols.; London: Macmillan, 1950–1953), Vol. II, p. 41.

THE UPRISING

Lenin had begun the revolutionary year with the slogan, "All Power to the Soviets." After the July Days he had renounced it in favor of armed uprising. When the Petrograd Soviet passed into Bolshevik hands in September, Lenin reverted to "All Power to the Soviets" without, however, abandoning armed uprising. In the Bolshevik party itself there was again, as in April, some reluctance to go along with Lenin's tactics. On October 23 there was a secret meeting of the Bolshevik Central Committee in the apartment of N. N. Sukhanov, a Left Menshevik, though it was his Bolshevik wife who acted as hostess. Lenin declared that the political situation was ripe for action, and that the foremost need was organization of the uprising. He recognized that the Constituent Assembly would not have a Bolshevik majority, and thus to await its meeting would "mean a complication of our problem" (a little later he did stake the success of the coup on the likelihood of the party's obtaining a majority in the II Congress of Soviets, scheduled to meet on November 7). Gregory Zinoviev and Leo Kamenev, two of the most influential leaders, warned of the risks and opposed Lenin on the vote, which was ten to two. The historic meeting not only decided on an uprising, but also chose the party's first Political Bureau of the Central Committee. The first Politburo consisted of Lenin, Trotsky, Stalin, Zinoviev, Kamenev, G. Y. Sokolnikov, and A. S. Bubnov. It seems, however, not to have been active in the events immediately following, and achieved importance only during the Civil War. Zinoviev and Kamenev took their objections to the coup to the party press, thereby revealing its imminence to the public, although in any event it was an ill-kept secret.

Amid the turmoil of October the very decision to convene a II Congress had to be forced on the Soviets' Central Executive Committee. On October 24 a Soviet congress was held for the northern region alone, and the Bolsheviks triumphantly assumed control over it. Two days earlier they had managed to push through the Executive Committee approval of the setting up of a Military Revolutionary Committee to control the Petrograd and nearby garrisons. This body was actually employed as the "general staff of the insurrection." Colonel Polkovnikov, the government's commander of the Petrograd military district, at first hoped to avoid bloodshed by simply ignoring the existence of the Committee. However, on November 5 the Provisional Government made another about-face in its attitude to the Bolsheviks and ordered the rearrest of Bolshevik leaders free on bail as well as the carrying out of other legal steps against the party. Simultaneously loyal troops were to be concentrated in Petrograd.

November 6 brought a showdown. Cadets of the military schools patrolled various key points in the city. The crew of the cruiser *Aurora,* who were pro-Bolshevik, brought their ship into the Neva River to anchor near the Winter Palace, seat of the Provisional Government, and defied orders to put out to sea. In the afternoon the Council of the Republic adopted its resolution for immediate action on the issues of peace and land (see p. 145). Its wording led Kerensky to take offense, and he declared he would resign. However, the events already afoot both led him to change his mind and made his resignation superfluous. Kerensky fled the next morning to seek loyal troops, his automobile accompanied by a casually commandeered embassy car flying the American flag.

On the night of November 6 Bolshevik troops began seizing public buildings and other key points in Petrograd. There was a fight for the Winter Palace, but in the early morning of November 8 it was overrun by soldiers led by Antonov-Ovseenko. The ministers of the Provisional Government, headed after Kerensky's flight by A. I. Konovalov, were removed to cells in the Fortress of St. Peter and St. Paul. Sukhanov, a member of the Soviet Executive Committee, encountered insurrectionary troops on the afternoon of November 7 (October 25, O.S.; the accepted date of the "October Revolution") and chatted with their commander, who declared:

> "Incomprehensible! The order was to march. But why—no one knows. Against one's own people, after all. All rather strange. . . ." The Commander smiled with embarrassment, and it was evident that he was indeed rather baffled by everything. There was no doubt about it: there was no spirit; such troops would never fight; they would never fight; they would scatter and surrender at the first blank shot. But there was no one to do any shooting.[2]

THE II CONGRESS OF SOVIETS

On the same afternoon, the II Congress of Soviets convened. Lenin's calculations on obtaining a majority of delegates proved justified. Out of about 650 delegates, 390 were Bolsheviks. The Mensheviks and orthodox Socialist Revolutionaries walked out in protest at the armed insurrection, but the Left S.R.'s, who had by now broken off and formed a separate party, remained. As Sukhanov says, they "had no objection to being the sole representatives of the peasantry."[3] Their usefulness to

• [2] Sukhanov, *The Russian Revolution, 1917,* p. 624.
• [3] *Ibid.,* p. 654.

Lenin was considerable; the Bolsheviks stood for the "proletariat," the Left S.R.'s for the "poor peasantry." This uneasy and unequal partnership lasted only a few months, but upon the participation of the Left S.R.'s for even that short a time hung both Lenin's claim to have realized his slogan of "dictatorship of the proletariat and the poor peasantry" and his contention that there was a *Soviet* government rather than a purely Bolshevik government in power.

How broad was Lenin's support at the time of the October Revolution? He could not even claim a clear majority in the Soviets. Although the Bolsheviks were the largest faction at the Congress of Soviets of Workers' and Soldiers' Deputies, the Soviets of Peasant Deputies returned an anti-Bolshevik majority at their meeting several weeks later. Any doubt about the attitude of the people as a whole was shortly to be dispelled by the elections to the Constituent Assembly. However, not long before, Lenin had made it clear that majorities were not of primary importance to him. In the pamphlet, *Will the Bolsheviks Retain State Power?* he declared that 130,000 landlords had been able to govern Russia after the Revolution of 1905, and certainly 240,000 Bolsheviks would be able to govern "in the interests of the poor and against the rich . . . The state is an organ or instrument of violence of one class against another. While it is an instrument of violence used by the bourgeoisie on the proletariat, the proletarian slogan can only be *destruction* of that state. But when the state becomes proletarian, when it becomes an instrument of violence used by the proletariat on the bourgeoisie, then we will completely and unconditionally stand for strong state power and centralism."[4] In other words, the new government would be a dictatorship, and indeed it was.

The cabinet of the new regime was announced at the II Congress of Soviets on the evening of November 8. It was called a Council of People's Commissars—the word "minister" was rejected as redolent of bourgeois governments. The chairman, or prime minister, was Lenin; Alexis Rykov was commissar of interior; Trotsky foreign commissar; agriculture went to V. P. Miliutin, labor to A. G. Shliapnikov, education to Lunacharsky, nationalities to Stalin.

The main business of the Congress was to pass a Decree on Peace and a Decree on Land. The Decree on Peace simply proposed ending the war "without annexations and indemnities," which had been the formula of the Soviets in the spring. Neither did the Decree on Land enact the Bolshevik program. The measure transferred private and church lands

• [4] V. I. Lenin, *Sochineniia* (4th ed.; 35 vols.; Moscow, 1941–1950), Vol. XXVI, pp. 87 and 92.

to land committees and the Soviets of Peasant Deputies, declared the abolition of private property in land, and fixed a "toiling" norm for actual peasant holdings—a peasant was to hold only as much land as he could till himself. Certain delegates hastened to point out that this was nothing more or less than the S. R. land program. Lenin replied, "Life itself is the best teacher, and it will show who is right; let the peasants solve this question from one end and we from the other. It isn't important whether the problem is solved in the spirit of our program or in the spirit of the Socialist Revolutionary program." Chernov, leader of the orthodox S.R.'s, complained bitterly, "Lenin copies out our resolutions and publishes them in the form of 'decrees'," but he could do nothing to stop it. The Left S.R.'s, now in coalition with the Bolsheviks, retained the old land program of the S.R. party, and they were pleased to see it enacted into law. After passing the two decrees, approving the new government, and electing a new Central Executive Committee composed of 62 Bolsheviks and 29 Left S.R.'s (there were, however, no Left S.R. commissars in the cabinet at first), the II Congress of Soviets dispersed.

After they walked out from the Congress, the Mensheviks and orthodox S.R.'s organized, with the co-operation of the old Soviet Central Executive Committee, a Committee for the Salvation of the Country and the Revolution. The Committee did little but urge government employees to refuse to co-operate with the newly-installed commissars. The Menshevik and S.R. leaders declared that the II Congress of Soviets was merely a private meeting of Bolshevik deputies. They thought the Bolsheviks were behaving badly but seemed to have no conception of the magnitude of the change that had occurred. They continued to demand that a "broad" (including Bolsheviks) socialist government be formed, and indeed a number of Bolsheviks were willing. They worried, as did the Bolsheviks, about rumors that "counterrevolutionary" troops were en route to Petrograd. Few realized that a new era had opened in Russian history, and that the Bolsheviks were already on the way to the establishment of a single-party dictatorship.

Kerensky had managed to find help from General P. N. Krasnov at Pskov, and with a few hundred Cossacks had advanced to Tsarskoe Selo. However, the troops were routed at a skirmish at Pulkovo, twelve miles from Petrograd, and Kerensky fled, this time abroad. Meanwhile, after a week's fighting, the Bolsheviks took control of Moscow. Within a month or two, local Bolshevik detachments of workers and soldiers seized power in most of the cities of Russia. In the industrial town of Ivanovo-Voznesensk the take-over was easier than in Petrograd; in Kazan there was fighting, as in Moscow. With or without bloodshed, the Bolshevik power spread over most of the urban centers. However, the Cossack atamans kept their authority in the southeast; Kiev remained in the hands of the Ukrainian Rada; and, not very far from Petrograd, General Dukhonin at Supreme Headquarters in Mogilëv refused to recognize the Bolshevik coup.

PEACE

There no longer existed any dependable armed force at the disposal of either the Bolsheviks or their opponents. Lenin's government attempted to implement its promises as well as to ward off any possible danger of attack by army units loyal to the Provisional Government, by ordering General Dukhonin to begin negotiations for peace with the enemy high command, but he refused. N. V. Krylenko (who with Antonov-Ovseenko and P. E. Dibenko made up a sort of triple-headed commissariat for military and naval affairs) was sent to replace him, and Dukhonin was lynched by the soldiers. Krylenko ordered subordinate units to make their own cease-fire arrangements, simultaneously offering the Germans general peace negotiations. On December 5 a preliminary armistice agreement was reached at Brest-Litovsk.

Soon after Krylenko assumed command the old army dissolved entirely, many of the officers trying to reach anti-Bolshevik centers, the soldiers streaming homeward. The Bolsheviks were left with no weapons but those of diplomacy in facing the Germans. It was now the turn of Trotsky, as foreign commissar, to achieve "peace." His view of his functions was reflected in the remark attributed to him by friends, "I will issue some revolutionary proclamations to the peoples and then shut up shop." The Soviet Government was not created to make agreements with bourgeois regimes but to overthrow them. However, the first task was to prevent the Imperial German army from advancing; "our final negotiations," Trotsky declared hopefully, "will be with Karl Liebknecht" —the leader of the German Communists.

On December 22 parleys began at Brest-Litovsk between the Soviet Government (the delegation was at first headed by Adolf Joffe, then by Trotsky himself) and the Central Powers (the main figures were German Foreign Minister von Kühlmann and General Max von Hoffmann). Hoffmann made it clear at once that the price of peace was Bolshevik surrender of German-held territory. He introduced representatives of the Ukrainian Rada into the negotiations as an example of the way he interpreted the phrase "no annexations"—that is, he demanded that any borderlands which desired should be permitted to secede from Bolshevik Russia. On January 18 Hoffmann pointed to a line on the map which was both the boundary of opposing forces and, he said, the future boundary of Russia. At this Trotsky decided to return home for discussions.

By now the Bolsheviks were deeply split about how to attain "peace." Nicholas Bukharin and others, especially in the Moscow party organization, advocated rejection of Hoffmann's ultimatum and wanted to proclaim a "revolutionary war." Lenin believed that the need of the Bolshevik regime for a breathing spell overshadowed all else. Although the expected socialist revolution in the West "must and will come," he declared, it might be delayed for a time. Attempts to fight on would not only strengthen the Anglo-French "imperialists," but would also imperil the popular acceptance of the Bolsheviks and of the Soviet power. Zinoviev, Kamenev, and Stalin concurred. Trotsky attempted a dialectical resolution of this disagreement by offering the formula, "no war, no peace," which was no solution at all. On January 21 in Petrograd a Bolshevik conference considered the matter and voted 32 for Bukharin's proposal, 16 for Trotsky's, and 15 for Lenin's. However, three days later the Bolshevik Central Committee canceled out that verdict in favor of Trotsky's formula by a nine-to-seven vote, and a joint Bolshevik-Left S.R. session assented the next day.

Trotsky returned to Brest-Litovsk hoping to play for more time, trusting that propaganda and agitation among German and Austrian troops might yield results. On February 9 Hoffmann produced a peace treaty with the Ukrainian Rada—at the moment, as it happened, when the Bolsheviks were occupying Kiev. The next day Trotsky invoked his "no war, no peace formula"; he refused to agree to the German demands, announced that the war was at an end, and left Brest. Trotsky's gesture had the sole effect of eliminating his formula from further serious discussion by Bolshevik leaders. Within a week the Germans launched a new offensive which moved forward unopposed. On the day it opened, February 18, Lenin's demand for acceptance of the German terms was narrowly adopted by a seven-to-six vote of the Central Committee. The Germans, however, replied by new and harsher terms. Lenin insisted that they be accepted, threatening to resign if they were not, and the party leaders, realizing there was no alternative, agreed. On March 3, 1918, a Bolshevik delegation signed the Treaty of Brest-Litovsk. Trotsky thereupon yielded the foreign commissariat to Gregory Chicherin and became war commissar.

THE SIGNIFICANCE OF BREST-LITOVSK

The Allies had done their best to prevent Russia from signing a separate peace. It was in direct response to an appeal by an American agent in Russia, Edgar Sisson, to "restate anti-imperialistic war aims and democratic peace requisites of America . . . in short, almost placard paragraphs" that President Woodrow Wilson delivered his "Fourteen Points" speech on January 8. Wilson's sixth point was a demand for evacuation of all Russian territory and a call to give Russia "a sincere welcome into the society of free nations under institutions of her own choosing; and, more than a welcome, assistance also of every kind that she may need and may herself desire."

Such influential though only quasi-official diplomats as Colonel Raymond Robins, head of the U.S. Red Cross Mission, R. H. Bruce Lockhart, British special agent, and Captain Jacques Sadoul of the French Military Mission attempted to sound out Trotsky on the possibility that the Bolsheviks might continue the war with Allied aid. When this question was discussed in the Party Central Committee on February 22, Lenin sent his proxy: "I ask to add my vote in favor of taking potatoes and arms from the bandits of Anglo-French imperialism." Although Trotsky kept up contacts with Robins and Lockhart even after the peace treaty was signed, nothing came of them. The IV Congress of Soviets (which ratified the treaty) replied to a friendly message from Wilson with a statement of "its firm conviction that the happy time is not far away when the working masses of all bourgeois countries will overthrow the yoke of capital and establish the socialist order." In those days the Communists were more direct, as their immediate expectations were greater.

By the Treaty of Brest-Litovsk Lenin's government lost Poland, the Baltic states, much of Belorussia, the Ukraine, Finland (which had already been given its independence), and a strip of territory on the Turkish border of Transcaucasia: in total, about 1,300,000 square miles and 62 million people. On March 9 another treaty between the Central Powers and defeated Rumania also sanctioned the latter's annexation of Bessarabia. Lenin's concessions were certainly necessary. However, the calculations on which he based his surrender to German terms were erroneous. Although he talked of a "Tilsit peace," comparing Brest-Litovsk with the treaty of 1807 between Alexander I and Napoleon, he did not expect renewal of the war (as in 1812) but rather the speedy overthrow of the Imperial German government by a Communist revolution. The treaty was indeed to be torn up very soon, but for a quite different reason: Germany's surrender to the Western Allies.

The Brest peace had immediate consequences for the Bolshevik regime.

The new frontier was perilously close to the capital, and the government was promptly transferred from Petrograd, where it had been for over two centuries, to Moscow, where it had been in the days of the Muscovite Tsars and where it has remained. The popular response to the peace was mostly apathy, although it is likely that an attempt to pursue any kind of war would have produced a sharply negative reaction. Within the Bolshevik and Left S.R. ranks there was open opposition to the treaty. The VII Congress of the Bolshevik party (which incidentally renamed the party "Communist" as Lenin had demanded in the April Theses) met March 6–8 and ratified the treaty; the IV Congress of Soviets did so again a few days later. However, Bukharin openly attacked the treaty, particularly for its provision compelling the Communists to renounce propaganda against the Central Powers, and others were at best sullen in their acquiescence.

The Communists' junior partners, the Left S.R.'s, showed no such restraint. In March their representatives resigned from the cabinet and the Central Executive Committee of Soviets in protest at Lenin's peace. By July they had an additional grievance, the activities of the Communist-directed "Committees of Poor Peasants" (see p. 163). Thereupon they resorted to their old and preferred weapons against their former allies. A Left S.R. named Blumkin, hoping to provoke a renewal of hostilities, assassinated the German ambassador, Count von Mirbach, and there were several attempts at insurrection. On August 30 Left S.R.'s wounded Lenin, inflicting an injury from which he never fully recovered, and killed two other Communist leaders. To this effort to overthrow the Communist power and reopen the war, the now single-party government retaliated swiftly. A Red Terror was launched by the Extraordinary Commission for Struggle with Counterrevolution and Sabotage ("Cheka" from the initial letters of the first two words in Russian) under Felix Dzerzhinsky.

DESTROYING THE OLD STATE

The Cheka had been established in December, replacing the Petrograd Military Revolutionary Committee as the agency of revolutionary force. Its creation was but one of a series of measures by which the Bolsheviks sought to destroy the old state and build a new one—to use the formulation which came out of Marx's analysis of the Paris Commune of 1871 and was restated in Lenin's pamphlet of 1917, *The State and Revolution*.

Much was to be done to achieve such an objective. Even the Provisional Government was not finally disposed of by the October Revolution. The socialist ministers were soon released, and they proceeded to meet as a government, issuing orders which affected state institutions. On November 30 they even proclaimed themselves the "sole legitimate organ of power," spoke of the Bolsheviks as "rebels," and urged support of the Constituent Assembly. Lenin's government promptly deported them to Kronstadt, and the last remnant of the Provisional Government disappeared. The anti-Bolshevik Petrograd and Moscow municipal councils were dissolved. On December 7 the Senate, which had been in effect the Imperial supreme court, placidly pronounced the Bolshevik regime illegal and was thereupon abolished. Not for another month did Lenin get around to dissolving the zemstvo organs of local self-government, including the township zemstvos created by the Provisional Government. The crumbling army was pushed to complete disintegration by decrees ordering election of officers (but now called "commanders") and abolishing all ranks and decorations. What units were left in being were speedily demobilized. Neither Reds nor Whites managed to take over the old army; it simply ceased to exist.

The old marriage and divorce laws were repealed. Only civil marriage was to be officially recognized, illegitimacy was to entail no disabilities, divorce might be had by either partner for the asking. On February 14, 1918 (February 1, Old Style), the Gregorian calendar was adopted, and the Julian calendar was abandoned by all except the ecclesiastical authorities.[5] Even the old Cyrillic alphabet was purged of dispensable letters, although there was no attempt—as in Turkey, for example—to adopt a Latin alphabet.

The Russian Orthodox Church, the official religious institution of the old regime, was attacked, not with the intent of destroying it instantly but rather of penning it into a corner where, it was hoped, it would wither and die. On February 5, 1918, the government proclaimed the "separation of the Church from the state and from the schools." Actually the separation of the Church from the control which the state had exercised, through the Holy Synod, had already been begun under the Provisional Government. The Church itself had taken the initiative in summoning a council and in restoring the Patriarchate which Peter the Great had abolished. However, the Communists had never made any secret of their belief that religion was ideologically pernicious and institutionally an instrument of the exploiting classes. It was not "separation" but destruction which they planned for the Orthodox Church and all

• [5] This accounts for the discrepancy between the dates of the "Russian" Christmas and other religious holidays and the dates on which they are celebrated in the West.

other religious institutions and doctrines. Nevertheless Lenin had repeatedly cautioned against a premature frontal attack on the "superstitions" of the masses. The Communists believed that the overturn of the economic foundation would undermine the "superstructural" institutions, including religion, of a bygone time. Time would show that they had grossly underestimated the magnitude of their task in obliterating religious belief.

THE CONSTITUENT ASSEMBLY

One institution which the Provisional Government had promised and had finally prepared to convene still plagued the Bolsheviks. That was the Constituent Assembly. There had never been such a thing, and yet as a slogan it had a history of several generations and widespread popularity. Like all the other opposition parties, the Bolsheviks had always claimed to support it, although as long ago as 1903 Plekhanov (in his fleeting Bolshevik phase) had declared that if a good assembly was elected, it would be kept, if a bad one, it would be dispersed. Even though Kerensky's government had at last fixed the elections to the Constituent Assembly, the Bolsheviks had charged that he intended to subvert it, and immediately after the October Revolution, *Pravda* had declared, "Comrades, by shedding your blood you have assured the convocation . . . of the Constitutent Assembly."

The elections were held as scheduled on November 25, with the exception of a few districts. It is impossible to give a precise and complete tabulation of results, but the general picture is clear enough. In the large cities the Bolsheviks polled the most votes, with the Kadets a reasonably close second, but in the smaller towns and the countryside the S.R.'s won enough to give them a majority in the election as a whole. Radkey's study yields roughly the following figures: S.R.'s and Ukrainian S.R.'s 17,100,000, Bolsheviks 9,800,000, Kadets 2,000,000, Mensheviks 1,360,000 out of a grand total of 41,700,000 (including a number of nationalist or minority groups).[6] Out of 703 deputies, 380 were regular S.R.'s (Russian and Ukrainian), 39 Left S.R.'s, 168 Bolsheviks, 18 Mensheviks, 17 Kadets and Rightists, 4 Popular Socialists, 77 minority group representatives.

The elections were carried out under conditions wherein freedom of campaigning was partially (for the Kadets very severely) curtailed, and the results were undoubtedly clouded by the prevailing political con-

• [6] Oliver Henry Radkey, *The Election to the Russian Constituent Assembly of 1917* (Cambridge: Harvard University Press, 1950), esp. pp. 16–17.

fusion, misinformation, and uncertainty. The Bolsheviks did not try to make a case that the country was really in favor of their party, but they argued that the Left S.R.'s were not adequately represented since they had broken off from the rest of the party after the electoral lists had been drawn up, and thus that the peasants had no opportunity to distinguish between the Bolsheviks' allies (the Left S.R.'s) and their enemies (the orthodox S.R.'s). However, according to Radkey, those who did attend the assembly as Left S.R. deputies sometimes managed to do so only because the new party had obtained control of certain party organizations and "rigged the lists." In that way their participation in the Soviet Government certainly offset to a considerable extent the handicap to which the Bolsheviks pointed.

In any case Lenin did not much care what the elections proved, as his attitude toward the Constituent Assembly was purely instrumentalist. He had desired to postpone the elections but had been outvoted on that. When the results he feared had come in, he tried in several ways to render the assembly impotent. He arrested a few deputies, dispersed forty-three of them who invaded the Taurida Palace on December 11 (the date set by the shadow Provisional Government) and tried to hold a session. He outlawed the Kadets and arrested two of their leaders who were deputies to the assembly, A. I. Shingarëv and F. F. Kokoshkin, who were murdered in a detention hospital a few weeks later. In December Uritsky (himself to be assassinated by the Left S.R.'s within a few months) spoke for the Bolsheviks: "Shall we convene the Constituent Assembly? Yes. Shall we disperse it? Perhaps; it depends on circumstances." In *Pravda* Lenin made it clear that the only way the assembly might survive would be to vote confidence in the Soviet Government.

On January 18 the Constituent Assembly met for the first and last time in the Taurida Palace. The session was dominated by the leaders of the S.R. and Menshevik parties, Chernov and Tsereteli. Chernov was elected president of the assembly over Maria Spiridonova, a Left S.R. leader fronting for the Bolsheviks, by a vote of 244 to 153. Three measures were adopted: a Land Law, an appeal for peace (which deprecated the separate-peace character of the Soviet-German negotiations then in progress and proposed an international socialist conference to realize a "general democratic peace"), and a decree proclaiming Russia a democratic federative republic. At 5:00 A.M. on January 19 a sailor informed Chernov that the "guard is tired," and requested the deputies to disperse. The assembly adjourned until noon, but the delegates were prevented by force from reassembling. Bolshevik troops fired on street demonstrators in favor of the Constituent Assembly, but there was little popular reaction to the dissolution.

It is difficult to prove from these events that the "people" supported the Bolsheviks, the Constituent Assembly, or anything else. The assembly had the same leadership as the Soviets in early 1917—the Mensheviks and S.R.'s (even though actual Menshevik strength in deputies was negligible, the plurality of their S.R. friends accounted for the continued partnership). The leaders of the two parties had persistently refused to recognize the problem of power and continued to do so. They had been unwilling to countenance the creation of police or military forces which might have prevented the Bolshevik coup, and as a result no force existed sufficient to defend the Constituent Assembly. It has been argued that the failure of the assembly proved that the Russian people were unready for democracy. More concretely and perhaps more accurately, it showed that the leadership of the assembly had learned little from the success of the Bolshevik coup. The Menshevik and S.R. leaders, with some exceptions, remained ambivalent about whether democracy is justified in using arms in self-defense, and many of them readily accepted the contention that their own weaknesses were at root the fault of the peoples of Russia.

With the Constituent Assembly there disappeared virtually the last institutional toehold for the political forces opposed to Bolshevism. Thenceforth the only alternative appeared to be an attempt to build a territorial base on the periphery of the country from which to attack the Bolshevik-controlled center.

BUILDING THE NEW STATE

As Lenin well realized, the creation of new institutions was a much more difficult task than the destruction of old ones. If, as John Reed reports, his first words to the II Congress of Soviets were, "We shall now proceed to construct the Socialist order!"[7] he still recognized that such construction would take some time. It was the Bolshevik view that the building of a new state structure was already well begun at the time of the October Revolution. The Soviets, organized in many divergent and informal ways in different parts of the country, were to be the building blocks of the new edifice.

However, certain of the blocks required some reshaping. Although the

• [7] John Reed, *Ten Days that Shook the World* (New York: International Publishers, 1919), p. 126.

Workers' and Soldiers' Soviets fell completely into Lenin's hands at the moment the Mensheviks and S.R.'s walked out of the II Congress, thus saving the Bolsheviks much trouble, the Peasant Soviets were a more serious problem. In early December a Congress of Peasant Deputies was summoned in Petrograd; it promptly voted confidence in the orthodox S.R. leader, Chernov, and no confidence in the Bolshevik-Left S.R. coalition. Lenin and Maria Spiridonova, who owed her leadership of the terrorist Left S.R.'s to notoriety earned by her own past murder of a Tsarist general, thereupon forced a split in the Congress. This time, in effect, the majority walked out. The remaining delegates fused with the Workers' and Soldiers' Soviets and elected several members to the Central Executive Committee. From then on the Peasant Soviets were safely Bolshevik-controlled, by exclusion of opponents. There was never any pretense that "Soviet democracy" was going to mean that any Soviet body could override the will of the Bolshevik party Central Committee. Legislation might or might not be formally ratified by one of the Congresses of Soviets or the Soviet Central Executive Committee between sessions of the Congresses, but it was initiated in the top party echelons.

The recasting of the economic system began slowly. On November 11 the eight-hour working day was universally introduced. Two weeks later "workers' control," the slogan advanced by the Bolshevik-led factory committees earlier in the year, was enacted, and workers' committees were thereby awarded the right to oversee all steps in production. On December 14 a new organ, the Supreme Economic Council, was created to supervise the whole national economy. Shortly afterward banks were nationalized, and in February all debts of the Tsarist regime were cancelled. Nevertheless, except for a number of arbitrary financial levies on businessmen which were carried out in many cities, there was little effort at this stage to disturb private enterprise as a whole.

In the spring of 1918 the Communists were apparently solidly in power. Enough of the old structure had been wrecked or undermined to make its restoration very difficult, and enough enthusiasm had been aroused among veteran and recently recruited Communists to make it hard for any non-Communist group or coalition to build a corps of comparably dedicated leaders. The Russian people were still mostly peasant and Christian, but the Communists had not as yet made it clear that their real objective was to tear the people away from their own soil and their ancestral religion.

The masses knew that the "Revolution" had become very puzzling indeed, that it was hard to tell who was really in favor of it and who was not, and that the government in Moscow was quite unpredictable, unlike the Tsarist regime which, although often oppressive, was at least familiar. The politics of the Revolution had passed beyond popular comprehension:

From house to house
A rope is strung,
A sagging placard on it hung:
"All Power to the Constituent Assembly!"

A bent old woman, tearful, trembly,
Stares at the placard in despair.
Her blear eyes see
How many fine foot-clouts could be
Cut from the canvas wasted there,
While the children's feet go bare. . . .

The masses shed few tears for the "old" regime, and many of the youth (and by no means only the Communists) ripped into what was left of it with gusto:

Comrades, show spunk, take aim, the lot!
At Holy Russia let's fire a shot,

At hutted Russia,
Fat-rumped and solid,

Russia the stolid![8]

Millions hoped the powerful would be brought low and the wretched would be exalted, but after the miseries of three years of war and another year of revolutionary turmoil, they were confused and weary. What awaited them, however, was not peace and a resumption of their quest for human dignity and security, but three more years of civil war.

• [8] From Alexander Blok, *The Twelve,* trans. Babette Deutsch in Avrahm Yarmolinsky, ed., *A Treasury of Russian Verse* (New York: Macmillan, 1949), pp. 155 and 159.

The Civil War:
the White Challenge
(1917–1919)

★
★
★
★
★
★
★
★
★
★

CHAPTER 11

"WAR COMMUNISM"

From the start Lenin's efforts to establish a new political and social order in Russia were severely hampered by war and domestic chaos. Both problems were in part legacies from the Tsarist regime and the Provisional Government, but they were soon aggravated by developments of the winter of 1917–1918. Even before the Treaty of Brest-Litovsk brought Russia's participation in World War I to an end, anti-Bolshevik forces had been assembled which were to launch a Civil War lasting three more years. The economy was already disorganized by the events of 1917; workers had spent much time on demonstrations and meetings and little at their jobs, the transportation and communication systems were near a breakdown, food shortages were spreading, and sporadic local seizures of property were occurring all over the country. Much war industry was dismantled before the magnitude of the needs of the Civil War was clear, and as a result unemployment spread.

However, it was plain that some kind of army would be needed by the new government, and the old army had ceased to exist. In January 1918 a decree provided that any Soviet citizen eighteen years of age or over could volunteer for the new Red Army, if vouched for by a trade-union or an army committee, for a three-month period, at a salary of a hundred and fifty rubles per month. Tens and then hundreds of thousands of recruits responded, but they remained a rabble, not an army. After Brest-Litovsk Trotsky became war commissar, and in April he began to create a regular army based on conscription, authority, and discipline—of a "new" sort, of course. In April compulsory military training was ordered for all workers and for peasants who did not hire labor. The honor of military service was denied members of the "bourgeoisie" (which sometimes meant, in practice, simply those who wore coats), but they were conscripted for labor service. The death penalty, for which Kornilov had asked in vain before the Bolshevik coup, was restored. Deserters were sometimes shot, although more often they were sent into punishment units. Election of officers was terminated, and army committees were given to understand that their period of decision-making was past. Trained officers had to be found for the new army, and Trotsky not only accepted officer volunteers from the old army, but even conscripted old officers, warning them frankly that desertion would result in harm to their families. In order to counter the objections of worried Bolsheviks and recalcitrant worker-soldiers, Trotsky described this device as building socialism with bricks left over from the demolished old order. Almost fifty thousand officers of the old army were used by the Reds in the Civil War.

In order to prevent what were presumably the officers' real views from interfering with their command duties, Trotsky appointed political commissars to watch the officers, as well as to carry out propaganda among the recruits. Through the work of the commissars, a full-fledged Party hierarchy was built into the army at every level. There seemed adequate justification for using political spies on officers who might have monarchist sympathies, but, once instituted, the commissar device survived long after none but loyal Communists supposedly remained anywhere in the army. The commissars were only a small percentage of the Party members in the new army; perhaps as many as half of the total Party membership served in the Red Army during the Civil War. Such soldiers fought with devotion to their cause, for they believed that torture and death awaited them if captured by the Whites, and they thought that their victory would inaugurate the millennium.

The economic situation deteriorated further in the summer of 1918. The government adopted a number of measures which, however, tended to worsen rather than alleviate it. On June 11 the decision was taken to establish all over Russia "Committees of Poor Peasants," whose task was to "carry the class war to the village" by fighting "kulaks" (rich peasants), and at the same time to requisition the grain needed to feed the cities. Among a peasantry where there were no recognized class distinctions and almost everyone was a smallholder to some degree, such an order provoked chaos. E. H. Carr, who is generally sympathetic toward the Bolsheviks, acknowledges that although the committees did provide some informers, they were handicapped by the fact that the "poor peasants" proved "less numerous than the Bolsheviks had supposed."[1]

More often than not the "class struggle in the village" and the requisitioning were actually carried out by Communists from the cities, and the peasantry was deeply embittered. The declaration was often heard—and not only in the countryside—"I am for the Bolsheviks, but am against the Communists." The peasants' confusion was understandable. They knew that the Bolsheviks had sanctioned land division, and they also saw that the Communists were trying to loot their property and disrupt their villages. The only item of information lacking was that the two groups were identical, since the Bolshevik party had in the meantime renamed itself Communist. Peasant risings against the Reds multiplied in July and continued into the fall of 1918. In June the city of Tambov was the scene of a briefly successful anti-Red revolt.

In July 1918, at the V Congress of Soviets, despite Communist manipulation of seats, the Left S.R.'s had a large delegation (all orthodox S.R.'s and Mensheviks had been expelled from the Soviets in June). The Left S.R. spokesmen at the Congress bitterly attacked the Committees of Poor Peasants as committees of "village loafers," and protested the requisitioning detachments. Two days later the Left S.R.'s killed the German ambassador and attempted an uprising (see p. 155). Their party was promptly expelled from the Soviets. At the same moment a former S.R., Boris Savinkov, who had been Kerensky's assistant for military affairs, organized a revolt which seized the city of Yaroslavl and held it almost two weeks. It was in such an atmosphere of domestic crisis that local Communists in Ekaterinburg carried out the murder of the entire Imperial family. By this time the Cheka had unleashed the full force of the Red Terror against active and potential enemies alike, seeking not to win friends but to frighten enemies into submission.

On June 28, some two weeks after the Committees of Poor Peasants were established, the Soviet government nationalized all major industries without compensation and placed them under the Supreme Economic Council. Management, nominally in the hands of *Glavki* or main departments of the Council, was at first actually left to workers' committees. The only difference from the earlier regime of "workers' control" was

• [1] *The Bolshevik Revolution, 1917–1923,* Vol. II, p. 158.

that now the managers were gone. The consequent disorganization of industry was such that soon new ones had to be appointed. Again "bricks of the old order" had to be used; many new managers were the old ones back again, watched over like the army officers by political appointees.

The measures of the spring and summer of 1918 inaugurated the period of so-called "War Communism." Such measures neither won the government popularity nor stimulated production and trade. It was thought that they would enable the government to prosecute the Civil War more effectively, although it is doubtful that they did so. In any case "War Communism" constituted an attempt, which proved premature, to realize the Party's stated ideological goals.

On July 19, 1918, there was promulgated the first Soviet Constitution, intended to reflect the Marxist-Leninist principles which underlay the government's policy. The "bourgeoisie" was excluded from voting, and urban residents were given a considerable preponderance in suffrage over village dwellers. The objective of the regime was said to be "the pitiless suppression of exploiters, the socialist organization of society, and the victory of socialism in all countries." Provided Lenin's definitions of the words "exploiters" and "socialism" be accepted, this was a very fair description of what the Communists were doing in Russia and what they hoped to do abroad.

The Constitution of 1918 and subsequent constitutions prescribed suffrage for Soviets which had no power and guaranteed rights which were not implemented. In any case, Lenin did not pretend that the Soviet Constitution was the fundamental law of the land. It was designed merely as a description of the landmarks at a given point on the route which the Communists were traversing, and that route was given not by the Constitution itself but by the principles of Marx and Lenin.[2]

THE WHITES IN THE SOUTH: THE EMERGENCE OF DENIKIN

Immediately after the Bolshevik coup, anti-Bolshevik leaders began to plan and organize a movement of opposition to the new regime. Such leaders fell into three groups: the non-Bolshevik Russian party politicians, the former officers of the army of the Empire and of the Provisional Government, and the nationalists seeking independence or autonomy for the minority peoples. Not all the non-Bolshevik party leaders were disposed to resist. Generally speaking the Mensheviks held aloof from

• [2] For a discussion of the role of the Constitution of 1936 in the Soviet system, see pp. 283 ff.

the struggle; by temperament and outlook they were linked more closely with their former Bolshevik comrades than with the chieftains of the White cause. The orthodox S.R.'s suffered, as will appear, from feelings of ambivalence toward both sides in the Civil War, although at first many took the road of resistance. The Kadets leaned to the White side with varying degrees of commitment. The party politicians were uneasy at the abandonment of the old opposition shibboleth, "No enemy on the Left," and were not trained to engage in armed struggle themselves or accustomed to countenance it except when it had been directed against the old regime. Although many were drawn into the White camp, since they were disinclined to exercise the weapons of power themselves, they were soon reduced to criticizing the military leaders who were willing to do so. The nationalists were fighting their own battles; when their own lands were not involved, they could only temporarily and conditionally be prevailed upon to fight. The military commanders thus became, virtually by default, the moving spirits in the White camp whose only unifying principle was a desire to overthrow Bolshevik rule, although for the most part its leaders were agreed on the establishment of some kind of republican and representative government in its stead.

The first military leader to emerge was the former commander-in-chief, Kornilov, who following the "affair" of September had been under arrest in Mogilëv along with several other generals. Friendly guards allowed him and his fellow officers to escape just before Krylenko arrived to replace Dukhonin as commander-in-chief. They made their way to Rostov-on-Don, where General Kaledin, the Don Cossack ataman, had succeeded in weathering the October Revolution and where he gave promise of establishing a base for anti-Bolshevik resistance. Such party leaders as the Kadet Miliukov and the Octobrist Michael Rodzianko also appeared in Rostov. Like Kaledin at Rostov, local Cossack authorities had maintained control over Ekaterinodar, capital of the Kuban Cossack territory, and also Orenburg. Russia's southeastern frontier seemed to be the best hope of the Whites.

Between the Cossacks at Rostov and the Bolsheviks in Moscow lay the Ukraine, where the situation remained fluid for several months after the October Revolution. The regime of the Ukrainian Rada had to face an abortive Bolshevik attempt to seize Kiev but succeeded in reasserting its authority by the use of some Ukrainian troops. On November 19 the Rada proclaimed the Ukraine a People's Republic[3] and a component part of a projected Russian Federation. However, in and near the Donets Basin to the east, where there were more Russians and more industrial

• [3] Not to be confused with the later Communist employment of this phrase.

workers, the Bolsheviks had greater strength. They managed to establish a Ukrainian Soviet regime in Kharkov, and for a brief period the Ukraine was in effect partitioned between west and east. With a small and untrained force, the Bolshevik Antonov-Ovseenko was sent to curb the Rada and harry Kaledin in Rostov. On February 8, 1918, Bolshevik troops took Kiev. On the same day, however, the Ukrainian Rada's delegation at Brest-Litovsk was signing a separate peace with the Central Powers, and on March 3 the Germans entered Kiev, nominally restoring the power of the Rada. Within two months they reversed themselves, dispersed the Rada, and replaced it with a puppet regime headed by Hetman Pavlo Skoropadski. For eight months German occupation removed the Ukraine from the arena of the Civil War. Popular discontent with the brutality of the military authorities spread rapidly, and the Germans were kept too busy in the Ukraine to be able to have much influence on the course of events to the east.

Meanwhile in the Rostov area a serious effort to build an anti-Bolshevik army and center of power was launched. General M. V. Alexeev, who had been chief of staff to the Tsar while he had supreme command and in the early months of the Provisional Government was commander-in-chief, arrived in Novocherkassk, near Rostov, on November 15, 1917. Immediately he set about to create a new Volunteer Army, performing such unaccustomed tasks as scrounging a few bedsteads here, a few rifles there. Six weeks later Kornilov arrived from Mogilëv and took command. There was issued a public appeal for the "creation of an armed force which could be opposed to the impending anarchy and to the German-Bolshevik invasion," and for the defense of liberty and the Constituent Assembly. General Kaledin, the host, as it were, of the Volunteer Army, tried to rally his Cossacks and win the support of the peasants, whose grievances against the Cossacks were numerous.

By the beginning of February the Whites already faced a crisis. As Red forces from the Donets Basin were approaching Rostov, Kaledin resigned as Cossack ataman and committed suicide. The Bolsheviks occupied Rostov and captured a Cossack center farther east at Orenburg. The Volunteer Army, only some three or four thousand men strong, retreated toward the single remaining Cossack stronghold at Ekaterinodar in the Kuban, only to find it taken by the Reds. Kornilov, commander of the Volunteer Army, rallied the Kuban Cossacks who had evacuated Ekaterinodar and planned an attack on the city. However, he was killed by shellfire on April 13, and the plan had to be abandoned.

Kornilov's place was taken by General Anton Denikin, a republican and a moderate. His Kadet colleagues distrusted him as too conservative, while some of his conservative associates suspected him of being pro-Kadet. He was never comfortable in dealing with political issues, and his military capacity is debatable. His first task was to save the Volunteer Army. In a cruelly difficult campaign lasting almost three months, which became known as the "icy march," he led his forces back to the Don-Kuban border, where they could rest and recuperate. The march took the army seven hundred miles by foot and resulted in severe losses; nevertheless enough recruits joined them so that Denikin ended with a larger force than he started out with. For the time being the Whites in the south had salvaged their hopes of further struggle, and during the months which followed anti-Bolsheviks of varying political coloration were attracted to Denikin's cause.

THE CZECHOSLOVAK RISING AND ALLIED INTERVENTION

Although the Volunteer Army had survived, its prospects in the spring of 1918 remained doubtful. In other widely scattered regions there was chaos but little effective resistance to the Communists. At that moment the forces of Denikin were heartened by the uprising of the Czechs, which opened up a great new front of the Civil War in Siberia, precipitated more or less serious Allied intervention, and alarmed the Communists sufficiently to hasten the creation of a new Red Army.

The Czechoslovak brigade which had fought in the World War with the Russian Army had survived the collapse of the front, and after the February Revolution had been augmented by volunteers from Austro-Hungarian prisoners of Czechoslovak origin. The Czech nationalist leader, Thomas G. Masaryk, desired to send this corps—as it had become by the autumn of 1917—to France to fight for Allied victory and Czechoslovak independence, despite the hopes of General Alexeev and others that it might remain in Russia to fight for Russian freedom against the Communists. Such hopes appeared ill-founded in any case, for the Czechs had helped Red forces resist the German advance into the Ukraine, and their relations with Moscow were cordial. On March 26 the Soviets, the Czechs, and Allied representatives signed an agreement by which the Czech corps would be transported as "free citizens" to Vladivostok and thence to France. The corps was to travel with minimal armament; the rest of its arms were to be turned over to the Soviets in Penza, where the agreement was signed.

By this time the Czech soldiers were debating among themselves what they ought to do. Communist propagandists were trying their best to persuade them to join the Red Army, while pro-Allied officers warned them against surrendering their arms. The Allied government to which the Czechs were closest and whose advice they most often heeded was that of the French. On May 2 the French were instrumental in arranging a change of route for those Czech troops who had proceeded no farther east than Omsk. In order to reach the Western front faster, they were to be taken out through Archangel instead of Vladivostok.

Rumors spread among the Czechs that this decision was made on Soviet rather than Allied initiative, and their fear of being disarmed deepened. On May 14 an accidental brawl between Czech soldiers and Hungarian war prisoners at the railway station in Cheliabinsk, in the Urals, led to an open break between the Reds and the Czechs. The Cheliabinsk Soviet arrested some Czechs, but their comrades promptly released them by force. In response to news of the incident, War Commissar Trotsky ordered, on May 25, that the Czechs be disarmed and that any Czech who was found armed should be shot forthwith.

Beginning on May 25 armed clashes occurred between the Czechs and the Reds all along the Trans-Siberian Railway. By June 8 the Czechs had seized a series of towns from Penza in south-central Russia through Samara on the Volga to Omsk and Tomsk in central Siberia. Within the following month they had established contact between most of the towns captured, although it was not until late August that eastern Siberia was cleared of Reds.

When the French realized what had happened, they urged the Czechs to remain where they were and to prepare the way for Allied intervention. Allied landings had already begun in March in Murmansk and were followed by others in Archangel and Vladivostok. Their stated purpose had been merely to safeguard war supplies in order to prevent their falling into German hands, but the Czech rising changed the picture drastically. Hopes spread in certain Allied quarters that Russian troops, aided by the Czechs, could overthrow the Communists without direct additional support other than that of a moral and logistic kind. French, British, Japanese, and a few other national contingents landed on the coasts of the White Sea, Black Sea, and Sea of Japan.

The Allied statesmen and military men who made and executed intervention policy were far from unanimous in their conception of the aims of intervention. Some were firm in their belief that the Communists had to be overthrown to protect their own governments from the specter of revolution, or to safeguard their nations' economic or political interests at various points, or to aid the cause of Russian freedom, or (in 1918) to restore an Eastern front or at least to prevent the Germans from strengthening their armies by way of Allied-produced munitions or their power by way of Russian resources. Intervention was prompted by a mixture of motives, compounded differently in the individuals, groups, and powers concerned. In each Allied country, moreover, there were influential men who from the start opposed the idea or were at least ambivalent toward it, and believed that the Communists could be brought to "listen to reason" or that they were actually dedicated to peace, freedom, and the welfare of the Russian people. America's General Graves and France's General Janine had grave doubts about the Whites and questioned the wisdom of the whole intervention. Those who favored it were often hampered by a faulty comprehension of Russian affairs in general and inadequate intelligence reports: Britain's Lloyd George once publicly referred to "Kolchak, Denikin, and Kharkov [*sic*]" as leaders of the White movement.

The Allies were thus by no means solidly committed to the overthrow of the Communist regime. Probably there was broader agreement on an objective somewhat similar to what later would be called "containment"; that is to say, the need to prevent a Bolshevik regime, even if victorious in Russia, from expanding westward by taking advantage of the spreading chaos in central Europe and supporting Communist revolutions in the West. The effect of the halfhearted intervention which did take place was to enable the Whites to manage for a time without any kind of satisfactory industrial base or source of supply, and to provide opportunities which greater political sagacity on the part of the White leaders might have turned to account. As Miliukov recognized very early, if the Allies wished the Whites to win the Civil War, they should either have given them much more assistance or none at all. In the event, the Communists were able to undermine White support by using the slogan of defense of the homeland against foreigners, while the Whites received no decisive aid to offset that psychological disadvantage.

THE WHITES IN THE EAST: THE EMERGENCE OF KOLCHAK

The Czech rising threatened the regime of the Russian Communists, but only Russian anti-Communists could overthrow it and install a new government. In April the Volunteer Army appeared the only possible nucleus for such an effort. However, Socialist Revolutionaries who distrusted the generals in the south were already preparing to strike in the east when the Czech rising eased their task. It appears that the gifted and energetic Czech Captain Gajda (soon to become a general) was in touch with S.R. and other organizations in the area, and the Czech occupation of Samara was in fact instigated by a local S.R. leader.

In the wake of the Czech rising two governments were established in the area wrested from Red control. On June 1 at Omsk a West Siberian Commissariat proclaimed the autonomy of Siberia under a special white and green flag, symbolizing snow and forest. It claimed continuity with the Siberian Regional Duma, a body elected by universal suffrage which had set up a shadowy regional government in February 1918 before being dispersed, like the Constituent Assembly, by the Bolsheviks. The West Siberian Commissariat announced support of the Constituent Assembly and gave as its aims the restoration of local self-government and the re-establishment of normal conditions of trade.

Siberian regionalism had been developing rapidly during the previous decades, spurred by the enormous influx of immigrants from European Russia. As Siberia was almost wholly a peasant land, the Bolsheviks could mobilize little support among their usual targets, the industrial workers;

moreover, Bolshevik land policy won few peasant adherents since the Siberians had ample land to begin with and there were no large estates to divide. On the other hand, during their few months as rulers of Siberia, the Bolsheviks had made few enemies. The peasant population stood aside from the struggle as the urban intelligentsia, having expelled the Reds, argued about what sort of government Siberia should have.

At first the S.R.'s controlled the West Siberian Commissariat, and they were inclined to keep the Soviets of 1917 in existence, although not to use them as organs of government. However, on June 30, 1918, they were supplanted by a new Siberian Government led by the moderate liberal Peter Vologodsky. The new regime, which had support among the officers, suppressed the Soviets, sanctioned the formation of non-political trade-unions, and undertook to raise an anti-Communist army by conscription.

The second government which profited from the Czech rising was the S.R.-dominated Government of the Committee of Members of the Constituent Assembly (*Komuch*). Five S.R. deputies took over Samara, ordered reinstatement of local self-government, and like their Siberian comrades called for resumption of meetings of the Constituent Assembly to which they had belonged. Under such capable commanders as Colonel Kappel, they mustered a force which advanced westward and on August 6 captured the city of Kazan. There they found the former Tsarist government gold reserve, valued at well over half a billion rubles. The next day anti-Red revolts occurred in the nearby centers of Izhevsk and Votkinsk, among workers and peasants who had experienced Bolshevik requisitioning. The prospects for an anti-Communist offensive looked bright; however, political objectives remained obscure. Within the Samara camp, as a participant points out, "The Government was Socialist Revolutionary, unconciliatory even with the Kadets, and the armed force, in its majority, consisted of right-wing elements, hostile to the Socialist Revolutionaries."[4]

Between Samara and Omsk, not to mention lesser centers of resistance, there was ideological distrust and power rivalry. Under the impatient pressure of the Czechs, an effort was made to harmonize the differences among the Whites in the east by calling a State Conference at Ufa on September 8. The news of the Red capture of Kazan pressed the S.R.'s on the one hand and the Kadets and officers on the other into a compromise agreement. The Conference established a "national" government to sit at Omsk, called the Directory and consisting of two S.R.'s, Avksentiev

• [4] P. Petrov, *Ot Volgi do Tikhago Okeana* (Riga, 1930), p. 17, quoted in Chamberlin, *The Russian Revolution, 1917–1921,* Vol. II, p. 18.

and Zenzinov, and three liberals, Siberian Premier Vologodsky, the Kadet Vinogradov, and General Boldyrev.

However, the Ufa State Conference did not and could not reconcile S.R.'s, who thought of themselves as socialists and in moments of irritation remembered that the Bolsheviks were socialists, too, with the moderates who believed that the Bolsheviks must be overthrown before any sweeping reform program could be safely undertaken. Moreover, the S.R.'s did not forget that they had been the majority party in the Constituent Assembly and thus claimed to represent the "people's will," while the moderates contended that another election carried out after almost a year of Bolshevik-Left S.R. rule might well reflect a change in the popular support of all parties and groups.

The possibility of White success depended less on political compromise than on postponement of political debate until the military situation was clarified. None of the White leaders tried to dispense with the announcement of political principles and objectives; some kind of policy statements were essential in order to rally popular support. Therein lay the dilemma, for any political formulation whatsoever provoked angry debate. Generalities about political democracy and social reform were not enough to establish unity. The S.R.'s were no mere reformers but believed that class struggle in order to establish a new toilers' state was inevitable and desirable, while the moderates reproached them for such views, and the officers impatiently wondered when and how they could ever get on with the struggle.

On October 9, 1918, the Directory assumed authority in Omsk in an atmosphere of confusion and intrigue. Various Russian personalities and parties exchanged rumors and contrived plots. Czech, British, American, French, Polish, Rumanian, Italian, and Japanese agents, officers, and troops made no secret of their alarm over the situation and offered a multitude of conflicting suggestions. The old Siberian Government, despite its acknowledgment of the authority of the "national" Directory, retained great local influence and frustrated the S.R.'s at every turn, while the S.R.'s were regarded with suspicion by many moderates and conservatives who knew that a number of members of the S.R. party elsewhere in Russia were invoking a plague on both Reds and Whites or even joining the Communist side.

On October 11 the Central Committee of the Socialist Revolutionary party, situated at Ekaterinburg, protested the conservative tendencies of the Omsk authorities and summoned the party to "resist" the "counter-revolutionary organizers of civil war in the rear of the anti-Bolshevik front." Most of the Czechs, fatigued, confused, and to some extent influenced by S.R. and even Communist propagandists, agreed with the Central Committee's protest. The moderates were disheartened, the conservatives furious.

By this time a newcomer in Omsk, Admiral Alexander Kolchak, had attracted favorable attention from moderates and conservatives. Kolchak, the former commander of the Black Sea Fleet, had made his way to the Far East and thence to Omsk with Allied encouragement and aid, intending to reach the Whites in the south. The moderate General Boldyrev invited him to remain in Omsk as war minister for the Directory. In November, one week after the armistice ending World War I, the conservatives carried out a *coup d'état* in Omsk, arrested the S.R. leaders, and offered Kolchak the posts of "Supreme Ruler" or dictator and commander-in-chief of all land and naval forces of Russia. Although he apparently had not connived in the coup, he accepted. The Czech National Council denounced the action, declaring that it "violated the principle of legality," but the Czech General Gajda supported Kolchak, as did the British General Knox and other Allied officers. Naturally the S.R.'s were hostile to him, but the Kadets favored him. It was clear that for the time being the fate of the Whites in Siberia would depend largely on the success of his leadership.

THE END OF WORLD WAR I

The Czech uprising had dealt a heavy blow to the Communist cause, and for several months the Whites in the east had things their own way. However, in late August the tide of civil war turned as Trotsky himself hastened to the Kazan front and rallied Red forces at Sviazhsk. This skirmish has been called the "Valmy of the Russian Revolution," recalling the first check to foreign armies by French Revolutionary troops, although it should be remembered also that the Whites at Sviazhsk were not foreigners. On September 10 the Red Fifth Army, whipped into order by Trotsky, recaptured Kazan. On October 8 Samara, capital of the *Komuch* regime, fell, and much of the Volga region soon followed. The Whites in the east were forced back to the Urals.

During the spring and summer of 1918 the Whites in the south, having barely survived the previous winter, tried to broaden their base of operations. After the suicide of Kaledin, he was succeeded as ataman of the Don Cossacks by General P. N. Krasnov, who had tried to fight back into Petrograd with Kerensky after the Bolshevik coup. Krasnov's relations with the Volunteer Army were soon strained. Generals Denikin and Alexeev kept aloof from the Germans who were occupying the

Ukraine, and before undertaking any adventure northward wished to recapture the Kuban, where the Cossacks were friendly. Krasnov accepted assistance from the Germans and hoped to make contact with the Whites in Samara by an offensive to the northeast.

With German aid Krasnov cleared the Reds from the Don area and, failing to persuade the Volunteer Army to help him, attacked toward Tsaritsyn with his own troops. The Reds in Tsaritsyn were led by Stalin and, by chance, some of his old Baku comrades: Kliment Voroshilov, Sergo Ordzhonikidze, and Semën Budënny, founder of the Red cavalry. Tsaritsyn (later to be renamed Stalingrad) was labeled the "Red Verdun" for its successful defense against Krasnov. Although he failed to capture the city, Krasnov maintained the pressure until German evacuation of the Ukraine exposed his left flank to Red attack from the Donets Basin.

Meanwhile Denikin was pursuing his own plan. In June he plunged into the Kuban and by August 16 managed to throw the Bolsheviks out of the capital, Ekaterinodar. Ten days later he entered Novorossiisk, too late to prevent the Russian Black Sea Fleet there from being half scuttled. His base had been satisfactorily broadened, and he was ready for an attempt to link up with the Whites in the east. However, before any large-scale offensive it was obviously desirable to clarify the political picture.

The collapse of the Central Powers was now under way. Austria-Hungary was dissolving into its component nations by the summer of 1918. The Allies recognized Czechoslovak and Yugoslav independence, and German Austria and Hungary prepared to form separate states. At the end of September Bulgaria surrendered, a month later Turkey followed suit, and on November 3 Austria-Hungary signed an armistice. On November 11 the armistice with Germany took effect; the Emperor had already abdicated.

The end of the World War had an important influence upon the Russian Civil War. The Allies had no further need to try to restore an Eastern front; they might concern themselves with German and Turkish evacuation of the former territories of the Russian Empire, and they might then either consider that their interests in the Russian struggle had ended, or launch an all-out effort against the Communists. The Central Powers could no longer influence the Russian scene. Both Reds and Whites were cheered by the armistice. On October 22 Lenin had declared that "we were never so near to international proletarian revolution as we are now," although he warned of the continuing domestic danger. Two days before the German-Allied armistice, Trotsky told the VI Congress of Soviets, "We must slip in between departing German militarism and approaching Anglo-French militarism." The Reds were overjoyed by the news that the Hapsburg and Hohenzollern monarchies had crumbled, that what they hoped would prove "Kerensky-type" socialist regimes had succeeded them, and that Soviets had appeared in Berlin, Munich, Warsaw, and Riga. Lenin could now tear up the Treaty of Brest-Litovsk, and the Communists hoped to pursue the retreating German armies into Europe. The Whites likewise hoped to take over the western territories to be evacuated by the Germans, and, more important, looked for large-scale Allied assistance in a concerted effort to overthrow the Reds.

Immediately after the armistice, a conference of well-known Russian political figures, who ranged in political coloration from monarchist to moderate socialist, was summoned at Iasi in Rumania, where it sat from November 14 to 23, 1918. The participants were unanimous in appealing for Allied military aid, and they sent a delegation to the Western capitals which met only a lukewarm and noncommittal reception. The Iasi conference was unable to reach agreement about what type of regime the Whites should form, but a majority was willing to accept Denikin as temporary military dictator.

The coup of November 18 in Omsk elevated Kolchak to prominence, and during the next few months the White leaders formed a common front under his leadership. Within a few weeks Sazonov, one of the last of the Tsar's foreign ministers, was recognized as representative of all White regimes in Paris. In April 1919 General Eugene Miller, who, much as Kolchak had done in Omsk, had assumed power in Archangel after the collapse of a local S.R. government there, acknowledged Kolchak's authority as "Supreme Ruler," and in June Denikin did likewise. Surprisingly, there was no attempt by the White leaders to compete for primacy.

The Whites were concerned with the situation in Russia; so were the Reds, of course, but they saw their immediate opportunity, on the aftermath of the armistice, in Western and Central Europe. Therefore they made strenuous efforts through the Allies to arrange an armistice in the Civil War so that they would have a free hand in the West. President Wilson, who remained unsure whether or not Russian Communism contained an admixture of democracy, and Prime Minister Lloyd George were responsive; the French and Italians much less so. On January 21, 1919, a decision was taken to invite both Red and White representatives to Prinkipo Island, near Constantinople, for armistice talks.

The Whites rejected the invitation; the Reds, after some delay, accepted it, simultaneously offering territorial concessions to the Allies.

This Red effort to treat the Allies like the greedy monsters Marxism-Leninism presumed them to be and to offer them appropriate fodder was too much for Wilson. On February 5 Sazonov notified Kolchak that the Prinkipo proposal was being given up. In March an American emissary, William C. Bullitt, was sent to Moscow; he obtained another Soviet peace proposal amounting to a cease-fire which would have left the Whites in control of the territories they currently occupied. However, Wilson had lost interest by that time, and not all of the other Allies had ever agreed that it was wise to try to mediate the conflict.

The Russian Civil War was to continue. By an agreement of December 1917 confirmed immediately after the armistice, the British and French divided the western borderlands into two spheres of operation. The British were allotted the Cossack areas, the Caucasus, and Kurdistan; the French were to operate in Bessarabia, the Ukraine, and the Crimea. The British landed in Baku and Batum, the two main ports of the Caucasus on the Caspian and Black seas, and assumed the task of supplying Denikin; in addition they were active in Estonia, where General Yudenich was to organize an army, the White Sea region, where General Miller ruled, and Kolchak's Siberia. Both Whites and Reds girded for the battles of 1919, which were to decide the Civil War.

THE WESTERN BORDERLANDS

Even before the armistice was announced, the German-supported regime of Skoropadski began to collapse, and the Ukrainian Communists, newly organized as a separate party,[5] prepared to make a bid for power. The party was sharply divided between a left wing, headed by Gregory Piatakov, and a right wing, led by Fëdor Artem and others. The Leftists desired to seize power directly, while the Rightists, supported by Moscow, advised caution. The Ukrainian radical nationalists identified with the earlier Rada regime, headed by Vinnichenko and Petliura, intended to establish an independent Ukraine, as did also the unruly peasant partisan leaders, Makhno and Hryhoryiv (Grigoriev). Already, in the fall, the former leaders of the Rada had set up an underground Directory of five men, in which Vinnichenko was chairman but Petliura the most powerful figure. A few weeks before the armistice the Moscow government, through its agent Dmitry Manuilsky, agreed to support the installation of the Directory as the government of the Ukraine.

In this decision Moscow followed the cautious line of the right wing

• [5] At length it was decided, however, that the party would be a constituent part of the Russian Communist Party.

of the Ukrainian Communists, but in November it hedged by ordering a concealed Soviet government to be set up under Piatakov, the leader of the left wing, in Kursk, just east of the Ukrainian border. After some fighting the Directory assumed power in Kiev on December 14, 1918, and Skoropadski fled. However, a few days earlier Piatakov had proclaimed his Kursk regime and invaded the Ukraine with Red troops. The Directory was dumfounded by reports of the Communist offensive. Vinnichenko protested bitterly to Moscow, but Foreign Minister Chicherin blandly assured him that the Russian government had nothing to do with Piatakov's offensive.

In January 1919 the Communists entered Kharkov. Moscow now replaced Piatakov as head of the Red regime with Bulgarian-born Christian Rakovsky, who had, according to Pipes, "publicly expressed extreme skepticism concerning the very existence of the Ukrainian nation."[6] The Directory responded to the fall of Kharkov by declaring war on Moscow, but its resistance was feeble. Petliura's troops were deserted by the peasant partisans of Makhno and Hryhoryiv, who were attracted to the demagogic slogans of the Communists. In February the Red Army captured Kiev, from which they had been expelled by the Germans a year earlier, and became masters of most of the Ukraine.

The second Red regime in the Ukraine was to last little longer than the first. Rakovsky's government promptly alienated the population by pursuing a policy of immediate collectivization of land and by displaying open contempt for Ukrainian nationalism, thereby flouting Lenin's generally cautious formulations on the national minorities as well as his specific directives for the Ukraine. Makhno and Hryhoryiv now turned on the Communists and launched a partisan campaign against "Communists, Jews, and Russians" under the slogan, "Long live the rule of true Soviets!" By the spring of 1919 the Ukraine was in chaos.

To the north, in Belorussia, the Germans had permitted the formation of an independent Belorussian National Republic. It had no real authority, however, and departed in the baggage of the German army when it evacuated the region following the armistice. The Red Army immediately occupied Belorussia. Despite protests from Belorussian nationalists, even those who were pro-Red, Moscow converted the predominantly Great Russian Smolensk Communist organization into a "Communist Party of Belorussia." In February 1919 a combined Lithuanian-Belorussian Soviet Republic (*Litbel*) was formed in Vilna. Like its Ukrainian counterpart, the regime pursued an uncompromising policy, beginning at once to nationalize great estates. However, in April the

• [6] *The Formation of the Soviet Union,* p. 141.

armies of newly-independent Poland (so recognized by the Provisional Government and also by the Soviet negotiators at Brest-Litovsk) occupied most *Litbel* territory and the republic disappeared.

Just after the October Revolution Finland had achieved—and maintains to this day—the distinction of being the only country previously belonging to the Russian Empire to which the Soviets granted independence.[7] In December 1917 Commissar of Nationalities Stalin authored Soviet recognition of independent Finland as an application of Lenin's doctrine of national self-determination, and this circumstance has been urged as part of the explanation of Stalin's seeming leniency toward Finland during and after World War II. However that may be, in January 1918 Stalin decided that it was necessary "to limit the principle of free self-determination of nations, by granting it to the toilers and refusing it to the bourgeoisie." The Soviets tried to correct their error by aiding Finnish Communists who seized Helsinki and set up a Socialist Workers' Government. In May 1918 Finnish anti-Communists drove out this regime with the help of German troops which landed to assist them, however, and Moscow did not try again until 1939.

The Baltic states had also proclaimed their independence—Lithuania in December 1917 and Latvia and Estonia in February 1918. Although prevented by German occupation from invading Lithuania, Red forces drove out the Latvian and Estonian governments only to be in turn expelled by a renewal of the German offensive. Following the armistice Soviet troops returned and proclaimed the Baltic states Soviet republics, but once again they were driven out by a combination of native forces, the Northwestern White Army just forming under General Yudenich, and the Iron Division of Count von der Goltz. The Iron Division consisted of volunteers from the German occupation army and the local "Baltic barons," the heirs of a Germanic domination in the Baltic which dated from the time of the Teutonic Knights. By May 1919 these forces had cleared Latvia and Estonia and were ready to take the offensive.

The stage was set for the decisive battles of the Civil War.

• [7] As just pointed out, in the case of Poland the Soviets recognized an independence already granted by their predecessors.

The Civil War:
the Red Victory
(1919–1921)

★
★
★
★
★
★
★
★
★
★

CHAPTER 12

KOLCHAK AS "SUPREME RULER"

By the early months of 1919 there were four White armies in being, commanded by Denikin in the Azov region, Yudenich in Estonia, Miller in Archangel, and Kolchak in Omsk. Denikin's and Kolchak's armies were the most important, and the possibility of a link-up between them encouraged the Allies and frightened the Communists. General Alexeev, a wise old man devoted to freedom, had died in October 1918, and his loss was deeply felt in a camp where political sagacity was not plentiful. Following Alexeev's death Denikin assumed both political and military leadership in the south. After the armistice Red forces had turned the flank of Krasnov's Cossacks near Tsaritsyn, and the defeat in combination with Cossack unrest led Krasnov to resign as ataman in February 1919. He was replaced by General Bogaevsky, whose relations with Denikin were harmonious and who was willing to co-operate with his forces. In January a Volunteer Army unit under General Baron Peter Wrangel had won an important victory by breaking through Red lines to the east and destroying the North Caucasian Red Army. Denikin was now in a position to strike northward in a large-scale offensive.

In the meantime Kolchak was attempting to strengthen his base of operations. On assuming the post of "Supreme Ruler," he had publicly renounced both reaction and "the fatal road of party partisanship" and set as his goal "victory over Bolshevism and the establishment of law and order, so that the people may choose the form of government which it desires without obstruction and realize the great ideas of liberty which are now proclaimed in the whole world." He tried to set up a dictatorship, but he claimed that his objective in so doing was to achieve, through military victory, the possibility of democracy. His enemies naturally charged that he simply veiled autocratic principles in the cloak of democratic phrases; however, the evidence indicates otherwise. Baron Budberg, a bitter critic of Kolchak's, writes that he was devoid of selfishness and "passionately desires everything good," and others who knew him well depict a man who was puzzled and bewildered by his inability to make things go the way he felt they should. His own capacity for leadership was limited, but even more important was the difficulty which plagued all the White generals, that of finding trained and principled leaders to assist him in both military and political affairs.

A naval officer, Kolchak had no special competence in land warfare, and even failed to assure the delivery of British supplies to the front. Politically he had little experience or skill. In this respect he was like the other old officers around him, whose training had not equipped them to deal with politics. Even their military efficiency was meager, partly because the new commands were too heterogeneous to permit them to operate under the kind of discipline to which they had been accustomed. The Whites suffered from the fact that they had to operate on the territorial periphery of the country, where the transportation network was thin, the industrial base inadequate, the lines of communication long and strained to the utmost; but most of all they were hampered by lack of leadership. It was their misfortune that they had to fight an enemy which, despite some difficulties with defection, corruption, and disobedience of orders, still had a corps of trained and disciplined men all over the country in the form of the Communist Party.

Kolchak had to deal with much inner dissension in his camp. Only a month after the coup of November 18, an anti-Kolchak rising in an Omsk suburb resulted in the unauthorized shooting of fifteen S.R. and other prisoners. Kolchak disapproved of the shooting and remained convinced that it was the result of a plot to discredit him. All he asked of the S.R.'s was that they forget political partisanship until victory, but he had no success. While the S.R.'s detested him, they split on what to do about it. Some, under Volsky, made their peace with the Reds and obtained a hollow promise to legalize the S.R. party on Red territory;

others, following Chernov, adopted the slogan of "a struggle on two fronts," damning Reds and Whites alike, although a party conference in the spring of 1919 went further and decided that the S.R.'s should cease to combat the Reds and fight with all possible weapons against the Whites. In the Far East Kolchak had to contend with a very different sort of problem. An anti-Bolshevik leader, Ataman Gregory Semënov, had taken power in Chita under Japanese sponsorship, and his brutality had become widely known. Kolchak demanded that Semënov submit to his authority and when the latter refused, he threatened attack. However, the ataman's Japanese protectors prevented any such action, and Kolchak had to be satisfied with a nominal acknowledgment of his supreme authority. Another Japanese puppet, Ataman Kalmykov in Khabarovsk, never did submit, even verbally, to Kolchak.

Kolchak's main immediate task was military victory, and he achieved certain successes within a few months of his *coup d'état*. By the beginning of 1919 the right wing of the Siberian armies, under the Czech General Gajda, had captured Perm. The left wing fared less well; soon afterward the Whites lost Orenburg to the Reds. Although the left flank pointed toward the important objective of a link-up with Denikin, the successes of Gajda led Kolchak to concentrate instead on an effort to make contact with Miller and the British in Archangel. By the end of April Gajda captured Glazov, a town halfway from Perm to Viatka, and it appeared that his troops might soon reach their goal.

The Allies were watching Kolchak's offensive with close interest, and their enthusiasm for his cause was reinforced by alarm over Red successes in the West. While prospects for the Communist revolution in Germany on which Lenin and Trotsky counted looked rather dim, elsewhere the Reds were doing better. In March 1919 in Moscow there was held the founding Congress of the Communist International (or Comintern). The new organization, which made reality of the last of Lenin's April Theses, proclaimed world revolution as its objective. The Comintern included, in addition to the Russian Communists, the newly formed Communist parties of Central and Eastern Europe, and was joined by the Swedish Left Socialists, the Norwegian Labor Party, and the Italian Socialist Party. At the moment of the I Congress of the Comintern the Reds were fighting for control of Finland and Latvia. By April the Hungarian Communists under Béla Kun had proclaimed a Soviet Republic, and Bavaria followed suit. Communist hopes soared, and in the spring of 1919 there was a revival of the conviction that the world revolution was finally on its way.

Although these particular Red adventures soon failed, they spurred the Allies to action. On May 27 Premier Clemenceau, on behalf of the Allied Supreme Council, sent a note to Kolchak in which he promised official recognition provided certain conditions were fulfilled. They included the reconvening of the Constituent Assembly, recognition of the independence of Poland and Finland and of the autonomy of other minority nationalities, and repudiation of any aim to restore the old regime. Kolchak had already expressed himself on similar lines, except that he was unwilling to concede Finnish independence in advance of the Constituent Assembly.

Whatever Kolchak expected the Constituent Assembly to do, his policy in Siberia in regard to the problems of minority nationalities—and also the land problem—was indecisive and unwise. His relations with the Cossacks and the Turkic peoples of Asiatic Russia were at best lukewarm, and his refusal to acknowledge the formal independence of faraway Finland was only one example of shortsightedness on the nationalities issue. As for the land question, Siberia was already a country of relatively well-to-do peasants, but the problem was a burning one in European Russia, which the White armies were entering in the spring of 1919. However, a declaration of April 8 on the land question merely indicated a gingerly acceptance of the status quo as far as divisions of estates already carried out were concerned, and warned against any further disturbance of land titles prior to the Constituent Assembly. It was not a document calculated to win fanatical support from the peasantry; nevertheless many peasants who had experienced Communist land policy received the Whites with favor.

The Allies were not disposed to examine Kolchak's Siberian policies closely, and they declared themselves satisfied by his reply to the note of May 27. They did not, however, extend official recognition. The reason was not political but military. Immediately after Gajda's capture of Glazov, Michael Frunze and the Reds launched a counteroffensive. It rolled the Whites back toward the Urals, and in June Ufa fell to the Reds. In Moscow the leaders debated whether to pursue Kolchak, as Lenin thought wise, or to shift forces to meet Denikin, whom Trotsky considered the greater danger. It was decided to press the offensive against Kolchak. The Reds pushed east of the Urals, where a Siberian peasant partisan movement began to harass Kolchak's rear. Gajda resigned his command and left Siberia. Kolchak, although not yet defeated, was deprived of any part in the decisive battles of the autumn. His chances of reaching Denikin had vanished permanently.

THE OFFENSIVES OF DENIKIN AND YUDENICH

At the very moment Kolchak's armies were hurled back, the forces of Denikin began to win significant victories. In the spring of 1919 the Reds faced formidable adversaries in the south. Formerly greatly outnumbered, the Volunteer Army, now renamed the Armed Forces of South Russia, had built up its strength and was reinforced by British tanks (though no Allied troops). In addition the Reds had to contend with a more or less regular army of Don Cossacks northeast of Rostov and the peasant partisans of Hryhoryiv in the Ukraine.

In late May and June the Whites smashed three Red armies and occupied a fan-shaped area reaching from Kharkov in the eastern Ukraine to Tsaritsyn on the Volga. Denikin's right wing, the Army of the Caucasus, was led by Wrangel, who was a brilliant cavalry commander. After the capture of Tsaritsyn, he advocated a dash up the Volga valley to link up with Kolchak. It is tempting to speculate what the effect might have been if Gajda, Kolchak's best officer, had commanded the southern rather than the northern sector of the front during those months and had attempted to reach Wrangel and Denikin. By June, however, Kolchak's armies were retreating, and Denikin rejected the proposal to try and overtake them in favor of the objective of capturing Moscow. On July 3 he issued an order for an advance on Moscow in three directions: Wrangel was to move up the Volga; General Sidorin, commanding the Don Cossacks, was to strike north from Rostov; and General Mai-Maevsky, whose troops were drawn mainly from the original Volunteer Army, was to attack from Kharkov, simultaneously attempting to take Kiev.

The offensive made most progress in the west, and by the end of August Odessa, Kherson, Nikolaev, and Kiev were in White hands. An attempted Red counteroffensive was forestalled, largely by the daring raid of the Don Cossack General Mamontov, who penetrated all the way to Tambov before returning south to rejoin the main White armies. However, he failed to raise a revolt in the Red rear areas; his Cossacks were intent on plundering, not on psychological warfare. The White forces moved forward to Kursk on September 20, Voronezh on October 6, and Chernigov on October 12. On October 13 Orël fell to Denikin, and White advance guards approached Tula, the last large city before Moscow.

At the same moment General Yudenich and his Northwestern Army, based in Estonia, were making a desperate attempt to take Petrograd. Here also there was British support and some British-made tanks. On

October 11 Yudenich captured Yamburg on the Luga River, less than a hundred miles from Petrograd. Gatchina, thirty miles from the former capital, fell on October 16. The first sign of trouble came when a White commander, ordered to cut the only remaining railway southward (to Moscow), disregarded his instructions. Trotsky hastened to Petrograd to rally the disorganized defenders. On October 20 the Whites besieged Pulkovo, on the southern outskirts of the city, but there the Reds held. Yudenich was forced back to Gatchina, and faced with Red troops at his rear, he retreated by November 14 to his starting point at Yamburg. His army crossed into Estonia and was rapidly disbanded. Lack of co-ordination with the British and the White army of Colonel Bermont in Latvia, which chose the moment of Yudenich's offensive to attack the Latvians in Riga, contributed to the failure. However, at best Yudenich's effort was a long shot, for he was outnumbered from the start and lacked reinforcements and adequate supplies.

In the middle of October 1919 it appeared that Petrograd and Moscow might fall simultaneously to the Whites, but within a few days the whole picture changed. Denikin, his troops outnumbered and extended over a seven-hundred-mile front from Kiev to Tsaritsyn, came to a halt. On October 20 he lost Orël, while to the east Budënny's cavalry recaptured Voronezh. The White collapse followed swiftly. On November 17 Kursk was lost. General Mai-Maevsky, a confirmed drunkard who made little attempt to keep discipline among his troops, was replaced by Wrangel in the central sector, but it was already too late. The Communists advanced with their regular forces and successfully employed peasant partisans to harass the retreating White army. In December the Ukraine was reoccupied, and a reorganized Red regime under Rakovsky resumed power in Kiev. In January 1920 the Whites and Cossacks made a desperate but unsuccessful stand around Rostov. By the end of March Denikin was penned into the port of Novorossiisk, from which the British helped evacuate his troops. He crossed into the Crimea, the only territory in Russia remaining in White hands (in February Kolchak had been shot and Miller's regime at Archangel had fallen), and resigned his command in favor of Wrangel.

Denikin had committed several military errors, but perhaps his decisive weakness was political. In many ways he was like Kolchak: a republican, without the political capacity or an effective corps of assistants to establish the kind of regime he desired, and an officer who was unable to enforce discipline or pursue a consistent military objective. Even more than Kolchak he was an uncompromising Russian nationalist, as shown by his slogan, "Russia shall be great, united, undivided." Just as Kolchak could not get along with his minorities, Denikin was constantly at odds with the Cossacks, Ukrainians, and Caucasian peoples. Like Kolchak, he advocated restoration of a Constituent Assembly, introduction of civil liberties, decentralization of government, and the enactment of land reform and labor legislation, but he did not go beyond promises.

For a time Denikin's government seemed to have some merit. He set up a Special Conference of twenty-four men to act as a sort of cabinet.

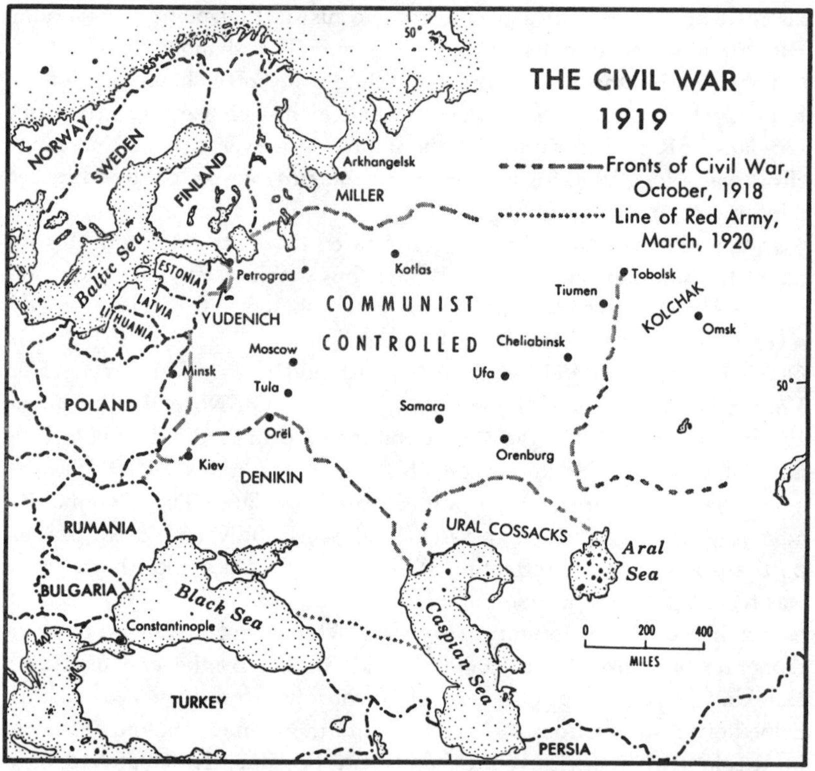

It had three factions: the generals, except for the liberal chief of staff, General I. P. Romanovsky, were conservatives; a group of bureaucrats was less so; the Kadets were liberals. There were disputes at least some of which might have been resolved by a strong leader, but Denikin was not that. He made a number of fair enough policy statements, but did little to translate them into reality. Under his regime Professor Bilimovich drew up a reasonable land program securing peasant homesteads, but by the time it was ready the White armies were retreating toward the sea. The notorious lack of discipline in the ranks of the army, especially under Mai-Maevsky, led to pillaging and pogroms while the Whites were occupying the Ukraine, and under such conditions it would have been most difficult to interest the peasants in the White agrarian program. It would have taken great abilities to take advantage of all the opportunities, but Denikin did not have them.

By the end of 1919 Kolchak, already driven back into Siberia, suffered final defeat. His commander-in-chief, General Diederichs, wanted to evacuate Omsk and was dismissed for the proposal, but on November 14 the capital fell nevertheless. Kolchak's cabinet established itself in Irkutsk, where at the end of December it was overthrown by a group of non-Bolshevik radicals. On January 4, 1920, Kolchak abdicated his post of "Supreme Ruler" in favor of Denikin and made the gesture of appointing his old enemy Ataman Semënov as commander of Russian forces in the Far East. The French General Janine and the Czechs handed Kolchak over to the radical regime in Irkutsk, which was supplanted by a Red government on January 21. Its agents interrogated Kolchak at length but could not even wait until he had finished his testimony before shooting him, along with his Kadet Prime Minister Pepeliaev, on February 7. The White cause in Asiatic Russia was lost. Thousands upon thousands of the educated and wealthier classes—and poorer people—of Russia and Siberia made their way out to Manchuria, China, and elsewhere.

The Czechs completed their evacuation of Russian territory, and Allied intervention for the most part came to an end. The French did give some help to Wrangel in 1920, and the Japanese remained in the Russian Far East. The Japanese puppet, Semënov, plainly had no future and in October 1920 abandoned Chita and went to Manchuria, where he was caught and executed by Soviet forces at the end of World War II. Moscow handled the situation in the Far East adroitly. In April a curious figure named Krasnoshchëkov, who had returned to Russia from Chicago, had been encouraged by Lenin to proclaim a kind of "people's republic" in the region east of Lake Baikal. This "Far Eastern Republic" formally established diplomatic relations with Moscow, negotiated with the Japanese army which remained on its territory, and sent delegates who gained widespread American sympathy at the Washington naval conference. Under resulting United States pressure, the last Japanese forces left the mainland in October 1922. Instantly the Republic dissolved itself and the Communists extended their control to Vladivostok.

THE CRISIS OF 1920

In 1920 the Reds faced an internal situation verging on total catastrophe. Hunger and disease were widespread, and industry and trade were at a virtual standstill. Trotsky attempted to meet the crisis by applying the methods he had used successfully with the Red Army: he inaugurated mass labor conscription and "militarization of labor." Armies of workers marched to the tunes of martial music and reported their achievements in military fashion. The device was colorful but ineffective.

Meanwhile there remained formidable external threats. Wrangel still led a White army in the Crimea; it was disorganized, but it worried the Red leaders. Even more serious was the danger from newly independent Poland, where the ex-socialist Joseph Pilsudski had established a regime with the avowed aim of recreating the "Poland of 1772," that is, before the time of the First Partition among the three eastern monarchies. It seemed an overly ambitious goal, but in fact Polish forces had been drawn up on a line in places coinciding with the 1772 frontier, and in the western Ukraine only about a hundred miles away from it.

In the spring of 1920 Moscow suggested negotiations to Warsaw and tried to make friendly gestures toward Pilsudski. The Poles paid little attention, continuing to prepare for attack. On April 25 the Polish army opened an offensive west of Kiev and on May 6 swept into the city. Although in 1919 Pilsudski had rejected Denikin's proposal to join forces against the Reds, since he disliked Russians of any political stripe, in 1920 he co-operated closely with Petliura, leader of the Ukrainian nationalist regime which had been expelled by the Reds. Pilsudski calculated that if an independent Ukraine were established, Russia—whether Red or White—would be reduced to the level of an inferior power. Nevertheless the Ukrainian population, also remembering the past, showed unfriendliness toward the Poles, and Pilsudski thought it wise to halt his troops at Kiev.

Once again the Reds invoked nationalist slogans, as they had done with success against the Allied interventionists and the Whites whom the Allies had supported. They managed to attract to their side such former Tsarist generals as Brusilov, who assumed leadership of a special military council to advise the Red high command. However, they did not lose sight of their Marxist goals. They appealed to the Polish "toiling masses" to help establish a Polish Communist state, and they prepared the nucleus for a Red government which they hoped to install in Warsaw.

In May General Tukhachevsky launched a counteroffensive. Budënny's cavalry broke through Polish lines in June and forced the enemy back from Kiev. The Reds pushed forward, approaching Warsaw from two directions. Although in 1919 Denikin's advance had deprived them of the chance to help the Hungarian and Bavarian Communists, it seemed in 1920 that the Red Army might after all assist a Red revolution in Germany to succeed. The Allies were alarmed; on July 12 British Foreign Minister Lord Curzon hastily proposed a truce along a roughly ethnic border which has been known ever since as the Curzon Line, but Moscow was not interested in a truce. Already a Polish government headed by the Polish Communist Marchlewski had been set up in Bialystok, and by August Red troops were approaching Warsaw. Pilsudski and his recently arrived French military adviser, General Weygand (later to become French commander-in-chief during the last weeks of resistance in 1940), prepared a counterattacking force and at the crucial moment sent it into the battle. The Poles advanced and soon had virtually routed the Red Army. Now that hope of reaching Warsaw and Berlin was gone, the Reds quite meekly accepted an armistice in October. Its provisions, confirmed by the Treaty of Riga in March 1921, left many Belorussians and Ukrainians in Polish territory.

During the Polish-Soviet war, Wrangel hoped in vain for a joint effort with Pilsudski against the Reds. Wrangel had assumed command in the Crimea in the early months of 1920, when it appeared as if the best that could be hoped for was orderly evacuation. He soon surprised everyone by restoring discipline in the ranks of the remaining White troops and re-establishing civil order in the peninsula. Since the Crimea had no significant industrial base, no large-scale offensive was possible without Allied supplies. The British refused any further aid to the Whites, but the French for a time showed interest in Wrangel's efforts. After he had won minor victories on the battlefield against the Reds, France extended *de facto* recognition to his regime as the Government of South Russia; however, the munitions necessary for an offensive were not forthcoming.

Wrangel, although more conservative than either Kolchak or Denikin, was a most capable man who fully understood the needs of the moment. He established iron discipline in the army and ended the pillaging and plundering which had damaged White chances under Denikin's command. He enlisted the services of such able civilian officials as Stolypin's former assistant, Krivoshein, who became his prime minister, and Peter Struve, former Marxist, whom he made his foreign minister. Wrangel devoted much effort to a land reform program which was applied in 90 out of 107 counties under his occupation during the few short months he was in power, and established the zemstvo on the canton (*volost*) level, as the Provisional Government had attempted to do with scant success. By July his chief of staff told him with enthusiasm, "The population is on our side now; they have faith in the new regime, and realize that it is fighting to free Russia and not to punish her." Wrangel himself claimed, perhaps justifiably, that if the "conditions of harmony between the Army and the wishes of the peasants [which prevailed in 1920] had been achieved at the time when the Russian Army was advancing victoriously on Moscow and nearly half of Russia was freed from the Red yoke, the fate of the White movement would have been quite different."

On June 6 Wrangel launched an offensive northward; he broke out of the Crimea and occupied the entire Northern Taurida region. Next he tried to strengthen his hand by seeking an agreement with the Ukrainian partisans, but Makhno simply hanged his envoy. He had better luck with the Don and Kuban Cossacks, and in August he sent an invasion force into the Kuban. His subordinates hesitated at the wrong moment and were forced to evacuate, but they brought out a larger army than they took in. At the same time Wrangel tried to break across the Dnieper to link up with the Poles, but the death of his commanding officer in that sector led to failure. At that moment the news of the armistice between Moscow and the Poles arrived. The Reds could now concentrate all forces on Wrangel, and they sent Frunze to finish the job. On October 28 the final battle began on the Northern Taurida front. Wrangel was forced back, but he kept his armies in order and fought on for two weeks before withdrawing into the southern Crimea. He evacuated a hundred and fifty thousand troops and civilians to Constantinople. The veterans of the White struggle in European Russia were dispersed to Belgrade, Berlin, Paris, London, and New York.

THE CIVIL WAR IN THE CAUCASUS

After the Bolshevik Revolution a combination of loyalty to the Provisional Government, antipathy to Communism, and local nationalism led Transcaucasia to break away from Bolshevik Russia. For a time the Communists hung on in the northeastern region between the Caucasus Mountains and the Caspian Sea by forming a coalition regime, in which they shared power with Mensheviks, S.R.'s, and local parties. This government, established at Vladikavkaz, called itself the Terek People's Soviet Socialist Republic and lasted from March to August 1918. It is of some interest as apparently the first "people's republic"—that is, a regime in which Communists accepted a temporary coalition arrangement in a region where they were as yet too weak to rule alone.[1]

The Terek "people's republic" was overthrown by Terek Cossacks who disliked the land socialization policy which the regime was pursuing. However, Ordzhonikidze arrived on the scene and made an arrangement with the two mountain Moslem tribes, the Chechen and Ingush, to reestablish Communist rule, this time as part of Soviet Russia. Although the Chechen and Ingush were to be liquidated by Stalin in World War II for alleged treason, during the Civil War they were loyal to the Reds, largely because the lands and goods of the mutinous Terek Cossacks were turned over to them as the Reds' part of the bargain. Soviet rule in the Terek region foundered with the defeat of the North Caucasian Red Army in January 1919, but was restored when the Reds conquered most of the Caucasus the following year.

The chief Caucasian nationalities, the Georgians, Armenians, and Azerbaijani, were included in a Transcaucasian Federative Republic proclaimed on April 22, 1918, with the Georgian Menshevik Chkhenkeli as president. However, it fell apart after only a month. On May 26 the Georgians, led by Chkhenkeli, declared their independence, accepting German control as a lesser evil than the Turkish conquest which then appeared imminent. Georgia was the only place where the Mensheviks, who disdained power in Russia proper for theoretical reasons, established a government. While they nationalized almost all industry and communications, they wisely carried out land reform. Partly in order to fill a depleted treasury, they first leased plots to the peasants, and then in 1919 sold them outright. At the time of the World War I armistice Chkhenkeli, who had become identified with the German occupation, was replaced as prime minister by Gegechkori, while the old Menshevik, Noah Zhordania, became president. The British arrived, and for the moment preserved the independence of Georgia.

Azerbaijan and Armenia declared independence two days after Georgia. In Moslem and Turkic-speaking Azerbaijan the Mussavat party of nationalist socialists had the ascendancy. However, in March, two months before the proclamation of Azerbaijani independence, the Communists had seized the oil city of Baku, using Armenians in a coup in which some three thousand Moslems were killed. Under the Communist Stephen Shaumian, a Bolshevik-Left Menshevik government was set up, despite the fact that those two groups were in a minority even in the Baku Soviet. This regime lasted less than four months. Shaumian fled and was killed, and the S.R.'s, taking over, invited in the British General

• [1] Pipes, *The Formation of the Soviet Union,* p. 197.

Dunsterville to defend Baku against the approaching Turks. It was too late; the city fell to the Turks on September 15, 1918.

The Mussavat party led the country into alliance with the same Turks whom the Christian Georgians and Armenians feared and hated. However, the Turkish occupation forces halted all reform measures and alienated the Mussavat leaders. After the armistice, the British General Thomson landed in Baku. He was sympathetic to reform and at once re-established labor unions, but he had no use for the Azerbaijani nationalists and declared it his task to help General Denikin. Nevertheless he recognized a government formed in December 1918 which was headed by Fathali Khan-Khoisky, a former liberal Duma deputy who had held office under the May 1918 Mussavat regime. Independent Azerbaijan was rich in oil, but under conditions of civil war it was next to impossible to obtain revenue by making oil deliveries abroad. The tiny nation stood aside from the Russian struggle as long as it could.

Armenia was the orphan nation of the Caucasus in 1918—the Georgians had the Germans and the Azerbaijani had the Turks, but the Armenians had no one. The country defended itself successfully in 1918 mainly because the Turks were less interested in capturing Erivan than Baku, which they took, or Tiflis, which they were denied by the presence of their German allies. Armenia was poor and hungry, and the government, dominated by the radical nationalist Dashnaktsutiun party, was unable to accomplish anything important. After the armistice the Armenians made contact with Denikin and, unlike the Georgians and Azerbaijani, they supported the Whites as they had the Provisional Government. As the White cause faltered, they turned to the United States hoping to persuade it to assume a League of Nations mandate over the country. Although such efforts failed, Armenia did manage to escape the worst consequences of famine by means of American relief aid.

At the beginning of 1920 the Allies recognized the *de facto* independence of Georgia, Armenia, and Azerbaijan and persuaded the defeated Denikin to do the same. However, the intervention was over, and neither the Allies nor the League of Nations were willing to do anything further. The Caucasus now seemed fair game for Moscow. The Communists eliminated the only possibility remaining for the Caucasians to obtain outside aid by a quiet rapprochment with the Turkish revolutionary regime of Mustafa Kemal. In the spring the Reds moved in, under the military leadership of General Tukhachevsky and the political direction of Ordzhonikidze. In April the independent government of Azerbaijan capitulated before a Red ultimatum, and Ordzhonikidze entered Baku. The Red forces started for the remaining two capitals, but they were halted in May because of the crisis attending the war with Poland. Moscow abruptly recognized Georgian independence and opened negotiations with Armenia, although they reached no conclusion.

The Communists gave the Caucasus only a temporary respite. In August they made clear their continuing interest in Asia near and far by way of a Red-sponsored Congress of the Peoples of the East in Baku. In September Armenia made the mistake of becoming embroiled in a shooting war with the Turks over Armenian-inhabited areas of eastern Anatolia. The Armenian forces were badly mauled by the troops of Mustafa Kemal, and the Soviets chose this opportunity to issue a flat ultimatum to the weakened government. On December 2, 1920, Armenia was compelled to yield power to the Reds, who had almost no native strength at all. After hesitating for a time for fear of Turkish reactions, Moscow took the risk of attacking Georgia in February. After bitter fighting, during which the Armenians revolted (and had to be suppressed after Georgia was subdued), the Reds under Ordzhonikidze entered Tiflis (soon to be given the Georgian name Tbilisi) and in March 1921 completed the conquest of the last Caucasian state.

THE MOSLEM BORDERLANDS OF THE EAST

At the time of the October Revolution the Bolsheviks had seized power in Tashkent and a few other centers, but generally their control over the Moslem areas of the southeast and Central Asia was nominal or nonexistent. Such areas were the targets of passionate Bolshevik appeals which promised protection of their political and religious autonomy. An all-Russian Moslem Assembly known as the Medzhilis, sitting in Kazan, rejected these overtures and supported the Constituent Assembly. In February 1918 a Medzhilis committee decided to form an autonomous Volga-Ural Moslem state, but the Reds in Kazan prevented the fulfilment of the plan.

The Moscow government attempted to subvert the Moslem autonomist movement from within. Commissar of Nationalities Stalin made a Tatar, Mulla Nur Vakhitov, chairman of a newly-established Moslem Commissariat. In May 1918 Vakhitov was told to set up under Communist auspices a state with the same territory as that envisaged by the Medzhilis, and he proclaimed an Autonomous Tatar-Bashkir Republic. However, the Czech rising in this area, which included Ufa and Kazan, put an end to Vakhitov's plans, and he was executed. Now that the territorial base of the Tatar Communists had vanished behind White lines, Moscow dealt with them with scant ceremony. In the spring of 1919 the Moslem

Communist organization was absorbed into the Central Bureau of Communist Organizations of Peoples of the East, and Soviet pseudo-pan-Islamism was brought to an abrupt halt.

In late 1919, when Red troops entered the Tatar-Bashkir region, the Turkic peoples there were wooed by the establishment of not one but five separate administrative areas. The Orthodox Christian Chuvashes and Maris were given Autonomous Regions; the Moslem Tatars (of the Kazan area), Votiaks, and Bashkirs got Autonomous Soviet Socialist Republics. Red rule was, however, not gentle. The especially rough treatment given the Bashkirs led to a serious anti-Red uprising in late 1920, and when formally organized, the Bashkir ASSR had no Bashkirs at all in its government. Not long before, a Communist spokesman had told a Bashkir delegation in Moscow, "That whole autonomous republic, which you take so seriously, is only a game to keep you people busy."

To the south of Bashkiria, the Kazakh-Kirghiz area was dominated by the native party called the Alash-Orda. In 1918 it collaborated with the Whites and continued to do so after Kolchak's coup in Omsk. However, when Red troops penetrated the region in mid-1919 and invited members of Alash-Orda to join them, many did so. A few (as individuals, not as members of the Alash-Orda party) were taken into the government of the Kirghiz (Kazakh) Autonomous SSR, which was proclaimed in October 1920. A very severe famine, which also extended into Bashkiria and facilitated the establishment of Red control there, struck in 1921 and cost over a million native lives. It had the double effect of postponing the formation of an effective government and of paralyzing native resistance to the Communists.

Still farther south, in Turkestan, the Bolsheviks held the most important center, Tashkent. The Tashkent Communists were mostly Russian and showed little inclination to conciliate the Turkic peoples of Turkestan. In February 1918 the Tashkent Reds attacked the nearby city of Kokand, where liberal Moslem groups had founded an autonomous regime. Much of the city was destroyed and uncounted people massacred. The Tashkent forces next attacked Bukhara, which under the Tsars had been a semi-independent emirate, but they were repulsed. By this time there had appeared many partisan bands, calling themselves the Basmachi, who challenged the authority and resented the brutality of the Tashkent regime. Moscow, alarmed at the spread of resistance, ordered Tashkent to seek native support by establishing a Turkestan Autonomous SSR. In April 1918 one was proclaimed, but it existed mainly on paper.

The armistice brought British troops into Central Asia as it had into the Caucasus, although not enough of them to accomplish any important objectives. A weak S.R. regime had been set up in Ashkhabad in Turkmenistan, and it invited the British General Malleson to come in to help resist the Tashkent Reds. He did so, but evacuated his forces in April 1919, and two months later the Communists captured Ashkhabad.

The penetration of Red forces into the steppe in mid-1919, in pursuit of Kolchak, enabled Moscow to put a bridle on the uncompromising Tashkent leadership. In February 1920 a Turkestan Commission, including Michael Frunze, commander of the Red Fourth Army, and Valerian Kuibyshev, his political commissar, arrived in Tashkent. They promptly adopted a "soft" policy, by which they hoped to cut the ground out from under the Basmachi. For a time this tactic appeared to yield some results, but the partisan bands remained in existence. The Red capture of Khiva in February and of Bukhara in August provoked the Basmachi to renewed activity.

In the fall of 1921 Enver Pasha, a formerly influential Turkish minister who had fled his country and gained Red confidence, was sent to Turkestan to put down the revolt. Instead he joined the Basmachi himself and became their leader. In 1922 he captured the town of Diushambe (later Stalinabad), but in October of the same year he was killed by the Reds. Although the Basmachi did not cease resistance until 1926, in 1923–1924 the Communists crushed the backbone of the movement. Khiva became the People's Socialist Republic of Khorezm and Bukhara also was designated a PSR.

By the spring of 1921 the Reds were victorious almost everywhere in the territories of the old Russian Empire. The exceptions were Finland, Estonia, Latvia, Lithuania, and Poland, which had become independent states; Bessarabia, which had been ceded to Rumania, and parts of Belorussia and the Ukraine, ceded to Poland; the Amur region, where the Far Eastern Republic could not yet be liquidated in the face of Japanese occupation; and Bukhara, where the last organized resistance to the Communists had not yet been stamped out. Moscow retained the core area of Great Russia, most of the Ukraine, some of Belorussia, the Caucasus, Siberia, and Central Asia. But although the Civil War was at an end, there was still no revolution in the West, and there was serious trouble inside Russia.

Lenin and the New Economic Policy

CHAPTER 13

"THE PEASANT BREST"

Just before the X Congress of the Party in early 1921, Lenin declared that socialism could be built in Russia only on one of two conditions: if there was an international socialist revolution, or if there was a compromise with the peasant majority within the country. The essence of the "New Economic Policy" which he adopted soon afterwards was acceptance of a compromise with the peasantry. The Bolshevik theoretician Riazanov labeled the NEP "the peasant Brest"; that is to say, a temporary truce was concluded with the peasant adversary, as with the German Empire at Brest-Litovsk, but its purpose was *reculer pour mieux sauter*.

In reluctantly accepting the terms of Brest-Litovsk, Lenin had not given up hope that a revolutionary situation would still develop in the West. In 1919, when Communist regimes appeared briefly in central Europe, and in 1920, when Red armies were approaching Warsaw and hoping to reach Berlin, such hopes revived. However, even though the Comintern tried twice more to foment a revolution in Germany, by 1921 it was plain enough that the Russian Communists could not count on their foreign brethren to solve their immediate problems.

These problems were domestic. Peasant risings had erupted in the south and east of Russia, for centuries the regions from which *jacqueries* had sprung. As demobilization of the Red Army got under way in September 1920, rural riots, the most serious led by Antonov in Tambov, broke out and continued to smolder despite punitive measures. Tambov was in fact not pacified until 1924, and months after the promulgation of the NEP, the army general staff reported that twenty thousand "bandits" were operating throughout south Russia and the Ukraine. The climax of anti-Communist unrest, involving as Lenin himself admitted "discontent not only among a considerable part of the peasantry but among the workers as well," came with the uprising in Kronstadt in March 1921.

Kronstadt had been a great Tsarist naval base, but during 1917 its sailors had become one of the strongest bulwarks of the Bolshevik cause. Its location on an island in sight of Petrograd made the political orientation of its garrison most important. During the Civil War, many of the most active leaders during the 1917 events had gone off to become Red political and military officers in various districts, and in 1921 most of its personnel consisted of new peasant recruits. The uprising in March fleetingly threw off Communist rule and proclaimed the slogan, "Soviets without Communists." Opposition elements of all kinds, in Russia and among the *émigrés,* from Mensheviks to monarchists, pricked up their ears. Red forces moved in, shot down thousands, and quelled the revolt. But Lenin understood well enough that Kronstadt was no isolated or accidental outbreak, but evidence of widespread popular discontent.

He appeared before the X Congress of the Party in March 1921 and proposed a far-reaching measure, that the requisitioning of agricultural surpluses, which had been part of War Communism, be abandoned in favor of a tax in kind set at a fixed percentage of production. Only a year earlier Trotsky had proposed just such a measure, but it had been blocked by his colleagues, including Lenin. However, Lenin now pushed it through, and thereby inaugurated the "New Economic Policy"—although the actual phrase seems to have been first used in May, without capitals or quotation marks, and with them only several months later.

Lenin had evidently decided that a serious and many-sided retreat from Communist objectives (although a conditional and temporary one) was essential if the regime was not to be endangered by revolt from within by the very elements who had adhered to the Red side during the Civil War. His own formulation was that the reason for the NEP was "the maintenance of the alliance of the proletariat with the peasantry, in order that the proletariat may keep the role of leadership and state power." The economy was prostrate, and the food tax could reasonably be expected to revive agricultural production and trade by providing the peasant with an incentive and security hitherto lacking. Nevertheless the economic motive was not the crucial one; as Lenin said, the question of the new tax was "pre-eminently a political question, since it is essentially a question of the relation of the working class to the peasantry." The peasantry, he declared candidly, "cannot be driven out as we drove out and annihilated the landowners and the capitalists. It must be transformed with great labor and great privations."

Maxim Gorky was blunter and more pessimistic in confiding to a French visitor, that same summer:

> "In the struggle which, since the beginning of the revolution, has been going on between the two classes, the peasants have every chance of coming out victorious. . . . The urban proletariat has been declining incessantly for four years. . . . The immense peasant tide will end by engulfing everything. . . .The peasant will become master of Russia, since he represents numbers. And it will be terrible for our future."[1]

Gorky thus asserted that there was a class struggle under way between the proletariat and the peasantry and had been since 1917, but that nevertheless the proletariat, instead of struggling, persisted in melting into its adversary. Obviously the real opponents of the peasantry were the Communists, not the proletariat, who were (as Lenin said) discontented with their urban situation—in fact, sufficiently so (as Gorky said) to return to the villages from which many of them originally came.

Lenin had long realized that the peasantry as a whole did not thirst for socialism, but he had counted on the "poor peasantry" to come to the Communists' aid. In 1918 he had tried to use them in the Committees of Poor Peasants, but the device had been a resounding failure (see p. 163). In November 1918 the Committees had been abandoned, and the decision was taken to work temporarily with the "middle peasants" instead.

At that moment Lenin had scarcely finished saying, "Things have turned out just as we said they would. . . . *First,* with the 'whole' of the peasantry against the monarchy, against the landlords, against the medieval regime (and to that extent, the revolution remains bourgeois, bourgeois-democratic). *Then,* with the poorest peasants, with the semi-

[1] To A. Morizet, quoted in E. H. Carr, *The Bolshevik Revolution, 1917–1923,* Vol. II, p. 291, note 1.

proletarians, with all the exploited, *against capitalism,* including the rural rich, the kulaks, the profiteers, and to that extent the revolution becomes a *socialist* one."[2] As he soon learned, those assertions were premature, to say the least. But they were no empty words; they represented Lenin's basic solution to the dilemma posed by the attempt of the Communists to take power in an agricultural country. If "poor peasants" could not be found to perform their allotted tasks at the proper time, they must be found later. The stubborn refusal of the Russian peasantry to "split" and conduct its own civil war was a great blow to Lenin. However, he was prepared to wait for it, as he awaited the revolution in the West.

For the moment, in any event, the "poor peasants" remained a mirage. As E. H. Carr puts it, instead of a split in the peasantry between rich and poor, there had occurred "a striking equalization of the size of the unit of production . . . the smallholding worked by the labor of the peasant and his family . . . already typical in 1917, had become by 1920 the predominant unit in Russian agriculture."[3] Therefore the Communists had to compromise with the "middle peasants"—that is, the overwhelming majority of the Russian people. In March 1919 Lenin defended such tactics by declaring that the middle peasantry "does not belong to the exploiters, since it does not draw profits from the labor of others," but it was not exploited either, since it was self-employed. Lenin never came closer to an admission that a Marxian class analysis simply did not apply to the country where he had sought to lead the world's first Marxist revolution.

In fact Lenin did not "compromise with the middle peasant" in 1919; his talk of doing so was translated into action only in 1921 when he inaugurated the NEP. By that time he had largely ceased to talk about the "middle peasant" and simply referred to "the peasantry." NEP, like Brest-Litovsk, was an admission of defeat; however, neither was intended as a surrender, but rather as a tactical maneuver to be pursued only until the inevitable change of conditions which would make victory possible. NEP was like Brest-Litovsk in another respect: the end of the compromise was not that foreseen by Lenin. What enabled him to tear up the treaty was not a Communist revolution in Germany, but Allied victory. What enabled Stalin (Lenin had died in the meantime) to abandon NEP was not a split of the peasantry into rich and poor—to

• [2] V. I. Lenin, *Selected Works* (2 vols.; London: Lawrence & Wishart, 1947), Vol. II, p. 414. The pamphlet was *The Proletarian Revolution and the Renegade Kautsky.*

• [3] E. H. Carr, *op. cit.,* Vol. II, p. 168.

which sanction for a capitalist development in the villages was supposed to lead—but the accumulation of sufficient power in the Communist state to do the job which the "poor peasants" were supposed to do, namely, liquidate the kulaks and establish collective farms.

LIMITED FREEDOM IN THE ECONOMY

In 1921 the economy of Russia lay in ruins. Seven years of war and civil war had produced catastrophe. Industrial production stood at thirteen per cent of prewar volume; the grain harvest had fallen from 74 million tons in 1916 to 30 million tons in 1919 and continued to decline still further. Inflation was rampant, and although the Communists hated and feared it, they saw no alternative but to contribute to it by printing paper money. The immediate economic measures taken to meet the crisis could not be directly financial, nor could they involve any plans for extensive change in the structure of the economy. They aimed merely to persuade people to work and produce more, in the city or in the village, so that some kind of regular trade could be resumed, the urban masses fed, and the villagers supplied with the goods for which they would willingly exchange their grain.

Although as indicated the food tax was prompted by basically political motives, it also initiated the revival of the economy. The law provided that the peasant must pay the government a tax in kind consisting of a certain percentage, varying somewhat from region to region, of his produce; he could then dispose of the remainder on the free market. A year later the tax was fixed at a standard ten per cent. In 1922 also the peasant was permitted to lease land and hire labor, although purchase and sale of land were still prohibited. By the Fundamental Law on the Exploitation of Land by the Workers, enacted in May 1922, the government guaranteed the peasant freedom of choice of land tenure—individual, communal, or other. Thus the villager was permitted, within rather broad limits, to manage his own economic life as he saw fit.

The small businessman was also granted a measure of economic freedom. Although the state retained in its hands the ownership of the so-called "commanding heights"—including the largest enterprises, railways, and banks—private entrepreneurs were permitted to resume management of smaller concerns, to hire labor, and to trade more or less freely with the goods produced. The new class of small urban capitalists, who became known as "Nepmen," suffered from social pressures from which the peasants were exempt. It was difficult for them to obtain credit at the banks, the rentals for their apartments were often

Nepman
L small urban capitalists

higher than their neighbors', their children had to pay higher tuition fees at schools. Many of them expressed their suspicion that their situation was precarious and temporary by free spending and high living.

The new era of "free enterprise" benefited not only the peasants and small businessmen, but also the industrial workers. The trade-unions, organized under the leadership of Michael Tomsky, were permitted to strike against the private capitalists, and accordingly it was thought necessary that they be allowed to strike against state enterprises also, even though they were urged not to do so and reminded that by so doing they were by definition striking against themselves.

Under the new dispensation, the economy began to revive. Lenin addressed himself to the disagreeable topic of gold, and he announced that in the future gold would be used to construct public lavatories in the streets of the great cities of the world, but that for the time being orthodox principles of finance, as well as of trade, must be taken seriously. He handed the slogan, "master trade," to the rank-and-file Communists, who picked it up in a generally uneasy and gingerly fashion. State industries and state farms were now commanded to show profit and to operate on commercial principles generally. Financial stability was slowly recovered. By the end of 1922 a third of the government revenue was coming from the food tax, one third from a variety of direct money taxes, and one third from the issuance of bank notes. As a result of the growing tax yield, in 1924 a new currency (the unit was the *chervonets,* which means "red") could be introduced and the old note issue gradually abandoned.

However, by this time a crisis had arisen in urban-rural trade. The new nationalized industry was producing again, but its costs were much higher than prewar levels and thus the prices of manufactured goods were high. As the marketing of agricultural produce was resumed, the greater supply drove grain prices down. The terms of trade thus moved against the countryside. Whereas the peasant had formerly been able to get a shirt for thirty-odd pounds of rye or the equivalent, by 1923 he needed two hundred and fifty pounds. The result was the "scissors crisis," so called from a diagram Trotsky used in a speech, which showed the intersection of a falling rural price curve and a rising urban price curve. The curves intersected, said Trotsky, in September 1922.

Thereafter the "scissors" continued to open until October 1923, when the gap was widest. The government took energetic action to force industrial prices downward. Direct pressure was exerted on the national-ized trusts to lower prices. Credit rationing, price regulation, and even the importation of lower-priced goods from abroad were employed. In consequence the gap began to narrow after October, and the crisis was surmounted, although many Party members resented the leaders' firmness with the state enterprises.

By 1923–1924 it was apparent that the regime was managing to stabilize itself, at least for the time being, as the economic revival made headway. The open although limited encouragement given to private enterprise led many in and out of Russia to conclude that "capitalism" had returned for good, and that the Communists had jettisoned their long-proclaimed ideological objectives, which might never have been seriously meant anyhow. The introduction of the NEP was the first in a long series of occasions in Soviet history when foreign observers decided that Communist doctrine was ceasing to be significant in influencing the Soviet leaders.

No doubt many of the peasants expected NEP to be permanent, and although the Nepmen had fewer such illusions, they too hoped the policy would last for some time. Many Communist Party members feared that NEP might be prolonged and fought to end it before it got out of hand. Perhaps indeed it might have lasted somewhat longer than it did, if it had not been for certain developments which restricted political freedom, in and out of the Party, at the very time when the regime was experimenting rather boldly with economic freedom.

THE END OF ORGANIZED OPPOSITION

The first measures to silence opposition were directed against the remaining non-Communist parties. The Left Socialist Revolutionaries were briefly tolerated even after their resignation from the government at the time of Brest-Litovsk, but after they resorted to violence against the regime in late summer, they were sternly repressed. The Kadet party was declared illegal before the end of 1917. Certain Kadet leaders were placed on state-appointed committees to deal with problems of the severe famine of 1921–1922, but already by then the party as such had disappeared from the Russian scene.

Orthodox Socialist Revolutionaries and Mensheviks were still permitted to attend the VIII Congress of Soviets of Workers', Soldiers', and Peasant Deputies in December 1920, although there was no pretense that they were present on the same footing as the Communist deputies. The chief Menshevik leaders still inside Russia were allowed to emigrate to Berlin in 1921, and Berlin became a sort of Menshevik capital (until the rise of Hitler, when the exile center moved to New York). However, the Socialist Revolutionary leaders did not receive the same courtesies. In

1922 a number of them were put on public trial and charged with counterrevolutionary crimes. Foreign radicals interested themselves in the case, and the Belgian Socialist, Emile Vandervelde, was allowed to undertake their defense. Despite findings of guilt, several S.R. leaders were permitted to go abroad after short prison terms, and they proceeded in stages to Berlin, Paris, and New York. After 1922 no organized non-Communist political organization was tolerated on Soviet soil.

Sharp differences of opinion had appeared within the Communist party itself during the Civil War. In 1918 the "Left" Communist faction, following Bukharin, had opposed the Brest-Litovsk peace and demanded a revolutionary war. After the treaty was signed many of Bukharin's followers, who included Radek, Lomov, Uritsky, V. M. Smirnov, Bubnov, and Piatakov, resigned posts of prominence in protest, but they remained in the Party. At the VIII Party Congress in March 1919, a new Party program was adopted, replacing the old one of 1903. It proclaimed that the "dictatorship of the proletariat" had been brought into being in Russia, based on the Soviets, and among other things reasserted the right of national self-determination (see p. 44). Bukharin and the "Left" Communists objected. Lenin replied, "Scratch certain Communists and you will find a Great-Russian chauvinist." That may well have been true; however, the militant "Lefts" did not defend Russian pre-eminence, but the primacy of the international proletariat over any nation, in tactics as well as doctrine.

At the IX Party Congress in April 1920, many former "Left" Communists appeared as the "Democratic Centralism" group. Led by Osinsky, Sapronov, and V. M. Smirnov, they criticized the growth in power of Communist bureaucrats and their use of "bourgeois" specialists. By the time of the VIII Congress of Soviets in December 1920, the conflicts in the Party came to center on the question of the dangers of "bureaucracy." Trotsky was quite willing to have strict central control and quasi-military discipline; in fact, he was enthusiastic about "labor armies" and "shock methods," as a result of his experience as war commissar. However, he was concerned about the power of the bureaucrats, which he proposed to curb by turning trade-unions into organs of state, while carefully selecting leading personnel through what he called "sandpapering" the unions.

Those who feared state control most deeply were now forming a group known as the "Workers' Opposition," led by Shliapnikov, the colorful Mme. Kollontai, and others, who urged that the existing state organs turn their powers over to the trade-unions. Lenin disagreed with both Trotsky and the Workers' Opposition. He insisted that the trade-unions must remain separate from the state (because the poor peasantry was "represented" in the state but not in the trade-unions, and therefore it had to fall to the unions to defend the class interests of the proletariat alone). He also expressed reservations on the use of military methods. While Lenin disagreed with Trotsky, he did not denounce him but he promptly branded the Workers' Opposition as anarchist or anarcho-syndicalist, which to a state socialist is a very bad name.

At the X Party Congress in 1921 Lenin obtained the adoption of NEP, which both Trotskyites and the Workers' Opposition opposed in whole or part as involving undue concessions to the peasantry. But Lenin led the Party to stigmatize the Workers' Opposition as a "deviation towards syndicalism and anarchism." At the opening of the Congress, he declared, "We are going to put an end to opposition now, to put the lid on it; we have had enough of oppositions!" The Congress proceeded to do just that. All factional groups within the Party were "dissolved" and prohibited. In a secret resolution, the Central Committee was given the power to expel Party members (including members of the Central Committee itself) for engaging in factionalism.

In the summer of 1921 a nation-wide purge of the Party was carried out which resulted in the reduction of Party strength from 730,000 (at the time of the X Congress) to 530,000. Almost one-third of the Party members were thus expelled. Such measures might have been expected to "put the lid" on any opposition beyond doubt; but more was to come. The following year the Cheka was abolished and replaced by the GPU (*Gosudarstvennoe Politicheskoe Upravlenie* or State Political Administration), which was given the right to arrest Party members—a right not possessed by the Cheka. The creation of the GPU was announced at the XI Party Congress in March 1922.

The XI Congress was the last Lenin attended. Addressing it, he forecast decisive battles with foreign capitalism, but these were far ahead, while the one "in the near future" would be with "Russian capitalism . . . which grows out of petty peasant economy"—in a word, with the peasants. Lenin defended the necessity of using "bourgeois specialists," declaring that Communists in Russia were only "a drop in the ocean of the people." He discussed the *émigré* Kadets and others who had published a symposium entitled *Change of Signposts (Smena Vekh),* in which they declared that the Soviet regime was undergoing an evolution into a new "national" and normal regime meriting the support of all Russians. This current had found support also within the country. Lenin declared himself willing to use such ideological fellow travelers (however mistaken their analysis) for Communist purposes in the same way as the "bourgeois specialists" were being used already.

Taking note of the fact that "former" members of the Workers' Opposition had taken their grievances to the Comintern, charging that the Russian Party leaders had become isolated from the workers and were paying undue attention to the peasantry, the XI Congress cracked down again on dissidents, and meted out further expulsions from Party ranks.

THE EMERGENCE OF STALIN

Shortly after the Congress ended, Lenin suffered a stroke of arteriosclerotic paralysis. Suddenly the ranks of the highest Party and state leadership were thrown into confusion. As long as Lenin was at the helm, everyone in the Party, even including the members of the opposition, knew where he was, what arguments he might urge with some hope of success, what the consequences might be. With Lenin removed from effective leadership even temporarily, all was uncertainty.

Virtually from the moment of the Bolshevik revolution, the actual governing body of the country had been the Politburo (Political Bureau of the Central Committee of the Party). During the Civil War the Politburo was composed of five men: Lenin, Trotsky, Stalin, Kamenev, and Bukharin. Its functions were to settle policy questions; such decisions were then communicated to the Orgburo (Organization Bureau of the Central Committee) to be translated into action by the assignment of jobs to specific persons. The liaison between the two bureaus was effected by Stalin, who from the first had been given "practical" jobs, often the ones nobody else among the theoretically-minded leaders wanted.

In 1919 Stalin had become commissar of the Workers' and Peasants' Inspectorate (*Rabkrin*), whose job was to combat corruption and inefficiency in all branches of the government. One month before Lenin's stroke, Stalin was also made general secretary of the Central Committee, with his old colleague, Viacheslav Molotov, and Valerian Kuibyshev as his assistants. The functions of the Secretariat included the composition of the agenda for the Politburo, which had now added Zinoviev and Tomsky to the five of the Civil War period. The Secretariat had also to co-ordinate the joint sessions which the Central Committee and the Central Control Commission (a new body created by the XI Congress) began to hold and, in general, smooth the relations between them. The Commission had been proposed, paradoxically enough, by the Workers' Opposition, which envisaged it as a means of keeping the Party pure of careerist and bourgeois infiltration and therefore truly proletarian. However, it was a weapon which was soon turned on its authors and all other dissidents from Politburo policy; Stalin's powers in it were very great.

From the first Stalin had also been commissar of nationalities. As such he was responsible for the Red Army invasion of Georgia and the destruction of its Menshevik-led independent government in the early months of 1921. He seems to have been determined not to allow the right of "self-determination," in the name of which he had countenanced the secession of Finland from Russia, to be invoked in any other case where a country sought to escape Soviet power. Actually he could support his position on Marxist grounds. The Marxian analysis was a class analysis, and the category "nation" had to be reduced to class terms. "Self-determination" for a nation was thus bound to mean self-determination for that nation's proletariat, which would of course be Communist, unless duped or seduced by the bourgeoisie into a misapprehension of its true interests. The Communist leaders' patience with backward proletarians who failed to grasp their own interests fluctuated, but no principle of Marxism-Leninism excluded the possibility of the Soviets' "coming to the aid" of local Communists anywhere. This was Stalin's justification in the case of Georgia, although the brutality of the conquest of his own native country provoked some puzzlement and criticism among his colleagues.

In mid-1922 Stalin intervened in a dispute over the government of the Ukraine, and again there was criticism from within the Party leadership. Soon afterward he attempted to bolster his prestige by coming up with a proposal for a constitutional change fixing the relationship between Russia and the various non-Russian Soviet "republics." Lenin supported the idea and at first defended Stalin against his critics. However, by November Lenin's whole attitude toward Stalin was apparently shifting. In December he suffered another stroke, and this time he was sufficiently convinced that he was near death to dictate a will which dealt not with his private affairs but those of the Party and government.

In this will Lenin emphasized again the necessity of agreement between the peasantry and the working class which he believed indispensable to the survival of Communism in Russia. However, the danger which concerned him was not a class antagonism but a personal one: that between Stalin and Trotsky, whom he called "the two most able leaders of the present Central Committee." Trotsky he declared to be the more able of the two, but he thought he had recently shown "too far-reaching a self-confidence and a disposition to be too much attracted by the purely administrative side of affairs." On the other hand, Stalin had "concentrated an enormous power in his hands; and I am not sure that he always knows how to use that power with sufficient caution." Lenin recalled Zinoviev's and Kamenev's hesitation on the eve of the October Revolution and Trotsky's tardy adherence to Bolshevism, but he said these facts ought not to be used against the men personally. Bukharin he labeled "the greatest and most valuable theoretician," but lamented "something scholastic" in his make-up.

Thus Lenin's will did not point to any single individual as unqualifiedly worthy of his mantle; in fact, he seems to have taken care to emphasize that each one had strengths and weaknesses. However, only ten days later he added a postscript in which he singled out one man as currently causing the most trouble in the Party. Stalin, he wrote, "is too rude, and this fault . . . becomes unbearable in the office of General Secretary. Therefore I propose to the comrades to find a way to remove Stalin from that position and appoint to it another man . . . more patient, more loyal, more polite and more attentive to comrades, less capricious, etc." This remark was dictated on January 4, 1923.

While Lenin lived the whole document remained known only to his wife, Krupskaia, and his secretaries; but Lenin went on to attack Stalin publicly. In *Pravda* he sharply criticized Stalin's conduct of the Workers' and Peasants' Inspectorate. He followed this up by a promise to the disgruntled Georgian Party leaders to support them against the "arrogance of Ordzhonikidze and the connivance of Stalin and Dzerzhinsky"; finally he wrote Stalin that he "broke off" all personal relations with him. He was preparing to launch an open onslaught at the XII Congress, scheduled for the spring of 1923, for which he had concerted measures with Trotsky, but on March 9 he suffered his third stroke and never recovered from it.

THE CONSTITUTION OF THE USSR

Stalin was aware of at least part of his danger, but he also knew that if attacked he was entrenched in a multitude of important and powerful Party posts. However, he did not confine himself to manipulation behind the scenes, but sought to enhance his public prestige. As commissar of nationalities, he was able to take credit for the constitutional "reform," by which in December 1922 a Union of Soviet Socialist Republics was established.

Up to that time the formal Constitution had been the one adopted July 10, 1918, by the V Congress of Soviets for the "Russian Socialist Federated Soviet Republic." It had begun with a Declaration of Rights of Toiling and Exploited People, and had gone on to legalize the "government" (as distinguished from the central organs of the Communist Party, which were actually running the country) which had come into existence at the time of the October Revolution.

The supreme authority was said to be the periodic meeting of the All-Russian Congress of Soviets, elected by a system under which the urban population considerably outweighed the rural in representation; moreover, the rural deputies were elected only indirectly. Between meetings of the Congress, power was wielded by a Central Executive Committee (VTsIK), a very large "committee" of not more than two hundred members elected by the Congress. This committee was supposed to appoint the Council of People's Commissars (*Sovnarkom*), a sort of cabinet. A hierarchy of local and regional soviets was also written into the Constitution. The Constitution of 1918 made no mention of the Communist Party, and in general bore only the vaguest relationship to the actual facts of governmental life at the time. The reality was a highly centralized state—even the provisions of the Constitution made that clear—in which no fundamental questions were to be subjected to popular will, nor were significant decisions to be made by any level of the imposing and intricate "governmental" machinery.

Decision-making rested with the central organs of the Communist Party. In theory "democratic centralism" characterized the process of arriving at decisions. That is to say, free discussion of any particular issue—to be sure, within the limits of the basic Bolshevik viewpoint—was supposed to be permitted at all levels of the Party until the national Congress pronounced upon it. From that moment all Party members were bound to accept the decision and act on it without question. Structurally "democratic centralism" was and is supposed to be assured by election of all "leading Party bodies, from the lowest to the highest," periodic reports of such bodies to their organizations, strict Party discipline and "subordination of the minority to the majority," and "the absolutely binding character of the decisions of higher bodies upon lower bodies." "Democratic centralism" actually did operate in some such fashion in the Party during the early years of the Soviet regime. However, the central organs, headed by the Politburo, soon in fact acquired more power than the Party Congresses, and after the ban imposed on "factions" at the XI Congress, it became increasingly difficult for dissenting opinions of any kind to obtain a hearing. But whether the central organs submitted to guidance from the rest of the Party or not, the Party decisions from the very first determined governmental policies and practices.

Besides the description of governmental machinery, the Constitution

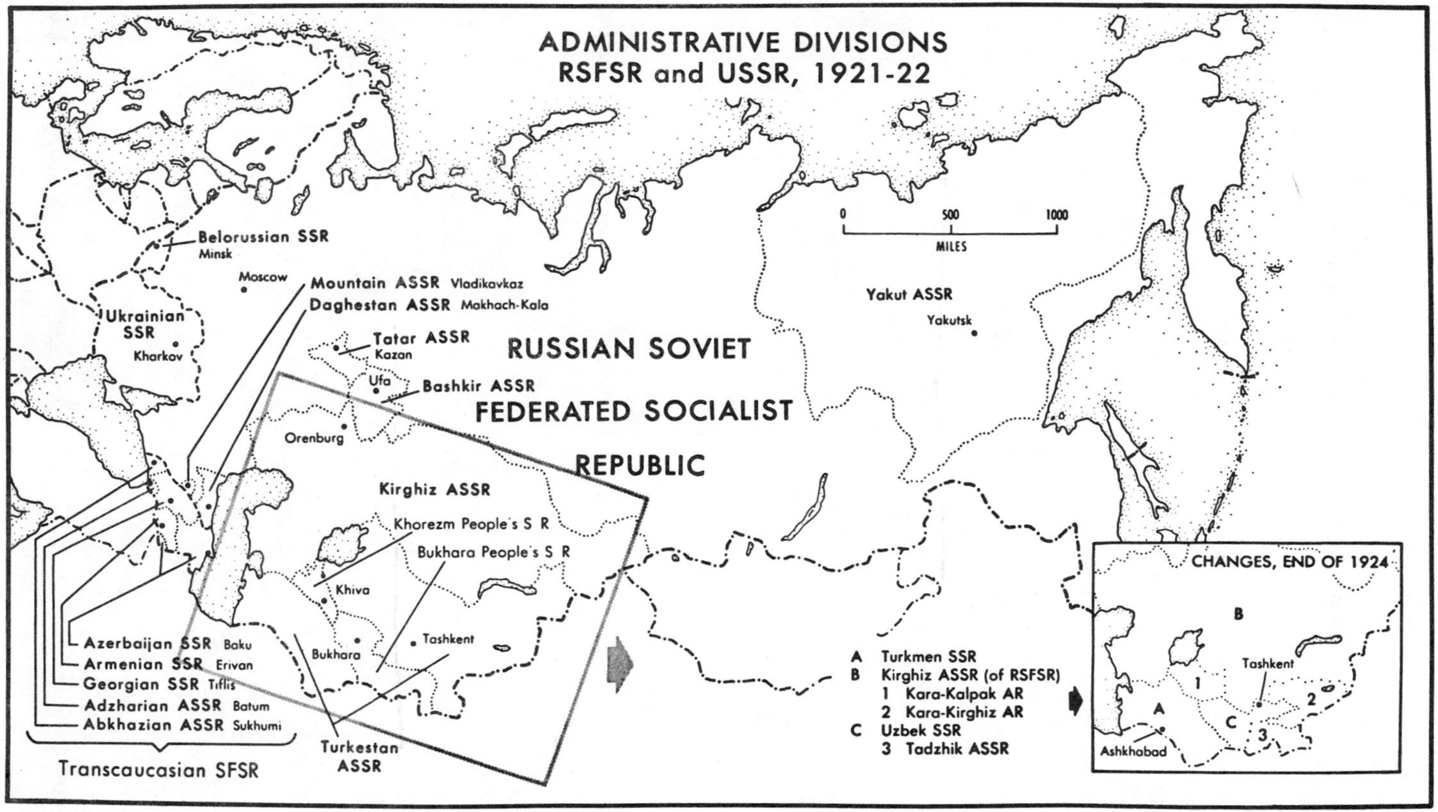
ADMINISTRATIVE DIVISIONS
RSFSR and USSR, 1921-22
0 500 1000
MILES
Belorussian SSR
Minsk
Moscow
Ukrainian SSR
Kharkov
Mountain ASSR Vladikavkaz
Daghestan ASSR Makhach-Kala
Tatar ASSR
Kazan
Ufa
Bashkir ASSR
Orenburg
RUSSIAN SOVIET
FEDERATED SOCIALIST
REPUBLIC
Yakut ASSR
Yakutsk
Kirghiz ASSR
Khorezm People's S R
Bukhara People's S R
Khiva
Bukhara
Tashkent
Turkestan ASSR
Azerbaijan SSR Baku
Armenian SSR Erivan
Georgian SSR Tiflis
Adzharian ASSR Batum
Abkhazian ASSR Sukhumi
Transcaucasian SFSR
A Turkmen SSR
B Kirghiz ASSR (of RSFSR)
1 Kara-Kalpak AR
2 Kara-Kirghiz AR
C Uzbek SSR
3 Tadzhik ASSR
CHANGES, END OF 1924
B
Tashkent
1
2
A
C
3
Ashkhabad

included the Declaration of Rights already mentioned. Freedom of speech, press, association, assembly, and access to education was guaranteed, but only to the "working class." Church was said to be separated from state, and school from church (that is, the Russian Orthodox Church, for a thousand years the national religion of the Russians, Belorussians, and Ukrainians), and all citizens were assured freedom to conduct religious and antireligious propaganda. Discrimination against national minorities was forbidden. "Regions with special usages and national characteristics" were authorized to unite in "autonomous" groupings to be admitted to the Russian Soviet Federated Socialist Republic. The duty to bear arms, and the duty to work—"he who does not work shall not eat," a very fair rendition of 2 Thessalonians 3:10—were also specified.

By 1921 there nominally existed six separate Soviet republics: Russia, Belorussia, Ukraine, Azerbaijan, Georgia, and Armenia. In late 1922, at Stalin's behest, the last three were amalgamated into a Transcaucasian Republic, despite stiff opposition from several Georgian Communists. The resulting four were to be formed into a union. In March 1921 the X Party Congress had already set the stage by declaring for a "union of the several Soviet republics." Actually all four already had representation in the All-Russian Congress of Soviets when, in December 1922, that body was superseded by the I Congress of Soviets of the USSR, of similar composition. The December Congress declared a Union of Soviet Socialist Republics to be in existence, and approved a new draft constitution.

However, the national issue, already settled in theory, caused sharp debate within the Party through the early months of 1923. Again Stalin rode down opposition, especially from the Ukrainian Party leaders headed by Rakovsky, and pushed through his own final version of the Constitution. "Nationalist in form, socialist in content," was the accepted formula for uniting several nationalities under Communist rule—and one honest enough when it is remembered that for a Marxist content is everything. The Ukrainians in particular urged large minority-republic representation in a second legislative chamber and Union-republican (rather than Union) control of foreign affairs, but in vain. Stalin's Constitution, as finally approved by the Central Executive Committee in July 1923 and ratified by the II All-Union Congress of Soviets in January 1924, made no substantial changes in the Constitution of 1918. A provision was inserted insuring the right of each republic to "secede freely," but it was repeatedly made clear that a request for secession could only arise from class feelings hostile to those of the proletariat, and such a demand has indeed never been expressed.

The remainder of the governmental structure was not revised in any essential particular. The Congress of Soviets, Central Executive Committee, and Council of People's Commissars were now "All-Union" instead of "All-Russian." The Central Executive Committee was divided into a Council of the Union, with numerical representation only, and a Council of Nationalities composed of five delegates from each union republic—which provision, unmodified, would have left the Russian Republic greatly outnumbered—and also five from each autonomous republic and one from each autonomous region. At this stage the Russian Republic had seven autonomous republics—the Turkestan, Bashkir, Tatar, Kirghiz, Daghestan, Mountain, and Yakut republics—and ten autonomous regions, while all the other union republics together had a total of two autonomous republics and two autonomous regions. Not that the make-up of the Council of Nationalities made much practical difference, but psychological factors were at stake.

The Constitution contained lists of the cabinet ministries (that is, the People's Commissariats), in which certain offices, such as Foreign Affairs, and Military and Naval Affairs, were present only at the All-Union level; certain others, such as the Supreme Council of National Economy, at both All-Union and Union-republic levels; and still others at the Union-republic level only, such as Internal Affairs, Justice, and Education. There was a new provision for a Supreme Court and a procurator, but they were in law as well as in fact made subject to the Central Executive Committee, and there was no pretense of any kind of judicial independence. Like the 1918 Constitution, the Constitution of the USSR made no mention of where the real power lay, or in fact referred to the Communist Party at all.

This document was touted by Stalin as an achievement equal in importance to the organization of the Red Army in the Civil War, an implied assertion that he was at least the equal of Trotsky. He praised the constitutional reform as a "decisive step on the road toward uniting the toilers of the whole world into a World Soviet Socialist Republic." Although Lenin had, some time after his first stroke, approved the principles of Stalin's plan for a new constitution, he was pointedly silent about the whole business in December 1922 when the USSR was being formally proclaimed. His break with Stalin remained, however, unknown to the public and to all but a few individuals at the top levels of the Party.

THE TRIUMVIRATE

The final attack of Lenin's illness forced his colleagues to seek a substitute for the single leader whose word had become, although it had not always been, final. The Politburo did not formally select any successor, but in fact Zinoviev, Kamenev, and Stalin began to act together as such. The bond that seemed to unite them was their "old Bolshevik" status, reaching all the way back to the schism of 1903, against the "ex-Menshevik" and newcomer to the party, Trotsky, whose brilliance, personality, and achievements seemed to match if not surpass Lenin's. Zinoviev was a successful speaker and effective with crowds; he had strong local power in Petrograd as chairman of its renowned Soviet, and as president of the Comintern he had wide prestige. Kamenev probably had the stronger intellect; he had enjoyed a close association with Lenin as his assistant and held considerable power as chairman of the Moscow Soviet. Stalin's many offices have already been cited; it should be added that as commissar of nationalities he had come to have great influence in the outlying areas of the country, where his colleagues had little. Zinoviev and Kamenev still had a tendency to regard Stalin as the junior partner and glorified errand boy, but for the moment they could all work in harness. Together they could manage the Politburo, and the Politburo could manage the Party.

That did not mean that all of the Party was yet willing to be managed. The XII Congress in April 1923, at which Lenin and Trotsky had planned to attack Stalin (see p. 207), was instead marked by the triumvirate's victory over its opponents, in which Trotsky assisted the triumvirs. On the eve of the Congress the "Workers' Truth" group, following A. A. Bogdanov (whom Lenin had attacked in *Materialism and Empirio-Criticism*), were denouncing NEP as a simple return to capitalism. The "Workers' Group," led by Miasnikov (who had earlier been expelled from the Party for advocating freedom of speech for all "from monarchists to anarchists"), also attacked NEP, declaring it ought to stand for "new exploitation of the proletariat." At the Congress, both Zinoviev and Trotsky anathematized these two groups. Stalin forcefully invoked the shade of the not-yet-dead Lenin, and the Party opposition outside the Politburo was effectively trampled down. For the moment, the antagonism among the leaders seemed to recede into the background.

However, it broke out afresh in connection with the new economic crisis provoked by the Party's attempt to solve the "scissors" problem (see p. 201). In the spring of 1923 industrial enterprises were feeling the pressure exerted to bring prices down; credit was being curtailed, and low wages and unemployment were widespread. Although Trotsky did not raise the economic issue, he chose the moment of crisis to give point to an attack on "bureaucratization" in the Party. Hard upon his heels, forty-six prominent Communists echoed his criticism in a public "platform." A number of the signers of this declaration had been associated with the earlier small opposition groups. Although there was no direct evidence of collusion between Trotsky and the "forty-six," the substance of the criticism was the same. Thus, as Isaac Deutscher points out, Trotsky "had the worst of both worlds":[4] that is to say, he had not approved of the pressure on state industry, but had remained silent until the opposition groups which had been publicly objecting were crushed; thus it was too late to find allies outside the Politburo, while he was already isolated within it.

The triumvirate nominally bowed to the criticism by announcing a Party discussion on all issues about which members were concerned. Trotsky was thereby provoked into writing an open letter, on December 5, 1923, to the Communists of Red Presnia, the section of Moscow in which the armed uprising of December 1905 had occurred. In the letter he warned against the possible degeneration of the revolutionary "old guard" into bureaucracy. The conflict behind the scenes was thus made public, and there was open hostility between the triumvirs and Trotsky.

Zinoviev even urged the arrest of Trotsky, but Stalin was for restraint. For one thing, Trotsky retained immense popularity within the Party, even if it was not organized. Stalin contented himself with further thunder at the "opposition," choosing to be ambiguous about whether he included Trotsky in it or not, and taunting him with refusing to identify himself clearly with either the Politburo or the opposition. On January 21, 1924, Lenin finally died. Trotsky himself was not well, and perhaps his illness had something to do with the apparent indecision he displayed during the last months of 1923. At the moment of Lenin's death he was absent from the capital. Probably this coincidence was not decisive, although it gave Stalin the chance he needed to identify himself publicly with the heritage of the fallen leader. Five days after Lenin's death, Stalin addressed the II All-Union Congress of Soviets and delivered a remarkable statement:

> We Communists are people of a special mold. We are made of a special stuff. We are those who form the army of the great proletarian strategist, the army of Comrade Lenin. There is nothing higher than the honor of belonging to this army. There is nothing higher than the title of member of the party whose founder and leader is Comrade Lenin. . . .
>
> Departing from us, Comrade Lenin adjured us to hold high

[4] I. Deutscher, ***Stalin: a Political Biography*** (New York: Oxford University Press, 1949), p. 260.

> and to guard the purity of the great title of member of the Party. We vow to you, Comrade Lenin, that we will fulfill your bequest with honor! . . .
>
> Departing from us, Comrade Lenin adjured us to guard the unity of our Party as the apple of our eye. We vow to you, Comrade Lenin, that this behest, too, we will fulfill with honor! . . .
>
> Departing from us, Comrade Lenin adjured us to guard and strengthen the dictatorship of the proletariat. We vow to you, Comrade Lenin, that we will spare no effort to fulfill this bequest, too, with honor! . . .
>
> Departing from us, Comrade Lenin adjured us to strengthen with all our might the alliance of the workers and the peasants. We vow to you, Comrade Lenin, that this behest, too, we will fulfill with honor! . . .

Stalin's oath, cast in the form of a church litany, grated on a number of old Bolsheviks and puzzled a number of others. The triumvirate's decision to place Lenin's body in a mausoleum in Red Square also was repugnant to many. The changing of the name of Petrograd to Leningrad—the first city to be renamed by the Soviets—seemed more in the revolutionary tradition and served as a precedent for similar changes. Ekaterinburg became Sverdlovsk, after Sverdlov, who had died in 1919. Shortly afterward, Elizavetgrad became Zinovievsk, honoring a leader who was still very much alive. Still playing the role of caution and modesty, Stalin waited until one of his fellow triumvirs was so honored before he allowed Tsaritsyn to be renamed Stalingrad, in April 1925.

However, Stalin had made it clear that he aspired to be Lenin's heir as he claimed to have been his true disciple. And although it was true that before he died Lenin had in some sense disowned Stalin, it was also true that Stalin had done Lenin's bidding, had never embroiled himself in a conflict with him on either principle or tactics—unlike Trotsky, Zinoviev, or Kamenev—and in the famed "oath" presented, in however crude a manner, a digest of the essentials of Leninism. On such factors rested his title to succeed Lenin.

The last words of Lenin himself were not spoken until, in May 1924, the will was read aloud in the Central Committee. The scene was one of consternation. Stalin and Trotsky sat silent, wrestling with their emotions, while Zinoviev referred obliquely to the "oath" that had been taken to execute Lenin's wishes, adding, "we are happy to say that in one point Lenin's fears have proved baseless. I have in mind the point about our General Secretary. You have all witnessed our harmonious co-operation in the last few months; and, like myself, you will be happy to say that Lenin's fears have proved baseless." The will was not published, and Stalin was saved. Zinoviev would live to regret his statement, but it was not yet the power of Stalin, only his adroitness, which had led Zinoviev to make it. Not fear of Stalin but assurance that they could make good use of him led the other two triumvirs to preserve the third. The moment was decisive for Stalin's rise to power; for Trotsky, it was virtually the last chance, which went by without an effort to seize it.

In the fall of 1917 power in the former Russian Empire had passed to the Communist Party; by 1922 it had passed into the hands of Lenin and the other leaders of the Central Committee; by 1924 it lay at the disposal of the three men who dominated the Politburo. It was to narrow further. However, much more than personalities was at stake. All the leaders, despite the hostility among them, were committed to the realization of the Communist program at home and abroad, and the struggle for personal power was at the same time a debate on the best and fastest way to realize that program.

Stalin, Trotsky, and Bukharin

TRIUMPH of Stalin

★
★
★
★
★
★
★
★
★
★

CHAPTER 14

DZHUGASHVILI AND BRONSTEIN

Joseph Stalin, born Dzhugashvili, and Leon Trotsky, born Bronstein, were the same age, and both had been from early youth members of the Russian Social Democratic party. As dedicated Communists, they had a common basic outlook: they were philosophical materialists, committed to the unity of theory and practice and bent upon spreading Communism throughout the whole world. While Lenin was alive (at any rate until 1922) both men had a secure place in his favor and therefore in the party as a whole. Stalin had always adhered closely to Lenin's most cherished principles and practices. Since 1917, at least, Trotsky had supported Lenin on the main issues and seemed to have more of his candor and flexibility than Stalin. However, as Lenin sickened and died, the mutual antagonism between Trotsky and Stalin, who had never been compatible, deepened into a life-and-death struggle.

It is difficult to compare the later lives of the two men, for Stalin achieved sole power and Trotsky was exiled, and since Trotsky thus escaped Stalin's dilemmas, it is uncertain how he would have responded to them, although he detested Stalin's rule. Stalin hated his adversary so deeply that he caused his name to be written simply "Judas Trotsky" in officially commissioned books, but he borrowed many of his ideas and methods. Their earlier lives, however, suggest something of the personal differences which were to be complicated by disagreements over doctrine and practice.

Stalin was the eldest surviving child of the shoemaker Vissarion Dzhugashvili of Gori in Georgia. Today the hut in which he was born is preserved by a temple-like structure erected over it. As a boy he attended a church school in Gori and then the theological seminary in Tiflis. Today the seminary has been converted into a museum of medieval Georgian art. Young Joseph joined a Marxist society known as Mesame-Dasi while a student at the seminary, but it is not clear whether this had anything to do with his expulsion in 1899. During the next two years his Marxism crystallized, and his first Marxist essays appeared in a Georgian newspaper in 1901. At that time he was already an enthusiastic defender of Lenin and the other orthodox Marxist exiles who published the newspaper *Iskra*. His literary style was not then distinguished; in fact, it never got much better.

Stalin was active in the revolutionary movement in Tiflis, Batum, and elsewhere, not as Dzhugashvili, nor yet "Stalin," but as "Koba." This meant something like "courageous" in Turkish, and it was also the name of a fabled Georgian freebooter; it is uncertain which the nickname first signified. Later he was called, indeed, practically dubbed himself, the "Lenin of the Caucasus." However, he was not necessarily the most outstanding leader of the Caucasian Social Democrats, nor even of the Georgian Bolsheviks after the party split in 1903. The great majority of the Marxists in Georgia became and stayed Menshevik; among the Bolsheviks Stalin was prominent, but that did not mean a great deal. Very soon after the news of the London Congress of 1903 reached the Caucasus, he took a firmly pro-Bolshevik stand, and he continued to do so in 1905. It seems that it was at the Tammerfors Party conference at the end of 1905, that Stalin first met Lenin.

After the Revolution of 1905, in defiance of the ban of the then Menshevik-controlled Party, "Koba" led "fighting squads" in raiding banks in order to augment scant Party funds. In one raid in Tiflis a squad seized a quarter of a million rubles. This is the basis of the legend that Stalin was a bank robber; but he did not act as gunman, and he did not pocket the proceeds. He spent much of the period between revolutions in jail or in exile, but made a few important trips abroad in 1912. By this time the Bolshevik organizations in Russia had been gravely weakened, and the Bolsheviks of the Caucasus had assumed an importance quite out of proportion to their numbers. Stalin had become editor of the Party newspaper, *Pravda,* and he was co-opted by Lenin onto the Party Central Committee just after the Prague conference of 1912, at which the Bolsheviks broke permanently with the other Marxist factions. He visited Lenin in exile and spent some time with him. As a result of their talks, he wrote an essay on the "nationalities question" which led Lenin to inform Gorky that a "wonderful Georgian" had done a fine job on the subject. The pseudonym with which the pamphlet was signed was "K. Stalin."

At the outbreak of World War I Stalin was in Siberian exile, sharing a hut with Sverdlov, future Chairman of the Presidium ("president") of the Soviet republic, who, it seems, found Stalin an uncomradely hut partner. Stalin chose not to try to escape during the war. In 1916 he was summoned to Krasnoiarsk to be drafted but was found physically unfit for military service owing to his withered left arm. During the war period he apparently wrote next to nothing.

Liberated by the February Revolution, Stalin hastened to Petrograd and, as the only member of the Central Committee on the spot, assumed temporary leadership of the Bolshevik Party. Like almost all other Bolsheviks, he became identified with the movement for reunification with the Mensheviks. When Lenin arrived and sharply castigated such tendencies to compromise, Stalin was as dumfounded as anyone else, but he took his scolding without protest. He owed his position in the Party to the fact that he worked hard and did not argue with his comrades, especially Lenin.

Trotsky, like Stalin, was born in 1879. His real name was Lev Davidovich Bronstein; his father was a well-to-do Jewish farmer in the Ukrainian province of Kherson. He attended school in Odessa, developing an early brilliance and bookishness. He reports his observation of the composition of his class: "the tale-bearers and envious at one pole, the frank, courageous boys at the other, and the neutral, vacillating mass in the middle." He was to apply the same threefold classification to his fellow revolutionaries and fellow citizens of the Empire and the world. In his teens he went to Nikolaev, met a number of populists, became enamored of a girl in the group, and accepted the populist doctrine. Soon, however, he became converted to Marxism, engaged in revolutionary activity, and for it spent his eighteenth birthday in jail. He was exiled to Siberia but soon escaped and arrived in London in 1902 to join Lenin. In Western Europe he met another young lady. The girl from Nikolaev was known as Mrs. Bronstein, the Parisian as Mrs. Trotsky, and neither seemed to complain.

After the II Congress in 1903 Trotsky was for a time associated with the Mensheviks, but in 1905 he developed an independent doctrinal line (see p. 62) and between revolutions belonged to neither the Bolshevik nor the Menshevik wing. In 1905 he won renown for his brief chairmanship of the St. Petersburg Soviet of Workers' Deputies. During the next few years he tried to reunite the Party and for that reason refrained from trying to build a faction of his own. None of the other groups found this pose to its taste. During the years just before World War I Trotsky's anti-factionalist stand became in effect an anti-Leninist one. After the war began he went to New York, and it was from there that he traveled to Russia in the spring of 1917. During the summer he joined the Bolshevik Party, although he clearly implied that his only reason for doing so was that the Party had belatedly adopted the analysis and tactical line which he had espoused all along.

His ability and his logic did not always endear him to his comrades, but his oratorical and practical gifts did win him broad popularity among the urban workers and soldiers in late 1917 and during the Civil War. Having failed as foreign commissar to put into effect his dialectical but quixotic policy of "no war, no peace," he had become war commissar, and his most brilliant success was achieved in organizing the finally victorious Red Army. As war commissar he clashed with Stalin, who ensconced himself at Tsaritsyn with some of his old friends from Caucasus days and flouted Trotsky's authority. However, Stalin was as yet no adversary in the field of theory and policy, which Trotsky considered fundamental.

As the triumvirate took form, Trotsky was plainly the most important figure outside it; but no one regarded Stalin as the most eminent of the three. Zinoviev, especially, had an international prestige which Stalin lacked, while both Kamenev and he were regarded as theorists in a way Stalin was not—and a Communist leader had to be a theorist. As the struggle developed between Trotsky and the triumvirs, Stalin counted less on his own influence than on Trotsky's vulnerability. He did not at first try to turn the struggle into a personal contest; an eye witness has told the story of how Zinoviev and Kamenev would snub Trotsky in Politburo meetings, while Stalin would greet him warmly.

TROTSKY AGAINST THE TRIUMVIRATE

On the eve of Lenin's death, the Thirteenth Party Conference published, on Stalin's motion, the decision empowering the Central Committee to expel Party members for factionalism. At the moment the leader died a new sanctity enveloped his every word and deed, including this decision, in which Lenin had taken part. Simultaneously the triumvirs decreed a new recruiting campaign, nominally with a view to strengthening the actual worker element in Party ranks. Actually Stalin, as general secretary, was able to bolster his own influence by guiding the Party machinery in selecting new members. In a few short weeks nearly a quarter of a million men and women were admitted in the new "Lenin enrollment."

At the time of the XIII Party Congress in May 1924, the economic situation was improving sufficiently to enable the triumvirs to call their critics to account. Zinoviev openly attacked Trotsky and demanded that he retract his "errors." As Stalin had only shortly before opposed Zinoviev's demand for Trotsky's arrest, he found it wise to remain in the background. Trotsky replied to Zinoviev with a *cri de coeur* which went to the root of his whole position, morally requiring him to sit passive in the face of doom:

> The party in the last analysis is always right because the party is the single historic instrument given to the proletariat for the solution of its fundamental problems. I have already said that in front of one's own party nothing could be easier than to say: all my criticisms, my statements, my warnings, my protests—the whole thing was a mere mistake. I, however, comrades, cannot say that, because I do not think it. I know that one must not be right against the party. One can be right only with the party, and through the party, for history has created no other road for the realization of what is right.

The Congress was unmoved. It promptly took steps to discipline the Russian Trotskyites, as well as dissidents in the other parties of the Comintern.

After the XIII Congress, as far as could be seen the chief antagonists were Trotsky on the one hand and Zinoviev and Kamenev on the other. In the autumn of 1924 Trotsky published *The Lessons of October,* in which he distinguished between objectively revolutionary situations and subjective failures of revolutionary leaders in such situations. As illustrations of the latter, he cited Zinoviev's and Kamenev's opposition to Lenin's decision to launch an armed uprising in the fall of 1917—thus reopening an extremely ugly wound—and he also implied that Zinoviev was largely responsible for the failure of the German Communist revolt of 1923. Trotsky restated his old theory of "permanent revolution," with its emphasis on the world leadership of the proletariat and its implicit challenge to the Leninist position on the role of the poor peasantry in building socialism. "October," said Trotsky, was the crucial stage in the history of the Party; "October" meant to him the time when Lenin adopted Trotsky's theory of permanent revolution—at least in the sense of rapid passage from the bourgeois to the socialist stage.

Trotsky had made a tactical error. By his emphasis on "October" he opened the way for Zinoviev and Kamenev to retaliate by reminding the Party again of Trotsky's sharp disagreements with Lenin prior to 1917. Stalin's caution had reaped its reward. Since he was not directly drawn into this controversy, he was in a position to make public statements in November which in effect forgave Zinoviev and Kamenev for their earlier mistakes—he even acknowledged some of his own—but forcefully recalled to his hearers the fact that Trotsky was, after all, a newcomer in Party ranks.

Meanwhile Stalin unleashed a new weapon, which Trotsky probably had not considered him capable of producing. He set forth a theoretical position of his own from which he could challenge Trotsky. In order to do so he had to reverse himself within the space of a few months. In *Foundations of Leninism,* published early in 1924, he had denied that a proletarian dictatorship could establish socialism before the victory of the world revolution. A few months later, in *Problems of Leninism,* he advanced his theory of "socialism in one country." [*socialism in one country* — handwritten margin note]

The theory was an innovation and a repudiation of some things which Lenin had said years earlier; but it was a perfectly logical extension of what Lenin had said and done in 1917 and later. If the Russian Communists were not to be indefinitely bogged down in the NEP stage, they must push on to socialism, even if the world revolution was still further delayed. Authority for such an effort could be found in Lenin. Like Lenin, Trotsky believed the building of socialism could be begun in Russia alone; but what Stalin did was to assert that it could be completed with success and to furnish reasons for his contention. Russia was an enormous country, rich in natural resources. Provided that "capitalist" intervention was not renewed, the Russian proletariat, drawing on Russia's great potential wealth and protected by its vast spaces, could accomplish the task.

For a time, however, the theory of "socialism in one country" was over-shadowed by the acrimonious personal struggle between Trotsky and the two most prominent triumvirs. In January 1925 the Central Committee removed Trotsky from the War Commissariat, even through he remained in uneasy possession of a seat on the Politburo. This was the decisive blow. Although he was still not completely crushed, Trotsky receded to the background. If he had been another kind of man, he might have tried to use the Red Army against his adversaries, but his loyalty to the Party was paramount, and he accepted his deposition without trying to resist.

Although Trotsky was defeated, Zinoviev and Kamenev soon discovered that the victory was not theirs. In March 1925 the Fourteenth Conference of the Party accepted Stalin's theory of "socialism in one country," while Zinoviev and Kamenev paid little attention. Soon afterward Stalin was able to break up the triumvirate quietly. Too late Zinoviev and Kamenev attacked Stalin's new theory. By the middle of 1925 he had found new allies in Bukharin, Rykov, and Tomsky, who accepted "socialism in one country." Far from yet aspiring openly to individual power, Stalin chose to be regarded as a mediator, and he asserted that "after Ilich [Lenin]" collegial—or what would later be called "collective"—leadership was the only conceivable way of running the party.

STALIN ALLIED WITH THE RIGHT

Rykov had become Lenin's successor as chairman of the Council of People's Commissars; Tomsky was the leader of the Soviet trade-unions; Bukharin, the "Left" Communist of 1918, was now, like Rykov and Tomsky, on the "right" and the leader of those who felt that the NEP was a success, and while indeed socialism might be built in Russia, the ground was secure and there was no great need for haste. Zinoviev and Kamenev, on the contrary, were profoundly uneasy about the continuation of the NEP, but they had been abruptly thrust into the minority. In the autumn of 1925 Zinoviev published his *Leninism,* attacking NEP as a policy of "continuous retreat," and demanded a renewal of the "policy of 1918" directed against the kulak. Zinoviev managed to use his position in Leningrad to rally the powerful Party organization there to his support, in opposition to the new Politburo majority.

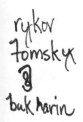

Zinoviev and Kamenev tardily recognized Stalin as the man from whom they had most to fear and carefully prepared an attack on him for the XIV Party Congress, to be held in December 1925. However, the plan completely miscarried. Kamenev, who spoke most sharply in criticism of Stalin at the Congress, was punished by demotion from full member to candidate member of the Politburo. As reconstituted just after the Congress, the Politburo had three new full members: Molotov, Voroshilov, and Kalinin, all loyal henchmen of Stalin's. Stalin also added several supporters to the list of candidate members of the Politburo and to the newly enlarged Central Committee. Shortly before, Voroshilov had replaced Michael Frunze, who had been named Trotsky's successor but had died soon afterward, as war commissar. Stalin had established a formidable position of strength within both Party and government. Leningrad remained the only stronghold of resistance, and Stalin followed up his victory at the XIV Congress by sending Sergei Kirov to replace Zinoviev as Party leader there, ordering him to clean out the opposition.

Only then, in the spring of 1926, when the supporters of all three had been scattered, did Zinoviev and Kamenev make common cause with Trotsky. Stalin's reaction was, "Ah, they have granted themselves a mutual amnesty"—since a few short months earlier they had been bitterly attacking each other. The three were united enough in their opposition to continuance of the NEP and the "alliance with the middle peasantry" on which it was based; but their past personal antagonisms made their alliance an uneasy and incongruous one.

In the meantime the Right wing of the Politburo was championing the NEP and all that it implied. Bukharin advised the peasants, "Enrich yourselves," which was a phrase Guizot had used under the French monarchy of Louis Philippe, whatever Marxist glosses might be given it. At the XIV Congress Bukharin had set forth the basis on which he accepted Stalin's theory of "socialism in one country": "We shall creep at a snail's pace, but . . . we are building socialism and . . . we shall complete the building of it." This amounted to a frame of mind to which the NEP idea was congenial, rather than something uneasily and temporarily accepted for tactical reasons.

For the time being, however, Stalin was less concerned about policy than with getting rid of his enemies in the Left Opposition led by Zinoviev and Trotsky, which was not hard for him to do. In July 1926 Lashevich, a Zinovievite who was Voroshilov's deputy war commissar, was accused of organizing oppositionist groups within the Red Army and was dismissed. Stalin seized the opportunity to expel Zinoviev from the Politburo. On October 4 all the major opposition leaders replied with a statement admitting violation of Party statutes and pledging disbandment of the opposition, but they could not refrain from repeating their policy criticisms of the Politburo majority. Stalin's reply was to remove Trotsky from the Politburo and Zinoviev from the presidency of the Comintern. However, lesser figures in the opposition leadership were allowed to recant and to obtain well-publicized rewards for their submission. At the end of October 1926 the Fifteenth Party Conference sanctioned all these maneuvers and applauded Stalin's description of the opposition leaders as "Social Democratic" deviators who were reverting to the line of the Second International.

By the beginning of 1927 the Left Opposition had thus lost any immediate hope of success, but its leaders were not yet silenced. Trotsky and his colleagues attacked the Politburo for "Thermidorism, degeneration, Menshevism, betrayal, treachery, kulak-nepman policy against the workers, against the poor peasants, against the Chinese revolution," as the Stalinist writer Popov sums it up.[1] The opposition leaders were able to blame the Politburo majority for a series of foreign setbacks: Britain's rupture of diplomatic relations with the USSR, the assassination of the Soviet ambassador in Warsaw, and especially the crushing of the Chinese Communists by Chiang Kai-shek.

In an article submitted to *Pravda,* Trotsky climaxed opposition criticism by calling on his adherents to follow the example of Clemenceau (who had opened the way to take over as French premier by attacking his predecessor's failures in World War I) in case war engulfed the USSR (a prospect taken seriously by the Communists in 1927) (see page 240). However, advocating a change of government was dangerous in the Soviet Union. If, as all good Communists agreed, the existing regime represented the proletariat, then any move to change it was bound to be antiproletarian and therefore treasonable. For that reason Stalin promptly engineered the expulsion of Trotsky and Zinoviev from the Central Committee. After the two men led street demonstrations on the tenth anniversary of the October Revolution (November 7, 1927), they were expelled from the Party.

The way was now clear for Stalin to oust the opposition from the Party en masse. The XV Congress, in December 1927, decreed as much. It might have been expected that Stalin's tactics would have drawn his opponents together, but on the contrary, the result was that they were neatly split down the middle. Trotsky refused to accept the Congress decision and was thereupon exiled to Alma Ata in Central Asia. But Zinoviev and Kamenev submitted and renounced their earlier-stated views; they were permitted to crawl back into the Party.

TROTSKY DEFEATED

As far as the Soviet Communist Party and the Comintern were concerned, the controversy between Stalin and Trotsky was now at an end; the followers of Trotsky left what they henceforth called "Stalinist" ranks and attempted to build their own parties and organize them into

• [1] N. Popov, *Outline History of the Communist Party of the Soviet Union* (2 parts; Moscow-Leningrad: Cooperative Publishing Society of Foreign Workers in the USSR, 1934), Part II, p. 313.

a Fourth International. The dispute shook and divided the Communist parties throughout the world as no such controversy before or since ever did (the immediately ensuing struggle between Stalin and Bukharin had fewer repercussions abroad, for it seemed to center on the peasant, for whom most Communists never had any use). By 1927, however, Trotsky and his sympathizers had given up any immediate hope of overcoming Stalin's ascendancy from within the Russian Party. They declared that a "bureaucracy" had come to power in the USSR, and that it must be eliminated. This assertion was difficult to explain on Marxist grounds, unless it were to be on the basis of Marx's analysis of Oriental society, and the Trotskyites shrank from that. Since Trotsky continued to believe that a distorted socialism still existed in the USSR, it was also difficult to think of any way through which the Stalinist leadership could be displaced without disturbing the economic foundation. As a result the Trotskyites had to retreat into a position comparable to that of the prewar Social Democrats, opposing all existing governments and declaring that there could be no basic improvement unless they took power. They never managed to do so anywhere.

The rank and file of the world's Communists had little chance to observe the personal differences and antagonisms between Stalin and Trotsky, and supported one or the other on the basis of his theoretical position. The differences may be briefly formulated thus: Trotsky declared that it was impossible to build socialism in Russia because the peasants did not want it; that it would only be possible to do so if the workers of the West revolted, and he was right. Stalin declared that it was impossible to wait for the Western workers to revolt before building socialism, because they were not likely to revolt in the immediate future. Therefore socialism could be built in Russia only if the Party used the peasantry, and he was also right. However, that the Western workers were not Communist, Trotsky could never admit; he could only assert that they would be soon. That the Russian peasants were not Communist, Stalin could never admit, but he could try to compel them to be. As a result Trotsky retreated into utopianism, while Stalin proceeded to establish a minority dictatorship built on terror.

BUKHARIN DEFEATED

The XV Party Congress heard Stalin declare that since the economy had been essentially restored to the prewar levels of production, the next task was to alter its character. The fundamental objective was to change agriculture, since it still included the great majority of producers.

The "way out," said Stalin, was to "amalgamate the small and tiny peasant farms gradually but steadily, not by means of pressure, but by example and persuasion, into large-scale undertakings. . . ." At the same time efforts already begun to construct new factories and expand the industrial base were to be redoubled. In retrospect the First Five-Year Plan seems to have been foreshadowed clearly enough in those decisions, but what they would mean in practice was still uncertain.

In early 1928 the Rightist adherents of "snail's pace" construction of socialism tended to think that the victory against Trotsky and Zinoviev had been theirs; indeed, the latter had predicted that it would be. Kamenev had disappeared from the ranks of the Politburo two years earlier, and Trotsky and Zinoviev had been removed shortly before the XV Congress. After the Congress the Politburo received two new recruits, Rudzutak and Kuibyshev. Added to the veterans, Stalin, Bukharin, Rykov, and Tomsky, and the three additions from the XIV Congress, Molotov, Voroshilov, and Kalinin, that made a total of nine. As it became clear that Stalin had anything but a "snail's pace" in mind for the future, Bukharin and the Right tried to win over Voroshilov and Kalinin, but in vain. Bukharin is said to have complained, "Stalin has some special hold on them that I do not know of." Both the defeated and the presumed victors were wrong. Stalin clearly dominated the new Politburo, and the three veterans of the Right were completely isolated.

During 1928 the major economic problem which the Communist leadership faced was, or was said to be, grain collection. Already in January grain purchases were short, and in the spring and summer "emergency measures" were decreed in order to obtain the grain. Stalin blamed the "kulaks," and in July ordered the Party to "strike hard at the kulaks." At this point the Right, already uneasy, was seriously alarmed. Bukharin now approached Kamenev, his erstwhile opponent, with a proposal to make common cause against Stalin, whom he termed the "Genghis Khan" of the General Secretariat. The conversation came to light, and Bukharin was compelled to make a humble apology to the Politburo.

It is hard to see what common ground Bukharin and Kamenev could have found. Although not long before Stalin had been hewing to the NEP line and denouncing supporters of "super-industrialization" and hasty economic transformation, he now appeared in the role of foe of the independent peasantry. His supporters tried to turn this *volte-face* to advantage. They approached the adherents of Trotsky and Zinoviev, urging them to come back and help do what they had—only slightly prematurely—wanted to do all along. (Trotsky had predicted that the

XV Congress would be followed by a "swing to the right" and the "restoration of capitalism"; he was completely wrong.) Delighted with the prospect of at any rate a theoretical victory, many of the former opposition responded favorably, though not Trotsky or his close colleague Rakovsky, who had been exiled to Astrakhan at the same time Trotsky was sent to Alma Ata. In a party where inconsistency could always be explained away on dialectical grounds, Stalin's tactics were able to achieve remarkable success.

Although outnumbered in the Politburo and now facing again some of their former opponents on the Left who had recovered their voice (though not their power), the Rightists had what seemed formidable support at their disposal. Bukharin had replaced Zinoviev as president of the Comintern; Tomsky counted on the backing of the trade-unions which he headed; Rykov as chairman of the Council of People's Commissars held great prestige in the administrative apparatus. Moreover, the Right had adherents in many Party organizations.

In November 1928 Stalin courted a test of strength with the Rightists. Within the Moscow Party organization, once Kamenev's province, a Rightist named Uglanov was chief. Stalin attempted to remove him, and succeeded. In April 1929 Uglanov was stripped of other posts, and Stalin quickly followed up his advantage. Bukharin was removed from the Comintern presidency, Tomsky from the trade-union leadership. In November 1929 Bukharin was ejected from the Politburo; at the XVI Congress in June 1930 Tomsky was also removed. The last of the Rightists, Rykov, lost his membership on the Politburo in December 1930, and simultaneously was replaced by Molotov as chairman of the Council of People's Commissars. The Politburo was now composed of Stalin, Voroshilov, Kalinin, Kuibyshev, Rudzutak, Kaganovich, Kirov, S. Kosior, and Ordzhonikidze. All were Stalin's supporters.

Although Stalin did not finish disposing of his Rightist adversaries until the end of 1930, his victory in both Party and governmental apparatuses was secure over a year earlier. In January 1929 he had won approval from the Politburo for the expulsion of Trotsky from the Soviet Union, Bukharin alone dissenting. Trotsky had proved not only Stalin's most capable opponent, but the only one among the first rank leaders to refuse to submit when he was beaten. He went first to Prinkipo Island, near Constantinople, then to Norway, and finally to Mexico. As Stalin's chief foe, he was punished first, which proved a blessing in disguise, for it was only later that Stalin began to execute his enemies. Trotsky enjoyed more years of freedom and eventually three years more of life than his colleagues who groveled before Stalin and remained in Russia.

From his successive places of exile, Trotsky edited his *Bulletin of the Opposition,* copies of which found their way to Moscow and were carefully scanned by the men he attacked. In somewhat similar fashion Alexander Herzen, Tsarist Russia's first internationally renowned exile, during the 1850's had published a newspaper, *The Bell,* which his Tsarist adversaries at home had eagerly devoured. There was a world of difference between Alexander II and Stalin; there were also many differences between Trotsky and Herzen, one of which was that Trotsky remained ambivalent about what should be done with Stalin, while Herzen wished to sweep away Tsarism root and branch. Trotsky regarded himself as a Communist until his death. He believed that a proletarian revolution had occurred in Russia; that the tender shoots of socialism had only been stunted and not uprooted; and that attempts to overthrow Stalin by force would only contribute to the cause of counterrevolution. However, Trotsky's restraint did not prevent Stalin from eventually murdering him.

In December 1929 the Soviet Party and government led the celebration of Stalin's fiftieth birthday. The slogan, "Stalin is the Lenin of today," was widely and incessantly employed. In some sense, indeed, it was factually correct; in any event, from 1929 to 1956 no one in the Soviet Union was suffered to deny it, or to raise openly any questions about its accuracy.

Finding A Soviet Foreign Policy (1917–1927)

CHAPTER 15

FOREIGN POLICY AND WORLD REVOLUTION

The phrase, "Soviet foreign policy," is a self-contradictory one. The adoption of the very name, "Union of Soviet Socialist Republics," from which the word "Russia" was absent, was designed for the administrative convenience of the Communists in handling the anticipated world-wide revolutions of coming years. The Russian Bolsheviks thought they were merely doing their part in a universal upheaval whose completion could not be long delayed. Trotsky expressed this early optimism when he declared that as foreign commissar he would simply issue a few revolutionary proclamations and then "shut up shop." While he was negotiating with the Germans at Brest-Litovsk, he was so confident of imminent victory throughout the world that he divulged the Bolshevik anticipations and plans to General Hoffmann. The general regarded the revelations as a curious form of madness and little more. Hoffmann's reaction was a natural one; however, even after the Soviets had spent two generations making their intentions plain, no one seemed to take them seriously. At a cocktail party in 1957, for example, Khrushchëv taunted Western envoys, "We will bury you!" but the remark was interpreted chiefly as an instance of the Soviet leader's well-known personal boorishness.

Over the four decades between 1917 and 1957, the Russian Communists have not visibly changed their objectives, but their tactics have undergone some transformation. Lenin always denounced the idea of "spontaneity" as used by the Mensheviks and emphasized in contrast the principle of organization, insisting that the Party had to lead the masses to revolutionary victory. Nevertheless, he believed in trying to gauge whether a "revolutionary situation" had developed in which the Communists might usefully act, and warned against adventures in revolution in countries where the proletariat was not yet "politically conscious." Although he was excited by the prospects when the German Communists raised minor rebellions in 1919, 1921, and 1923, the Hungarian and Bavarian Communists effected briefly successful coups in 1919, and the Polish Communists rode toward Warsaw in the baggage of the Red Army in 1920, he did not believe such attempts could succeed unless supported by the mass of the proletariat.

In the Communist planning of the 1950's, "world revolution" no longer necessarily implies mass uprisings. Lenin's reliance on old-style insurrection has been to a large extent replaced by another set of tactics, based on the armed seizure of power from above. To be sure, Lenin (for example, in 1920) did not overlook the utility of military action in bringing Communists to power, while Stalin (for example, in Eastern Europe in 1944–1946) did not neglect to use whatever semblances of mass organization he could find; but the shift in emphasis is considerable.

Means may alter ends, and no doubt the Communist regime in Poland in 1946 had a relationship to the masses very different from that of the Russian regime of 1918. But although Lenin emphasized consent (of the proletariat, not necessarily of the majority of the people), he also and more strongly emphasized Communist power, and the aim of Lenin, Stalin, and Khrushchëv has been Communist power throughout the world. When Lenin declared that the Party spoke for the proletariat, the way was clear doctrinally for the Party to do anything it pleased, the Marxist trappings of analysis being dragged along by simple definition.

When a chorus is announced, and only one singer appears on the stage, he has the choice of calling off the concert or singing alone. The latter is the alternative the Russian Communists chose, temporarily, even though they were forced to wait decades for anyone else to appear. The course of both internal and external policy was determined by the fact that the Communists came to power in Russia and nowhere else for twenty years. Domestically the result was "socialism in one country"; internationally the result was "Soviet foreign policy." In both cases the Communists accepted a tactical compromise whose end was hoped for at any moment; but if it was deferred indefinitely, so must they prolong the compromise, without forgetting the final and unchangeable objective.

The long period of waiting did have one important effect on the picture which Lenin envisaged. He warned the Bolsheviks to be prepared for the time that Communism won elsewhere and Russia again became a relatively "backward" country in the Communist camp. But during the period when Russia alone was ruled by Communists, Russia acquired prestige and seniority and above all became a strong enough industrial and military power to be able to enforce its mandates within the Communist camp when it grew rapidly after 1945. Khrushchëv gives little evidence of taking Lenin's warning seriously any longer.

ATTEMPTS AT COMMUNIST REVOLUTION IN GERMANY

From the moment the Bolsheviks came to power in Russia, they glued their eyes on developments in Germany. Here were the strongest Marxist party in Europe, the most politically-minded working class, and the most prominent leaders outside the Russian Party who sympathized with Communism, the Spartakist chiefs, led by Karl Liebknecht and Rosa Luxemburg.

On November 10, 1918, a Council of People's Commissars was established in Berlin, consisting equally of Social Democrats (led by Friedrich Ebert, who was also chancellor) and Independent Social Democrats (who had broken off from their more conservative fellows in 1916, and among whose ranks the extreme leftist Spartakist Union had been formed). Ebert, however, was far from being a Bolshevik, or even an orthodox Marxist, and called on the army General Staff for support. The Independent Socialists were divided; some leaned more toward Ebert, while others sympathized with Liebknecht. The Liebknecht faction soon withdrew from the government, and at the end of December 1918 the Spartakists entirely severed their connections with the Independent Socialists. Assuming the name "Communists," they led riots in Berlin in January but were gravely weakened by the assassination of both their leaders, Liebknecht and Luxemburg.

There followed the holding of free elections for a national assembly at Weimar, from which Ebert's Majority Social Democrats and the Catholic Center party emerged with the strongest representation. In the spring of 1919, while the new assembly was in session, new Communist outbreaks occurred in several cities. Shortly after the Communists under Béla Kun seized power in Budapest, Munich was the scene of a successful coup by Bavarian Communists led by Eugen Levine. The newly-founded Comintern hailed the revolutions in Hungary and Bavaria, but Moscow was unable to send aid, and after a few weeks the Communist regimes in central Europe were overthrown.

The German Communists were still weak, but Moscow was able to provide political, if not military, assistance. In October 1920 the Independent Socialists were debating whether they should try to overthrow the Republic or defend it from the threat from the Right. The Rightist threat seemed serious; a few months earlier the government of the Weimar Republic had managed to suppress the Kapp Putsch only with great difficulty. Zinoviev appeared at the Independent Socialist conference and forced the secession from the party of the pro-Communist elements. Taking the latter into the KAPD (*Kommunistische Arbeiterpartei Deutschlands* or Communist Workers' Party of Germany), he more than doubled its membership, at a stroke converting it into something like a mass party. Moscow hoped that German Communism was now ready for a real revolution, but the first effort of the augmented party miscarried. During the Kronstadt crisis of March 1921, Béla Kun arrived from Moscow with instructions to organize a "diversion." The German Communists struck in the Ruhr with the Mansfeld "March Action," but it was a total failure.

The III Congress of the Comintern, which met in June 1921, thereupon executed a change of front. Lenin declared that the time for hunting out "Centrists" had passed, and that the important thing was now to obtain majority support among the workers. The policy of "united front" with non-Communist workers' groups was proclaimed, and it was to be used many times during the decades to follow. With this slogan Lenin in effect confessed that expectations of "world revolution" had to be deferred for a time. The "united-front" period of Comintern tactics fitted well into the domestic needs of Russia as expressed in the NEP. Many foreign governments, businessmen, and others were ready to interpret both tactical shifts as permanent, and to seek a "business-as-usual" arrangement with the Soviet regime.

DIPLOMATIC RELATIONS WITH THE "CAPITALIST" WORLD

The Soviets established diplomatic relations with a foreign power for the first time by the Treaty of Brest-Litovsk, but the Imperial German signatory was swept away only a few months later, in November 1918. The first treaty which lasted for some years was signed in February 1920 with the independent government of Estonia—a treaty which, according to Foreign Commissar Chicherin, prepared the way for "the first experiment in peaceful coexistence with bourgeois States." The British watched closely as Lithuania followed suit in July, Latvia in August, Finland in October, and Poland in March 1921. In the latter month they signed an Anglo-Russian trade agreement.

The Communists had not troubled to make it easy for the British. At a Congress of the Peoples of the East, held in Baku in September 1920, Zinoviev had said that the Comintern "turns today to the peoples of the East and says to them, 'Brothers, we summon you to a Holy War first of all against British imperialism!' " At this there were cries of "Jehad, Jehad!" and much brandishing of picturesque Oriental weapons. However, Moscow followed up this colorful beginning in Asian foreign relations not with an Eastern crusade, but instead, in February 1921, with treaties with Afghanistan and Persia, where British interests were considerable. Thereupon the Anglo-Russian trade agreement went forward to signature. Similar commercial treaties were promptly negotiated with a number of other European states. The blockade of the Civil War period was at an end, and economic relations of sorts between Soviet Russia and the "capitalist" world were launched.

In the Far East, as in the Middle East and Europe, the stabilization of the international situation was accompanied by Soviet economic overtures. At that time (and in fact up to 1945) regarding the United States as having been more ambivalent in its participation in intervention than other powers, the Soviet regime counted on America to keep a rein on Japanese ambitions in the Far East. There was discussion with two American businessmen about concessions in the Far East; Vanderlip was to be granted oil, coal, and forest rights in Kamchatka and eastern Siberia, and Sinclair to get oil rights in north Sakhalin. It seems that Lenin regarded such proposed concessions as devices bound to insure United States governmental support for Soviet interests in the Far East, since United States capitalists were thought to control their government. Actually American pressure played a decisive part in bringing about Japanese evacuation of the Russian mainland in 1922, but it was not until 1925 that Japan recognized the Soviet regime and evacuated north Sakhalin, for which not Sinclair but Japan received the oil concession. By that time the Soviets had regained the ascendancy which Tsarist Russia had enjoyed since 1912 in Outer Mongolia, and in 1924 a Mongolian People's Republic was established under Soviet auspices. However, it was not formally annexed to the USSR.

As for China, by the time of the Russian Revolution its central republican government, established by the anti-Imperial revolt of 1911 led by Sun Yat-sen, had fallen into a state of disintegration. At the time of the Chinese Revolution Lenin had greeted it, along with comparable uprisings in Turkey and Persia, as the beginning of a great movement of "advanced Asia" against the plundering imperialists of "backward Europe." After the October Revolution in Russia, Lenin renounced on behalf of the Soviets the "unequal treaties" which had bound China, and called on it to join "its only allies and brothers in the struggle for liberty"—namely, the Russian Communists. Sun Yat-sen, who by this time had become established in the Canton region in an effort to lead the Chinese Nationalist party (Kuomintang) in overthrowing the war-lord regime in Peking, in turn responded to the October Revolution with enthusiasm. He welcomed the Soviet government as the product of a revolution which marked the breakaway of the Slavs from the "white races" and could make them the chief allies of the Chinese, just as Lenin had contended.

In 1921 the Comintern established a tiny Communist party in China—as in many other countries of both Asia and Europe, for the Comintern soon became a creator of parties rather than a union of previously existing ones. Soon Stalin was to put the new "united-front" policy into practice in earnest in China. However, as in Germany, the Soviet foreign office sought "friendly relations" with the same government the Comintern was trying to overthrow, to last until it should succeed in doing so. In May 1924 the Soviets and the Peking government signed an agreement by which the Communists in effect recovered the Tsarist rights over the Chinese Eastern Railway through Manchuria, and later in the year the *de facto* dictator of Manchuria, Chang Tso-lin, accepted the arrangement in a supplementary agreement.

ANTI-VERSAILLES DIPLOMACY

The Soviets correctly interpreted their improved relations with the British, resulting from the Anglo-Russian trade agreement, as the beginning of regularization of diplomatic contacts with the other Western powers. When the Allied Supreme Council met at Cannes in January 1922 and planned a European Economic Conference at Genoa later in the year, Lenin accepted with alacrity an invitation to take part. At Cannes the Allies even obligingly endorsed Chicherin's "coexistence" thesis, declaring that "It is for every nation to choose for itself the system (of ownership, internal economy, and government) which it prefers. . . ." Although the United States did not take part in either the

Cannes meeting or the Genoa conference, Britain dragged a reluctant France into sitting down with the Communists (and with the Germans as well, which was even more repugnant to France's Poincaré).

At Genoa the Russian delegation appeared in top hats and cutaways, which surprised and pleased a number of Western representatives and which they took as further evidence that the Russian Revolution had run its course and that its leaders had settled down to be reasonable and businesslike. Nothing came of the Genoa conference itself, but the Soviet and German delegates went farther up the Italian Riviera to Rapallo and there signed an agreement of considerable significance. By the terms of the Treaty of Rapallo (May 1922) the Soviets canceled their war claims based on destruction caused by the German army, while the Germans canceled Tsarist debts to their government on condition that the Soviets paid no other government debts. Thereby Soviet-German diplomatic relations, established officially at Brest-Litovsk, were resumed, and the two outcasts of European power politics found solace in each other.

The kind of friendship the Soviets were seeking with the "bourgeois" German Republic was obviously a limited one; the Communists had already tried repeatedly to overthrow it, and were to try again in a few months. Nevertheless the Treaty of Rapallo did inaugurate a period of relatively extensive commercial and military intercourse between the two countries. From 1922 to 1934 Soviet relations with Germany were closer than with any other power.

However, the significance of the treaty to Soviet foreign policy was broader than any "friendship" with Germany resulting from it. Official Soviet doctrine on international relations emphasized the "two camps"; there was the camp of "capitalism" and the camp of socialism (the USSR only). In the former, it was argued, existed exploitation, misery, and aggressive tendencies; in the latter, the opposite. However, the evil capitalist world was not to be treated as a single unit. The Soviet doctrine of diplomacy has always held that when the USSR enters into relations with the capitalist powers, it behaves as they do (although that has, to be sure, often meant behaving like a caricature of how capitalist governments are mistakenly thought to behave). As soon as the Soviets accepted the necessity of having a foreign policy, what they tried to do, beginning at Rapallo, was to restore something like a balance of power in Europe.

In 1922 the European diplomatic scene was dominated by France, as one of the victorious powers of World War I and the peace of Versailles. By then the United States had defected from the Allied coalition and Britain was reluctant to accept postwar continental commitments. France had labored to construct an alliance system in which the *cordon sanitaire* of Poland, Czechoslovakia, and Rumania was to check Germany—and Soviet Russia as well. Therefore the Soviets attempted to offset that system by agreement with "bourgeois" Germany—hoping it would soon be replaced by a Communist Germany—victim of Versailles. They tried to do something similar in the Middle East, where French influence was newly installed in Syria but where British power continued to be strong, by agreement with the new nationalist regime of Mustafa Kemal which had arisen in defeated Turkey. Similar calculations went into the collaboration with Sun Yat-sen's Kuomintang, which sought power in China, where British interests were also considerable. For more than a decade after 1922 Britain and France, the architects of intervention and the chief capitalist powers, were the chief targets of Soviet diplomacy; the other arm of Moscow in foreign affairs, the Comintern, impartially tried to foster revolution against all bourgeois governments.

THE RUHR CRISIS

In 1923 the Communists thought their hour had struck in Germany. Poincaré answered German default on reparations by French military occupation of the Ruhr, the industrial heart of Germany and all Europe. The inhabitants of the Ruhr responded by passive resistance, but the Germany economy was hard hit, and inflation reached an extent unparalleled in any other industrial country in recent times. The "united-front" policy was invoked by Moscow's German specialist, Karl Radek, in an astonishing manner. The extreme Right in Germany was in the forefront of the outcry against French occupation, and it was in that direction that Radek made overtures. A nationalist, Albert Leo Schlageter, who had been shot by the French for sabotage, was hailed by Radek as a martyr. The new line of "National Bolshevism," in which Germany was depicted as the suffering semi-colony of France, shocked the doctrinaire Communists without evoking much response from the Right. However, there was without doubt deep popular discontent and many strikers were evincing a militant mood. In Moscow there was some dissension about how to act. Zinoviev, Radek, and Trotsky were in different ways inclined to hope for great things from a German uprising, while Stalin believed insurrection foolhardy at the moment.

Karl Radek

At length the leader of the German Communists, Heinrich Brandler, was given a set of confused instructions, which were executed in an equally confused manner. In October 1923, when the worst of the crisis had already passed, the Communists attempted, by entering "united-front" governments with Social Democrats in the states of Saxony and Thuringia, to work from the country in toward the capital. They were smashed in the provinces. Adolf Hitler seized the occasion to launch his beer-hall putsch in Munich, invoking the Communist danger and attacking the Republic as well, but his Rightists were suppressed too for the time being. It seemed that the German Republic had weathered the worst and survived. Brandler lost his leadership in the KAPD. In June 1924 the V Congress of the Comintern decided that the remedy lay in "bolshevization" of all Communist parties—that is, for them to be modeled more closely on the lines of the Russian Party—but the "united-front" line was not changed.

THE "UNITED FRONT" IN BRITAIN AND CHINA

The two countries where the "united-front" tactic was used with most determination were Britain and China. Britain's first Labor Government, formed in 1924 under Ramsay MacDonald, extended diplomatic recognition to the USSR, despite the King's undimmed memories of how the Bolsheviks had dealt with his late relatives, Nicholas II and his family, not to mention very strong political pressures. The MacDonald government did not last out the year. The Conservatives published a letter which was alleged to be from Zinoviev to the British Communists urging forcible overthrow of the government, and the "Zinoviev letter" hastened MacDonald's fall.[1]

Although elections removed the Labor Government, a section of British workers continued to move leftward, in part as a result of economic depression. In 1925 there was established an Anglo-Russian trade-union committee. Among its wider aims was that of bringing about fusion between the International Federation of Trade Unions, sponsored by the socialist or "Amsterdam" International, and the weak Communist league of unions called the Profintern.[2] The committee's chance for revolution in Britain seemed at hand in May 1926. A general strike erupted, with the Communist-infiltrated coal miners taking a

• [1] It also may have hastened Zinoviev's fall in the USSR, and he himself suspected that Stalin's secret police planted the forged document where the Tories would find it. See Ruth Fischer, *Stalin and German Communism* (Cambridge: Harvard University Press, 1948), pp. 458–463.

• [2] The Russian use of the phrase *professionalnyi soiuz* (abbreviated *profsoiuz*) to mean trade-union originated in the period of the Revolution of 1905, when the first large national unions formed were actually unions of professional men rather than of workers.

prominent role. However, the strike proved a great disappointment to the Communists. The disciplined Londoners tried to walk to work even though the subway ("underground") had ceased to operate. Worst of all was the sort of social cohesion shown in the famed football game played in Plymouth between the strikers and the police, in which the chief constable's wife kicked off. The strike soon collapsed, and the leaders in Moscow argued over who was to blame. Trotsky ascribed the failure to the tactic of collaboration with the British Laborites, but Stalin denied it and insisted on continuing the alliance until the British unionists themselves abolished the Anglo-Russian committee in 1927.

Many Communists hoped that the chief capitalist stronghold, Britain, could be stormed by way of China. The report of the Sixth Plenum of the Executive Committee of the Comintern (February 1926), published under the title *The Itinerary of Revolution,* suggested as much. While prospects of success in Europe had dimmed, much was expected, in Zinoviev's words, from "a new, exceptionally important factor . . . *the movement in China,* which is fraught with many surprises." At that stage the Communists were less interested in the repercussions which success in China might have on the rest of Asia than in the effects on Europe. What excited them was the hope that if the tentacles of British imperialism could be cut off in China, the helpless body in the home island could be speared easily.

By 1926 the Russian Communists were already deeply embroiled in Chinese events. Five years earlier one of the Comintern's Far Eastern specialists, G. Maring, had talked with Sun Yat-sen in the Canton region. Maring was a former Dutch teacher, whose real name was Sneevliet. In Java he had observed the local Communists work with some success within the Javanese nationalist organization, *Sarekat Islam.* He recommended a similar tactic for China: co-operation between the tiny Chinese Communist party and Sun's Kuomintang. Adolf Joffe was sent by Moscow to continue talks along such lines. In 1923 he concluded an agreement with Sun by which the Chinese Nationalists on the one hand and Moscow and the Chinese Communists on the other were to work together to overthrow the Peking government. That September Michael Borodin was sent from Moscow to China with the mission of putting the agreement into effect. He was supported by ample funds and a host of Russian experts, advisers, and military men.

Sun responded by sending many Chinese, including Chiang Kai-shek, to study in the Soviet Union, and many returned, as did Chiang, to attempt to incorporate their experience in action. "In reorganizing the party," said Sun, "we have Soviet Russia as our model, hoping to achieve a real revolutionary success." To a correspondent who inquired what Borodin's real name was (it was Gruzenberg), Sun replied, "His name is Lafayette." Sun, whose own political conceptions were always vague and eclectic, began to mix Marxism into his philosophy during his last months. However, his real bond with Moscow was an organizational rather than ideological one, and the organizational ties between the Kuomintang and the Communists continued after his death in 1925.

Stalin's ideological program for China was to secure the "hegemony of the proletariat" within the "bloc of four classes" (proletariat, peasantry, petty bourgeoisie, and national bourgeoisie) which the Kuomintang as a whole was deemed to represent in the struggle against imperialism. Stalin argued that China internally was on the threshold of a "bourgeois-democratic" revolution, complicated by a common national antagonism to foreign imperialism. Therefore, he contended, the Chinese situation was in important respects parallel to that in Russia on the eve of 1905.

However, Trotsky dissented sharply from this view. He had the same scorn for any possible allies of the Communists within China that he had had for any within Russia. He argued that capitalism was already strong in China, that it was necessary to strike for Communist power and a socialist economy, and that to collaborate with the Chinese bourgeoisie was "Menshevism"—which, in a way, it was. Thus the prerevolutionary polemics of the Russian Marxists were revived in a context where they bore an even dimmer relation to reality than they had in Russia. The important difference was that in 1925–1927 Stalin and Trotsky were engaged in a struggle for power in an existing Communist government, and theoretical successes or failures in China might have immediate power implications in Russia as well as China.

In 1925 the revolutionary tide seemed to be rising in Chinese cities, and the preparations of the Nationalist-Communist alliance were beginning to bear fruit. As Sun had demanded, the Kuomintang had been reorganized on the lines of the Soviet Communist Party. The Nationalist army had been revamped with a new officer corps trained at the military academy established at Whampoa near Canton under Chiang Kai-shek, assisted (and sometimes resisted) by the Soviet General Bliukher (called Galen in China). The allies were ready to advance north to take over the entire country.

However, there were signs that Sun's successor as Kuomintang leader, Chiang Kai-shek, lacked enthusiasm for the alliance with Moscow. In March 1926 he purged a number of Chinese Communists from high political and military posts and even arrested some Russians. Borodin tried to patch up the rift by going along with what Chiang had done, and surface harmony was restored. Since only a month earlier the Kuomintang had actually been admitted to the Comintern as a "sympathizer-member," Moscow chose to believe that all was well.

In the summer of 1926 the Nationalists marched north. One column, headed by the more leftist Kuomintang leaders, Borodin and the Russians, and some Chinese Communists, moved inland through Wuhan. Chiang led another column to Nanchang, and then headed for the coast. The evidence suggests that he was hoping to rid himself of the Soviet connection and obtain Western aid. He paused in his march to take over Shanghai and in so doing crushed the Communists there in April 1927. The conflict between Chiang and the Wuhan group now came into the open, and as Chiang established his capital in Nanking the break was complete.

Amid a confused series of negotiations and struggles, the Wuhan government broke up, and in July 1927 Borodin returned home. By 1928 Chiang completed the unification of China under his own leadership. Whatever Trotsky's plan for China might have achieved, Stalin's efforts had failed completely. Moscow now repudiated the Kuomintang, and ordered the Chinese Communists to conduct an insurrection against Chiang. This was the affair of the "Canton Commune" in December 1927, resulting in a final and bloody defeat for the Communists. The fiasco to which Stalin's tactics had brought Communism in China—and which Trotsky had virtually predicted—was an important factor behind Trotsky's fall from power; Stalin could not permit him to claim events had proved him right.

Trotsky had hastened his own political ruin by his "Clemenceau statement," issued during the synthetic "war crisis" of 1927 (see p. 224). As the Soviets had admitted their intention to use China as a means of weakening Britain, the British grew restive. After conducting a raid for documents on the Arcos trading company in May 1927, Britain's government broke diplomatic relations with the USSR. Paris followed suit by a *de facto* break. The assassination in June of Voikov, the Soviet minister in Warsaw, was the climax to a series of diplomatic disasters.

In July Stalin spoke of a "real and actual threat" of an anti-Soviet war by the capitalist powers led by England. The "war scare" of 1927 had no substance whatsoever in fact, although it may have assisted Stalin in disposing of the opposition within the Party and diverted attention from the failures of Soviet foreign policy. In 1927 the only bright spot abroad was Central Asia, where a series of interlocking pacts among the USSR, Turkey, Persia, and Afghanistan were signed from late 1925 to late 1927. Otherwise the record of both the Soviet foreign office and the Comintern seemed to be one of general catastrophe. At the beginning of the period of his personal rule, Stalin found the slogan, "socialism in one country" especially useful, for it did not look as if Communists were going to succeed in taking over any other country in the near future.

The Revolution,
the Arts,
and the Church (1917–1927)

CHAPTER 16

THE REVOLUTION AND THE ARTS

In Lenin's view, art and nothing else could serve as a substitute for religion. Since he believed religion ought to be and would be destroyed in the future, he considered the role of the arts to be of great importance. Amid the heated debates and revolutionary intoxication of the first years of the Soviet regime, he told Clara Zetkin, "Every artist, and every one who regards himself as such, claims as his proper right the liberty to work freely according to his ideal, whether it is any good or not. There you have the ferment, the experiment, the chaos. Nevertheless, we are Communists, and must not quietly fold our hands and let chaos bubble as it will. We must also try to guide this development consciously, clearly, and to shape and determine its results."

Lenin recognized the fact that the artist claimed creative liberty, but he declared that the regime, not the artist, should and would determine the outcome in the arts. He himself was far from being a cultural revolutionary in the sense of wishing to break all the artistic images of the Tsarist period and build *de novo*. Of the cultural "isms" which churned around him, he said, "I do not understand them. I take no joy in them."

It is well known that he preferred Pushkin, who wrote a century earlier, to his contemporary Mayakovsky, even though the latter became a sort of quasi-official bard of the Bolshevik Revolution. Lenin's personal esthetic preferences ran to a kind of Russian Victorianism, as did Stalin's; the difference was that Lenin did not try to enforce his preferences. He looked for new and exciting developments in the arts, but he did not pretend to know exactly what they would be like, and while he lived he attacked what he regarded as "unhealthy" schools of the arts without prohibiting other artists from working.

During World War I, many writers and artists had been swept into uniform or war work and added patriotism to their other attitudes with which Bolshevism was incompatible. On the morrow of the October Revolution, few of them adhered to the Bolshevik regime. During the five years following many of the most outstanding emigrated, including the prose writers Bunin, Andreyev, Kuprin, Merezhkovsky, Remizov, Gorky, and Alexis Tolstoy, the poets Balmont and Ilia Ehrenburg, and the artists Repin, Benois, Somov, and Korovin. Others, including the Acmeists Akhmatova and Mandelshtam, fell silent but remained in Russia. Several prominent symbolists, especially Blok, Bely, and Briusov, and the young "peasant poets," Sergei Esenin and Nicholas Kliuev, made peace with the regime, "accepting" the Revolution as a merited catastrophe for the social order they had known, and an event which brought Russia a new hope to which they ascribed a mystical or religious character. The Futurists, led by Mayakovsky, threw themselves boldly into the Bolshevik camp. However, genuine Bolshevik artists were rare indeed. Even Gorky, who had been a friend of Lenin's and a Bolshevik sympathizer for years, went back to Italy, maintaining an ambiguous kind of link with the regime. The only prominent Old Bolshevik artist to remain in Russia was Demian Bedny (pseudonym of E. A. Pridvorov), a poet of peasant origin and strong atheist convictions.

The ideological *mariages de convenance* entered into by the non-Bolshevik poets were ill-fated from the start. In his remarkable poem of 1918, *The Twelve,* Blok celebrated the Revolution in a non-Marxian vein. The same year, in *The Scythians,* he sang of Russian self-sufficiency and greatness as well as his own scorn for the West. In 1921 he commemorated Pushkin's birth in a public address, charging that freedom—not "the freedom of being a liberal," but "the freedom of creation, the secret freedom"—was being taken away in Russia; he continued, "And the poet dies because he can no longer breathe: life has lost its meaning." A few months later Blok died. Briusov died in 1924; Bely lived until 1934, although he ceased to write poetry and turned to novels and memoirs. In 1925 Esenin committed suicide, writing in his own blood his last poem:

> My poems are no longer needed here.
> And I too—by your leave—I am no longer needed. . . .

The individualistic poets of the Silver Age stifled under the Soviet regime and disappeared. There survived from that period Boris Pasternak, one of the greatest lyricists of the twentieth century, and the aging Akhmatova, both trying to work under Soviet rule, but no later poet of comparable gifts has appeared.

THE CIVIL WAR PERIOD: THE PROLETKULT

Not merely the coming of the Bolsheviks, but also the hunger, cold, and misery of the Civil War transformed the conditions under which artists had to work. What it meant for the artist—or any man—to survive the winters of 1918–1919 and 1919–1920 in the great cities is well shown in Eugene Zamiatin's short story, "The Cave." Although during these grim years little creative work could be done, the lines were drawn for the ideological struggle over what sort of art was proper to a Communist system. In 1919 and 1920 the writers gathered at their preferred cafes in Petrograd and Moscow to declaim their works, debate the shape of the art to come, and revel in what many regarded as new-found freedom. Mayakovsky in his "Left March" produced a revolutionary ode characteristic of this dissonant period, which fairly begs to be shouted:

> Deploy in marching ranks!
> There is no room for verbal tricks.
> Silence, you orators!
> Your turn to speak,
> Comrade Rifle.
> Enough of living by the law
> Given by Adam and Eve.
> We will ride the mare of history 'till she drops.
> Left!
> Left!
> Left! . . .[1]

However, the creative artists, exhilarated with revolution and drunk with history, were not to be the ones to decide what a Communist esthetic

• [1] Translated by D. W. T.

should be like; that was already being debated by the ideologists. The group around the magazine *Proletarskaia Kul'tura,* or *Proletkult,* led by A. A. Bogdanov, laid claim to express proletarian interests in the sphere of culture as the Party did in social and political matters and the trade-unions (so Bogdanov said) in the realm of the economy. This amounted to a demand that *Proletkult,* free from Party control, should itself be allowed to act as collective dictator over the arts. *Proletkult* labored assiduously at organizing writing schools for workers in many Russian towns, and in these schools Bely and Briusov, Zamiatin, Gumilëv (who was to be shot in 1921 for alleged counterrevolutionary activity), and other prominent writers served as instructors. Lunacharsky, the people's commissar for education, took the organization under his protection, although he had a milder attitude toward the great art of the past than some of the spokesmen of *Proletkult.* At this point Lenin saw a danger of revival of the old currents of 1909, then supported by the same Bogdanov and Lunacharsky, against which he had inveighed in *Materialism and Empirio-Criticism.* In December 1920 the Central Committee attacked *Proletkult* as a cover for the philosophical deviation of "Machism" and subordinated the group to state control.

Proletkult was composed of theoreticians rather than artists and did not include the extreme radical wing of the writers, who talked of uprooting all the culture of the past. Such men belonged to the Smithy-Cosmist (*Kuznitsa-Kosmist*) group, so called from their organizations in Moscow and Petrograd respectively. One of their number, Vladimir Kirilov, in a poem entitled *We,* called for the proletariat to destroy museums "in the name of our Tomorrow." The same title, *We,* was given by Eugene Zamiatin to a novel he wrote during the Civil War period, but it was a humanist attack on Soviet Utopianism, which Zamiatin already foresaw would lead to a dehumanized monster state and what would later be called totalitarianism.[2]

THE NEP PERIOD: THE FELLOW TRAVELERS

The coming of the NEP marked a sharp turn in cultural as well as political and economic policy. In February 1921 there was formed a group of young men, for the most part writers of prose, called the Serapion Brothers. When asked whether they were for or against the Revolution, they replied that they were "for the Hermit Serapion"—a character in a story by the German writer E. T. A. Hoffmann. However,

• [2] Aldous Huxley's *Brave New World* and George Orwell's *Nineteen Eighty-Four* later followed the pattern of Zamiatin's *We* very closely.

the Formalist critic and extreme Westernizer, Leo Lunts, added that this did not mean indifference to politics: "Each of us has his own ideology, each paints his hut in his own color." Indeed the more prominent members of the group, Michael Zoshchenko, Constantine Fedin (at thirty their oldest adherent), Vsevolod Ivanov (who pioneered the literary treatment of Asiatic Russia), and others, were of such diverse persuasions that, as one scholar puts it, the Brothers constituted "a defensive alliance rather than a literary school."[3]

To such writers who were willing to go along with the regime but eschewed ideological battle either for or against it, Trotsky sympathetically applied the word, "*poputchiki*" (fellow travelers)—a term which was to find a much wider usage abroad. Many of the fellow travelers found haven in the pages of a new "fat monthly" (*tolstyi zhurnal*), *Red Virgin Soil* (*Krasnaia Nov'*), edited by A. A. Voronsky. Voronsky was a Marxist critic who agreed with Trotsky's opinion that art had its own "peculiar laws," in opposition to the militant ideologists who argued that art should merely reflect life mechanically. Both *Red Virgin Soil* and the large publishing enterprise named *International Literature,* under pressure from Gorky and supported by Trotsky, gave the nonpolitical writers both protection and subsistence.

The "literary NEP" produced a modest quantity of good, rather than great, writing. Boris Pilniak, in his novel of 1922 called *The Naked Year* (*Golyi God*), employed the artifices and stylistic idiosyncrasies of prerevolutionary times and interpreted the Revolution in a neo-populist manner as a resurgence of the native tradition. Eugene Zamiatin, in *We* (which he read aloud in public but which remained unpublished in Russian until an *émigré* edition of 1952) and other satirical novels and stories, combined experimental craftsmanship with the ideology of the non-Communist Left. Other satirists, such as Valentine Katayev and the team of Ilia Ilf and Katayev's brother, "Eugene Petrov," produced amusing and biting works which were officially approved in the NEP atmosphere, where both survivals of a "presocialist" past and unavoidable present concessions to "capitalism" were recognized to exist and to merit the writer's scourge.

From 1923 to 1925 the debate over literary ideology reached its height. In March 1923 the so-called LEF ("Left Front of Literature") movement, composed largely of Futurists following the lead of Mayakovsky, founded a journal called *LEF.* It was backed not only by writers but also by men from the theater, especially the two wayward pupils

• [3] Victor Erlich, *Russian Formalism: History-Doctrine* (The Hague: Mouton, 1955), p. 127.

of the great producer Stanislavsky, Meyerhold, who wanted to introduce "the October Revolution into the theater," and Vakhtangov. LEF came under fire from two directions. It was too authoritarian to suit the fellow travelers in its ideological demand for "integration of literature into life"; while the militant proletarian writers attacked it for its "decadent" roots and "intellectual-bourgeois" membership.

The proletarian writers launched their attack on LEF in a magazine called *On Guard* (*Na postu*), which began to appear in the summer of 1923. The *Napostovtsy* proclaimed the "primacy of content" over artistic form, and proceeded to bait not only the avant-garde Futurists and non-political fellow travelers, but also ideologically-minded critics who disagreed with them. LEF was torn apart, and its magazine disappeared in 1925; Mayakovsky attempted to revive it in 1927 as the *New LEF,* but in vain.

The militants of *Na postu* were finally bridled, as the *Proletkult* had been, by the regime itself. In January 1925 the I All-Union Congress of Proletarian Writers was held; it passed a resolution denouncing the line of Trotsky and Voronsky, who defended the fellow travelers. However, the militants were soon chastised. In July the Party Central Committee issued a warning against a "frivolous and disdainful attitude toward the old cultural heritage and toward literary specialists"—that is, toward the fellow travelers. The resolution was drafted by Bukharin, who believed that "snail's pace" progress toward socialism left ample time for the development of a "proletarian culture" and thus, like Trotsky, wanted to refrain from cultural controls.

For the next three years the fellow travelers—not, it should be made clear, anti-Communist writers—were relatively free to write what they liked. Publishing houses multiplied, newspaper circulation mounted rapidly, and the normal academic life of the universities was resumed. Already in 1923 relations with *émigré* writers in Berlin, Paris, and Prague had become possible, and in that year Ilia Ehrenburg and Alexis Tolstoy returned to the USSR. Many artists took advantage of the opportunity of visiting the West and of entertaining Western visitors in Russia. Along with economic recovery seemed to come a hope of a newer, brighter future, purged of the old evils and entailing a better life and broader cultural interests for the masses.

Under the new atmosphere the great tradition of the Russian novel seemed to stir again in Isaac Babel's *Red Cavalry* (1926), which depicted the savagery of the Civil War along with the nobler emotions, and Leonid Leonov's *The Thief* (1927), which appeared to owe part of its inspiration to Dostoevsky. Despite the thrusts of Communist critics,

Pasternak continued to write fine poetry and some prose, and the poet Nicholas Tikhonov passed through a period of exoticism and experimentalism before 1930, when he turned to convert his talent into a weapon on the "ideological front."

The later NEP was a time of innovations and ferment in the other arts as well. The greatest Soviet film-maker, Sergei Eisenstein, produced *Potëmkin,* praise of which sounded around the world. In the theater Meyerhold and Vakhtangov attempted to develop new types of play production, and while Stanislavsky was aging, his old collaborator, Nemirovich-Danchenko, continued to work to preserve his techniques and achievements. In the field of music, an early Group of Revolutionary Composers, comparable to *Proletkult* in literature, was followed in 1925 by a Group of Young Professional Composers, led by A. A. Davidenko. The young militants criticized the composer Dmitry Shostakovich (also young, but not then militant) for his kinship to the modern musicians of the bourgeois West, but he continued to work, and in 1927 one of the greatest living Russian composers, Sergei Prokofiev, returned from exile. In the realm of the arts all was ferment, as Lenin expected. Much of the diversity and talent of the Silver Age had been lost, but some of it remained or had been restored, and the spread of theaters and schools throughout the country and the appearance of new writers and artists even from the backward eastern borderlands argued that culture was more widely diffused than before. So far the state had intervened chiefly to prevent rather than to enforce cultural dictatorship, even though the noisy ideologists who had governmental connections could still make it difficult for real artists to do their work. Under Stalin, however, the state was shortly to assume quite a different role in the arts.

THE REVOLUTION AND THE CHURCH

In an article written in 1905, Lenin restated succinctly the Marxist view of religion:

> Religion teaches those who toil in poverty all their lives to be resigned and patient in this world, and consoles them with the hope of reward in heaven. As for those who live upon the labor of others, religion teaches them to be charitable in earthly life, thus providing a cheap justification for their whole exploiting existence and selling them at a reasonable price tickets to heavenly bliss. Religion is the opium of the people. Religion is a kind of spiritual

> intoxicant, in which the slaves of capital drown their humanity and their desires for some sort of decent human existence.[4]

Lenin not only criticized the social effects of religion as he saw them, but as a philosophical materialist he objected to any kind of religious belief in principle. However, in the same article he warned that "the religious question must [not] be pushed into the foreground where it does not belong. We must not allow the forces waging a genuinely revolutionary economic and political struggle to be broken up for the sake of opinions and dreams that are of third-rate importance . . . and which are being steadily relegated to the rubbish heap by the normal course of economic development."

After taking power, Lenin applied the same caution in approaching problems affecting religion and the churches. He preferred to let the churches "wither away" along with the state as the economic "foundation" of society was transformed. However, he did so not because he minimized the importance of religious belief as an obstacle to Communism but because he was wary of its surviving strength among the Russian masses and preferred to avoid direct combat with it.

While the Russian peasants and many of the urban groups held fast to Orthodox Christianity, the intelligentsia had in large part defected from religion before the Revolution, accepting philosophical materialism and socialism in one form or another (see p. 31). Even some of the advanced clergy had embraced variations of a "social gospel" and even socialism. There had been countercurrents; some former radicals such as Nicholas Berdiaev and Sergei Bulgakov had embraced Christianity, and there were elements among the clergy striving for a genuine theological revival which would restore to the church some of the vigor it had lost during the two centuries it had lain under state domination. However, the leadership of the Russian Orthodox Church in general remained weak, and in 1917 it appeared divided between a dominant group which resisted any kind of change and a party of dissidents who were willing to compound with the Communists.

The overthrow of the monarchy hurled the clergy into a situation for which they were ill prepared. The Provisional Government was largely composed of men who were hostile or indifferent to religion, but outside

• [4] From the article "Socialism and Religion," written for *Novaia Zhizn'*, No. 28, December 16, 1905, and reprinted in Volume 7 of "Little Lenin Library," *Religion*, by International Publishers in 1933. The phrase, "Religion is the opium of the people," was earlier used by Marx.

of proclaiming freedom of religion in July (including that of altering one's denomination or professing no religion at all), it left the Orthodox Church for the most part to its own devices. In the first few months after the February Revolution several clergymen who had been compromised by association with Rasputin resigned or were eased out of posts of influence. The clerical leaders then set about to convene an All-Russian Church Council (*Sobor*), the first since 1681. It met in Moscow in August 1917.

At the council a new dissident current was in evidence. There had arisen around the Theological Academy in Petrograd a League of Democratic Clergy and Laymen, led by Dean Alexander Vvedensky and others. It was linked with the socialist clerical groups of the prerevolutionary period, and certain members of the Provisional Government worked closely with it. Some of its representatives spoke publicly and to soldiers at the front, favoring continuation of the war and attempting to counter Bolshevik agitation.

However, the Petrograd liberals were outnumbered at the council by traditionally-minded conservative clerics. Although there was no official expression of the council's view, the dominant conservatives there voiced open sympathy for General Kornilov before and after his attempted march on Petrograd. Over the objections of the Petrograd liberals, the council proceeded to elect (again for the first time since Peter the Great) a Patriarch, who, unlike the early patriarchs, was to be merely *primus inter pares* in relation to the other bishops and responsible to periodic church councils. Three candidates were chosen by vote of the delegates; the name of one of the three was then drawn by lot. Metropolitan Tikhon of Moscow was proclaimed Patriarch, and he was invested in November.

In the meantime the Bolsheviks had come to power. Lenin's policy toward the Orthodox Church at first was as cautious as his earlier pronouncements on religion. In January 1918 the Soviet government decreed the separation of "church from state, and school from church," and for the time being did not attack the church directly, although there was some official seizure of church properties. Patriarch Tikhon anathematized the Bolsheviks and condemned the peace of Brest-Litovsk, and he was echoed by other members of the church council. In August the council dissolved itself; Tikhon was left in control, assisted by the Holy Synod and the Higher Church Administration also chosen by the council.

In October 1918 Tikhon boldly denounced Communist rule: "Where is freedom of speech and of the press? Where is freedom of religion?"

The government retaliated by placing him under house arrest. During the Civil War Lenin stepped up the seizure of church properties, which netted the regime over seven billion rubles, and dissolved the monasteries, at the same time exposing a variety of "relic frauds" in which purportedly miraculously preserved saints' corpses were revealed to be wax images and the like.[5] During the same period the Communist Party sometimes had to prescribe expulsion for young male members who yielded to their brides on the question of church weddings and other religious observances (such measures had to be invoked into the 1950's to restrain the weak from ideological compromise). Many priests sympathized with White forces, and some even fought in their ranks. However, in September 1919 the Patriarch called for submission to the temporal power and dissociated the church from the White cause. Plainly the Soviet regime was going to last longer than the church council had anticipated.

During the famine of 1921 which followed the Civil War, the high clergy undertook to organize relief for the starving. However, the state itself took over the relief organization and began to requisition church treasures for the purpose. The Patriarch acquiesced but insisted that consecrated articles be exempt from requisition. *Pravda* admitted that the Soviets' main interest was not in obtaining the consecrated articles themselves but in making their confiscation "serve to sunder the crumbling body of the former state church." Charged with withholding the sacred vessels, collusion with the monarchist ecclesiastical council held in Sremski Karlovtsy in Yugoslavia in November 1921, and other anti-Soviet activities, Patriarch Tikhon was arrested in May 1922.

At the same moment a group of Petrograd liberals, including Dean Vvedensky but now headed by Father Krasnitsky, organized a movement called the "Living Church." They established an irregular Temporary Higher Church Administration, which received Communist recognition. The emergence of the Living Church originally reflected, in part, a desire among the parish priests to curb the power of the monks and the bishops (who were drawn from the ranks of the monks), and in part a genuine wish among the clergy for liberalization of church regulations and practices. However, the movement was utilized by the regime, in particular the secret police, for political purposes. As a Soviet official declared, the regime intended to "profit by the discord existing among

• [5] Such exposures seem to have had only limited effect on the faithful, for forty years later the Soviets were still prominently displaying "relic frauds" in the museums attached to the few surviving monasteries, suggesting that simple piety still retained an attachment to such relics.

the clergy with the sole purpose of drawing the people away from all and every religion."

At first the Living Church was allowed to convene a council, in April 1923, which declared Tikhon unfrocked and abolished the Patriarchate. The Soviet regime accepted these decisions; nevertheless, immediately after the council met, it released Tikhon from arrest in return for his confession of error and a promise not to oppose Soviet rule. Apparently with the approval of the authorities, Tikhon promptly embarked on a struggle with the Living Church, which was by this time also beset from within by its own dissident and splinter movements. The reformist groups, nevertheless, continued to believe that they had governmental support, and they managed to take over control of about one-third of the Orthodox churches in the whole country.

In April 1925 Tikhon died. A gathering of bishops named Metropolitan Peter head of the "Patriarchal" Church, but he was arrested in December and in the summer of 1926 exiled to Siberia. Peter was replaced by his own choice as deputy, Metropolitan Sergei of Nizhny Novgorod. Sergei was also arrested in early 1926 but was soon released. In June he appealed to the government for recognition of the Patriarchal Church. Shortly afterwards a group of bishops who were in exile at the Solovetsky Monastery in the White Sea issued a remarkable statement on church-state relations. The Solovetsky bishops attacked the reformists for making "pitiful attempts to instill into the consciences of the faithful the idea that Christianity in its essence did not differ from Communism," but they warned that reconciliation between the Patriarchal Church and the regime was necessary to prevent the schismatic reformists from becoming a "state church" and called on the clergy and faithful to render allegiance to the Soviet power while retaining their doctrinally orthodox belief.

In May 1927 Sergei was recognized by the regime, and the Living Church was allowed to die unregretted. A large number of the clergy went along with the conditional reconciliation, although many abroad accused Sergei of having surrendered the church to the secret police, whose influence on clerical appointments mounted rapidly. It seems that two different types of "conciliators" were to be found among the clergy: one, following the reasoning of the Solovetsky bishops, accepted what they considered the lesser evil out of repugnant practical necessity but disdained theoretical compromise; the other, of which Sergei was an example, soon grew hazy as to where compromise stopped and integrity began, and ended by serving as pliant tools of the Communists.

Although the Soviet regime recognized Sergei, it was far from surrendering to religion. The government's manipulations of the various church groups had gone along simultaneously with a campaign of antireligious propaganda and agitation. In 1922 there began to be published a newspaper called *The Godless* (*Bezbozhnik*), and such books as Sir James Frazer's *The Golden Bough* and the works of the French materialists of the Enlightenment were issued in Russian editions for antireligious purposes. In 1925 a group around the newspaper *The Godless* organized itself as the League of the Militant Godless, and by 1929 it claimed close to half a million members. Emelian Yaroslavsky, Demian Bedny, and other leaders of the league wrote treatises and satires attacking religion, which were widely distributed.

A decade after the Bolsheviks took power, the Russian Orthodox Church was functioning on a scale not much smaller than that of 1917, and Islam and other religions retained much of their former following. However, the evidence suggests that antireligious propaganda had made a good deal of headway among the youth of the cities, and the organized religious bodies had been shrewdly weakened and divided. Believing that religion had already been undermined by being deprived of its influence on the young people and by suffering disruption of its institutional leadership, Stalin prepared to launch the kind of direct attack on the churches against which Lenin had warned.

Part THREE

Stalin's Rule Before World War II

Stalin and the First Five-Year Plan (1928–1932)

CHAPTER 17

THE END OF THE BREATHING SPACE

Under the New Economic Policy the ordinary citizen of the USSR had obtained a partial respite from state interference in his life, and the economy had undergone substantial recovery from the collapse brought on by World War I and the Civil War. By 1928 the indices of production were generally back to what they had been in 1914. Although a severe struggle was still raging at the top levels of Party leadership over who and what policy would determine the fate of the people, for seven years they had been for the most part left alone to lead their own lives.

The results were examined under peculiar circumstances by an old monarchist, V. V. Shulgin. In 1926 he was approached by the purported representatives of monarchist groups inside Russia with an invitation to return clandestinely and visit the country and his political confreres. He accepted, talked with circles in Russia which appeared to be monarchist, and returned to Western Europe, only to find that he had throughout been the guest of the secret police. In any case he saw something of Russia and reported that the country "is just the same, only shabbier." During NEP an American, Calvin Hoover, asked peasants if they had more freedom or less under the Communist regime and frequently received in essence the same answer: that the peasant after the Revolution had more freedom, since he obtained land. This was not necessarily a stupid reply, for although land was not the same as freedom —and the old peasant revolutionary tradition had always distinguished between the two in its slogan "land and liberty"—the peasant in fact had considerable freedom as well as the land under NEP conditions.

The ordinary man was free even to indulge in political criticism. Men and women who retained openly anti-Soviet views were barred from holding certain jobs but otherwise were not sharply penalized. An aphorism was current that there was any number of political parties in the USSR, but one was in power while the others were in jail. Not only many supporters of non-Communist parties, but some Communist dissidents, were in prison—but by no means all of either, and some prisoners might look for release in the near future. Moreover, although many were in jail, they were not in the cemetery, which was a decade later to be the destination of not only dissidents, but multitudes who were not opponents of the regime at all.

Undoubtedly many of the common people responded favorably to what appeared to be the Communist program as enunciated by Bukharin. The peasants should "enrich themselves," the country would "creep at a snail's pace" to socialism, and whatever exactly socialism would be like, no doubt it would be very fine. Some enthusiasm for the Soviet regime was reflected in the names given newborn babies, such as Vladlen (from Lenin's first and last names), Barrikada, Antichrist, Elektrifikatsiia (Lenin had declared that "Soviet power plus electrification equals socialism"), and Diamata (from *dialekticheskii materializm*). In a country where babies' names had always come exclusively from saints' names, this was a remarkable development.

It is difficult to find a parallel for a regime or a party which held power for ten years, biding its time until it felt strong enough to fulfill its original program. It had been observed that West European Marxism had been tamed when its representatives obtained governmental posts, and Western commentators were inclined to discount any possibility that the original Communist program could somehow be kept in cold storage for some time in Russia, to be defrosted and served up again in the future. Thus the coming of the *velikii perelom* ("the great change"), "Russia's Iron Age" (W. H. Chamberlin), or the "Second Revolution" (B. H. Sumner) startled foreign observers and produced a mass of admirers of the gigantic "Soviet experiment." The "Second Revolution" began with the First Five-Year Plan (1928–1932) in both industry and

SOVFOTO

TWO CITIES

TOP–Red Square, Moscow
BOTTOM–Nevsky Prospekt, Leningrad (St. Petersburg)

SOVFOTO

THREE TSARS

Peter I

SOVFOTO

Ivan III

SOVFOTO

"The Conquest of Siberia by Yermak,"
Painting by VASSILI SURIKOV

"Ivan IV and His Slain Son," *Painting by* ILIA REPIN

SOVFOTO

SEVERAL BOOKS THAT SHOOK THE WORLD

Title Pages of Some of Lenin's Chief Works

BETTMAN

THE LATE EMPIRE: A Family and a Palace

TOP–Nicholas II and and His Family in 1917
BOTTOM–Petrodvorets (Peterhof)

SOVFOTO

THE REVOLUTION OF 1917

SOVFOT

TOP–Demonstration in Petrograd, July 1917. Banners read "Immediate End to the War," "We Demand a III International," "Land and Liberty," "All Power to the Soviets," etc. BOTTOM–"The Attack on the Winter Palace, October 1917," *Painting by* V. KUZNETZOV

SOVFOTO

LEADERS OF THE REVOLUTION

Included are Trotsky, Zinoviev, Lenin, Kalinin, Chicherin, Rykov, Dzerzhinsky, Bukharin, Radek, Lunacharsky, Kollontai, Demian Bedny / *From F. A. MacKenzie,* RUSSIA BEFORE DAWN. *London: T. Fisher Unwin, Ltd. Courtesy of* ERNEST BENN, LTD.

SOVFOTO

WHEN THE REVOLUTION WAS YOUNG

TOP—A Bolshevik Propaganda Train

BOTTOM—Tatars Examining the Map of Their New Autonomous Republic

SOVFOTO

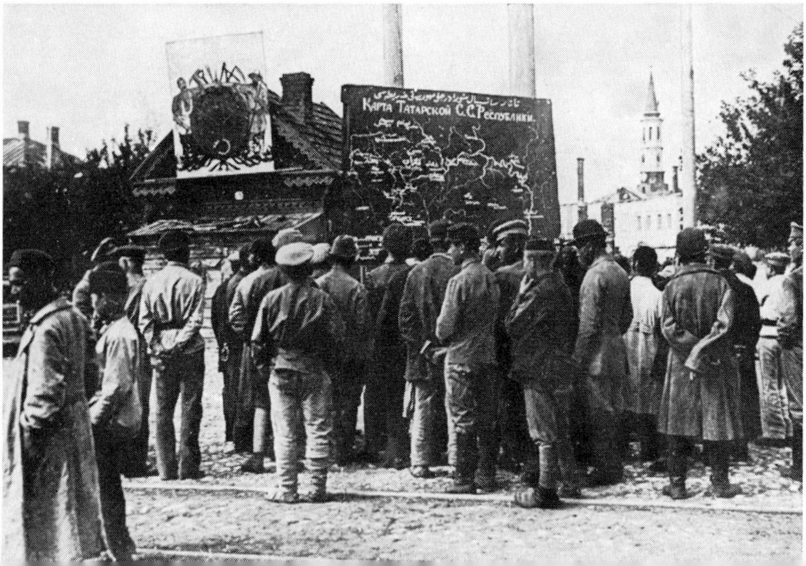

LENIN AND THE MASSES

Lenin Addressing a Meeting in Tverskaya with Kamenev and Trotsky Beside Him / *From F. A. MacKenzie,* RUSSIA BEFORE DAWN. *London: T. Fisher Unwin, Ltd. Courtesy of* ERNEST BENN, LTD.

GERMAN VICTORY AND DEFEAT

TOP–German Entry into Minsk BOTTOM–German Prisoners Being Sent to the Rear by Soviet Troops in a Recaptured Village / *From* DER ZWEITE WELTKRIEG IN BILD, *ed. Dr. Franz Burda. Offenburg, Germany: Burda Druck und Verlag. Courtesy of the publishers.*

SOVFOTO

Beria, Molotov, and Stalin as Pallbearers for Kalinin at His Funeral in June 1946

Mao Tse-Tung and Khrushchëv at the Anniversary Celebration of the October Revolution in Moscow, 1957

agriculture, which was attended by political and cultural changes as well.

When the economic offensive began in earnest, the political struggle had already been decided. Stalin and his supporters had rendered impossible any serious challenge from the Right Opposition led by Bukharin, while the members of the former Left Opposition of Zinovievites and Trotskyites were at least initially persuaded that Stalin had simply adopted their earlier demands as his own policy—although they too were powerless to impede Stalin's policies if they had wished to do so. This was something of a paradox, for the Stalinists interpreted the new offensive as the practical embodiment of the theory of "socialism in one country," which had served Stalin as a weapon in the fight with Trotsky. In any event, it was clear that the NEP line of compromise with the peasantry, which the Right had wished to extend and prolong, was being discarded.

The decision was taken to industrialize rapidly and to industrialize the countryside as well as the city, by converting the peasantry into a landless agricultural proletariat. This program was to be carried out by employing all the power of the Communist state, in such a way as to strengthen state control over all branches of economic, social, and cultural life. Technically the First Five-Year Plan was a purely economic scheme; in actual fact it inaugurated a new phase in Russian history, in which governmental fiat invaded every area of life in a manner unparalleled in the history not only of Russia but of any other country up to that time. The First Five-Year Plan marked the real beginning of Soviet totalitarianism.

Before launching an effort of the magnitude of the First Plan, Stalin had taken pains to prepare to meet all foreseeable opposition inside and outside the Party by silencing all open criticism of himself among the Party leaders as well as among the rank and file, and by constructing an apparatus by which he could enforce his orders on the masses.

THE SECRET POLICE

The necessary apparatus, outside of the Party organization itself, consisted mainly of the secret police and the army. The first secret police organization had been the Cheka (see p. 155), which had earned for itself a fearsome reputation. Especially after the Cheka order of February 1918 to local Soviets to shoot on sight all "counterrevolutionaries" or those who aided and abetted them, such a reign of terror developed that even local Communist authorities complained. In February 1922 the Cheka was abolished and replaced by a GPU, renamed OGPU *(Ob"edinënnoe Gosudarstvennoe Politicheskoe Upravlenie),* or Unified State

Political Administration, at the time the RSFSR was reorganized as the USSR.

Unlike the Cheka, which was completely independent, the GPU was subordinated to the Commissariat of Interior, at that time under Rykov. It was entrusted with the tasks of suppressing "open counterrevolutionary outbreaks" (rather than indiscriminate shooting of all individual "counterrevolutionaries," as informally and arbitrarily defined) and of administering international border control, along with some vaguer functions. Moreover, the GPU was compelled either to release prisoners after two months or remand them for trial to courts under the jurisdiction of the Commissariat of Justice. It seemed as if the wings of the secret police had been clipped somewhat; however, the GPU obtained the power of arresting Party members, which the Cheka never had.

During the NEP period the operations of the secret police were on a fairly limited scale. Most often arrests fell into one of two categories: first, the so-called "KR's," or "counterrevolutionaries," including former members of the Kadet party and all parties to the right of the Kadets as well as non-party supporters of the pre-Communist regimes, prominent churchmen, and the children of "exploiters"; second, the so-called "politicals," comprising members of the non-Communist Left—Mensheviks, S.R.'s, and anarchists. Generally the "politicals" received better treatment than the "KR's," including that *sine qua non* of the political exile, the privilege of having access to books and writing materials, which the Tsarist regime also had granted its political prisoners.

During the intra-Party battles of the 1920's the successive chiefs of the OGPU, Felix Dzerzhinsky and (after Dzerzhinsky died in 1926) V. R. Menzhinsky, put the agency increasingly at Stalin's disposal. The OGPU arrested or cowed dissident Party members and kept a watch on industrial performance and suspected opposition in the armed forces. It spied on all foreigners in the Soviet Union, and its Foreign Section organized espionage abroad and carried out surveillance of Soviet diplomatic agents as well as Russian *émigré* groups.

The secret police acquired special troops of its own, some of which were used to operate the concentration camps for "KR's" and "politicals" and for the most dangerous (nonpolitical) criminals. Among the most important OGPU camps were those on or near the island of the former Solovetsky Monastery in the White Sea. Many prisons and camps remained outside OGPU jurisdiction, and under the NEP, the secret police was used much more to keep an eye on the economic and political leadership than to terrorize the mass of the people directly. However, its apparatus had been built up to considerable dimensions and lay safely in the hands of Stalin's men, ready for the larger-scale operations which began with the First Five-Year Plan.

From 1928 on the OGPU was called upon to arrest Nepmen (private entrepreneurs), "kulaks," and members of the old intelligentsia. The police had little interest in the Nepmen; the purpose of seizing their persons was to lay hands on their wealth, especially gold and foreign currency needed for purchases abroad. The specialists who came from the old intelligentsia, however, were often brought before "show trials," a device which Stalin used for the first time during the First Five-Year Plan. Persons known to be innocent of the charges against them were tried and sentenced in order to intimidate critics of the regime and to evoke greater efforts from those who feared similar treatment. During the First Plan there were three especially publicized "show trials." These were the 1928 trial of engineers from Shakhty, in the Donets coal basin, who were accused of "wrecking" for Germany; the trial in 1930 of the so-called "Industrial Party," including Professor Ramzin and other engineers, accused of working for France; and in 1931 the trial of a number of ex-Mensheviks headed by Professor Groman of the State Planning Commission, who were said to have acted for *émigré* Mensheviks.

The accused were intimidated, but not liquidated. Stalin was merely trying to frighten the specialists trained in prerevolutionary days into doing what he demanded of them. In June 1931 he was ready to call off Menzhinsky and the OGPU. In his "Six Points" speech, Stalin declared that the period when "wrecking" had been in fashion and had necessitated stern measures had passed, and that a section of the old intelligentsia had shown itself ready to work loyally for the regime. He therefore called for a new attitude toward the intelligentsia. In part the speech signified that he thought the managers and technicians could now be controlled more effectively with cajolery than with intimidation; in part he was thrusting at poor labor discipline among the trade-unionists, who in the early years of the Soviet regime had thought that since they were in control, it was their prerogative to treat the "bourgeois" managers or engineers as they pleased.

THE UNIONS AND THE ARMY

The trade-unions for a decade had enjoyed considerable power of their own. They were supposed to represent the proletariat, and some of their defenders had even suggested that since this was so, they ought to run the government. Although they achieved no such power, they had a good deal of weight in the state industries and, paradoxically, the reemergence of some private industry under the NEP had strengthened the independence of the unions. Since they had the right to organize and strike against Nepmen employers, and it was regarded as unwise to try to prevent them from acting also to protect workers in state enterprises, the disappearance of the Nepmen would therefore mean circumscription of the rights of unions.

As Tomsky saw that headlong, state-controlled industrialization would threaten union prerogatives, he resisted such proposals along with the rest of the Right Opposition. In 1929 he was removed from the leadership of the unions; his nominal successor was Nicholas Shvernik, but the reins actually passed to one of Stalin's trusted men, Lazar Kaganovich. For two years longer Stalin was willing to encourage the workers to bully the old technicians. When Stalin thought he had the old intelligentsia intimidated, in his "Six Points" speech he called off the workers, and his control over the union apparatus was sufficient to enforce his demand. He was telling the workers to get back to work and stop interfering with decisions of an engineering or management character; moreover, that all decisions affecting industry were to be made neither by the unionist rank and file nor by the "bourgeois" technicians but by the state apparatus. By the end of the First Plan, the trade-unions had been converted into an organ of state control over the industrial workers.

Under the NEP the Red Army also remained partly outside direct control by the Party leadership. The Political Administration of the army, which since 1919 had been charged with safeguarding its ideological purity and either making or transmitting major policy decisions on its organization, was far from subservient to the triumvirs of the Politburo. The political commissars were in no one's pocket, but for the most part they supported Trotsky, who was war commissar from 1918 to 1924, in his struggle with the triumvirs. Only when Voroshilov took over the commissariat in 1925 did Bubnov become chief of the Political Administration and proceed to replace the political commissars, where necessary, with reliable Stalin men.

The Political Administration of the army worked energetically to indoctrinate new recruits, especially those taken in at the close of the Civil War, who were mostly peasant boys who neither knew nor cared what "ideology" was. Still more intensive efforts went into rebuilding the officer corps; the political commissars managed to remove over ninety per cent of the ex-Tsarist officers who had been coaxed or blackmailed into serving during the Civil War. It was easier to rid the army of the old officers than to find reliable new ones. Political indoctrination of the officer corps and the enlisted men was a long-term job, but the main thing was that the Political Administration, by the beginning of the First Plan, was rapidly becoming Stalinized, and thus the whole army was being brought under closer control of the Party leadership.

By 1928–1929 Stalin had substantially completed taking over the secret police, the trade-unions, and the army, through adroit use of the Party apparatus. Some of his critics within the Party he had won over; others he had not, but he was able to keep watch on what they were saying and doing. He counted—rightly—on winning over many by the magnitude of the effort to carry through the "Second Revolution." He also calculated accurately that resistance would be met from the masses, and that the apparatus would be powerful enough to overcome it.

AIMS OF THE FIRST FIVE-YEAR PLAN

Why did the "Second Revolution" occur? Partly because Stalin found it expedient to launch it, but the deeper reason was, as one well-known economist says, that without such an effort it would have been "impossible to solve those ideological problems for the sake of which the Revolution had been made."[1] An attempt was to be made to transform the economy and to increase the production of capital goods and other items. But that was not the chief purpose of the First Five-Year Plan. The essential point was to convert the entire labor force, rural as well as urban, into employees of state-controlled enterprise.

The assumption was that once the economic "foundation" was changed, the noneconomic "superstructure" would change correspondingly. Once the economy was put into a state socialist mold, men's minds would come to accept that mold. No longer would the regime be troubled by the attachment of the peasantry to its land, the ambivalence on the part of the workers as to what their "real" interests were, the persistence of religious belief, the survival of prerevolutionary values in the family, and in general mass indifference or hostility to the aims of the materialist and socialist Soviet state. Stalin and the Russian Communists expected some resistance and were ready for it, repeating to each other that "one cannot make an omelet without breaking eggs." Nevertheless, it is doubtful that anyone realized in 1928 quite what the human cost would be, since the human factor was left out of the oversimplified ideological equation.

The First Five-Year Plan was not an inflexible blueprint prepared in advance and inaugurated at a given moment. Soviet economic planning—though the planning was never exclusively economic—has always been

• [1] Alexander Baykov, *The Development of the Soviet Economic System* (Cambridge: Cambridge University Press, 1946), p. 158.

characterized by a periodic revision of goals. Such revision might have scaled down targets as unforeseen obstacles were encountered; instead, more often the targets have been revised upward. It has been argued that in the strict sense the USSR has never employed "planning" at all: overfulfillment of goals has always been praised, underfulfillment criticized or punished, yet the former is no more reconcilable with the original "plan" than the latter and may lead to serious distortion in resource allocation. In this light Soviet "planning" appears not as a rationalized method of the satisfaction of human wants, or even of the demands of the regime (which intentionally subordinates the welfare of the consumer to the task of strengthening its own military strength and potential), but as a means of universal and permanent intimidation of the labor force.

In 1926 the State Planning Commission, headed by Professor Strumilin, was first entrusted with the task of preparing an over-all plan. The plan as actually instituted is known as the "August version," presented in August 1928 and covering the period through August 1933. It was predicated on four assumptions: that there would be no serious crop failure, that world trade would increase (since the USSR could, it was hoped, export more and obtain more foreign loans), that "qualitative indices" (cost of production and individual laborer productivity) would show improvement, and that the proportion of expenditure for national defense would fall.

These expectations were all disappointed, in part because of the Soviets' own mistakes. The Great Depression, beginning in 1929, which brought on a catastrophic decline in world trade, was not the Soviets' fault, nor was the Japanese invasion of Manchuria in 1931, which occasioned an increase in Soviet military spending. But the famine of 1932–1933 was largely man-made, and the failure of costs to decline and of productivity to rise as expected was the result of a combination of the managers' inexperience and ignorance with the regime's disregard of human welfare and the incentives for which men may be induced to work. It was planned that productivity would rise twice as fast as wages; instead the wage rise was over twice the rise in productivity. In consequence many more workers were taken on than intended and the urban demand vastly increased, pushing up prices and forcing the regime to introduce rationing once more, as in the time of the Civil War. The real miscalculation was not in any of these specific respects. It lay in the attempt to use political fanaticism as a substitute for rational principles of management, and in the failure to grasp the limits of what brute force could achieve when inspiration and persuasion failed.

THE FIVE-YEAR PLAN IN INDUSTRY

The First Five-Year Plan was formally adopted in April 1929 by the Sixteenth Party Conference. The XV Congress had merely considered a draft plan, and one generally much more modest in its goals than the "August version" finally instituted. The objectives were stunning: total industrial output was to increase by 250%, that of heavy industry by 330%; output of pig iron was to be nearly tripled, that of coal more than doubled, that of electric power to increase more than four times. Agricultural production was scheduled to increase 150%, and 20% of the peasant farms were to be collectivized.

Bukharin and the Right were at that time still resisting such targets. Stalin repeatedly accused Bukharin of wanting to "put the brake on the revolution . . . surrender the position to the capitalist elements." There was a grain of truth in what he said. Of course Bukharin was a Communist and not a defender of "capitalism" at all; but his voice was the last raised in open defense of at least the economic freedom of the Russian people, against which large-scale violence was about to be used. When he called for "normalized" conditions of trade, when he cited Lenin as urging caution in regard to the peasantry, when he spoke of "military-feudal" exploitation of the villagers, he was to be sure not speaking for the "kulak," as Stalin charged, but he was expressing for the last time in the USSR doubts about the advisability of crushing the independent peasantry which still made up the bulk of the Russian population.

Far from paying any attention to Bukharin's insistence that the targets of the "August version" were too high, the Party Central Committee in the summer of 1929 raised them still higher. In November Bukharin was removed from the Politburo and was no longer in a position to protest; in fact, he joined the other Rightist leaders in a public recantation of error. No one was left to urge putting on the "brakes." By the end of the year the pace of industrial construction and especially of collectivization had reached breakneck speed. In November 1929 Stalin declared, "We are advancing full steam ahead along the path of industrialization to socialism, leaving behind the age-long 'Russian' backwardness . . . when we have put the USSR in a motor car and the muzhik upon a tractor . . . we shall see which countries may then be classified as backward and which as advanced."

Optimism surpassed all limits. The XVI Party Congress, held in June and July 1930, adopted the slogan, "the Five-Year Plan in four years"

—although five years had seemed a short enough time for the realization of Stalin's announced objectives. The Congress also approved a revision of the plan for agriculture so as to bring about wholesale collectivization of peasant farms within the next few years. A further decision was taken to create a "Ural-Kuznetsk Combine," based on the exchange of Ural iron for Kuznetsk Basin coal, which would place an especially heavy strain on the whole transportation system.

In 1930 signs of trouble were beginning to appear. Factories were erected for which no machines were available; machines were delivered to plants unable to house them; hastily recruited and untrained workers ruined shiny new machines in one place, while skilled workers elsewhere sat idle for want of equipment. In the last quarter of 1930 there was an attempt to overcome all difficulties at once in connection with a statistical change-over from the agricultural (autumn to autumn) to the calendar year: October, November, and December were proclaimed a special "shock quarter." (This was one of many cases in which Stalin borrowed Trotsky's device of using military terminology in nonmilitary situations for propaganda purposes.)

The "shock quarter," Stalin's efforts to wheedle and frighten workers and technicians into greater exertions (see p. 261), and all other expedients were not enough. In 1931 something went wrong, and from that year onward the USSR ceased to publish price indices. At the end of 1932, when four and a quarter years had elapsed, the First Five-Year Plan was declared to have been fulfilled, but the claim had a hollow ring. Stalin contended that production of machinery and electrical equipment had risen 157%, but it was admitted that output in heavy metallurgy (iron and steel) had increased only 67%, coal output 89%, and consumer goods 73%, and even these figures are questionable.

No doubt in the First Plan great industrial expansion occurred, and in subsequent plans has continued to occur, whether or not goals are precisely fulfilled. That the Communists can get "results" from their methods is not in doubt; but the "results" are designed not to build a healthy economy, but to strengthen the totalitarian system, to which end the physical and moral well-being of the Soviet worker and consumer is ruthlessly sacrificed.

The underlying assumption of certain students of the Five-Year Plans, and of many influential persons in the so-called "underdeveloped areas" in recent years, has been that the chief Soviet objective is "economic development." Yet the Communists have never contended that their main aim was to increase output, nor does the evidence indicate that it has been such in fact. Their aim has been rather to achieve a transformation of society in which industrial growth is only one aspect, related to a much broader and more fundamental set of changes in men's way of life, attitudes, and allegiances.

By 1931 the headlong rush of the "Second Revolution" had evoked alarm among the technicians who were accustomed to operate on the basis of costs and rational calculations in general. Addressing a group of industrial managers in February of that year, Stalin admitted, "It is sometimes asked whether it is not possible to slow down a bit . . . ," but he declared that on the contrary a still swifter pace was dictated by the Party's "obligations to the workers and peasants" of the USSR and its "still higher" obligations to the world proletariat. He continued, "We are fifty to a hundred years behind the advanced countries. We must cover this distance in ten years. Either we do this or they will crush us."[2]

Thus Stalin stated the doctrine of no respite which thereafter was not only to govern the effort to increase industrial production, but was to become the keynote of all sides of life under Soviet totalitarianism. A Communist is always at war. There may be periods of calm on the front, but the battle is still waiting—for the millions of unwilling fighters who make up the Soviet citizenry as well as for the Party leadership.

THE FIVE-YEAR PLAN IN AGRICULTURE

The aspect of the "Second Revolution" which was the most dramatic and sweeping—indeed it was laden with sheer horror—was the collectivization of agriculture. The problem of the "alliance between the proletariat and the peasantry," which Lenin considered so crucial to the Russian Communists, was to be solved by the elimination of the peasantry in its hitherto familiar form. The class struggle which Lenin had in 1918–1919 tried in vain to foment within the village was to be carried into the village, if necessary, from without. The kulaks or rich peasants would be destroyed; the "poor peasants," carrying with them a portion of the "middle peasants," would emerge victors from the struggle. They would then establish collective farms in token of their achievement of the attitude proper to a proletariat.

Who were the kulaks? By the 1927 census estimates, the peasantry was divided into "proletarian" peasants (without land or livestock), who

• [2] This statement has been interpreted as a prophecy of Hitler's invasion in 1941. However, it should be noted that in 1931 Soviet relations with the Germans were better than with either the British or French. As far as Hitler was concerned, moreover, Moscow and the German Communists were for their own purposes co-operating with his Nazis against the forces supporting the Weimar Republic. See pp. 309 ff.

made up about 4% of the total, and "independent" peasant smallholders, who constituted the remaining 96%. Of the "independent" group, about 5% were classified as "kulaks"—defined as those who owned property worth roughly $800 and who hired labor for fifty days out of the year. By the Marxist definition, exploiters are those who own the means of production but do not work it themselves; Stalin's census-takers had used criteria bearing only the feeblest and most distant relationship to those of Marxism. Stalin could not be entirely blamed, however, for such ideological dubiousness. Long ago Lenin had also used a distinction resting on wealth rather than on economic function in trying to discover classes within the peasantry when he calculated "rich" and "poor" peasants on the basis of number of horses owned. As for Marx and Engels, they were fortunate enough not to be writing about countries in which the peasants made up the majority of the people. Although they did not embarrass themselves with attempts to divide the rural masses into "exploiters" and "exploited," they provided justification for collectivization by holding that the peasantry as a whole represented a survival of feudalism and would disappear in the modern world. Engels had indeed advised giving the small peasant plenty of time to ponder whether he was ready to enter a co-operative farm, but the assumption was that he ought to and would be ready sooner or later.

In December 1929 Stalin quoted those very lines of Engels but asserted that they were inapplicable in the situation existing in the Soviet Union. Although in May 1928 he had declared that the "expropriation of the kulaks would be folly," in the summer of 1929 he had ordered Party workers to "liquidate the kulaks as a class." In December he went still further. It was ridiculous, he said, to suggest that after being expropriated the kulaks should be allowed to join the collectives. That was unequivocal language, and the result in the winter and spring of 1929–1930 was bloodshed and chaos.

When traveling with Rykov in the Volga region in the mid-1920's, William Reswick, a foreign correspondent, heard the peasants question Rykov anxiously: "What is a kulak? Can it be a muzhik who owns a horse, a cow, and some poultry?" Rykov replied that a kulak was simply a village usurer—which was indeed the original meaning of the word, but was not the meaning employed by Lenin and the Communist Party. The Communists meant by "kulak" a peasant who had more property than his neighbors and therefore might exploit them in some way. It is doubtful that the criteria of the 1927 census were ever taken very seriously in determining who a kulak was, and in many cases no economic criteria were applied at all. It is reported, for example, that Uzbek peasants were catechized: "What is socialism?" and "When was Darwin born?" If a recalcitrant peasant failed to give a satisfactory answer, he might be branded a kulak.

It remained for Tito, many years later, to confess that Communists defined a kulak to mean any peasant opposed to "socialism," but Soviet collectivization had already put that definition into practice. Peasants who resisted inclusion in collective farms were uprooted and transported away from their homes, often to the far north in unheated freight cars. Many times whole villages were simply surrounded and attacked. During this period an OGPU colonel confided to a foreign journalist, "I am an old Bolshevik. I worked in the underground against the Tsar and then I fought in the Civil War. Did I do all that in order that I should now surround villages with machine-guns and order my men to fire indiscriminately into crowds of peasants? Oh, no, no!"[3] The peasants who could not fight openly resorted to passive resistance by killing their own livestock and burning their own crops. They were able to do grave economic damage to the regime as well as to themselves, but they could not halt the pursuit of the political objective of creating collectives.

On January 20, 1930, there were slightly over four million peasant families in collective farms, most of them having been taken in during the previous year or two. By March 1 of the same year the number had risen to over fourteen million—fifty-five per cent of all peasant families. There were supposed to be over a hundred and ten thousand collective farms, but it would be more accurate to say that fourteen million peasants had surrendered and were awaiting the orders of the terrible and incomprehensible invaders of their countryside. Then, abruptly, on March 2 Stalin published an article in *Pravda* entitled "Dizziness from Success." In it he contended that "the fundamental turn of the village toward socialism may be already considered secured," but he warned, "It is impossible to establish collective farms by force. To do so would be stupid and reactionary."

The peasants who were heard later saying that things improved when Stalin got over *his* dizziness from success were quite right. Stalin in the *Pravda* article tried to blame the chaos in the village on Party underlings, but for the most part they had merely tried to obey his orders. At any rate the Communists who were carrying on the virtual civil war in the countryside responded at once. By May 1, 1930, it was reported that the number of peasant families on collective farms had fallen below six million. However, Stalin had made it clear that the objective was

• [3] Deutscher, *Stalin*, p. 325, n. 1.

unaltered. By the end of 1932 sixty per cent of peasant families were reported collectivized. One can only conjecture what brutality, suffering, and bewilderment lay behind the fantastic fluctuation in these statistics.

The political victory was substantially won, but the economic consequences were disastrous. In 1933 the number of horses in the Soviet Union was less than half the 1928 figure; during the period from 1929 to 1931 alone, the number of cattle fell by one-third, the number of sheep and goats by one-half. It was intended that the horses, which had been used as draft animals, should be replaced by tractors, but they could not be supplied in anything like the quantity needed. Nothing could replace the other animals. Tractors do not give milk, furnish meat, or produce manure. Politically, however, the introduction of tractors had great significance. They and other agricultural machines were pooled in Machine-Tractor Stations (MTS's), each of which served several collective farms. The MTS became the political headquarters of the victorious Communists in the defeated countryside, where records were kept and orders were received from above and transmitted to the collectives.

The new collective enterprises were of two basic types: the state farm *(sovkhoz,* short for *sovetskoe khoziaistvo)* and the collective farm *(kolkhoz,* short for *kollektivnoe khoziaistvo).* The state farm was (and is) the full property of the Soviet government; its manager operated it with hired labor, in accordance with the directives of the Ministry of State Farms or any other ministry to which the farm in question was allotted. The state farm, as a "factory in the field," was and remains the Communist objective for agriculture; there the peasant is truly a proletarian with no property of his own.

In contrast, the collective farm was supposed to be a self-governing co-operative made up of peasants who voluntarily pooled their means of production and divided the proceeds. The first collectives were of various kinds of which three were the best known. The "commune" (not to be confused with the prerevolutionary village commune) was the closest to the state farm; all implements and livestock were owned in common by the members, who lived in communal buildings. The *toz* (or "society for joint land cultivation") was the loosest type of collective; it was a production co-operative, in which each peasant family kept title to its own plot of land, livestock, and implements, and joined with others to work the land and buy machinery. Intermediate between the "commune" and the *toz* was the *artel* (not to be confused with the prerevolutionary craft association). Under the *artel* the peasant retained possession of his own livestock and a small garden plot, on which he might raise crops either for his own use or for sale on the market.[4]

The resistance of the peasants to collectivization was not entirely in vain, for it forced the Communists to accept the *artel* as the prevalent, in fact, almost universal, type of collective. At the beginning of the plan Stalin, although he did not expect *state* farms to be set up everywhere immediately, continually referred to "state and collective farms" as the goal of the collectivization campaign. After the disastrous first quarter of 1930, however, he reversed the order of priority, and began to speak of the goal as "collective and state farms." A considerable number of state farms were actually dissolved and their holdings turned over to collective farms. The type of collective farm to which Stalin gave his support in the "Dizziness from Success" article and which the XVI Congress approved two months later was the *artel.*

The Communists viewed the *artel* as a temporary compromise. The XVI Congress's resolution declared that the *artel "does not complete, but is only the beginning* of the creation of a new social discipline, of the task of teaching the peasants socialist construction." In the continuing struggle on the agricultural "front," it might be said that the state had won the "commanding heights"—to borrow a phrase from the NEP period. Most of the land was held by the *artel,* and that "collective sector" of the land was tilled in common. The *artel* was clearly dependent on the state: the state agency, the MTS, dealt with the *artel,* not the individual peasant, furnishing the machinery required to sow and harvest. In the apportionment of the proceeds, the compulsory grain deliveries had first to be made to the state—this was called the collective farm's "First Commandment." Next the MTS had to be paid for the machinery the farm had used, and only then was the residual share divided among the individual households. However, the peasant retained his own tiny garden plot and his livestock, and thus every day he was able, even compelled, to compare the advantages of individual and collective farming, since he engaged in both. The *artel,* wholly satisfying the aims of neither the Communists nor the peasants, thus contained a built-in contradiction. Since by 1933 over ninety-six per cent of all collective farms were of the *artel* type, and the state farms included only a very small proportion of the tilled land, the contradiction within the *artel* affected most of Soviet agriculture.

• [4] It should be noted that none of these types of collective resembled the pre-revolutionary commune, wherein each peasant family had its own house and land, which it worked by its own labor even when the land lay in widely scattered strips.

The economic and human costs of collectivization had to be set alongside the substantial, if incomplete, political victory which the regime had gained. By 1937, it has been computed, the over-all pre-1928 per capita level of all agricultural production was barely regained, but in food production alone, it is doubtful that the pre-1928 per capita level has ever been exceeded since. The human losses were colossal. At least five million peasants died in the process of collectivization and the resultant famine of 1932–1933 (the figure Stalin revealed to Churchill at Yalta was ten million). No wonder that there were Russians who survived the horrors of World War II who could not talk of their experiences years before, during collectivization, without losing their composure.

It is difficult to compute the economic results or the human casualties with precision. More fundamental than such computation is the question of what possible moral and political justification could be found for completely overturning the lives of a hundred million people, in peacetime, in the name of a goal which was anathema to them. Stalin admitted that collectivization entailed a "revolution from above," although he insisted that it was supported "from below" by the "poor peasants." Certainly it involved a struggle—but chiefly one between urban Communists and the villagers; the "poor peasants" proved as much of a will-o'-the-wisp as they had in 1918 (see p. 163). Although the victory of the Party over the peasantry was incomplete, it was decisive enough that a battle of such dimensions did not need to be fought again. The collectivization of agriculture had vast economic consequences in that it enabled the regime to obtain much of the capital desired for industrialization from the defeated village (largely by selling the compulsory grain deliveries, received at a nominal valuation, at high prices). The political consequences were still greater. Collectivization was the decisive step in the building of Soviet totalitarianism, for it imposed on the majority of the people a subjection which only force could maintain.

OTHER ASPECTS OF THE PLAN

During the First Five-Year Plan rationing was introduced, not as a means of keeping the cities from starvation as during the Civil War, but as a system of differential privilege which provided extra-monetary income for technicians, skilled workers, and other groups essential to the fulfillment of the plan. Rationing was again abolished in 1935, when the Stakhanovite movement (see p. 291) was launched to achieve some of the same objectives.

Pressure was exerted in a variety of ways to obtain a stable labor force.

In October 1930 it was announced that unemployment had ceased to exist, and unemployment relief was cut off. Excessive demands for manpower or failure to enforce discipline on the part of managers were defined as criminal offenses. In November 1932 workers guilty of one day's voluntary absence from the job were ordered to be dismissed and deprived of their housing, which, the regime openly admitted, might mean starvation. In 1930 and 1931 legislation provided that a worker must go where he was sent by the authorities. In 1932 the passport system, which had been adopted by the Tsars as a means of catching runaway serfs, was restored, and thereafter individuals could move only with police consent. All such measures served to reduce absenteeism and labor turnover but did not eliminate them.

Even if all workers currently employed in industry could have been made to stay on the job, they would have been too few to satisfy the plan's needs for labor. Other workers had to be found, and from 1928 on the system of "organized intake" of labor was introduced. By this system industrial managers might conclude "agreements" with collective farm chairmen under which the latter undertook to furnish "redundant" collective farmers as new urban laborers. In the following decade millions of peasants were conscripted into industry by way of this system.

Open compulsion might prevent workers from leaving the job and obtain additional workers, but to raise productivity other methods were necessary. In 1929 the Soviet regime resorted, at first cautiously, to the device of competition. To begin with, groups of laborers were authorized to engage in what was called "socialist emulation," which was ordered "not to impinge upon the solidarity" of the proletariat. By 1931 the regime decided to sanction competition between individuals. Wage differentials and payment of piece work were gradually introduced, and since then no comprehensive wage statistics have been published.

In all these changes the trade-unions had no voice at all. Working conditions and wages were fixed by the regime, either in the Five-Year Plan or in supplementary legislation. In 1933, when a law abolished the signing of collective bargaining agreements between unions and managers, the unions had already lost most of the substantive rights they had possessed.

The First Five-Year Plan witnessed a transformation of the Soviet financial structure. At the end of 1930 a new tax, called the "turnover tax," was introduced, and it soon became the cornerstone of all state receipts, providing the largest part of the Soviet budget. The turnover tax was levied as part of the wholesale price on all goods—thus the wholesale price consisted of cost price plus planned profit plus turnover tax. In recent years foreign travelers in the USSR have reported that many Soviet citizens are unaware of the existence of any such tax. An income tax is also levied, but its rate is very low. This is the tax which the Soviet citizen knows he pays, but it is not a major source of state income.

Russia's "Second Revolution" was thus infinitely more far-reaching in its scope than the Revolution of 1917. Certain scholars, such as Isaac Deutscher, although acknowledging the human sacrifices and brutality which accompanied the First Plan, have mustered some sympathy for "the rulers' determination to overcome at any cost the prodigious difficulties involved in the mobilization, training, and education of many millions of raw, undisciplined peasants."[5] All industrial revolutions, it is said, have their casualties. In Russia under the First Five-Year Plan there were certainly casualties, and there was an industrial revolution; but even more important, Stalin achieved an unparalleled degree of state control over the peoples of the USSR, and individual freedom, political, economic, and other, fell near the vanishing point. State-controlled industry was greatly expanded, but it was only one building block in the growing edifice of Soviet totalitarianism.

• [5] *Soviet Trade Unions: Their Place in Soviet Labour Policy* (London: Royal Institute of International Affairs, 1950), p. 138.

The Consolidation of Totalitarianism (1933–1941)

★
★
★
★
★
★
★
★
★
★

CHAPTER 18

THE DILEMMA OF THE OLD BOLSHEVIKS

Stalin and his colleagues were somewhat shaken by the upheavals which their own policy had produced. In November 1932 Stalin's own wife, the former Nadezhda Allilueva,[1] spoke up bluntly in a small gathering about the misery the country was suffering; Stalin retorted with abuse, and the same night she died, apparently by suicide. Victor Serge tells a widely accepted story that about this time Stalin offered his resignation to the Politburo. Two of his formerly trusted henchmen, Syrtsov and Lominadze, had shortly before been jailed for suggesting that the Central Committee depose Stalin as general secretary, and no Politburo member would risk urging that the offer of resignation should be taken seriously. After a strained silence, Serge reports, Molotov said, "Come, come! You have got the party's confidence. . . ."[2]

The members of the former Left and Right oppositions watched with mixed feelings the travails which the country was undergoing. Some of

• [1] His second wife. The first, Ekaterina Svanidze, died during the Revolution of 1905, leaving one son who was raised in the Caucasus by her parents. Stalin married Allilueva in 1918.

• [2] *Portrait de Staline* (Paris, 1940), p. 95.

the Left had demanded that a "Second Revolution" be launched earlier, but none had clearly envisaged the extent of the violence, waste, and suffering which actually took place. In any case neither the Left nor the Right could very well deny that the cause of socialism—defined as the extension of control over the economy by the alleged "proletarian" state—had been advanced, whether or not they lamented the cost. Even Trotsky, writing from Prinkipo in his *Bulletin of the Opposition,* said in the fall of 1932 that the overthrow of Stalin "would almost certainly benefit the forces of counterrevolution."

In 1932 Zinoviev, Kamenev, and others were exiled to Siberia, but in the spring of 1933 they recanted once more and were allowed to return, shortly after Rykov, Tomsky, and Bukharin had added recantations to their own records. The opposition could not bring itself to do any more than grumble and hope for the best. Its members could bring themselves neither to admit nor to deny fully that the regime of Stalin and the casualties of the "Second Revolution" were logical consequences of the single-party oligarchy—one which they themselves had labored with great pains to create—which was attempting to create state socialism in a deeply anti-socialist country. As Marxists, they could not admit that the person of Stalin, or any other individual, could be decisive in history. Although Trotsky abroad and others inside Russia might talk of "bureaucratic deformation," Marxism itself could not explain how a proletarian dictatorship could be converted into something else without a change in the ownership of the means of production. Trotsky himself believed that the Soviet worker retained some power and some liberty under Stalin's rule. In 1934 Trotsky's stalwart supporter, Rakovsky, previously the most prominent figure in either the Left or the Right Opposition to refuse to submit, gave in and won release from prison by recanting his "errors."

"CADRES DECIDE EVERYTHING!"

At the end of 1932 the First Five-Year Plan was declared to have been fulfilled. Immediately the Second Plan, covering the years 1933–1937, went into effect, although it was not formally adopted until January 1934 when the XVII Party Congress met. By that time, it was reported, ninety-nine per cent of all Soviet industry was controlled by the state, while the *kolkhozes* and *sovkhozes* included ninety per cent of the total crop area. Private business and trade had virtually come to an end in the USSR, with the exception of the peasant markets for garden-plot produce and the illegal (but more or less tolerated) black market, both of which survive today.

The aim of the Second Plan was purportedly "to eliminate completely the capitalist elements" in the USSR. The implication was that they were substantially gone already. If the First Plan had been an era of "shock" methods, the second was to be a time of consolidation. The previous emphasis on quantity was to be replaced by stress on quality. "Gigantomania" became an epithet applied to the fascination for the big and the dramatic which had characterized the First Plan. The approved new slogans were "consolidate the gains already won" and "master the technical base." In his characteristically spare and elementary style, Stalin declared,

> Formerly we used to say that "technique [that is, machinery and capital goods] decides everything." This slogan helped us to put an end to the dearth in technique and to create a vast technical base . . . . That is very good. But it is not enough, it is not enough by far . . . . In order to set technique going and to utilize it to the full, we need people who have mastered technique, we need cadres capable of mastering and utilizing this technique according to all the rules of the art. . . . [The old slogan] must now be replaced by a new slogan, the slogan "cadres decide everything." That is the main thing now.

Cadres meant simply people able to do their jobs. The feverish efforts of the First Five-Year Plan had produced a broader "technical base"; they had also done much to develop a system of central economic controls and, above all, political controls based on the Party machinery and supplemented by the secret police, army, trade-union and other apparatuses. The systems of control depended on the individuals who operated them. For the apparatus of totalitarianism to function, *apparatchiki* were indispensable. In the early 1930's such a group did not need to be created; it already existed. What it needed was to be expanded, rewarded, prodded, intimidated, and terrorized. Only then would it become a completely reliable instrument.

THE GREAT PURGES

In 1934 the XVII Party Congress was held. It was called the "Congress of Victors," in ostensible reference to the achievements of the Five-Year Plans. The "victors" in fact were those who, following Stalin's lead, had beaten into silence the Party dissidents. At the Congress, Stalin announced complacently, "There is nothing more to prove and, it seems, no one to fight," and he appeared to be right. The terror directed against the enemies of the Party or simply those outside it, that is, the mass of the people, was not at an end, but its objective had evidently been achieved. The peasants and workers had been starved, killed, or frightened into submission.

However, the Party elite remained a problem, not because any of them resisted Stalin openly, but for other reasons; some murmured their dissatisfaction in private; others, who seemed satisfied, were relaxing and becoming complacent. It has been argued that totalitarianism cannot accept a situation where there is "no one to fight." In any case during the 1930's the target of the ruling faction changed somewhat. The mass terror, of which the clearest example was collectivization, yielded to the mass purge of the Party itself. The purge actually began before 1934 and the terror continued afterward, but the shift in emphasis was noteworthy. Having silenced its opponents, the apparatus turned on itself.

By the early 1930's, the Politburo consisted of Stalin, Molotov, Voroshilov, Kalinin, Rudzutak, Kuibyshev, Kaganovich, Kirov, Kosior, Ordzhonikidze, and Andreyev. None had belonged to either the Left or the Right Opposition; all were Stalin's trusted henchmen. But there remained questions of timing and emphasis in the execution of Stalin's policy which contained overtones of the earlier issues between Stalin and the opposition. It appears, for example, that Rudzutak, who had been charged with certain responsibilities regarding the trade-unions, reported and reflected some of the unrest among the workers. War Commissar Voroshilov did the same for the soldiers, and obtained exemption of the Far East from collectivization on General Bliukher's insistence that otherwise defense capabilities there would be completely undermined. Kalinin, himself of peasant origin, may have voiced the need for relative restraint with the countryside. Kirov, who had been sent to Leningrad to "clean up" Zinoviev's supporters there, seems to have passed on the discontent of those around him. In short, here were the worries of the Right Opposition reproduced, in however muted a fashion, by men who had backed Stalin against both Right and Left.

On December 1, 1934, Sergei Kirov, then rumored to be Stalin's chosen heir, was assassinated in Leningrad. The assassin was a young man named Nikolaev who had earlier had connections with Zinoviev. "Objectively," therefore, Zinoviev was said to be responsible. By the logic he himself used in his later confession, "The former activity of the former opposition could not, by the force of objective circumstances, but stimulate the degeneration of those criminals." A rising young star in the

Party apparatus, Andrei Zhdanov, was promptly sent to replace Kirov, and in the early months of 1935 whole trainloads of "Kirov's murderers" were deported from Leningrad to Siberia.

The official story was thus that the old Left Opposition had struck at Stalin through Kirov. The truth cannot be established beyond a doubt, but evidence has been offered in recent years, some of it by Khrushchëv in his "secret speech" of 1956, that Stalin himself instigated Kirov's murder. The episode was only the curtain raiser for the epic drama to follow. From the middle of 1935 to the middle of 1936, arrests of real or alleged supporters of Zinoviev and Trotsky continued, but on a relatively limited scale. It seemed during those months as if an era of relative relaxation was indeed at hand. In 1935 a new constitution was called for, and much publicity attended its preparation under the guiding hands of Bukharin and Radek. Stalin made many public appearances, smiling at little children and bestowing awards.

Then in August 1936 came the public trial of sixteen Old Bolsheviks, of whom the most prominent were Zinoviev and Kamenev. Although the target still appeared to be the former Left Opposition, the fabricated "confessions" of the accused tarnished the old Right as well. In September Henry Yagoda was removed as head of the NKVD *(Narodnyi Kommissariat Vnutrennykh Del* or People's Commissariat of Internal Affairs, into which the OGPU was changed in July 1934), along with some of his closest assistants. He was replaced by N. I. Yezhov. According to one account, Yezhov thereupon reported to the Party Central Committee that the executed defendants in the "trial of the sixteen" had implicated Bukharin, Rykov, and Tomsky—that is, the leaders of the former Right Opposition; however, Bukharin replied sharply, and the report was rejected by a majority which included five members (or candidate members) of the Politburo. It is at least certain that the five believed to have acted thus—Kosior, Rudzutak, Chubar, Postyshev, and Eikhe—were all purged in the blood bath which followed, and that they all were rehabilitated in Khrushchëv's "secret speech." (In fact, those five, all trusted Stalinists throughout the fight with the opposition, were the only top leaders killed during the purges whom Khrushchëv did rehabilitate.)

In January 1937 came the trial of the so-called "Anti-Soviet Trotskyite Center," consisting of seventeen lesser-ranking but still prominent opposition leaders, including Piatakov and Radek. It appears that in the February–March 1937 Plenum of the Central Committee Stalin overrode opposition to the broadening of the purges, and the real *Yezhovsh-*

china[3] rolled into high gear. On the eve of the plenum, Ordzhonikidze was said to have died of "heart disease"; we know that this was false, but it is still uncertain whether he was hounded into committing suicide or was murdered. In either case Stalin was responsible for his death.

Although only a year earlier the army had been reorganized in a fashion presumably more acceptable to the military leadership (ranks and discipline were restored and five marshals were appointed), in June 1937 the chief army generals, headed by the chief of the general staff, Marshal Tukhachevsky, were tried and executed. In March 1938 came the turn of the Right Opposition leaders (and some others) in the trial of the so-called "Anti-Soviet Bloc of Rights and Trotskyites." Tomsky killed himself before the trial; Bukharin, Rykov, Rakovsky, Yagoda, and others were tried and executed.

Altogether the accused included all members of Lenin's Politburo except Stalin himself (even Trotsky was tried *in absentia*), one ex-premier (Rykov), two former chiefs of the Comintern (Zinoviev and Bukharin), an ex-chief of the trade-unions (Tomsky), an ex-chief of the general staff (Tukhachevsky), and two ex-chiefs of the secret police (Yagoda and Yezhov—the latter was not tried publicly). However, the Great Purges by no means stopped with the elimination of the Bolshevik old guard and many of the newer Stalinite henchmen. The victims included seventy per cent of the members (and candidates) of the Party Central Committee elected in 1934, the great majority of the highest officers of the army, over ninety per cent of the central trade-union committees, and many managers, intellectuals, and Party and Comintern functionaries. In addition a multitude of ordinary citizens were accused; orders went out to the secret police to arrest a certain percentage of the whole population, varying slightly from district to district. It has been estimated that eight million people were arrested, and the actual total may well be higher still.

In July 1938 Yezhov himself was shunted aside by the appointment of Lavrenty Beria as his deputy, and in December Beria replaced him outright (Yezhov was later arrested and shot). This was the signal for the end of the mass purges. The mass purge and the show trial fell into disuse, but individuals—sometimes large numbers of them—continued to be arrested, shot, or sent to concentration camps. Those liquidated

• [3] In Russian the suffix *-shchina* means roughly, "the wicked deeds of" the person whose name precedes it. By this token the word *Stalinshchina* would be more accurate for the bloodiest phase of the purges, especially since Yezhov himself became one of the victims, but it is too late to change the terms.

were dealt with secretly, though sometimes their fate was publicized. During the 1930's Stalin used another device for getting rid of inconvenient persons in high places: murder coupled with public eulogy and grief. Among those who fell in this way may be counted Kirov, Kuibyshev, and Ordzhonikidze, all Politburo members, and Maxim Gorky, dean of Soviet writers.

The show trials themselves, conducted under the direction of Procurator General Andrei Vyshinsky, amazed and puzzled the world. In only one case, that of Krestinsky in the trial of March 1938, did a defendant repudiate a confession in open court, and a night with the NKVD sufficed to change his mind once again. The defendants uniformly confessed to the crimes with which they were charged, which included plotting with the secret services of foreign powers to overthrow Stalin and the Communist Party, "restore capitalism" in the USSR, and cede territory to Germany and Japan. A number of specific acts which the defendants admitted were shown by independent investigation—much of it undertaken by a private commission established under the chairmanship of John Dewey to probe the truth behind the trials—to have been physically impossible: meetings at hotels long since dismantled, landings at airports where no such planes had landed, and so forth.

Why Stalin conducted the blood bath, and why the defendants confessed to lies are questions which have been widely debated. Isaac Deutscher, while acknowledging the falsity of the charges, has argued that they "were based on a perverted 'psychological truth.' . . . [Stalin's] reasoning probably developed along the following lines: they may want to overthrow me in a crisis—I shall charge them with having already made the attempt . . . if they succeed, they may be compelled to . . . agree to a cession of territory. . . . I shall accuse them of having entered already into a treacherous alliance with Germany (and Japan) . . . . No milder pretext for the slaughter of the old guard would have sufficed . . . . It is not necessary to assume that he acted from sheer cruelty or lust for power. He may be given the dubious credit of the sincere conviction that what he did served the interests of the revolution and that he alone interpreted those interests aright."[4]

The sort of diabolical rationality which Deutscher imputes to Stalin may well account for the "slaughter of the old guard." But how then are we to account for the murders of the hitherto devoted Stalinists and the hounding of millions of puzzled little people, some of whom begged their fellow prisoners to tell them enough about the ideological sins with which they were charged (Zionism, for instance), but of which they had

• [4] *Stalin,* pp. 377–378.

scarcely heard before, so that they could make their confessions plausible? What of those who were innocent—as far as one could humanly judge—of even any oppositional thoughts, let alone acts? The only hypotheses so far advanced which account for such facts as the order to arrest a fixed percentage of the population are two: that Stalin was utterly mad, or that he realized that under totalitarianism anyone at all is potentially disloyal, and that therefore the regime would be secure only if everyone was sufficiently terrorized to become incapable of acting independently. Perhaps Stalin was deranged, but he was certainly attempting to secure the totalitarian regime.

A quite different question is what motives led the defendants to confess. The simplest explanation is that they succumbed to physical torture and the psychological pressure of the "conveyor"—endless interrogation of the victims while they were in a physically weakened condition. A more complex suggestion was offered by novelists—Charles Plisnier in *Faux passeports* (1938) and Arthur Koestler in *Darkness at Noon* (1941). The best of the accused, Koestler contended, signed confessions "in order to do a last service to the Party. . . . They were too deeply entangled in their own past, caught in the web they had spun themselves, according to the laws of their own twisted ethics and twisted logic; they were all guilty, although not of those deeds of which they accused themselves." Some certainly confessed without torture, hoping to save themselves or their families. After Khrushchëv's "secret speech" and the liberation of Cardinal Mindszenty, we can be certain that torture indeed was used on the chief defendants, some of whom went to their deaths with their bodies shattered but their minds intact. No doubt the perverted use of psychiatry to make minds sick instead of well, a technique further perfected by the Chinese Communists later, was first worked out in its fundamentals by the NKVD in the course of the Great Purges. Probably all these techniques were used, in varying combination.

The result was that a very substantial proportion of the entire leadership of the Soviet system was eliminated, and the whole population of the USSR was more or less successfully intimidated into acquiescence. Although Stalin announced at the XVIII Party Congress in March 1939, "Undoubtedly we shall have no further need of resorting to the method of mass purges," it was not forgotten that son had informed against father, father had been executed simply because he was the son of grandfather, and that whether there were "mass purges" again soon or ever, there was no such thing as a safe statement on public affairs, whether made to family or friends or fellow workers—indeed, in the USSR there was no safety for the individual at all.

Certain of the chief state institutions had been gravely weakened. The high command of the army had been decimated through the use of forged documents turned over to Stalin's secretariat by the Nazis. Although it is not certain that Stalin accepted them as genuine, he found that they served his purpose well. The Party, the trade-unions, the factory managements, and even the secret police itself had suffered from arrests of their leaders. All of the basic institutions of the totalitarian system had been shaken; however, by the same token they were less capable of independent stands, more reliable instruments of the remaining elite, and therefore more totalitarian, than before. Whether or not Stalin had sought more power for himself as his sole or chief end, his personal power was infinitely greater, and his apparatus was supreme. From 1933 to 1938 around one million technicians, administrators, and professional men had been graduated from the secondary schools, and they were used to replace the victims of the purges—thus, in *Darkness at Noon,* does Gletkin, the "Neanderthal" Stalinite, replace Ivanov, the cultured Old Bolshevik.

The last death sentence of the Great Purges was not carried out in 1938, but two years later. Trotsky, who had fled from Prinkipo to Norway to Mexico, trying to create a Fourth International, writing furiously, inveighing against Stalin but refusing to advocate his overthrow, was the last victim. He was murdered in Mexico in August 1940. The assassin, about whose person but not about whose crime there is much that is unknown, remains in a Mexican jail to this day.

THE "STALIN CONSTITUTION" OF 1936

At the moment when the Great Purges were swelling to their full fury in November 1936, Stalin appeared before the VIII All-Union Congress of Soviets to present for formal approval the new "Stalin Constitution." Already in June the Constitution had been published in draft form and a public discussion of its contents was invited. It is reported that 154,000 amendments were proposed, of which only 43 were adopted. The form of the document was obviously influenced by, and intended to be interpreted by those familiar with, the constitutions of "bourgeois democracies." However, the basic prerequisite for understanding the Stalin Constitution—which, with subsequent amendments, remains officially in effect—is that it neither purports to be nor is in fact the fundamental law of the USSR. The official ideology of the Soviet state, "Marxism-Leninism," is nowhere mentioned. At one point, in Article 126, the locus of power is indeed clearly indicated: "the most active and politically-conscious citizens in the ranks of the working class and other sections of the working people [that is to say, the workers are still distinguished from the peasants] unite in the Communist Party of the Soviet Union, which is the vanguard of the working people in their struggle to strengthen and develop the socialist system and is the leading core of *all* organizations of the working people, both public and state" (italics added). But this is the only mention of the Party.

The stated reason for the new Constitution was to give legal expression to the new stage of development which, it was contended, the USSR had reached by 1936, namely the completion of the building of "socialism" as distinguished from "communism," a distinction first set forth in Marx's *Critique of the Gotha Program.* Under "socialism," it was argued, exploitation had come to an end, and the principle "from each according to his ability, to each according to his work" was to be applied. Class antagonism had disappeared, but not classes *per se.* There were now two "friendly" classes, workers and peasants, with a stratum (not a class) known as "intelligentsia" overlying both. The state, which, it had been supposed, would "wither away" under socialism, was obviously and admittedly no weaker than before (actually it was immensely stronger than it had ever been). This was explained by the persistence of "capitalist encirclement," the continuing external danger which had its counterpart in the efforts of foreign governments to subvert the regime by utilizing domestic malcontents, who were by definition themselves "bourgeois survivals." As long as the Communists had not come to dominate the whole world, the Soviet state would accordingly persist.

The Constitution of 1924 had provided for an indirect suffrage, weighted in favor of the proletariat. The new Constitution provided for a suffrage which was equal for citizens of both sexes eighteen years of age or over, universal except for insane persons and convicts, direct in electing deputies to the new USSR Supreme Soviet, and secret. Thereby it seemed that the old revolutionary demand for "Four-Tail" (universal, equal, secret, and direct) suffrage—then projected for a constituent assembly—had been realized. However, the use of the secret ballot, which was made optional (booths being provided for those who desired to exercise their constitutional right), was taken as evidence that the voter had something to hide, and has remained a dead letter. Since 1936, it is true, suffrage has been universal, equal, and direct, but that fact has had no significance to the voter. He votes for deputies to the Supreme Soviet, which has no power, and he has no alternative to voting for the Party nominees except that of crossing out their names, an empty gesture risked by an utterly negligible percentage of voters.

The Constitution declares the Supreme Soviet to be the "highest organ of state power in the USSR," and it is entrusted with all governmental functions which do not "come within the jurisdiction of organs of the USSR that are accountable to the Supreme Soviet of the USSR." Such organs are the Presidium of the Supreme Soviet,[5] the Council of Ministers,[6] and the ministries themselves. The Supreme Soviet has two chambers, the Soviet of the Union (one deputy for every 300,000 voters) and the Soviet of Nationalities (deputies represent administrative units; there are 25 from each union republic, 11 from each autonomous republic, and so forth). A simple majority is said to be sufficient to pass laws, and there are provisions for disagreement between the chambers. In actual fact there has never been any other vote on a substantive question than a unanimous one in either chamber. What is of even more fundamental importance is that the Supreme Soviet is as a rule presented with *faits accomplis* for approval; even if the proposal in question has not actually gone into effect, "debate" on the floor is confined to laudatory remarks about what the leaders have handed in, and there is no pretense of consulting the deputies in drawing up any proposals nominally submitted for their vote. The Supreme Soviet has been called the "world's dullest parliament." It is dull because it has no power, and its sessions must be devoted to attempts to conceal the fact.

The Supreme Soviet elects its own Presidium, headed by a chairman, often referred to as "President" of the USSR, who is technically chief of state and carries out such duties as conferring honors and receiving ambassadors. The Supreme Soviet "appoints" the Council of Ministers of the USSR, the ministries being enumerated in the Constitution. Therefore whenever they are changed, as has happened many times, the Constitution must be amended. Sometimes such amendments come years after the changes are in fact made.

The Supreme Soviet "elects" the Supreme Court and Special Courts of the USSR and "appoints" the procurator general of the USSR. No powers are listed in the Constitution for the Supreme Court, and there is no procedure for finding any law "unconstitutional." The procurator general is given "supreme supervisory power to ensure the strict observance of the law by all Ministries and institutions subordinated to them, as well as by officials and citizens of the USSR generally." Article 112 states that "judges are independent and subject only to the law"; a Soviet jurist declares that this article "expresses the subordination of the

• [5] Not to be confused with the Presidium of the Central Committee of the Communist Party, by which name the Politburo has been known since 1952.

• [6] Until 1946 known as the Council of People's Commissars.

judges to the policy of the Soviet regime, which finds its expression in the law. The demand that the work of the judge be subject to the law and the demand that it be subject to the policy of the Communist Party cannot be in contradiction in our country."[7] Here is a good example of the fact that the Constitution cannot be taken at face value; its interpretation requires a knowledge of both the official ideology (as in this case) and actual Soviet practice.

Much was made of Soviet "federalism" in the new Constitution, and Stalin pretended to insist to the VIII Congress of Soviets that the union republics be given the right to secede from the USSR. In 1929 the original four republics (Russian, Ukrainian, Belorussian, and Transcaucasian) had acquired three new sister republics: the Uzbek, Turkmen, and Tadzhik SSR's. At the time of the adoption of the Stalin Constitution, the number was raised to eleven as the Transcaucasian republic was dissolved into its Georgian, Armenian, and Azerbaijani components, and the Kazakh and Kirghiz Autonomous Soviet Socialist Republics were raised to union-republic status. Each of these union republics was given the right of "secession," although it has been plainly stated that any attempt to exercise this right would be evidence of bourgeois nationalism directed against international proletarian solidarity.

The Constitution enumerates a number of "fundamental rights and duties of citizens," including the right to work, to rest and leisure, to maintenance in old age or in case of sickness or disability, and to education; and equality of rights for women and all nationalities or races is specified. Freedom of "religious worship and antireligious propaganda," speech, press, assembly, and of "street processions and demonstrations" is guaranteed. As the Constitution states, these freedoms are granted only "in order to strengthen the socialist system," and do not exist for anyone who, in the view of the regime, wants to weaken it. However, persons who accept the regime do not have the free exercise of these rights either; for example, a group that wished to demonstrate its loyalty in a manner and at a place and time inconvenient for the regime would encounter serious difficulties; the regime prescribes the conditions under which all such "rights" are to be implemented. As Fainsod puts it, "the right to work is not a right to choose one's work freely but a duty to work in disciplined subordination to state purposes"[8] and for several millions, to work in concentration camps. Article 127, which guarantees "inviolability of the homes of citizens and privacy of correspondence,"

• [7] N. N. Poliansky, in *Vestnik Moskovskogo Universiteta,* November 1950, as quoted by Merle Fainsod, *How Russia is Ruled,* p. 317.

• [8] *Ibid.,* p. 318.

has always been a dead letter. A few miscellaneous articles, on such matters as coat of arms, flag, and capital, complete the document.

Although understanding of the actual operation of the Soviet system cannot be gained from a study of the Constitution alone, Stalin and his henchmen employed a good deal of frankness in glosses which they publicly gave the document. In his speech to the VIII Congress of Soviets Stalin declared, "I must admit that the draft of the new Constitution . . . preserves unchanged the present leading position of the Communist Party of the USSR . . . . In the USSR only one party can exist, the Communist Party, which courageously defends the interests of the workers and peasants to the very end."

Why then was the Constitution so phrased as to slur over such important points, which Stalin was willing to mention in public? For one thing, it was realized that many more people would read the Constitution than would hear or read the commentaries. The phrasing of the Constitution was thus designed to appeal to Russians and minority peoples who had fought and hoped for democracy in the past, and it was intended to be misconstrued by statesmen, scholars, and ordinary citizens in Western countries which Soviet foreign policy, by way of the Popular Front, was at that time attempting to influence. The latter aim, to be sure, was widely achieved.

THE POSITION OF THE COMMUNIST PARTY

As Stalin said, the new Constitution left unchanged the role of the Communist Party in providing the direction of the whole Soviet system. It was argued that the Party "represented" the working classes. Stalin's view of the matter, perhaps, was that the Party thought what the workers ought to have been thinking and might be brought to think—or in any event to refrain from openly denying—and acted accordingly. But the Soviet people were not asked what they thought, although Stalin probably knew pretty well. Both Stalin and Andrei Vyshinsky (who in his *The Law of the Soviet State* provided authoritative commentary on the operation of the Stalin Constitution) contended that the Party "persuades" the majority, but "coerces" the minority, of the people outside its ranks. In this formulation, as in the Party Rules' definition of "democratic centralism" within the Party—which includes the phrase "strict Party discipline and the subordination of the minority to the majority"—the words "majority" and "minority" are fictions. The leaders tell the Party rank and file what to do, and they pass the word on to the masses. The operative phrase in the Party Rules' definition is "the absolutely binding character of the decisions of higher bodies upon lower bodies"—this principle is in effect in and out of the Party.

During the early years of Communist rule, there was a good deal of open discussion in the lower Party units and in the Party congresses, which remain in theory the governing body of the Party as a whole. Although already in Lenin's time "factions" were prohibited, they did in fact exist during the period of the NEP. While they could not count on a fair hearing, their spokesmen could obtain the floor (despite frequent heckling) and they could record their votes. By the time of the XV Congress in 1927, even these possibilities existed no longer. Subsequent congresses became fully subservient sounding boards for Stalin's clique, which summoned them with ever-decreasing frequency.

The original notion of "democratic centralism" was that decisions made by congress majorities must bind the Central Committee, other central organs, and all the rank and file. Stalin simply transferred the process of decision-making to himself and his own picked Politburo. The Party structure was not formally changed, but the views of no Party organ but the Politburo counted, and during the Great Purges several members of the Politburo itself were liquidated. The only security from execution, imprisonment, or dismissal was Stalin's unpredictable personal favor.

Having destroyed so many of the leaders of the Party, Stalin was naturally at pains to try to produce a leadership more amenable to his desires. The militant, even military, character of the Communist Party became fully developed during the thirties. Stalin tried to create a reliable new generation of Party members by emphasizing indoctrination in the principles of *partiinost'* ("party" converted into a generic noun; literally, "party-ness"), discipline, and self-criticism (*samokritika*). An attempt was made to create an atmosphere of unceasing combat, whether against "enemies of the state" or foreign "capitalists," or for the fulfillment of the goals of the Five-Year Plans or achievement of the objectives of Party propaganda and agitation (*agitprop*). A proliferation of "feeder" organizations was developed and expanded. The Little Octobrists for children eight to eleven years of age, the Pioneers for those ten to sixteen, and the Komsomol (Communist Union of Youth) for persons aged fifteen to twenty-six were together designed to produce adults who accepted the fundamental ideological commitments and values of the Party proper and were habituated to its standards of unquestioning discipline.

The cessation of the purges at the end of 1938 was a signal that two processes were nearly complete: members of a suspected older generation had been wiped out or terrorized, and also a younger and presumably more reliable generation had assumed the posts vacated by those purged or new posts established to perfect the control of Stalin's apparatus over all branches of Soviet life.

In that apparatus the Party was both in theory and practice the paramount and central mechanism, and the Constitution was quite accurate in stating that it was the "leading core of all organizations" including the "organs of government." But the Party itself had been converted into an instrument of Stalin and his clique. The Party members as a group were more privileged and more powerful than any other. Within its hierarchy there was a series of gradations of prestige and authority, but even the top functionaries were subject to Stalin's supreme power, and the word *Vozhd* (Leader) came to be used openly to acknowledge and proclaim that fact. In George Orwell's *Animal Farm* all of the animals were equal, but some were more equal than others; in those terms, Stalin was the most equal of all. By 1939 (and there were no further changes until 1946) the Politburo had come to consist of Stalin, Molotov, Voroshilov, Kalinin, Kaganovich, Andreyev, Mikoyan, Zhdanov, and Khrushchëv, while candidate members Malenkov and Beria also wielded considerable power. At the time of Hitler's invasion, probably Zhdanov was closest to being a Number Two man in Stalin's Politburo.

ECONOMIC GROWTH IN THE THIRTIES

The human casualties of the Great Purges were very great, but those executed comprised only a small proportion of the eight million or so arrested. Most of the victims went into the concentration camps. It was during the thirties that the NKVD became the largest single employer in the Soviet Union. The 1941 economic plan for the Soviet Union, captured by the Nazi armies and later released by the U. S. Government, showed that about one-sixth of all new construction in that year was entrusted to the NKVD. Since the document did not include material on armament production, gold output, or NKVD labor subcontracting to other enterprises, it is a safe conclusion that the share of the NKVD in the entire Soviet economy was much greater than the over-all figure of one-sixth. In certain industries for which detailed figures were given, the proportion was considerably higher: for example, the NKVD share in chrome-ore production was forty per cent. Even if the figures were complete, they would not convey adequately even the economic (let alone the political or moral) significance of the NKVD's gigantic prison labor force, which has been estimated by the most thoroughgoing study available as numbering around ten million.[9]

• [9] David J. Dallin and Boris I. Nicolaevsky, *Forced Labor in Soviet Russia* (New Haven: Yale University Press, 1947), pp. 49–87.

The Soviet Union naturally endeavors to conceal the role of the secret police in its economy, but its statistics on over-all economic growth also reflect a series of intentional deceptions which make it very difficult to evaluate them. There is no doubt that the industrial expansion of the USSR from 1928 to 1941 was very considerable indeed. One may credit this to the Soviet regime in approximately the same sense that one may credit the Pharaohs with the Pyramids or the Chinese emperors with the Great Wall; it was done for the power and glory of the regime, at the sacrifice of the welfare of the people. But in measuring that expansion it is necessary to note certain points about the official figures (the only ones available, although a few scholars have tried to correct them as best they can through a process of informed guesswork). First, all figures involving monetary value were computed in terms of 1926–1927 prices; during that fiscal year a wide range of goods which appeared under the Five-Year Plans had not been produced at all or had not had the improvements or models used in the later period, and such products were assigned the value of the price they sold for in the first year they were turned out. This tended to inflate greatly the real increases as represented in monetary indices. Second, the shift to large-scale enterprise meant that figures for the Five-Year Plans, under which production was fully (or even exaggeratedly) reported, were compared with totals for the NEP period, when small producers (both urban and rural) were able to conceal a portion of their output from state agencies. There are other difficulties with Soviet statistics; the system is one in which emphasis falls not on accurate reporting of the facts, but on matching and exceeding predetermined quantities of output, with the manager's job or even his life at stake if he does not produce or at least claim to produce his quota, while great benefits may accrue to him if he greatly exceeds it. A million terrified little men may greatly distort Soviet statistics even if the government reports correctly what it is told.

Taking 1913 as the base year, in 1940 national income was officially claimed to be 611%, gross industrial output 854.9%, and gross farm output 184.1% of the pre-World War I Tsarist figures. From a total of 170 million in 1913 the population declined sharply to 147 million in 1926, owing to World War I and Civil War losses, famine, and collectivization, and did not reach 170 million again until 1939 (actually this amounted to a slight increase, since the 1939 borders were inside those of 1913 at certain points). Thus no considerable rise in population accounts for the percentage increases in the indices mentioned. Soviet sources claim that coal production (in millions of metric tons) rose from 29.1 in 1913 to 166 in 1940, oil production from 9.2 to 31, steel production from 4.2 to 18.3, and electric-power production went from 1.9 to 48.3 billion kilowatt-hours. Whether or not these figures are entirely accurate, there has unquestionably been a very significant rise in the output of heavy industry, including armaments.

The capital which made this increase possible was amassed by intensive exploitation of the ordinary Soviet citizenry, especially the peasantry. The regime made the deliberate decision to hold down the production of the necessities of life, not to speak of luxuries. According to Soviet sources, in 1928 "means of production," or capital goods, accounted for about 46% of all industrial production, consumer goods about 54%. This was at the very beginning of the Five-Year Plans. The plan for 1953, as announced by Malenkov (who was at that moment endeavoring to increase consumer-goods production somewhat), was for about 70% means of production, 30% consumer goods; thus during the 1930's the figures were doubtless even more lopsided. As a result, in the judgment of one prominent specialist on the Soviet economy, the standard of living in 1940 "was probably little if any improved over that of the late 1920's."[10] Other studies have indicated that the real earnings of Soviet workers declined very steeply after 1928 and did not approach the level of that year again until the 1950's. Those who have been in shops and in the homes of even privileged persons in the USSR after the resumption of tourism in 1956–1957 can testify that, whatever was the case in any past year, "consumer goods" remains a grotesque euphemism for the type of purchases available for the health and comfort of the ordinary Soviet citizen.

INDUSTRIAL LABOR

To achieve the priority goals of Soviet heavy industry, the regime adopted a series of measures to elicit the maximum effort from the workers. During the First Five-Year Plan limited competition was tried, and official attacks were made on the concept of "equalitarianism." Certainly if, under socialism, pay was to be scaled "according to work," there was no reason why differences in quantity and quality of work done should not be reflected in differences in income.

On August 31, 1935, a new expedient was launched. It was reported that one Alexei Stakhanov, a coal hewer in the Donets Basin, had hewed 102 tons of coal in one shift and thus had overfulfilled his quota by fourteen hundred per cent. This news was soon followed by other astound-

[10] Harry Schwartz, *Russia's Soviet Economy* (2nd ed.; New York: Prentice-Hall, 1954), p. 133.

ing reports of overexertion, and the word "Stakhanovite" came to be applied to all workers who achieved such staggering records of output. These workers were paid very highly and rewarded with various honors and decorations. It is true that such records could not be and were not actually achieved by a single unaided man, and that his fellow workers had to set up tools and conditions by means of which he could chalk up vast overfulfillments of quota. This circumstance led to natural resentment among non-Stakhanovites, and intentional frustrations, attacks, and even slayings of Stakhanovites by their fellows occurred. Nevertheless, a considerable part of the new record was the result of the Stakhanovite's own labor, and it is common knowledge in the USSR that the life expectancy of many of them was shortened by their glories.

The regime did not trust simply to the inspiration produced by the new records. Usually after a Stakhanovite demonstration the old "norm" was raised, not, to be sure, to the level of the new record, for all workers could not furnish set-ups for each other, but to a point midway between the old norm and the new record. In other countries the device is known simply as the "speed-up." The opposition to Stakhanovism was, though unorganized, widespread. It is probable that the purge of the overwhelming majority of the members of the trade-union central committees in 1937–1938 was particularly intended to crush such opposition. Simultaneously the regime began to give strong emphasis to piecework, so that by 1938 only sixteen per cent of the workers received ordinary wages, the remainder of the wages being some combination of simple-piece, progressive-piece, and bonus.

However, incentives of this kind were not sufficient to produce the results the regime demanded. From 1938 to 1940 the most stringent compulsion was applied to the labor force. In December 1938 one law provided that every worker must have a labor book in which his whole employment history was recorded, to be presented to the authorities whenever required. Another defined "absenteeism" as constituting any unauthorized absence from the job, be it as little as arriving twenty minutes late for work, and four cases of such "absenteeism" in two months entailed dismissal of the offending worker. In June 1940 the worker was prohibited from leaving his job without permission. Any attempt to obtain dismissal through intentional "absenteeism" was forestalled by a provision that the latter offense should henceforth be penalized by compulsory work in the same enterprise, at three-quarters of the usual wages. By a law of October 1940 the regime could transfer skilled workers anywhere at will. Legally all labor thus became compulsory in the sense that no worker could select or change his own job, although in fact many violations of labor legislation did occur owing to the feverish efforts of Soviet managers to fulfill their quotas under conditions of labor shortage, and their willingness to countenance infractions to that end.

By the end of the 1930's the system of "organized intake" of "redundant" rural labor (see p. 273) was proving unsatisfactory, often because the laborers drafted not only lacked the requisite skills but might be too old to acquire them easily. Therefore in October 1940 a new system known as the State Labor Reserves program was inaugurated. Close to a million boys aged fourteen to seventeen were drafted annually for skilled training in special schools, and girls aged sixteen to eighteen were added during World War II. The training was to be followed by four years of obligatory work on assigned jobs, after which military service had to be discharged.

At every stage the Soviet worker was closely subjected to state control. The trade-union structure gave him no protection. In 1933 collective agreements between trade-unions and managements were abolished, strikes were at an end, and the trade-unions had no say whatsoever regarding wages or hours, as they were fixed by law or the central planning machinery. The unions' functions were reduced to such things as deciding which workers were to go to which sanatoriums—the nearest Soviet equivalent to a Western "vacation"—for short periods, conducting propaganda among the workers in a given enterprise, and watching the towel supply in the washrooms.

THE PEASANTRY

By the end of the First Five-Year Plan the basic structure of Soviet agriculture had been largely decided upon, but efforts were needed to bring all the farms into that structure and to enforce its regulations. By 1938, 93.5% of all peasant households had been collectivized. Most of these were on collective farms (*kolkhozy*); state farms (*sovkhozy*) remained small in proportion (10%) to the total sown area and grain output. Individual farming was still practiced by 6.5% of all households under sharply discriminatory conditions, and was soon to disappear.

The Communists had compromised on the *artel* form of *kolkhoz* (see p. 271). By the new Model Statutes of the Agricultural Artel of 1935, the regime confirmed the *kolkhoznik's* ownership of garden plot and livestock. The collective farms were now permitted to readmit "kulaks" who gave evidence of "reform," and the farms settled down to an uneasy calm. The collective farmer and his wife and children worked as long and hard as they could on their garden plot and as little as they were able to manage on the "collective sector" of the *kolkhoz* land. As a result, in 1937 the tiny plots accounted for an amazing one-fourth of the gross farm output of the USSR. At the XVIII Party Congress in 1939 it was openly admitted that in many places private farming was the peasant's chief concern. In order to combat this, two measures were enacted. First, the regime abandoned all pretense that the farmer worked willingly on the collective sector and established a legal minimum of eighty "work-days" (*trudodni,* often more than chronological days, but variously defined) per year; if the *kolkhoznik* did not fulfill that requirement, he could be expelled from the collective farm, which the regime openly admitted would mean starvation. Second, a new survey was ordered to confiscate any land in each garden plot in excess of a prescribed maximum, usually about one acre. As in urban industry, however, the laws and regulations were by no means always observed. One example is provided by Fedor Belov in a revealing appendix, headed "Bribes to Raion [Regional] Officials in 1948," to a useful sketch of life on a collective farm during these years and later.[11]

Long before, in 1920, Trotsky had declared that Soviet methods "are not less varied than those used by the bourgeoisie, but they are more honest, more direct and frank, uncorrupted by mendacity and fraud. The bourgeoisie had to pretend that its system of labor was free. . . . We know that every labor is socially compulsory labor. Man must work in order not to die. He does not want to work. But the social organization compels and whips him into that direction." No doubt the Stalinist regulations for the workers and peasants were not what Trotsky had in mind, but the statement is a suggestive forecast of what actually happened in the USSR by 1941.

THE INTELLIGENTSIA

According to Stalin, over the worker and peasant classes in the new socialist society there existed a stratum which he called intelligentsia.[12] "No ruling class," Stalin declared, "has ever managed without its own intelligentsia, and there are no grounds for believing that the working class of the USSR can do so." In 1939 Molotov reported that just under ten million Soviet citizens should be classified as members of this "stratum"; he included in it administrators, industrial managers, collective-

• [11] *A History of a Soviet Collective Farm* (New York: Praeger, 1955).

• [12] Soviet usage of this term should not be confused with its meaning which refers to the pre-1917 revolutionaries; see p. 33.

farm chairmen, engineers, doctors, teachers, accountants, army officers, and technicians of all kinds.

Many of these persons were members of the Communist Party, but the majority were not. Party membership (both full members and candidates) fell from 3,500,000 in January 1933 to 1,920,000 in January 1938, in the midst of the Great Purges; even though the purges continued through 1938, during that year the membership began to increase once more. By January 1939 the total was 2,306,000; by January 1940 it was 3,400,000, of whom forty per cent had been recruited in the previous two years. It is impossible to establish exactly how many Party members came from the "intelligentsia," but certainly it was a large proportion. In general the intelligentsia, overlapping with the membership of the ruling Party, formed the peak of the pyramid of Soviet society.

As in other Soviet social groups, there were gradations within the intelligentsia. David J. Dallin provides an example in reference to medical care: each of the highest officials has his own physician who has no other patients; for the second rank of Kremlin employees there is a doctor to each five or six families; in the third rank, one per fifteen to twenty families. For the ordinary population of Moscow there is a "dispensary" (usually one doctor) for every two thousand to three thousand people.[13] A Spanish former Communist who was employed by the Comintern in the USSR during this period writes, "In the Comintern there were three categories: A, B, C. In the Lux Hotel [for the most privileged foreign Communists] there were three categories: A, B, C. In the hospitals also there are three categories: A, B, C. Why do they call it a classless society?"[14]

Why indeed? The Stalinist argument ran as follows. The means of production were in the hands of the regime which was assumed to "represent" the "proletariat," or, as was sometimes said, the "toilers" (including the peasantry). Since there was no private ownership, and no class antagonism arising from such a basis remained, there could be no exploitation. Each was paid "according to his work"—as determined by the regime. Therefore Soviet society was both classless and socialist. Any manifestation hostile or unacceptable to the regime was explained on the basis of "capitalist survivals," or the machinations of foreign capitalists. It was all a matter of simple logic, and indeed, given the assump-

• [13] *The New Soviet Empire* (New Haven: Yale University Press, 1951), pp. 140–143.

• [14] Enrique Castro Delgado, *J'ai perdu la foi à Moscou,* trans. from Spanish by Jean Talbot (3rd ed.; Paris: Gallimard, 1950), pp. 115 and 177. English trans. by D.W.T.

tions, the conclusions followed. All that was necessary was to ignore the evidence.

Stalin's objective was not merely economic transformation or concentration of political power or dictation over thought and the arts. It was all of those things, but it was also much more. It was the alteration of human nature, or, as the official phraseology had it, the creation of the "new Soviet man." In 1941 Stalin, his Politburo, and the upper echelons of the Communist Party—even some of those who regretted the casualties and feared or even hated Stalin—appeared convinced that this goal was in sight. Stalin and his ideologists cited Marxism to prove that the goal would inevitably be achieved, because the economic foundation of society had been transformed. However, the totalitarian dictatorship had been sufficiently consolidated to ensure that all the power at its disposal would be utilized to hasten the inevitable.

Stalin and the Borderlands

CHAPTER 19

THE MINORITY NATIONALITIES

From the first Stalin's specialty in Party affairs had been the "nationalities question" (see p. 218), and he did not neglect it after his rise to supreme power. Each of the hundred and eighty nationalities which existed in the USSR, or at least the forty or fifty which were large enough to have some political significance, required separate study before the Party was able to formulate a policy to achieve its desired ends. The Commissariat of Nationalities and other governmental and state-run academic bodies accomplished prodigious labors to make this possible. The past and present of each people had to be examined seriously and factually, in order to discover which traits had to be suppressed and which encouraged, which traditions and cultural artifacts had to be expunged and which distorted to serve the needs of central control of the borderlands. In more than one case Moscow's busy specialists rediscovered virtually forgotten figures and events of a nationality's past to which they could attach some merit for propaganda purposes, only to castigate admiration for them as ideologically harmful a few years later.

Stalin's chief objectives in relation to the borderlands were four: 1. to eliminate any threat of centrifugal pressures by stifling local nationalism and substituting as an object of allegiance "Soviet patriotism," or, when that failed, enforcing as a dogma belief in the eternal brotherhood of the nationality in question with the Great Russians; 2. to influence and attract the USSR's neighbors by open and concealed subversion carried out by members of a given local nationality, as well as by propaganda about the alleged economic, political, and cultural gains of that nationality under Soviet rule; 3. economic and social transformation designed to destroy the previous native society and to substitute a social system susceptible of control by Moscow; 4. outright economic exploitation of the borderlands. All of these objectives served Stalin's purpose in establishing totalitarian control over the entire USSR and attempting to extend it beyond Soviet borders.

Stalin's theoretical position in relation to the nationalities was restated at the XVI Party Congress in 1930 and reiterated at the XVII Congress of 1934 and subsequently. He declared that "survivals of capitalism in men's consciousness are much more tenacious in the sphere of the national problem than in any other sphere." On the national question, he contended, there were twin dangers: "Great Russian chauvinism" and local nationalism. Either one might at a given moment or place be the more threatening to the foundations of the "fraternal" union of nationalities in the USSR.

Actually, "Great Russian chauvinism" never threatened Stalin's domination (though he sometimes pretended that it was the offense for which he removed or punished maladroit functionaries in the borderlands). He was able to decide how and when he would use this or that old Russian hero or writer for his own purposes. There was never any possibility that any genuine Russian nationalist could achieve any power in the Russian republic, or that the Great Russians could somehow break off from the Communist center—they were in it for as long as the regime should hold together. What threatened the totalitarian control was local nationalism, which might be found intertwined with devotion to Communism in the border regions and in that form was regarded as especially dangerous.

THE UKRAINE AND BELORUSSIA

The Ukraine was the most difficult region for Stalin to deal with simply because it was the biggest. In his "secret speech" of 1956, Khrushchëv drew nervous laughter from his audience by declaring that the Ukrainians avoided the fate of small peoples liquidated during World War II "only because there were too many of them and there was no place to which to deport them. Otherwise, he [Stalin] would have deported them also." This sally might have been more effective if Khrushchëv himself had not been one of the key men in Stalin's repressions of the Ukraine during the 1930's, but the words doubtless had some truth in them.

The Ukraine was also the most important of the border regions. It was not only the most populous republic (next to the Russian), but its rich store of raw materials and heavy industry and its strategic location *vis-à-vis* the Black Sea and eastern Central Europe gave it a decisive significance for the whole USSR.

During the NEP Lenin's policy of restraint toward the minorities and his belief that Communism could thrive in the borderlands, if the local language and traditions were converted to its needs, were in the ascendant in the Ukraine as well as in most other border regions. In 1923 a policy of "Ukrainization" was announced; it meant expanding the use of the Ukrainian language in the schools and government and placing Ukrainians in positions of authority (in a republic set up by a Bulgarian, Rakovsky, with all too prominent Russian participation). For a time "Ukrainization" flourished, and indeed if such a policy ever had a chance it was in the Ukraine, where the national religion was the same as that of the Russians and the language was closely related to Russian, and where, in contrast to such ancient nations as Georgia, Ukrainian national or even cultural self-consciousness was only recently and incompletely developed.

However, reflecting both the popular discontent with the Soviet system and their own nationalist aspirations, the Ukrainian intellectuals took advantage of the "Ukrainization" policy to speak out. In 1925 Mykola Khvylovy began to publish a weekly in which he attacked what he termed the rebirth of Muscovite messianism in Communist guise, styled Moscow the center of "all-Union Philistinism," and, declaring that "The ideas of the proletariat we all know without the guidance of Moscow," called on the Communist Ukraine to turn away from the East and to draw nearer to the "progressive" West of Newton, Darwin, and Marx. Khvylovy's "Away from Moscow" slogan was sharply denounced and in 1926–1927 he was silenced. In 1928 Mykhailo Volobuev, a writer on economics, criticized what he already recognized to be Moscow's exploitation of the border regions, the Ukraine in particular, for the benefit of the center. He also was at once attacked, and he recanted.

The Ukrainian republic's commissar for education, Alexander Shumski, a former Borotbist (Ukrainian Left S.R.), was a prime mover in the campaign for "Ukrainization," and complained to Stalin in a personal interview that the policy was being implemented too slowly, adding other grievances. This smacked of a political deviation, and Shumski was attacked. Although he recanted partly several times and fully in 1930, he was arrested in 1933 and disappeared.

Shumski was succeeded as commissar of education by Mykola Skrypnyk, a staunch Communist but likewise a supporter of Ukrainian cultural nationalism. Skrypnyk led the Ukrainian Communist party during the period of collectivization, which was perhaps more brutal and more sharply resisted in the Ukraine than anywhere else in the whole USSR. Several alleged (and very possibly real) anti-Soviet conspiracies were uncovered and the participants tried, especially forty-five members of the Union for the Liberation of the Ukraine (*Spilka Vyzvolennia Ukrainy* or S. V. U.) in 1930. Other such trials followed, and in June 1933 the Russian Paul Postyshev and the Pole Stanislaw Kosior attacked Skrypnyk in a meeting of the Ukrainian party Central Committee for coddling Ukrainian nationalist deviation. A few weeks later he killed himself. Khvylovy's suicide had preceded Skrypnyk's by two months.

Postyshev and Kosior now launched a campaign against "over-Ukrainization" and repressed the Ukrainian intellectuals. In 1937 Stalin, evidently still dissatisfied, liquidated virtually the entire leadership of the Ukraine. Within a year a galaxy of prominent Communists, including three successive Ukrainian prime ministers, the entire Ukrainian Politburo, and Postyshev and Kosior themselves, were eliminated. Apparently only one of the top leaders survived, Gregory Petrovski, president of the Ukrainian republic, who was released from a concentration camp in 1953. In 1938 Nikita Khrushchëv was given charge of the Ukrainian party. He promptly began to enforce the compulsory teaching of the Russian language in the schools, and there was no more talk about "Ukrainization."

Belorussia was a smaller, poorer, and less strategically located republic. This was fortunate for Stalin, since the Belorussian intelligentsia was even less enthusiastic than the Ukrainian about Soviet control. In the 1920's there was a move among the intellectuals to abolish even the name "Belorussia" because it had the word "Russia" in it, and to replace it by "Krivia," taken from a tribe which had inhabited roughly the same area at the dawn of Eastern Slavic history. During the First Five-Year Plan alleged Belorussian nationalist conspiracies were discovered, but only after 1933 did the persecution of the Belorussian intellectuals become intense. In 1937 the chief of the purgers, N. F. Gikalo, was himself purged along with the prime minister, Nicholas Goloded, the president of the Belorussian republic, and many others.

THE CAUCASUS

The region north of the Caucasus Mountains constituted a mosaic of peoples who had practically nothing in common except a detestation of Communism. They clung stubbornly to their own traditions: during collectivization the Ossetians, for example, converted the task of determining who was a "kulak" into a weapon of clan warfare. A clan which managed to win Communist favor would find no kulaks in its midst, while a neighboring clan might be discovered to consist entirely of kulaks.

The problem of Daghestan, the eastern part of that region, was one to make any administrator despair; its population of one million comprised thirty-two nationalities living in an area about the size of the state of Maryland. These peoples shared an attachment to Islam, the use of Arabic as a literary language, and veneration of the memory of Shamil, fighter against Tsarist armies of conquest. Arabic, as the literary vehicle of the Moslem religion, was to be wiped out; to this end the Soviets tried first to substitute Turkish, then eight selected Daghestani languages, and finally Russian. N. Samursky, head of the Daghestan party committee, tried his best to fight Islam and Arabic against fantastic odds, but in 1937 he was himself executed as a "bourgeois nationalist."

South of the Caucasus Mountains lay the three union republics. Although Stalin himself came from Georgia, the country had not only fought Soviet invasion in 1921 but was also the scene of a mass uprising against Moscow in 1924. The Georgian Communist party leaders, chief of whom was Budu Mdivani, the vice-premier of the republic, did not get on well with Stalin and were purged in 1937. Apparently Ordzhonikidze, though he had been Stalin's trusted lieutenant and seemed no more squeamish about the sensibilities of his fellow Georgians than Stalin, opposed the liquidation of Mdivani and his colleagues, and so perished at the same time (see p. 280).

In Georgia deep resentment was felt against Moscow's insistence on the expansion of tea and citrus farms, when what the country needed was more food. Similar unrest was created in Azerbaijan by central compulsion to grow more cotton, as a result of which the grain acreage substantially decreased. In Azerbaijan "national deviation" was punished repeatedly, by Kirov in the mid-1920's and by Beria in the period of the Great Purges just before he became chief of the NKVD.

Despite troubles with Azerbaijan, Moscow used it with some success as a magnet for interesting the youth among Turkic peoples everywhere in Communism. Armenia, although not Turkic like Azerbaijan, was also a thorn in Turkey's side because Turkey still had a small Armenian minority, but even more because it had a large area in which Armenians had once lived and which they might claim (including Mount Ararat, which is ambiguously shown on the coat of arms of the Armenian SSR). The Armenians were useful to the Soviets especially for their long-developed talents as traders and travelers, and Armenians rose to the Politburo (Anastas Mikoyan) and to the top level of army generals (Ivan Bagramian). However, their ancient nationalism and their Christian religion—although the hierarchy of the Armenian Church was, like that of the Georgian and Russian Orthodox churches, finally forced to serve the ends of the Soviet regime—remain as continuing obstacles to the attainment of Moscow's objectives.

THE MOSLEMS

Except for the Azerbaijanis and the Crimean Tatars, most of the Moslem peoples in the USSR lived in Central Asia and a contiguous wedge of territory bending northwest from it to Kazan. For the most part the Moslems were ethnically Turkic, and the Turkic peoples were Moslem, although there were a few exceptions: the Tadzhiks were Moslem but Iranian, the Chuvash (just west of Kazan) were Turkic but Christian. Some, such as the Kazakhs, were nomads, while others, like the Uzbeks, were settled peoples; some had rich and ancient traditions, such as the Tadzhiks, linked with the culture of Persia, while others had scarcely any written literature of their own. Most of them were united in their devotion to Islam and their use of the Arabic script for writing their Turkic languages.

The assault on the old societies therefore started with an "alphabetic revolution," which was begun in Azerbaijan in 1925 and gained momentum after the Turkological Congress in Baku in 1926. It consisted of the replacement of Arabic script, sometimes overnight, by the Latin alphabet. The object was simultaneously to isolate the Moslems from their co-religionists south of Soviet borders and to undermine Islam, whose sacred and legal texts were all in Arabic script. In 1928 Mustafa Kemal also adopted Latin letters for Turkey, thereby undercutting the Soviet desire to prevent cultural intercourse. However, too much effort and expense had gone into the change-over for it to be replaced immediately by some other system, and the vital aim of secularization (which was also Kemal's) was still served by it.

After 1928 Islam was assaulted frontally, along with pan-Islamism, pan-Turkism, and local nationalisms. The Kazan Tatars resisted the new script especially strongly, and Mirza Sultan-Galiev, first prime minister of the Tatar ASSR, who had been arrested six years earlier, was tried for "nationalism" in 1929. About the same time the prime minister of the Crimean ASSR, several prominent Bashkirs, and other Turkic leaders were prosecuted for national deviation.

Simultaneously Stalin advanced to assault the basis of the old societies outright. Elsewhere in the USSR collectivization created great misery and starvation; in Central Asia it threatened to wipe out whole peoples. Until 1928 the old, in some places still tribal, life had scarcely been touched; now it was broken up. Clan leaders were wiped out, nomads were forcibly settled, and an effort was made to uproot Islam and all its institutions. According to Soviet admission, the Kazakh population decreased by almost a million and came to be outnumbered by Russians (as occurred in a number of other "national" units, usually more gradually) in the Kazakh SSR. The republic's livestock losses amounted to 73% of the cattle, 87% of the sheep, and 83% of the horses. In the settled area of Uzbekistan, Moscow demanded, as in Azerbaijan, that more cotton be grown, and the food supply accordingly fell off. The Soviet regime built a number of railways and canals (although they announced with much fanfare far more of both than they actually completed), and created much new industry. But the whole economy of Central Asia was disrupted, and the people were terrorized and bewildered.

Stalin had won a victory of sorts, but he rightly reckoned it as far from complete. In 1937 he conducted a thorough purge of national "deviationists" in Central Asia as elsewhere. Already at the end of the First Five-Year Plan, in Kazakhstan and Tadzhikistan, the chief Communists had been eliminated for failing to execute the plan's directives successfully. Nevertheless their replacements were among those who were branded as "traitors" in 1937–1938. They included the Armenian leader of the Kazakh party C. I. Mirzoyan, Tadzhik prime minister Abdullah Rakhimbayev, Uzbek prime minister Faisulla Khodzhaev and party leader Akmal Ikramov, Turkmen president Nederby Aitakov, Kirghiz State Planning Commission member Abdukerim Sydykov and prime minister Yusup Abdurrakhmanov, and many others.

The Great Purges drove home the necessity of obeying Moscow's political and economic policies; now Stalin attempted once again to enforce his cultural policy through a second "alphabetic revolution." Only three years earlier it had been triumphantly announced that sixty-nine new alphabets had been constructed in Latin letters. However, in March 1938 Moscow issued a decree requiring that the Russian language be taught in all non-Russian schools. In order to make it more accessible by making Russian letters familiar, the regime threw out the new Latin alphabets for the indigenous languages (although the Balts and Finns were left their Latin letters, which they had always used) and replaced them by still newer alphabets in Cyrillic letters. The newest change was immensely costly, difficult, and repugnant to most of the peoples concerned. The Chuvash, Ossetians, and a few other small groups had used the Cyrillic alphabet before 1917, but even they must have regarded its restoration after a decade of Latinization as a mixed blessing. In some cases the second "alphabetic revolution" was not completed until after World War II. Its ultimate purpose, to isolate the borderlands from foreign influences (Central Asia being the chief area affected) and to draw them closer to the center, was not new. However, the behavior of Central Asian soldiers during the war and other developments made it clear that neither that nor the other objectives of Sovietization had been fully achieved.

THE JEWS AND OTHER MINORITIES

There were somewhat less than three million Jews in the Soviet Union. The Russian Empire had generally restricted them to a Pale of Settlement in the Ukraine and adjacent areas (large numbers also lived in Russian Poland), but by 1921 much of the old Pale was west of the Soviet border. Around forty per cent of the Jews who remained in the USSR left the former Pale area before 1939, many to enter the cities, some to take up agriculture.

Both Lenin and Stalin denied that there was a Jewish "nation," Stalin emphasizing that the reason for this was the absence of a large Jewish agricultural population. Nevertheless, at the time of the October Revolution the Jews received all the rights accorded other minorities, and indeed the Revolution was welcomed as an act of liberation by many Russian Jews, perhaps more enthusiastically than by any other national group. Jewish schools which taught Yiddish (the language of most Russian Jews) spread rapidly; a Jewish press sprang into existence, and by 1918, 81 Yiddish and 10 Hebrew newspapers were being published; a Jewish theater backed by the state flourished and produced such great figures as the actor Solomon Mikhoels; and Jewish Sections were organized in the Communist Party. To be sure all of the cultural growth had to be Communist in orientation, and the Judaic religion was attacked in the schools, but often by Jews themselves. Moreover, although popular anti-

Semitism, strong in Russia as in other East European countries, persisted even among some non-Jewish Communists, during the 1920's the Soviet government combated it with vigor.

Jewish agricultural settlement was encouraged by Kalinin and others. In scattered areas of the Ukraine and Belorussia Jewish farmers through their hard work gained acceptance by their peasant neighbors, who often were at first suspicious. In 1927 the distant and forbidding Far Eastern region of Birobidzhan was reconnoitered for possible Jewish colonization. Soon afterward immigrants began to move, and in 1934 a Jewish Autonomous Province was created there. However, it proved a failure; Jews remained in the minority in the province, and those who came stayed chiefly in the towns.

During the middle 1930's the campaign against "national deviation" manifested itself in the beginnings of official anti-Semitism, cloaked in the concepts of Marxism-Leninism. The Judaic religion had always been anathematized along with all other religious faiths, but in addition ties with foreign Jews and Jewish culture, and Zionism in particular, were condemned as consorting with the "capitalist" enemy. The Jewish press collapsed, cultural life withered, and Birobidzhan virtually disappeared from official propaganda. In 1926 the Jewish Sections of the Communist Party had ceased to meet, and not long afterward they were disbanded. In 1937 Semën Dimanshtein, the party secretary of Birobidzhan, who had been Stalin's own assistant in the Nationalities Commissariat, and other prominent Jews fell in the purges.

Moscow's public policy of anti-Nazism, which attracted and misled many Jews abroad, was perhaps for a time some consolation to Soviet Jews. However, after the Nazi-Soviet Pact Stalin assumed a position of official neutrality toward Nazi ideology and prohibited attacks upon it. Thereby, as a prominent authority says, the regime "blinded Soviet Jews to the mortal danger threatening them";[1] and in the early stages of Hitler's invasion the Nazis overran multitudes of Jews who were quite unprepared for their swift and gruesome fate.

There were other small national groups which Soviet nationality policy was able to turn to account. The Volga German ASSR, set up in 1924, boasting such towns as Marx and Engels, for years served as a show window for the Germans at home. Although it met strong opposition here as elsewhere, collectivization in the ASSR was almost completed by 1931, ahead of any other district in the whole country. In 1937 "national

• [1] Solomon M. Schwarz, *The Jews in the Soviet Union* (Syracuse: Syracuse University Press, 1951), p. 310.

deviation" brought about the purge of the prime minister, A. Welsch, and the president of the ASSR, but Soviet propaganda continued to sing the republic's praises. No one would have thought that the Volga Germans were fated for genocide a few years later.

Although before 1939 there were few Poles in the USSR, the Soviets found thirty Polish villages in a Volhynian marsh which they proclaimed a "Polish National District" in 1925 to attract support from across the western borders. Although the Baltic states were annexed only in 1940, Communists from there had risen high in the Soviet system, especially the Latvians Janis Rudzutak and Robert Eikhe, who reached the Politburo, and Robert Eideman, president of *Osoaviakhim,* the civil defense organization; all three were purged in 1937–1938. Whether a particular minority was large or small in number, whether it had many or few kinsmen beyond Soviet borders, whether it was organized in a republic or lesser administrative unit, its leaders met the same fate.

Stalin's policy toward the borderlands had its successes and failures. The destruction of the existing societies among the minorities, as among the Russians, was largely achieved. The prevailing institutional patterns were broken up and the religions and traditional cultures were wrecked or perverted to Soviet use. While formal acknowledgment of "statehood" for many minorities was made and proclaimed abroad, any kind of regional combination was broken up or prohibited (as in Transcaucasia and Central Asia), and while usually the minorities' own nationals were made figureheads in the republics, Moscow's trusted men, usually Russians, stood at their elbows in a totalitarian version of old-style colonialism. Local nationalisms were not wiped out, but they were silenced at great human sacrifice. Representatives of minority peoples were used as foreign agents abroad and authors of propaganda for foreign consumption with varying yet considerable success. Economic transformation was carried out with the utmost thoroughness (even reindeer hunting, as among the Samoyeds or Nentsy, was forcibly collectivized). The borderlands were exploited ruthlessly, if not efficiently, for the benefit of the center (Russian Communists turned the Pechora region, inhabited by the Komis, into a coal basin supplying Leningrad, and converted much of Bashkiria into an oil center which was called the "Second Baku").

The result was not the "new Soviet man" in the borderlands any more than in the Russian areas. Many of the minority peoples, faced with the dictation and brutality of Russian Communists, concluded that prerevolutionary Russian colonialism was back, only increased a hundredfold in severity. They failed to give much thought to what Stalin and his cohorts had done to Russian national traditions, institutions, and religion, and what they were doing to the Russian people. It was natural, for the minorities had seen horror to equal the worst that Oriental empires had been able to mete out for thousands of years past to the inhabitants of the vast area now known as the USSR.

Stalin's Diplomacy and World Communism (1927–1935)

CHAPTER 20

STALIN AND THE RISE OF HITLER

At the end of 1927 ten years of Soviet foreign policy had seemed to produce a general fiasco. At that juncture Stalin's assumption of supreme power in the Soviet Union led to two significant developments in the USSR's international position: he secured Soviet (and at the same time his own) domination of the Comintern, and he reversed the previous "united front" line in attempting to spread Communist power.

Until 1927–1929, opposition was tolerated within the Comintern as within the Soviet Communist Party, although it was increasingly outnumbered and treated more and more roughly as the twenties wore on. In the Comintern, as in the Soviet Party, the Right Opposition was given two more years of grace than the Left Opposition. The chief Rightist, Bukharin, still appeared at the VI Congress of the Comintern in the summer of 1928 as Comintern president, and although he was already a helpless hostage of Stalin's, he was not removed from the post until 1929. At that time no new president was officially selected; Molotov formally took over the functions for a time, but Dmitry Manuilsky actually assumed the direction of Comintern affairs.

At the VI Congress the Comintern, under Stalin's direction, adopted the most uncompromising public position of the entire period of its existence under that name. The congress's resolution repeated the fantasy that the capitalists were preparing to attack the USSR, but interpreted this alleged fact as an effect of growing contradictions—that is, weakness—within the "imperialist" camp. The slogan "class against class" was proclaimed; in other words, an attack was to be launched on all forms of bourgeois political activity. Such forms were said to include social democracy and fascism, the former seeking to subvert the proletariat from within, the latter to destroy it from without. However, as suggested by the fact that Communist use of the phrase "Social Fascist" now was standard, the Social Democrats became the chief enemy.

By 1928 a declaration of war on all socialists could have little effect except in Germany. Most of the Communist parties of all other countries were still little larger than the tiny groups which had joined the Comintern at the time it was founded or had later been formed by Moscow agents (these were chiefly outside Europe). Only the German party was strong enough to have any independent influence on the course of events, and the abandonment of the "united front" policy left Germany as the only country outside the USSR in which Communist acts, as distinguished from words, could be expected to achieve anything without direct Soviet assistance.

In Germany the effects of the Great Depression were more serious than in any other industrial country. The ruin of much of the middle class, begun during the inflation of 1923, seemed on the verge of completion. For a younger generation looking for jobs and recognition, the prospects were bleak. As Bertolt Brecht, a gifted and embittered poet who became the Communists' chief artistic conquest in Germany, put it in the popular *Die Dreigroschenoper* (*The Threepenny Opera*) of the period, "Erst kommt das Fressen und dann die Moral" ("First a man must feed his face; right and wrong come later"). Profound cynicism and disillusionment were widespread.

The Weimar Republic was defended by the Social Democrats, the Catholic Center party, and the Liberals; it was attacked by the Communists and the Nazis. In May 1928 Reichstag elections had given the Nazis 13 seats, the Communists 54. The Social Democrats, the strongest single party, had many prominent members who wanted to make common cause with the Communists against any further gains by the Nazis, and they repeatedly made overtures to this end during the next few years.

However, the Communists were instead pursuing the anti-S.D. tactic of the VI Congress of the Comintern. In 1929–30 they joined the Nazis and other extreme Rightist groups in public attacks on the Young Plan for a reparations settlement, and on the S.D.'s for attempting better relations with the Western powers. In the September 1930 elections the Nazis obtained 105 seats in the Reichstag, while Communist strength increased only slightly, to 77. The Eleventh Plenum of the Comintern, in March–April 1931, labeled the Social Democrats as the most active party in Germany in preparing war on the USSR. When the Nazis and Nationalists demanded a referendum for removal of the Prussian government, which was a bulwark of the Republic's strength, the Communist leaders supported the campaign. The referendum took place, although the proposal failed. In July 1932 another Reichstag election was held, bringing the Nazis to 230 seats and the Communists to 89. A few months later the two parties co-operated in a big transport strike in Berlin. In November elections were held once more. This time Nazi strength fell to 196 seats, while the Communists won 100. The Communists redoubled their efforts to bring down the Republic.

In February 1933 the Social Democrats made a final effort to win over the Communists to an agreement to stop the Nazis. The German party leadership replied, "The Nazis must take power. Then in four weeks the whole working class will be united under the leadership of the Communist Party." Actually Hitler was appointed Chancellor on January 30, but he remained a minority prime minister. Not until another election in March 1933 gave the Nazis and Nationalists together a bare majority—in an election marked by widespread intimidation and fraud—did Hitler manage, after excluding the Communist deputies from voting, to get the Reichstag to abdicate its powers "for four years." He thereupon proceeded to construct the Nazi totalitarian state. The German Communists were among the first to feel the full force of Nazi terror, and the party was soon destroyed.

The Social Democrats, Trotsky, and others have blamed the Communists for the rise of Hitler, citing their refusal to ally with the Social Democrats as well as their open co-operation with the Nazis. Franz Borkenau dissents from this view, declaring that the "longing for a United Front expressed a feeling of helplessness on the part of the liberal intelligentsia, a profound distrust of its own forces, an abandonment of its own cause." If the Communists *had* supported the Social Democrats, he believes, many of the unemployed who voted Communist would have voted Nazi instead, since, in his opinion, the Communists could not carry their really radical voters into any alliance with the status quo.[1] Nevertheless, the Communist leaders clearly failed to mobilize all their voters in the campaign against the existing Prussian government, so Borkenau's

• [1] *European Communism* (New York: Harper, 1953), pp. 75–76.

speculation seems not well founded. Whether or not the German Communists could have done something different, Moscow refused to urge or permit them to try. The two totalitarian parties recognized their own kinship in detesting liberal government and scorning the "bourgeois law" which sustained it—that is to say, the anti-S.D. tactic of the VI Congress found some solid basis on which to operate. However, the Communists failed to see that after the Republic was brought down, one of the two totalitarian parties would certainly try to destroy the other, and that if the Nazis took power, as the Communists explicitly predicted would happen, the Nazis might succeed in destroying them.

As late as April 1933 Eugene Varga, an authoritative Soviet spokesman, declared that the victory of Hitler was a hopeful sign, to be explained away as a result of the terror of the bourgeoisie at the rise of German Communism. The theme of the first Soviet reactions was that Hitler would be swept aside by "history." It was reminiscent of Radek's similar expectations for Pilsudski, who had seized power in Poland in 1926 with Communist support. Pilsudski was not Hitler, but the Communists' refusal to reckon with the possibility that Hitler could, as Pilsudski had done, remain in power and do what he wanted to do, was in both instances a combination of stupidity and a compulsion to justify the Comintern policy. Even as late as December 31, 1933, *Bolshevik,* the Russian Party's theoretical organ, declared, "In Germany the proletarian revolution is nearer to realization than in any other country. . . ."

To be sure, there were influential individuals in Germany (such as the geopolitician Haushofer and the philosopher-historian Spengler) who had no use for Communist ideology, but still thought in terms of a national German-Russian collaboration. However, the specious nature of Hitler's "nationalism" soon became as clear as that of Stalin's. The Nazis did—while destroying the German Communists—protest their desire for good relations with the Soviet Union as well as with all other countries, and in May 1933 they actually ratified a renewal (pending since 1931) of the 1926 neutrality treaty with the USSR. However, by the end of the year Moscow's spokesmen were compelled to refer publicly to the Nazis' continued use of the unequivocally anti-Soviet propaganda line of Hitler's *Mein Kampf,* and it seemed that they had at least perceived, without admitting, their mistake.

LITVINOV AND SOVIET DIPLOMACY

In the late 1920's Foreign Minister Chicherin was ill, and his assistant, Maxim Litvinov, took over more and more of his duties, officially becoming foreign commissar in 1930. At the end of 1927 Litvinov had appeared at the deliberations regarding disarmament being conducted by the League of Nations (which the I Congress of the Comintern had termed a "Holy Alliance of the bourgeoisie for the suppression of the proletarian revolution," and there was no indication of an official change of view since 1919). Litvinov presented to the League a draft convention for immediate disarmament, making clear as he did so that the objective was not to limit weapons. Certain statesmen had argued that disarmament could not be risked because the USSR would refuse to take part. Litvinov merely wished, by undermining this excuse, to prove that the "bourgeois" powers did not take disarmament seriously. Two years later the Soviet Union offered to take part in pan-Europe discussions, again not out of any interest in the ostensible aims of the European Commission, but, as Moscow declared, "By taking part . . . the Soviet Union will wreck the plans of the leaders of the Commission, plans for the secret elaboration of anti-Soviet projects."[2]

When the Kellogg-Briand Pact for the renunciation of war as an instrument of national policy was proposed by the American and French foreign secretaries, the Soviet Union undertook to utilize it for its own purposes by means of the Litvinov Protocol, signed in Moscow in February 1929. The effect of the protocol was to bring the pact into operation on a regional basis without awaiting all the ratifications to the pact itself. The USSR signed along with Poland, Rumania, Latvia, and Estonia, and within a few months Lithuania, Turkey, Persia, and the Free City of Danzig had added their signatures. The protocol continued the pattern established by the 1926 treaty with Germany and the Middle Eastern pacts of the same period. Another wave of comparable agreements came with the signature of non-aggression treaties with Poland, the Baltic states, Finland, and France in 1932. Only with Rumania did negotiations founder, as they had repeatedly done before, on the question of Bessarabia, whose annexation by Rumania the Soviets refused to recognize.

However, none of this apparently peace-loving activity was intended to alter the basic lines of Soviet foreign policy. Under Stalin as well as Lenin it remained based on the effort to mobilize the anti-Versailles powers against Britain and France in the European balance, without assuming either that eternal friendship was possible with the one group of powers or that armed hostilities were inevitable with the other. (Thus there was even a rationale for agreement with Hitler, who was in any

• [2] The more recent Soviet application to join the North Atlantic Treaty Organization might appear more comprehensible when such statements are taken into account.

case regarded as merely another "bourgeois" leader.) The public trials of the First Five-Year Plan period, which involved accusations of complicity with Britain and France in anti-Soviet activity, served to underline this policy. In October 1929 the USSR resumed relations with Britain as a result of MacDonald's and Labor's return to power, but no dramatic change in Anglo-Soviet relations ensued.

At the end of 1933 there occurred a diplomatic development which in itself brought no shift in Soviet policy, but which was both dramatic and, once the Soviet about-face of 1934–1935 had taken place, significant in its results. This was United States recognition of the Soviet Union. Among the obstacles to the establishment of relations had been American resentment at Soviet debt repudiation and confiscation, but the chief deterrent to recognition, in the view of Secretaries of State Hughes, Kellogg, and Stimson, was Communist propaganda inside America. American commercial and other contacts—the American Relief Administration effort under Herbert Hoover during the famine of 1921–1922 being the most important—proceeded despite the absence of diplomatic relations (a precedent not always remembered during later discussions about the advisability of recognizing Communist China). None of the other American states except Mexico and Uruguay had recognized the USSR, and Mexico had broken relations in 1930, but it was plain that many Latin American governments would follow the U.S. lead if Washington decided on recognition.

It was during the World Economic Conference, held in London in the summer of 1933, which otherwise had negligible results, that contacts were made between Soviet and American representatives which led to recognition. William C. Bullitt, Wilson's envoy of 1919, talked to Litvinov in London and visited the Soviet Union a few weeks later. Finally in November Litvinov himself came to Washington in response to President Roosevelt's invitation to the Soviet Government. In the same month diplomatic relations were established between the U.S. and the Soviet Union, each nation pledging to abstain from hostile propaganda against the other. The USSR acknowledged the religious and legal rights of Americans in the country and waived all claims originating with U.S. intervention in Siberia, thus underlining the factor which they indicated as their chief motive for seeking U. S. recognition, namely, fear of Japan in the Pacific. Bullitt went to Moscow as ambassador. However, although a trade agreement was concluded in 1935, debt negotiations foundered, and soon Bullitt himself became soured on his post as well as on the Soviet Union in general, for which he had felt a good deal of sympathy.

FAR EASTERN WEAKNESS

In the Far East there was real ground for Soviet concern. Before the Japanese attack on Manchuria in 1931, Britain was regarded, there as elsewhere, as the chief enemy. Stalin even suggested that the Japanese might fight alongside Britain in a possible Far Eastern conflict with the United States. It does not seem that the Soviet leaders felt any serious concern about a British "threat" to them in the Far East, although they had counted (in vain) on doing the British harm through their partnership with the Kuomintang in China.

The weakness of the Soviet position in the Far East was partly the result of the failure in China in 1927. The chief asset Moscow retained was the Chinese Eastern Railway through Manchuria. In May 1929, however, Marshal Chang Hsüeh-liang, the *de facto* ruler of Manchuria under nominal Nationalist suzerainty, seized the railway and expelled the Soviet personnel. In July Soviet-Chinese diplomatic relations were officially severed. In November General Bliukher, lately Soviet adviser to the Kuomintang armies, led a military expedition against Chang and repossessed the railway.

However, in September 1931 the Far Eastern situation was completely upset again by the Japanese invasion of Manchuria. The Japanese soon overran the area of the railway as well as the whole province, establishing a puppet regime calling itself the "Government of Manchukuo." The League of Nations debated the question of Japanese aggression at length, but did nothing. The Soviets could not hope to succeed with the tactic of outright attack used on Chang Hsüeh-liang, at least not without courting full-scale war with Japan. Therefore Moscow blustered a good deal but soon accepted negotiations for sale of the railway to the Japanese. By an agreement finally reached in March 1935 it was sold, and cheaply at that. The Soviets did not discount the Japanese danger, however, and in December 1932, not long after the invasion of Manchuria, they reestablished relations with China.

Of course, neither Moscow nor the Chinese Communists gave up their hostility toward the government of Chiang Kai-shek, who had broken the alliance with the Soviets, nor did Chiang give up his war on the Chinese Communists. Beginning in November 1930 he launched a series of "extermination campaigns" against them, the fourth and last coming to an end in October 1933. After the debacle of 1927, the first Chinese Communist leader, Ch'en Tu-hsiu, was made the scapegoat and replaced by Li Li-san, who was himself purged and recalled to Moscow in 1930.

In the meantime a new leader, Mao Tse-tung, a former librarian who came from a Hunan peasant family, made his appearance. Sent in 1927 to investigate a peasant revolt in his home province, he returned to Peking placing much stock in the peasants' role for the future. They were to serve as a mass army for what he called the "national" revolution—that combination of "anti-imperialist" and "anti-feudal" insurrections which would, in Marxist terms, bring about the completion of the "bourgeois" phase and make possible a transition to the "proletarian" one. This was a thoroughly Leninist and Stalinist position, presented with generous invocations of Communist scripture. Mao's reaction to the Hunan riots is reminiscent of Lenin's reaction to the Ukrainian peasant disturbances of 1902.

What was new in the Chinese Communist movement after 1927 was neither some kind of organizational split from Moscow nor any sudden theoretical discovery of the peasantry; it was the disappearance of the urban movement with which the Communists had made a good deal of headway in the mid-1920's. However, the doctrine that the immediate goal was a "democratic dictatorship of proletariat and peasantry" (in Lenin's phrase)[3] or a "people's democratic dictatorship" (Mao's term) remained unchanged even when the Chinese proletariat—in any case small in number—vanished from Communist reach, as it had remained in force when, to facilitate the tactic of co-operation with the Kuomintang, Communist leaders publicly disavowed the utility of peasant uprising.

In the autumn of 1927, following the break with Chiang, Mao was commissioned to organize peasant risings in Hunan. However, he failed to do so and was penalized by dismissal from the Politburo of the Chinese Communist party. He retreated eastward toward Kiangsi province and in the spring of 1928 was joined there by Chu Teh, along with a group of Communist officers who had been trained at the Whampoa academy. Mao assumed political and Chu Teh military leadership, and in November 1931 the two together proclaimed a "Chinese Soviet Republic" in Kiangsi. By that time Moscow had purged Li Li-san and replaced him with Mao as party leader. It was this southern nest of Communists which Chiang from 1930 to 1933 tried in vain to dig out, foiled by the guerrilla warfare so skilfully carried on by Chu Teh's troops.

Although the Kiangsi regime "declared war" on the Japanese in 1932 in order to exploit national feeling against the invasion of Manchuria, Mao and Chu Teh continued to follow the current Comintern policy of refusing to co-operate with "bourgeois" groups. In November 1933 a

• [3] The phrase was also used in the 1931 Constitution of the Chinese Soviet Republic, headed by Mao.

group of dissident Nationalists seized parts of Fukien province and called for a common front with Mao's Communists, but Mao did not respond and allowed Chiang to suppress the revolt without trying to interfere.

Chiang's pressure was not enough to crush the Chinese Communists, but by 1934 it led them to evacuate their Kiangsi base. In October of that year Mao and Chu Teh led over ninety thousand men on the well-known "Long March," a six-thousand-mile movement west and north to Yenan in Shensi province. In October 1935 a remnant of twenty thousand arrived there and established a new base. Here the Communists found themselves close to their Soviet mentors, with their backs to Soviet-controlled Mongolia, west of which lay the nominally Chinese but strongly Soviet-infiltrated province of Sinkiang.

It appears that Chiang Kai-shek regarded Mao's new location as an advantage to his own government. He hoped that the force could be driven to cross over into Soviet territory and thus that his troops might be spared further efforts to cope with the Communist guerrilla tactics used in Kiangsi. But neither Mao nor Stalin was inclined to oblige Chiang by abolishing the Chinese Communist army, government, or party. They had important and immediate tasks to perform. While the Long March was under way, the Comintern line had shifted sharply. In the summer of 1935 the Chinese Communists had halted en route northward to hold a conference in Szechuan in order to repeat the changed policy for Chinese consumption, and to call for a united national effort against the Japanese. In Europe the new tactic was called the "Popular Front."

THE POLICY SHIFT IN FRANCE

Since the Communists declared that Nazism was merely an alternative type of capitalist regime, and since Soviet preference for close relations with Germany had been based on opposition to Britain and France, not fondness for the Weimar Republic, its fall was unlamented in Moscow. The destruction of the German Communist party was a blow; Litvinov declared, "We of course sympathize with the sufferings of our German comrades, but," he added, "we Marxists are the last who can be reproached with allowing our feelings to dictate our policy."

Certain early Nazi statements indicated that they were willing not to hold the German Communists, whom they were busy executing, against the Soviet regime. Actually a certain amount of the co-operation that was begun during the Weimar period carried over for a time into the Nazi era. In 1934 Germany took a considerably larger slice of Soviet exports than in 1933, and her imports from the USSR did not fall sharply until 1936, while Soviet imports from Germany were still considerable in 1937. The collaboration between the German and Red armies continued into 1935.

However, in December 1933 Litvinov publicly distinguished between capitalist states on the basis of their foreign policy. There were, said he, "actively aggressive," "passively indifferent," and "actively co-operative" bourgeois powers. He left no doubt that the Soviet regime had become concerned about the likelihood of Nazi aggression eastward. Finally, in February 1934 came an abrupt about-face by the French Communist party which was the harbinger of a worldwide shift in Soviet policy.

On February 6, in the wake of the Stavisky financial scandal, the Communists in Paris co-operated openly with the French extreme Right—as the German Communists had done with the Nazis—in a successful riot before the Chamber of Deputies designed to overthrow Daladier's Socialist-Radical[4] government. However, only six days later the Communists threw in their lot with the socialist trade-unions to lead a big strike directed against the Right. Lest the wrong conclusions be drawn, the French Communist chieftain, Maurice Thorez, warned in the party organ, *Humanité,* in April, that "all gossip about a marriage between Communists and Socialists is fundamentally alien to the spirit of Bolshevism." However, before the end of the month he was summoned to Moscow, and he returned with new instructions. Without any apparent embarrassment he now called for the very "marriage" he had scorned a few weeks earlier. The French Socialists, who had just lost much of their right wing in an interparty battle, accepted with alacrity. In July a pact, providing among other things for mutual abjuration of criticism, was signed between the two parties. This was the first "Popular Front" agreement. In November Thorez proposed the formation of a Popular Front government; this offer the Socialists received with some wariness. However, parallel diplomatic developments forced their hand.

In May 1934 Litvinov and J. L. Barthou of France met in Geneva. Already proposals for a Franco-Soviet mutual assistance pact were being considered, and at the May meeting Barthou suggested that the USSR also enter the League of Nations. At first the two diplomats tried to construct a broad security-treaty network which would include most of the East European countries. However, Poland and other nations were reluctant, and so a simple Franco-Soviet Pact was decided upon. Signed in May 1935, it provided for mutual "aid and assistance" in case of un-

• [4] This party is often called "Radical Socialist" in English, but since in French the modifier follows the substantive, this is a mistranslation; even the accurate rendition misrepresents the real character of the party, but not as grossly.

provoked attack by a third power. In the same month a Czechoslovak-Soviet Pact was concluded, providing for mutual assistance only in the event that France aided the country attacked. It is uncertain which country was responsible for inserting this provision, but it had uses for both sides.

On May 16, 1935, the French press published a declaration by Stalin giving unreserved support to "the policy of national defense followed by France so as to maintain her armed forces on the level necessary to maintain security." In late May and June, on the heels of the agreement with the Socialists and the Communist defensive stand taken with Moscow's express sanction, the French Communists scored heavy gains in local elections.

By now Thorez was extending the hand of co-operation not only to the Socialists, but also to the Socialist-Radicals, puzzling and alarming many Socialists whose ideology remained genuinely leftist. On Bastille Day (July 14), 1935, Thorez, Léon Blum (the Socialist leader), and Edouard Daladier (Socialist-Radical) marched side by side at the head of the parade in Paris—the first time since 1889 that the French Socialists had celebrated the bourgeois national holiday; but the presence of the Communists seemed even more astounding. It appeared to many that the French (and therefore all other) Communists had abandoned revolutionism in favor of the defense of the USSR against the threat of Hitler and the support of any other government which was disposed to resist the Nazis.

THE VII CONGRESS OF THE COMINTERN

The French united-front agreement, by now an obvious success, may be considered the test run for the policy newly adopted by the VII (and last) Congress of the Comintern, held in Moscow in July and August 1935. There was proclaimed the policy of the Popular Front, wherein the Communists expressed willingness to co-operate, not merely with the "masses" in spite of and against the "reformist" leaders whom they might be following, as in the 1920's, but also with the leaders of any group, socialist or rightist, which took a line of resistance to the Nazis or to the Japanese militarists who had taken control in Tokyo.

The Popular Front tactic was linked to the Bulgarian George Dimitrov, who had attracted worldwide attention by his outspoken conduct in the Reichstag fire trial of 1933; he became general secretary of the Comintern at the congress. However, there was no pretense that personalities or factions were at odds in the change of policy; the VII Congress was, as Max Beloff points out, "the first Congress at which a complete display of unanimity was achieved"[5]—put another way, complete subservience to Stalin. Stalin had reversed himself; he had simultaneously recognized the bankruptcy of the "go-it-alone" tactic of 1928–1934, the danger from the new factor introduced into German and European politics by Nazism (whose "newness" Moscow had previously denied), and the gains which might be made by a call to resist "war and Fascism."

It remains obscure whether Stalin ever had any serious intention of collaborating with Britain and France against Hitler, or whether he ever gave up hope (before 1939) that collaboration with Hitler could be arranged. The defected Soviet intelligence chief for Western Europe, General Krivitsky, declares that Stalin never took the Popular Front seriously nor used it as anything but a bargaining counter in the game with Hitler. In any case it is clear that as the anti-Versailles diplomacy of the pre-1934 period reflected no fondness for the Weimar Republic, so the pro-Versailles policy adopted in 1934 was not based on any love for bourgeois France or Britain. The Soviet chose between groups of "capitalist" powers not on the basis of ideological compatibility—none were compatible—but from considerations of power.

However, it appears that Stalin miscalculated the relative strengths of Hitler on the one hand and the British and French on the other, and that he did not fully grasp Hitler's inflexible hostility to the USSR and his designs on Soviet territory. During the period of the Popular Front, there were indications that Stalin expected nothing from a tie with the English and French; however, there were also moves apparently inexplicable on any other ground but Stalin's desire to create or strengthen such alliances. Probably the truth is that the Popular Front offered an opportunity to the Soviets to gain much foreign popularity and influence at slight cost, whatever the progress of a diplomatic alignment with the West, while Moscow's public pronouncements during the period had the effect of leading many to justify Stalin's domestic brutalities as made necessary by the Nazi danger. Thus although few actual Popular Front agreements or governments came into existence, and none provided a direct bridge to Communist power, the psychological effects of the policy were far-reaching, and Stalin may well have reckoned it an over-all success. Perhaps even he did not look for the effects to be so immediate; in fact, the virulent anti-socialist and anti-liberal campaigns led by Moscow during the previous six years were rapidly forgotten by many of the persons and groups Stalin sought to influence most.

• [5] *The Foreign Policy of Soviet Russia, 1929–1941* (2 vols.; London: Oxford University Press, 1947–49), Vol. I, p. 190.

At the VII Congress, the then obscure Wilhelm Pieck (later president of the East German Communist state) gave the opening report, castigating foreign Communists for a "mechanical" interpretation of the 1928 resolutions which led them to scent fascism where it was not and fail to recognize it where it was. Pieck also denounced the "sectarian" views of those who did not defend the "remnants of bourgeois democracy" against war and fascism. Dimitrov discussed the new Popular Front tactic, making clear that the aim of the Communists remained to assure their own pre-eminent leadership over the "masses," but calling for more agreements with non-Communist parties along French lines.

Thorez explained the success the Popular Front had already gained in France, and spoke in reverent terms of the French Encyclopedists and the *Marseillaise,* as did Earl Browder of the American Revolution and the Civil War. Dimitrov concluded that "*national forms* of the proletarian class struggle" furnished the proper means through which the "*international interests* of the proletariat can be successfully defended." However, Palmiro Togliatti, leader of the Italian Communists, explained that even capitalist powers which had signed pacts with the USSR had not come to terms with their own working class; thereby he made it plain that neither bourgeois France nor any other non-Soviet power could enjoy more than conditional support from the Communists. However, the fine print largely escaped the serious attention of the reformist leaders with whom the Communists proclaimed a desire for alliance, and Communism was launched into the period of its greatest international popularity.

Stalin's Diplomacy and World Communism (1936–1941)

CHAPTER 21

THE POPULAR FRONT GOVERNMENT IN FRANCE

Following the VII Congress of the Comintern, the French Communists, exploiting their earlier successes, managed to create the first Popular Front government. In the May 1936 elections the Communist vote almost doubled and for the first time passed the million mark. Although the Socialists made virtually no gains, their leader, Léon Blum, was designated premier in June. The Communists supported his ministry, on the condition that he carry out the Popular Front program, but they refused to enter it. At the moment Blum was taking office a wave of "sit-down strikes" (then a novel weapon) under genuinely revolutionary leadership broke out, and the Communists aided his government by helping to force the end of the strikes.

The course of the French Popular Front government was stormy. Unending squabbles raged between Communists and Socialists, full of accusation and recrimination. They fought over domestic issues, over French policy toward the Spanish Civil War just beginning, over the Great Purges in the USSR, which the Socialists denounced. Although the Communists had helped Blum into power, they embarrassed his government by leading successive waves of strikes and contributing to a series of financial crises which brought about his fall in June 1937.

The heritage of the first Popular Front government was a forty-hour week (which under existing conditions barred any effective French rearmament), industrial chaos, and political bitterness. A coalition of Socialists and Socialist-Radicals continued in power with the Socialist-Radical Camille Chautemps as premier. Thorez repeated the same sort of pledge of support he had given Blum; however, in December the Communists led further strikes, while another financial crisis was impending. Chautemps's cabinet fell in March 1938. Next came the brief tenure of a second Blum government, more Communist-led strikes, and again the fall of the cabinet, followed by a Socialist-Radical ministry under Edouard Daladier. After helping him into power, the Communists soon attacked him as they had his predecessors. By the summer of 1938 the Popular Front in France was at an end.

At the time of the Munich Agreement in the fall the French Communists were again paralyzing rearmament efforts through strikes. However, in November Daladier finally used the army to recapture seized plants. The united *Confédération Générale du Travail,* formed two years earlier by amalgamation of the Socialist and Communist trade unions, suffered a great loss of membership. Once again the French Communist party was deprived of any important influence in the country, but it was France as a whole which suffered most from the turmoil of these years.

POPULAR FRONT AND CIVIL WAR IN SPAIN

Two Popular Front governments were formed outside France: in Spain and Chile (in a few other cases, Communist support was of marginal significance). In both France and Spain, international issues vital to the USSR were at stake, but in Spain these issues became entangled in the large-scale fighting of the Civil War, the European dress rehearsal for World War II.

In 1930 Spain was a country in many ways socially more backward than Russia in 1917. The Roman Catholic Church had a cultural monopoly and economic power greater than the Russian Orthodox Church had had; the peasantry was much more downtrodden; the economic stagnation of the whole country contrasted with the growth of the economy under Nicholas II. The Spanish monarchy had collapsed not long after the seven-year dictatorship of Primo de Rivera, and a republic had been proclaimed in 1931, but national unity was lacking. There was strong autonomist feeling in the Basque northwest and the Catalan northeast;

there were large and fanatical groups of anarchists, especially in Catalonia, socialists with much strength among the Madrid workers, a tiny Trotskyite group called P.O.U.M. (*Partido Obrero de Unificación Marxista*), and an even tinier Spanish Communist party (in March 1936 its strength was estimated at only three thousand).

Elections in November 1933 had installed a Rightist regime, against which bloody but unsuccessful revolts were raised in October 1934 by the Asturias miners and the Barcelona workers. Shortly afterward the forces of the political Left reached a Popular Front agreement, intended to avert a Spanish fascism. The participants were two Republican groups, the Catalan Left (*Esquerra*), Socialists, and Communists. Even the anarchists supported the Popular Front list, which in February 1936 elections won a big majority of deputies in the Cortes, though by a narrow margin of the popular vote. The Republican regime which thereupon took power was faced in July by an army revolt started in Spanish Morocco by General Francisco Franco and others. The Republican leaders wavered as to how to meet it, but some army units remained loyal, others were hastily assembled by various Leftist parties, and in Catalonia and eastern Spain the revolt was crushed. However, the rebels captured most of the west.

Stalin thereupon faced a grave dilemma. Soviet military intervention in Spain might frighten the British and French into making a compact with the Nazis, thus confronting the USSR with a formidable bloc of "capitalist" powers, or, if one is to credit such assertions as Krivitsky's, that Stalin's unchanging aim throughout this period was to reach agreement with Hitler, Soviet intervention might imperil the possibility of doing so. On the other hand, if the Spanish Republic were to be quickly crushed, Soviet prestige would be damaged and the infant Popular Front policy might be wrecked.

According to General Krivitsky, the Soviet Politburo decided on August 28, 1936, in favor of intervention in Spain. The USSR would send arms aid; it would also support the Spanish Communists in assuming a more prominent role in the government (indeed, the Russians soon took over a large share of that task themselves). The Communists declared that resistance to Franco should not be confused with social revolution, and called for order and defense of the Republic, thus attracting the favorable notice of the more conservative Republicans. In Catalonia the Communists had increased their strength slightly by amalgamating with local socialists in the P.S.U.C. (*Partido socialista unificado Catalan*), which they controlled, and the unified party entered the autonomous Catalan government. In September the Socialist, Francisco Largo Caballero, formed a national Popular Front government into which went two Communists, Uribe and Hernandez. This was not enough for Moscow; in the same month the NKVD set up a Spanish section, entrusted by the Politburo with control over all Communist activity in Spain. Within a few months the NKVD was carrying out its own arrests and executions on Spanish soil—not of Franco's agents, but of the Trotskyites of the P.O.U.M., anarchists, and socialists, especially in the army.

The Spanish Republic had hoped for Western, particularly French, aid. Stalin also hoped such aid would be forthcoming, as it would spare the Soviets the embarrassment of acting alone and would also commit Britain and France against the Axis. The French Communists from the start demanded Western intervention. However, Britain and France invoked a policy of "nonintervention" to secure peace in Europe and clung to it although Germany and Italy, which also belonged to the nonintervention committee, almost at once sent air and ground forces into action on Franco's side. The Spanish Republic had to accept Soviet aid or go under, and it chose to accept. Some of its leaders recognized the attendant dangers, but were powerless to counter them, while others discounted them altogether.

Once Communist power obtained a foothold in Spain, Soviet armed aid was forthcoming. By November 1936 the International Brigade, recruited first from foreign Communist refugees in Russia and supplemented by genuine volunteers from Western Europe and the U.S., was sent into the line just in time to save Madrid. The same month much of the Spanish gold reserve was sent to the USSR to clinch the bargain. Largo Caballero's war minister, Julio Alvarez del Vayo, accepted the introduction throughout the army of political commissars, who were Communists almost to a man.

By the beginning of 1937 the Communists were ready to provoke a crisis to enforce their demands for centralization, discipline, and no quarter for revolutionism. They chose Catalonia to make a stand, since it was least threatened by the rebel advance and also was the stronghold of anarchism and revolutionary extremism in Spain. The Communists armed the P.S.U.C., and their demands were supported by Indalecio Prieto and Juan Negrín (two Socialist ministers), other Right Socialists, and the Republicans. However, Prime Minister Largo Caballero and his Left Socialists supported the opposing Catalan anarchist union, the C.N.T. (*Confederación Nacional del Trabajo*). When street fighting between the P.S.U.C. and the C.N.T. broke out in Barcelona in May 1937, Largo Caballero hesitated, but finally suppressed the Trotskyite P.O.U.M.

as a concession to the Communists and their more conservative allies. Nevertheless he was still forced out of office.

The Communists had gained a good deal. Juan Negrín, a Right Socialist, took office, and Prieto became war minister. While Prieto believed in the necessity of discipline and postponement of social changes, he tried to resist Communist efforts to establish themselves in the decisive organs of control, especially in the army; he was forced out of the war ministry in April 1938. That spring Franco's army reached the eastern coast south of Barcelona and cut off Catalonia from the rest of republican Spain. By this time many of the chief Soviet agents in Spain, including Antonov-Ovseenko (the hero of the storming of the Winter Palace in the October Revolution), General Kléber (Stern) of the International Brigade, and others, had been recalled to Moscow and purged. Nevertheless it was after Prieto's resignation, under the clique of Negrín, del Vayo, and Uribe, that the Communists reached the highest point of their influence. They controlled almost the entire army through the commissars, they ran the government propaganda department and the new Spanish political police (although the NKVD was much more powerful, more active, and more efficient in exterminating the Communists' enemies of the Left). For a time after Prieto resigned, President Manuel Azaña resisted the Communists, but he was silenced by Negrín.

For a few months the Communists were in firm control of the remnant of republican Spain. However, Stalin had plainly decided to end Soviet intervention, and in November 1938 he withdrew the International Brigades and ended arms shipments. In February 1939 Franco took Barcelona. During the last months of the Civil War the military command in Madrid and the Right Socialists joined to send the Communists packing and attempted in vain a negotiated peace with Franco. In March 1939 Madrid surrendered, and Franco mercilessly punished the former defenders of the Republic. The Spanish Communist leaders escaped to Moscow, where Stalin promptly decimated them. The foremost figures were executed or sent to concentration camps, with the connivance of the renowned "La Pasionaria" (Dolores Ibarruri). She emerged as the new Spanish Communist leader, but she had virtually no followers left, either in Spain or the USSR.

It is difficult to say whether Stalin achieved his aims in Spain or not. Certainly Soviet intervention against Franco did not prevent Hitler, who made Franco's victory possible, from signing a pact with Stalin. The Soviets' conduct in Spain, above all their ruthlessness against their fellow defenders of the Republic, alarmed many in the West, but Stalin must have counted that a loss only if he still (or ever) hoped for a real agreement with Britain and France. Stalin had delayed Franco's victory until the uses of the Popular Front were near an end, and his agents had gained experience in warfare and in successful political infiltration which was to be useful in the future.

As Borkenau points out, a number of foreign Communist parties emerged from the Spanish events with a sort of double leadership, one set having had experience in Spain and another having spent much time in Moscow.[1] He might also have pointed out that in each case the Moscow-trained man won out over his rival—Ulbricht over Dahlem in Germany, Togliatti over Longo in Italy, Tito over Gorkić in Yugoslavia, Rákosi over Rajk in Hungary. Although the foremost Soviet agents in Spain were purged, it is not clear that the reason lay in the course of events there; most of the victims of the Great Purges had no connection with Spain, including many prominent foreign Communists living in the USSR. (Among them were Hungary's Béla Kun, Germany's Heinz Neumann and Hugo Eberlein, and virtually the whole leadership of the Polish Communist party, which was soon afterwards formally dissolved. It is ironic that many Communists from democratic countries escaped because the Soviets were then concerned not to provoke their governments, which might well have intervened to protect their citizens despite the latter's commitment to overthrow them.)

Outside of France and Spain, no Popular Front governments were formed in Europe. However, Popular Front party agreements won the Communists increased influence in Yugoslavia, Czechoslovakia, and elsewhere. Even more significant, Soviet prestige and Communist popularity reached a peak in the United States, Britain, Scandinavia, Poland, and other countries, embracing many people unaffiliated with the Communist or even any other political party.

POPULAR FRONT IN CHINA AND WAR WITH JAPAN

The Popular Front policy was formulated in opposition to both German Nazism and Japanese militarism. Accordingly its effects were also important in Asia, perhaps as important as those in Europe. It restored Chinese Communism to a level of strength it seemed to have lost permanently and set Mao Tse-tung on the road to power, and it gave Communism increased influence among the intellectuals of other Asian countries, especially India, Japan, and Indonesia.

The new policy had been proclaimed in Moscow while the Chinese

• [1] *European Communism*, p. 173.

Communists were engaged in the Long March northward. Their call while still en route in the summer of 1935 for "all classes" to fight Japan evoked no immediate response. However, shortly after Mao's columns reached Yenan, there were demonstrations by the Peiping students under patriotic and anti-Japanese slogans, and the spread of militant nationalist feeling was utilized by the Communists in their agitation for a Popular Front.

Developments in Japan warranted the concern which was felt by growing numbers of Chinese. After a period of party government in the 1920's, during which business interests and the bureaucracy helped restrain the armed forces, the army had launched a bid for power. The conquest of Manchuria in 1931 in effect gave the army a province to rule as its own and greatly strengthened its domestic prestige. During 1935 the Japanese military entered into closer contacts with the Nazis, who shared their scorn for politicians and businessmen. In February 1936 the army carried out a *coup d'état* in Tokyo which led to a cabinet which was virtually controlled by the new war minister, General Terauchi. Although the cabinet lasted less than a year, the military dominance remained through World War II, and the political parties were deprived of any important influence. The tiny Japanese Communist party under Sanzo Nozaka was repressed more severely than ever; its nucleus found refuge with Mao in Yenan by 1943, as did the leading Korean Communists.

In August 1936 the Chinese Communists repeated their offer to Chiang Kai-shek of a united-front agreement. The signing of the Anti-Comintern Pact between Japan and Germany in November, in which Communism was named as the ostensible enemy at a time when Japanese forces were actually attacking non-Communist Chinese areas, helped to suggest that all Chinese must resist Japan together. By this time the Japanese had marched south from Manchuria to occupy much of North China. However, while Chiang was ordering Marshal Chang Hsüeh-liang to attack the Communists at Yenan, he was still engaged in negotiations with the Japanese. In December Chiang flew to Sian to try to enforce his orders to Chang. Instead a curious incident occurred; he was "kidnapped" (that is, detained) by Chang's forces, who were already affected by Popular Front agitation. The Communists were instrumental in arranging for Chiang's release at the price of his accepting co-operation with them and agreeing to lead a united struggle against Japan. Chiang flew back to Nanking amid public rejoicing. In February 1937 the Chinese Communist party and the Nationalist government exchanged messages indicating a general line of agreement.

In July the Japanese attack on the Marco Polo bridge near Peiping launched the eight-year undeclared Sino-Japanese war. A month later, the USSR signed a nonaggression pact with Chiang Kai-shek's government. The Soviets promptly began to send in arms aid through Sinkiang which continued until Hitler invaded the USSR in 1941, meanwhile using the opportunity to strengthen their control over that nominally Chinese province. The League of Nations again discussed Japanese aggression with no result, but in June 1938 Litvinov spoke publicly of the Japanese as aggressors with designs on the USSR. Chiang dismissed the German advisers whom he had been using, and again Soviet advisers came to China. Soviet-Chinese co-operation was also marked by a trade treaty, signed in June 1939.

The Japanese were watching Soviet-Chinese relations closely. In June 1937 there was a skirmish with Soviet forces on the Amur River, which separated the Japanese puppet state of Manchukuo and the USSR. In July 1938 the hill of Changkufeng, near the Soviet-Manchurian-Korean border, was the scene of fighting, and in May 1939 at Nomonhan, near the border between Outer Mongolia and Manchuria, the most serious of such incidents occurred. Each side seemed to be testing the other's determination and military efficiency. While plainly neither was at that time disposed to engage in all-out war, there was a sort of mutual notice of preparedness should a real conflict break out later.

NATIONALISTS AND COMMUNISTS

Two months after the Japanese war began, the Chinese Communist party announced the formal abolition of the Chinese Soviet Government and the Chinese Red Army, and the acceptance of Sun Yat-sen's Three People's Principles (nationalism, democracy, and livelihood) as China's most important current need. Sun's principles, which remain to this day the foundation of Kuomintang ideology, are not adequately indicated by three words. Sun had declared that "nationalism" meant that "we . . . must break down individual liberty and become pressed together into an unyielding body like the firm rock which is formed by the addition of cement to sand . . . on no account must we give more liberty to the individual; let us secure liberty instead for the nation." "Democracy" meant to Sun the masses' acceptance of the leadership of a wise elite. The meaning of "livelihood" was obscure, but one of the chief measures designed to implement it was to be a Henry George-like "equalization of landownership." The Nationalist land law of 1930 had fixed a maximum land rent of thirty-seven and a half per cent of the peasant's main crop, presumably as a first step toward Sun's goal, but even that law remained a dead letter.

If Mao had in reality adopted such a hodgepodge of authoritarian and reformist aims as Sun's, that would have been news indeed. It is true that Communist tactics (not aims) did change after 1937. The party ceased land confiscation and other revolutionary actions. The Communists began to enforce the Nationalist thirty-seven and a half per cent maximum rent law in the rural areas which they controlled, especially in such border regions as that of Hopei-Chahar-Shansi, in the vicinity of Peiping and nominally controlled by the Japanese, and thereby won the support of many peasants. The tactic was reminiscent of Lenin's adoption after the October Revolution of the land program of the Russian S.R.'s, who had shared power for months previously without enacting it themselves. However, its employment no more converted the Chinese Communists into Nationalists (or "agrarian reformers") than Lenin's action had made him an S.R.

The theoretical implications of the Communist policy were explained by Mao in his work, written in 1939 and published the following year, entitled *On the New Democracy.* Using the conceptual framework of the Russian Communists, Mao declared that China had been a feudal society[2] which had become a semi-colony of the Western imperialist powers. The first stage of revolution must then combine the overthrow of the power of "feudal" landlords with destruction of the Western imperialist influence and those Chinese elements associated with it. In this "bourgeois-democratic" stage, the peasantry would furnish the main force, but the leadership would come from the "proletariat" (that is, the Communist party). This stage would merge directly into the "socialist revolution," but until that time leadership would be assumed by a "joint dictatorship of all revolutionary classes" (the proletariat, peasantry, "petty bourgeoisie," and "national bourgeoisie"). Thus Mao appealed to these groups to support the Communists instead of (and against) Chiang Kai-shek. The closest

• [2] This was not the view held by Marx or many early Russian Communists, but it was Stalin's. Marx spoke of China as possessing an "Asiatic mode of production," characterized by an all-powerful centralized despotism in which a bureaucracy ruled over a mass of scattered peasant producers. In his *Short Course* in the history of the Soviet Communist Party in 1939, Stalin omitted any reference to this Marxist category from his discussion of historical materialism. Since then the concept has been a *malum prohibitum* in the USSR; it might all too easily be converted into a weapon against the Soviet bureaucracy itself.

thing to an answer which Chiang attempted was the book *China's Destiny,* published three years later, in which he criticized virtually the whole Chinese intelligentsia for adopting "foreign theories" and castigated Chinese businessmen for their "quest for profit," suggesting that a planned economy of state capitalist type must supersede private enterprise. Thus Chiang unwisely attacked social groups which Mao was then trying to win over and which also happened to be those on which the National government had depended heavily for support.

To be sure, by this time many intellectuals as well as businessmen were behind Japanese lines and could not be of much help to the Nationalists even if they had wished (which many of them no longer did). The Japanese had rapidly conquered the Chinese cities. By the end of 1937 Peiping, Shanghai, and Nanking had fallen, and Hankow and Canton were taken in October 1938. The Chinese government moved inland to Chungking, taking with it considerable industrial machinery and many of the faculty and student bodies of the chief universities. Chiang was now far from the businessmen of the treaty ports and was thrown into the midst of the powerful landlords of Szechuan province. Seeking to combat Communist popularity as it grew as a result of the united-front policy, he had outlawed Communist-front organizations in August 1938, and became increasingly unwilling to tolerate any kind of criticism of his government. Those intellectuals from the universities who retreated with him to the interior reacted with rising hostility. Gloom and defeatism settled over Chungking.

Despite the Nazi-Soviet Pact of August 1939, the USSR continued arms shipments to China, and the Chinese Communists refrained from dismissing the Sino-Japanese War, as they did the war between Hitler and the West, as an "imperialist war," nor did they break openly with Chiang. However, even before the pact Mao's policy as stated in a secret document since smuggled abroad was "70% expansion, 20% dealing with the Kuomintang, and 10% resisting Japan."[3] The Communists were making special efforts to establish themselves in the crucial area between Nanking and Shanghai, and in January 1941 the Nationalists attacked their forces in an attempt to drive them to the north. After the Soviet-Japanese neutrality pact of April 1941 the Communists made even less effort than before to resist Japan. As the impact of the Hitler-Stalin Pact was less dramatic in Asia than in Europe, so was the effect of the Hitler-Stalin war beginning in June, and Communist-Nationalist relations remained near the level of armed truce.

• [3] See F. F. Liu, *A Military History of Modern China, 1924–1949* (Princeton: Princeton University Press, 1956), pp. 205–206.

POPULAR FRONTS IN SOUTH ASIA

In two cases of note Popular Front agreements were made in South Asian countries, and elsewhere local Communists gained in strength during the period. In 1917 an Indo-Chinese Marxist group had been organized in Paris among Indo-Chinese students by Ho Chi Minh (pseudonym of Nguyen Ai Quoc), but the Vietnamese Communist party was founded only in 1930 in Hong Kong, after the collapse of the first Nationalist-Communist alliance in China, during which Ho Chi Minh had served as assistant to the Soviet adviser Borodin. In 1936 the Vietnamese Communists, whom the French treated more leniently than the nationalists, set up a Communist-controlled "Democratic Front." In May 1941, at a meeting in the Chinese province of Kwangsi, the front was converted into the Vietnamese Independence League or Vietminh. After the fall of France in 1940, the Vichyite governor of Indo-China had accepted Japanese protection. At first occupying only a few key points, the Japanese forces by July 1941 occupied the whole of Indo-China, and thenceforth the local resistance to the Japanese and to the still formally sovereign French were one and the same.

In the Philippines the government ended the previous illegal status of the Communist party in 1938. It managed not only to merge the Socialist party into its ranks, but also ran many successful candidates on a Popular Front ticket in local elections in 1940. The Popular Front became a fighting force when, after the Japanese invasion in December 1941, the Communists created the Hukbalahap ("People's Anti-Japanese Army") movement. A Communist-led party in Burma, the "Our Burma National League," placed three deputies in the parliament elected in 1937. In Indonesia the Communist party, after a period of some success, had been banned by the Dutch authorities in 1926, and although during and after the war it revived rapidly, in the thirties its action was much less important than the growth of Marxism and admiration for the USSR among Indonesian intellectuals. In India, during the twenties M. N. Roy had attained considerable prominence in the Comintern, but his expulsion in 1929 as a Bukharinist was a severe blow to the Indian party, and, as in Indonesia, the popularity of Communism among Indian intellectuals during the thirties could not be credited to the local party.

In none of these countries was the Communist party strong enough to seize power unaided, but in each it was ready, as a trained and disciplined organization, to exploit the turmoil which resulted when Japanese armies overran Southeast Asia. On the eve of World War II the Communists were in a similar position in many of the Middle Eastern, African, and Latin American countries, but during the war they were rarely able to increase their strength substantially outside of areas occupied by Axis or Japanese troops.

SOVIET DIPLOMACY AND COLLECTIVE SECURITY

While Communist parties everywhere were endeavoring to put Moscow's Popular Front policy into effect, Soviet diplomacy was attempting to exploit the shifts in the European balance of power which resulted from Axis gains.

In 1933 Hitler had inaugurated a Nazi foreign policy by withdrawing from the League of Nations, and he began his attempts at expansion with a *Putsch* in Austria in 1934. Although Britain and France had bound Austria by the peace treaties never to join Germany, they took no action, and Hitler was forestalled only by Mussolini's mobilization on the Brenner Pass. In 1935 Hitler repudiated the disarmament clauses of the Treaty of Versailles; instead of trying to enforce them, the British signed a naval agreement with Germany. The same year Hitler obtained the Saar, not by conquest but by League of Nations plebiscite. In 1936 he flouted the Versailles treaty again by sending troops into the demilitarized Rhineland. Simultaneously he denounced the Locarno treaties of 1925, by which Germany had accepted her Weimar borders, on the grounds of France's "military alliance" with the USSR, which he described as "exclusively directed against Germany." Although Hitler had ordered his troops to withdraw if resistance was encountered, neither the French nor the British tried to stop them.

In October 1935 Mussolini had embarked on his own adventure of conquest by invading Ethiopia. This time the League of Nations, which sat generally bemused before the spectacle of Japanese and Nazi aggression throughout the 1930's, invoked sanctions on the aggressor, but they were not pressed, and after an embarrassingly long bout against troops often armed only with spears, Mussolini won his war by May 1936. In June Count Ciano, Mussolini's son-in-law, became Italian foreign minister and helped to effect a Nazi-Fascist partnership, which grew closer when both powers intervened in the Spanish Civil War which broke out in July. In November 1937 Italy adhered to the Anti-Comintern Pact which Germany and Japan had signed in November 1936. Mussolini had become Hitler's junior partner, and within three years Hitler had come to overshadow him completely.

Litvinov expressed the Soviet reaction to these events by repeated calls in the League of Nations for "collective security," denunciations of the so-called "nonintervention" policy toward the Spanish War, and, especially in 1937, approaches to France and Czechoslovakia which were designed to build the Soviet-French-Czechoslovak pacts into the military alliance which Hitler had wrongly asserted them to be. It is difficult to determine how seriously any of these diplomatic maneuvers was intended. Plainly the "appeasement" policy of Neville Chamberlain (who became British prime minister in May 1937), pointing toward an understanding with Hitler and Mussolini, was not designed to facilitate Soviet-British collaboration; nevertheless Anthony Eden (foreign secretary from September 1936 to February 1938) was known as a defender of the policy of "collective security," which was Litvinov's public doctrine. The evidence suggests that Soviet policy was not determined by the relative "friendliness" which the various powers displayed toward the USSR. When Stalin finally did sign a definite agreement, it was with Hitler, whose soldiers had fought against the Soviet-supported side in Spain and whose public statements had all along been unswervingly anti-Soviet, although at that moment Stalin had the option of signing a pact proffered by Britain and France, where much public and official sentiment had approved—even demanded—such an alliance.

Whether or not the Soviets could have been brought into an alliance to resist Nazi aggression, it is plain that Chamberlain and the French premier, Daladier, failed to understand that "appeasement" of Hitler was impossible. The French had been too seriously weakened by internal dissension to do more than follow London's lead. Although France was the power which had signed a pact with the Soviets, the link remained fragile, as shown in December 1937, when Foreign Minister Yvon Delbos toured the East European capitals of Warsaw, Bucharest, Belgrade, and Prague without visiting Moscow. The effect which the Western powers judged the 1937 purges had had on the Red Army made it less likely than ever that anything would be done to give real substance to the Franco-Soviet agreement.

In January 1938 both Zhdanov and Molotov, obviously men more powerful than Litvinov in the Soviet hierarchy and clearly acting with the approval of Stalin, publicly criticized the Foreign Commissariat for failing to take France to task for the "anti-Soviet activity" of "criminals of Russian or non-Russian bourgeois origin" in France. The reference was to a French police investigation into the NKVD abduction of a former White leader, General Miller, in Paris, so it might seem that the USSR was the real offender in the incident, but the important thing was that Stalin had called into question the whole public policy of current Soviet diplomacy. However, there was no suggestion of a response from

Hitler in his speech of February 20, 1938, the most openly anti-Soviet thus far: "There is only one State with which we have not sought to establish relations, nor do we wish to establish relations with it: Soviet Russia. More than ever do we see in Bolshevism the incarnation of the human destructive instinct. . . ."

By 1938 the USSR thus appeared throughly isolated. On the day after Hitler's speech (which was also the day after Eden's resignation), Chamberlain declared that peace would depend on "the four major powers of Europe: Germany, Italy, France and ourselves." It seemed a forecast of the Munich Agreement. In March came Hitler's annexation of Austria, now blessed by Mussolini. Britain and France did nothing, but as Hitler began to threaten Czechoslovakia there was a flurry of diplomatic activity. Austria was made up of German-speaking people; so were the western marches of Czechoslovakia, called the Sudetenland. Hitler talked as if it were merely a problem of applying a Wilsonian right of self-determination until all Germans lived within a single border, when all would be well, and Chamberlain appeared to believe him. Yet on May 28 Hitler ordered that by October 2 preparations to attack Czechoslovakia should be completed.

The summer and fall were a diplomatic nightmare. The Soviets claimed that they were ready to honor the Czechoslovak commitment, provided the French did. Perhaps they felt sure that contingency could be ruled out, for there was no evidence of unusual Soviet military preparations in 1938. Refusing to abandon the hope of "appeasement," Chamberlain personally flew to confer with Hitler in September, first to Berchtesgaden, then to Bad Godesberg, and at the end of the month to Munich, where it was decided that a conference of what Chamberlain had called "the four great powers" was to assemble.

At Munich Chamberlain and Daladier consented to the partition of Czechoslovakia and Hitler's annexation of the Sudetenland, and gave the Czechoslovaks nothing but a solemn guarantee of the integrity of the remnant. Prague felt obliged to acquiesce; the Czechs feared that accepting only Soviet aid would convert their country into another Spain (always assuming it would have been forthcoming, which the Soviets never promised unless France also helped), and they dared not fight alone if the British and French washed their hands of them. Chamberlain arrived home with the unfortunate phrase, "peace in our time," and the conviction that appeasement had succeeded. Whatever his conviction, it was sadly true that Britain and France were in no military position either to fight or to bargain effectively. Many in the West were ashamed of Munich; many Czechoslovaks never forgot the experience of being sacrificed to their enemies by their friends. Hitler, who had received as a gift what he had been prepared to fight for, was jubilant.

SOVIET NEGOTIATIONS WITH BOTH SIDES

The deception of Munich was soon exposed. In October and November the helpless Prague government had to cede Teschen as the result of a Polish ultimatum, yield a strip of territory holding a million people to Hungary, and grant full autonomy to Slovakia and Ruthenia (now renamed "Carpatho-Ukraine"). For a time Ruthenia was the scene of much real or alleged pan-Ukrainian agitation under Berlin sponsorship, which seemed to portend grave Nazi-Soviet tension. Nevertheless Stalin, in his report to the XVIII Party Congress on March 10, 1939, brushed aside Western forecasts of trouble over the Ukraine as designed "to provoke a conflict with Germany without any visible grounds." Declaring that the "nonaggressive" states were "unquestionably stronger than the Fascist states," he argued that their failure to resist Hitler was motivated not by weakness but by desire to embroil the Nazis with the Soviets. He warned against "war-mongers who are accustomed to have others pull the chestnuts out of the fire for them," and proclaimed the Soviet intention to stay out of a "new imperialist war" which was "already in its second year." The Soviet *Political Dictionary* of 1940 described Stalin's report as raising "the question of the good neighborly relations between the USSR and Germany. This declaration of Comrade Stalin," the article added, "was properly understood in Germany."

It is now known not only that this assertion was true but also that Stalin's declaration fell on already receptive Nazi ears. Until the end of 1938 Hitler hoped for a compact with Poland at Soviet expense, in which he would receive Danzig and the Corridor in exchange for supporting Polish gains in the Ukraine. When Poland did not respond, he was turning to the idea of a partition of Poland in concert with the USSR.

On March 15 Hitler sent German troops to occupy Bohemia and Moravia, set up Slovakia as an "independent" state, but sacrificed his tiny Ukrainian "Piedmont" by giving it to Hungary. Thus he simultaneously made clear to the West that his ambitions exceeded the boundaries of German-speaking lands and to the USSR that his much-bruited "designs on the Ukraine" might at least temporarily be laid aside for purposes of diplomatic discussion.

Much British opinion was now clamoring for an end to "appeasement" as well as an approach to the USSR. After the occupation of the core of Czechoslovakia, even Chamberlain lost his illusions about Hitler. He asked the Soviets what their attitude would be if Rumania were attacked and thus launched a series of Anglo-Soviet exchanges which continued into the summer. On March 31 he guaranteed Poland against attack and, after Mussolini seized Albania, on April 13 he guaranteed both Greece and Rumania. Meanwhile Hitler had extorted Memel from Lithuania by simple ultimatum, and he now began to demand Danzig and the Polish Corridor from Poland openly.

In September 1938 the USSR had been isolated and ignored. Beginning in March 1939 she was ardently courted as a likely ally by both the Western powers and the Nazis. On May 3 Stalin replaced Litvinov with Molotov as foreign commissar; thus departed the man publicly identified with the policy of "collective security." Nevertheless the British and French pushed on with negotiations for a pact to halt further Nazi aggression. In the meantime discussions about a Nazi-Soviet trade pact were proceeding. On June 15 the Soviet chargé d'affaires in Berlin passed on a message to the Nazis that the USSR was trying to decide whether to conclude the pact with the British and French, drag out negotiations further, or undertake a rapprochement with Germany, adding that "this last possibility, with which ideological considerations would not have to become involved, was closest to [Soviet] desires."

Thenceforth the USSR was negotiating secretly with the Nazis and openly with the British and French at the same time. If it had chosen to take it, the West had ample warning of what was in store. Molotov continually raised the Soviet price for a pact, but the plainest danger signal was an article by Zhdanov in *Pravda* on June 29, in which he said he could not agree with his friends who thought Britain and France were sincere in the negotiations which were taking place. The British and French did not exhibit any hastiness, at any rate; when they sent a military mission to Moscow in August, it went by leisurely boat.

However, Hitler was in a great hurry. An attack on Poland was scheduled for late August, and by the end of July the Nazis realized that they must reach agreement with the Soviets very soon if these plans were to be safely implemented. It seems fairly clear that on the night of August 3 Hitler agreed to pay the Soviet price for a pact. Mussolini was left in the dark about his plans. The Italians learned only on August 11 that Hitler was bent on war, and the news threw them into a panic. On the night of the nineteenth the Nazi-Soviet trade treaty was signed. The next day Hitler telegraphed Stalin with a request that he see Ribbentrop on August 22 or 23. When he received Stalin's assent, Hitler pounded on the wall with his fists and shouted, "I have the world in my pocket!" On the night of August 23, 1939, the pact was concluded; it contained the provision which only totalitarians could insert, that it was to take effect as soon as it was signed.

THE NAZI-SOVIET PACT AND THE BEGINNING OF WORLD WAR II

The public text of the Nazi-Soviet Pact was simply an agreement of nonaggression and neutrality, referring as a precedent to the German-Soviet neutrality pact of 1926. The real agreement was in a secret protocol which in effect partitioned not only Poland (along the line of the Vistula) but much of Eastern Europe. To the Soviets were allotted Finland, Estonia, Latvia, and Bessarabia; to the Nazis, everything to the west of those regions, including Lithuania; and each was to ask the other no questions about the disposition of its own "sphere of interest." The pact, coupled with the trade treaty and arrangements for large-scale exchange of raw materials and armaments, amounted to an alliance.

When confronted with the public text of the pact, the Western emissaries could only creep home quietly. For the moment the Soviet obtained immunity from attack by Hitler, the opportunity for considerable expansion, and noninvolvement in the war which opened with Hitler's blitzkrieg against Poland on September 1, and which Britain and France entered on September 3. On September 17 the Soviets announced they were entering eastern Poland. Actually the line of the secret protocol was now shifted by mutual consent. The Nazi-Soviet boundary in Poland became the Bug instead of the Vistula; in exchange the Soviets were allotted Lithuania. The Polish state disappeared. The USSR handed Vilna to Lithuania and acquired an area whose western boundaries were roughly the same as the Russian frontier of 1795, plus eastern Galicia. For the moment World War II had no front, except for what was derisively called the *sitzkrieg* or "phoney war" in the West, where neither the French nor the Germans attempted any serious offensive. In September and October the USSR forced the three Baltic states to sign mutual assistance pacts, but for the moment left them independent.

The foreign reaction to the Nazi-Soviet Pact and the annihilation of Poland was one of shock and rage. The Communist parties abroad, which had no official warning of the Soviet switch, reacted with confusion. On September 6 Thorez and other French Communists joined their regiments, calling for aid to Poland, only to desert at Moscow's behest a few days later. Harry Pollitt, the British Communist leader, wrote a pamphlet unfortunately titled *How to Win the War,* and after two weeks both he and his pamphlet had to drop from public gaze. The German Communists in exile made strange noises suggesting that the Allies were worse than Hitler. The general line was that already stated by Stalin in March, that the war was an "imperialist" one for the redivision of the world. The Communists said much more about Allied than about Nazi "culpability," and demanded "peace."

The Soviets brought pressure on Finland for a pact comparable to those signed by the Baltic states, but Finland refused and on November 29 was invaded by the Red Army. Otto Kuusinen, a Finnish Communist in Moscow's reserve for such emergencies (he was to be elevated to the Soviet Party Presidium in July 1957), was brought out and made head of a puppet government which conceded all Soviet demands. The Soviets thereupon declared that they were not at war with Finland at all. Western sympathy for the Finns mounted as they successfully resisted the Reds. In 1939 the USSR was expelled from the League of Nations. Britain and France, observing the apparent weakness of the Red Army, debated sending troops to aid the Finns, and actually decided to do so a few days before a Soviet-Finnish peace was concluded in March 1940. The Nazis also took note of Soviet military weakness and filed it for future reference. The peace was an important factor in Daladier's replacement by Paul Reynaud as French premier, just in time to be faced with a new Nazi offensive in the West.

On April 9 Hitler occupied Denmark and invaded Norway, where British forces landed and tried to resist. When they had been defeated and withdrawn from southern Norway (although troops remained in Narvik a month longer), public opinion forced Chamberlain from office and on May 10 Winston Churchill became British prime minister, heading a coalition government including Labor. The same day Hitler attacked the Netherlands, Belgium, Luxembourg, and France. A break-through at Sedan was followed by a Nazi advance which reached the Channel on May 21, splitting Allied armies and compelling the British evacuation of Dunkirk. The Dutch had already been overrun, and the Belgian king surrendered on May 28. On June 10 Italy belatedly declared war on Britain and France. The French army was already shattered, and on June 16 Reynaud yielded the premiership to Marshal Pétain, who sued for peace at once. Churchill's Britain was left alone.

NAZI-SOVIET TENSIONS

The Soviets reacted sharply to the fall of France even before the signing of an armistice. Stalin ordered military occupation of Estonia, Latvia, and Lithuania, and all three were "admitted" into the USSR as constituent republics in July. In late June the Soviets also annexed Bessarabia and northern Bukovina (the latter going beyond the line of the secret protocol of the pact with Hitler) by way of ultimatum to Rumania, and most of the annexed territory became a new Moldavian SSR.[4]

The Nazis as well seemed to be closing up to their side of the protocol line. In August and September they began to occupy the rest of Rumania, partitioned its Transylvanian province and gave much of it to Hungary, and forced the Rumanians to cede the southern Dobrudja to Bulgaria. In July 1940 Hitler had secretly decided to prepare to attack the USSR. In September a German-Italian-Japanese Tripartite Pact was signed, and although it stipulated that it would not affect the relations of any of the three powers with the Soviets, a certain deterioration in Berlin-Moscow amity had become apparent. In November 1940 Molotov visited Berlin for further discussions of a vague and grandiose kind, but Hitler did not cancel his plans for attack. On December 18, 1940, he issued the directive for Operation Barbarossa, the code name for the invasion of the USSR, to be launched in the middle of May 1941.

Beginning in August the Nazis were launching large-scale air attacks on Britain; they were also consolidating their influence in the Balkans. The line of the secret protocol ended where Bessarabia touched the Black Sea, and south of that point neither Nazis nor Soviets could formally object to what their partners did. Hitler now extended the Tripartite Pact (often called the Rome-Berlin-Tokyo Axis) by obtaining the adhesion of Hungary, Rumania, and Slovakia in November, and after some tension with Moscow over Bulgaria, the latter too signed in March. German troops went where the pact did.

In late March 1941 Yugoslavia added its signature, but the government was promptly overthrown by a pro-Western coup. Immediately Hitler attacked and overran Yugoslavia, and Greece as well (thereby incidentally extricating Mussolini from a gravely embarrassing position; after his declaration of war in June he had attacked Greece from Albania, but had been forced to retreat under successful Greek counterattack). The brief Balkan campaign compelled Hitler to postpone Operation Barbarossa for a month, but its success left him in control of the whole continent up to the Soviet border, either directly or by way of his allies Mussolini and Franco, except for neutral Portugal, Sweden, and Switzer-

• [4] In 1924 a Moldavian Autonomous SSR had been created within the Ukrainian SSR on the left bank of the Dniester to put pressure on Rumania. In August 1940 the Moldavian ASSR was transformed into the new SSR, but with mostly different territory; over half of the former ASSR was transferred to the Ukrainian SSR, which also received the southern strip of Bessarabia, the rest of which made up most of the area of the new SSR.

land. Even in Finland the government had accepted his aid in joint preparations for attacking the USSR.

Western sources warned the Soviets that Nazi attack was imminent. It is still uncertain whether Stalin and his colleagues expected the attack. Evidently the Soviets were still thinking in terms of better relations with the Nazis, deliveries to whom were maintained with scrupulous fidelity throughout the period of the pact, as well as with Hitler's Japanese allies. In the spring Foreign Minister Matsuoka came to Europe, and in April a Soviet-Japanese neutrality pact was signed, acclaimed by *Izvestiia* as an "historic reversal in the relations between Russia and Japan." Stalin conducted a remarkable public demonstration of affection for all Germans and Japanese who were in sight as he was bidding farewell to Matsuoka at the railway station. At that moment the Nazi attack was two months away. The Soviets, of course, did not know that; for that matter, neither did the Japanese.

The night before the attack, Molotov summoned Count Schulenburg, Nazi ambassador in Moscow, told him that there were indications that the Germans were dissatisfied with the Soviets, and begged him to explain what had brought about the existing state of affairs. Schulenburg professed himself unable to say, and departed. A few hours later, however, he was back with a declaration of war on the USSR. The Nazi invasion occurred, with Finnish, Rumanian, and other aid, all along the front from the Arctic Ocean to the Black Sea, on June 22, 1941.

Stalin's Cultural Policy (1927–1945)

CHAPTER 22

THE ARTS AND THE FIRST FIVE-YEAR PLAN

During the "Second Revolution" the arts were hurled into an atmosphere of combat. In April 1928 a second All-Union Congress of Proletarian Writers (the first had attacked the fellow travelers in 1925) was convened. The Russian Association of Proletarian Writers (*Russkaia Assotsiatsiia Proletarskikh Pisatelei,* or RAPP), the new name of the former All-Russian Association (VAPP), now emerged alongside a number of other regional writers' groups in one all-embracing All-Union Organization of Associations of Proletarian Writers (VOAPP). However, it was RAPP which became, for the four years following, the arbiter of Soviet literature. Its real chief was Leopold Averbakh, whose brother-in-law was Yagoda, chief of the secret police. Calling for the creation of a "literary front" in the struggle to fulfill the First Five-Year Plan, Averbakh inaugurated what soon became a literary dictatorship. Mayakovsky, declaring that he had "stepped on the throat of his own song," left a poem ending, "No need itemizing mutual griefs, woes, offenses. Good luck and goodbye"; and shot himself. There was no room for anything but "realism," the "social command," and "shock workers" of "artistic brigades."

In 1929 warning was given errant writers by quasi-official condemnation of the "mistakes" of two prominent novelists. Boris Pilniak was chastised, nominally for publishing a novel abroad and for other failings. He attempted to set things right by a larger work glorifying the Five-Year Plan called *The Volga Falls to the Caspian Sea*. However, the death of his hero, "a Communist of the year 1919," in the waters of a newly-completed dam, left no doubt that Pilniak thought the "new" was indeed destroying the old—but that he considered it a catastrophe for Russia. Eugene Zamiatin was attacked for the publication of a shortened Russian version of *We* in a Prague journal, but although he declared he was not responsible for the publication, he refused to grovel. In 1931, probably through the intercession of Gorky, he was allowed to emigrate and died in France six years later.

Thus the disappearance from the Soviet scene of Trotsky and Bukharin was followed by notice to the fellow travelers whom they had, for different reasons, defended, that the period of relative freedom was at an end. The writers who wanted to go on publishing hastened to write "Five-Year Plan novels": Fëdor Gladkov produced *Cement* and *Energy;* Valentine Katayev wrote *Time, Forward!* The process of collectivization was depicted in Fëdor Panfërov's *Bruski,* but it remained for Michael Sholokhov to perform the same task with honesty in *Virgin Soil Upturned* (*Podniataia tselina*),[1] a matchless social document filled with a horror which the author does not try to conceal.

As the First Five-Year Plan neared its end, in April 1932 the Party Central Committee again intervened on the literary scene. RAPP (along with VOAPP and the others) was abolished and replaced by a single Union of Soviet Writers "with a Communist fraction therein." The policy of Averbakh as leader of RAPP was condemned by Paul Yudin (who had been elevated to Party spokesman in the field of philosophy a year earlier, at the time of the attack on Deborin and the other editors of the philosophical journal, *Under the Banner of Marxism,* for their alleged overvaluation of Plekhanov and imputed leanings toward idealism and Menshevism). Yudin particularly attacked the Averbakh slogan of "the living man," his emphasis on individual psychology, and his brand of realism. He also criticized RAPP's strictures on fellow travelers. All this harmonized with Stalin's expressed willingness to "forget" the past errors of the old intelligentsia and utilize them for "socialist construction." Moreover, it conformed with his not yet fully stated line that when socialism was built (as it was declared to have been in 1936) and class struggle disappeared, there was to be no room for "proletarian" par-

• [1] The British edition bears the correct translation as given; the American translation is entitled *Seeds of Tomorrow.*

ticularism; all "socialist" and "Soviet" intellectuals should serve the interests of the system and think in terms of the interests of the USSR rather than any segment of its population. However, although the new policy appeared in the guise of softening the cultural dictatorship, it was immediately to be made plain that the dictatorship was only being taken away from RAPP and placed in the hands of the Party, which would apply it to all artists with an unprecedented rigor.

At the same time the "proletarian" music association was dissolved and replaced by a Union of Soviet Composers. In 1936 the musicians, together with theater artists, painters, and sculptors, came under one Central Art Committee which arranged all contracts for their work. All writers and artists had come under state control, and the period of warring factions ended. No matter how ardently one or another group might support the regime, all intellectuals were to be told what was required of them. Even those artists who were willing to compromise or corrupt themselves by servility to the Party in order to be allowed to work—and, if they were, to be rewarded by increasing privileges—were far from immune to the risk of denunciation, but only the Party was to decide when to denounce and how to punish. However firm the artist's feelings of loyalty to Stalin might be, he spoke his mind at his peril.

THE PARTY TAKES OVER: "SOCIALIST REALISM"

By the end of 1932 the slogan of "socialist realism," a phrase attributed to Stalin himself, was *de rigueur* in literature and increasingly in the other Soviet arts as well. According to Radek, "Socialist realism means not only knowing reality as it is, but knowing whither it is moving. . . ." In other words, authentic "realism" was suspect because its test was truthfulness. What was demanded of the Soviet artists was didacticism, the portrayal less of what was than of what ought to be. They had to become, as Stalin put it, "engineers of human minds."

In August 1934 at the first Congress of the new Union of Soviet Writers, Zhdanov declared, "Soviet literature must know how to portray our heroes, it must be able to look into our tomorrow." The speech was followed by "confessions" of error by Vsevolod Ivanov, Olesha, and other fellow travelers, but in their statements they still endeavored to preserve dignity. Radek indicated the relationship of the new literary doctrine to the Popular Front policy abroad by declaring, "Foreign literature which is still hostile to the revolution but is already hostile to Fascism is of great importance to us." However, he made clear the official attitude to *nonpolitical* foreign literature by calling the work of James Joyce "a heap of dung" and by denouncing the "morbid interest" of certain Soviet writers in Joyce, as well as in John Dos Passos and Marcel Proust.

The use of literature as a "weapon" took a new turn with the 1934 campaign against the historical views of the chief Soviet historian, Michael Pokrovsky, who had died two years earlier. The campaign was launched by Stalin, Kirov, and Zhdanov. Pokrovsky, who had been highly praised by Lenin, had gone to extreme lengths in denigrating the personal lives and reigns of past Tsars and in condemning Tsarist annexation of territory and rule over minority peoples, in a manner indeed not necessarily Marxist. The new policy demanded that the contributions of certain Tsars who were "progressive for their time" be studied, and that the Tsarist annexations be regarded as the "lesser evil" confronting small nationalities placed between larger powers. The first demand was in principle quite compatible with Marxism; the second was in itself not Marxist, although authority might be found in Marx's works for asserting the beneficial influence of conquest in introducing higher modes of production (for example, by the British in India).

Many foreign observers erroneously concluded from the new policy that Russian nationalism was replacing Marxism as the basis of Soviet ideology. The important feature of the change, however, had little to do with whether Pokrovsky or Stalin should be regarded as the better Marxist, or even whether Marxism should be used as a political weapon (Pokrovsky so held, and Stalin, although he was shameless enough to attack Pokrovsky for that very view, obviously used it as one). The difference between the periods before and after 1934 in the writing of Soviet history was between an individual's use of Marxism (albeit Pokrovsky was an individual with great academic influence) as an instrument of interpretation on the one hand, and on the other a despotic state's use of Marxism as an instrument of the current needs of policy and severe punishment of those who did not co-operate in such use to the state's full satisfaction. As a result independent Marxists were entitled to claim that the doctrine had been perverted, but not that it had been abandoned. In fact, Stalin's own contribution to the perversion of history, the *Short Course* in the history of the Soviet Communist Party (1939), insisted as strongly as ever on the necessity of interpreting all phenomena in the light of "Marxism-Leninism."

The selective use of Russian nationalist themes was permitted and even demanded, but they had to be themes which served the ends of Stalin and the Soviet state at the moment: defense of the fatherland, ruthlessness against domestic enemies, and the benefits of Moscow's rule for the borderlands. Party policy in literature (as well as history and other branches of writing) used such themes to justify Stalin's cruelties and stimulate "Soviet patriotism" by ostensibly expatiating on the heroic deeds of Ivan the Terrible, Peter the Great, and other early practitioners of social transformation by force. Alexis Tolstoy's unfinished novel, *Peter the Great,* was begun with no such intention in evidence in the late 1920's, but the later portions clearly show the effects of the new policy. During World War II Tolstoy wrote two plays about Ivan the Terrible, in which the elements of apologia for Stalin show clearly through the guise of the sixteenth-century setting. During the 1930's a number of novels of the same kind were written, which attempted to meet the requirement of a "positive" attitude toward the Soviet state, and dealt with either the past or the present in terms of what the regime wished had been the case or wanted it to be in the future.

Despite the growing output of politically motivated trash, a chosen list of West European classics, such as Shakespeare and Molière, and later works of some "social" significance, such as Dickens, Balzac, and Mark Twain, continued to circulate by the millions. The same was true of certain great Russian authors such as Pushkin and Leo Tolstoy (though much less so, or during certain periods not at all, such writers as Tiutchev or Dostoevsky). The works of Michael Sholokhov, a Communist, but one who maintained artistic integrity up to a point, were published in quantity, and his four-volume work *The Quiet Don* (*Tikhii Don*), probably the outstanding prose work produced by a Soviet writer, became perhaps the most popular single work of Soviet literature. It was a genuinely realistic novel about the Civil War, especially successful in its treatment of the Cossacks, and its characters, both Red and White, have human strengths and weaknesses. However, the first three volumes were written during the First Five-Year Plan, before the Party assumed control of literature.

After 1932 the ideological night closed in rapidly over the Soviet literary scene. In Alexis Tolstoy's *The Road to Calvary (Khozhdenie po mukam)*, begun in the 1920's and completed on the day Hitler invaded Russia, one can trace by stages the gradual replacement of creativeness by political hack work, the sort of decline which overtook Soviet literature in general. After Tolstoy's death in 1945, Eugene Lyons repeated what Tolstoy had told him in the privacy of his room years before: "When I enter this room I shake off the Soviet nightmare, I shut out its stink and horror. . . . Some day, believe me, all Russia will send *them* to hell. . . ."[2] While he lived, however, Tolstoy, like many of his

• [2] *Our Secret Allies: the Peoples of Russia* (New York: Duell, Sloan and Pearce, 1953), p. 371.

colleagues, publicly prostituted himself in return for a luxurious life and the opportunity to write.

In 1936 the artists felt the first tremors of the coming Great Purges. In January *Pravda* attacked Shostakovich's opera based on Leskov's story, *Lady Macbeth of Mtsensk,* for its "purposely harsh and discordant stream of sounds," and condemned such musical "Leftism" as comparable to that of Meyerhold (who had already fallen from favor) in the theater. Demian Bedny was denounced for his libretto to the opera *The Bogatyrs* for failing to evaluate positively the contribution Christianity made to Russia in the tenth century. Marx was quoted—and aptly—in the denunciation, but what worried the genuine artists was not whether Bedny was a good Marxist, but whether the state should determine what art might be allowed to reach an audience.

In 1937 some of the foremost writers of the NEP period, such as Isaac Babel and Boris Pilniak, disappeared, as did D. S. Mirsky, the foremost historian of Russian literature, a former prince who had been converted to Communism while in Britain and had thereupon returned to his homeland. Artists who fell from favor were accused of "Formalism"—and indeed the school of Formalist criticism had been influential even into the early thirties. Although certain of its prominent adherents, such as Roman Jakobson (at present a professor at Harvard) had emigrated, others, such as Victor Shklovsky, Boris Eikhenbaum, and Victor Zhirmunsky, remained, compromised, and still influenced the study of language and literature for a time. However, the word "Formalism" as used by the Soviet cultural dictators became only an epithet to justify punishment of artistic offenders of quite diverse kinds, to crush any kind of experimentalism (which was suspect of kinship with the "decadent" West), and to drive home the regime's demands for esthetic didacticism.

THE BREATHING SPACE OF WORLD WAR II

The coming of World War II abruptly inaugurated a period of relative freedom for the writer. The regime encouraged the literary use of nationalism, religion, love, anything which might sway the emotions of the reading public into identifying themselves with the struggle against Hitler, with scant effort to apply ideological criteria. At the writers' congress of April 1942, the poet Nicholas Tikhonov declared that Soviet literature "is understanding of and sympathetic to suffering because it has an intense interest in man's inner world and in changes brought about by the war. . . ." This sounded a new key, indeed. A multitude of novels, plays, and poems which dealt with the war either with honesty or, if with bombast, then of a nationalist rather than Communist kind, poured forth in edition after edition.

Among such works were those of Constantine Simonov, who wrote, in *Days and Nights* (1944), a popular tale of the inferno through which the defenders of Stalingrad lived, and also produced simple lyrics of "man's inner world" such as "Wait for Me and I'll Return":

Wait for me and I'll return.
Only just you wait . . .
Wait, when melancholy brings
Saffron-colored rain,
Wait, when snows have fallen,
Wait, when the season's warm,
Wait, when others do not wait,
Forgetting bygone days.
Wait, when letters fail to come
From distant, far-off lands,
Wait, when others waiting too
Have ceased at last to hope.[3]

Ilia Ehrenburg, like Alexis Tolstoy a man personally fond of the Bohemia of the West but willing to pay the price for privilege in the USSR, was able to produce a novel called *The Fall of Paris,* which was completed before the invasion of Russia and was doctrinally orthodox, yet in its setting managed to escape some of the strictures courted by novels of Soviet life. Alexander Fadeyev's *The Young Guard* (1945) dealt with life under German occupation in such a fashion that later the book was attacked for minimizing the Party's role in the events described, and Fadeyev was forced to "revise" the novel accordingly. During the war the first-rank poets Pasternak and Akhmatova published a few pieces, but Akhmatova's poems ignored the war, as did the novel of Michael Zoshchenko, *Before Sunrise* (*Pered voskhodom solntsa*).

In 1946 Akhmatova and Zoshchenko were attacked by Zhdanov (see p. 451); at the same time Tikhonov was removed as leader of the Union of Soviet Writers. He was replaced by Fadeyev, who had undertaken to correct his "mistakes" and had not been caught talking publicly about "man's inner world." The brief wartime interlude of relaxed controls was over. It had revealed that when controls were loosened and artists were allowed to choose their own subject and manner of treatment within

• [3] Translated by D.W.T.

much wider limits than before, few artists of stature remained to exercise a choice.

SOVIET EDUCATIONAL POLICY

Stalin's cultural policy aimed at forcing into the service of the state not only the talent and training of professional writers and artists, but of teachers and scholars, and the entire educational system. In a country where mass education was only in the planning stage on the eve of the Revolution, one of the major aims of the Communists was to bring about a physical expansion of the school system to include all the people. Illiteracy of those over ten years of age was reported to have dropped from 49% in 1926 to 19% in 1939, and since then has declined to perhaps 5–10%. Education through the seventh grade has remained free; higher education was also free until 1940, when tuition was introduced on the secondary and college levels. At that time the system of state subsidies for living costs was restricted to those "students of higher schools who excel in their studies." Actually such subsidies were part of a contractual obligation into which students entered which obliged them to pursue certain specified work, often in particular enterprises, for a period of years after graduation. Also in 1940, the system of State Labor Reserves schools was established, providing for the conscription of one million students per year into these vocational training centers.

In consequence of such measures as these, there is no doubt that most children in the USSR who combine ability with demonstrated political reliability can obtain both advanced education and a privileged position in the Soviet state thereafter, and, moreover, that there is available in certain fields, among them many of the pure sciences and many branches of technology, training of high quality, little hampered by ideological interference. On the other hand, it is a fact that in all fields Soviet scholars, scientists, and teachers are subject to direct personal surveillance by the Party and the secret police. Beginning in the 1930's, but especially since World War II, the Party has repeatedly intervened not only to formulate an obligatory policy on academic issues, but also to silence all views other than its own. Furthermore, the Party line has changed several times without warning, so that even those who are willing to accept the Party as the arbiter of all truth cannot protect themselves from the shifting winds of doctrine or from consequences which have included academic discrimination or dismissal, confinement in a concentration camp, or execution, for ideological deviation.

The education policy of the Soviet regime has evolved through stages comparable to its policy toward the arts. During the 1920's a good deal of experimentalism was permitted. In part the Soviets were employing trial and error to find the kind of education which suited their needs; but at the same time the scholastic innovations served the useful purpose of destroying the old habits of discipline and hierarchy and the type of curriculum which had prevailed in Tsarist times. This is not to say that the old education system had been chiefly intended to further the ends of the regime; the Tsarist government did not regard education as a means of political indoctrination, and while it tried various ways to combat the phenomenon, the student bodies of higher schools and universities had become open strongholds of political opposition.

In the first decade Soviet educational theorists drew heavily on the ideas of John Dewey and other Americans who espoused "progressive education." Such influential men as S. T. Shatsky and Paul Blonsky emphasized "freedom for the child" and dropped such traditional subjects as Latin from the school curriculum. However, in the middle thirties the Party intervened to restore a differential grading system, classroom discipline, and some of the traditional subjects—taught in a far from traditional way with emphasis on ideological goals. In 1936 Blonsky was attacked by the Party Central Committee and promptly vanished. The notion of group "socialistic competition" in education, popular under the First Five-Year Plan, was dropped. As in all other respects, in his education the individual was to be at the mercy of the state, with as few intermediary agencies as practicable. His position in the school was to be such that his reliability could be constantly tested and rewarded or punished, without reference to a group with which he might be working. Stalin made no secret of his view of education (which Lenin had shared): to H. G. Wells he declared, "Education is a weapon, whose effect depends on who holds it in his hands and who is struck with it."

The Soviet state makes no attempt to claim credit for the advancement of truth, knowledge, and art for their own sakes. Any effort to interpret those values as of inherent worth or of some significance independent of the needs of the Soviet state is branded as "bourgeois objectivism" or even, in certain cases, treason. The intent of the Soviet regime is not to educate, but to indoctrinate through a culturally totalitarian system of controls which produce, in the words of Stalin, a group of intellectuals who are "engineers of human minds," and for the rest, minds capable of being engineered. In this manner it is intended to create the "new Soviet man."

Nevertheless there is evidence that the proliferation of schools, books, newspapers, theaters, art galleries, concert halls, and the like has not always had the effect the Soviet state desired. In 1956, according to Soviet statistics (which must always be used with caution, since they are specifically and officially required to serve state interests), 54,000 book titles were published in over a billion copies, 9,000 titles of newspapers and journals were being issued, and over 35 million young people were studying in various levels of the Soviet educational system. By comparison, in 1914–15, 28,000 book titles were issued in something over 100 million copies, 2,000 titles of newspapers and journals were published, and less than 9 million people were studying in the schools of the Russian Empire. Those were no mean educational achievements, but under the Soviets information, skills, and cultural opportunities were made available to much greater numbers of people. Despite formidable efforts to use broader education for its own purposes, the Soviet regime has unleashed forces which are not completely susceptible to the controls at its disposal. Even the older generation of artists and scholars had not entirely forgotten the meaning of art and knowledge, as shown by the intensity of the campaign of ideological repression which the regime felt it necessary to carry out after World War II, while the younger generation of intellectuals and students, although it has had to formulate its questions and demands for itself, has in the middle 1950's attracted the attention of the whole world by its search for answers more plausible than those given it by the regime.

STALIN'S POLICY TOWARD RELIGION: FRONTAL ATTACK AND COMPROMISE

When Stalin became unchallenged master of the Soviet Union, the regime was still pursuing the dual policy of attempting to spread militant atheism on the one hand and pursuing a *divide et impera* line toward the Orthodox Church. With the coming of the First Five-Year Plan, the situation changed abruptly, and a large-scale offensive against religion was launched. In May 1929 the Constitution was amended to omit the previous guarantee of the right of religious propaganda, leaving "the right of professing a religion and of antireligious propaganda." Great numbers of churches were closed, church bells were seized (ostensibly to provide tin and copper for industrial use), and many of the remaining monasteries and nunneries were dissolved. The antireligious significance of the introduction of the "continuous" work week (ending the regular Sunday work holiday) was heavily emphasized in the official press.

By January 1930 the League of Militant Godless claimed two million members. Yaroslavsky, its leader, was accused by certain of his enthusiastic followers of unwarranted moderation because he hung back from abolishing all religion by fiat. Early in 1930 the Party criticized overly impatient "Left deviationists" in the antireligious campaign, and Yaroslavsky kept his authority. However, the Party action did not mean the abandonment of the campaign, any more than Stalin's "Dizziness from Success" article had meant abandonment of collectivization (see p. 269). In 1931 it was reported that there were thirty-two hundred "Godless shock brigades" operating among the industrial workers. By 1932 the League claimed a membership exceeding five million. In the same year much fanfare attended the conversion of the Kazan Cathedral in Leningrad into an antireligious museum (which it remains), and several dozen other such institutions were created.

The leadership of the Russian Orthodox Church indicated by its reaction to the antireligious campaign how far it had already gone in subservience to the Communist Party. In 1930 Metropolitan Sergei asserted that the church retained thirty thousand parishes (as compared with almost fifty thousand which had been functioning in 1914), and he not only refused to criticize the regime for its offensive against religion, but even attacked Christians abroad who had voiced alarm. The campaign continued for some time after Sergei's declaration, but it lost momentum and plainly fell short of success. Yaroslavsky lamented the decline in antireligious activities among League members, and in the middle thirties he admitted that approximately half of the population remained "believers." In 1934 the newspaper *The Godless* discontinued publication, and the decline in militant atheism was plain.

Nevertheless the regime refused to admit defeat. Early in 1936 the Party Central Committee surveyed the situation and demanded a renewal of antireligious efforts. In 1938 *The Godless* was revived. A number of high clergy fell during the Great Purges. Just before 1941 the membership of the League of Militant Godless, having slumped to below two million, rose above three million again. The prewar situation may be summed up in the episode of the census of 1937, which included a question about religious belief. The entire census results were branded as faulty, and they were not published. Part of the reason for their suppression was certainly the population deficiency they recorded, which resulted from collectivization and the early stages of the purges. However, persistent rumors suggested that another important reason was that forty per cent of the population had declared their religious belief. That some such embarrassing figure had been obtained was suggested by the omission of the question from the census of 1939.

Until the war the Orthodox Church continued, in obviously difficult circumstances, under the leadership of Metropolitan Sergei. After talks with Stalin, he was elected Patriarch in September 1943, in a dramatic reversal of Soviet policy toward religion. It is uncertain whether by that time Sergei remained in any sense a free agent; certainly the concordat between church and regime was the product of Stalin's and not Sergei's decision. Along with Soviet resumption of relations with the Orthodox Church went strict governmental controls over its clergy and the properties allotted for its use, controls which, it appears, are actually exercised by the secret police. In May 1944 Sergei died and was succeeded by Metropolitan Alexis of Leningrad, who was elected Patriarch early in 1945. Patriarch Alexis has taken a prominent part in Soviet "peace" campaigns, but the more powerful cleric seems to be Metropolitan Nicholas of Krutitsa, who attacked American Christians for countenancing "germ warfare in Korea." Such yeoman service to the regime on the part of the Orthodox hierarchy has not, however, been rewarded by the termination of antireligious activity, which the Soviet press has continued to emphasize.

When the imprisoned bishops of Solovetsk recommended reconciliation with the state power (see p. 252), they insisted on the retention of the Orthodox faith and on the understanding of its incompatibility with Communism. Patently the present leadership of the church has failed to follow the Solovetsk injunctions. The high clerics of Russian Orthodoxy have been willing to serve as instruments of Soviet state policy in both domestic and foreign affairs as the price of being permitted to resume for the time being their functions as the leaders of an officially tolerated religious institution. During the war the leadership of the Orthodox Church of Georgia, the Armenian Church, the (Protestant) Baptists and Evangelical Christians, and the Moslems accepted a similar status (the Roman Catholics have not done so, while the Jews have suffered more than any other religious group).

The success of such arrangements, from the Soviet viewpoint, is illustrated by the adherence of other Eastern Orthodox Patriarchs to a number of pronouncements by the Patriarch of Moscow, the political effects of the resumption of pilgrimages to Mecca by Soviet Moslems in November 1944, and the favorable reports about the state of religion in the USSR rendered by uninformed clergymen visiting from the Western countries during the last decade and a half. For some time to come it is unlikely that the details of the real relationship which exists between the various religious leaderships mentioned and the regime will become known. No doubt there are men of integrity, deeply devoted to their professed beliefs, among the officially approved clergy, as there are clearly others who, like Soviet intellectuals in general, have submitted completely to the state. Some clergymen may have done so to preserve their own privileges; others may have hoped merely to keep the faith of the people alive through the holding of religious services, even though the teachings of their religion must be mutilated or suppressed.

PART FOUR

The War and Postwar Period

The USSR in World War II: The Military Crisis (1941–1943)

★
★
★
★
★
★
★
★
★
★

CHAPTER 23

A DIPLOMATIC REVOLUTION

On the day before the Nazis invaded the Soviet Union, Stalin was still acting as if he considered Hitler to be his partner. The USSR had protested the British blockade of Germany, exerted pressure on Turkey to reject a pact with Britain and France, and bitterly attacked the United States program of Lend-Lease to Britain. Foreign Communists, although damning both sides in the "imperialist war," reserved their sharpest denunciations for Britain and (before her defeat) France. On Moscow's orders, the Communists in Norway, Denmark, and the Netherlands had at first been willing to accept the ambiguous status of being tolerated by the Nazi occupation forces, and in Belgium they were clearly favored, all other parties having been banned. Although by the autumn of 1940 the Nazi-Communist honeymoon was over in Western Europe, even after the Nazis overran Yugoslavia and Greece in the spring of 1941 Moscow was unwilling to give the Balkan Communists the signal to resist. The British, still smarting from the humiliating circumstances in which they had learned of the Nazi-Soviet Pact and well aware of Stalin's aid to Hitler, along with their supporters in America and elsewhere, regarded the Soviets with bitter hatred.

However, within twenty-four hours of the invasion, Churchill declared that although "no one has been a more consistent opponent of Communism than I have been for the last twenty-five years," nevertheless "any man or state who fights on against Nazidom will have our aid." The United States, still a neutral, extended Lend-Lease to the USSR. Communists abroad abruptly announced that the conflict had become a "people's" war, and gave verbal support to the British war effort and American Lend-Lease policy. Nevertheless even in that hour of the USSR's greatest peril, the Communist doctrine of old did not disappear. British Communists called on Labor for a common front against "Toryism"—to which Laborites Harold Laski and Emanuel Shinwell responded by advocating a merger between the Socialist International and the Comintern—but still directed its sharpest attacks at the Labor party. The apparently contradictory policy was reminiscent of the Popular Front period, and indeed the professed aims of the Popular Front seemed at last to have been achieved—an alliance was formed between Communists and all anti-Fascist political groups, and between the USSR and all anti-Nazi governments. To be sure, the Popular Front's slogan was "against war and Fascism"; but no Communist (any more than any British Tory) professed to be anything but a fervent supporter of the war until Hitler should be completely crushed. In his first speech to the Soviet people, Stalin referred "with gratitude" to the "historic utterance of the British Prime Minister, Mr. Churchill, regarding aid to the Soviet Union and the declaration of the United States government" regarding Lend-Lease. It seemed that the diplomatic revolution was complete, and, many Westerners thought or hoped, permanent.

THE CAMPAIGN OF 1941

Hitler's objective, as stated in the directive for Operation Barbarossa, was "to crush Soviet Russia in a quick campaign before the end of the war against England." As the invasion opened, he announced that the Soviet Union was dissolved, and the first few days of fighting suggested that he would achieve his aims in 1941. The Nazis achieved virtually complete tactical surprise, destroyed much of the Red air force on the ground by bombing, and their initial onslaught crashed clear through Soviet lines.

Whether strategic surprise was achieved remains uncertain. In his speech of July 3, 1941, Stalin implied that it was when he said that the Nazis attacked "suddenly and treacherously," which meant, if true, that he had ignored the warnings of the British that attack was imminent, and

Khrushchëv accused him of precisely such blindness in his "secret speech" of 1956. However, Stalin had mobilized a hundred and seventy divisions and placed most of them near the frontier, which argues against the "surprise attack" explanation. In any event, he acted swiftly after the invasion. The Third Five-Year Plan, begun in 1938, was shelved. A State Defense Committee, consisting of Stalin, Molotov for diplomacy, Beria for the secret police, Malenkov for Party matters, and Voroshilov for the army, was established. In addition Voroshilov commanded the northern front, while Timoshenko and Budënny were the field commanders in the center and south. For the duration of the war there was little pretense that anyone but Stalin made the decisions.

Hitler's plan of attack was predicated upon the rapid collapse of both the Red Army and the Soviet regime. He had rejected the more cautious proposal of General Marcks to hold the main Soviet armies north of the upper Dniester while a single great southern offensive struck east to Rostov and then north to Moscow and Leningrad, saving the main Nazi armies for annihilation blows once this offensive was well under way. Instead Hitler ordered an all-out frontal assault by three army groups, the northern under Field Marshal von Leeb toward Pskov (headed for Leningrad), the central under Field Marshal von Bock toward Minsk and Smolensk (headed for Moscow), and the southern under Field Marshal von Rundstedt in two wings converging on Kiev.

Within two weeks, owing largely to the speed of Guderian's tank forces, Army Group Center had surrounded and captured almost three hundred thousand Soviet troops near Minsk, and Guderian's columns had reached the Dnieper. Ten days more, and he was through Belorussia into the territory of the RSFSR at Smolensk. Bock and Guderian were eager to strike on to Moscow at once. However, on July 19 Hitler ignored their pleas and made the fateful decision to disperse his tank forces to keep both flanks moving forward. Guderian was ordered to turn south to assist Rundstedt in the Ukraine, while another large armored group was to aid Leeb's advance in the north. It is possible that the outcome of the Nazi-Soviet war was decided then and there. Besides being of immense psychological importance, Moscow was the center of a highly centralized regime, the hub of all Russian railways, and the transshipment point for the supplies which would soon be flowing in quantity from the U.S. and Britain by way of the White Sea and Vladivostok. The capture of Moscow within the first two or three months of the campaign, Guderian was sure, would have had such an effect that the risks attending a single massive armored thrust toward the capital were well worth taking.

At any rate, Guderian's southward movement soon resulted in another

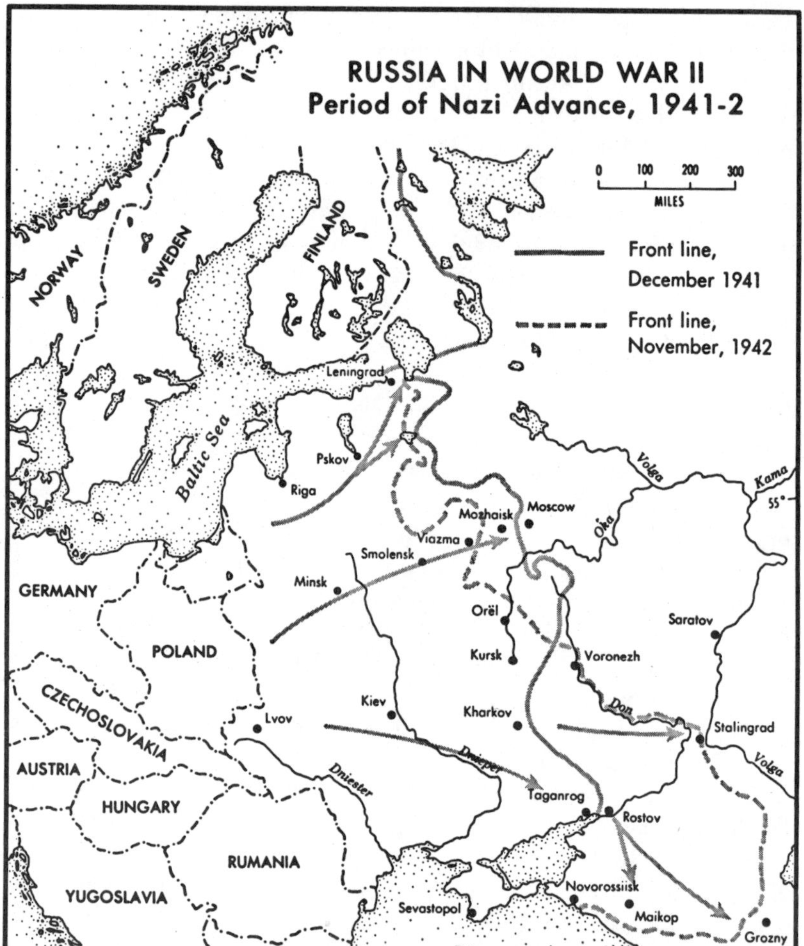

great victory. On September 14 his tanks met those of Army Group South east of Kiev and surrounded six hundred thousand Soviet soldiers. Budënny's army was virtually dispersed, and he was replaced by Timoshenko (Zhukov took over Timoshenko's post on the central front). Rundstedt continued his advance to Kharkov and Taganrog on the Sea of Azov. Nearly the whole of the Ukraine had been conquered in four months.

Leeb had succeeded in reaching Leningrad in the middle of September, and in conjunction with Field Marshal Mannerheim and the Finns, invested the city from north and south, but was unable to capture it.

Hitler had consented to return Guderian's tanks to Army Group Center when the Kiev operation was complete, but Bock was not ready to resume his advance until October 2. Almost at once another gigantic encirclement was achieved near Viazma, and another mass of six hundred thousand prisoners was taken. On October 15 Bock's armor reached Mozhaisk, sixty-five miles from Moscow. But now winter was descending, earlier than usual as in 1812—a precedent German officers had increasingly on their minds. On November 15 another attempt was made; the Nazis floundered through snowy mud for two more weeks, but they remained twenty miles from the city. A last effort began on December 2, and German advance guards actually penetrated the suburbs of Moscow, but the main force made little headway. On December 8 the German army announced suspension of operations on account of winter. Hitler's generals begged him to consent to a retreat, since the troops had no winter clothing or equipment and their positions were unsuitable for defense against the counteroffensive the Soviets were now launching all along the line, but he refused. Thereupon Rundstedt, Bock, Leeb, and the army commander-in-chief, Brauchitsch, resigned. Hitler himself assumed the command and dismissed Guderian. Thus a clean sweep of the field leadership was made.

The Nazi military victory had been great, but Hitler's plan to crush the USSR "quickly" had failed. Guderian's scheme of a massive thrust to Moscow might have achieved the victory on which Hitler counted. Instead he had used the tactic of an in-line advance. Such a scheme was bound to require more time, and yet, in the months of October and November, three things happened for which he had not prepared. Winter came, and the troops, already fatigued, had insufficient clothing to protect them from the cold. The roads became impassable for wheeled vehicles, although if tracked transport had been available, the advance might have continued. The Soviets had time to bring up reserves, whose size the Nazi command had discounted, and the combination of factors spelled failure. The military mistakes were Hitler's; however, he may well have been right in refusing to retreat once the failure was plain. The news that blitzkrieg had miscarried for the first time, coupled with the realization of what United States entrance into the war (December 7, 1941) might mean, had already deeply damaged domestic morale. The psychological and political effects of a withdrawal to the Polish borders might have had further serious consequences.

For the winter German troops were withdrawn into "hedgehogs" (*Igels*), fortified centers with defenses all around their perimeters, in order to prevent surprise attack from the rear by infiltrating forces. The Germans were unable to keep the Soviets from regaining contact with besieged Leningrad through the construction of a road across the ice of Lake Ladoga in January (nevertheless, more than half a million Leningraders starved to death during that winter). On the central front they lost Mozhaisk to Soviet counterattacks, while in the south the Red Army made some gains in the Crimea, but failed in an effort to retake Kharkov. From February to May 1942 the front was fairly quiet.

HITLER AND THE SOVIET PEOPLES

Just before the invasion, Hitler had written, "We do not want to convert the Russians to National Socialism, but to make them into our tools." In the "Commissar Decree" of May 1941 he ordered that all "political officials" and army political commissars were to be killed on capture. Heinrich Himmler, one of the chief Nazis and master of both the dreaded SS formations and the Gestapo, wrote contemptuously of the *Untermensch,* the subhuman Slav whose fate was to serve Germany or die. The Nazi doctrine on the Soviet minorities was somewhat less savage in tone, and Hitler even regarded the Moslems with some favor, but there was to be no nonsense about "equality" of any of the peoples with the Germans.

In practice, competition and conflict among Nazi agencies—Hermann Goering's economic staffs, Joseph Goebbels's propaganda ministry, Alfred Rosenberg's Ministry for the Eastern Territories, Himmler's empire of picked savages, and the army—prevented a policy of extermination, or any other policy, from being consistently carried out. The main difference in emphasis lay between the SS (until 1944) and political officials who were ideologically committed to the notions of "master race" (*Herrenvolk*) and *Untermensch,* and the army, whose officers judged alternative policies in terms of their effects on the tasks of mounting military operations and administering rear areas, and thus leaned toward less brutality and more "realism." In the army and in the Foreign Office there was even a handful of men who combined sympathy for the Soviet peoples with opposition to Hitler's rule in Germany, although they couched their pleas in "realistic" terms. However, although the army was able to circumvent or thwart certain of Hitler's directives, Hitler never was willing to countenance any real recognition that the peoples of Russia were human beings, and thus the foundations of Nazi policy were never altered. This policy was, from the Nazi standpoint, suicidal, but it is difficult to see how it could have been changed substantially unless Hitler had been overthrown in the course of the war, or the Nazis had ceased to be what they were.

More often than not, the peoples of the Soviet Union at first received the Nazi invaders as liberators. The peasants of Belorussia, the Ukraine, and Great Russia met the Germans with the traditional token of welcome, bread and salt. Many collective farms in areas overrun by the *Wehrmacht* were instantly and spontaneously abolished by the farmers themselves. Many churches were reopened by the Russians, and although the German army was not authorized either to abolish collectives or reopen churches, at first they did not try to prevent the local inhabitants from doing so. As Rosenberg wrote, the Germans found in the USSR, "in contrast to the West, a people who went through all the terror of Bolshevism, and who now, happy about their liberation, put themselves willingly at the disposal of Germany . . ."[1] yet they were treated far worse than the people of Western Europe.

Rosenberg was referring chiefly to the Ukrainians. He hated Great Russia (he was of Baltic German origin himself) but attempted to foster separatist movements and anticipated the organization of "Greater Finland," "Baltica," the Ukraine, and the Caucasus as German satellites. The Ukraine seemed the most promising region in which to employ local separatists, and the Nazis had shown Ukrainian nationalist leaders some favor after they conquered western Poland in 1939. At that time Stephen Bandera and others were released from Polish prisons. Bandera criticized the older nationalists, led by Colonel Andrew Melnyk, and the factions which crystallized around the two leaders remained at odds during the war with the USSR.[2]

At first the Ukrainian nationalists hoped for real Nazi support. When the Germans occupied Lvov on June 30, 1941, the Banderists promptly moved in and proclaimed a Ukrainian state, but the SS immediately arrested them. When Kiev was captured in September, the followers of Melnyk attempted to take in hand the organization of Ukrainian public life, but they in turn were shunted aside by the Nazis. A third group, connected with more moderate Ukrainian *émigrés,* and led by Taras Borovets (he took the *nom de guerre* "Taras Bulba" after a Gogol hero), was permitted to organize a partisan force to fight Soviet stragglers. However, after German repressions in the Ukraine in the winter of 1941–1942, Borovets began to fight the Nazis. The Ukrainians also fought among themselves. The two extreme nationalist groups formed partisan units of their own and squabbled instead of co-operating; in the summer

• [1] Quoted in George Fischer, *Soviet Opposition to Stalin* (Cambridge: Harvard University Press, 1952), p. 9.

• [2] The OUN (*Organizatsiia Ukrainskykh Natsionalistiv* or Organization of Ukrainian Nationalists) split into the OUN-B and the OUN-M, the letters after the hyphens standing for the names of the two leaders.

of 1943 the Banderists used force to take away the followers of both Melnyk and Borovets and came to dominate the Ukrainian nationalist movement. By this time, as a partisan congress in August 1943 indicated, the Ukrainian leaders had decided on all-out resistance to both Nazis and Soviets.

The Ukrainian nationalist leaders broke with the Nazis less because they had been personally ill-treated than because the occupation policy had revealed its full savagery. A brute named Erich Koch, who scorned even the plans for a Ukrainian satellite of his nominal chief, Rosenberg, was named *Reichskommissar* of the Ukraine. A crucial question in occupation policy was recognized to be that of the collective farms, and plans for their dissolution by Nazi decree had been discussed for months. In October 1941 Hitler had disapproved of the idea, but in February 1942 Rosenberg managed to get his sanction for issuance of a Law for Restoration of Private Land (*Reprivatisierungsgesetz*). However, the law envisaged only "gradual and orderly transition" to co-operative farms, and in the few places where it was implemented the peasant was scarcely able to tell the difference from the Soviet collectives. In any case Koch and others sabotaged any serious effort to put even this weak measure into effect. The reopening of churches, although sometimes permitted by the army, was not made part of occupation policy, and Hitler's fear of nationalism as well as the Nazi hostility to Christianity prevented any propagandistic exploitation of the actual partial revival of religious worship which took place here and there behind Nazi lines. Hitler also decreed that only the most fragmentary education was to be given the occupied peoples.

The Russians, Belorussians, and Ukrainians in occupied areas hoped for real restoration of individual farming and the Christian religion. The Nazis not only failed to restore them, but earned the hatred of the people by the shooting of non-Communist hostages beginning in October 1941, mass deportation of civilians as a penalty for terrorism or sabotage, and mass recruitment of forced labor which began in March 1942 under the direction of the infamous Fritz Sauckel, former *Gauleiter* of Thuringia. After generally unsuccessful efforts to incite the local inhabitants to conduct pogroms, the Nazis simply exterminated the Soviet Jews by the tens of thousands. The civilians also observed the inhuman treatment of prisoners of war. Many were shot before their eyes for lagging behind, and yet it was forbidden to give them food, even to save the starving. When the prisoners reached camps in the rear their treatment defied description. In 1941 over three and a third million Soviet prisoners had been captured (the total captured during the war was close to six million).

During the last four months of 1941 alone, half a million prisoners died of hunger and cold in Nazi camps, and of those who remained alive only a small fraction were able to work. The SS was responsible for much of this slaughter and suffering, but the army bore its share of responsibility also. However, a number of high officers soon came to advocate milder treatment, realizing that the immense group of prisoners could provide a great reservoir of trained troops many of whom were eager, despite the treatment they had received at Nazi hands, to fight the Soviet regime alongside the Nazis.

In early 1942 Nazi brutality had already begun to turn the civilians in the occupied areas against the regime, and Soviet partisan activity, at first negligible, had increased markedly. The Germans estimated that in August 1941, 10% of the forests behind their lines were infested with partisans; by October 1942, 75%. By the autumn of 1943, 10% of all German field divisions in Russia were fighting partisans. Partisan units could grow only if a sizable proportion of the civilians would join or support them in some manner. Although Moscow tried its best to obtain and keep control over the partisan units and many of them (not the Ukrainian nationalist ones) were nominally pro-Soviet in allegiance or leadership, others were opposed to both totalitarianisms, and there is evidence that there were many partisan units behind Soviet lines which gave Moscow much trouble. At any rate, it was clear that the occupied areas were becoming actively hostile to the German armies.

Yet during the first weeks of the fighting it had been revealed that the millions ruled by Stalin hated the regime, and as popular feeling began to turn against the Nazis, a number of voices were raised to persuade Hitler to alter his policy at least verbally, or to allow the army to turn to account the willingness to co-operate with the Nazis which remained among many war prisoners. In Rosenberg's *Ostministerium* Otto Bräutigam called for a "Russian de Gaulle" (whatever the appropriateness of the slogan). A memorandum by a certain Captain Strik-Strikfeldt in the army propaganda office calling for a Russian "army of liberation" and government-in-exile was actually approved by Brauchitsch, shortly before he was removed in December 1941. The commander of the largest army rear area declared he could not fight partisans successfully unless the Nazis promised a future Russian state and put into effect a policy of decollectivization and religious restoration. The quotation from Schiller's *Demetrius,* "Russia can be defeated only by Russians," was frequently employed by the "realists." However, none of these proposals had any result.

Without authorization, the army had begun to use some of the thousands of Soviet prisoners who begged to be allowed to fight Stalin as *Hilfswillige* or "Hiwis" ("Volunteer Helpers"), chiefly for noncombat duties behind the lines. Beginning in November 1941 battalion-size combat units of *Osttruppen* were also being formed, and even Hitler went back on his own order that none but Germans should be armed in order to sanction the organization of Turkic and other non-Slavic "legions." But Slavic *Osttruppen,* some of them called "Cossack" to avoid the use of the word "Russian," also were formed in considerable numbers. By 1943 perhaps half a million to a million "Hiwis" and a quarter of a million *Osttruppen* were being used by the Nazis. Since Soviet citizens were also used widely as individual replacements, it is very difficult to determine the total of such auxiliaries.

In July 1942 the Nazis had captured Lieutenant General Andrew Vlasov while he was commanding an army trying to relieve Leningrad. He was generally recognized as the most suitable candidate available to lead an anti-Soviet Russian army, if one were to be organized. For two years, however, Hitler forbade the creation of any such force (see p. 386). Even the national committees of the minorities which Rosenberg had assembled in his *Ostministerium* were vouchsafed no official notice. Until it was too late, there was no Nazi policy toward the peoples of the USSR but one of terror and exploitation. Scarcely knowing which was the frying pan and which the fire, the Soviet citizenry wrestled with the dilemma posed by the discovery that the Nazis came as anything but liberators. Hitler's political errors were perhaps no less decisive in the long run than his military miscalculations.

STALIN'S RESPONSE

From June 22 until July 3, 1941, Stalin did not utter a word in public. He then admitted the "grave danger" to the Soviet Union, and although he falsely asserted that the best of the Nazi armed forces had been already destroyed, he called for a "scorched-earth" policy during the continuing retreat and summoned the people to conduct guerrilla warfare in Nazi-occupied areas. Invoking the precedent of 1812, he declared that now as then Russia was waging a "national patriotic war," and the official Soviet name for the war became the "Second War of the Fatherland" (not World War II; that was something being fought elsewhere).

Conceding that it might be wondered how the Soviet government could have "consented" to sign a pact with "such perfidious people, such fiends as Hitler and Ribbentrop," he gave his answer: "We secured to our country peace for a year and a half and the opportunity of preparing our forces." A little later Stalin himself hinted the truth, that Hitler had used the time to much greater advantage in "preparing forces" than the Soviets had. He charged that Hitler wished to turn the Soviet peoples "into the slaves of German princes and barons"; and here, the noble titles aside, was the bald truth. In Stalin's speech lay in germ the propaganda tactic of nationalism which he was to unfold in the coming months.

Stalin doubtless knew that multitudes had defected to Hitler and that many more were awaiting the opportunity to do so. In his speech he warned that "there must be no room in our ranks for whimperers and cowards, for panic-mongers and deserters." There is evidence that thousands of prominent political prisoners, who might conceivably emerge as popular leaders if the regime cracked, were hastily executed, and that local draft commissions were guided by the NKVD to select for front-line service in especially dangerous sectors those who were suspected of potential disloyalty. To prevent the population from hearing German propaganda, radio receivers were gathered in wholesale. Soviet citizens of German descent were rounded up. The entire population—almost half a million—of the Volga German ASSR, which had been vaunted as a showpiece of nationality policy, was uprooted and "deported" by methods which few survived. Stalin's fear was plain. It was reflected in his offer to Harry Hopkins, the special envoy of President Roosevelt, in late July 1941, to "welcome" American troops under their own command anywhere on the front, and his similar invitation to Lord Beaverbrook four months later for British troops to take over part of the Ukrainian sector. When Stalin had recovered a little of his confidence, he would not even allow foreign observers near the front.

Nevertheless, from the time of the invasion Stalin attempted to maintain the appearance of loyalty and solidarity with Britain (on the eve of June 22 the only state at war with Hitler) and the United States (still technically a neutral but deeply committed to aid Britain in her fight). Churchill's blunt remark, "I unsay no word that I have spoken" about Communism, had been coupled with a firm resolve not to say any further words on the subject which would embarrass the Soviets and interfere with the prime objective of defeating Hitler. None of the Allied representatives attempted to disturb Stalin with questions about his past role and future aims.

By tacit common consent, it was assumed in London and Washington that as a result of the grave crisis into which Stalin had blundered, he would shelve all the tiresome nonsense of Marxism-Leninism and assume the role of genuine leader of the Russian nation. As some of the less cautious critics of the Soviets had damned both Tsarist and Soviet "expansionism" as part of the same phenomenon, so other careless commentators began to find heroism and humaneness equally in the Russian past and the Soviet present. It was assumed that Communist power and Stalin's dictatorship were at worst a passing phase in Russian history, and that the Soviet leaders were Russian nationalists in a cumbersome and now happily outmoded ideological guise. As not only British and American leaders but Allied public opinion took up this view, Stalin reciprocated by playing the role to the hilt, appearing as "old Joe," the man with the smile and the pipe. The Allied leaders were not shocked, but were even relieved, when he made demands or promises on behalf of the government without pretending—except on the rare occasions when it suited him—that he had to ask someone else's consent. What they asked of him was not that he be a democrat, but only a *nationalist.*

In a speech delivered on November 7 in Red Square to troops marching directly to the front outside the city of Moscow, Stalin invoked the shades of medieval saints and Tsarist generals in an unequivocal appeal to Russian nationalism: "Let the manly images of our great ancestors—Alexander Nevsky, Dmitry Donskoi, Kuzma Minin, Dmitry Pozharsky, Alexander Suvorov, and Michael Kutuzov—inspire you in this war!" In effect he begged his soldiers to fight for Mother Russia, not for Communism. Stalin thus assumed the pose which he recognized as his best hope of salvation in the effort to persuade the people to fight for the regime; it was also the attitude which promised to be most useful to him in relations with the Allies. Soviet propaganda actively employed, in its appeals to the peoples behind Nazi lines, the fact that democratic Britain and America supported the USSR. By seeming to behave like a Russian Tsar, he might secure for himself the maximum Allied aid for the conduct of the war and the fullest hearing at the peace tables if the war could be won.

On July 12, 1941, Ambassador Cripps, who had talked to Churchill just before his famous speech offering Stalin aid, was instrumental in the conclusion of an Anglo-Soviet mutual assistance pact renouncing any separate peace with Hitler. The former United States ambassador, Joseph E. Davies, expressed sufficient optimism about Soviet capacity to resist so that President Roosevelt thought it important to obtain a direct report. For that purpose Harry Hopkins was sent on a special mission in the last days of July, and he conducted amiable talks with Stalin. Before he went, however, orders had already been given to prepare Lend-Lease shipments to the USSR.

In September W. Averell Harriman was sent to report on Soviet needs, accompanied by the Briton Lord Beaverbrook. During this mission, agreement was reached for America to supply over a billion dollars' worth of goods in 1942. Stalin also presented the Allies with his first demand for a "second front," and was to repeat it many times during the next two and a half years. As far as is known, no Allied representative ever suggested that the Russian front itself was the second of the war (leaving aside the Polish and Balkan campaigns), and that the first, in Western Europe, had been overrun by the Nazis while the Soviets were their allies. It would have been not only tactless but pointless to mention that, but the Allied negotiators' patience and abstention from recriminations against the Soviets, throughout the war and afterward, were nevertheless remarkable.

As a result of the Harriman-Beaverbrook mission, in March 1942 Roosevelt ordered that the matériel promised to Stalin was to be delivered ahead of all other commitments including the requirements of American armed forces. In the course of the war 16½ million tons of goods were sent the USSR from America, of which more than 15 million tons were delivered safely. The items sent included railway cars especially built for the Russian broad gauge, trucks, oil, food, medical supplies, and many other goods, to the value of $11 billion.

The Soviets claimed to have moved more than a thousand war plants to the Urals and Siberia from the Ukraine alone from September to December 1941, and during the war the growth of new industrial production in the Soviet East was great enough to affect the geographical pattern of industry permanently. Nevertheless, by the end of 1941 the USSR had lost to Nazi occupation for the time being more than half of its previous coal and steel production, virtually all its ball-bearing production, and almost half of its railways—not to mention forty per cent of its total population. For this reason Allied shipments were of crucial importance, especially in 1942–1943. They were sent, moreover, at a time when it was far from clear whether the Soviets could stave off complete military defeat, in which case the supplies would have fallen into the hands of Hitler, who became America's enemy along with Japan and Italy after December 7, 1941.

THE CAMPAIGN OF 1942

In 1942 Nazi capabilities no longer included the power to mount a full-scale offensive all along the front, as in 1941; German losses had been too great. There were several alternatives: a war of attrition, which promised to make World War I look swift and painless by comparison, and was ruled out; another effort to take Moscow; or a campaign to seize the Caucasian oilfields with Baku as the final objective. Hitler decided on the last, and issued his order on April 5, 1942. As a preliminary, in May the Germans attacked and cleared the whole Crimea except for Sevastopol, which was not occupied until July 1. On May 12 Timoshenko unleashed another fierce attempt to retake Kharkov,[3] which probably delayed the main Nazi offensive for almost a month, but it resulted in severe losses and the capture of many of his troops by encirclement.

The main blow fell on June 28 near Kursk, where the Nazis broke through Soviet lines. On July 6–7 staunch Red resistance at Voronezh stopped the advance eastward toward Saratov on the middle Volga, but the southern armies moved forward rapidly, on July 27 taking Rostov and crossing the Don River there. Hitler decided to exploit the southern breakthrough with Field Marshal von Kleist's tank forces, meanwhile masking Voronezh without attempting to push through in that sector to the east. In so doing he left intact the railway network supplying Stalingrad and the south, thereby handing the Soviet high command a freedom of movement which may have been the decisive factor in the whole campaign.

In accordance with Hitler's new orders, one force crossed the Don at the bend near Stalingrad in August and on September 9 reached a railway just north of the city. At the same time Kleist's armor fanned out in the north Caucasus. On August 8 the Soviets destroyed and abandoned the Maikop oilfields, and by the end of the month the pursuing Germans were nearing the oil of Grozny. On September 10 they took the Black Sea naval base of Novorossiisk, but Kleist made no further progress in the Caucasus, partly because he ran out of gasoline, but chiefly because Hitler weakened his forces in order to reinforce the armies attacking Stalingrad.

Located on the Volga's right bank, Stalingrad was open to direct assault without a river crossing. The less costly tactic would have been to cross the Volga, cut off river traffic supplying the city, and force its surrender. Hitler chose not to cross the river but to storm the city directly. The attack began on September 15. The oil of Grozny and Baku remained in Soviet hands, and Hitler seemed to have forgotten his objective. Stalingrad possessed nothing of importance to Hitler except its name; the "city of Stalin" had to be taken at all costs. Two weeks earlier General Halder, chief of the General Staff, had tried to persuade Hitler to abandon the assault on Stalingrad and to retreat to the line Kiev-Riga, but he failed to do so and was dismissed into the bargain.

• [3] Evidently it was this unsuccessful attack from which Khrushchëv, in his "secret speech" of 1956, claimed he tried in vain to dissuade Stalin.

All available forces were hurled into the attempt to storm the city, which continued day after day for a whole month. The new chief of the Soviet General Staff, Vasilevsky, General Zhukov, and Malenkov were all sent to the Stalingrad front, and the Soviet armies under General Chuikov were ordered to defend the city to the last man. Stalingrad was shelled and bombed into a heap of rubble, in which the Soviet garrison hid and inflicted disastrous losses on the attacking enemy. The whole war seemed, to millions of people in various countries, to hang in the balance. Constantine Simonov's *Days and Nights* and Theodore Plievier's *Stalingrad* are two novels which have given the world something of the feeling of what it was like for the Nazi soldier to attack senselessly and endlessly and for the Soviet soldier to hold out in a hell of fire, deprived of reinforcements and supplies, while the situation of both the besiegers and the defenders seemed to grow more and more desperate.

On November 19, 1942, a Soviet force counterattacked heavily on both flanks of the narrow Nazi salient whose apex was Stalingrad. The flanks were held by Rumanians and Italians, and both were pierced deeply with little difficulty. General Rokossovsky (who had been imprisoned in the Great Purges and released just before the war) cut off any possible retreat by General Paulus (now named field marshal by Hitler as a reward for his impending sacrifice). Field Marshal von Manstein assembled a relief force and attacked eastward, but by December 27 he was brought to a standstill. Kleist, by a military miracle, extricated his armies from the Caucasus through Rostov, although the Soviets threatened to capture the city and cut him off. The plight of Paulus's surrounded army, again without winter clothes and short of food and ammunition, was hopeless, yet Hitler ordered the troops to fight on. Finally, on January 31, 1943, Paulus was captured, and the last of the pocket was mopped up two days later. Hitler sacrificed the surrounded army in the belief that annihilation was preferable to retreat for psychological reasons. The Soviet high command had not dreamed that the sacrifice would be made and expected their double flank attack to force Paulus's withdrawal immediately.

The Soviet forces continued the attack westward. On February 7 the Kursk "hedgehog" fell; on February 14, Rostov; on February 16, the "superhedgehog" of Kharkov. Hitler then temporarily yielded the command to Manstein, who mounted a counterattack on February 21, and, retaking Kharkov on March 15, was halted only by the coming of the spring thaw. But the Nazi defeat at Stalingrad could not so easily, or in fact ever, be undone.

There has been some dispute about how decisive the battle of Stalingrad was in the whole Russo-German war. Experts have contended that the war was really lost before Moscow in the fall of 1941; that the crucial moment was Stalingrad; or, as Liddell Hart argues, that it was post-Stalingrad events which made Nazi defeat certain.[4] It seems likely that at Moscow the best Nazi chance to win was missed, and perhaps any chance of *victory* became slim; furthermore, that wiser strategy even after the loss of Paulus's army might have staved off complete Nazi *defeat,* at least for some time, but that nevertheless, both militarily and psychologically Stalingrad was the beginning of the end for Hitler, just as it seemed to the ordinary newspaper reader of the time.

In other theaters of war Stalin's allies were experiencing varying degrees of success. In the Pacific, the United States was just beginning to win victories. Japan's crippling of the United States fleet at Pearl Harbor had inaugurated a period of months of disaster for the West. The Japanese had conquered Malaya and Singapore, the Philippines, the Netherlands East Indies, and Burma; invaded New Guinea and the Aleutian Islands; and threatened Australia and India. Under the slogan of a "Greater East Asia Co-Prosperity Sphere," the Japanese invited and obtained collaboration of substantial elements of the population in occupied areas, directing their animus against white imperialism and ostensibly treating the other Asians as equals—an occupation policy whose apparent success excited Nazi envy as they contemplated the growing resistance of the Soviet peoples.[5] Not until the middle of 1942 was the Japanese advance finally halted with American naval victories in the battles of the Coral Sea and Midway Island and the landing of an expeditionary force on Guadalcanal in August. However, Japan controlled most of the south and east Asian mainland and most of the Pacific islands, and all that could be said by the end of the year was that the farthest tip of the Japanese thrust had been blunted.

In Africa, however, the picture had brightened enormously. From the time when Italy invaded Egypt from Libya in the fall of 1940, the desert battle had seesawed back and forth. Early in 1941 the British counter-attacked; in the spring the Nazis rescued the Italians in Libya (as in Albania) and after more skirmishing the Axis troops under General Rommel were approaching the Suez Canal in the autumn of 1942, while the Nazis were thrusting toward Stalingrad and the Caucasus. This was the most dangerous moment of the entire war for the anti-Hitler coali-

• [4] B. H. Liddell Hart, ed., *The Soviet Army* (London: Weidenfeld and Nicolson, 1956), pp. 114–116.

• [5] See, for example, *The Goebbels Diaries, 1942–1943,* ed. and trans. by Louis P. Lochner (Garden City: Doubleday, 1948), p. 348.

tion, when there appeared to be a serious possibility that Rommel from Egypt, the German armies in the Caucasus, and the Japanese from India would make contact somewhere in the Middle East and thereby effect the subjugation of the whole Eastern Hemisphere.

However, the tide turned dramatically in North Africa at almost the same moment that the Germans were defeated at Stalingrad. In October 1942 General Montgomery counterattacked and drove Rommel out of Egypt. On November 8 an Allied force under General Eisenhower invaded Morocco and Algeria, and the two forces met in Tunisia, clearing Africa of Axis troops by May 1943. The diplomatic repercussions were great. Franco's Spain began to cultivate a sedulous neutrality, Turkey showed increasingly open sympathy toward the Allies, Hitler's occupation of Vichy France merely strengthened the French will to resist, and Mussolini had all too plainly lost his nerve.

By the first months of 1943 it was clear to Hitler that military victory was virtually impossible. Thereupon he tried to stave off complete defeat by seeking to split the coalition facing him and playing on European fears of Soviet Communism. As early as December 1942 it appears that a German approach to Soviet agents was made in Stockholm, proposing a separate peace, and there were further talks in the summer and fall of 1943. It is uncertain how seriously either party took these overtures, which both may have hoped to use as a means of putting pressure on the Western Allies in discussions thereafter.

STALIN'S PROPAGANDA OFFENSIVE

During the last months of 1941 Stalin's regime had tottered on the brink of collapse and yet survived. But survival was one thing and victory quite another. While the Soviets bent every effort to train larger armies, produce more war matériel, and carry out military preparations for any eventuality, Stalin was also mounting a political offensive—and this was a type of fighting at which he was far more adept than Hitler. His propaganda was directed toward three audiences. To begin with he sought to persuade the Soviet citizens behind Nazi lines to resist Hitler; he did so by spreading word of German atrocities and the desperate economic situation in the occupied areas (which by 1942 the people needed no persuasion to believe), by reminding them that the Allies were on his side, by repeatedly promising that the Soviets would return (which played an important part in determining the people's actions, whether out of fear or hope), and by portraying his regime in new and attractive colors, implying that things would be different after the war was won. To the populace which remained in Soviet territory, he addressed exhortations to fight, using Allied aid and the hints of a changed policy as support. For the benefit of the Allies, as for the ears of the Soviet peoples, he suggested that Communist ideology was being replaced by the cause of the nation. He intended his propaganda to contrast sharply with Hitler's occupation policy and Nazi propaganda, and it did. If the reverse had been true—if Hitler had adopted different propaganda, and Stalin had not changed his line—it is possible that Soviet Communism might not have survived. But fortunately for him, Stalin knew better than most men the uses of political warfare.

In a speech of 1941 he had already asked himself, "Can the Hitlerites be regarded as *nationalists?*" He replied, "No, they cannot. Actually, the Hitlerites are now not nationalists but *imperialists.*" His implication was clearly that to be a nationalist was a good thing—contrary to all Communist teaching of the evil character of "bourgeois" nationalism—and that the nationalism of Russia, at least, was an admirable phenomenon. The openly nationalist slogan, "Death to the German invader!" came to be widely used, and even replaced "Workers of the world, unite!" on the masthead of *Pravda.*

Especially after the battle of Stalingrad, Stalin developed the nationalist doctrine more fully. The Communist Party slogans for the commemoration of the October Revolution (November 7) in 1942 omitted any reference to world revolution. Stalin especially tried to use the army and the church, the two institutions with the strongest links to the nation's past, in his propaganda tactics. In October 1942 the political commissars with the armed forces were formally abolished (even though they survived as "Deputy Commanders for Political Affairs"). The next month *Pravda* declared flatly that the soldier had no socialist obligations, only the duty to defend his fatherland as his ancestors had done. In March 1943 Stalin himself assumed the title of marshal—as if to lend the rank honor—and gave both promotion and publicity to his top officers by the hundred. Epaulettes and saluting were restored; a sense of hierarchy and discipline was widely emphasized. The army, and in particular its high officers, were singled out as the defenders of the native soil and for the moment the most honored institution in the country.

Stalin even pretended to restore the Russian Orthodox Church to favor. During the first days of the invasion, the highest clerics had called for national defense. Evidently the public enthusiasm at being permitted to reopen churches behind Nazi lines spurred the regime to its first gestures in religious policy; it also had Allied opinion in mind. In September 1941 the League of Militant Godless was disbanded—Harriman thought this was because he had transmitted Roosevelt's suggestion to that effect—and the League's printing shop was used to publish a lavish volume inaccurately entitled *The Truth About Religion in Russia,* which was sold for export only.

Nevertheless, a public reconciliation was delayed for some time. In connection with the celebration of the Revolution in November 1942, for the first time Metropolitan Sergei and Stalin exchanged telegrams of felicitation. Only in September 1943, however, did Stalin receive Sergei and other clerics for a talk. As a result a meeting which claimed to be a church council was hastily summoned; it elected Sergei Patriarch—an office vacant since the death of Tikhon in 1925. While the "reconciliation," far from resulting in freedom of religion, actually led to the conversion of the church into a tool to regain the loyalty of the Orthodox laity in the USSR and, later, to assist in the Sovietization of the Balkan Orthodox countries, it was widely misinterpreted at the time both at home and abroad.

What seemed to the Western Allies conclusive proof of Stalin's change of heart was the dissolution of the Comintern in May 1943. "Dissolution," to be sure, did not even lead to the dispersal of the Comintern staff in the USSR, let alone disturb Soviet control of its foreign apparatus or weaken the loyalties of foreign Communists to the USSR. It may in fact have strengthened the Kremlin's hand by reducing lateral communication between parties while leaving vertical lines of authority from Moscow untouched. By that time, however, the alleged conversion of Stalin into a "nationalist" leader was a widespread article of faith in the West. Those who knew little of the USSR—except perhaps, as some had learned in school, that "Trotsky wanted world revolution, while Stalin only wanted socialism in one country"—found it easy to believe or did not dare to doubt that Stalin was a Tsar in commissar's clothing.

It would be most difficult to generalize on what the Russian people thought of the purported about-face of the government. It appears, however, that some thought Stalin had perceived the error of his ways, and all would be well; others welcomed the concessions of the present while realistically reserving judgment about the future; still others doubted that the leopard had changed his spots, but worked to defeat Hitler, assuring themselves that they could "pull up the weeds . . . afterwards"[6] —that is, drive out the Communists. The Soviet peoples had ample experience with the meaning of temporary Communist shifts in tactics. They perceived that although for the moment Stalin was glorifying the

• [6] The phrase comes from Michael Soloviëv's novel, *When the Gods are Silent.* See the discussion by Eugene Lyons in *Our Secret Allies,* pp. 228–235.

army and showing the church public respect in the name of the nation, winking at all sorts of violations of regulations by workers and collective farmers and deviations from Party orthodoxy by intellectuals, and saying little about Communism, still he had not promised to abolish the single most hated economic institution, the collective farm, or to end the totalitarian system of controls. Stalin was not about to grant his peoples freedom.

THE CAMPAIGN OF 1943

In the spring of 1943 Hitler, having resumed command in the East, was still determined on an offensive, partly because he retained confidence in his own power to do the impossible, partly because he had been unwarrantably cheered by Manstein's brief post-Stalingrad counterattack. However, he faced a bigger Red Army and a more experienced group of generals, while Nazi reserves were nearing exhaustion. The Reds shrewdly waited until Hitler had committed most of his remaining armor in an effort, beginning on July 5, to reduce the Kursk salient by double envelopment. After the Nazis suffered heavy tank losses, the Soviets launched an offensive of their own on July 12. By the first week of August they recaptured Orël and Belgorod and began to move forward on a front extending all the way south to the Black Sea. On August 23 Kharkov was retaken, this time permanently; by mid-September Novorossiisk and the Taman Peninsula were occupied. By the end of September Poltava and Smolensk had fallen and the Nazi "Winter Line" at the Dnieper River had been reached.

The Soviets crossed the Dnieper almost without a pause. Rokossovsky, Vatutin, and Konev led their army groups across on October 5–6 both north and south of Kiev. To the southeast, Malinovsky's and Tolbukhin's groups reached the bend of the river at Dnepropetrovsk and neared the Isthmus of Perekop, thereby threatening both the German forces to the north in the Dnieper bend and those to the south in the Crimea. At the beginning of November Manstein delayed the Soviet advance by a strong counterattack south from the bend position. Although the Germans lost Kiev on November 4 and were pushed back to Zhitomir a week later, they mounted another counterattack on November 19 which halted the Soviet westward thrust, recaptured Zhitomir, and made some further progress before being stopped by mud. Farther north the Soviets tried to advance along the Moscow-Minsk road, but they were repulsed time after time by the German defenders, despite the fact that the latter were outnumbered more than five to one.

RUSSIA IN WORLD WAR II
Period of Soviet Advance, 1943-5

At the close of the 1943 campaign the Germans continued to hold the greater part of the Ukraine, although the line from Zhitomir to the Dnieper bend ran east and west for roughly three hundred miles, and south of it was an exposed salient which clearly would be difficult for the Nazis to hold. Hitler's armies were still capable of fierce and clever defense, but their losses in manpower could no longer be made up, and they were outnumbered more decisively every month. In contrast, Stalin had managed to patch up domestic controls and morale somewhat, and as for the people in the occupied areas, although they might hate the

Communists as much as ever, they were faced with the likelihood that Stalin would, as he had promised, soon be back. Now that the flood of American supplies was continuous, and the output of men from the recruit training centers and matériel from the war plants in the Soviet East was steadily rising, Stalin correctly began to scent victory.

THE DIPLOMACY OF THE "SECOND FRONT"

Evidently taking seriously the possibility that the Western Allies might make a compromise peace with the Nazis, or even join them in an attack on the USSR, Stalin from 1941 on called for a "second front" by way of guarantee against such eventualities. Of course, an Allied landing in Europe would also have great military significance, but the political factor seems to have been uppermost in Stalin's mind throughout. Until the end of 1943 Stalin held aloof from any top-level meeting with Western leaders, plainly awaiting developments.

In the meantime, however, the Soviets endeavored to stay in the picture of Allied plans for the peace. Stalin authorized Litvinov, now his ambassador in Washington, to sign the United Nations Declaration (a sort of expanded Atlantic Charter) (see p. 379) on January 1, 1942, along with twenty-five other nations. In May 1942 Molotov visited London and signed an Anglo-Soviet Alliance, valid for twenty years. At that time the ambiguous public announcement was made that the two powers had reached agreement on the "urgent tasks of opening a Second Front in Europe during 1942." Therefore Churchill, when he visited Moscow in August, had the unpleasant task of explaining that an invasion which had been publicly described as likely, and privately (to Molotov) said to be possible, would not take place. Stalin expressed resentment and a general lack of confidence in Allied promises.

When the Allied invasion of North Africa occurred in November 1942, the West made some effort to label it a "second front," but the Soviets refused to acknowledge it as such. Roosevelt and Churchill, when they met at Casablanca in January 1943, had the problem in the forefront of their minds. The chief Casablanca decisions were military: for the time being the war in Europe was to be pressed at the expense of the war in the Pacific, and preparations were ordered for an invasion of northern France in the summer of 1944. However, political questions were also seriously considered. The two Western leaders proclaimed "unconditional surrender"—a phrase which General Grant had used at Fort Donelson in the Civil War—to be the objective of the war in Germany, Italy, and Japan.

As far as the countries subjugated by the Axis were concerned, the goals of peace had already been set forth in the Atlantic Charter, drawn up by Roosevelt and Churchill at a meeting off Newfoundland in August 1941, which promised to all nations self-determination, equality of economic opportunity, and the like—in effect restating the principles of Wilson's Fourteen Points of 1917. "Unconditional surrender," however, implied a very different fate for the peoples of the enemy countries. It clearly suggested to them that they had no alternative but to fight to the bitter end without hope of quarter or compromise, and that any effort to change their rulers in order to bring about peace was useless. But the slogan was not aimed at the enemy peoples; it was intended to strengthen the determination of all Allied nations, and "above all," as Chester Wilmot writes, "as an assurance to Stalin that the inability to open a Second Front in 1943 did not indicate any weakening in the resolution of the Western Allies."[7]

Stalin welcomed the verbal commitment of the Casablanca conference, and must also have felt satisfaction that the Western Allies seemed to have renounced any attempt at political warfare at the very moment that Field Marshal Paulus, whom he was to make the chief of a "Free German Committee," had fallen into his hands.[8] However, the "unconditional surrender" slogan was not enough to eliminate Western-Soviet tensions, which grew more serious in 1943. Rumors of Nazi-Soviet peace feelers aroused suspicions. Stalin rejected an American offer to mediate in bringing about peace between the USSR and Finland.

The most severe strains up to that time followed the Nazi announcement of the discovery of the graves of a large number of Polish officers at Katyn, near Smolensk. As early as July 1941 the USSR and the Polish (and also the Czech) government-in-exile in London had signed an agreement providing for the formation of national troop units on Soviet territory and dealing with other matters. From the first Soviet-Polish relations had been fragile because of the Soviet part in the destruction of Poland, Soviet refusal to confirm Polish borders as of 1939, and, most urgent of all, Moscow's professed inability to solve the mystery of what had happened to almost fifteen thousand Poles interned by the Soviets in 1939. Repeated Polish inquiries about the men failed to elicit any information. After the Nazis discovered the bodies at Katyn, a German-appointed commission, including some neutral experts, investigated and concluded that the men had been executed in 1940—therefore by the Soviets.

• [7] *The Struggle for Europe* (New York: Harper, 1952), p. 123.

• [8] Actually the committee never came to much, but it was only the beginning of Stalin's political efforts in Germany.

On April 17, 1943, Prime Minister General Sikorski of the Polish regime in London publicly requested the International Red Cross to investigate, whereupon the USSR immediately broke relations with the Poles. Whatever the suspicions of Churchill, who regarded Britain as having special obligations to Poland, he regarded the matter as secondary to the war effort and tried to smooth things over—but quite in vain. After the Soviets recaptured the Smolensk region, they announced that a commission of their own had decided that the murders were committed by the Nazis. However, at the Nuremberg war crimes trials the Soviets did not repeat this contention, and subsequent evidence indicates that they were indeed the executioners.

Shortly after the Katyn revelations, an angry exchange between Stalin and Churchill led to the recall of Ambassadors Maisky and Litvinov from London and Washington. This caused the abandonment of a plan, which had been the result of a mission by former Ambassador Joseph E. Davies, for a meeting between Roosevelt and Stalin in July. Instead Churchill and Roosevelt together proposed a meeting of the three foreign ministers, Eden, Hull, and Molotov. Stalin's assent arrived during the Anglo-American conference at Quebec in August 1943. At the meeting the news was also received that General Eisenhower, whose troops had vaulted from North Africa to Sicily and thereby precipitated the resignation of Mussolini and his replacement by Marshal Badoglio, had been informed by Badoglio that the imminent landing on the Italian mainland would bring about Italy's surrender.[9]

The diplomatic picture had brightened somewhat. The foreign ministers met in Moscow in October, and Eden and Hull were able to notify the Soviets that the cross-Channel invasion was being planned for the summer of 1944. It was agreed that on the conclusion of peace Germany was to be completely disarmed and was to be compelled to pay reparations for the physical damage inflicted upon all Allied nations. The question of the military and political partitioning of Germany and Europe was raised without being settled. The chief result of the foreign ministers' conference was that a meeting of the "Big Three"—Roosevelt, Churchill, and Stalin—was arranged to take place at Teheran one month later. Although the war was far from over, the prerequisites of victory—at least in Europe—were already visible, and the Teheran conference inaugurated the period in which the considerations of postwar politics came rapidly to the foreground of Stalin's relations with the Western Allies.

• [9] This was hardly the whole story. During the weeks that Badoglio and Eisenhower had been fencing verbally about what "unconditional surrender" meant, the Nazis had poured troops into Italy and met the Allied invasion force with a rude surprise which set the stage for a long, tortuous, and indecisive Italian campaign.

The USSR in World War II: Political Successes (1943–1945)

★
★
★
★
★
★
★
★
★
★

CHAPTER 24

THE TEHERAN CONFERENCE

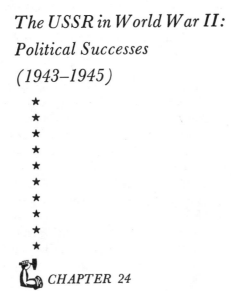

Three of the dominant personalities of the twentieth century confronted one another for the first time at the Teheran conference of November–December 1943. No wonder the reports of every smirk and toast were eagerly devoured by the public in Allied countries, weary of war and defeat, but now scenting victory. Not long before the conference Roosevelt told former Ambassador Bullitt, "I have just a hunch that Stalin doesn't want anything but security for his country, and I think that if I give him everything I possibly can and ask nothing from him in return, *noblesse oblige,* he won't try to annex anything and will work for a world of democracy and peace." The illusions, by no means confined to Roosevelt, of the Allied leadership at this point could scarcely be more succinctly phrased. A document of alleged "military" authorship which Harry Hopkins had brought to the Quebec conference said, "Since Russia is the decisive factor in the war, she must be given every assistance and every effort must be made to obtain her friendship. Likewise, since without question she will dominate Europe on the defeat of the Axis, it is even more essential to develop and maintain the most friendly relations with Russia." This sounded a more hardheaded note; nevertheless the estimate shared Roosevelt's basic assumption that Stalin was a nationalist speaking for a nationalist regime, and was chiefly concerned with the national security of Russia. Stalin had labored long to achieve Allied acceptance of this image, and he played the role throughout the "Big Three" conferences with success.

In accordance with his hopes, Roosevelt tried his best at Teheran to establish close personal ties with Stalin. He even used Churchill as a foil for this purpose, deliberately evoking Churchill's frowns as a spur to Stalin's grins. Stalin appeared to respond to these overtures, persuading Roosevelt to move to the Soviet Embassy as security against a "German plot." The conferees discussed military questions first. On Roosevelt's invitation, Stalin voiced the opinion that Italy and the Balkans promised little advantage to the Allies, linked a promise to join the war against Japan (after Hitler's defeat) with a demand for a strong cross-Channel invasion of France, and hinted that the one might depend on the other. Churchill had in mind objectives in northern Italy and the Balkans; Stalin bluntly insisted that if anything further was to be done in the Mediterranean, it should be an invasion of southern France in addition to the Channel crossing.

The political implications of this exchange, hinging on the distance which the Allied armies would be kept from Eastern Europe, were plain at least to Churchill and Stalin. The decision was for a southern France landing, more or less coinciding with Operation Overlord, which was to be launched against northern France in May 1944. One agreement of chiefly political character was reached: the British and Americans accepted the Curzon Line (see p. 189) as the future Soviet-Polish border. The London Polish regime, it was virtually certain, would not accept this frontier, and only a month after Teheran, Stalin established a Polish Communist junta in Moscow which would.

After the period of heated debates had passed, the conference closed in a spirit of camaraderie. Churchill presented Stalin with a gem-encrusted sword sent by George VI for the city of Stalingrad, and Stalin bowed to kiss it. Stalin toasted Churchill's birthday with a reference to his "great friend." The conference communiqué affirmed, "We came here with hope and determination. We leave here friends in fact, in spirit and in purpose." Immediately afterward, Roosevelt confided to Frances Perkins at some length how he thought he had won Stalin's friendship.

SOVIET ARMIES ADVANCE BEYOND SOVIET BORDERS

The coming of winter in December 1943 did not halt the fighting on the Eastern front. Hitler's troops now not only faced a numerically stronger Red Army, but also were subjected to formidable harassment from partisan units, which in January 1944, on the central sector alone, were estimated to number close to a hundred and fifty thousand men. In several areas partisan sabotage created serious difficulties in moving up reinforcements and supplies. Hitler was no longer capable of mounting a major offensive, and the most he could do was to break the tips of the Soviet spearheads. The vast exposed southern salient which the Nazis still held was especially difficult to defend.

At the end of December Vatutin enveloped Zhitomir, at the base of the salient, from both sides and thrust northwestward to Sarny, just south of the Pripet Marshes. Simultaneously he struck south to Vinnitsa, threatening the Odessa railway and making the big Nazi salient less tenable than ever. In January 1944 the northern armies relieved Leningrad and advanced almost to Pskov. In February Konev encircled most of a German army on the flank of the salient near Korsun, while Vatutin drove westward close to Kovel, and Malinovsky cut off the eastern tip of the salient at Krivoi Rog.

All these blows were preliminary to the main offensive of 1944. In March it was launched by Zhukov, who had replaced Vatutin as army group commander, with an advance toward Tarnopol. At the same time Konev overran an important Nazi base at Uman and cut the Odessa railway. The salient was now collapsing everywhere. By the end of March Zhukov had crossed the Dniester on a broad front and taken Czernowitz, and both Konev and he reached the Prut River, the border between Rumania and Soviet-annexed Bessarabia. Malinovsky mopped up the remnants of the salient. The Nazis in the Crimea were ordered to make a stand but were overrun in April and May.

As the summer began, the Soviets enjoyed a three to one over-all superiority in manpower, and—thanks to American supplies—an estimated five to one advantage in equipment. The Nazi reserves were exhausted. The 1939 borders had been reached or crossed on most of the front, and the Soviets had the military capability of capturing virtually any objectives in Eastern and Central Europe which they chose. Four days after Operation Overlord struck Normandy, in June, a sector-by-sector Soviet advance was begun. First the Mannerheim line was breached and Finland effectively knocked out of the war, although fighting continued until September. On June 23 four army groups with one hundred divisions struck westward on the central front. Minsk fell on July 3, Vilna on July 13, and the Niemen River was bridged three days later. At that moment another large-scale offensive in the north was launched, which swung north to Pskov before bearing down on Dvinsk and sweeping westward to Siauliai in central Lithuania on July 27. Soon afterward the Germans began to withdraw from Estonia and Latvia.

Further south Marshal Konev enveloped Lvov and captured it on July 25, continuing on to Rzeszow. Soviet thrusts from several directions passed through Bialystok and Brest-Litovsk and by July 31 reached points only a few miles northeast and southeast of Warsaw. At this moment the Polish resistance army under General Tadeusz Bor-Komorowski, expecting the Soviet forces to continue into Warsaw, attacked the Germans inside the city. Marshal Rokossovsky, himself a Pole by birth, led his Soviet troops close to the scene, but was halted temporarily by counterattacks. On August 15 he occupied Praga, Warsaw's suburb east of the Vistula, but he made no attempt to cross.

With Soviet forces in plain sight, the insurgents fought on without aid until October 5, when the Nazis completed mopping up and in revenge systematically destroyed the city of Warsaw block by block. Out of a population of a million, some ten thousand remained huddling in the ruins at the end of the war. It has been suggested that if Polish Communists had led the rising, Stalin would have ordered a crossing to assist them; the point is rather that Polish Communists would not have acted at all in the absence of orders from Stalin. It is clear, at any event, that Stalin shed no tears for the destruction of the non-Communist Polish fighters in Warsaw, since he refused even to allow British or American planes which were attempting to drop supplies to the insurgents to land on Soviet airfields.

The Soviet forces made no effort to cross the Vistula during the rest of 1944. The next offensive was directed at Rumania. On August 20 Tolbukhin struck out of his small Dniester bridgeheads, while Malinovsky drove beyond the Prut to Iasi. On August 23 King Michael of Rumania arrested his Nazi-collaborator prime minister, Marshal Antonescu, and pledged co-operation with the United Nations on condition that the portion of Transylvania which Hitler had given Hungary be returned to Rumania. No one raised any quibbles about "unconditional surrender," and the Soviets officially declared that they aimed neither at annexation of Rumanian territory (except for Bessarabia and northern Bukovina, which they considered Soviet soil) nor at "altering the social structure of Rumania as it exists at present." Soon afterward King Michael declared war on Germany. The German armies in Rumania collapsed swiftly. By the end of August the oil city of Ploesti and Bucharest, the capital, had been occupied. On August 26 Bulgaria withdrew from the war, and on September 16 Soviet forces occupied Sofia. At this point the Nazis were frantically trying to extricate themselves from Greece.

By the time that Soviet armies reached the Balkans, the USSR and the Western powers seemed to have reached full agreement about their fate. Continuing to play the role of a ruler primarily concerned with national security, Stalin had made gestures in regard to Western Europe which appeared to lend striking confirmation to the virtually-settled Western interpretation of his motives. In March 1944 the Soviets had recognized the Italian regime of Marshal Badoglio and had compelled the Italian Communists to cease demanding the removal of both Badoglio and King Victor Emmanuel III. Similarly in France, where, as in Italy, the Communists were emerging as the strongest single party, they were told to hold their hand and not to insist on control of the police and the justice ministry.

In June 1944 there was some amicable discussion regarding the division of Europe into spheres of influence, and when Churchill visited Moscow in October he proposed (and Stalin accepted) an oddly arithmetical formula: in Rumania the Soviets would have a "90–10" preponderance, in Bulgaria "75–25," in Yugoslavia and Hungary influence would be shared "50–50" with Britain, while in Greece the British would have a "90–10" voice.

Churchill also raised the question of Poland. When Soviet troops had crossed into Polish territory, the Polish Communist junta had been installed in Lublin, and soon afterward Stalin officially recognized it as the legitimate government of Poland. In July Stanislaw Mikołajczyk, the leader of the Peasant party, who had become premier of the London Polish regime after the death of General Sikorski, was persuaded by the British to visit Stalin. On his arrival he was informed of Soviet recognition of the Lublin junta, with which he was amicably advised to conduct his own talks. At this very moment the Warsaw uprising broke out, and Mikołajczyk appealed to Stalin to assist it. At length Stalin promised aid, but he gave none. In October, when Churchill tried to put the case for Mikołajczyk's regime, Stalin would not budge an inch.

However, as far as Churchill could see, Poland was an arena where British and Russian national interests clashed, and little more. Stalin raised no ideological questions; he might appear blunt, peevish, or stubborn, but thus far he had not discarded the pose of hardheaded bourgeois-nationalist statesmanship. In April 1944 he even descended to the level of comedy by receiving personally a bewildered but well-intentioned Roman

Catholic priest, Father Orlemanski of Springfield, Massachusetts, and entrusting him with a message of reconciliation with the Vatican (which had no results except to get Orlemanski into trouble with his superiors). It seemed that Stalin had no ideological enemy left on earth.

VLASOV AND THE NAZIS

By 1944 defeat stared Germany in the face. Goebbels's propaganda machine did its best to counter the deterioration of morale, especially emphasizing the bleak prospects with which the "unconditional surrender" slogan confronted the German people. On July 20 a few army officers and government officials attempted to kill Hitler and overthrow the Nazi regime, but the plot miscarried and merely resulted in the liquidation of the chief non-Nazis anywhere near the summit of power.

Opportunely for Goebbels came Allied publication of lists of "war criminals," the mass proscription of the German General Staff, and the approval of the "Morgenthau Plan," which envisaged the destruction of German industry and the conversion of all Germany into "a country primarily agricultural and pastoral in character," at the second Quebec conference in September 1944. Goebbels declared, "It hardly matters whether the Bolshevists want to destroy the Reich in one fashion and the Anglo-Saxons propose to do it in another." Doubtless the Morgenthau Plan did much to confuse those Germans who might be thinking of surrendering to the West while holding out against Stalin, and thus Stalin could only profit by its dissemination by the U.S. and Britain.

At virtually the same moment that the Allies were endorsing the Morgenthau Plan at Quebec, the Nazi regime turned in desperation to a weapon which, if used earlier, might indeed have had great effect on the outcome of the war, but what the Nazis did with it in 1944 was too little and much too late. General Vlasov, who had been captured two years earlier (see p. 366), was to be transformed from a pawn of Nazi propaganda into the leader of a real Soviet anti-Stalinite army and government.

Vlasov who was born in 1900, the son of a peasant family of Nizhnii Novgorod, had risen in Red Army ranks. A Party member since 1930, he had been Soviet military adviser to Chiang Kai-shek in 1938–1939, decorated in 1940, and in the autumn of 1941 one of the chief army commanders in the defense of Moscow. Apparently he possessed great personal magnetism, integrity, and ability. Of the most influential men who joined his cause, probably the ablest was the brilliant but mysterious

Milenty Zykov, who had been assistant editor of *Izvestiia* under Bukharin and for a time had been exiled by Stalin. When captured he claimed to be serving as a battalion commissar, but it was suspected that he was much more.

By the end of 1942 Captain Strik-Strikfeldt of the German army propaganda section was planning to establish a Russian National Committee led by Vlasov at Smolensk. The plan was vetoed from above, but in December the formation of the committee was proclaimed on German soil instead. Vlasov published a statement of his aims, and he was allowed to tour occupied Soviet areas, meeting a considerable popular response. In April 1943 an anti-Bolshevik conference of Soviet prisoners opposed to Stalin's regime was held in Brest-Litovsk. After Vlasov declared that if successful he would grant the Ukraine and the Caucasus self-determination, Rosenberg was persuaded to support the committee. However, in June 1943 Hitler ordered that Vlasov was to be kept out of the occupation zone, and that the movement was to be confined to propaganda—that is, promises which Hitler could ignore later—across the lines to Soviet-held territory.

During 1943 Vlasov's circle, under the protection of Strik-Strikfeldt's section at Dabendorf just outside Berlin, was allowed to carry on remarkably free discussions about a future non-Communist government for Russia and to publish two newspapers in Russian, one for Soviet war prisoners and another for the *Osttruppen*. The political center of gravity at Dabendorf fluctuated between the more socialist-inclined entourage of Zykov and the more authoritarian-minded group close to the *émigré* anti-Soviet organization, N.T.S. (*Natsionalno-Trudovoi Soiuz* or National Toilers' Union). Of course political arguments among Soviet *émigrés* were nothing new; what was new was the hope of imminent action, utilizing the five million Soviet nationals in Germany, to overthrow Stalin—either with Hitler's support or, if he should fall, perhaps in conjunction with the Western Allies. Despite arguments, a fair degree of harmony was maintained among the Russians at Dabendorf. Especially noteworthy was the extent to which Vlasov and his followers succeeded in preventing themselves from being compromised by Nazi ideology and in maintaining the integrity of their own effort to win Russian freedom.

Until 1944, however, the Vlasov circle was confined to discussion and publication. Although the phrase, "Russian Liberation Army," and its Russian abbreviation, ROA (for *Russkaia Osvoboditel'naia Armiia*), were much used in propaganda—with Hitler's approval—there was in fact no such army. "ROA" was only a shoulder patch which the *Osttrup-*

pen, scattered in small units throughout the Nazi army, were permitted to wear. In the summer of 1944 the ablest intellectual of the Vlasov group, Zykov, was abducted and almost certainly murdered forthwith by the SS.

Nevertheless it was Himmler, chief of the SS, who not long afterward achieved the reversal of Nazi policy toward Vlasov. In a meeting with Vlasov in mid-September 1944, Himmler agreed to the formation of a Committee for the Liberation of the Peoples of Russia (*Komitet Osvobozhdeniia Narodov Rossii* or K.O.N.R.), which would have the potentiality of a government, and an actual army. It appears that Hitler consented to Himmler's new policy chiefly because his suspicion of other Nazi officials who opposed it was by 1944 greater than his fear of arming enemy nationals—a fear which, it must be said, was justified from the Nazi standpoint. The concrete results of Himmler's decision were meager, largely because the Russians could not, amid the disintegration which overtook the Nazi system during the last months of the war, obtain the material aid they needed to implement their plans.

However, in November 1944 in Prague the K.O.N.R. was officially established at a meeting which issued the so-called "Prague Manifesto." This document, declaring that the irruption of the Red armies into Eastern Europe revealed more clearly than ever the Soviet "aim to strengthen still more the mastery of Stalin's tyranny over the peoples of the USSR, and to establish it all over the world," stated the goals of the K.O.N.R. to be the overthrow of the Communist regime and the "creation of a new free People's political system without Bolsheviks and exploiters." It proclaimed recognition of the "equality of all peoples of Russia" and their right of self-determination as well as the intention of ending forced labor and the collective farms and of achieving real civil liberties and social justice. If such a document had been widely disseminated two or three years earlier and given some substance in Nazi occupation policy, the results might have been important or even decisive; coming in 1944, it had no observable effect on the Soviet peoples.

The Prague meeting did stimulate certain Nazi officials to make efforts to put the minorities into the picture with political committees and armies. A year earlier the Nazis had finally organized a Ukrainian SS division which bore the name "Galicia," but although it fought hard and well at the battle of Brody, on the Rovno-Lvov road, in July 1944, when it was finally overrun there, it dispersed to join Ukrainian partisan forces behind Red lines. In October an SS official, Dr. Fritz Arlt, attempted to secure the consent of the Ukrainian nationalist leaders to the formation of a Ukrainian national committee. To avoid being overshadowed by Vlasov, Bandera and Melnyk agreed to the setting up of such a committee, nominally headed by General Paul Shandruk. Melnyk protested the Prague Manifesto, but many Ukrainians nevertheless joined the Vlasov movement, along with representatives of other minorities.

In January 1945 the formation of the Armed Forces of the K.O.N.R. was announced; however, only two divisions were actually activated and mobilized. The First Division, under the command of a Ukrainian, General S. K. Buniachenko, was committed in April on the front near Frankfurt on the Oder, but the unit refused to fight under existing circumstances, and amid the Nazi military collapse moved south toward Czechoslovakia. At the call of the Czech resistance leaders in Prague, the division moved into the city and on May 7, with Czech aid, captured it from the Nazis.

However, in the Europe of the spring of 1945 there was no place for an anti-Soviet Russian army. The generals, including Vlasov, were turned over to the Soviet command by American and British forces, with or without authorization to do so. In February 1946 the remainder of the army was handed over by U.S. authorities without warning to Soviet repatriation officers at Plattling, Bavaria. In August *Pravda* announced the execution of Vlasov and his fellow officers, describing them as "agents of German intelligence" and failing to inform the Russian people that they had organized a movement to overthrow Stalin.

THE DEFEAT OF NAZI GERMANY

In the summer of 1944 the Allies had landed in Normandy and on the Riviera and rapidly cleared most of France and Belgium of Nazi forces. By September the American troops had crossed the German frontier. The British and Americans tried and failed to cross the Rhine at Arnhem. Farther south the advance halted when they ran out of gasoline. Ground transport was powerless to keep the front supplied, and there was not enough air transport to make good the difference. A Western front thereupon came into existence and lasted until spring.

Meanwhile the Soviet armies, having conquered Rumania, plunged into Central Europe. The strategic result of the "unconditional surrender" policy, in the view of General Fuller, was that "the Soviet war aim was rapidly expanded from the defeat of Germany into the conquest of Eastern Europe, the strategic key of which is Vienna and not Berlin."[1] There was no need for the Soviets to hurry to Berlin, since "unconditional surrender" precluded the possibility that Hitler or any other Germans

• [1] Major-General J. F. C. Fuller, *The Second World War, 1939–45* (New York: Duell, Sloan and Pearce, 1949), p. 281.

could capitulate to the Western Allies alone, and, moreover, Stalin had been promised, by the time of the Yalta conference in February 1945, that Berlin was to be well inside his zone of occupation. He could then proceed to strengthen his political position to the south by moving Red troops there as rapidly as possible. Hitler could still mount counterattacks but in general lacked the power to stop him.

In September 1944 Marshal Malinovsky's forces struck westward, from a line running from the Iron Gate of the Danube to Czernowitz, toward Hungary. Rumania, in the hope of regaining the lost portion of Transylvania, had also declared war on Hungary. On October 5 Malinovsky crossed the Hungarian border near Arad, while Marshal Tolbukhin advanced from Bulgaria across the Danube into Yugoslavia, made contact with Tito's partisan forces, and on October 19 captured Belgrade. On October 11 Malinovsky crossed the Tisza River at Szeged and turned north toward Budapest, which he was approaching in early November. By the beginning of December he had linked up with General Petrov on a line from Miskolc to Košice in Slovakia but then halted, as the Germans concentrated strong forces for a last-ditch stand northeast of Budapest.

Simultaneously Soviet forces in the Baltic states launched an offensive. On September 21 they captured the Estonian capital, Tallinn, and occupied Oesel (Estonian, Saare) and the other Estonian islands. Other troops neared Riga from the northeast and east. At this point the Nazis decided to withdraw toward East Prussia. On October 10 the Soviets succeeded, by reaching the Baltic coast north of Memel, in cutting off any retreat by land. Three days later Riga fell. However, many of the isolated German troops were withdrawn by sea. Not stopping to clean up the pocket, the Soviets attacked into East Prussia. They moved up to the Angerapp River before fierce Nazi resistance halted them on October 25.

Between the Danubian and the Baltic fronts, the Soviet armies in Poland remained stationary from August 1944, when Rokossovsky reached the Vistula opposite Warsaw, until January 1945. At the end of November 1944 the Danubian campaign was resumed with twin offensives by Tolbukhin and Malinovsky toward Budapest from the southwest and east. Moving up the west side of the Danube, Tolbukhin met Malinovsky north of Budapest and surrounded the city. Despite a strong German counterattack, they continued onward to occupy the Hungarian capital by February 13, 1945.

Meanwhile, in mid-January, four Soviet army groups attacked all the way from the Baltic to the Carpathians. In southern Poland Konev and Zhukov struck together across the upper Vistula. Zhukov moved north toward Warsaw from the rear, forced the Nazis to evacuate, and occupied the city on January 17. Two days later Konev took Cracow. Cherniakhovsky and Rokossovsky attacked through East Prussia and, by reaching the Baltic near Elbing on January 26, created another pocket of Germans. Konev reached the border of German Silesia, crossed the upper Oder, and took Bunslau on February 15, while Zhukov surrounded Posen (Poznań) and on February 10 reached the Oder River north of Frankfurt. Farther north, Rokossovsky stormed Danzig on March 30. The Germans in East Prussia continued to fight fiercely. On February 17 Cherniakhovsky was killed and replaced by Marshal Vasilevsky, who pushed on to capture Königsberg on April 9.

In Western Hungary, on March 3, 1945, the Germans opened a great counterattack comparable to the Ardennes offensive of Marshal von Rundstedt in December 1944. The blow was actually spearheaded by the German Sixth SS Panzer Army, which had led the thrust into the Ardennes. The Germans broke through the Soviet front between lakes Balaton and Velence toward the southeast and came near to reaching the Danube. However, as in the Ardennes offensive, the tanks ran out of gasoline, and by the middle of March the Nazi salient was eliminated. Counterattacking almost at once, Tolbukhin and Malinovsky advanced together, and their opponents began to retreat in disorder. On March 29 the Austrian frontier was crossed at Köszeg, and Tolbukhin from the south and Malinovsky from the east attacked Vienna, using much the same tactics that they had used against Budapest. However, Vienna was easier prey, and by April 13 it was completely occupied. Central and Eastern Europe was in Soviet hands.

In February and March Allied forces, continuing to advance in a cautious and even line, closed up to the Rhine and crossed it. By the first week in April the front had collapsed. The Ruhr was the object of a gigantic and successful double envelopment, and on April 18 the trapped German forces surrendered. At that moment there were sharp verbal exchanges between the British, who wanted to occupy Berlin for political reasons, and the Americans, who believed it militarily necessary to halt the advance at the Elbe while swiftly thrusting into the so-called "National Redoubt" in the Alps, where the Germans were supposed to be preparing a do-or-die defense—but they were by this time quite incapable of doing so. Eisenhower, supported by Roosevelt, pursued the latter strategy. Both Berlin and Prague were left to the Soviets.

On April 17 the final Soviet offensive began. Eight days later Zhukov and Konev encircled Berlin and Konev's patrols linked up with the U.S. First Army at Torgau on the Elbe. On April 30 Hitler committed suicide in his bunker, and two days later the remainder of the troops in Berlin surrendered. As the Allied forces in Italy advanced toward Austria, Mussolini was caught by Italian partisans and executed on April 28. Eisenhower halted his troops on the Elbe and at a line a few miles inside Czechoslovakia. The Soviet forces closed up to the Elbe and entered Prague, already freed by Vlasov's troops. On May 7 a document of "unconditional surrender" was signed, and the war in Europe came to an end at midnight of the next day, but by that time there was virtually nothing left to surrender. The war was ended by complete Allied occupation of German territory before the termination of the armistice formalities.

THE BEGINNING OF PEACEMAKING

For a time after the Teheran conference, the course of Soviet relations with the Western Allies was smooth. The Soviets hailed the Normandy invasion as the "Second Front" for which they had been waiting, and they followed its progress with great interest. However, when the Allied advance was halted on the German frontier in the fall of 1944 Stalin showed no great concern. It is doubtful that he would have welcomed an Anglo-American thrust into the heart of Germany before the Soviets were ready to move in from the east. By that time the outcome of the war was certain, and Stalin, like Churchill—but unlike Roosevelt—was thinking more in terms of the postwar political situation than of the remaining battles which had to be fought.

The Allies began long-range planning for the peace at the conferences held at Bretton Woods in July 1944, where the delegates discussed the establishment of an International Monetary Fund and an International Bank for Reconstruction and Development as means of solving postwar economic problems, and at Dumbarton Oaks in August and September, where the shape of the proposed United Nations organization was debated. However, agreement could not be reached on whether a great power should be entitled to exercise its veto on the Security Council in disputes to which it was a party (none of the Big Three would consider giving up a veto entirely). This question remained to be solved at the highest levels.

At the end of 1944 the most vexing diplomatic problem remained that of Poland, which had been left out of the informal Anglo-Soviet agreement on zones of influence in postwar Europe. After the Soviet refusal to help the Warsaw insurgents, there was little hope of reconciliation between the London regime of Prime Minister Mikołajczyk and Stalin, who had his own men established in authority on Polish soil. In October 1944 Churchill did manage to arrange a meeting with Stalin and Mikołajczyk in Moscow. There Mikołajczyk finally agreed to accept the Curzon Line as Poland's eastern frontier, provided it was modified in the south to leave Poland the oilfields of Galicia and the city of Lwów (Lvov). However, he could not obtain the backing of his London colleagues for this concession and thereupon resigned. Reporting these events to the House of Commons, Churchill argued the "reasonable and just" character of the Curzon Line as a frontier. He did not report that during the October meeting, Stalin had for the first time urged an Allied descent on Yugoslavia and an offensive northward toward Austria. The reason for this unexpected plea may have been the hope that German forces would thereby be drawn away from the Russian front. Stalin may have felt that such a move would force the unruly Tito into a closer dependence on Moscow, or it is even possible that, feeling certain no such proposal would be acted upon at that stage, he hoped by making it to disarm Churchill's suspicions of Soviet designs in Central Europe.

For some time discussions regarding arrangements for a second Big Three meeting had been in progress. During the Ardennes offensive, Stalin proposed to meet Roosevelt and Churchill in the Crimea in a month or two, and both agreed. A few days later, in January 1945, the USSR extended diplomatic recognition to the Lublin (Communist-led) committee as the legitimate government of Poland. In the same month the Soviets occupied most of the country within pre-1939 borders, and by early February they had reached the Oder. In any talks about Poland, Stalin was certain to be negotiating from strength.

At a conference at Malta, Roosevelt and Churchill discussed tactics for the Big Three meeting at Yalta to which they were proceeding. Churchill was eager for a closely concerted plan of action, but Roosevelt was cool. He wished to play the mediator between the British and the Soviets. His conduct was deeply influenced by his constantly expressed belief that while British imperialism remained a serious problem for the postwar world, that of the Soviets did not. As he told Mikołajczk, "of one thing I am certain, Stalin is not an Imperialist." Roosevelt's close confidant Harry Hopkins was expressing views held also by his chief when he wrote that "Russia's interests, so far as we can anticipate them, do not afford an opportunity for a major difference with us in foreign affairs," that the United States and the USSR were economically "mutually dependent," and that "above all, they—the Russians—want to maintain friendly relations with us. . . ."[2] The conviction that British imperialism was wicked, while Soviet imperialism did not exist, had already led to severe Anglo-American friction over internal developments in Italy and Greece but protected Roosevelt from any deep concern over Poland.

THE YALTA CONFERENCE

As at Teheran, Stalin at Yalta appeared to respond to Roosevelt's efforts to achieve "man-to-man" understanding with him, and again Stalin opened the conference by proposing that the President act as chairman. After an exchange of military reports, the Big Three discussed the problem of the veto in the U.N. Security Council and decided that it should not apply to procedural matters. Stalin advanced and then withdrew a proposal to seat all sixteen Soviet republics in the General Assembly. Roosevelt, although plainly embarrassed, finally agreed to "support" at the forthcoming United Nations conference a Soviet demand for separate seats for the Ukrainian and Belorussian SSR's only.

The conferees turned next to German problems. Since he had been informed that American troops would not stay in Europe longer than two years, Churchill pressed hard for a French seat on the proposed Allied Control Commission for Germany and a French zone of occupation in order to strengthen the position of the West vis-à-vis Stalin. He succeeded in obtaining the one at Yalta and the other later. Proposals for the dismemberment of Germany into small states and the levy of heavy reparations were discussed; Stalin favored both, Churchill neither, while Roosevelt as on other disputed points suggested a compromise. The proposals were not adopted, but Stalin did not allow Roosevelt to forget his acceptance of Stalin's suggested figure of twenty billion dollars for German reparations, even though it was only as "a basis for discussion." It was agreed that all citizens of the Allied powers found on enemy-occupied soil would be repatriated to their homelands—by implication, through the use of force if necessary.

At Yalta the question of Poland occupied more time than any other. It was agreed that the Curzon Line would be the basis for the new Polish frontier. However, Roosevelt said he was "suggesting" but not "insisting" that the line be modified so that Poland could keep Lwów (Lvov) and Galician oil (this had been Mikołajczyk's last line of diplomatic defense,

• [2] Robert E. Sherwood, *Roosevelt and Hopkins: an Intimate History* (New York: Harper, 1948), pp. 922–923. Although the memorandum cited was written after Roosevelt's death, it reflects rather opinions held at Yalta and earlier, about which Roosevelt felt increasing doubts in the last weeks of his life (see p. 398).

for which his colleagues had repudiated him) (see p. 393). Churchill was already publicly committed to the Curzon Line, so he could not openly support this suggestion, but he made his sympathy for it plain. However, he concentrated his demands on an issue even more fundamental for Poland, the guarantee of a "fully representative Polish government" which would hold free elections. Stalin declared that if he conceded modifications of the Curzon Line, his peoples would say he was a "less reliable" defender of Russia than the Briton, Lord Curzon. He rejected Roosevelt's "suggestion," but he urged that Poland be compensated with German territory up to the line of the Oder and Neisse rivers. Churchill disagreed, asserting that "it would be a pity to stuff the Polish goose so full of German food that he will die of indigestion." There was no final agreement on the frontier, but the phrase in the protocol, "substantial accessions of territory in the North and West," left the way open for Stalin to assign the territory east of the Oder-Neisse line to "Polish administration."

On the question of a Polish government, the agreement ran: "The provisional government which is now functioning in Poland [the Communist junta formerly at Lublin] should . . . be reorganized on a broader democratic basis with the inclusion of democratic leaders from Poland itself and from Poles abroad"; after reorganization, the government should hold "free and unfettered elections" on the basis of universal suffrage and secret ballot as soon as possible. Roosevelt declared, "I want the election in Poland to be beyond question, like Caesar's wife. I did not know Caesar's wife, but she was believed to have been pure." To this Stalin replied with a smile, "It was said so about Caesar's wife, but, in fact, she had certain sins." A declaration on policy toward liberated European areas, phrased in general terms, was also adopted.

In the agreements on Poland and Eastern Europe, the Western leaders felt they had achieved all they could. The alternative would have been to withhold recognition, to which the Soviets obviously attached much importance (since it would suggest to the Poles and others that the Allies were not going to help them, and many were still hoping for Western aid), unless governments were established which were willing to submit to popular decision. Yalta did not provide in advance for *de jure* recognition of the satellite regimes. However, the agreements reached committed the United States and Britain to support the Communist junta as soon as it included a cabinet minister from London, and this commitment was in fact to be honored.

The last issue discussed at Yalta concerned the conditions under which the Soviets would take part in the Pacific war. As early as October 1943

Stalin had volunteered to Secretary of State Hull a promise to join the fight against Japan after Germany was defeated. At Teheran Stalin had linked such a promise with his expectations for a cross-Channel invasion of France and American aid to the USSR. At that time Roosevelt had on his own initiative mentioned Dairen and free access to warm waters as possible compensation for Soviet participation in the war with Japan. At Yalta, in bilateral Soviet-American discussions, it was agreed that the USSR would enter the war within "two or three months" after the surrender of Germany, provided that: 1. "the status quo" (*i.e.,* Soviet control) be preserved in Outer Mongolia. 2. the Kurile Islands be "handed over" to the USSR. 3. "the former rights of Russia violated by the treacherous attack of Japan in 1904 shall be restored": these were itemized as the restoration of southern Sakhalin, internationalization of the port of Dairen, lease of Port Arthur as a Soviet naval base, and joint Sino-Soviet operation of the Manchurian railways in such a manner as to safeguard "the pre-eminent interests of the Soviet Union," although China was to "retain full sovereignty in Manchuria." It was agreed that "these claims of the Soviet Union shall be unquestionably fulfilled after Japan has been defeated," and although it was stipulated that "the President will take measures in order to obtain . . . concurrence" of Chiang Kai-shek in respect to Outer Mongolia and the "ports and railroads" concerned, it was crystal clear that neither Roosevelt nor Chiang would have any alternative but to confirm the concessions listed.

All this was contained in a "top secret" protocol, which Eden tried to dissuade Churchill from signing. However, Churchill believed that the security of "the whole British Empire in the Far East" compelled Britain to share in the agreement. Churchill signed, although he had taken no part in the discussion except to listen to a remarkable exchange in which Stalin declared, "I only want to have returned to Russia what the Japanese have taken from my country," and Roosevelt responded, "That seems like a very reasonable suggestion from our ally. They only want to get back that which has been taken from them."[3] Roosevelt recognized Stalin, not as the chief of the world Communist movement, but as the legitimate heir of Nicholas II, who had lost the possessions and rights itemized under 3. above.

Subsequently the secret promises to Stalin of Far Eastern gains were the most sharply criticized provisions of the Yalta agreement. The fact that they were kept secret is not surprising: their publication would have invited Japanese attack on the USSR before troops could be transferred

• [3] Stalin actually got more than had been taken from the Russian Empire, as the Kurile Islands had never formally been Russian territory.

eastward, and in any case would have destroyed any Soviet chance to attack Japanese forces with the benefit of surprise. Their substance is another matter. The "realists" have argued in their favor that they granted the Soviets nothing more than they could have taken anyway. This argument begs the moral question; it is difficult to justify giving away things which belong to other people, at Munich, Yalta, or elsewhere. But the "realists" also overlook the erroneous analysis on which the promises were based. The American government assumed that the USSR desired only to regain the position of power and security in the Far East which Imperial Russia had lost. This assumption could be supported not by the record of Soviet statements and actions (at least prior to 1941) or by the conclusions of the best expert opinion, but only by trust that Stalin and his regime had undergone some kind of inner transformation—a trust that proved unwarranted. Moreover, the military leadership, including the Joint Chiefs of Staff and General Douglas MacArthur, United States commander in the Pacific, overestimating both the Japanese strength and morale which remained, anticipated a bitter and bloody struggle for capture of the home islands of Japan and believed Soviet aid of great importance in reducing possible American losses. They did not suggest that any particular price should be paid for such assistance, but they indicated that it needed to be bought. This also proved an erroneous estimate of the situation. However, since Roosevelt and Churchill had volunteered consent to Soviet acquisitions in the Far East as far back as the Teheran conference, the military estimate presented at Yalta cannot be regarded as decisive. The ultimate responsibility at the conference was that of the American and British governments, whose leaders there made agreements which, whatever their moral or political justification, were certainly based on a mistaken appraisal of Soviet intentions.

POST-YALTA TENSIONS

Although in order to win the European war first, the Allied governments had kept their Pacific forces in short supply of men and matériel, a series of hard-won successes had been achieved. Beginning with the invasion of Guadalcanal in August 1942, the "island-hopping" operations led by General MacArthur had moved westward along two axes of advance. One was from Guadalcanal to New Guinea to the Philippines, recaptured from October 1944 to July 1945; the other was to the north, from the Marshall Islands to the Marianas to Iwo Jima, taken in February and March 1945, and Okinawa, in April to June. Meanwhile, the British under Admiral Mountbatten reconquered Burma from August

1944 to May 1945 and reopened land communications with China. By the summer of 1945 Japan was rapidly losing the outer reaches of her war-acquired empire and falling back on her home islands, even though her troops were still scattered over vast areas of Asia and the Pacific. However, the battles of Iwo Jima and Okinawa (where 110,000 Japanese had fought to the death and only 8,000 were captured) misled the Allied leaders into thinking that it would be necessary to overcome similar resistance on the soil of Japan proper before victory could be won. The problem of how to shorten the Japanese war without verbal abandonment of the "unconditional surrender" slogan was therefore raised at the Big Three conference at Potsdam in July 1945.

There were also political problems pertaining to Europe for the Potsdam conferees to consider; they were, in fact, inherited from Yalta. On February 27 Churchill told the House of Commons, "The impression I brought back from the Crimea . . . is that Marshal Stalin and the Soviet leaders wish to live in honourable friendship and equality with the Western democracies . . . . I decline absolutely to embark here on a discussion about Russian good faith." On March 3 Roosevelt told a joint session of the two Houses of Congress, "I am sure that—under the agreement reached at Yalta—there will be a more stable political Europe than ever before."

Nevertheless by March three developments had shaken Roosevelt's confidence in Stalin's intentions. On February 27 Deputy Foreign Minister Vyshinsky arrived in Bucharest and shortly thereafter delivered King Michael a face-to-face ultimatum to dismiss his prime minister, General Radescu, within two hours. Radescu was dismissed; another ultimatum then demanded the appointment of Petru Groza, a Communist tool, and he was sworn in on March 6. In vain the Western Allies referred the Soviets to the terms of the Yalta Declaration on Liberated Europe. Second, the reports of Ambassador Harriman from Moscow made it clear that Stalin was refusing to consider any genuine transformation of the Communist regime in Warsaw. Worse still, fourteen Polish leaders, given safe-conduct assurances by Stalin for the holding of talks, were arrested and held in Moscow despite Allied protests. In an exchange of messages among the Big Three, Stalin remained obdurate. The third incident concerned the arrangements under way for surrender of the German forces under General Kesselring in Italy to Field Marshal Alexander, the Allied commander-in-chief there. Stalin, charging that the British and Americans had promised Kesselring to undertake to soften the peace terms, in effect accused Roosevelt of falsification and bad faith. Roosevelt replied by expressing resentment of the "vile misrepresentations" of those who presumably had given Stalin reports on the Italian arrangements, and Stalin's next message was milder in tone. Meanwhile, Roosevelt had decided to send a joint message with Churchill on the Polish situation. While the message was being prepared, the President died on April 12, 1945, newly but deeply disturbed about the prospects for a just peace.

One of President Truman's first acts was to send Harry Hopkins (although he was seriously ill) to Moscow, requesting him to approach Stalin personally on the Polish issue and the question of waiving the power of procedural veto in the U. N. Security Council. On the latter point agreement was thought to have been reached at Yalta, but the Soviets had brought the San Francisco conference, then in session, to an impasse by refusing to yield on it as expected. However, when Hopkins appealed to Stalin, he gave way on the veto question, ostensibly after learning for the first time from Molotov on the spot how the matter stood. Hopkins also secured from Stalin a commitment to admit four non-Communist ministers into the Warsaw regime. Actually, Mikołajczyk, the leader of the Peasant party, was the only non-Communist of importance to be taken into the government. Nevertheless this was enough to obtain British and American diplomatic recognition for the "Polish Provisional Government," even though from the first Mikołajczyk found himself a helpless hostage of the Communists.

THE POTSDAM CONFERENCE

The strains among the Big Three, seemingly arrested by expressions of sentiment made on the occasion of President Roosevelt's death, appeared afresh at the Potsdam conference in July and August 1945. By the end of the conference two of the Big Three of Yalta were missing. President Truman represented the United States throughout. Midway in the talks, Churchill and Eden were thrown out of office by general elections. The new prime minister, Clement Attlee, and foreign minister, Ernest Bevin, took over the British delegation, on which they had been included from the start. The only thing new about Stalin was a title he had just conferred upon himself, that of "Generalissimo."

The conferees addressed themselves to the problems of a postwar settlement in Europe and the achievement of military victory over Japan. It was agreed to create a Council of Foreign Ministers which would draw up the peace treaties, deferring action on Germany until treaties were signed with Italy and Hitler's former Balkan allies. Western criticism of Soviet conduct in Eastern Europe and the character of the regimes which the USSR recognized there provoked sharp Soviet countercharges regarding Greece and Italy, followed by an agreement to drop complaints all around.

It was decided that Germany should be administered as a unit by the Allied Control Council, sitting in Berlin, and representing the U.S., Britain, the USSR, and France. Germany was to be decentralized, de-Nazified, and demilitarized. Beyond that the ACC's mission was vague. There was no final agreement on the extent of reparations; for the time being each power was authorized to satisfy its own demands from its zone of occupation, except that the USSR and Poland were to receive ten per cent of the war-industrial equipment from the three Western zones and an additional fifteen per cent in exchange for food and raw material shipments.

These agreements on Germany were only carried out for a short time, but the boundary arrangements—which were supposed to be temporary—proved to be more lasting. It was decided that the USSR would receive Königsberg and part of East Prussia. Stalin had already turned the region east of the Oder-Neisse line over to Polish administration, and it was agreed that that area and the part of East Prussia not annexed by the USSR should remain under Polish control until the "final" peace conference (which never took place). The powers agreed to the mass deportation of Germans—in a "humane" manner—by Poland, Czechoslovakia, and Hungary, and the ACC was ordered to distribute those expelled "equitably" among the four zones of Germany. This was as far as the Big Three powers ever got in making "peace" with Germany.

During the Potsdam conference the Japanese secretly requested Stalin to mediate in concluding peace in the Far Eastern war, but he rejected the overture before informing the Western leaders. Stalin was plainly not interested in concluding the war before Soviet troops went into action in the Far East. Truman now knew, on the basis of the New Mexico test, that the United States possessed an operational atomic bomb, and at Potsdam he informed Stalin of the fact, to which Stalin displayed only a casual reaction. Truman realized both the military effect which the bomb might have and the moral and psychological problems its use would create. It was agreed that before using it, the United States would join Britain and China in issuing a declaration to Japan which called for surrender with terms (although without relinquishing the phrase, "unconditional surrender"), and that the USSR might subsequently subscribe to it.

The Potsdam Declaration to Japan incorporated the principles of the Cairo Declaration, which had been issued by Churchill, Roosevelt, and Chiang Kai-shek after a brief meeting in November 1943 on the eve of the Teheran conference. The Cairo Declaration had stated that the three signatory powers "covet no gain for themselves," but would strip Japan of all Pacific islands acquired since 1914; that Manchuria, Formosa, and the Pescadores would be restored to "the Republic of China"; that Japan would be expelled from "all other territories which she has taken by violence and greed" (a phrase on which a justification of the secret concessions to the Soviets at Yalta might rest); and that Korea would become "free and independent." The Potsdam Declaration added the following peace conditions: as penalties, the limitation of sovereignty to the four main Japanese islands, the end of the military ascendancy over the government, the disarming and return to Japan of its armies abroad, the trial of war criminals, and the destruction of war industries, all to be achieved by a military occupation. However, the Japanese people were promised democratic institutions, no enslavement or destruction as a nation, and an eventual return to world trade and access to raw materials.

THE DEFEAT OF JAPAN

The Japanese overtures to Stalin were made both before and after the receipt of the Potsdam Declaration in Tokyo. The Emperor and the Supreme War Council, except for the two army and navy representatives, wished to accept it, but conceded to the army and navy a delay until word had been received from Stalin. None was. On August 6 the United States air force dropped the first atomic bomb on Hiroshima. The Soviets, who had already informed the Japanese in April that the neutrality pact of 1941 would not be renewed on its lapse in 1946, declared war on Japan on August 8. Under the direction of Marshal Vasilevsky, three army groups entered Manchuria from Mongolia, Vladivostok, and Khabarovsk and rapidly enveloped and defeated the Japanese forces there.

On August 9 the second atomic bomb was dropped on Nagasaki. Even the Japanese military now gave way but desired to add a number of conditions. Later in the day, however, an official communication announced Japanese willingness to surrender on the understanding that the Potsdam Declaration did not include any item which "prejudiced" the Emperor's prerogatives. The American reply, on behalf of the Allies, was sufficiently ambiguous so that the Japanese, including the Emperor himself, chose to interpret it as an indication that the Allies would not themselves depose Hirohito. A surrender note was dispatched on August 15 and General MacArthur accepted the signature of the surrender document on September 2 on the battleship *Missouri*, lying off Tokyo.

In his war proclamation Stalin had spoken of the "blemish on the tradition of our country" left by the Japanese victory in 1905 and had declared, "For forty years we, the men of the older generation, have waited for this day. Now it has finally come." In fact not only the Bolsheviks but the entire Russian opposition movement, including liberals, had openly espoused defeatism in the Russo-Japanese War, which had provoked the domestic crisis leading to the Revolution of 1905. However, the nationalist note in this hypocritical declaration served both Stalin's domestic and international interests of the moment.

No top-level international conference ever dealt with the problem of how defeated Japan should be treated. From start to finish the United States had borne the brunt of the Far Eastern war. The subsequent Soviet claim to have effected the defeat of Japan was perhaps the most grotesque case of falsification to which official history has descended in the USSR, but in 1945 Stalin did not press any such claims. Although he desired to have a double command in Japan, one of the commanders to be Russian, and a Soviet occupation zone in Hokkaido, those demands were refused, and Stalin had no alternative but to acknowledge General MacArthur as Supreme Commander, Allied Powers. However, after a moment of confusion, it became clear that MacArthur's jurisdiction would not run to Manchuria, where Marshal Vasilevsky's authority was supreme. Soviet representatives sat on an Allied Council for Japan, established in Tokyo, and a Far Eastern Commission set up in Washington, D.C., but the Soviets had no important influence over Japanese occupation policy.

The armistice with Japan, ending World War II, was signed on September 2, 1945, although in fact the fighting had been over for three weeks and in law the war would end only when peace treaties were signed. Stalin, who had faced utter ruin in the autumn of 1941, had managed to regain control of the situation, mobilize nationalist sentiment in Russia against Hitler, hurl Nazi forces back to Berlin and beyond, win the apparent confidence of the United States and obtain major diplomatic and territorial concessions from his wartime allies, and end the war with his control extending from central Germany to the middle of Korea. The Soviet armies and peoples ended the war believing that they had secured international peace, as well as the prospect of at least a degree of domestic freedom and the possibility of regular association with the individual citizens and governments of the Western countries. During the last two months of the war, the shadow of tension had fallen across British and American relations with the USSR, troubling many of the Western leaders, but even they continued to cling to the hope that with patience and firmness, all would be well in the postwar world.

Communist Expansion in Europe (1945–1953)

★
★
★
★
★
★
★
★
★
★

CHAPTER 25

COMMUNIST PARTISANS IN EASTERN EUROPE

As Stalin's alliance with the Western powers produced important Soviet gains by way of international diplomacy, so it gave the Communist parties throughout most of Europe (except Germany and Spain) an unprecedented opportunity to build up their strength and influence. During World War II they created their own armed forces and instruments of political control, which were ready for use in 1945, or even earlier, in establishing regimes subservient to Stalin's orders. Although while the war was still in progress the Communists devoted much effort to undermining or destroying their organized political competitors, in their public proganda they employed the slogans of national unity and antifascism in most European countries, achieving particular success with such methods in Greece and France.

In Greece, Yugoslavia, and Albania the Communists created strong underground regimes supported by partisan forces, while in France and Italy they mounted sizable resistance movements. Elsewhere in Europe they did what they could pending the time that Soviet diplomacy or the Red Army might come to their aid in establishing Communist control.

In Greece, in September 1941 the Communists had set up the first of the underground regimes, based on an attempt to revive the tactic of the Popular Front of the mid-1930's—which was in fact to achieve its greatest successes during the decade of the forties. The regime was called the EAM (*Ellenikon apelevtherikon metopon* or Greek Liberation Front); although it prominently featured non-Communist members, it was fully controlled by Communists. Its army was called ELAS (*Ellenikon laikon apelevtherikon straton* or Greek People's Liberation Army). Although it carried out isolated guerrilla actions against the Germans, it fought harder against non-Communist resistance forces. In October 1944, on the heels of the withdrawing Nazi armies, the British landed in Greece, and found most of the country in the hands of EAM-ELAS.

Although the Soviets had conceded British predominance in Greece (see p. 385), Stalin evidently told the Greek Communists to make a try for power on their own. Owing to the broad mass support they had obtained, their chances for success seemed bright. However, for several weeks after the British landing the Communists held their hand, apparently underestimating the resistance they would meet from the British as well as from non-Communist Greeks. It is quite possible that a coup in Athens in the fall might have succeeded, but fighting did not break out until December. The British, although they had to bring in two divisions of reinforcements, held off the Communists and in February compelled them to sign an agreement by which ELAS would be disarmed but democratic liberties would be guaranteed to all parties including the Communists. Greece remained in turmoil, and rightist vigilantes, ignoring the democratic government in Athens, took over much of the countryside for a time, but power had been denied to what was then perhaps the strongest Communist group in any European country.

In Yugoslavia the Communist leader who had been Moscow's instrument in purging most of his colleagues in the local party leadership in 1937, Joseph Broz (Tito), began to organize his partisans in Serbia after the Nazi attack on the USSR. He had to compete with the Chetnik (in peacetime, a sort of National Guard) units of General Draža Mihailović, who had been fighting the Germans since they invaded the country in the spring, and who was soon made war minister by the Yugoslav government-in-exile under King Peter II. Driven from Serbia by 1942, Tito's partisans retreated to Bosnia and there, in November 1942, formed a Popular Front regime called AVNOJ (Anti-Fascist Council of National Liberation of Yugoslavia). The AVNOJ included a few genuine democrats, such as the Serb Agrarian party leader Dragoljub Jovanović, but it was under firm Communist control. A year later it was converted into a provisional government. Tito and Mihailović fought hard to crush each other, but Tito was the more successful in winning support, even among the Chetniks. His popularity was in part the result of his policy of amity—based on the doctrine on nationalities which Lenin had advanced and to which Stalin still verbally adhered—among the Serbs, Croats, and other Yugoslav peoples; many Yugoslavs were horrified by the atrocities of Croat Fascist puppets of the Italians and troubled by Mihailović's narrow Serbian nationalism. Moreover, Mihailović had ceased to fight the Germans by early 1943, and was even willing to collaborate with Axis forces, being more concerned about possible postwar Communist efforts to take power and being convinced, quite wrongly, that the Western Allies secretly understood and agreed with his views.

In the early stages of fighting the British had furnished supplies to both Tito and Mihailović. Tito embarrassed Moscow by taking a sharply anti-Western line and evincing calculated rudeness toward his British benefactors. Although Stalin urged Tito to play the game of harmony more adroitly and not to show his colors prematurely, Tito's unruliness in fact convinced the British that, although they knew him to be a staunch Communist, he would be likely to take an independent line in the future. In the spring of 1943 the British ceased to support Mihailović altogether. As they abandoned the staunchly anti-German and pro-Allied Albanian resistance leader, Abbas Kupi, at the same moment, it is doubtful that Mihailović could have saved himself by resuming attack on the Nazis at that stage. Tito did not bother with any displays of gratitude toward the British, even when they saved him after the disastrous German parachute raid on his headquarters in 1944 and helped him reconstruct his movement.

With British aid and much popular approval, Tito managed to take over much of Yugoslavia with his own forces by the time the Soviet armies entered the country in September 1944. Tito secured Soviet agreement that they would not move into the western part of the country, and thus Zagreb became the last (along with Prague) of all European cities to be taken from Axis control. By March 1945 Tito had already obtained the withdrawal of Soviet troops from Yugoslavia. In the closing stages of the war he kept his reputation for unruliness by clashing with New Zealander and British forces in Trieste and Austria, backing down only under threats of force.

In March 1945 a Yugoslav government was re-established in Belgrade. Nominally its membership implemented the December 1944 agreement between Tito and the non-Communist prime minister of the Yugoslav government-in-exile, Dr. Ivan Šubašić. Western pressure had forced Tito to sign the agreement; however, as in the case of Poland, the West failed

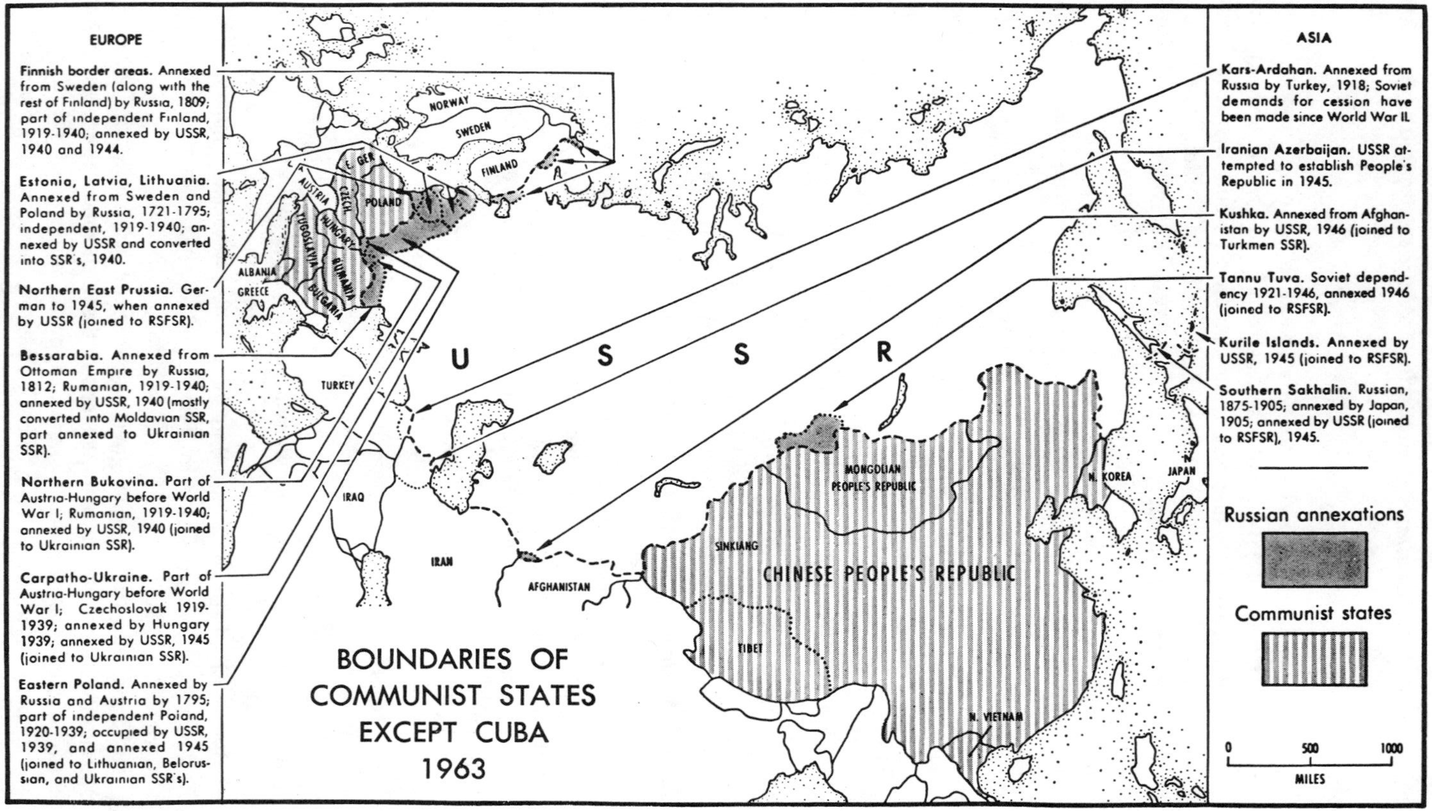

EUROPE
Finnish border areas. Annexed from Sweden (along with the rest of Finland) by Russia, 1809; part of independent Finland, 1919-1940; annexed by USSR, 1940 and 1944.
Estonia, Latvia, Lithuania. Annexed from Sweden and Poland by Russia, 1721-1795; independent, 1919-1940; annexed by USSR and converted into SSR's, 1940.
Northern East Prussia. German to 1945, when annexed by USSR (joined to RSFSR).
Bessarabia. Annexed from Ottoman Empire by Russia, 1812; Rumanian, 1919-1940; annexed by USSR, 1940 (mostly converted into Moldavian SSR, part annexed to Ukrainian SSR).
Northern Bukovina. Part of Austria-Hungary before World War I; Rumanian, 1919-1940; annexed by USSR, 1940 (joined to Ukrainian SSR).
Carpatho-Ukraine. Part of Austria-Hungary before World War I; Czechoslovak 1919-1939; annexed by Hungary 1939; annexed by USSR, 1945 (joined to Ukrainian SSR).
Eastern Poland. Annexed by Russia and Austria by 1795; part of independent Poland, 1920-1939; occupied by USSR, 1939, and annexed 1945 (joined to Lithuanian, Belorussian, and Ukrainian SSR's).
NORWAY
SWEDEN
FINLAND
E. GER
POLAND
CZECH.
AUSTRIA
HUNGARY
YUGOSLAVIA
RUMANIA
BULGARIA
ALBANIA
GREECE
TURKEY
IRAQ
IRAN
AFGHANISTAN
U S S R
MONGOLIAN PEOPLE'S REPUBLIC
SINKIANG
CHINESE PEOPLE'S REPUBLIC
TIBET
N. VIETNAM
N. KOREA
JAPAN
BOUNDARIES OF COMMUNIST STATES EXCEPT CUBA 1963
ASIA
Kars-Ardahan. Annexed from Russia by Turkey, 1918; Soviet demands for cession have been made since World War II.
Iranian Azerbaijan. USSR attempted to establish People's Republic in 1945.
Kushka. Annexed from Afghanistan by USSR, 1946 (joined to Turkmen SSR).
Tannu Tuva. Soviet dependency 1921-1946, annexed 1946 (joined to RSFSR).
Kurile Islands. Annexed by USSR, 1945 (joined to RSFSR).
Southern Sakhalin. Russian, 1875-1905; annexed by Japan, 1905; annexed by USSR (joined to RSFSR), 1945.
Russian annexations
Communist states
0
500
1000
MILES

to bring about a real broadening of the government, and the result was only to legitimize the Yugoslav Communist regime. King Peter II was persuaded with difficulty to transfer his powers to a regency, Šubašić was taken into the government as foreign minister, but Tito did not yield any of his power. As before, he completely controlled the secret police, whose chief was Alexander Ranković, the army, and all effective government in Yugoslavia. Moreover, Albania, where a Communist government headed by Enver Hoxha had taken over after the Nazi evacuation in October 1944, was for the time being administered as a kind of satrapy of Tito's.

COMMUNISTS IN THE AXIS SATELLITES

In the rest of Eastern Europe the local Communists were installed in power with the aid of Soviet armies. In Rumania, Bulgaria, and Hungary the regimes, although they collaborated with the Axis during the war, were headed by men who had no love for Hitler and had tried vainly since 1943 to get out of the war by surrendering to the Western Allies, but all such overtures were rejected. In Rumania and Bulgaria the Communists had established Popular Front juntas. The chief Rumanian democratic leader, Iuliu Maniu of the National Peasant party, rejected an invitation to join because the Communists insisted on ceding Bessarabia, which he with some justice regarded as Rumanian, to the USSR. As a result the "National Democratic Front" included no important non-Communist groups. The tiny Ploughman's Front, headed by Dr. Petru Groza, which was included in the Communist-led junta, did make some independent gains in peasant support, but was soon taken over by Communists without hindrance from Groza. In March 1945, after Vyshinsky's ultimatum to King Michael, Groza was installed as prime minister of a National Democratic Front government, in which all vital posts were held by Communists (see p. 398).

In Bulgaria an underground Fatherland Front had been formed, including along with the Communists the powerful Agrarian Union, led by Dr. G. M. Dimitrov and Nikola Petkov, the quasi-socialist "Zveno" party, led by Kimon Georgiev, and some Left Social Democrats. In September 1944 the Front took over the Bulgarian government by *coup d'état* in the presence of Soviet power. The boy king, Simeon, was expelled, and Kimon Georgiev, like Groza a pliant Soviet tool, became prime minister. In January 1945 Dr. Dimitrov was forced to resign as leader of the Agrarian Union, and the Communists seized control of the party a few months later. In August Petkov and the Social Democrats unwilling to take Communist orders resigned from the government, which by that time was clear of any opponent of the real leader, the veteran Stalinist George Dimitrov.

In Hungary a genuine coalition provisional government, with General Miklos, a late defector from the Nazi-collaborating Hungarian General Staff, as prime minister, was set up in December 1944 and reached Budapest in April 1945. Along with the Communists were included the Social Democratic party, delivered into Communist hands by a new leader, Arpád Szakasits; a small National Peasant party, which the Communists tried unsuccessfully to convert into their rural affiliate on the model of the Russian Left S.R.'s of 1917; and the strong Small Farmer's party under Zoltán Tildy and Ferenc Nagy, which kept aloof from the Communists. The nation—especially the city of Budapest—had been ravaged by war and looting, and the Small Farmers became the focus of both urban and rural resentment at Soviet conduct. The Communists held the police, agriculture, and other ministries but for the time being were unable to control the government. The agriculture ministry, crucial because of the justifiable popular demand for land reform, was given to Imre Nagy, who was later to win fleeting fame in the Hungarian Revolution of 1956 (see p. 483).

To some extent the success of the Small Farmers in temporarily preventing Communist dictatorship was accidental. In the fall of 1945 the Communists, presenting a joint list with the Social Democrats, agreed to the holding of free elections in the city of Budapest. They counted on sweeping the polls; however, instead the Small Farmers won an absolute majority. As a result of this miscalculation Marshal Voroshilov, chairman of the Allied Control Commission and in effect Soviet viceroy for Hungary, felt compelled to permit free national elections. The Small Farmers won 57% of the popular vote and the Communists only 7%. Tildy became prime minister and then president of the newly-proclaimed Hungarian Republic, at which time Ferenc Nagy succeeded him as prime minister. Stalin and his Hungarian Communist puppet, Mátyás Rákosi, chose to bide their time.

COMMUNISTS IN POLAND AND CZECHOSLOVAKIA

Poland and Czechoslovakia were more difficult than the Axis satellites to subject to Soviet power, since they were Allies and were also much better known to the West. After Harry Hopkins had managed to get Mikołajczyk, leader of the People's (Peasant) party, included in the Communist-controlled Polish regime, Western recognition had been extended to it in July 1945. The Communists in Poland depended on

Soviet bayonets to a greater extent than in any other Eastern European country. Since the old Polish Communist party had been destroyed by Stalin himself, a new "Polish Workers' Party" had had to be organized in 1942. It controlled the police and army, and for good measure many Soviet officers were transferred directly into the Polish forces. However, since the West was watching closely and popular hostility was so strong, the Warsaw regime moved slowly at first. It attempted to trade on the nationwide satisfaction at the annexation of all lands east of the Oder-Neisse line, but at the same time set up a virtually separate adminstration for the "Regained Territories" under the Communist Władysław Gomułka which undertook to establish there the type of totalitarian control which could later be extended to the whole country. Underground resistance to the Soviets continued, and from the first Mikołajczyk was accused of connections both with anti-Soviet guerrillas inside Poland and with General Anders's Polish forces in exile, who had fought with the British and refused in large numbers to return home.

The example of Poland was in the mind of President Eduard Beneš of Czechoslovakia in his dealings with the Soviets. He also knew that Klement Gottwald and other Czechoslovak Communist leaders were in Moscow, ready for whatever use Stalin wished to make of them. Nevertheless he did not act entirely unwillingly when he acquiesced in the establishment of a People's Front government on Czechoslovak soil at Košice in March 1945. He had long sympathized with "Russia" (which he did not clearly distinguish from the USSR) and hoped for the best from co-operation with Stalin. Beneš had to agree to forget any notion of a "Czechoslovak" nationality and distinguish Czechs from Slovaks in the restored republic. The Košice regime included "Czech parties" (the Communists, Social Democrats, National Socialists,[1] and the People's [Catholic] parties) and "Slovak parties" (Communists and Democrats). Thus the Communists alone enjoyed the advantage of being a "national" party through their inclusion on both lists.

The Communists held the control of the police, army, information and agriculture ministries, and other vital agencies. A Communist enclave, similar to that in the new western territories of Poland, was created in the Sudetenland, from which the Germans were expelled. Like the Bulgarians and Serbs, the Czechs had a tradition of pro-Russian feeling, which the Communists exploited with some success, and little was said in public about the government's cession of Ukrainian-speaking Carpatho-Ruthenia to the USSR in June 1945. In December both Soviet and American forces (the latter had occupied the strip west of Plzeň) with-

• [1] Not to be confused with German National Socialists or Nazis.

drew from the country. For the moment the Communists in Czechoslovakia, despite their great power, behaved with greater restraint than anywhere else in Eastern Europe.

COMMUNISTS IN FRANCE AND ITALY

In Western Europe the Communists had a real chance of taking power in only two countries, France and Italy. The French Communists' most formidable rival was General Charles de Gaulle, who had organized French resistance from British soil after 1940. They were therefore even willing to play a strange game of supporting General Giraud during the confused weeks when President Roosevelt, who was skeptical of de Gaulle's promise as leader of French resistance, sought to use Giraud as a counterweight to de Gaulle. The Communists would have nothing to do with the Gaullist underground army when it was formed in October 1942, but established their own partisan forces (F. T. P. or *Francs-Tireurs Partisans*). The Communist partisans ignored Allied pleas not to act until their forces landed, as partisan activity was a useful means of preparing the ground for a seizure of power. In September 1943 the Communists, in close co-operation with Giraud, carried out the seizure of the island of Corsica just in advance of commando landings and there unleashed a wave of executions of their enemies which served as a rehearsal for the similar killings (which counted many thousands of victims) undertaken after the Allied landings on the mainland.

In April 1944 de Gaulle had accepted two Communists as ministers in his Algiers regime. He had few illusions about their intentions, but the party was thereby given an aura of legitimacy which it needed. The Communists profited greatly from their record of open resistance, regardless of the fact that the non-Communist underground forces had been much more numerous and quite as valorous when their services were called for. They also exploited the cathartic effect on frustrated public feelings induced by Communist-led violence against "collaborators"—many of them quite innocent—following the liberation. For these and other reasons, in the elections of October 1945 the party emerged as the strongest in France, polling five million votes. De Gaulle, now chief of the government, took in five Communist ministers, but resolutely refused to let them have the foreign affairs, interior (police), or war ministry. Although Léon Blum and the Socialists were again, as during the thirties, willing for a time to risk an on-and-off type of co-operation with the Communists, they ended the new Popular Front in the summer of 1946. About the same time the Communist-controlled trade-union organization split and a Socialist wing broke away. Finally, on the heels of the Truman Doctrine, in the spring of 1947, the Socialist premier, Paul Ramadier, dismissed the Communist ministers. The French Communists' opportunity to take power had passed.

Palmiro Togliatti, the Italian Communist leader, was more capable than Thorez in France, and Italian Communism had the additional advantage that Pietro Nenni had in effect delivered the Italian Socialist party into its hands. By his curious pseudo-monarchism of 1943–1944, Togliatti had managed to convince many conservatives that the party was really made up of good patriots. However, for the May 1946 referendum on the monarchy he switched to professed republicanism and provided the margin of the republic's victory. The simultaneous parliamentary elections gave the Communists together with Nenni's Socialists 219 seats to 207 for Premier Alcide de Gasperi's Christian Democrats. Togliatti set forth demands which did not go beyond economic improvements in the existing system and held the trade-unions in the north. For a time it appeared as if the Communists might slip into power. However, Giuseppe Saragat weakened the Communist-Socialist coalition by leading a schism of fifty deputies out of the Nenni-controlled party, and early in 1947 de Gasperi succeeded in removing Nenni as foreign minister and the Socialist Romita as interior minister. The Truman Doctrine laid down the gauntlet; Togliatti attacked the position of the Roman Catholic Church in Italy, indicating the end of any attempt to influence Catholics, and de Gasperi provoked the remaining Communists and Socialists to resign in May 1947. The postwar Popular Front came to an end in Western Europe. The Communists controlled the minuscule statelet of San Marino until 1957, but with that picturesquely irrelevant exception, the Communist bid for power west of the Iron Curtain had failed.

THE COMING OF THE "COLD WAR" IN EUROPE

The failure of the Communists in Western Europe coincided with and was partly caused by the break-up of the wartime alliance between the Western powers and the USSR. It was contemplated, at least by the West, that this alliance would continue to operate in two forms: in the military and diplomatic machinery for the occupation of Germany and Austria and the making of peace with those two countries, Italy, Finland, and the former Axis satellites, and informally as a harmonious nucleus of the new United Nations organization.

Peace treaties were actually signed with Italy, Rumania, Hungary, Bulgaria, and Finland, and later, in 1955, with Austria. In a series of meetings from September 1945 to October 1946, the Council of Foreign Ministers of the Big Three, deputized for this purpose, worked out the provisions of the treaties, which were signed in Paris in February 1947. Italy lost her colonies, the hinterland of Trieste to Yugoslavia,[2] and minor bits of territory to France and Greece (the Dodecanese Islands). Rumania lost Bessarabia and northern Bukovina to the USSR and southern Dobrudja to Bulgaria, but regained northern Transylvania from Hungary. Finland lost the northern district of Petsamo (giving the Soviet Union a common frontier with Norway), the territory west of Lake Ladoga including Viipuri, and yielded the Soviets a fifty-year lease of the base of Porkkala on the Gulf of Finland.[3] All except Italy had to pay considerable sums in reparations to the USSR. The conclusion of the treaties chiefly signified a recognition of the power realities of the moment, wherein the Soviets were in a position to do more or less what they liked with the three East European Axis satellites, but were barred from doing so in Italy, while they chose to let Finland pay heavily, as it was prepared to do, for its continued independence.

Turning next to the problems of Germany and Austria, the Council of Foreign Ministers met in March 1947 in Moscow at the moment of the issuance of the Truman Doctrine, and discussions made no further progress. Actually the fate of Germany, at least for the next decade or so, was by then already decided. The Allied Control Council for Germany had never functioned as intended, and the only fruit of four-power (including France) action was the trial of the major "war criminals" at Nuremberg. The Soviets had proceeded to run their zone of Germany as a satellite. They had forced the large Socialist party to merge with the tiny Communist one, creating a Socialist Unity party (*Sozialistische Einheitspartei Deutschlands* or S.E.D.), and used it as a tool. By May 1946 Soviet stripping of the Eastern zone had alarmed the Western powers sufficiently to bring them to cease delivery of additional equipment from their zones to the USSR, as provided by Yalta.

By this time reports of Soviet ruthlessness, impediments placed in the way of Western representatives, and restrictions on freedom in Eastern Europe were overwhelming. In March 1946 Winston Churchill, in a speech at Fulton, Missouri, said publicly what had been plain to the informed for many months past: "From Stettin in the Baltic to Trieste in the Adriatic, an iron curtain has descended across the the continent." He recommended closer Anglo-American co-operation as a safeguard against

• [2] Trieste became a "Free Territory" until 1954, when by agreement Italy annexed the city and Yugoslavia most of the rest of the Free Territory.

• [3] The USSR relinquished the lease in 1956.

any "temptation to ambition or adventure"—on whose part he did not say, but his meaning was clear.

Not long afterward George F. Kennan, the chief United States State Department expert on the USSR, wrote, under the pseudonym "X," an historic article in *Foreign Affairs* which set forth a basic element of United States foreign policy from that time until the present: "a long-term, patient but firm and vigilant containment of Russian expansive tendencies. . . ." Secretary of State James F. Byrnes, in a speech at Stuttgart in September, renounced the Morgenthau Plan for the economic pauperization of Germany, which the Soviet press in the Eastern zone was using extensively in its anti-American propaganda, and he unequivocally promised U.S. support for German reconstruction and affirmed the intention of the United States to defend West Germany from any encroachment from the East.

These statements expressed an underlying, although perhaps tardy, American realization that whether or not the problem of Communism in Europe was conceived solely in terms of Russian power, effective opposition to Soviet expansion in the postwar era could come only from the United States. Stalin understood this fact well enough, as shown by the Soviet campaign of denunciation of America which had been under way for many months. Considering the Soviet-annexed territory behind the "Iron Curtain" to be at least temporarily unredeemable, the United States began gradually to assume the leadership of the opposition to any further Soviet expansion in Europe. The Soviets thus found their westward political offensive checked, but while they turned to complete the building of Communist control east of the curtain they did what they still could to the west of it.

In Germany Stalin evidently still hoped to take over the entire country. When the British and Americans merged their occupation zones to produce "Bizonia" in December 1946, the Soviets nevertheless confined themselves to protests. Stalin apparently was counting on the French, whose fear or hatred of the Germans was stronger than that of the other two Western powers, to obstruct or prevent the establishment of a unified West German state. However, in June 1948, as it became clear that the French were wavering, Stalin cut off all overland contact between the Western occupation zones and the city of Berlin, which was under quadripartite administration, in an effort to intimidate the West sufficiently to make it abandon the plan to set up a West German republic. It was only by dint of great exertions, no doubt unexpected by the Soviets, that the West managed to maintain air contact with the city and thereby to supply it. However, the air lift succeeded in frustrating the intended purpose of the Berlin blockade, and in May 1949 the Soviets raised it.

At the same time the Council of Foreign Ministers, which had adjourned sine die after the failure of its December 1947 meeting in London, was convened in Paris for a resumption of talks. However, there was still no progress made. In May a constitution for a Federal Republic of Germany was prepared and in the fall the republic was proclaimed, including the French zone along with "Bizonia." Once the possibility had disappeared of a unified German state which they might hope to take over, the Soviets converted their zone, with half the territory and less than half the population of the other three zones, into a German Democratic Republic, whose fortunes followed those of the other East European satellites of the USSR. Any hope of a common Soviet-Western policy in establishing a Germany which was both unified and free vanished.

In the United Nations organization, deliberations immediately revealed that the Big Three coalition, upon which the hopes for harmony and stability in the U.N. had rested, was destined soon to weaken or to break up altogether. In January 1946 the first complaint which the U.N. had to handle was that of Iran against the USSR for its refusal to evacuate the northern region, which had been occupied in wartime for the purpose of insuring the supply line from the Persian Gulf, and for its attempt to establish a local Communist-front government there. Under United States pressure the Soviets finally did evacuate Iranian Azerbaijan, but the Communist-run Tudeh party continued to cause trouble in Iran.

In few instances did the Soviet and the American delegates in the Security Council or General Assembly ever vote on the same side. Paradoxically, in view of later events, such an instance was the approval of the partition of Palestine and the founding of the state of Israel in May 1948. If the Soviet motive, as some have speculated, was not to support Israel (indeed the treatment of the new Israeli envoy in Moscow and the Soviet press campaign against Israel confirm that it was not) but rather to provide a permanent focus of Arab nationalist discontent which the Communists might exploit, then the paradox may be understood.

SOVIET EXPANSION IN EUROPE CHECKED

Although the Communist opportunity in France and Italy was already passing, in Greece the party made another try for power, coupled with Soviet diplomatic pressure on Turkey (where internal Communist strength was virtually nil). The Communists boycotted the Greek elections of March 1946, and the Soviets refused to join the Western Allies in sending observers. However, the Allied Mission reported that although about forty per cent of the voters did not cast ballots, less than half of those abstained as a gesture of support for the Communists. In the summer the Communists retaliated by reopening the Greek Civil War from bases in Macedonia, where they could use Yugoslav, Albanian, and Bulgarian territory to train, rest, and obtain arms. Greece took the question of foreign Communist intervention to the U. N., whose investigators confirmed Greek charges in June 1947. Two months earlier President Truman had proclaimed the Truman Doctrine of support to free countries threatened by "armed minorities or by outside pressures," and had secured Congressional approval for immediate aid to Greece and Turkey. Thereupon the United States assumed the British commitments in Greece. American advisers entered the country to try to help defeat the Communist insurgents and bring some political and economic order into the Greek scene.

In December 1947 a Communist "democratic Greek government" was proclaimed under Markos Vafiades, wartime ELAS commissar for Macedonia. It was the Communists who threw down the gauntlet; up till October Communist newspapers had been allowed to publish in Athens, and the party had had freedom of open action in government-held territory. American assistance was not enough to secure victory as long as the rebels could cross over the border to evade pursuit and attack southward at another point the next day. However, the Truman Doctrine also had an important indirect effect which hastened the end of the rebellion. It influenced the outcome of the Tito-Stalin conflict by securing Tito's rear and enabling him to defy Stalin's wrath with greater confidence because the United States military was near. Conversely, the break between Belgrade and Moscow confused the Greek Communists and led to Tito's closing of the Yugoslav-Greek frontier in July 1949. As a result Greek government forces rapidly mopped up the rebel centers, and the leaders ended the fight. In the elections of March 1950 the Greek moderates overshadowed the Right, and some degree of political as well as economic stability gradually returned to the country. Meanwhile Turkey, strengthened by American aid, rejected Soviet diplomatic demands. The Truman Doctrine had succeeded in its immediate aims.

After 1947 West European leaders were becoming increasingly aware of Soviet intentions, and, partly following the American lead, they began to make common efforts at economic stabilization and military defense. The new American secretary of state, General George C. Marshall, announced the "Marshall Plan" in June 1947. It was enthusiastically welcomed by West Europeans, who set up an Organization of European Economic Cooperation (OEEC) to plan its operation. The early Franco-

British alliance of Dunkirk, signed in March 1947, was supplemented by the adherence of the "Benelux" nations (Belgium, the Netherlands, and Luxembourg) in the Treaty of Brussels of March 1948, and further broadened by the North Atlantic Treaty of April 1949, in which Italy, Portugal, Denmark, Iceland, Norway, Canada, and the United States also joined.[4] The signatories established a common defense command, whose first chief was General Eisenhower.

In September 1947 the Soviets countered by announcing the formation of a Communist Information Bureau (Cominform), with headquarters in Belgrade, replacing the "dissolved" Comintern. In January 1949 they established a Council for Mutual Economic Assistance (the so-called "Molotov Plan") for the satellites, and in May 1955 they set up a Communist counterpart to NATO in the Warsaw Treaty, placing all satellite forces under Marshal Konev. Such measures had some propaganda use, but little practical effect: the planning of the East European economy and the organization of the Communist armed forces did not depend on any treaty. However, they suggested that the Soviets had for the time being been thrown on the diplomatic defensive in Europe.

THE SOVIETIZATION OF EASTERN EUROPE: POLAND AND CZECHOSLOVAKIA

According to Hugh Seton-Watson, the Sovietization of Eastern Europe generally proceeded in three stages. First, genuine coalition, in which the regimes undertook measures against Axis collaborators and introduced social reforms, and limited freedom only to the extent of forbidding criticism of the Soviets, but in which Communists came to control the police, army, and propaganda machine. Second, "bogus coalition," in which the non-Communist parties no longer chose the men who held the ministries assigned to represent them in the "coalition" cabinets, but instead the Communists handpicked nominal members of the other parties for such appointments, while the peasant and moderate parties were crushed and only a few shreds of freedom remained to the opposition. Third, the "monolithic" regime, in which there emerged a "single communist-managed 'front,' with one hierarchy, one centralised discipline and one organisation."[5]

For all practical purposes the first two stages were skipped by Yugo-

• [4] Greece and Turkey joined NATO in 1951 and the Federal Republic of Germany in 1955.

• [5] *From Lenin to Malenkov* (New York: Praeger, 1953), pp. 248–249.

slavia and Albania, and Poland missed the first one. The third stage, complete Soviet control, was reached throughout Eastern Europe during the year which followed the establishment of the Cominform in September 1947 (however, by the end of that year, in Tito's Yugoslavia there was indeed a monolithic regime but not one subject to Moscow). The Western Allies vainly tried to create or broaden genuine coalitions. At the Moscow conference in December 1945 they had secured the admission of real opposition leaders into the Rumanian government, and the Soviets were forced to invite such men to join the government of Bulgaria, but the Rumanians were as helpless as Mikołajczyk and the Bulgarians refused to become hostages. The West protested continually over the progress of Sovietization, which violated the Yalta Declaration on Liberated Europe, not to mention specific undertakings on Poland, Rumania, and other countries, but did nothing more.

In each of the East European countries (except Albania), the opposition which the Communists had to crush centered in the peasant parties and the Christian churches—especially the Roman Catholic, since the Rumanian, Bulgarian, and Serbian Orthodox churches succumbed to the sort of infiltration tactics earlier employed on the Russian Orthodox Church, whose official clergy were in fact important instruments in bringing the Balkan churches to heel.

In Poland Mikołajczyk and his Polish People's (Peasant) party requested that national elections be held within a year of the Potsdam conference, as there decided, but the Communists postponed them until January 1947. Varied techniques, such as arrest of People's party candidates, arbitrary disqualification, and "voluntary" open voting, were used to render the elections fraudulent and to prevent the People's party from proving itself to be, as it clearly was, the focus of the national (urban as well as rural) resistance to Sovietization. Learning secretly in October 1947 that he was to be subjected to a faked trial and executed, Mikołajczyk escaped abroad. By December 1948 the regime became "monolithic" with the forced fusion of the last remaining separate party, the P. P. S. (Polish Socialist party), with the Polish Workers' party. The premier, the former Socialist but now Soviet tool Cyrankiewicz, was less important than President Bierut, Jakub Berman, and other Communists.

In Czechoslovakia genuinely free elections were held in May 1946 and yielded the Communists thirty-eight per cent of the popular vote. The size of their poll may be explained in part by peasant gratitude for the postwar land reform (carried out under Communist auspices as in all other East European countries)[6] and in part by a widespread nonideological overoptimism about the prospects of Soviet-Czechoslovak relations, colored by memories of the West's betrayal of Czechoslovakia at Munich. However, much opposition remained. In the spring of 1947 the execution of Msgr. Tiso, Hitler's wartime puppet ruler of "independent" Slovakia—a measure disapproved even by many who believed he should be punished—deepened Slovak discontent. In the summer occurred the degrading episode connected with the Paris conference on the Marshall Plan. Prague first accepted a Western invitation to attend, then withdrew its acceptance on Soviet ultimatum. As a result, the regime was thrown into prolonged crisis.

The Czechoslovak Communists, led by Premier Gottwald (Eduard Beneš had remained president), now doffed the kid gloves with which they had generally handled forms of legality, and the Communist Minister of Interior Nosek proceeded unabashedly to pack the police with his own men in preparation for new elections. In February 1948 all non-Communist ministers except the Social Democrats (already seriously infiltrated, thanks to the Soviet puppet Zdeněk Fierlinger) resigned in protest at Nosek's conduct. Unfortunately they did so without preparing themselves for either further constitutional action or armed defense against the Communist vigilantes who now began to employ open terror. After four days of hesitation, the troubled Beneš yielded to the Communist demand for a new government in which the non-Communist ministers should be chosen not by their own parties but by the Communists. Only Jan Masaryk, son of the founder of the republic, remained as a genuinely non-Communist minister—for two weeks, when he died in circumstances officially described as suicide. Beneš resigned in June and died in September, when Gottwald became president and Zápotocky premier.[7] The events of February 1948 have been interpreted as Communist "seizure" of Czechoslovakia. This is misleading to the extent that Communists had for three years previously held crucial ministries and had been gradually introducing measures of Sovietization.

• [6] The peasants were in any case unable to vote for the Agrarians, who had been strong in the countryside in the prewar period, as the Communists had suppressed them for "collaboration."

• [7] In March 1953 Gottwald was said to have died of pneumonia contracted while attending Stalin's funeral. It is remarkable how dangerous Moscow visits became for satellite Communist leaders. The reported circumstances of the death of President Bierut of Poland, just after attending the XX Congress of the Soviet Party in 1956, were almost identical. The Bulgarian satrap George Dimitrov had also died in Moscow in 1949. It is impossible to say whether in all these cases we confront a satellite phenomenon, involving murder-cum-eulogy, of the sort used earlier in the USSR (see p. 281).

THE SOVIETIZATION OF THE OTHER EAST EUROPEAN SATELLITES

Through the lucky accident of the Budapest and subsequent national elections, Hungary seemed to have the best chance of any East European country of retaining its independence. However, the Small Farmers' party's powers of resistance were weakened by President Tildy's responsiveness to Communist pressure. Furthermore, although the party had no single predominant leader who had been in wartime exile, like Mikołajczyk, upon whom Communists could focus their propaganda attack, the Small Farmers were beset by false charges and invented conspiracies, and their leaders were blackmailed. By May 1947 Prime Minister Ferenc Nagy, who had emerged as the party's strongest leader, was compelled to resign while in Switzerland on holiday and was replaced by a Soviet tool. The Communists then proceeded to break the Small Farmers' resistance successfully. However, even in the partly rigged elections of August 1947, the remaining opposition to the Communists polled thirty-five per cent. By 1948 the last independent party, the Social Democrats, was forced into fusion with the Communists, after those Social Democratic leaders resisting the merger had been expelled from membership (including Anna Késthly, whom the Hungarian revolutionary government of 1956 was to send in vain to the U.N. as its representative). Communist domination of Hungary was complete.

In Rumania the first elections, in November 1946, were already rigged. The National Peasant party was suppressed in June 1947, and its leader and the focus of popular opposition, Iuliu Maniu, was put in solitary confinement for life. The other parties were suppressed, except for the Social Democrats who in November 1947 merged with the Communists to form a United Workers' party. King Michael, the last remaining monarch behind the Iron Curtain, was compelled to abdicate. If Stalin had not publicly decorated him for his services in surrendering Rumania and thereby opening Central Europe to the Soviet armies, he probably would not have lasted that long. By early 1948 the regime was "monolithic," and the real Communist leaders, Ana Pauker and Gheorghe Gheorghiu-Dej, now openly assumed prominent posts.

The Bulgarian elections of November 1945, like those in Rumania, were fraudulent. After a second rigged election in October 1946, the Communist chief, George Dimitrov, became prime minister. The leader of the Agrarian Union, Nikola Petkov, was arrested and executed in September 1947. The last non-Communist party, the Socialist, was taken over in August 1948, and the "monolithic" stage was reached. When

Dimitrov died in 1949 while undergoing "medical treatment" in Moscow, he was replaced as prime minister by Vlko Chervenkov, who remained in office until 1954.

The Yugoslav Communists made shorter work of their non-Communists than any other East European regime except perhaps that of Albania, which was closely tied to Tito (up to the time of the Tito-Stalin break). Šubašić, the only non-Communist minister of consequence, resigned as early as September 1945. In July 1946 General Mihailović was executed. In September 1947 the Serbian Agrarian leader Jovanović, after offering mild objections to the regime, was arrested and imprisoned. However, he had been elected deputy on the Communist-front list and neither held a ministry nor had any party still in existence to support him. Tito's "monolith" was quickly hewn.

EASTERN EUROPE'S "SECOND REVOLUTION"

With the task of crushing political opposition achieved, the new Communist regimes could proceed to the stage of social transformation on the lines of the "Second Revolution" in the USSR. All agriculture was to be collectivized, all industry was to be taken over by the state, and heavy industry especially was to be expanded. Nationalization of industry had already begun, but collectivization would have to reverse the previously pursued program of land division.

Immediately after the war the Communists had sponsored land reform all over Eastern Europe. It may be argued that the break-up of the estates of the East German Junkers, the Hungarian magnates, and the Polish landlords was warranted in its economic and social aspects and made for long-run social stability, but in Yugoslavia and Bulgaria the farms had long consisted predominantly of small-scale peasant holdings, and much land reform had been carried out by the interwar regimes of Czechoslovakia and Rumania. The important thing was that the Communists were interested neither in social stability nor in land reform as ends in themselves. By carrying out land division, they hoped to gain peasant good will, since everywhere it was Communist ministers of agriculture who supervised the operation, and at the same time to undermine peasant support for the peasant parties which were their chief political opponents, often attracting also the votes of workers and other townsmen. Far from bringing the real agrarian objectives of Communism closer, land reform produced formidable obstacles to collectivization, since the peasants tried to defend what they had so recently been given as their own. However, land reform served the immediate and basic political needs of the Communists. Stalin's policy in the satellites reflected the lesson which Lenin had learned in Russia in 1917–1918: it is much easier to take over political control of a peasant country if land division is sanctioned at the beginning, and once such control is firmly established, collectivization can be carried out even in the face of overwhelming peasant opposition.

Nationalization of industry had proceeded at varying speeds, beginning with the seizure of all Axis-controlled property, then that of (elastically-defined) "collaborators," and finally all other industries. Only in Czechoslovakia, and to a lesser extent in Poland, was there enough industry in existence to make this operation very extensive or difficult. The great industrial effort was focused on new construction. In 1947–1948 short-term recovery plans were launched by most of the countries. Yugoslavia undertook a regular Five-Year Plan as early as 1947. The others adopted Five-Year Plans (in the case of Poland, a Six-Year Plan) a little later: Czechoslovakia and Bulgaria in 1949, Hungary and Poland in 1950, and Rumania in 1951. Using the usual percentage figures, the Communist leaders boasted great industrial achievements. In the USSR a poster was widely displayed in 1956 showing the growth in industrial production of the individual East European satellites. Since it was not production figures but percentages of increase which were shown, the increase appeared startling. The column for Albania, whose backwardness led Hugh Seton-Watson to call it the "Kirghizistan of the Adriatic," completely dwarfed the others. Percentage figures of this kind are quite valueless as a basis for evaluation of industrial expansion in countries which have little or no industry to begin with. Industry has been developed in certain East European countries with some success, though there are indications that the USSR is not satisfied with the progress.

If accurate, figures on the extent of collectivization of agriculture may be more useful than percentage statistics on the progress of industrial production, since they give proportions of a substantially stable total of arable area. By 1953–1954 collectives plus state farms were reported to account for 62.7% of Bulgarian arable, in Czechoslovakia 43%, in Hungary 30.5%, in Poland 20.2%, in Rumania 20%. From 1947 onward collectivization was embarked upon at an irregular pace, with several temporary retreats, much talk about "voluntary" collectivization intermingled with physical pressure and force to bring it about, and other features familiar from Soviet agricultural policy. But there was no blood bath comparable to that of the early 1930's in the USSR. That was another lesson which Stalin seemed to have learned, although the price paid was a level of achievement far short of his goals.

STALIN AND TITOISM

Tito's Yugoslavia advanced into its "Second Revolution" ahead of any other Soviet satellite, but the tempo was reduced after the break with Stalin in 1948. Although the split between Stalin and Tito was to affect the whole Communist movement, neither party desired the outcome which resulted from it. Tito and the Yugoslav party leaders were Stalin's picked men; they loved the USSR and took their Communism with the utmost seriousness, and they did not want to be cut adrift from their comrades. Stalin certainly did not want Yugoslavia removed from his control; his intention was to bring it into line with the other satellites. He hoped that the Yugoslav Communists would quickly depose Tito and his close associates, once the voice of Moscow (through the Cominform) had spoken. But Stalin made a serious miscalculation. He failed to perceive that the Yugoslav party was as firmly in Tito's hands in 1948 as the Russian Party had been in his own hands twenty years earlier.

The Cominform's denunciation of Tito in June 1948 climaxed a series of tensions which sprang from the fact that Tito and his partisans won substantial control of Yugoslavia for themselves during the war, unlike any other European Communist party. Tito's proposal for a Balkan Communist federation, which had led to negotiations with Dimitrov and the Bulgarians as early as November 1944, alarmed Stalin—although plainly not at first, but only when Tito began to be touchy about Soviet agents in Yugoslavia and gave signs of building up his own machine with success. In January 1948 *Pravda* rather abruptly attacked the federation scheme as "problematical and artificial."

In March the Soviet Party complained in a letter that the Yugoslavs refused to give the Soviets all the information they had asked for. At this point Tito arrested Andrija Hebrang, chief of the State Planning Commission and perhaps Moscow's most influential supporter in the Yugoslav party. In May the Soviet Party complained that collectivization was proceeding too slowly in Yugoslavia. In June the Cominform's public denunciation followed, repeating the earlier charges and adding that the Yugoslav party was run dictatorially. The last charge was, of course, quite true—the V Congress of the party, which met in July, was the first in twenty years—but the Soviets were scarcely in a position to criticize another Communist party for such a defect.

However, Tito did not deserve the Cominform's charge that his policy toward the peasantry was milder than that of the other satellites. Before 1948 he had pushed collectivization more vigorously than any other East European regime had done. There was no significant disagreement between Tito and Stalin over ideology or even tactics; at root the conflict was one of power. Tito, having retained his own secret police and system of controls, was in a position to prevent the Soviet personnel in Yugoslavia from running the country as they did the other satellites, and yet he could maintain appearances since he was, after all, pursuing the Communist program with as much or more vigor than any of the other satellite leaders. However, Stalin not only demanded that the Soviet pattern be followed but also that it be imposed and checked by Soviet agents. Since Tito refused to permit this, Stalin decided that he must be removed. He apparently believed that the Cominform denunciation would be sufficient to bring down Tito. If he planned other concrete measures, either they miscarried or Tito managed to frustrate them. The Yugoslav party, aside from Hebrang and one or two other highly placed leaders, rallied behind Tito. The Yugoslav people, grievously oppressed by Communists of their own nationality, undoubtedly preferred not to have Soviet commissars added to their burdens. As a result, Tito survived.

What has been called "Titoism" was an effect, not a cause, of Stalin's excommunication of Tito. As Adam Ulam points out, only after the break did the Yugoslav regime "begin to exhibit some of the characteristics of which it was wrongly accused in 1948. . . ."[8] In 1950 Tito slackened the pace of collectivization and in 1951 called off the drive (for the time being). He made efforts to apply the carrot rather than the stick to his workers by economic (but not party) "decentralization" and "workers' control." He accepted aid from the West, but avoided any commitments which would require him to change internal conditions. Milovan Djilas, one of the two Yugoslav party secretaries at the time of the break and also minister of propaganda, criticized the USSR for alleged bureaucratism, state capitalism, and imperialism, and helped to forge a "Titoist" ideology of sorts, claiming for it the quality of being "truly Leninist." All this sounded a good deal like Trotskyism, but Tito, attempting to appeal to other Communists who had fought with Stalin against Trotsky, avoided any identification with his name. As for Djilas, he went on from attacking Stalin to attacking Tito and Communism in general and ended in a Yugoslav prison. However, Tito held on to "Titoism," claiming that Stalin, not he, was the one who had ceased to be a good Communist. He managed to resist Moscow's wrath and the peril of invasion, induce the West to conclude that his Communism was at least different from Stalin's and perhaps even a sham, and meanwhile maintain firm control over Yugoslavia, until Stalin died and the prospects changed.

• [8] Adam B. Ulam, *Titoism and the Cominform* (Cambridge: Harvard University Press, 1952), p. 137.

PURGES IN EASTERN EUROPE

Tito's successful defiance of Stalin's ban had a great impact on the other satellites. Stalin recognized in Tito a grave danger to his entire system and redoubled his efforts to transform East European society and establish totalitarian controls—in part merely in continuation of what he had already begun, but also in feverish haste lest Tito find successful imitators in other countries of Eastern Europe.

A number of Communists in the satellites were accused of "Titoism," but there is no clear evidence that any of them had any particular attachment to Tito, except perhaps in Albania. Certainly some of the leaders were guilty, if not of the crimes with which they were charged, then of the modest wish that they could obtain a degree of independence from Moscow approaching that which Tito had enjoyed before 1948. But Tito had managed to survive Stalin's denunciation and thus escape Moscow's control only because he had an apparatus loyal to him personally, and since not a single satellite leader had such a machine, it would have been foolhardy indeed for any of them to risk provoking Stalin's wrath as Tito had done. In any case, during 1949 the Albanian Koçi Xoxe, the Bulgarian Traicho Kostov, and the Hungarian László Rajk were executed for "nationalist deviations," that is, "Titoism." The Pole Władysław Gomułka escaped with imprisonment and lived to fight another day. The Bulgarian George Dimitrov, who died in Moscow in 1949, had earlier had good relations with Tito, and may have owed his demise to that fact. The Czechoslovaks Novy, Clementis, and others were purged from the party.

Since 1947 the most publicized and most important victims of the Communist regimes in Eastern Europe have been Communists themselves. However, high clergy of the Roman Catholic Church, who remained staunch opponents of Communism (and had resisted Communist infiltration into the church hierarchy more successfully than the leaders of any other organization), were also prominent among those attacked. Tito placed the Croatian Archbishop Stepinac under house arrest as early as 1941 and after the war sentenced him to prison, although in December 1951 Tito released him, obtaining favorable publicity abroad. The Czechoslovak Archbishop Beran was interned in March 1951, and the Polish Cardinal Wyszynski was arrested in September 1953 (after Stalin's death). But the most publicized case of a clergyman was that of Cardinal Mindszenty of Hungary, arrested in December 1948 and forced through torture to "confess" to a series of crimes.[9] The next highest-ranking

• [9] He was released during the Hungarian Revolution, and after the uprising was put down obtained asylum in the American Embassy in Budapest.

Roman Catholic cleric of Hungary, Archbishop Groesz, was arrested and "confessed" in June 1951. Many lesser priests were dealt with more harshly and less publicly. The Communists made strenuous efforts to create "national Catholic" movements by using collaborating priests, but such attempts came to little. The Roman Catholic Church remained an unsolved problem, as serious as that of peasant smallholding, for the satellite satraps.

During the last year of Stalin's life the only slightly veiled anti-Semitism shown in Soviet policy counted victims in the satellite countries. Leading Communists who were Jewish, such as Ana Pauker in Rumania and Bedrich Geminder in Czechoslovakia, disappeared. The most publicized case was that of the general secretary of the Czechoslovak party, Rudolf Slansky. By this time the alleged failings of the purged satellite leaders had become a little mixed. In November 1952 not only Slansky, who had the reputation of being a "Muscovite" (that is, a docile tool of Stalin) and who was Jewish, but also Clementis, who was accused of "Slovak nationalism" and who was not Jewish, were tried in Prague and hanged. Clementis was apparently left over from the earlier purge of "Titoists," while Slansky was accused of "cosmopolitanism," "Zionism," and other offenses which were being attributed to persons being purged in the USSR during the same period.

The satellites had advanced far enough along the road to "socialism" to enjoy the blessings of Five-Year Plans, collectivization, and purges. Such was Stalin's contribution to Eastern Europe.

Communist Expansion in Asia (1945–1957)

★
★
★
★
★
★
★
★
★
★

CHAPTER 26

COMMUNIST RESISTANCE MOVEMENTS

During the war in Asia, as in Europe, the Communists achieved a prominent place in the resistance movements against Axis occupation. However, in Europe the Communists were unable to use their prestige in the resistance to obtain power, except in Yugoslavia; in all the other satellites Communist regimes were installed by Soviet troops. In Asia the Chinese and Vietnamese Communists were able to move on from positions of strength in resistance movements to take power; in North Korea the Communist regime was installed by Soviet troops; elsewhere the Communist bid for power failed, at least for the time being, as in Europe.

Nevertheless, the West reacted to the rise of Asian Communism in a rather different manner than it did to the European Communist successes. Debate raged at length as to whether Mao Tse-tung and Ho Chi Minh were really Communists at all and even if so, whether they were or would be friendly or subservient to Moscow. Kim Il Sung's North Korean regime was instantly recognized to be similar to the puppet juntas of Eastern Europe, but the other Asian Communists were often regarded as somehow more "reformist" or "nationalist" than European Communists. Many Asian intellectuals and other social groups were similarly confused. They often knew less about the USSR than Europeans did, and in particular the Communist use of anti-imperialist slogans appealed to them strongly and made them more willing to accept the party's claims to represent the real interests of Asians. Both Western confusion and Asian ignorance of Communist aims and techniques in Asia facilitated the party's task. But the effect on the peoples over whom control was obtained was substantially the same in Asia as in Europe, and Moscow's prestige and power were even more greatly enhanced by the Asian results.

China and Indo-China were the chief countries where Communists built up solid strength for themselves in the resistance period; to a lesser extent they succeeded in doing so in the Philippines, Burma, and Indonesia. The most important were of course the Chinese Communists. During the war they managed to set up, behind Japanese lines in north China (insofar as there were any lines), authorities similar to Popular Front regimes in which the openly Communist membership was restricted to one-third and the other representatives were selected by Communists from small peasants and landlords. In the realm of agriculture, the chief economic activity, the Communists confined themselves to a rent-limitation program (see p. 329) and temporarily muted the ideological note in their public statements and actions. Nevertheless a Party Reform (*Cheng-feng*) movement, directed against both Left and Right "deviationists," was carried out by Mao within Communist ranks during 1942–1943, while the war was in progress.

Despite Nationalist-Communist clashes, Chiang Kai-shek went on record with the view that the Chinese Communists were a "political" problem, and in May 1944 talks began on the relationship of the Communist army and regime with the Chungking government. In September General Patrick Hurley was sent to Chungking as a special American ambassador to assist in these discussions, in order to try to foster a consolidated anti-Japanese war effort. General Hurley, who expressed the belief that the Chinese Communists were something like "Oklahoma Republicans," had little effect on the negotiations. In November the Communists declared that they desired a new coalition government, not entrance into the single-party Nationalist regime. Chiang's representatives proposed to convene a "Political Consultative Conference" to discuss the formation of a genuinely unified and constitutional government as well as other matters.

In August 1945 a treaty was concluded between the USSR and the Chinese Nationalist government in which Chiang, bowing to the inevitable, honored those Yalta commitments of President Roosevelt which had been made at Chinese expense. However, the treaty also bound the Soviets to continue to recognize Chiang as the leader of China's only legal government. The Chinese Communists thereupon agreed to the Nationalist proposal for a Political Consultative Conference.

THE AFTERMATH OF JAPANESE SURRENDER

At this point in the negotiations between Chiang and Mao the surrender of Japan changed the whole situation. It was agreed that Chinese troops would accept Japanese surrender in China (except for Manchuria) and northern Indo-China, Soviet troops in Manchuria and Korea north of the thirty-eighth parallel, American troops in Japan, south Korea, the Philippines, and other areas, British troops in southern Indo-China and Indonesia, and so forth.

In Indo-China, where only as recently as March 1945 the Japanese had taken over the country entirely from the French, Ho Chi Minh proclaimed the "Democratic Republic of Vietnam" in September. Chiang's forces in northern Indo-China were reluctant to permit the French to restore their control; furthermore, curiously enough, they were quite willing to co-operate with Ho Chi Minh's regime. The British turned the south over to the French, but not until February 1946 did the Chinese allow the French to regain the north. Having already agreed to concede the kingdoms of Cambodia and Laos a measure of autonomy, the French, finding Ho Chi Minh in control of much of Vietnam and remaining in some doubt about his real aims, decided to negotiate with him as well. Early in 1946 Ho Chi Minh expanded his Popular Front regime considerably and in May signed an agreement with the French for the inclusion of an independent Vietnam within the French Union. However, when the French attempted to present Ho Chi Minh with the *fait accompli* of a government for Cochin China (the most solid French stronghold in Indo-China) separate from Vietnam, armed clashes resulted. By December 1946 Ho Chi Minh's government of Vietnam and the French were engaged in a full-fledged war which was to continue for eight years.

In Japan the Communists for the moment employed only parliamentary tactics. In the Philippines, under Luis Taruc, they had taken over the largest resistance group on Luzon island, called the Hukbalahaps (abbreviation of a Tagalog name meaning "Anti-Japanese Resistance Society"), and the "Huks" continued sporadic, small-scale rebellion against the newly independent (1946) Philippine Republic. Similarly, in Burma the anti-Japanese resistance movement gave the Communists their opportunity. They were influential in the federation of resistance organizations, the A.F.P.F.L. (Anti-Fascist People's Freedom League), which immediately after the war demanded independence for Burma from the British. Negotiations for this objective, begun in February 1946, encountered obstacles. The less disciplined wing of the Burmese Communist party thereupon broke off from the official organization, taking the name "Red Flag" Communists as against the Moscow-oriented "White Flag" Communists, and began armed resistance to the British. In September, when negotiations with Aung San, chief of the A.F.P.F.L., appeared on the verge of success, the "White Flag" group broke off relations with the nationalists and soon were in open rebellion. Burma entered a period of prolonged chaos. In Indonesia the Communists had taken part in the resistance movement, some of their leaders keeping the public coloration of "nationalists," and they fought alongside the real nationalists against the Dutch from the moment that the latter started to take over from the British, who had accepted Japanese surrender. Immediately after the surrender, in August 1945, an Indonesian Republic had been proclaimed. After much inconclusive skirmishing, the Dutch granted the Republic a grudging and uneasy kind of recognition in March 1947. The Communists remained in the nationalist movement, holding their hand for the time being.

In Korea and China (by way of Manchuria) the Soviets were directly involved in the effort to spread Communist control in Asia. In both Korea and Manchuria the Japanese surrender was accepted without incident. However, north China promptly became the scene of a feverish race for territory between the Nationalist government and the Communists, the Japanese frequently managing only with difficulty to surrender to the former as they were ordered. U.S. air forces aided in transporting Chiang's troops to the Shanghai and Peiping areas.

In December 1945 was held the Moscow Council of Foreign Ministers conference, which considered the problem of internal affairs in China and Korea. For Korea, a Joint Soviet-American Commission was established to form a provisional government and to prepare a plan for a four-power trusteeship for a period up to five years. The Commission accomplished literally nothing and even failed to agree to submit two contradictory reports with a covering joint letter reporting failure to agree. The Soviets, permitting no Westerner to enter north Korea, proceeded to establish Popular Front organizations and a puppet provisional government, which in February 1946 was renamed the "Provisional People's Committee of North Korea." It was headed by Kim Il Sung, a veteran Communist who, like other prominent members of the regime, had been trained in Moscow. The North Korean government proceeded to institute land distribution and nationalization of industry, establish government-controlled "trade-unions," hold fraudulent elections, and introduce a constitution modeled on that of the USSR.

The foreign ministers also discussed China. The Soviets, who had watched United States assistance to Chiang with alarm, demanded American withdrawal from China. The United States and the USSR thereupon agreed that the troops of both powers should be evacuated as soon as possible; furthermore, that neither power should interfere in Chinese affairs, although they expressed the joint expectation that Chiang would introduce "democratic elements" into his government. The Soviets, and indeed the Americans also for the next few months, interpreted this phrase to mean inclusion of Communists. In order to implement these decisions and to prevent the civil war which seemed likely to break out as a result of the scramble for north China, President Truman sent General George C. Marshall to Chungking in January 1946. Truman simultaneously declared that it was the United States' wish to see in existence a strong Nationalist government; Secretary of State Byrnes added that the government should be broadened to include the "so-called Communists."

THE CHINESE CIVIL WAR

As General Marshall was arriving in Chungking, the previously agreed-upon Political Consultative Conference was meeting. With Marshall's help, it reached agreement on a military truce and the maintenance of the political status quo. A genuinely constitutional and parliamentary regime was to be set up in stages, and if that was done, the Communist armies were to be integrated into the national army.

However, the status quo was shattered a few months later when the Soviet troops began to withdraw from Manchuria. This rich province, on which Chiang was counting heavily to restore his grave financial and economic position, was systematically looted by the Soviet army. Midway through the looting operation, the Soviet command offered Chiang joint Sino-Soviet management of the remaining industry, but he refused, and the Soviets completed the inflicting of damage amounting to an estimated two billion dollars. Manchuria was not included in the military truce agreement secured through the mediation of General Marshall. As the Soviet forces withdrew, the all-important character of that omission became clear. The USSR technically adhered to an agreement with Chiang covering terms of withdrawal, even postponing for three months its evacuation of Mukden and Changchun when the Nationalists, blocked by the Chinese Communists, were unable to keep to the schedule which had been arranged. However, the Soviets also rendered vital aid to the Chinese Communists, turning over to them vast stores of surrendered Japanese arms and permitting them to move at will into areas under their control. As the armies of Chiang forced their way into the chief cities, they found themselves virtually besieged by the Chinese Communists, compelled to rely on uncertain rail traffic for supplies, and no better off than the Japanese had been in many Chinese areas they had "occupied." The military mistake (pointed out by American advisers at the time) involved in Chiang's unsuccessful effort to regain Manchuria soon became plain, especially since he committed his best troops for the task and left the Communists still in control of much territory between Manchuria and south China, where his power was more solidly based.

By the summer of 1946 the situation was rapidly deteriorating. The USSR had begun a broad-gauged attack on American policy, concentrating much attention on the Far East. The Soviets were also publicly attacking the "Kuomintang" regime which they still recognized as the only legal government of China, and supported the Chinese Communist cause with increasing frankness. General Marshall's efforts to patch up violations of the truce brought him little thanks from either the Nationalists, many of whom desired an all-out attempt to destroy the Communists, or the Communists, who accused him of all manner of misdeeds.

In November 1946 Chiang held a National Convention, which was boycotted by the Communists and certain other parties, but which nevertheless adopted a constitution in the spirit of the PCC agreements, thanks largely to the efforts of the Social Democratic leader, Carsun Chang. The Social Democrats and the Youth party joined the new government established by the constitution, but the "Democratic League" of other smaller parties defected to the Communists. In this government Chiang was elected president by the National Assembly, but the opposition candidate for vice-president, General Li Tsung-jen, won.

At the start of the Marshall mission the Nationalist government had been warned that United States aid would be contingent on a settlement with the Communists and the introduction of reforms. Since these conditions had not been met, in August 1946 the United States embargoed all arms assistance to Chiang,[1] just at the moment that the Chinese Com-

• [1] The embargo was lifted in May 1947, but still no substantial U.S. aid was forthcoming.

munists had received from the Soviets the arms taken from the Japanese in Manchuria, and quite possibly substantial shipments of United States Lend-Lease war matériel stockpiled at Vladivostok.[2] Chiang was also experiencing grave domestic difficulties. Emphasizing loyalty above efficiency, he did little to check corruption and maladministration in his regime. Private business was hurt by the necessity of competing with the government-favored monopolies of the Soong and Kung families. The intellectuals were increasingly alienated from the Nationalist government, which used police measures against university faculties and student bodies as the Civil War got under way. General Marshall believed that his mission could not be achieved. In January 1947 he was recalled to become secretary of state, and shortly after his departure full-scale civil war broke out.

In the Chinese Civil War the Nationalist government suffered a virtually unbroken series of defeats as the victorious Communist armies marched southward. The Nationalist strategy was generally to capture cities rather than to destroy enemy forces, which was virtually no military strategy at all. Chiang's best armies were bottled up in Manchuria, where by the summer of 1948 they had to be supplied by air. By that autumn they had been forced to surrender, and Peiping capitulated soon afterward. Although still faced by superior Nationalist equipment, the Communists skillfully maneuvered and routed an army of over a million men at Tungshan, just south of the Grand Canal, in December 1948.

As a result Chiang retired from the presidency and General Li became acting president, but he had neither the prestige nor the funds to succeed. The Communists regrouped and crossed the Yangtze River in April 1949. The Nationalist government fled to Szechuan province, which it was forced to abandon in December. General Li escaped to the United States, while Chiang, who had already withdrawn to Formosa with the government's financial reserves (which Li had needed so badly) and many troops, took over the presidency again in March 1950.

The Chinese Communists proclaimed Peking (formerly Peiping) capital of their new government in September 1949. Maintaining the Popular Front facade, they called representatives of the Democratic League and a few defected Nationalists together with their own delegates to a People's Political Consultative Conference. This body set up a Central People's

• [2] The evidence on this point remains chiefly circumstantial, since naturally both the Soviets and the Chinese Communists would have been interested in concealing any such shipments which did occur. The evidence from Soviet sources is sifted in George Tokmakoff, "An Analytical Study of *Pravda* on Sino-Soviet Relations, 1945–1955" (Unpublished M.A. thesis, University of Washington, 1957).

Government of the People's Republic of China. Mao Tse-tung became chairman of the government and military council as well as chairman of the party. General Chu Teh was the effective chief of the military. Chou En-lai, as chairman of the State Administrative Council, was in effect prime minister. Liu Shao-ch'i, the party ideologist, held a number of important posts including the presidency of the Sino-Soviet Friendship Association, established in October 1949.

Any doubt as to the authenticity of the regime's "Communism" ought to have been removed by the signing of the Sino-Soviet treaty of February 1950, after a lengthy visit by Mao to Moscow. The treaty covered political, military, economic, and cultural matters. It provided for an alliance ostensibly directed against any possible further aggression by Japan or by any state joining Japan "directly or indirectly" in such aggression. The Soviets undertook to supply important industrial equipment to China, and to return to China the rights obtained at Yalta over the Manchurian railways, Port Arthur, and Dairen either at the time a Japanese peace treaty was signed or in 1952, whichever came first. The Soviets secured joint control with China over four companies to be set up in Sinkiang and Manchuria. But even before the treaty was signed, the USSR had gained in China—the most populous nation in the world, which totalitarian control promised to convert rapidly into a world power—something less than a satellite, something more than an ally.

THE COMMUNIST OFFENSIVE OF 1948

The launching of a full-scale Chinese Communist offensive in 1947 was immediately followed by a co-ordinated Soviet advance in Asia. The Far Eastern effort was managed by the Cominform, founded in September 1947, which, although nominally an association confined to European Communist parties, issued material and directives for Asia and elsewhere as well. In February 1948 the Cominform sponsored a Youth Conference in Calcutta which evidently served to prepare the beginning or intensification of armed Communist rebellions in India, Burma, Malaya, the Philippines, Indonesia, and Indo-China which occurred within the few months following. The great Communist Far Eastern offensive was climaxed by the direct armed aggression in Korea, which was from all indications intended to have a strong effect on Japan, if not to bring Communists to power there, and also to maintain the tremendous psychological momentum resulting from Chinese Communist capture of the entire mainland a few months earlier.

In India the strongest Communist provincial organization, that of

Andhra (since organized as a separate Indian state), was entrusted with the task of converting endemic peasant unrest in the Telengana district of Hyderabad into an armed uprising. By July 1948 the Communists claimed to have "liberated" twenty-five hundred villages, and they seemed to be on the way toward establishing an enclave of control similar to Mao's earlier inland domains in China. However, Nehru's India was not Chiang's China. In September the Indian government occupied the state of Hyderabad (whose Nizam was then still resisting incorporation within the new nation of India) and crushed the uprising by means of armed force.

In Burma the A.F.P.F.L. leader, U Nu (who had just inherited leadership when Aung San and all the other major figures except himself had been machine-gunned in a fantastic plot by a prewar Burmese leader), secured British consent to independence for the Union of Burma which was proclaimed in January 1948. He was immediately faced with a rebellion of Than Tun's "White Flag" Communists, who now joined the schismatic "Red Flag" Communists in open warfare against the new government. Revolt also flared among certain of the non-Burmese minority peoples. In March 1949 U Nu banned the Communist party and launched a concerted effort to suppress the rebels. The government began to gain ground in 1950, and after two more years was successful in pacifying most of the country.

In Malaya postwar British efforts to reach a political settlement providing for local self-government had been hampered by tensions between the Malays and the large population of Chinese origin. In February 1948 a step was taken toward self-government by the creation of a Malay Federation, which excluded the British crown colony of Singapore. Shortly afterward the Communists of Malaya (who were mostly Chinese) launched an attack on the British and the new government, combining guerrilla warfare with planned individual murders. In February 1949 the Communists proclaimed the formation of a "Malayan National Liberation Army" with the aim of establishing a Communist state of Malaya. The British tried several tactics, finally using a device similar to that used in the Philippines of resettling Chinese squatter-farmers in the guerrilla-held areas. By 1954 they had managed to reduce the Communist threat to a minimum, and the following June they felt confident enough to reject peace feelers from the "Liberation Army."

In the Philippines it appears that Moscow's orders to Luis Taruc and the "Huks" to launch a full-scale revolt arrived just at the moment when the new president, Elpidio Quirino, was attempting a peaceful settlement with them. Taruc broke off the talks abruptly, admitted he was a Communist, and proceeded to exploit agrarian discontent in order to spread his rebellion. The government tried to combat Taruc's revolt, but it had no success until the spring of 1950, when the new minister of defense, Ramon Magsaysay, embarked on a policy of resettling the peasant guerrillas and protecting loyal villages. After his election as president in 1953 he succeeded in capturing Taruc and in breaking up most of the remaining "Huk" forces.

In Indonesia the Dutch-Indonesian nationalist agreement of March 1947 broke down four months later when the Dutch launched a "police action" intended to restore their control over the archipelago. In January 1948 a United Nations-mediated truce was arranged on the basis of maintenance of the status quo by both sides. However, in September the Communists, led by Muso (who had just returned from Moscow), revolted against the nationalist government: The nationalists rapidly suppressed the uprising, killing in the fighting or executing the chief Communist leaders, including Muso. The Communists were decisively defeated, and the action of the Indonesian nationalists earned them strong American support. However, profiting from the confusion of the moment, in December 1948 the Dutch conducted a surprise parachutist attack which captured all the main nationalist leaders. American and other foreign pressure compelled the Dutch to release them and eventually, in November 1949, to recognize the Indonesian Republic as one of a number of states in a United States of Indonesia. Within a few months the other states dissolved themselves into the Republic, which in 1954 severed its last ties with the Netherlands. However, by that time the Communists had again emerged as a powerful force within the shaky parliamentary system. By 1957 President Sukarno was relying heavily on their support in his schemes for establishing "guided democracy" in Indonesia.

In Indo-China Ho Chi Minh's war on the French was intensified. Finally recognizing that Ho Chi Minh had managed to mobilize much of the force of Vietnamese nationalism on his side, the French attempted to counter with the establishment of an Empire of Vietnam under Bao Dai, who had collaborated at various times with the Japanese and Ho Chi Minh himself. The pyschological effects of this move were scarcely noticeable. In 1949 Chinese Communist victory led Ho Chi Minh to doff his nationalist mask and overtly express his Communist aims. In January 1950 the Peking regime accorded Communist Vietnam diplomatic recognition, and shortly afterward Moscow did the same. Southern

Chinese bases were made available for Vietminh armies,[3] which were joined by Communist Chinese military advisers who trained them in the use of Russian weapons. The situation in Vietnam resembled that in Greece three years earlier in that the strong Communist forces shifted back and forth between regular warfare and guerrilla tactics, using a base and a sanctuary across the border in neighboring Communist territory.

THE KOREAN WAR AND JAPAN

Korea was the country chosen for the risky adventure which marked the high point of the Communist Far Eastern offensive. After the stalemate on the Joint Soviet-American Commission, the case of Korea was taken to the United Nations, which in November 1947 passed a resolution calling for free elections for an all-Korean government. In 1948 a U.N. Temporary Commission was sent to supervise such elections, but the Soviets barred it from North Korea, and the Commission was able only to assist in the establishment of a Republic of Korea in the south, under Syngman Rhee as president. In October 1948 the Soviets recognized the North Korean government, and the United States recognized the Republic in January 1949. A few months earlier the USSR had withdrawn its troops from North Korea as a means of forcing the United States to do likewise in the south, and by June 1949 American troops evacuated Korea.

On June 25, 1950, the large North Korean army, trained and equipped by the Soviets, attacked, plainly on Stalin's orders, southward across the thirty-eighth parallel, advancing the palpably absurd claim that the South Koreans had attacked first. Two days later President Truman ordered United States air and naval forces to aid the Republic of Korea, and three days afterward United States ground forces were also committed. The United Nations Security Council considered the matter, and because the Soviet delegate had walked out in January 1950 in protest at the failure to admit Communist China, no Soviet veto could be cast to block the Council's decision to resist North Korean aggression. At U.N. invitation, President Truman appointed General MacArthur commander of United Nations forces and simultaneously announced an accelerated program of aid to the Nationalist government on Formosa, the Philippines, and France and the "Associated States" of Indo-China.

• [3] Short for Vietnam Independence League, the Popular Front organization set up in 1941. The name was kept for Ho Chi Minh's armed forces after a government was established.

For the first three months the Korean-U.N. defense was overcome by a speedy Communist advance to the perimeter of the southern port of Pusan. However, in September MacArthur mounted a double blow at the North Korean armies, counterattacking from Pusan while launching a seaborne invasion at the middle of the peninsula near Seoul. The Communists were rapidly ejected from South Korea, and with the implicit sanction of a resolution of the U.N. General Assembly, in October MacArthur's forces advanced into the north, nearing the Chinese and Soviet borders. After issuing a warning via Indian channels, in November Chinese Communist "volunteers" crossed the border to attack U.N. forces. MacArthur was compelled to retreat hastily to the south of the thirty-eighth parallel. In April 1951 he was relieved by President Truman, who was disturbed in particular by MacArthur's unauthorized invitation to the enemy command to negotiate an armistice, stipulating his own conditions.

The new commander, General Matthew Ridgway, slowly advanced his lines once more so that by June 1951 they were across the thirty-eighth parallel over most of the front. A stalemate ensued, in which the Soviet delegate to the United Nations suggested truce negotiations, and the United States and the United Nations accepted. Such talks began in July 1951 at Panmunjom, while fighting continued on a reduced scale. The talks dragged on for two years. It was at length decided that the truce line should generally follow the battle line, but no agreement could be reached on exchange of prisoners. Remembering the moral and psychological effect of the forced repatriation of Soviet citizens carried out by Western forces in Europe after World War II (see p. 448), the United States government insisted that prisoners on each side should be free to decide whether or not they wished to be returned to their former command. On this point the Communist negotiators refused to give way. The talks made no further progress during the last year of Stalin's life.

The North Korean attack had apparently been co-ordinated with an effort by the Japanese Communists, under Cominform instructions of January 1950, to disrupt the domestic political scene and to prepare for an opportunity to seize power in Japan. The Japanese Communist leader, Sanzo Nozaka (sometimes known as Okano), who had spent much of the 1940's at Mao's headquarters, was denounced for "Right opportunism" and his tactic of "peaceful revolution." Nozaka promptly admitted the charges and accepted the new policy, which required him and the other leaders to go underground while the open party took a militantly revolutionary tack. Attacks on American citizens in Tokyo in

May 1950 by Communist-led mobsters, coupled with agitation against both the Japanese government and the occupation forces, hastened the decision in Washington to draw up a peace treaty with Japan. In September 1951 a treaty was concluded, although the Soviet Union, the Communist and Nationalist Chinese governments, India, and Burma did not sign (Nationalist China and India signed separate treaties in 1952, and the USSR did so in 1957). In April 1952 sovereignty was restored to Japan. Although in 1951 the Japanese Communists succeeded in splitting the Socialist party into a left wing willing to collaborate with them to a certain extent and a right wing which refused to do so, they made little further headway in the country.

By 1951 the Communist Far Eastern offensive was temporarily checked (although the Communists were still to secure important gains in Indo-China three years later). Aside from Indo-China, the newly independent Asian nations had turned back their Communist uprisings. Nevertheless the balance of postwar developments in the Far East had been heavily in the Communists' favor. The fall of China to Communism was the greatest success the movement had achieved since the Bolshevik Revolution in Russia and was an event of sufficient magnitude to alter the whole political-power structure of Asia. It enormously increased Soviet prestige and contributed to the spread of Communist doctrines among the intellectuals, whose political importance in an unstable Asian country was perhaps as great as that of any other single social group in Asia. The United States resistance to the North Korean offensive for a time weakened the feeling among many Asians that it was wise or unavoidable to speculate on Communist success, but the Chinese Communist advance restored the position of early 1950, and the success of Asian armies in hurling back Americans had a great psychological effect throughout Asia. The Communists continued to push their political, commercial, and cultural offensive in the Far East, obviously concerning themselves for the time being with the long-term prospect rather than immediate power objectives.

FIRST STEPS OF THE CHINESE COMMUNIST REGIME

Beginning in 1949, the more than half a billion people of China experienced a rapid transformation closely patterned after that imposed upon the peoples of the USSR. Mao wrote, in his pamphlet *On People's Democratic Dictatorship,* published in July 1949, that "the Communist party of the USSR is our very best teacher, and we must learn from it."

The result, according to Richard L. Walker, has been an effort "to capsule over two decades of Soviet history into a few years."[4]

For the first three years one fundamental objective of Mao's regime was reconstruction: the restoration of financial stability, the railway, road, and water communications systems, and the prewar level of production of industrial goods. These measures were prerequisites to the successful application of the Communist type of totalitarian controls. At the same time, a series of mass "drives" was undertaken, designed both to remove inconvenient elements and to develop patterns of behavior which would be essential later on in programs of forced industrialization and social transformation. All such measures were accelerated during the Korean War and justified with reference to it.

In China a civil war preceded the Communists' assumption of control of the national government, in contrast to Russia where it came afterward. It can scarcely be said that any period comparable to that of the New Economic Policy (1921–1927) was to be found in China at all (or, for that matter, in the European satellites). The NEP had been undertaken primarily to conciliate and reassure the peasantry for the time being, for the initial land division sanctioned by Lenin in 1917 had been followed by a premature effort at rural class warfare and collectivization which miscarried, so that the measures of 1921 marked a retreat to 1917 on the "agricultural front." In China, as in the European satellites, land division was carried out by the Communist authorities themselves, utilizing its propaganda value among the peasants to the utmost, which Lenin had failed to do in Russia.

The Agrarian Reform Act, promulgated in June 1950, began to operate rather unobtrusively. However, after Chinese entrance into the Korean War, the pace was stepped up. Although the verbal pretense was maintained, for domestic as well as for foreign consumption, that there were only "volunteers" in Korea, governmental policy left no doubt that it was considered a national war effort. Countless landlords were killed under conditions designed to implicate as many villagers as possible in the violence and thus bind them to the regime. The Chinese land problem was a serious one, but it resulted largely from the pressure of a vast population on an insufficient tillable area, rather than from concentration of ownership in a few hands. Mao's assertion that a few landlords owned most of the land was sheer propagandistic invention.

In November 1950 there was launched the first of the great "drives" under the slogan of "Resist America, Aid Korea." It was accompanied by sweeping propaganda attacks on "American imperialism," as well as

[4] *China Under Communism* (New Haven: Yale University Press, 1955), p. 3.

arrests and falsified public trials of white foreigners, especially missionaries, and palpably lying charges of "germ warfare" by United States forces. Mao's apparent belief that such lies were needed suggests how widespread a sympathy for Americans remained among the Chinese people. The campaign had its simpler and more utilitarian side, however. In connection with the regime's stories that United States planes were dropping "germ-laden insects" on Chinese soil, a large-scale sanitation program was carried out, resulting in such picturesque claims as that eighteen and a half trillion "heads of mosquitoes and flies" were accounted for in 1952. Concurrently with the "Resist America, Aid Korea" drive came another for the "Suppression of Counter-revolutionaries," which term was very loosely applied.

A year after Chinese entrance into Korea, three more mass campaigns were begun. The "Three Anti" movement, whose avowed targets were "corruption, waste, and bureaucracy," had in view complete control of the administrative leadership at all levels. It had two aspects: removal of officials who had served under Chiang's government, and a purge of the Communist party, whose membership had risen from 1,200,000 in 1945 to 5,800,000 in 1951. The total now remained stationary for about two years before rising again toward the seven million mark. The "Five Anti" movement was said to be directed against "tax evasion, bribery, cheating in government contracts, theft of economic intelligence, and stealing of national property." Its actual object was the destruction of private enterprise. From confiscations of the property of large and small businessmen, with or without "show trials," the government realized the equivalent of about one billion American dollars. The most significant result of the campaign was not this financial gain, however, but the establishment of government ownership or control over all industry and commerce. The extent of the regime's progress in taking over the economy was suggested by the 1953 budget, which was twenty times the size of the last prewar Nationalist budget.

The third of the "drives" beginning in late 1951 was the "Ideological Remolding" campaign. The objective was to bring about the submission of the intellectuals, many of whom had so far gone along with the regime but had not been forced to conform precisely to the party line. The degree of positive and active assent to policy which was demanded of the Chinese intellectuals exceeded in breadth and depth anything so far exacted in the USSR, where the intellectuals in certain fields had enjoyed a conditional freedom of silence. In order to achieve the desired result, the element of "thought-struggle" (or, as the West has come to call it, "brainwashing") was strongly emphasized. Group discussions, in which confessions of error and positive protestations of adherence to the party doctrines were *de rigueur*, were held all over the country. Many intellectuals publicly submitted, others escaped to freedom, still others disappeared into concentration camps or were executed.

According to American estimates, all these campaigns together accounted for approximately fifteen million Chinese killed. Even prior to the all-out drive for collectivization beginning in 1955, it was believed that about twenty million Chinese were in concentration camps or were being used by the secret police for forced labor in gigantic construction projects. As in the case of the USSR, such estimates necessarily rest on incomplete information, but they are more than guesses, and the regime itself provided some of the evidence.

In the meantime the Chinese Communists had been occupying the last piece of territory accessible to them without large-scale warfare, namely Tibet. In October 1950 Peking had announced the invasion of that remote land, and in September 1951, after a cautious advance by stages, Mao's troops entered Lhasa, the capital. Occupation was followed by construction of a new road from Tsinghai province to Lhasa in 1953–1955. However, resistance by the Tibetans continued, and in 1957 the Chinese announced a partial withdrawal of troops and a temporary postponement of any extensive plans for social transformation.

Although India had at first reacted sharply to the conquest of Tibet, a pact between Peking and New Delhi was signed in April 1954 by which Prime Minister Nehru accepted the *fait accompli*. The agreement on Tibet was based on "five principles" of international co-operation, which were stated to be nonaggression, noninterference, mutual respect, equality and mutual benefit, and peaceful coexistence. The same principles were proclaimed, in a joint declaration of Chou En-lai and Nehru in June, to be a proper basis for a "peace area" made up of China and India, and later joined by Burma and Indonesia. The Soviet Union blessed the declaration, declaring that the "five principles" also expressed the foundations of Soviet policy. The dissemination of these "principles" in Asia and the attempt to identify them as the real basis of Communist Chinese and Soviet foreign policy were facilitated by the phrase *pañchaçīla* to refer to them. *Pañchaçīla* means the five commandments of Buddhism (and also Taoism). Thereby the Communists hoped to implant their "peace" campaign in the soil of Asian culture.

"SECOND REVOLUTION" IN CHINA

By 1953 the Chinese Communists were in a position to begin the kind of gigantic socio-economic offensive which Stalin had undertaken in 1928 in the USSR. The mass "drives" had aided in the establishment of a number of Communist-controlled mass organizations which boasted memberships running from the tens to the hundreds of millions. Aside from the Communist party and its youth "feeder" organizations, the Komsomol-age New Democratic Youth League and the Young Pioneers, there were the All-China Democratic Women's Federation, the All-China Federation of Trade Unions, the Peasant Associations, and the Co-operatives. The leadership of all these organizations was prepared to follow unquestioningly the directives of the regime.

In late 1952 a State Planning Commission was formed under the chairmanship of Kao Kang. Kao was not one of Mao's Kiangsi Communist clique, but he had been entrusted with the headship of one of the six quasi-military regional administrations which had been established immediately after the 1949 assumption of control, pending the setting up of reliable and smaller-scale provincial administrations. These regions were North China, East China, the Northwest, the Southwest, Central and South China, and the industrial heart of the country, Manchuria, which Kao Kang was allotted. The State Planning Commission prepared a Five-Year Plan, although it is doubtful whether the information was at hand even to determine accurately what the then existing economic situation was.

The plan went into effect in 1953 and was pushed ruthlessly despite the tremendous dislocation which resulted from the great floods of 1954, one of the worst such disasters in the annals of China. Collectivization was undertaken—scarcely three years after land distribution to private holders had taken place—simultaneously with a program of construction of heavy industry. Thus the plan followed the Soviet pattern, and, as in the Soviet case, it was admitted that grain production targets were those which fell the farthest short of attainment as the plan was put into effect. However, as Mao said, the Chinese party intended to "learn" from the Soviet experience, and as in the European satellites the process of collectivization was begun with caution. It was to operate in several stages: "mutual-aid teams" in agriculture, producers' co-operatives (in which income was still distributed partly on the basis of the lands privately held, even though already the labor expended was the chief determinant), and finally complete collective farms. In the summer of 1955, although it had been announced only a year earlier that the objective was limited to putting half of the peasants in producers' co-operatives by the end of the Plan in 1957, a gigantic speed-up was demanded. Mao now declared that collectivization was to be completed by 1957.

In September 1954 a National People's Congress was summoned, and it adopted a constitution for the Chinese People's Republic. The Constitution opened with a preamble declaring that "China has already built an indestructible friendship with the great Union of Soviet Socialist Republics and the People's Democracies." It proceeded to describe the central government. The National People's Congress had a position comparable to the Supreme Soviet of the USSR, with a standing committee, comparable to the Presidium of the Supreme Soviet, which was to operate between sessions. The National People's Congress elected Mao as chairman of the Republic and General Chu Teh as vice-chairman; the standing committee was headed by Liu Shao-ch'i. A State Council, headed by Chou En-lai, was similar to the Soviet Council of Ministers. There was also set up a Supreme Council of National Defense, headed by Mao. The Constitution contained a "bill of rights" much like that of the Soviet Constitution, making clear that "traitors and counter-revolutionaries" had no rights whatsoever.

The Constitution also restored the structure of local government, superseding the six regional administrations. In March 1955 Kao Kang, the former chief of the Manchurian region, was purged, and it was announced that he had committed suicide. There were other purges of high Communist leaders at the same time, including Jao Shu-shih, an important former member of the East China administration. At the time of the adoption of the Constitution a number of non-Communists who had held featured, if powerless, posts, were dropped. Among them was Mme. Sun Yat-sen, widow of the founder of the Chinese Republic and of the Kuomintang, although she had collaborated loyally with Mao.

The most prominent remaining non-Communist (although he was of course a loyal collaborator) was Kuo Mo-jo, who had long before achieved literary renown and retained an apparently important role in the management of cultural life. He assisted in the campaign against pragmatism (which had gained many adherents among Chinese intellectuals in the prewar period) and on all other non-Marxist doctrines in philosophy, historical interpretation, and literary criticism, which was inaugurated in October 1954 by way of a discussion in the Writers' Association. As Stalin had done in the USSR in the mid-1930's, Mao intervened to demand that, in accordance with Marxist canons as he interpreted them, historians point out the "positive" contributions of early figures and movements in Chinese history, such as Confucius and Taoism, in terms of the then prevailing historical "stages." Thus all the past had to be re-examined in terms of the needs of the by now firmly established totalitarian dictatorship. A writer and satirist named Hu Feng, despite the fact that he was a pupil of the regime's favorite author, Lu Hsün (sometimes called the

"Chinese Gorky"), was made the butt of a nationwide attack led by Kuo Mo-jo which was designed to frighten intellectuals into submitting to the new doctrine.

The Chinese Communist regime was rapidly moving in the direction of its chosen objectives. The speeches in February and March 1957 of Mao Tse-tung employing the slogan, "Let one hundred flowers bloom, let one hundred schools of thought contend," was misinterpreted by a number of non-Communist Chinese intellectuals, who proceeded to entrap themselves by relatively outspoken criticism of the regime. They were promptly made the target of sharp public attack, and it was even officially admitted that the slogans had been intended to entrap "enemies." In addition, it is likely that Mao hoped by the two speeches to open a controlled safety-valve for the mass discontent produced by the Chinese First Five-Year Plan and by the other measures taken to establish totalitarian control.

Mao remained unable to achieve his often-repeated aim of "liberating" Formosa. However, he succeeded in winning the admiration and cooperation of a number of non-Communist figures and groups in Asia (and elsewhere)—and, among other things, in persuading them that Communist occupation of Formosa was justifiable. A Peace Conference of the Asian and Pacific Peoples, held in October 1952 in Peking, was completely Communist-controlled but swayed a number of non-Communist delegates. In the wake of the joint "five principles" statement by Chou En-lai and Nehru (see p. 441), the Chinese Communists undertook to influence an international meeting of a much broader representation, the Asian-African Conference held in April 1955 in Bandung, Indonesia. Although the meeting was sponsored by the prime ministers of five free south Asian countries, and more than one influential speaker bluntly denounced Communist imperialism, Chou En-lai managed to score impressive diplomatic successes. He appeared to work closely with India's Prime Minister Nehru, and he associated Communist China with anticolonialist formulations which were adopted by the whole Conference, and which led many Asians to believe that the Peking regime supported the cause of freedom and independence. Despite the United Nations condemnation of Communist China as an "aggressor" in Korea, by 1957 a number of Eastern and Western nations (but not the United States, France, and others) had recognized the Peking regime as the legal government of China.

Under the Sino-Soviet treaty of February 1950, the Soviets had bound themselves to return their Manchurian rights and holdings by 1952 or by the time of a conclusion of a peace treaty. Since neither party had signed the 1951 treaty with Japan, the Soviets' obligation was to return them in 1952. They did return the railways, but on Peking's "invitation" they retained the Port Arthur naval base for the time being. The Panmunjom armistice negotiations dragged on; it is uncertain whether the Soviets or the Chinese Communists were the less willing to see them reach a conclusion. There Sino-Soviet relations rested at the death of Stalin in March 1953.

THE MOSCOW-PEKING RELATIONSHIP

It seems clear that although the establishment of Communist power in China was a tremendous victory for the Soviets, it brought them problems as well as advantages. The conquest of territory inhabited by people of dubious loyalty—as Communist regimes have always and rightly regarded the peoples under their control—in itself creates difficulties for the conqueror. Whatever the precise nature of the Moscow-Peking relationship, part of those difficulties in the case of Communist China became the USSR's to cope with.

But China presented the Soviets with special additional problems. China was unlike any other country which fell into Communist hands at the close of the war (except Yugoslavia) in that virtually all the fighting in the conquest of power was done by the forces organized by the national party, despite substantial aid given by the Soviets from surrendered Japanese or American-provided stocks of arms (this was somewhat different from Yugoslavia, where more arms aid was provided by Britain than by the USSR). Apparently Mao, like Tito, built up a reliable party machine of his own which he carried into power. In size and population, China was unique; China had more than twice as many people as the USSR. If the Soviets should try to force some issue, as they did with Tito, and the Chinese Communists should resist, Moscow could not count on a quick military decision, which Stalin may have considered seeking in Yugoslavia, and which the Red Army easily gained in Hungary.

The evidence is that the Chinese party before the conquest of the mainland in 1949 had a leadership quite as doctrinally and organizationally subservient to Moscow as that of the other "fraternal" parties, and that Mao did not claim to be or deserve to be regarded as a heretic in the camp of Marxist-Leninist orthodoxy. In many ways the links between Moscow and Peking were drawn tighter after 1949 as Mao's regime consolidated its power. From 1949 to 1957 the Soviets maintained a powerful hold on the Chinese Communists based on their acknowledged ideological supremacy and the seniority of the Russian Party and Soviet system, reinforced by the presumed indispensability of Moscow's financial, technical, and military aid and advice to the Chinese domestic transformation and of the Soviet alliance to the Chinese international position. The result was that the international Communist movement from 1949 to 1957 and in many ways thereafter (see Chapter 29) continued to operate as a generally coordinated and harmonious unit as its strength increased, especially in Asia, Africa, and Latin America.

It is true that a number of foreign observers had suggested in the 1940's that the West might hope to ally itself with the Chinese Communists, who were supposed not really to be Communists but something else, perhaps only "agrarian reformers," against the Soviets, who were real Communists. In the 1950's some hopes were expressed (in certain cases by the same people as before) that the West might succeed in allying itself with the Soviets, who had ceased to be truly Communists, against the Chinese, who had not. In neither case was there any substantial evidence for the assessments underlying these hopes. It is still not clear whether international Communist harmony in the period 1949 to 1957, insofar as it was accounted for by the Moscow-Peking relationship, was founded on a community of aims, Peking's subservience to Moscow, or both. In assessing the possibilities before and after 1957, however, it might do no harm to consider that power factors might have disrupted or might still disrupt the Moscow-Peking relationship without necessarily yielding any net benefit to the non-Communist world. In World War II, when the United States and Great Britain allied themselves with one totalitarian regime against another, the latter was destroyed, but the first succeeded in consequence in immensely increasing the power with which it sought to destroy its erstwhile allies. In Orwell's *Nineteen Eighty-Four,* the novelist envisages a world in which not two but three totalitarian states exist, all non-totalitarian regimes having disappeared from the planet, but the totalitarian states still wage war on one another incessantly, constantly altering their allies as they do so. The history and nature of totalitarianism to date suggest that when totalitarians fall out, others ought to beware of making confident assumptions about the probable result.

Stalin's Retrenchment (1945–1953)

CHAPTER 27

FORCED REPATRIATION

One of Stalin's most notable achievements was his success in concealing from the West the depth of disaffection which the Soviet peoples demonstrated in 1941 and later. At the end of the war in Europe, his first concern seemed to be to cover the traces of mass hostility to the Soviet regime. This required speedy repatriation of Soviet citizens still outside the zone of Red Army authority. Other domestic objectives could be deferred for a time.

On V-E Day there were more than five million Soviet citizens west of Soviet borders; of these perhaps three million were in territory occupied by Western military forces. They had been either prisoners of war, forced laborers, or simply civilians retreating from the front. Many of them had deliberately fled or surrendered to the Germans. A great many others, although captured in battle or sent into forced labor by the Nazis, were glad to have escaped the clutches of the Soviet regime. Most of them had family, friends, or at least familiar surroundings waiting for them hundreds or thousands of miles away in the USSR, while some scarcely knew what country they were in when the fighting stopped. For some, the attractions of home prevailed over hostility to the Soviet regime, at least at the start, but many such people re-defected, either en route or after they reached the USSR, when they found that the Soviet authorities looked on all of them with suspicion and regarded them as possible criminals. They had to be repatriated twice. Others were determined not to return home and to stay in the West at any cost.

At Yalta the Big Three had agreed that all citizens of Allied countries should be repatriated at the end of the war, and there was no provision for any alternative. The agreement chiefly affected the citizens of the USSR and countries newly occupied by Soviet troops where Communist regimes were being set up, since there were few Western nationals behind Red lines. There was no special discrimination against Soviet citizens. The Western commanders, like the Western statesmen at Yalta, took it for granted that everyone wanted to go home. If someone did not, it was often thought that he must have been a traitor who feared justice. Most American soldiers took this view readily, since they were thinking above all of home and how soon they could get back. Therefore the orders for repatriation of all Allied nationals were at first widely thought by Westerners to be self-evidently reasonable.

The Soviet citizens were herded into camps for "displaced persons" (DP's). Many successfully pretended to come from the Ukrainian areas of pre-1939 Poland, which exempted them from repatriation to the USSR, or the Baltic states, whose annexation by the Soviets had not been legally recognized by the United States, although no effort had been made at the Big Three conferences to secure their actual freedom. Other Soviet DP's said they were Poles, Czechoslovaks, or Yugoslavs. (Similarly, many Russians who had fallen into Hitler's hands had claimed to be Ukrainians or Cossacks to obtain the relatively preferential treatment accorded to the minorities.) Many others simply vanished into the local population. However, large numbers of Soviet citizens were so classified and placed in DP camps by United States army authorities for transportation to the USSR.

The camps were managed by the United Nations Relief and Rehabilitation Administration (UNRRA), under the direction of Fiorello LaGuardia, former mayor of New York. UNRRA employees were ordered to "try to persuade the DP's to agree voluntarily to proceed to Russia." Anti-Soviet propaganda in the camps was prohibited, although ample Soviet propaganda was made available, and mass meetings in the camps were discouraged lest they "provide an opportunity for dissidents, hecklers, and anti-repatriation organizers and . . . result in emotional mob action" against Soviet liaison officers. Mixed Soviet-Allied teams undertook to question those labeled as Soviet citizens and persuade them to accept repatriation. For the most part Western officers simply undertook to assist the Soviet officers in inducing the DP's to return, and if persuasion failed, used force.

Truly horrible scenes ensued. Men and women killed themselves in large numbers rather than be sent back. They fought soldiers who were trying to load them on trucks, threw themselves from moving trains, even burned themselves to death. One by no means unique incident occurred at Kempten, Bavaria, in August 1945. According to a report based on eyewitness accounts, "American troops drove up to the camp and ordered the inmates, who were mostly in church, to board the trucks for transportation to the nearest Soviet assembly point. When the Russians unanimously refused, the troops broke into the church, overturned the altar, manhandled the priest, dragged out men, women and children, clubbing them with rifle butts and throwing them into the trucks. Some of the women, to save their children, tossed them into a neighboring camp for Baltic refugees"[1]—where they were safe from forcible repatriation, at least.

Increasingly puzzled and alarmed by the response of Soviet citizens to the threat of repatriation, United States military authorities became less and less willing to co-operate with Soviet officers. In early 1947 forcible repatriation was officially halted. By that time the West had repatriated to the USSR over two million people, and the Soviets had repatriated from their own jurisdiction in Eastern Europe over three million. Thus well over five million had been restored to Soviet authority. There remained in the West, now apparently secure from being sent back to the USSR, but with uncertain futures, something like half a million "nonreturners" (*nevozvrashchentsy*). After talking to many of them, Louis Fischer wrote, "They love Russia and yearn for Russia. They are political fugitives . . . [they] demonstrate that when Soviet Russians had a choice they voted against the Bolshevik dictatorship. This is the most revealing fact I know about Soviet Russia."[2]

During these years Western forces discovered that defection from Soviet control had not ceased with the fighting. It has been estimated that twenty thousand Soviet soldiers deserted from 1945 to 1948; in early 1948 two American journalists, the Alsop brothers, reported that over thirteen thousand (including four thousand officers and two generals) had fled during the year just past. However, American and British forces were under orders to turn deserters over to their Soviet allies. Such action was usually followed by immediate execution of the men before the eyes

• [1] W. H. Chamberlin in the *New Leader*, as quoted by Eugene Lyons, *Our Secret Allies*, p. 264.

• [2] Quoted by Eugene Lyons, *op. cit.*, p. 257.

of their own units, as a warning to anyone else who thought of flight. Therefore many who escaped avoided Western headquarters and vanished into civilian life as many DP's had done. At the time of the Berlin blockade in 1948, the West generally ceased to turn deserters back to be shot.

While the Soviet army obtained Western co-operation in retrieving defectors, the secret police could not count on that. Nevertheless, under the cover of "Soviet military missions" to Paris and other cities, the Soviet secret police was permitted to operate for a time without serious interference, and in its efforts at "military repatriation" received from Western governments the same facilities given the Soviet army command. MVD[3] abductions from homes in the heart of Paris were frequent until the French press publicized some of the more notorious cases. From then on the MVD had to use greater caution, but still continued its work. As recently as the spring of 1956 such a kidnapping occurred in New York, under the very eyes of United States officials. Of course the Soviets do not manage to kidnap or murder all defectors or avert all defection, but there is no doubt about their determination to be thorough and not to overlook any individual, especially if he is prominent.

THE ZHDANOVSHCHINA

For the most part Stalin achieved his objective of reclaiming the masses of people who had been removed from Soviet soil and control during the war, getting them out from under Western observation, and then executing, punishing, or reindoctrinating them—in general an operation of "reconversion" beside which the restoration of Western soldiers to civilian life was a very minor one indeed. Returning Soviet soldiers, who had seen something of Central Europe while they were still under the regime's control, also required a good deal of reindoctrination. Soviet annexation of territory taken from Germany, Poland, and Czechoslovakia yielded additional millions among whom anti-Soviet attitudes were prevalent. Still vaster was the problem of the some sixty-five million who without moving at all had been for varying lengths of time under Nazi occupation, and there was finally to be considered the attitude of the remainder of the Soviet citizenry, who hoped for the gratitude of the regime which they had saved and expected it to take the form of concessions to freedom and democracy. Stalin had no such acts in mind.

Instead, he and his cohorts began a series of repressive domestic meas-

• [3] The NKVD was renamed MVD (*Ministerstvo Vnutrennykh Del*) at the end of the war when all People's Commissariats became "Ministries."

ures, coupled with the invention of a foreign danger which inaugurated the "Cold War." According to Soviet escapees, as early as 1944 the more reliable Party members were informed in closed meetings of the new slogan, "The war on Fascism ends, the war on capitalism begins." In August 1945 Kalinin, chairman of the Presidium of the Supreme Soviet and titular chief of state, declared to a meeting of rural Party workers that although some enemies had been defeated, others were still in existence. In February 1946 Stalin made a speech restating the old thesis of the inevitability of war as long as capitalism existed. The USSR, he asserted, remained a beleaguered fortress of socialism in a hostile world, and in particular it had to resist the false glitter of bourgeois culture to which many of its citizens were exposed during World War II.

In the summer of 1946 a full-scale ideological campaign was opened against those who had expressed admiration for the free culture of the West and therefore, by implication, dissatisfaction with the regime. The campaign was led by Andrei Zhdanov, who, although a junior member of the Politburo, had emerged from the war in the recognized position of Stalin's chief aide. Zhdanov thundered, "Does it suit us, the representatives of the advanced Soviet culture, to bow before bourgeois culture or play the role of its disciples? Our job is to scourge boldly and to attack bourgeois culture, which is in a state of miasma and corruption!"

At the start Zhdanov's fire was directed at literature; in particular he chose as scapegoats two writers who had gained renown already before the Revolution, the introspective poetess Anna Akhmatova, whom Zhdanov called "a harlot and nun who mixes harlotry and prayer," and Michael Zoshchenko, perhaps the most popular Soviet humorist, whom he labeled "a literary swindler." In August the Party Central Committee passed a resolution declaring that "Soviet literature neither has nor can have any other interests except those of the people and of the State." Neglect of ideology and subservience to Western influence were charged to men prominent in the other arts, including the composers Sergei Prokofiev and Dmitry Shostakovich, and the great film director Sergei Eisenstein, who confessed, "Like a bad sentry, we gaped at the unessential and the secondary, thus forgetting the main thing and abandoning our post." Not long afterward he died, plainly never having recovered from the shock of condemnation.

From the arts the campaign soon spread into other areas of creative and scholarly endeavor. The philosopher G. F. Alexandrov, himself a member of the Orgburo, was denounced for his *History of West European Philosophy*. The foremost Soviet economist, Eugene Varga, was attacked for questioning the certainty of an imminent depression in the United States.

The lash of official spokesmen, following the lead of *Culture and Life,* the organ of the Propaganda and Agitation Section of the Party Central Committee, fell on historians, geographers, architects, and even circus managers. The government called for "full unmasking of the cosmopolite-theoreticians and formalistic directors who have planted in the arenas of Soviet circuses alien bourgeois tendencies. . . ." From a host of different fields flowed a torrent of accusations, confessions, and promises to do better in the future.

In August 1948 Zhdanov carried his attack into natural science. At a congress of the All-Union Academy of Agricultural Science, a poorly educated plant breeder named Trofim D. Lysenko attacked accepted doctrines of genetics, labeling them as "metaphysical-idealistic," and declaring that the inheritance of acquired characteristics was possible. Lysenko's contentions were imposed upon the assembled Soviet biologists by his unequivocal announcement that the Party Central Committee had "examined and approved" his address. The chief "Mendel-Morganist" geneticists were liquidated. After crowning his work with this ideological coup, Zhdanov died suddenly on the last day of August 1948.

STALIN'S PSEUDO-NATIONALISM

However, Zhdanov's death by no means terminated the cultural purges which he had begun. In 1949 a gifted critic, Stein, announced in a writers' meeting that he had read twenty plays about collective farms, and that they all followed the same pattern:

> First Act. A *kolkhoz* which has suffered under the Nazi occupation: (a) there are no seeds; (b) there is no fuel; (c) the tractor station has been destroyed; (d) the chairman of the *kolkhoz* is either away or on a drinking bout, or he has lost faith, or he is simply a dolt. . . . Curtain of the First Act: (a) the district party secretary arrives on the scene; (b) also the assistant chief of the Political Department; (c) a war veteran is made chairman of the *kolkhoz*. . . . Second Act. The new chairman tells all the *kolkhoz* members "the earth is given us for our eternal use; we must gather in the harvest; comrades, let us work!"[4]

Stein had well summarized the havoc wreaked on the Soviet arts by the *Zhdanovshchina;* but he was savagely attacked for his remarks. He had

[4] Quoted by Edward Crankshaw, *Russia Without Stalin* (New York: Viking, 1956), p. 125.

implied that the "new Soviet man" was a fantasy; moreover, Stein was a Jew.

In the early months of 1949 the target of the campaign of ideological repression had been redefined as "bourgeois cosmopolitanism," a phrase to which the adjective "homeless" was often prefixed—and when it was, it referred to Jews. Penalties against Jews were not new in the Soviet Union. Large numbers had been disenfranchised during the 1920's and 1930's as "bourgeois," but at least the ostensible reason for penalties had been occupational rather than racial. During the period of the Nazi-Soviet pact, dismissals of Jews and restrictions on them had been increased, but they could be rationalized by reference to diplomatic necessity. However, in 1949 a quite unequivocal anti-Semitic campaign was launched.

The timing of the campaign is explained by the establishment of the state of Israel and the evident wish of many Soviet Jews to emigrate there, but in its aims it appeared to be an extension of the anti-Western propaganda policy laid down by Zhdanov three years earlier. Emphasis was placed on the Jewish names of many who, like Trotsky and Zinoviev, had adopted Russian aliases, and cartoons were published employing the grotesque features which anti-Semites have long labored to make recognizable as caricatures of their chosen enemies. It was hinted that Jews had some kind of inherent tendency to worship the West and should be "hounded out of Soviet life." The anti-Semitic campaign was to continue to mount in intensity until Stalin's death. However, there remained for the use of foreign apologists Kaganovich in the Politburo and Ilia Ehrenburg in the writers' organizations, proving that the Soviets were not anti-Semitic. After all, some of Stalin's best friends were Jews.

In 1949–1950 came the turn of physiologists, some of whom were accused of having turned to metaphysics from the study of the prescribed mechanistic teachings regarding the human mind produced by Ivan Pavlov, whose experiments with the conditioned reflex in dogs had brought him worldwide fame before the Revolution. In the summer of 1950 Stalin himself showed his hand in the campaign of repression, when he intervened in a "discussion" organized by *Pravda* on questions of linguistics.

The hitherto officially favored linguistic theorist, Nicholas Marr, who had died in 1934, interpreted language as part of the Marxian superstructure of society, and in effect forecast that when the socio-economic foundation was everywhere transformed, there would then emerge some kind of new "language of socialism." Stalin now denounced Marr, arguing that language was independent of social development, and that not a merger of languages but the triumph of a single (and by implication superior) language was to be expected in the future. It was not very obscurely hinted that that language would be Russian. Stalin thereupon came to occupy a paradoxical position in which not only did Soviet linguists hail his doctrine as one of "genius," but also Western linguists, who had long regarded Marr as more or less a charlatan, found themselves in agreement with much of what Stalin said about language—though not, to be sure, with his forecast of "victory" for the Russian language. Part of his pronouncements on this occasion, however, had nothing to do with linguistics (as indeed much of what he said about linguistics had no necessary connection with Marxism): he declared that the state would not wither away under the last stage, "communism," and that the superstructure, especially the state which forms a part of it, might act powerfully on the base which "produces" it. Thus the attack on Marr was accompanied by a new theoretical defense of the universal significance of the Soviet state. Moreover, the statement seemed to contain overtones of Russian nationalism.

Indeed, as the attack on the West mounted, the Party ideologists were apparently trying to pretend that all the important discoveries, inventions, and innovations of the past had been the work of Russians. It was quite true, and well known to Russians educated before the Revolution, that A. N. Ladygin had produced an electric light in 1874, four years before the news of Edison's lamp was published, that Alexander Popov in 1895 had demonstrated radio transmission independently of Marconi's work, and that a number of other discoveries had occurred very early in Russia, but had been virtually forgotten, partly because the technological basis for applying the inventions was still lacking in Russia at the time they were produced. However, the ideologists distorted these and other facts and apparently fabricated still other contentions out of whole cloth.

On the surface the whole campaign appeared to be similar to Stalin's invocations of Russian nationalism during World War II. However, there was in reality a significant difference. During the war Stalin did not need to create popular veneration for Alexander Nevsky and other national heroes; such an attitude already existed. What he did was to try to identify the regime with the traditions of pride in and defense of the motherland, and thus to make such traditions serve his own purposes. In contrast, the dubious existence of obscure eighteenth-century "inventors," for example, meant little or nothing to the people or to the scholars of integrity who remained. Interest in the great minds of the Western past could serve as a cover for interest in and admiration for the contemporary West, and as a substitute (however inadequate) for the contact with the outside world for which the Soviet intellectuals in particular had ardently hoped, and which had been temporarily and partially realized for a few months at the end of the war. This type of "cosmopolitanism" actually developed alongside the surge of genuine Russian national feeling among the people during the war and conflicted not with real nationalism but with the ethos of the Soviet regime. Stalin pretended to invoke forgotten or bogus Russian discoveries in order to try to stifle admiration of the West, suppress the nationalist aspirations of the minority peoples, and rally Russians to his support, while never verbally abandoning the Marxist doctrine of "two nations": "the Russian people, the Russian workers, peasants and the progessive elements of the Russian intelligentsia on one side and the Tsars, the Russian squires, the capitalists and the Tsarist colonial bureaucracy on the other." Nevertheless, the repressive measures which were designed to counter the wartime experience of relative freedom in certain aspects of life and of contact with Europe fell as hard on the Russians as on any of the other peoples.[5]

CHANGES IN THE PARTY AND THE GOVERNMENT

At the end of the war no time was lost in restoring the prewar structure of Party and government. In September 1945 the State Defense Committee was abolished and its authority distributed among the regular governmental organs. The jurisdiction of the military—in the USSR often less severe than civil courts—was ended in all districts except the western frontier regions. In February 1946 the first elections to the Supreme Soviet since 1937 were held. As before they yielded a virtually unanimous vote to the single list of candidates printed on the ballots. In March the Council of People's Commissars was renamed "Council of Ministers." Again the creation of new ministries and the abolition of old ones became frequent, and it was as difficult as ever to ascertain whether such changes involved real alteration of function or of the personal power of the ministers in question.

The Communist Party, which in 1940 had had 3,400,000 members and candidates, had undergone an enormous wartime expansion, ordered by the regime with a view to broadening its base of support. In January 1945 the total was 5,760,000; by September 1947, 6,300,000—approximately

• [5] Perhaps it should be said, of the other peoples who were left, for the Volga Germans, Crimean Tatars, Chechen-Ingush, Karachai, Kalmyks, and Balkarians were exterminated as ethnic units during the war. Khrushchëv, in his "secret speech" of 1956, criticized Stalin for the extermination of four of these groups; he was silent about the two largest, the Volga Germans and the Crimean Tatars, but the Crimean Tatars were subsequently rehabilitated.

half of whom had been admitted since Hitler's invasion. The Party was summoned to what was admittedly a herculean task, that of reindoctrinating the whole population in Communist ideology. In an article in *Pravda* in October 1944 it was contended, "During the occupation, the German invaders tried by every method to poison the consciousness of Soviet men and women. . . . It is the duty of party organizations to stimulate tirelessly the political activity of the workers. . . . Particular attention must be paid to the question of implanting in the population a socialist attitude . . . overcoming the private-property, anticollective farm, and antistate tendencies planted by the German occupants."

The swollen Party itself needed much political reindoctrination. Malenkov, in announcing the total of 6,300,000 in 1947, said ominously, "Quality is more important than quantity." However, no large-scale purge followed. Since the Party was highly centralized and dependent on orders from above, the Soviet leaders evidently concluded that it was wiser to keep the politically shaky newcomers in Party ranks and try to "train" them, than to expel them into the ranks of a populace evidently suffering from the ill effects both of Western "bourgeois" culture and "anticollective farm and antistate" attitudes (which, by the way, could scarcely have been legacies of the Nazis, who had refused to abolish the collective farms and were far from sympathetic to anarchist ideas). One indication that much work remained to be done within Party ranks is that no Party Congress was summoned until 1952 (the first since 1939).

Just after the war the Politburo itself was reshuffled. The membership of 1939, consisting of Stalin, Molotov, Voroshilov, Kaganovich, Mikoyan, Andreyev, Khrushchëv, Zhdanov, and Kalinin, lost two by death, Kalinin in 1946 and Zhdanov in 1948 (apparently Kalinin died naturally, but the circumstances of Zhdanov's death were most suspicious).

In 1946 Lavrenty Beria and Georgy Malenkov were raised to full membership. Beria, who had risen within the Party and secret police of his native Georgia and had been chief of the All-Union NKVD since 1938, was the biographer of his fellow Georgian, Stalin. Malenkov had been following in Stalin's own footsteps by promotion within the Party apparatus to Stalin's private secretariat, whose management he shared with Alexander Poskrebyshëv. During the war years he had been closely associated with Beria, while there were strong indications of rivalry between him and Zhdanov. After Zhdanov died Malenkov came into increasing public prominence, and in January 1952 his fiftieth birthday was given a degree of attention thus far reserved for Stalin alone.

In Stalin's lifetime three more members were added to the Politburo: Nicholas Voznesensky in 1947, Nicholas Bulganin in 1948, and A. N.

Kosygin in 1949. All three were identified with work in state administration. Voznesensky, whose rise to prominence had occurred under Zhdanov's auspices in Leningrad, had become chairman of the State Planning Commission (*Gosplan*) in 1938. In a book published in 1947 on the Soviet economy during the war, he had emphasized the primacy of the role of the state and state planning in the construction of communism, which seemed in harmony with Stalin's assertions in his attack on Marr's linguistics. Nevertheless, in July 1949 the Party Central Committee condemned his views as implying that the state could arbitrarily override economic laws. Voznesensky was removed from the Politburo and executed, as Khrushchëv confirmed for the first time in his "secret speech." At the same time certain other supporters of Zhdanov were liquidated in what has been referred to by Soviet leaders as the "Leningrad case," and thus the Zhdanovite clique followed their patron into the discard within an interval of a few months.[6]

Bulganin had followed the career of an administrator of industry during the 1920's and had been chairman of the Moscow Soviet in the thirties. For his work as political commissar on the Moscow front during the campaign of 1941 he was rewarded with the military rank of lieutenant-general. In 1944 he had replaced Voroshilov on the vital State Defense Committee, and in 1946 he had become head of the newly amalgamated Ministry of the Armed Forces and while in that post was promoted to the rank of marshal. Kosygin had been associated with administration in light industry and during the war was prime minister of the Russian republic.

All the men on the Politburo during the period were, at least at the time they were appointed, trusted henchmen of Stalin's. There was apparently a difference in either policy emphasis or in function between Zhdanov, who prosecuted the campaign of domestic repression and foreign intransigence with especial vigor, and Malenkov. As far as is known, however, each depended in turn entirely on Stalin's favor, and neither questioned Stalin's primacy or his authority to make all final policy decisions. It is quite clear that no one on the Politburo opposed Stalin openly; the assertion of Khrushchëv in his "secret speech" that the Politburo numbered many who opposed some of Stalin's measures privately but not publicly—either for fear of his wrath or out of concern that the "people" would not understand such opposition—rests on his

• [6] Victor Abakumov, minister of State Security at the time, was executed in December 1954 for his alleged responsibility for the "Leningrad case." It seems plain that Malenkov was influential in these executions, and Khrushchëv has since dropped some fairly definite suggestions that this was the case, without for the time being following them up.

completely unsupported testimony, uttered in circumstances which render its credibility profoundly suspect.

ECONOMIC RECONSTRUCTION

The Soviet Union suffered wartime losses which elude description. Much of the south and west of the USSR had undergone utter devastation, industry had been wrecked, and half of the total prewar railway network had been destroyed. The population losses were staggering; there were perhaps seven million civilian dead, an even larger number killed in the fighting, and taking into account the deficiency in births which might have been expected except for the war, the total loss ran between twenty and thirty million.

The purpose of the Fourth Five-Year Plan, to run from 1946 to 1950, was to make good the whole of the economic damage and raise the output of the economy higher than that of 1940 by a substantial extent. The Fifth Plan, which ran from 1951 to 1955, projected a continued sharp rise in the indices of production. In 1948 the inauguration of the "Stalin Plan for the Transformation of Nature" was announced, envisaging the creation of gigantic forest belts in the southern steppes, the construction of great hydroelectric stations on the Volga and the Dnieper, and long canals, in particular a Great Turkmen Canal in Central Asia. Much of this was before long quietly forgotten, although a Volga-Don canal was completed.

The volume of construction and the rise in industrial output during the period were indeed tremendous. The Soviet state, allocating its resources in a manner which only a totalitarian state can carry out, without regard to the needs of its people, achieved a level of industrial production approaching that of Western Europe, and in the output of aircraft and certain kinds of nuclear weapons and missiles matched or exceeded the United States. In all important sectors of the economy production in 1945 was well below that of 1940. However, steel production, which had been 18.3 million metric tons in 1940, rose to 38 million in 1953; coal production, 166 million metric tons in 1940, attained 318 million in 1953; oil output, which had been 31 million metric tons, reached 52.6; electric power production rose from 48.3 billion kilowatt-hours in 1940 to 133 billion in 1953. Although the official statistics may incorporate substantial inaccuracies as usual, other evidence confirms that heavy industry, including potential or actual war production, underwent a breathtaking rate of growth. However, light industry and the output of consumers' goods continued as ever since 1928 to lag sharply behind, and in the largest cities housing, shoes, furniture, and many types of food were harder to come by than during the 1920's.

In 1947 the regime introduced a currency "reform," requiring exchange on the basis of ten old rubles for one new one, which had a double effect. It supported the value of current income and thus encouraged persons who were idle or had been dislocated by the war to enter the labor force with vigor, and at the same time virtually wiped out the wartime savings of workers and peasants alike. The urban workers were as always directly at the mercy of the regime. In the summer of 1946 Stalin took severe measures to combat the wartime laxity in the use of the labor books, which were a principal control over labor turnover, and proceeded with a new sternness to punish absenteeism and similar offenses. As the regime recognized, the peasants presented a more difficult problem, both because of the war experiences and because of the loopholes remaining for their private endeavor in both agricultural production and trade.

FARM POLICY

In 1946 the implementation of Soviet agricultural policy was entrusted to A. A. Andreyev as chief of the Council on Collective Farm Affairs. He led the postwar crackdown on the common practice (dating from the thirties, but winked at by the officials during the war years) of "illegal land seizure"—that is, gradual and surreptitious enlargement of the private plots at the expense of the collective sector of the *kolkhozy*. At the same time Andreyev undertook the strict enforcement of the compulsory labor requirements on the collective farms. By a law of 1942 the minimum number of annual "work-days" (*trudodni*—units measuring work done which were quite independent of the chronological day) which a peasant had to perform on the *kolkhoz* was raised to between 100 and 150, depending on the region, for adults, 50 for boys 12 to 16 years of age, and the minimum was spaced throughout all four seasons of the year. If the farmer failed to meet the minimum, he was to be forced to work six months for the collective, for that period losing twenty-five per cent of his earnings. The requirements of the law were not always closely observed during the war period, but beginning in 1946 determined efforts at enforcement were made.

The regime waited three years before carrying out mass collectivization in the newly annexed Western regions. The largest part of this task was carried out in late 1948 and 1949. Although Andreyev apparently worked hard enough at all his politically defined tasks, he seems to have been guided also by a desire to restore production even at the cost of temporary neglect of political objectives. In early 1947 he criticized the state farms (*sovkhozy*) for overspecialization and other faults, and his report resulted in the allotment of about an acre of garden plot to each *sovkhoz* worker for private cultivation—a radical innovation in the state farm structure. For collective farm work, he sanctioned the employment of small "link" (*zveno*) work teams.

In February 1950 a *Pravda* editorial criticized Andreyev for the use of the "link" system on the collective farms and called for the reinstatement of the "brigade" (*brigada*), a team of from fifty to a hundred or more workers, as the basic work unit. Nikita Khrushchëv followed up with criticism of the size of collective farms, demanding their amalgamation into still larger enterprises. The amalgamation, carried out along with the break-up of "links" in favor of "brigades," proceeded very rapidly. At the beginning of 1950 there were 254,000 collective farms in the USSR; by the end of 1951 the total was a little over 100,000; in 1952 it fell below 100,000. Roughly speaking, the typical operation involved combining three farms into a single one—an administrative rather than a physical change, since there was no effort to move the farm installations. As a result, each Machine-Tractor Station came to serve about ten collective farms instead of thirty as formerly. Khrushchëv's original statement had complained of the number of *kolkhoz* chairmen who lacked higher education (which often went along with the Party membership), and press reports emphasized that the percentage of farms possessing Party units was rising sharply as amalgamation progressed. The whole campaign for amalgamation and "brigades" was aimed at strengthening the Party's control over agriculture and bringing the peasant's perennial aspirations toward economic independence still further under the regime's surveillance.

One aspect of Khrushchëv's proposals for agriculture proved premature. He had suggested that the objective ought to be the eventual formation of "agricultural cities" (*agrogoroda*), in which the peasants would live in central apartment buildings, with their private plots no longer in their back yards but together in a large common area (where it would be impossible to work unobserved). At the start *Pravda* took the unusual step of disassociating itself from this suggestion, though without explicitly repudiating it. At the XIX Party Congress in October 1952 Malenkov attacked Khrushchëv (though not by name) for proposing "forcing the pace" of amalgamation and thereby putting "consumer" tasks ahead of "production" objectives. The reference to "consumer" tasks was presumably meant to imply that the urban amenities of the "agricultural cities" were intended to result in excessive benefits to the peasants themselves.

It is extremely doubtful that this was either the truth or the peasants' interpretation of the proposal, but it is indeed probable that the operation would have brought about a decrease in production, as collectivization had done, and that either actual peasant resistance or anticipation of such resistance led the regime to postpone the attempt. There is no indication, however, of any repudiation then or since of Stalin's own acknowledgment that as long as the collective farms retained a shred of private enterprise in their structure, there remained unfinished business for the Party in Soviet agriculture.

THE XIX PARTY CONGRESS

In October 1952 the first Party Congress since 1939 was convened in Moscow. It was noteworthy by the indications of the rise of Malenkov to the clearly recognized position of Stalin's heir and by the announcement of a broad reshuffling of the Party machinery. During the four years since Zhdanov's death, henchmen of Malenkov had been placed in a series of high Party and government posts. At the Congress Malenkov was entrusted with the delivery of the main report, the first time since Stalin's power had been consolidated that anyone but he had given it.

The Congress announced the replacement of both the Politburo and the Orgburo by a Presidium of the Party Central Committee. Against eleven in the old Politburo, there were twenty-five full members of the new Presidium. Kosygin was dropped from full membership, and the following were added: V. M. Andrianov, first secretary of the Leningrad regional party committee; A. B. Aristov, secretary of the Central Committee; S. D. Ignatiev, minister of State Security; D. S. Korotchenko, prime minister of the Ukrainian SSR; V. V. Kuznetsov, chief of the Soviet trade-unions; O. V. Kuusinen, president of the Karelo-Finnish Republic; V. A. Malyshev, minister of Shipbuilding; L. G. Melnikov, first secretary of the Ukrainian party; N. A. Mikhailov, secretary of the Central Committee; M. G. Pervukhin, Soviet vice-premier; P. K. Ponomarenko, secretary of the Central Committee; M. Z. Saburov, Soviet vice-premier and chief of *Gosplan;* M. A. Suslov, secretary of the Central Committee; D. I. Chesnokov, chief editor of *Questions of Philosophy* and co-director of *Bol'shevik* (the Party's theoretical organ, which was renamed *Kommunist* after the XIX Congress); N. M. Shvernik, who had been president of the USSR since the death of Kalinin in 1946 and a candidate member of the Politburo since 1939; and M. F. Shkiriatov, chairman of the Party Control Committee of the Central Committee. Merle Fainsod points out that eighteen out of the twenty-five had joined the Party in

1924 or later and that of those eighteen, eight had not even been prominent enough to be named as delegates to the last previous Congress in 1939.[7]

The new and larger Presidium was notable for its inclusion of a number of the highest governmental functionaries in the highest *Party* body. This stratum of administrators was reputed to be especially close to Malenkov —somewhat paradoxically, since his rise had taken place within the Party rather than the administrative hierarchy. At the same time the number of Party secretaries, which had been five (Stalin, Malenkov, Khrushchëv, Suslov, and Ponomarenko), was increased to ten by the addition of Aristov, Mikhailov, N. G. Ignatov (party chief of Krasnodar), L. I. Brezhnev (from Moldavia), and N. M. Pegov. Indications then were that the Secretariat would be a much more important body than the unwieldy Presidium, but it is difficult to assess what was intended, since only a few months later there was another drastic reorganization of Party machinery.

On the eve of the Congress Stalin had published an article entitled "Economic Problems of Socialism in the USSR," which set the doctrinal tone for the Congress. Therein he discussed problems of the "transition from socialism [deemed to have arrived in the USSR by 1936] to communism," although he gave no date for the completion of that process. He seemed to change his emphasis somewhat; he talked less about the role of the state, on which he had said so much in his article on Marr's linguistics, and more about "objective" economic laws "which take their course independently of our will." This was consistent with the condemnation of Voznesensky in 1949, and it harmonized with an apparently less intransigent line in foreign policy, emphasizing the likelihood of conflict between different capitalist countries above that of "contradictions between the camp of socialism and the camp of capitalism." It was further implied that the revolutionary flood of the past few years might be followed by an "ebb." Anticipation of a slight *détente* with the chief Western powers, as well as a slight relaxation of the current Soviet posture of aggressiveness, were suggested also by the Congress's dropping of the name "Politburo," associated in Western minds with recent Soviet conquests, and the final discarding of the word "Bolsheviks" in parentheses from the official Party name, "Communist Party of the Soviet Union (Bolsheviks)."

At the Congress the slogan of "peace" was widely featured, not for the first time. In 1949 the Soviets had organized an international front group known as the "Partisans of Peace" (later renamed the "World Peace Council"). This group, meeting in March 1950, drew up the

• [7] *How Russia is Ruled,* p. 279.

"Stockholm peace petition," which obtained, according to Communist claims, almost half a billion signatures in the five years following. The "peace offensive" was an attempt to blame the Western powers for the so-called Cold War and to foster pro-Soviet sympathies among genuinely antimilitarist and pacifist groups and circles as well as among those who combined a fear of nuclear war with a low level of political sophistication. Such aims were broadly hinted by Stalin in "Economic Problems of Socialism in the USSR" when he wrote, "Under a certain confluence of circumstances, the struggle for peace may possibly develop in one place or another into a struggle for socialism"—that is, Soviet power.

The XIX Congress was not designed as the beginning of a period of retreat from the Party's objectives. That was evident from the adoption of a Fifth Five-Year Plan (for the period 1951–1955) which was replete with plans for gigantic hydroelectric and other projects whose implications for the Soviet nuclear program were plain, and which as before strongly emphasized heavy industry. Apparently the Congress was intended to begin a period of concentration on the assimilation of foreign conquests and consolidation of political and economic controls within the USSR.

STALIN'S LAST MONTHS

During the winter of 1952–1953, there occurred puzzling developments which plainly threatened to affect the chief aides of Stalin. In January *Pravda* announced that nine doctors, six of them Jewish, had been charged with assassinating, through medical mistreatment, a number of prominent Soviet figures including Andrei Zhdanov. The epithets "cosmopolitanism and Zionism" were again employed in discussion of the case, while similar phrases were used in the simultaneous trial in Prague of the Czechoslovak party's general secretary, Rudolph Slansky (see p. 425). At the same time the MVD, whose chief was Beria, was accused of insufficient vigilance in failing to detect the "doctors' plot." During the month of February the Soviet press sharply decreased the amount of attention paid to Malenkov, whose ties with Beria were thought to be close. There has been some speculation that Alexander Poskrebyshëv, the chief of Stalin's personal secretariat, was instrumental in these moves directed against Beria and possibly against Malenkov as well.

At this juncture, on March 4, 1953, it was abruptly announced that Stalin had suffered a stroke two days earlier, and then that he had died on the evening of March 5. The circumstances surrounding his death remain obscure. Since so many prominent persons in the Soviet hierarchy had previously been murdered, it is not surprising that the possibility was discussed that Stalin himself died by violence, or that his end was hastened in some way. Certainly Beria and apparently Malenkov benefited by Stalin's death at the time it came, and the instant disappearance of Poskrebyshëv and other persons known to have been personally close to Stalin was out of harmony with the official version of the time, that the beloved leader had died a natural death. Any further speculations cannot yet be fully supported by evidence.

It is reported that when, on March 9, Stalin was buried in the Lenin (now Lenin-Stalin) Mausoleum in Red Square, Molotov alone of the three funeral orators exhibited any grief, while Malenkov and Beria delivered impassive statements. The initial warning of these three men, who emerged for the moment as the top Soviet leaders, that the masses must avoid "confusion and panic" suggested that they were aware of how few tears would be shed by the Soviet peoples at the passing of their *Vozhd,* and knew that there were many who might try to seize the opportunity to rid themselves of the regime which he bequeathed them. Nevertheless Stalin had symbolized both Soviet power and Communist aspirations to rule the world, and among Party members, in particular foreign Communists, if not sorrow at least confusion was soon widespread indeed.

The Rise of Khrushchëv (1953–1957)

CHAPTER 28

THE ERA OF MALENKOV

Upon the death of Stalin in March 1953, speculation centered on who would succeed him as dictator, master of the Party and the government. At first it seemed that Malenkov would manage to do so. He had been designated heir by implication at the XIX Congress, and whether or not he had fallen into Stalin's disfavor since then, he was now featured by the Soviet press ahead of all other leaders. For ten days he held both of the most crucial posts, chairman of the Council of Ministers and senior Party secretary; it was then announced that he had yielded the latter (and historically the more decisive) job to Nikita Khrushchëv. Nevertheless, the triumvirate of Malenkov, Beria, and Molotov (in that order) continued to be treated in the press as the chief personalities of the Party and government.

In the Presidium as reconstituted after Stalin's death, the new roster of full members (reduced from twenty-five to ten) comprised, in addition to the triumvirate, Bulganin, Kaganovich, Voroshilov, Mikoyan, Khrushchëv, Saburov, and Pervukhin. The Party Secretariat was reduced from ten to five: Khrushchëv was assisted by M. A. Suslov, former head of the Agitprop Department of the Central Committee, P. N. Pospelov, N. N.

ADMINISTRATIVE DIVISIONS
OF THE USSR, 1963
LITHUANIAN SSR
LATVIAN SSR
ESTONIAN SSR
BELORUSSIAN SSR
Tallinn
Riga
Vilnius
Minsk
Karelian ASSR
Komi ASSR
Moscow
Kiev
Mari ASSR
Mordvinian ASSR
MOLDAVIAN SSR
Kishinëv
UKRAINIAN SSR
Chuvash ASSR
Tatar ASSR
Udmurt ASSR
Bashkir ASSR
Kalmyk ASSR
RUSSIAN
SOVIET
FEDERATED
SOCIALIST
REPUBLIC
Yakut ASSR
Buriat
ASSR
Tuvinian ASSR
Kabardino-Balkar ASSR
(Abkhazian ASSR)
Northern Ossetian ASSR
Chechen-Ingush ASSR
KAZAKH SSR
Tbilisi
Erevan
Daghestan ASSR
(Adzharian ASSR)
GEORGIAN SSR
ARMENIAN SSR
(Nakhichevan ASSR)
AZERBAIJAN SSR
Baku
(Kara-Kalpak ASSR)
UZBEK SSR
Ashkhabad
Tashkent
Alma Ata
Frunze
TURKMEN SSR
Diushambe
KIRGHIZ SSR
TADZHIK SSR
UZBEK SSR Union Republics
Yakut ASSR Autonomous Republics in RSFSR
(Kara-Kalpak ASSR) ASSR within SSR
0
500
1000
MILES

Shatalin, and S. D. Ignatiev, former head of the MGB.[1] Voroshilov replaced Shvernik as chairman of the Presidium of the Supreme Soviet (president of the USSR). A new Presidium of the Council of Ministers, consisting of the triumvirate plus Bulganin and Kaganovich, included the leading figures of the government proper, and, it appeared (with the exception of Khrushchëv), of the Party as well. The slogan of "collective leadership" was widely used to describe the new dispensation, but the fact that the same slogan had been used in Lenin's last days and the months after his death suggested that the arrangements of March 1953 might not be permanent.

During the following months Stalin's name was mentioned in the Soviet press with sharply fluctuating frequency. At one moment it might virtually disappear, the next it might be mentioned fairly often, though still much less obtrusively than during his lifetime. The frequent use of the phrase, "the cult of personality," in an unfavorable sense, cast a reflection at least on the outward conventions of the treatment of Stalin while he lived. Even more revealing were the policy statements made by Malenkov and Beria, which implied, if not direct criticism of Stalin's acts, at least an awareness that his policies had deepened popular discontent with the regime and a hope that a "new course" might evoke a different reaction from the Soviet peoples.

Malenkov identified himself with a promise of a higher level of production of consumer's goods, and the phrase "two or three years," which he used to suggest when such promises might be realized, became a public byword. Beria took an even more startling tack by suggesting that mild legal changes were in order. On April 3 he announced that the "doctors' plot" which had been "exposed" during Stalin's last days had been a hoax. Fabrication of the "plot" was ascribed to M. D. Riumin, who had been deputy minister of the MGB, and he was arrested, while Ignatiev, his chief, was sharply criticized. Beria further reported that "inadmissible" methods had been used by the police in handling suspects, called for revision of the criminal code to reduce the severity of penalties for minor crimes, and even spoke of the need for protecting the rights of citizens guaranteed under the Constitution.

These developments were reflected in various ways in the East Euro-

[1] In 1943 the NKVD had been divided into two commissariats, a new NKGB, which assumed the secret police functions, and the NKVD which retained the rest, including (after 1950) the supervision of special security troops. In 1946 the two commissariats, along with all others, were renamed ministries, becoming the MGB (*Ministerstvo Gosudarstvennoi Bezopasnosti* or Ministry of State Security) and MVD. After Stalin's death the two were combined once more, now under the control of Beria.

pean satellites. The precedent of the Soviet separation of Party and governmental leadership, at the time Khrushchëv took over the Party secretaryship from Malenkov, was followed in several satellite regimes. The death of President Gottwald of Czechoslovakia, reportedly from pneumonia contracted at Stalin's funeral, led to his replacement as president by Zápotocky and as party chief (under the title of First Secretary) by Antonín Novotny. In July 1953 Mátyás Rákosi yielded the premiership of Hungary to Imre Nagy, who inaugurated a "New Course" patterned after Malenkov's policy of increasing consumer goods production, but also permitted peasants to leave collective farms and released a number of political prisoners including the Socialist Anna Kéthly. In the early months of 1954 the separation of offices took place in other satellites, although unaccompanied by any such extensive shift of policy as in Hungary. The Bulgarian leader Vlko Chervenkov and the Rumanian Gheorghe Gheorghiu-Dej kept their premierships and gave up their party secretaryships, while the Pole Bolesław Bierut and the Albanian Enver Hoxha kept their party secretaryships (now everywhere the title became "First Secretary" instead of "General Secretary"—the title Stalin had used) and gave up their premierships.

Already by June 1953 the post-Stalin changes in leadership and policy had created a public impression of indecision and weakness at the top. In the satellites as well as the USSR, several demonstrations of unrest occurred within a few weeks of each other. On June 1 there were strikes in several Czechoslovak cities, occasioned by a financial "reform" which wrought much hardship on the industrial workers. In Plzeň the strikers held a political demonstration, seized the city hall, and demanded free elections, before secret police troops intervened. On June 16 an increase of labor "norms" in East Germany provoked a protest which rapidly turned into a revolutionary general strike in Berlin and other East German cities. Soviet troops were brought in, and the strike was crushed.

On July 10 it was announced that Beria, who had identified himself most clearly with the new measures and in particular with legal as distinct from economic changes, had been arrested. His appointee as East German police chief, Wilhelm Zaisser, and many of his Soviet henchmen were also purged. Although Khrushchëv later told a French Socialist visitor that Beria had been shot immediately after his arrest, it was not until December that it was publicly announced that Beria and six of his supporters had been executed without public trial—possibly because he had refused to "confess." Beria was charged with having attempted to seize power, acting as a "capitalist" agent, and so forth. It is impossible to know what his plans actually were, but the sequence of events clearly suggests that he was made the scapegoat for the East Berlin uprising.

In any event, no more was said in the USSR about legal or political changes, although Malenkov continued his policy of promising economic concessions, and the "New Course" was proclaimed in Hungary and to a lesser extent the other satellites *after* the Berlin rising. In some ways the most astonishing of the first series of post-Stalin demonstrations occurred in the Soviet Union itself a few days after Beria's arrest. In the concentration camp complex at Vorkuta, in the Pechora basin of northeast European Russia, there developed a mass strike of prisoners who voiced political demands. After initial hesitation, the strike was put down with mass executions.

THE RISE OF KHRUSHCHËV

Nikita Khrushchëv was born in Kursk, just northeast of the Ukrainian border, in 1894. He was a completely uneducated coal miner when he joined the Party in 1918. He attended a *Rabfak* or special worker's school and showed himself so apt in his training in Party work that in 1934 he became Kaganovich's assistant in running the Moscow Party organization and in 1935 succeeded him as its secretary. In 1938 he was placed in charge of the Ukrainian party (see p. 300), and except for 1946–1947 when Kaganovich replaced him briefly, he remained so until 1949. During his last two years in that post he conducted a mass purge of officials in the Ukrainian Republic. He became a full member of the Politburo in 1939, and remained in the Presidium when it was so renamed. In 1949 he returned to Moscow to take over the Party organization there once again, and became a secretary of the Central Committee. He had gained something of a reputation in the field of agricultural policy and had authored the *agrogorod* proposal in 1951. Since he suffered no demotion when it was withdrawn, it was thought that the Politburo had supported the proposal and allowed him to bear the public blame for "extremism" merely to save face. After the death of Stalin he had obviously achieved a place of great power by taking over the senior secretaryship of the Party from Malenkov.

In September 1953 Khrushchëv made an important statement on Soviet agriculture which indicated an increase in his power (ten days later he became "First Secretary" of the Soviet Party), and at the same time admitted more bluntly than ever before the horrifying state of the collective farms. Among other things Khrushchëv reported that the total number of cattle in the USSR was lower than it had been in 1916 under Nicholas II. The point of Khrushchëv's report was of course not to indict the *kolkhoz* system, but to evoke greater efforts on the "agricultural front." As a result, state-paid prices for compulsory deliveries were raised, the attempt to enforce the fixed minimums of compulsory labor (first set in 1942) by criminal prosecution was abandoned, and a good deal was said about "incentives" and "initiative."

Despite such apparent concessions to the peasantry, the regime strengthened its control over the collective farms still further. In mid-1954 the compulsory labor minimums were raised very substantially and enforced by means of greatly increased taxation on households any member of which fell short of his minimum. In addition a team of Party "instructors" was placed in each Machine-Tractor Station with powers to interfere in the collective farms which the MTS served (and which were virtually subject to its jurisdiction), and in April 1955 there was announced a mass replacement of collective farm chairmen (who had earlier been made openly subject to Party "confirmation") by urban Party workers. All these measures were identified with Khrushchëv, who evidently took over agricultural policy from Malenkov in September 1953.

In February 1954 Khrushchëv inaugurated as dramatic and sweeping a measure as the *agrogorod* idea would have been: in order to increase grain output it was ordered that an area later given as around seventy million acres of "virgin and idle lands" in the fertile but arid regions of Asiatic Russia was to be plowed up and sown. Thousands of young people and Party workers were dispatched as labor and supervisory personnel to do the job. In January 1955 Khrushchëv demanded that around seventy million acres be planted in corn (that is, maize) for fodder in order to increase livestock production. The resulting cornfields, on flat and hilly country, in cold and warm regions, earned him the nickname of *kukuruzchik* ("the corn enthusiast").

Khrushchëv's agricultural report and his elevation to the first secretaryship of the Soviet Party were the prelude to a number of personnel changes in the Party machinery which were reminiscent of the removals and appointments which Stalin had authored in the mid-twenties with a view to solidifying his own control of the Party. The fall of Beria was followed by a purge of the Georgian and Azerbaijani organizations (led respectively by G. A. Arutiunov and M. D. Bagirov, both of whom had criticized the *agrogorod* proposal), in which Beria's influence had been especially strong. In November V. M. Andrianov, the Leningrad party secretary, was removed, and about the same period the chiefs of the Moscow and other regional organizations were replaced. Apparently few of these men suffered execution, hitherto the usual fate of purged Party leaders. However, in 1954 two prominent men were shot: M. D. Riumin, who died in July, thus surviving his original accuser, Beria, by a few months, and in December Victor Abakumov, former head of the MGB, who was charged with framing the defendants in the so-called "Leningrad case" (see p. 457). Since this case involved the purging of Zhdanov's supporters, and thus presumably had the approval of Zhdanov's apparent rival, Malenkov, Abakumov's execution suggested that Malenkov's position had been seriously undermined.

Khrushchëv's ascendancy became plainer month by month. In November and December his signature appeared alone on certain decrees, and he made speeches and granted interviews on a variety of subjects. In December 1954 and January 1955 the Malenkov-Khrushchëv conflict erupted in public print in a fashion unfamiliar in the USSR for a quarter of a century. Whereas *Izvestiia,* the government organ and thus presumably controlled by Malenkov, emphasized again the need for consumer's goods, *Pravda,* the organ of the Party and thus, it seemed, the voice of Khrushchëv, attacked unidentified persons who wanted to encourage light industry as guilty of "a belching of the Rightist deviation . . . views which Rykov, Bukharin, and their ilk once preached." This was a clear declaration of war on Malenkov.

FOREIGN POLICY, 1953–1955

By this time Khrushchëv had also made his mark on Soviet foreign policy. The first notable act of the Malenkov-Beria regime in international affairs had been to consent to the signature, by the North Korean and Chinese Communist "volunteer" commanders, of an armistice in the Korean War, on July 27, 1953. This was made possible by Communist withdrawal of objections to the United States demand that the repatriation of prisoners be entirely voluntary; on this point negotiations had been stalled for a whole year. A neutral commission under an Indian chairman supervised the exchange of prisoners. Three-quarters of the Chinese prisoners of war, despite considerable pressure, decided not to go home and went to Formosa instead. By the truce the Soviets and the Chinese Communists thus accepted a noteworthy public humiliation, but the refusal of so many soldiers to return to Communist control had less effect on world opinion than American policy-makers expected.

In January 1954 the Council of Foreign Ministers, which had been inactive for years, was convened once again in Berlin to discuss peace treaties for Germany and Austria, again without result. In the spring another Soviet meeting with the Western powers was held in Geneva to consider the unification of Korea and an armistice in Indo-China. For the first time Chinese Communist delegates were included in a conference with the West. At the end of the meeting, the United States, which had only second-rank representatives present, made a separate declaration which gave implied assent to the main agreement reached by the participating powers, which was to partition Vietnam near the seventeenth parallel. Thereby the French yielded the north to Ho Chi Minh's Communist regime, while Communist guerrillas were to be withdrawn from the south. At the same time the French gave independence to Bao Dai's south Vietnamese regime, as well as to Cambodia and Laos; however, all three remained within the French Union.

The new prime minister of South Vietnam, Ngo Dinh Diem, managed to overcome warring factions in the south, expel Bao Dai after elections at the end of 1955, and resist the Communist demand that "free elections" (at Geneva it was agreed that such elections should take place within two years) be held, insisting that there be some prior guarantee that the elections in the north would be really free rather than Communist-style. The withdrawal of the French from the Red River delta, Hanoi, and Haiphong, under the Geneva agreement, marked the last Communist acquisition up to 1958.

Although intervention against the Indo-Chinese Communists had been discussed in the United States, no action was taken. However, there was a diplomatic effort to prevent further Communist advance in the region by the conclusion of a pact in Manila in September 1954 establishing a Southeast Asia Treaty Organization (SEATO). The new pact built on the groundwork laid by the "Anzus" treaty of August 1951 between the United States, Australia, and New Zealand, and the 1951 U. S. pact with the Philippines. These four powers were joined in the Manila treaty by Great Britain, France, Pakistan, and Thailand. The agreement was for common defense against Communist aggression and "internal subversion," a contingency to which such treaties as NATO had not applied. For the moment, at least, further Communist advance in eastern Asia appeared to be blocked, although Communists continued to gain strength inside Singapore, Indonesia, and elsewhere.

In the sphere of Sino-Soviet relations the Malenkov regime had signed an agreement in September 1953 to furnish further industrial aid. Khrushchëv, who had already begun his newsworthy travels with trips to Warsaw and Prague that spring, headed a Soviet delegation which visited Peking in September 1954 and concluded a second Sino-Soviet treaty (see p. 445). This pact yielded to Mao Soviet rights in Manchuria except for Port Arthur, which was returned in May 1955. Again the Soviets greatly increased their economic aid and technical assistance to the Chinese Communists; they also agreed with Peking to construct two long railways linking the two countries via Ulan Bator in Mongolia and Urumchi in Sinkiang. The Mongolian line was finished in 1955; the Urumchi route was scheduled for completion in 1961. The political, economic, and military significance of these communication links is potentially very great, especially considering the intensified Soviet interest in Central Asia manifested in connection with Khrushchëv's "virgin and idle lands" program.

CULTURAL POLICY

The developments after Stalin's death had a notable impact on Soviet cultural policy. In the fall of 1953 Ilia Ehrenburg and Vladimir Pomerantsev published articles questioning the propriety of Party dictation to the creative artist. Pomerantsev frankly advised the Soviet writers: "Don't think about prosecution [*sic*] . . . . Be independent." Soon afterward the outstanding Soviet composers Aram Khachaturian and Dmitry Shostakovich[2] spoke in comparable terms, emphasizing the right of the artist to "independence, boldness, and originality." In February 1954 a Party ideologist, P. K. Ponomarenko, who had been named minister of culture after Stalin's death, was replaced in that post by G. F. Alexandrov, whose *History of West European Philosophy* had been condemned in the Zhdanov period for undue favor toward his subject. In mid-1954 Ilia Ehrenburg published a novel entitled *The Thaw* (*Ottepel'*), in which he depicted realistically, if without particular literary skill, a number of Soviet types and suggested (as did the title itself, though the title also had its point in the story) that there had been a paralyzing freeze in Soviet life, but that with Stalin dead better things might be hoped for. All of these stirrings seemed to portend a thaw indeed.

However, the II All-Union Congress of Soviet Writers (the previous one having been held twenty years before), which met in September 1954, dashed many hopes. The foremost Soviet writer, Michael Sholokhov, repeated the standard formula that there could be "no contradiction" between what the Party and the individual (in this case the writer) wanted, because "our hearts belong to the party . . . ." There was to be no sharp change in the official policy. Nevertheless for the time being less severity was shown by the cultural dictatorship, and the plans announced in early 1955 for the re-publication of the great Russian novelist Dostoevsky and the early Soviet poet Sergei Esenin suggested that the fetters were to be loosened a trifle.

• [2] **The most gifted of them all, Sergei Prokofiev, died within a few hours of Stalin.**

In the spring of 1955 the grossest perversion of scientific truth perpetrated by Stalin and Zhdanov was repudiated when the official *Botanical Journal* labeled Lysenko's genetics as "factually unsound and theoretically and methodologically erroneous and . . . not of practical value . . . ." Two further developments were subject to two interpretations: the dismissal of Alexandrov from the Ministry of Culture in March 1955, and the reported suicide of Alexander Fadeyev, who had been the Party spokesman in literature for many years, in May 1956. Alexandrov was now denounced ostensibly for undervaluing Western culture in his work during Stalin's last years; whether that or his original work, which had been attacked for exactly the opposite reason, was the real cause of his dismissal is uncertain. Fadeyev's suicide might indicate either that he found life for the Soviet artist as unbearable as before, or that the regime had chosen to dispense with him in order to try a new tack in cultural policy. Whatever the intentions of the leaders at this point, the subsequent developments indicated that Soviet culture was not to be any further unfrozen for the time being (see p. 485).

KHRUSHCHËV AND BULGANIN IN POWER

On February 8, 1955, Georgy Malenkov resigned as chairman of the Council of Ministers, making an unprecedented statement in which he referred to his "inexperience," took on himself the "guilt" for what was admitted to be "the unsatisfactory state of affairs in agriculture" (which had according to all indications been managed by Khrushchëv, not Malenkov, for the past year and a half), and declared that the policy of founding the economy on heavy industry was the "only correct" one. On Khrushchëv's motion, the Supreme Soviet which heard the announcement of Malenkov's resignation promptly elected Bulganin as the new prime minister. Marshal Zhukov replaced Bulganin as minister of defense.

At that time the Party Presidium underwent no change, but at a Central Committee meeting in July 1955, two new full members were added: A. I. Kirichenko, first secretary of the Ukrainian party, and M. A. Suslov, one of the Party secretaries. The total was now eleven, the whole Presidium of March 1953 having been carried over except for the dead Beria (and one candidate member, M. D. Bagirov, who had been purged along with Beria). Three new men were named to the Secretariat: D. T. Shepilov, editor of *Pravda;* A. B. Aristov, party secretary of Khabarovsk province, who now became Khrushchëv's chief assistant for Party affairs; and N. I. Beliaev, party secretary of the Altai province—the latter two appointments apparentlv reflecting Khrushchëv's concern with the affairs of

Soviet Asia. Shatalin, reputedly a Malenkov supporter, disappeared from the list of secretaries. At the July Central Committee meeting it was also announced that the next Party Congress would be held the following February. As a result of the February and July reorganizations, apparently the single most important figure in the regime was Khrushchëv, with Bulganin second.

The leadership of Khrushchëv and Bulganin, however, was as yet far from secure. One known rival, Malenkov, retained sufficient power that he was not removed from the Presidium, and there might be others. The satellites had shown restlessness, and certain satellite leaders had evidently had close ties with Malenkov. In the background the specter of Stalin hovered over the Soviet leaders—for the Soviet people, an image associated with repression, terror, and want; for the foreign Communists, still an unbroken ikon; for the Western governments, a repugnant symbol but one which at the same time represented certainty about who could speak for the Soviet regime, a certainty which had been thrown into grave doubt. The first essentials seemed to be for Khrushchëv and Bulganin to establish clearly their authority over the East European satellites, remove the continuing danger to the Soviet orbit produced by the independence of Tito, and achieve recognition in international affairs. They attempted to postpone the more difficult problem of Stalin's ghost.

In the satellites, the chief example of a Malenkov-style "New Course" was the government of Imre Nagy in Hungary. In April 1955 Nagy was forced out of office and was replaced once again by Rákosi. After a conference between Rákosi and Khrushchëv in the summer, the Hungarian regime renewed its stress on collectivization of agriculture, with the added Khrushchëvian note of plans for more extensive corn production—for which Hungarian soil, at least, was suited. In May the Soviet hold on Eastern Europe was strengthened by the signing of the Warsaw Treaty for the fusion of satellite and Soviet armies under Soviet command (see p. 416). Despite this intransigent beginning, the next move of Khrushchëv and Bulganin was to make an astonishing visit to Tito in Belgrade. Khrushchëv arrived attempting to blame the dead Beria for the sad state of Soviet-Yugoslav relations. However, he found Tito would not swallow this tale, so after prolonged talks he made further concessions. On June 2, 1955, a joint declaration by the two governments stated that "differences in the concrete forms of socialist development are exclusively the concern of the peoples of the respective countries." Molotov, the surviving leader who had been most closely identified with the condemnation of Tito in 1948, and as Soviet foreign minister was presumably concerned with relations with Yugoslavia, was conspicuously absent from the Soviet delegation, while D. T. Shepilov seemed to take a prominent part in assisting the two chief leaders in the negotiations. In September a Moscow-Belgrade economic assistance pact was signed. In the same month Molotov was publicly criticized for an erroneous (and for any intelligent Communist, let alone a Communist leader, quite incredible) formulation about socialism in the USSR—suggesting that Tito's old enemy was about to fall from power.

THE "SPIRIT OF GENEVA"

In the summer of 1955 the international prestige of Khrushchëv and Bulganin was securely established. Already in June 1954 Winston Churchill had called for the West to make "a real good try" for "peaceful coexistence" with the USSR. President Eisenhower, using the phrase "deeds, not words," had summoned the Soviet leaders to show their "good faith" by signing an Austrian peace treaty and taking certain other steps before any "summit" meeting of the heads of government took place. In April the Soviets unexpectedly declared their willingness to sign an Austrian treaty, which was concluded the following month. Since the government in Vienna was already recognized as the legitimate government of all Austria (although its writ did not actually run in the Soviet occupation zone), there was no Soviet puppet regime in eastern Austria that had to be sacrificed. However, Soviet (as well as Western) troops evacuated their occupation zone, leaving an independent Austria committed to neutrality. There thus seemed no way for the U.S. to avoid the first meeting of the Big Three—this one included France, so was a Big Four meeting—since Potsdam, which none of the four (Eisenhower, Bulganin, Prime Minister Eden, and French Premier Faure) had attended as head of government, although Eden had started the Potsdam conference as Churchill's foreign minister.

The "summit" meeting was held in Geneva in July 1955. The questions of the reunification of Germany, European security, disarmament, and improvement in East-West relations were discussed without result. However, the "spirit of Geneva," as the atmosphere surrounding the resumption of talks of the leaders of the great powers was styled in popular parlance, netted Khrushchëv and Bulganin important propaganda benefits. The circulation of photographs showing Eisenhower and Bulganin engaged in amicable conversation, as well as various official Soviet statements, were intended to suggest to the peoples under the rule of the Kremlin that no hope of "liberation" (a word widely used in Republican foreign policy statements during the 1952 campaign, although not to mean the armed action which many abroad hoped or feared that it meant) by the United States was warranted. Furthermore, the intent was to persuade government leaders in both Western and uncommitted nations that contacts with the Soviet chiefs would not endanger the safety of such nations, and that the United States would be unlikely to prevent or penalize such contacts by the threat of withdrawal of financial aid.

The main issue which seemed to concern the Soviets at Geneva was American armed strength and participation in European defense arrangements by means of troops and bases. Therefore the Soviet announcement which followed Geneva by two months, that they would return the Porkkala base to Finland, was accompanied by pressure on the United States to do "likewise"—that is, withdraw from its bases in Western Europe. In a visit to Moscow in September, Chancellor Adenauer obtained Soviet recognition of the Federal Republic of Germany, but was unable to secure the release of all war prisoners still held by the USSR. Another meeting of the Council of Foreign Ministers, arranged at Geneva, was held in October and November, but it soon descended to the fruitless rancor of earlier sessions.

The more serious foreign activities of the Soviets in mid-1955 were being pressed at the very moment of the Geneva meeting but were pointed in a quite different direction. What that direction was could be discerned as early as April, when *Izvestiia* called for a revival in Soviet Middle Eastern studies, and Soviet publications began to devote increasing space to that region. Trouble had been smoldering in the eastern Mediterranean since the uneasy Arab-Israeli armistice of 1949, and the emergence in 1954 of Colonel Gamal Abdel Nasser as ruler of Egypt, strongest of the Arab countries, had tended to focus that tension on the Israeli-Egyptian relationship. However, there were also rivalries within the Arab League (a loose organization of Moslem states set up in 1944 under British encouragement; it then consisted of Egypt, Iraq, Syria, Lebanon, Jordan, Saudi Arabia, and Yemen, and later Libya and the Sudan were added). In February 1955 the strains between Iraq and Egypt were heightened when Iraq entered a defensive alliance with Turkey, later joined by Britain, Pakistan, and Iran, known as the Bagdad Pact. The next month Egypt and Syria countered with the signature of a Damascus Pact, soon joined by Saudi Arabia and Yemen.

In the summer of 1955 D. T. Shepilov, already identified as an important figure in Soviet foreign policy by his role in the talks with Tito, visited Cairo and arranged the purchase of considerable armament by Nasser, nominally from Czechoslovakia. Soviet propaganda and agitation in the Damascus Pact countries, especially Egypt and Syria, increased in late 1955, utilizing in particular the anticolonialist slogans popularized at the Asian-African conference which had been held at Bandung in April (see p. 444). In 1955, however, the Western leaders seemed to pay little attention to the developing Middle Eastern danger. The year closed with another Soviet diplomatic victory, which came on the heels of a triumphant tour by Khrushchëv and Bulganin in India, Burma, and Afghanistan: the admission into the U.N. in December of the East European satellites still outside it—Albania, Bulgaria, Hungary, and Rumania.

THE XX PARTY CONGRESS

At the XX Party Congress, held in February 1956 in Moscow, Khrushchëv dominated the proceedings as expected. The roster of the full members of the Party Presidium remained unchanged, but with the exception of Nicholas Shvernik, who was carried over, the alternate members were new. Ponomarenko was dropped, and four were added: Marshal Zhukov, Catherine Furtseva, first secretary of the Moscow party, L. I. Brezhnev, first secretary of the Kazakh party, and Nuritdin Mukhitdinov, first secretary of the Uzbek party (the latter two had just been given their posts in Soviet Asia, on the conclusion of Khrushchëv's and Bulganin's Asian tour). Brezhnev and Furtseva were also appointed to the Secretariat, making a total of eight secretaries of the Central Committee.

At the Congress the new personnel changes were formally approved, and the inauguration of the Sixth Five-Year Plan (for the period 1956–1960) was announced. In his public report, Khrushchëv made something like an open obeisance to Tito by referring to different "forms of transition of various countries to socialism" and citing Yugoslavia as an example of one such "form." He purported to revise the "Marxist-Leninist thesis that war is inevitable so long as imperialism exists" by declaring that since imperialism had ceased to be "an all-embracing world system" and since antiwar forces were stronger than before, imperialist war might be avoided. However, as he also reaffirmed "the Leninist thesis that in so far as imperialism exists the economic basis for war is preserved," the doctrinal "innovation" did not seem to come to much. The function of these involved remarks appeared to be to support a frank invitation to the "neutralist" leaders and countries of Asia to co-operate closely with the Soviet Union.

The most important development at the Congress was not made public at all, and if it had not been for the United States State Department's publication (in June) of Khrushchëv's "secret speech" at a closed session, the outside world might not yet have learned the details. In this speech, delivered the night of February 24, Khrushchëv itemized a good many of Stalin's crimes, chief among them being the murder of Party leaders loyal to him, and leveled other accusations against Stalin, such as responsibility for the break with Tito. Certain charges were palpably absurd, such as the assertion that Stalin could not read a map and planned military operations on a globe.

The reason for the timing and manner of the "secret speech" remains somewhat obscure. In his own public report to the Congress, Khrushchëv had called for a new history of the Communist Party to replace Stalin's *Short Course*. In another speech, on February 16, Mikoyan had criticized Stalin more bluntly than had hitherto been done by any Soviet leader, and at the same time had rehabilitated Kosior, whom Khrushchëv himself had helped purge in the Ukraine (see p. 469). Speculation was that Mikoyan's speech forced Khrushchëv to his scathing, if secret, attack; that Tito had successfully demanded the attack; that the Mikoyan speech was only a trial balloon connived in by Khrushchëv to test the reaction before going further; and there were other theories, none of which can be completely verified.

In general, however, Khrushchëv's motives seem clear enough. He was trying to exorcise the incubus of his dead master, whom he had loyally served so long, because of the massive unpopularity of all he stood for among the Soviet people, yet he wished to avoid calling into question the structure of the whole regime or opening the way to public queries about the role of the leaders of 1956 during the commission of the crimes which he detailed. Despite the attack on Stalin, Khrushchëv declared at the end of the "secret speech" that the "whole tragedy" lay in the fact that Stalin's errors were not "the deeds of a giddy despot," but that he "doubtlessly performed great services to the party, to the working class, and to the international workers' movement." The task of the Party was to restore "the victorious banner of our party—Leninism!" and under this slogan to eradicate the "cult of personality," strengthen "collective leadership" and criticism and self-criticism on all levels of the Party, and restore "the Leninist principles of Soviet socialist democracy" as expressed in the Constitution.

Following the Congress there were several public rehabilitations of Party leaders long dead, and even of a few who, such as G. I. Petrovski, who was in the Politburo in the 1930's, had somehow survived the purges. As word sifted down to the masses in the USSR and leaked out abroad that Stalin had been attacked at the Congress, there were two different sorts of responses. One came from foreign Communist leaders, who reacted with a mixture of shock and unwonted frankness. Palmiro Togliatti, the Italian Communist leader, hinted that he considered Khrushchëv's evaluation of Stalin unduly harsh, but that if it *had* been warranted, then the current leaders were also implicated. Other foreign comrades spelled out these hints. On June 30 the Soviet Party Central Committee felt obliged to speak. Brushing aside talk about confusion in Communist ranks as "fables," the Central Committee nevertheless admitted that certain comrades were "not completely clear on the question of the personality cult . . . ." By noting that the needs of Stalin's day included "iron discipline . . . vigilance . . . strictest centralization of leadership," the Central Committee clearly implied that the criticism had gotten out of hand and should cease.

REVOLUTIONARY STIRRINGS WITHIN THE SOVIET ORBIT

By this time a second type of response to Khrushchëv's speech had become manifest in the Soviet empire. Only weeks after the Congress, riots occurred in the Georgian capital of Tbilisi. The regime tried to convey the impression that the rioters had protested the desecration of Stalin's memory, but Stalin's past treatment of his own native land provided scant reason for Georgians to venerate him. Eyewitness accounts make it clear that opposition to the regime and Georgian nationalism played an important part in the disturbance, in which over a hundred were killed.

In the East European satellites, it had been expected that the May 1955 reconciliation between Tito and Khrushchëv would bring about a relaxation in Moscow's controls. When nothing of the sort was forthcoming, Poland led the way in open expressions of dissatisfaction. In August 1955 the official organ of the Polish Writers' Union published a remarkable *Poem for Adults* by Adam Ważyk, in which he wrote,

> We make demands on this earth,
> for the people who are overworked,
> for keys to open doors,
> for rooms with windows,
> for walls which do not rot,
>
> for hatred of little documents,
> for holy human time . . .[3]

Public discussion grew increasingly frank, and not long after the "secret speech," in May 1956, the chief die-hard leader of the Polish party,

[3] Translation of Lucjan Blit, *The Twentieth Century* (London, December 1955), p. 510.

Jakub Berman, was forced out of his posts. On June 28, while an international fair was under way at Poznań, factory workers organized a demonstration which developed into armed clashes with the police, resulting in the killing of perhaps a hundred (the government admitted fifty-three). Prime Minister Cyrankiewicz rushed to the scene and, ascribing the riots to "imperialistic agents," warned that anyone who dared "raise his hand against the people's rule" would "have his hand chopped off by

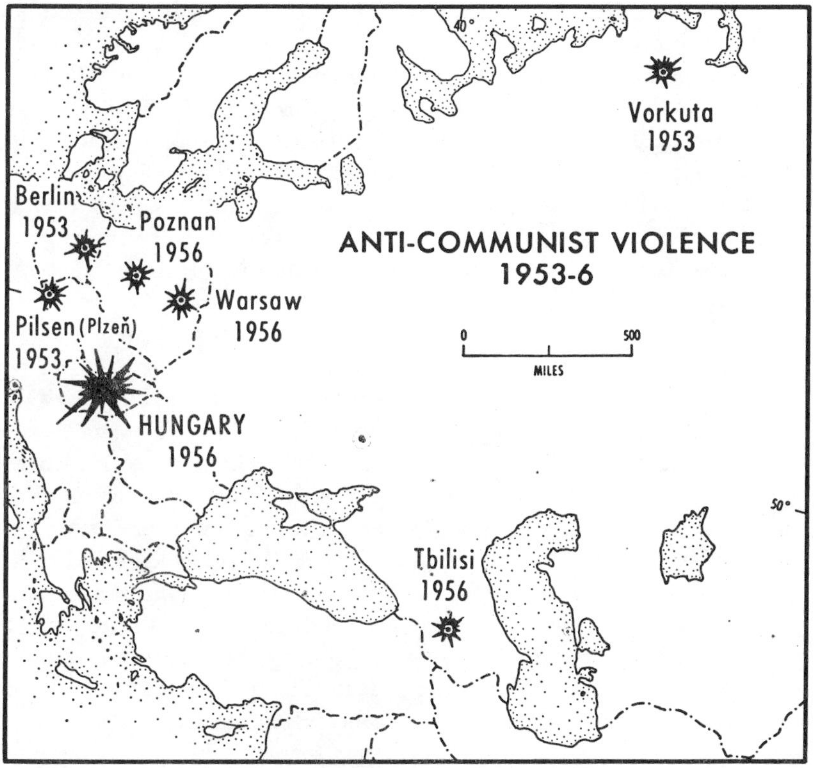

the authorities." Nevertheless the Poznań rioters who were given public trial received unexpectedly mild sentences, and criticism continued more and more openly, especially from the Polish writers.

Shortly before the Poznań riots, Khrushchëv had taken further steps in the *rapprochement* with Tito. The Soviet leader had paved the way in his "secret speech" by ascribing the break of 1948 to Stalin himself. In April 1956 the Cominform, the agency which had condemned Tito, was "dissolved"—although one may be certain that this measure, like the "end" of the Comintern, had little effect on Moscow's links with its foreign comrades. Two months later Tito returned Khrushchëv's visit by going to Moscow, and on June 20 a joint declaration of the two Communist parties repeated that "the path of socialist development differs in various countries and conditions," which suggested again that Tito had had his way. On the eve of Tito's visit to Moscow, Molotov had been dropped from the foreign ministry and replaced by Shepilov, who had gone to Belgrade with Khrushchëv the previous year. The *rapprochement* between Khrushchëv and Tito seemed to be proceeding with success, and the Poznań riots did not ruffle the calm.

In July, perhaps in consequence of Tito's visit to Moscow, the Hungarian party leader, Rákosi, was forced out and replaced by Ernö Gerö as first secretary. For some time public criticism had been sharpening in Hungary, especially in the "Petöfi circle" of Hungarian writers. Gerö criticized the circle in turn, but took no action against it. On October 6 the reburial of László Rajk (executed in 1949 as a Titoist) turned into a silent mass demonstration, and a week later Imre Nagy was publicly restored to party membership. The writers' discussions now broadened to include university students, who demanded and obtained, among other things, the end of compulsory Russian language instruction.

A few days later the Polish events reached a climax. Władysław Gomułka, who had been Poland's chief alleged Titoist but had escaped with imprisonment, had been reinstated in August. On October 19 a plenum of the Central Committee of the Polish United Workers' (Communist) party elected him first secretary and took a strong stand for further internal changes. Later the same day a Soviet delegation headed by Khrushchëv reached Warsaw. According to persistent reports, Khrushchëv and Gomułka had a stormy interview replete with threats, by the former to use the Soviet troops stationed in Poland, and by the latter to use Polish workers to impede communications. However, publicly it was stated simply that agreement was reached on problems of mutual interest. There were a number of public demonstrations, some of them erupting into violence, but on appeal from Gomułka—and from Cardinal Wyszynski, who had just been released from arrest—the Polish people refrained from pressing what seemed a clearly revolutionary situation into armed uprising.

THE HUNGARIAN UPRISING

In Hungary the crisis exploded into a revolution of the classic nineteenth-century type, which many historians had believed a thing of the past. It opened on October 23 with a demonstration organized by university students in support of the Poles, whose silent battle with the Soviets was being followed with intense interest in Hungary. The crowd later joined another group—the whole coming to two or three hundred thousand people, according to the later U.N. report—in front of the Parliament building in Budapest, and demanded to see Imre Nagy, who appeared briefly. The next day, October 24, the students approached the Radio Building seeking to have broadcast the demands which they adopted the day before, including immediate withdrawal of Soviet troops from the country, the reconstitution of the government under Nagy, free elections, free speech, and sweeping social changes. The students were fired upon by the Hungarian secret police (A.V.H.), and large-scale fighting broke out, which rapidly spread all over the country, against A.V.H. troops and Soviet forces which were sent into Budapest that night. The Hungarian army disintegrated and most of its men actively joined the rebels.

The same night the Hungarian Politburo named Nagy premier, but actually kept him under virtual arrest for three more days. On October 24 it was announced that the Hungarian government had called for Soviet military assistance under the terms of the Warsaw Treaty. There is evidence that Nagy on October 25 refused to sign such a document, which was dated the twenty-fourth when presented to him for signature. In any case Soviet troops arrived in Budapest before any such appeal was sent, even if the Communist version of its dispatch is to be believed. On October 25 Gerö was removed as first secretary, promptly disappeared, and was replaced by Janos Kadar, who had himself been imprisoned earlier. The following day revolutionary workers' councils—the first genuine Soviets to exist in the "Soviet" orbit for almost forty years, but like the Kronstadt Soviet of 1921, opposed to Communist dictatorship—began to be formed and continued to spring up all over Hungary. On October 27 the government was reorganized to include such genuine non-Communists as Béla Kovacs, former leader of the Smallholders' party. Imre Nagy, having escaped confinement, spoke the next day denying that a counter-revolution was in progress. In the last days of October the Soviet forces withdrew from most of Budapest. Nagy appeared to stand at the head of a regime of a successful popular revolution, and the Social Democrat Anna Kéthly entered his already multiparty government.

There followed a few days, filled with the exhilarating atmosphere of apparent victory, in which peace prevailed in Hungary and both democracy and national independence seemed to have been secured. On November 1 Prime Minister Nagy telegraphed to U.N. Secretary-General

Hammarskjöld notice of Hungary's repudiation of the Warsaw Treaty and declaration of neutrality, pleading with "the four great powers" to defend its neutrality, and requesting Hammarskjöld to place the problem on the U.N. agenda. Two days later nine Communist ministers resigned from the Hungarian government.

In the early hours of November 4, Soviet troops suddenly swept into Budapest. The Hungarians tried in vain to resist. Women and children in a bread line were shot down, an ambulance was destroyed, and many other noncombatants were killed. As the U.N. report puts it, however, "the whole population of Budapest took part in the resistance," and therefore it was impossible to distinguish between civilian and military personnel. On the same day Janos Kadar, who had remained until then a minister in the Nagy government, was installed by Soviet troops as prime minister of a new regime. That evening Imre Nagy and others found asylum in the Yugoslav Embassy. Some two weeks later, Nagy was seized by Soviet troops when leaving the Embassy under a safe-conduct from Kadar. Anna Kéthly escaped to protest in vain to the U.N. that she should be recognized as Hungary's U.N. delegate; tens of thousands of Hungarians fled across the border. The U.N. report accurately concludes that the Hungarian uprising "collapsed because of the Soviet armed intervention and because no support was forthcoming for them [the revolutionists] from abroad."

The U.N. did not take up the Hungarian affair, as Nagy had urgently requested it to do, until the uprising was already crushed. The United States was hampered in acting because it was in the last days of a presidential campaign; nevertheless, the U.S. delegation was active in the U.N. deliberations which occurred in those very days on the Suez crisis. On October 29 Israeli troops had suddenly attacked Egypt and rapidly neared the Suez Canal. Almost immediately Britain and France, still smarting over Nasser's seizure of the canal in July, in abrogation of an agreement which would have given him control over it by 1968, and irritated at United States Secretary of State Dulles's refusal to take the sort of line with Nasser which they felt necessary, bombarded Egyptian bases and landed troops near the canal. The USSR immediately demanded international action to stop the Israeli and Western invasion of Egypt. The Suez crisis was a godsend for the USSR in diverting world attention from Hungary, but quite aside from Hungary, the invasion would if successful have gravely threatened the Soviets' swiftly growing influence on the chief Arab countries. The United States took an equally strong line with the invading powers. The momentary United States-USSR partnership exerted pressure in and out of the U.N., which held noon-to-dawn sessions on the Suez crisis. Israeli, British, and French forces were compelled to withdraw from Egyptian territory, and the U.N. installed an international police force in the vicinity of the canal to keep peace. When it was too late to affect the outcome of the Hungarian uprising, the U.N. then turned to denounce, despite angry Soviet opposition, the USSR's actions in Hungary.

Shock and rage at the suppression of the Hungarian revolt swept the outside world. Such prominent Communists as Jean-Paul Sartre in France and Howard Fast in the United States tore up their party cards, and many lesser comrades defected. However, Tito held fast to his new relationship with Khrushchëv. In a speech on November 11 at Pula, although he declared that the Soviet intervention of October 24 was mistaken because no "counterrevolution" had yet appeared, he asserted of the attack of November 4 that if it "saves socialism in Hungary," then he had to say that "although we are against interference, Soviet intervention was necessary."

At this point a simmering unrest inside the USSR itself, manifested especially among the university students, took the form of public meetings in Leningrad, Moscow, and other cities. Angry questions about the Hungarian events were asked and the official answers scornfully rejected; basic doubts were voiced which, although often couched in the phraseology of official doctrine, by implication challenged many Soviet governmental practices or even the system itself. In October a full-fledged strike was reported in the Kaganovich ball-bearing works in Moscow, the first such manifestation by Soviet workers in decades. Although the Soviet writers as a group took no such defiant position as those in the Hungarian Petöfi circle, two or three had by this time risked much by producing frank novels about Soviet society as it was, not as it was ideally supposed to be currently or to become in the future. The most forthright of these works was Vladimir Dudintsëv's novel, *Not by Bread Alone*. In a public discussion held in May 1957, the book was sharply attacked by official spokesmen, but Dudintsëv for the time being refused to grovel, and a number of students, crowds of whom had come to defend the book, spoke bluntly in its favor.

From the Hungarian revolution to date (1963) there has apparently been no large-scale violence in the USSR or the Communist-ruled states of Eastern Europe. However, the upshot of the blood bath in Budapest has been that Khrushchëv had to face new facts about the position of the Soviet Communist leadership. What he might do in the USSR could no longer be done without serious consideration of its repercussions in the remainder of the Communist orbit and the whole international Communist movement. His "secret speech" of 1956 had led to armed uprising of the masses in Eastern Europe and grave concern about the implications of "de-Stalinization" in the leadership of Communist China. As events were soon to show, Khrushchëv was to face immediate and great danger in the USSR itself.

Khrushchëv in Power (1957–1963)

CHAPTER 29

THE DEFEAT OF THE "ANTI-PARTY GROUP"

Later historians will doubtless have an easier time perceiving when Khrushchëv's ascendancy was secured, but the precedent of the rise of Stalin suggests that fixing an exact moment may remain difficult. When Stalin was named general secretary of the Party, he was given a powerful organizational advantage over his rivals that he managed to use to decisive effect (see p. 205); something similar may be said of Khrushchëv's successful wresting of the first secretaryship from Malenkov's hands a few days after Stalin's death in 1953. Stalin's adroitness in seizing the occasion of Lenin's death in 1924 to deliver his "vow" helped his cause significantly, and made it easier for him to avoid any implementation of Lenin's testamentary recommendation that he be dismissed from his crucial post (see pp. 213–214); Khrushchëv's decision to take the leadership over the Stalin issue at the XX Congress gave him a program that had its risks but also important advantages, and that minimized the force of any hints his colleagues might make that he himself was implicated in Stalin's crimes. Stalin's defeat of the Left Opposition in 1927 (see p. 224) substantially consolidated his dictatorship; Khrushchëv's narrow victory of 1957 proved to be decisive for his own position. However, the outcome was scarcely a foregone conclusion.

What took place in the secret councils of the Kremlin during the Hungarian uprising remains unknown, but the indications are that Khrushchëv did not escape blame, either for the way he had handled "de-Stalinization," which had engendered the crisis, or for the way he handled the rising itself, or both. Speaking to a closed meeting of Party leaders, writers, and artists in May 1957, he used the accents of "thunder and lightning," as he said later, and is believed to have threatened that if Soviet writers should follow the path of the Hungarian writers, "my hand will not tremble." But at that moment his own control over the Soviet Party was in danger.

In December 1956 the Party Central Committee, apparently at the urging of Malenkov and the industrial managers, made a decision to strengthen the State Economic Commission, of which Pervukhin became chairman and apparently something like economic czar of the country. Khrushchëv was silent when this move was made and when it was ratified by the Supreme Soviet in February 1957. However, the very next day he launched a counterattack to cut down the Economic Commission in favor of a strengthened State Planning Commission (Gosplan), and proceeded to abolish 33 central ministries in Moscow in favor of 195 new regional Economic Councils (*sovnarkhozy*). The Supreme Soviet ratified these changes in May 1957. The measures were widely described in the foreign press as "decentralization," but this was a misnomer, since the new economic regions coincided in almost every case with the existing administrative districts (*oblasti*). The difference from the previous situation was merely that the managers were no longer subject to a managerial hierarchy, but instead were more directly than ever controlled by the still firmly centralized Party machinery. Under the guise of seeking a higher degree of technical efficiency in management—which was undoubtedly a real need of the regime—Khrushchëv thus struck a telling blow at his opposition.

It may be that Malenkov, Molotov, and Kaganovich decided then that they must strike back before it was too late. In June 1957 it was revealed that Khrushchëv had in unprecedented fashion taken a dispute from the Party Presidium into the Central Committee as a whole, and there won a decisive victory. It later became known that Khrushchëv had faced a seven-to-four majority, consisting of Malenkov, Kaganovich, Molotov, Bulganin, Voroshilov, Saburov, and Pervukhin, which had wished to depose him as chief of the Party. The Central Committee dismissed from the Presidium Malenkov, Molotov, Kaganovich, and Saburov, and the candidate member Shepilov, and demoted Pervukhin from full to candidate member. However, at this time Khrushchëv either did not feel strong enough or was too merciful to ask for more. Four candidates were raised to full membership: Brezhnev, Furtseva, Shvernik, and Zhukov. Five men were abruptly elevated to the highest Party body: A. B. Aristov (a close aide of Khrushchëv's in Party affairs) and N. I. Beliaev (who had previously been on the Secretariat), N. G. Ignatov, F. R. Kozlov, and the old-time Finnish Communist Otto Kuusinen, who was simultaneously raised to the Secretariat. Only one candidate member of the Presidium, Mukhitdinov,[1] remained, and seven new ones were appointed: P. N. Pospelov, earlier a Party secretary; D. S. Korotchenko, one of the chiefs of the Ukrainian party; J. E. Kalnberzins, first secretary of the Latvian party; A. P. Kirilenko; A. N. Kosygin (from 1949 to 1952 a full member); K. T. Mazurov, a Belorussian party leader; and V. P. Mzhavanadze, chief of the Georgian party.

Malenkov, Kaganovich, Molotov, and Shepilov were publicly stigmatized as an "anti-Party group," from which Khrushchëv claimed he had saved the party and country. Circumstances suggested that he owed part of his success to the backing of Marshal Zhukov and the army. Certainly Zhukov was the first fighting general (as distinguished from such political figures as Bulganin and Voroshilov) to become a full member of the highest Party body. However, Zhukov's pre-eminence lasted only a few months. In October he was dismissed from the defense ministry and shortly afterward from both Presidium and Central Committee, having been denounced for having fostered his own "cult of personality" in the armed forces.

Khrushchëv's ascendancy seemed secure. He apparently had a handpicked majority in the Presidium. With Zhukov out of the way, he seemed to have dispensed with the need of showing the generals special favor; with Malenkov exiled to a remote industrial installation, along with the managers who had been sent out of Moscow in May, the control of Khrushchëv's Party *apparatchiki* appeared to have been assured; with Molotov gone, the way was clear to further "de-Stalinization," improvement in relations with Tito, and emphasis on the policy of "peaceful coexistence" with the Western powers. Plainly he had more power than any one man had had since Stalin's death, and when he deposed Bulganin and himself assumed the office of premier in March 1958, he held the top posts in both Party and government, as Stalin had done.

Nevertheless, like the shade of the physically dead Stalin, that of the

• [1] In December 1957 Mukhitdinov was made a full member of the Presidium (which now numbered 15 again) and was also named to the Secretariat, as were Ignatov and Kirichenko.

politically dead Molotov threatened to return, in a Chinese if not a Russian guise, to bedevil Khrushchëv. The ideological mantle of Molotov seemed to pass to Mao Tse-tung, who was not within Khrushchëv's reach in the same way Molotov was. The danger signs appeared as early as 1957. Although Mao and the Chinese Communist leadership had made much of the "five principles" policy of peace in 1954–1955 and had made a deceptive gesture at domestic liberalization in the "hundred flowers" campaign in early 1957 (see p. 444) in the immediate aftermath of Hungary, there was no doubt that Peking's enthusiasm for Khrushchëv's attack on Stalin at the XX Congress in 1956 was considerably more restrained than that of most Russian comrades. Mao was senior to Khrushchëv as a first-rank leader in the international Communist movement, and, aside from whatever personal jealousies Mao may have felt, considerations of prestige, vital to any totalitarian regime, had to be reckoned with. As Mao moved into the period of "Second Revolution" (see p. 441) in China, the relevance of Stalin's writings and methods—indeed of his whole image—to Chinese Communist policies became more direct with every passing month, and Khrushchëv's attacks on Stalin, even though largely motivated by Soviet domestic problems, were bound to make the Chinese leaders uneasy. Khrushchëv faced the need to consolidate his own power, expand the economy, and establish the prestige of the USSR (and his own leadership) more firmly as a prerequisite to further expansion; all this required that the carrot be in the foreground, the stick in the background. Mao was entering the stage of creating a new society and a new economy, and the stick had to be his main device for some time.

Thus Khrushchëv and Mao responded differently to the tremendous soar in Soviet prestige produced when the earth satellites *Sputnik I* and *Sputnik II* (carrying a dog) were launched in October and November 1957. (The United States, in its feverish haste to match these feats, inadvertently contributed to the propaganda success reaped by the USSR by publicizing its own failures which preceded a successful firing in February 1958, and much of the American public treated Soviet scientific and educational achievements as a new revelation, overestimating them as greatly as the ill-informed had previously underestimated them.) Mao apparently concluded that the world Communist offensive might now be pressed with more open brandishment of weapons; Khrushchëv believed that it now did not need to be as openly aggressive as Mao tended to think. That did not prevent him from occasional and brutal threats to rain missiles on New York and London, but it seemed to set a divergence in foreign-policy emphasis between Moscow and Peking. One signal was the Rapacki Plan for "disengagement" of the powers in Central Europe, offered in October 1957 as a Polish scheme but plainly with Soviet backing. In November 1957 Khrushchëv summoned two consecutive conferences in Moscow, first one of 12 Communist and workers' parties in power, and then one of 64 parties from all parts of the world. Both conferences approved the Moscow line of re-emphasizing "peaceful coexistence." Khrushchëv's relations with Tito's Yugoslavia, which had after several ups and downs improved sufficiently in 1957 so that the Yugoslavs joined in the second Moscow conference, were strained again in early 1958. However, Mao went much further than Khrushchëv in attacking Tito.

The Moscow conferences were followed by a new Soviet drive for a summit conference, which did not succeed. The USSR had moved into the field of "economic aid," paying the United States the compliment of imitation, by an offer to build a steel plant in India after the Khrushchëv-Bulganin tour of 1955. In 1957 agreements were signed with Burma and Afghanistan, in 1958 the USSR loaned Egypt a sum sufficient to start the Aswan High Dam, and aid was subsequently extended to a number of African countries, including Ethiopia, Guinea, Mali, and Somalia. The opening of the institution soon to be called Patrice Lumumba Friendship University in Moscow in the fall of 1959 suggested the seriousness of the Soviet penetration into Africa, but also that it was to be "peaceful." That did not prevent the Soviets and Iraqi Communists from backing General Abdul Karim Kassem's coup in Iraq in July 1958, challenging Nasser's new (February 1958) United Arab Republic from the Left.

Mao, however, went home to Peking to dismiss Chou En-lai as foreign minister in February 1958 and to prepare for forceful action. More or less simultaneously he prepared to attack the offshore island of Quemoy and to push the "Second Revolution" into a tremendously accelerated phase. Apparently the Soviets assented to a probing operation against Quemoy but insisted on drawing back when U.S. forces showed themselves ready to fight, and Quemoy remained in the hands of the Nationalist Government on Taiwan. On the domestic front, Mao raised "three red flags": "the general line," "the people's communes," and "the great leap forward." Within a few months it was claimed that over 99% of the Chinese peasantry had joined the communes, in which private property and the family nearly disappeared, and there was stress on the formation of communal military units. By the autumn of 1958 the Chinese countryside was thrown into chaos similar to that of the early months of 1930 in the USSR. However, there soon came a withdrawal reminiscent of Stalin's "Dizziness from Success" statement (see p. 269): in December 1958 the Chinese

Communist Central Committee called for a temporary let-up in the drive for communes, and Mao Tse-tung resigned as chairman of the government. Initially the Soviets had praised the achievements of the "Great Leap," but as its pace had mounted, Moscow's tone changed, for the Chinese Communists were claiming that the Leap was taking them through socialism in the direction of pure communism, thus by implication carrying them past the stage of the USSR. Khrushchëv, Mikoyan, and others were at no pains to conceal their belief that the scope of the whole offensive was impossibly premature and doomed to fail. Moreover, they correctly saw in it a Chinese challenge to the Soviet leadership of the whole Communist movement.

THE XXI PARTY CONGRESS

The result was the XXI Special Party Congress, convened under extraordinary circumstances nominally to approve the new Soviet Seven-Year Plan, actually chiefly to demonstrate Khrushchëv's supremacy in the USSR and to assert again Soviet primacy in the international Communist movement.

In the preceding year two of Khrushchëv's domestic "reforms" suggested, as the decentralization of management in 1957 had done, that he continue to pursue the same goals as Stalin did but by the use of milder methods. In April 1958, just as the clamor in the United States for imitation of the Soviet educational system was reaching its height, he severely criticized Soviet schools for failing to meet the demands of socialist construction, and called for revamping the whole system. In December the Supreme Soviet approved a program in which much greater emphasis was laid on physical labor and actual part-time work in factories and plants as part of the curricular pattern. The humanities and social sciences were not to be taken out of mass education, but they were to take a definite second place to the scientific and technical subjects required to fill the jobs in the skilled labor force that were going begging. Since it had been revealed that only 55% of the children starting school actually had been reaching the eighth grade, despite previous claims that seven-year schooling was universal, the requirement that eight-year schooling should be "effectively enforced" on the whole school-age population itself was going to require great effort. Thus the needs of the state were placed first in a sweeping alteration of Soviet educational conditions. Here, incidentally, Khrushchëv seemed to be borrowing from Mao, for after 1957 there had been great emphasis on manual labor and practical work for the students of mainland China.

The second "reform" had been the abolition of the Machine-Tractor Stations (see p. 270), which appeared to suggest the reduction of Party controls over agriculture. Again appearances were misleading. As Khrushchëv said, it made no sense to have "two bosses on the land." As the number of collective farms, partly through amalgamation into larger units, dropped below 80,000 (1959; see p. 460), the MTS, which had served as intermediary agencies of control, could be dispensed with for the sake of more direct party supervision of the countryside. The continuing amalgamation of the collective farms had been accompanied by a gradual development of another sort: the steady increase of the acreage tilled by state farms, or "sovkhozization." The *sovkhozy* in 1957 embraced over 25% of the land as against 10% in 1952, in part because of the conversion of new *kolkhozy* in the Central Asian area of virgin and idle lands (see p. 470), but also because old collective farms were being turned into state farms. Collective farmers being converted into state farmers were promised that their private garden plots would not be diminished in the transfer, but the evidence suggests that the promise was broken, and that the size of the new state farmers' plots was soon reduced to that permitted to the industrial workers of the cities. The process of sovkhozization has continued despite a Central Committee warning in February 1958 that the conversion should not be too hasty; in March 1960, for example, over half of the Moscow *oblast* collectives were converted into state farms in a single month. The old Khrushchëv notion of the *agrogorod* (see p. 470), which he discussed again in a speech in his native village in October 1958, was still on the Soviet agenda.[2] These developments in the Soviet countryside, pointing in the same direction as the Chinese "people's commune," suggested that the dispute between Khrushchëv and Mao was not so much about goals as about whether Khrushchëv and the USSR were to be recognized as leading the way there.

The XXI Congress, in January–February 1959, represented Khrushchëv's attempt to reassert this principle against Mao's challenge. Ostensibly its task was merely to adopt a Seven-Year Plan, to run from 1959 to 1965. This was to replace the last two years of the Sixth Five-Year Plan, adopted at the XX Congress in 1956, and envisaged a substantially slower rate of growth. The Congress met against the background of successes for Khrushchëv. He had consolidated his victory over the "anti-Party group"

• [2] Meanwhile, especially in the first half of 1960, collectivization was "in the main completed" in most East European states (see p. 421). Collectives and state farms together reached 97% of the arable in Bulgaria, 91% in Albania, 86% in Czechoslovakia, 82% in Rumania. By the beginning of 1961 Hungary reported a figure of 82%. Only Poland and Yugoslavia constituted significant exceptions.

in 1957 by removing Bulganin from the Presidium in September 1958 (though without yet stigmatizing him as a member of the "anti-Party group") and by strengthening his control of the secret police by naming A. N. Shelepin as chief of the KGB[3] in December 1958, replacing General Serov. Shelepin, till then head of the Komosol, was replaced in that post by V. E. Semichastny.

Khrushchëv had other reasons for feeling confident. In 1958 the USSR had had the best harvest in its history. In November 1958 he had inaugurated a new Berlin crisis by threatening to hand the city over to the East Germans in six months, and had set off an alarmed diplomatic reaction in all Western capitals. In January 1959 Fulgencio Batista had been overthrown in Cuba by Fidel Castro with strong Communist support, and Castro acknowledged his dependence on it and his solidarity with the USSR.

The Congress itself was a sustained demonstration of Khrushchëv's increased power. Bulganin, Pervukhin, and Saburov were attacked as members of the "anti-Party group" by a number of speakers, and speech after speech paid tribute to the leadership of Comrade Nikita Sergeevich. However, the personnel changes at the Congress signified either Khrushchëv's moderation or continuing limitations on his absolute power, for Voroshilov remained a full member and Pervukhin a candidate member of the Presidium. The Presidium's full members remained the same as in June 1957 except for Bulganin's demotion and Mukhitdinov's elevation: they consisted of Aristov, Beliaev, Brezhnev, Furtseva, Ignatov, Khrushchëv, Kirichenko, Kozlov, Kuusinen, Mikoyan, Mukhitdinov, Shvernik, Suslov, and Voroshilov, 14 in all. There were nine candidate members: to the seven newly elected in June 1957 were added N. V. Podgorny and D. S. Poliansky. Beliaev and Kirichenko were dropped from the Secretariat; its membership now consisted of Aristov, Brezhnev, Furtseva, Ignatov, Kuusinen, Mukhitdinov, Pospelov, and Suslov.

Perhaps the most significant event at the Congress was Chou En-lai's speech, in which he renewed the same kind of acknowledgment of Soviet primacy in the Communist movement and leadership in building socialism that the Chinese had made at the 1957 meeting of Communist parties, without hinting that in the meantime Mao had challenged the Soviet

• [3] Under Beria (see p. 467), the MVD had temporarily absorbed the MGB. In March 1954 the MGB had been reconstituted under the name KGB (*Komitet Gosudarstvennoi Bezopasnosti* or Committee of State Security) and placed under General Ivan Serov, who had been noted for brutality, especially in carrying out deportations from the Baltic states after they had been annexed. In January 1960 the USSR MVD was abolished and its functions transferred to Union Republic MVD's, but the change was apparently more nominal than real.

position unsuccessfully. The atmosphere which the XXI Congress left behind is well characterized by the collective greeting sent Khrushchëv by the whole Presidium in April 1959:

> Our dear Nikita Sergeevich, on your 65th birthday we warmly and heartily greet you—our elder comrade and friend, true disciple of Lenin and outstanding leader of the Communist Party, the Soviet state, and the entire working-class movement.

This was not a recognition of Khrushchëv as the "Lenin of today" (see p. 228), as Stalin had been called on his fiftieth birthday, but it was still a remarkable notice of a birthday never previously celebrated in the USSR. Sharp-eyed foreign observers did catch one detail: the tributes were published two days late, in a country where such accidents rarely happen. Perhaps a few persons were reluctant to sign; if so, the fact still is that they did. Thus it may not be surprising that *Pravda* in December 1959 published an article commemorating Stalin's anniversary—his eightieth—for the first time in years, or that in 1959 the new *History of the Communist Party of the Soviet Union,* edited by a group headed by B. N. Ponomarev, and in preparation since Khrushchëv demanded it in 1956, considerably toned down its criticism of Stalin. At that point Stalin's strengths may have been especially attractive to his successor.

In 1959 one significant development was the extension of extra-judicial methods of compulsion and punishment for failure to do one's duty by the Soviet state. In April 1956 the Soviet worker had been relieved of some of the direst penalties of the Stalin era: prosecutions for absenteeism were stopped, the prohibition of unauthorized change of job was repealed, the compulsory transfer of workers from one plant to another was ended. This was, however, not the whole story. The plant manager still had at his disposition all sorts of instruments to keep the worker working: the labor book and the passport still recorded the circumstances of change of job, various economic privileges could be denied the laggard. In 1956 another device long intermittently used and formally revived in 1951 was put into operation once more: the comrades' courts, in which one's neighbors and fellow-workers might mete out certain punishments for social delinquency. In 1959 the comrades' courts were given much greater emphasis and scope than before. In March 1959 new volunteer squads called *druzhiny* were encouraged to form and act as guardians of public order and good conduct, hauling suspicious persons out of public places for questioning and combating "hooliganism." Labor discipline was the direct concern of a new series of judicial enactments, the "anti-parasite" laws passed in several republics in the late 1950's and in the RSFSR in May 1961, whose vague provisions made it difficult for a person thought not to be working properly for the good of society, if charged under such laws, to show he was not a "parasite." At the XXI Congress Khrushchëv had claimed that no "political prisoners" were left in the USSR. However, in December 1958, only weeks before, a law had extended the death penalty as a maximum punishment for a variety of "crimes against the state," which included economic and noneconomic offenses. In May 1961 the capital punishment provisions of the 1958 law were extended still further, and additional decrees followed the same trend. Under the May 1961 and subsequent legislation several hundred people have been executed and many more sent to detention, often for nominally "economic crimes." The prominence of priests, Jews, and medium-rank Party officials among the victims, however, suggests that the laws are being used as instruments of political policy. An especially clear example was the arrest of Olga Ivinskaia, close friend of Boris Pasternak, within weeks of the latter's death, nominally for financial misconduct.

CULTURAL POLICY, 1958–1963

The most sweeping challenge to the Soviet system from within the USSR for decades had been offered with Pasternak's great novel, *Doctor Zhivago,* published in Italian translation in November 1957. The author had announced in 1956 that he had finished a novel that would be simultaneously published in the USSR and in Italy (by the Italian Communist publishing house of Feltrinelli). In the summer of 1957 the Soviet literary authorities decided against publishing it, but Feltrinelli went ahead with his plans, and the Italian version was followed by translations into many other languages and by an edition in the original Russian, published in the United States and not permitted to circulate in the USSR. In *Zhivago* Pasternak gave the world his story of a man who comes from the intelligentsia, who is caught up in the Revolution, Civil War, and the building of the Soviet system, who retains his values of integrity and humanity amid the cataclysmic events of his time and is destroyed because of his detachment. Beneath the surface, the book is a prose poem about the meaning of life: "Reshaping life! People who can say that have never understood a thing about life . . . life is never a material, a substance to be molded . . . life is the principle of self-renewal, it is constantly renewing and remaking and changing and transfiguring itself, it is infinitely beyond your or my obtuse theories about it." Although Dr. Zhivago is killed, his spirit triumphs. The Christian that

Pasternak had become shows in the last stanza of the poems with which this thoroughly poetic book closes:

> I shall descend into my grave. And on the third day rise again,
> And, even as rafts float down a river,
> So shall the centuries drift, trailing like a caravan,
> Coming for judgment, out of the dark, to me.[4]

After Zhivago's death, his beloved Lara disappears into a concentration camp; the Soviet regime faithfully fulfilled this prophecy by arresting Ivinskaia.

Although the novel earned world-wide admiration, it did not reach the stage of open discussion in the USSR until 1958, when Pasternak was awarded the Nobel Prize and Khrushchëv compelled him to refuse it in exchange for being allowed to remain in the Soviet Union. He died within two years, himself assured of literary immortality, but after *Zhivago* he took no further part in the cultural life of the country.

The storm that broke over the treatment of Pasternak, however, was not to be quickly stilled. Disturbed by the manifestations of literary discontent of the past few years, and probably still mindful of the role of writers in the Hungarian revolution, Khrushchëv and his colleagues allowed the reactionary writers, led by such people as V. A. Kochetov, to lead the formation of a new organization, the Union of Writers of the RSFSR, in early 1959. However, the dissidents demonstrated such effective solidarity in the face of these efforts that the Party leaders found it expedient to back down. In March 1959 Kochetov was removed from the editorship of the *Literary Gazette* and in May, at the III All-Union Congress of Writers, Alexis Surkov was removed from the headship of the Union of Writers of the USSR and replaced by Constantine Fedin. Khrushchëv himself appeared at the Congress and almost casually made the notable statement, ". . . comrades, you should wash people's brains with your works," but he seemed as yet not to take any strong position in the struggle between reactionaries and dissidents.

The struggle continued with ups and downs for the writers seeking more freedom. It was well known to both sides that behind the dissident writers stood a large section of the generation of young people in their twenties, by now having enjoyed several years' exposure to Western jazz, modern art, and new ideas and fashions of all sorts by way of tourists

[4] Translated by Bernard Guilbert Guerney, in Boris Pasternak, *Doctor Zhivago*, trans. Max Hayward and Manya Harari (New York: Pantheon Books, 1958), p. 559.

from the West, Polish visitors, and underground exchange of their new discoveries. Behind the reactionaries, if it could be mobilized on their side, stood the whole power of the totalitarian state, which could publish or prevent publication, reward writers or exile or kill them if it wished. What a high Soviet official had told an American professor of law was in the minds of many: "If it becomes necessary, we shall restore the old methods. But I think it will not be necessary." In at least three or four cases, including those of Valery Tarsis and Alexander Esenin-Volpin (son of the peasant poet of the twenties), the regime seized the offenders and confined them on the grounds of "mental instability," thus recalling the treatment of Peter Chaadaev by Nicholas I in 1836. But these few were exceptions. The dissident writers knew they were on the perilous frontier of what little freedom was granted in the Khrushchëv era. They did not expect to be allowed to attack the regime or Communism; most of them demanded only the right to write of their private insights, feelings, and perceptions, instead of producing the vapid incantations the reactionaries demanded.

In September 1961 Eugene Evtushenko, along with Andrei Voznesensky one of the two most popular young dissident poets, published a poem entitled "Babii Yar," in which he referred to a famous mass murder of Jews by the Nazis near Kiev in order to strike at anti-Semitism in the USSR. Evtushenko became the idol and standard-bearer of the young radical writers and the thousands of young Russians who demanded more freedom. In 1962 the dissidents gained many positions of strength within the structure of Soviet publishing and editing. The climax came with the publication in November of Alexander Solzhenitsyn's novel *One Day in the Life of Ivan Denisovich,* which was a narrative of life in a Stalinist concentration camp, and created a tremendous sensation. In the same month *Izvestiia* published a poem by Boris Slutsky:

> My boss did not love me,
> Know, see, or hear me . . .
> Yet my whole life I worked for him,
> Late I went to bed and early rose.
> I loved him. And for him was wounded . . .
> And with each passing year less often
> Was hurt by his dislike . . .
> And now my mind is troubled not at all
> Since it is clear that from time's beginning
> For such as I bosses have borne no love.[5]

• [5] "Khoziain," *Izvestiia,* November 24, 1962. Translated by D.W.T.

November 1962 was a turning point, but in the direction of cultural repression. Apparently someone persuaded Khrushchëv to visit two exhibitions of modern art in Moscow at the end of the month, and he reacted, according to reports, with vicious and brutal denunciation and threats delivered on the spot to artists accompanying him. A reactionary, V. Serov, was immediately appointed President of the Academy of Arts. In March 1963, at a closed meeting in the Kremlin of high Party officials, Khrushchëv denounced abstract art and literary experimentation in the strongest terms, criticized Ilia Ehrenburg and Evtushenko sharply, and rejected what he termed "the moldy idea of absolute freedom," which he declared would not be introduced even under full communism in the future. There was no doubt that the problem of literary and artistic dissidence had not been solved.

Few of the young dissident writers and artists had religious convictions, but there had been enough indications that members of the younger generation were investigating religion to alarm the Party hierarchy. Since 1959 the antireligious campaign has mounted in intensity. Apparently two of the few surviving Russian Orthodox seminaries, those at Kiev and Saratov, were closed in 1959–1960. In February 1960 dissatisfaction with the existing management of church affairs was evinced by the replacement of G. G. Karpov by V. A. Kuroedov as Chairman of the Council for the Affairs of the Russian Orthodox Church. In June 1960 the first show trial of an Orthodox clergyman since 1927 was held; the defendant, the archbishop of Kazan, was sentenced to prison. The long-time mainstay of church collaboration with the regime, Metropolitan Nicholas of Krutitsa, fell from favor in 1960, apparently because he refused to cooperate with the new crackdown, and was deprived of his offices. Another show trial was held in November 1961, featuring the archbishop of Chernigov. Repeated statements by high Party officials unequivocally reminded the Soviet people that to be a Communist was to be an atheist.

THE XXII PARTY CONGRESS

In the early months of 1960 came more substantial personnel changes in the high Party leadership than were made at the XXI Congress itself. In May Kirichenko and Beliaev were fired first from the Ukrainian and Kazakh party secretaryships they respectively held, and then from the Presidium. Voroshilov was removed from the Presidium and from his post as titular head of state (Chairman of the Presidium of the USSR Supreme Soviet), which Brezhnev took over. Three new full members of the Presidium were named: Kosygin, Podgorny, and Poliansky. Furtseva and Ignatov fell from the Secretariat, and Kozlov was appointed to it. Of the full members of the immediate post-Stalin Presidium, only Mikoyan remained in addition to Khrushchëv himself. The last of the hostile majority of 1957, Voroshilov, had fallen. At the same time, Kirichenko and Beliaev had been close associates of Khrushchëv, and it was difficult to tell whether they had lost his favor or had been sacrificed to opponents who could not be identified.

Meanwhile Khrushchëv and his colleagues had attempted to follow up Chinese submission at the XXI Congress with action. Indications are that in July 1959 at a meeting at Lushan, Marshal P'eng Teh-huai and others, with Soviet backing, tried to remove Mao as chairman of the Chinese party. The attempt failed, and P'eng was purged.[6] But the Chinese internal offensive had encountered too many obstacles, and Mao was too weak to press a counterattack. His regime faced a full-scale revolution in Tibet in March 1959 which took months to put down. The Dalai Lama and many Tibetans fled into India, and though neither the United Nations nor any of the Western powers could be persuaded to take any official interest in the Tibetan blood bath, the result was unfavorable publicity abroad and intensive domestic precautions lest an echo of the rising should appear within China proper. In August the Chinese Central Committee issued "revised" figures for industrial and agricultural production in 1958, making clear that the Leap had failed to achieve its goals. Khrushchëv might not be able to force Mao out of power, but he may have thought that he could succeed in bringing him to heel by political and economic pressure.

In September 1959, after test visits by Mikoyan and then Kozlov, Khrushchëv visited President Eisenhower in the United States, arriving the day after a Soviet rocket hit the moon. Talks at the President's mountain hideaway produced the "Camp David spirit," which seemed as evanescent and intangible as the "Geneva spirit" attending the summit meeting of 1955. A full-scale summit meeting was planned for the spring of 1960. This meeting, however, was never held; Khrushchëv, arriving in Paris, produced the news that an American high-flying reconnaissance plane, or U-2, had been brought down over the USSR, and demanded an apology. Eisenhower, ignoring the ancient precedent that spies are not acknowledged when caught by the enemy, first denied the flight and then admitted it, but refused to apologize. Khrushchëv used the incident to justify calling off the meeting, although other evidence suggests that he intended to do so in any case. In September Khrushchëv appeared in New

• [6] See David A. Charles, "The Dismissal of Marshal P'eng Teh-huai," *China Quarterly*, October–December, 1961.

York at a United Nations General Assembly meeting, and made news by a fraternal meeting with Fidel Castro and by the astonishing act of taking off his shoe and pounding the table with it to show his disapproval of a UN speaker, thus producing a puzzled and fearful reaction from those delegates who attached meaning to the old-fashioned word, "gentleman."

Returning from these travels, the Soviet leader convened a meeting of 81 Communist parties in Moscow in November–December 1960. Again Mao knuckled under to Khrushchëv. In April the Chinese had put into a manifesto entitled "Long Live Leninism!" their objections to the Soviet line; in June at the Bucharest congress of the Rumanian party, where delegates of many foreign parties had been present, there had been angry words. In July and August the Soviets had withdrawn almost three thousand economic and military technicians and advisers from China. Soviet trade with China declined sharply in 1960 (and thereafter) from the peak of 1958–1959, in which period half of China's total trade was with the USSR. Confronted with such pressure, at the Moscow meeting the Peking delegates argued their position warmly, but finally signed the conference manifesto stating that the Soviet Communist party was the "universally recognized vanguard" of the international movement. There was one concession to the Chinese: it was predicted that all Communist-ruled countries would finally arrive at full communism in a "more or less simultaneous transition." In other words, at the finish line nobody would be in the lead. This was perhaps cold comfort for Mao. But he managed to accomplish one important thing: he detached Enver Hoxha's Albania from the Soviet camp. A convention was tacitly agreed upon that when Peking attacked "revisionism," it gave Yugoslavia and not the USSR as its example; when Moscow attacked "dogmatism," it mentioned Albania and not China. In the summer of 1961 Khrushchëv withdrew Soviet submarines and technicians from Albania, and a rupture of diplomatic relations followed not long thereafter. But Khrushchëv succeeded in offsetting this loss, more picturesque than substantial (even though embarrassing), by going on to pull Yugoslavia most of the way back into the Soviet camp, a task in which he was still engaged in 1963.

The struggle was now almost in the open. If the Soviets were going to keep their primacy and their lead, Khrushchëv had plainly to prepare forthwith for the "transition to communism," and that was the overt ideological purpose of the XXII Party Congress. In July 1961 a new Party program and a new set of Party rules were published in preparation for the Congress, to be held in the fall. The program envisaged the completion of the "transition" by 1980, which would not complete the building of communism, but would place the USSR in a position to embark on its construction. Among the delights that Soviet citizens were to enjoy by 1980 were separate apartments for every urban family, "including newlyweds," and "conveniences"—that is, indoor toilets—for most peasant families. What was planned for two decades hence was scarcely the earthly paradise, but no doubt Soviet citizens regarded the prospect as an improvement over what they now had. The rules contained an interesting new provision for compulsory rotation of Party officials, though loopholes permitted "exceptional" persons to avoid its application.

When the Congress was held in October, further de-Stalinization was proclaimed. The ancient Madame Lazurkina, a Party member since 1902, told of communing with Lenin's shade: "it was as if he stood alive before me, and he said: it is unpleasant for me to lie side by side with Stalin, who brought so much harm to the party." Following this spiritualist report to the materialist Congress, Stalin's body was removed from the mausoleum in Red Square, though not before Chou En-lai placed a wreath there in his memory. Stalin's crimes were further exposed by a number of speakers in a kind of detail that exceeded that of the 1956 "secret speech," and it was charged that several members of the "anti-Party group," especially Molotov, were deeply implicated in Stalin's offenses against the Party. According to reports made of Molotov's current position (not by Molotov himself, who did not speak), it closely approximated Mao's, and thus the battle with the Peking leadership seemed at least partly to merge with the problem of dealing with the "anti-Party group." What was especially interesting about these denunciations of men still at large in the USSR as criminals was that no immediately subsequent move was made to bring them to trial for the crimes with which they had been charged.

The Congress had been preceded by a large-scale shakeup of Party cadres. Of 9,746,000 members and candidates of the Party, more than one-third had joined since the XX Congress. Of the 4,813 delegates to the Congress, 19% had joined since the XX Congress and over 41% since World War II. One full member was added to the Presidium: G. I. Voronov, who had been credited with increasing agricultural production in the RSFSR, and had been made a candidate member in January 1961. Four were removed: Aristov, Furtseva, Ignatov, and Mukhitdinov. That made 11 full members: Khrushchëv, Kozlov, Mikoyan, Suslov, Brezhnev, Kosygin, Podgorny, Poliansky, Kuusinen, Shvernik, and Voronov. It was the smallest Presidium since 1953. Five candidates were dismissed: Kalnberzins, Kirilenko, Korotchenko, Pervukhin, and Pospelov.[7] V. V. Grishin (named in January 1961), Mazurov, and

• [7] Curiously, Kirilenko was suddenly elected full member of the Presidium in April 1962, making a total of 12 again.

Mzhavanadze were carried over, and S. R. Rashidov, chief of the Uzbek party, and V. V. Shcherbitsky, Chairman of the Ukrainian Council of Ministers, were added. The Secretariat was revamped and now consisted, in addition to Khrushchëv as First Secretary, of P. N. Demichev, Moscow's first secretary, L. F. Ilichev, Kozlov, Kuusinen, B. N. Ponomarev, Shelepin, I. V. Spiridonov, Leningrad's first secretary,[8] and Suslov. Immediately after the Congress V. E. Semichastny was appointed head of the KGB, replacing Shelepin—the second time running that the Komsomol had served as a direct springboard to the chieftainship of the secret police. The geographical implications of the Congress were realized as Stalino was renamed Donetsk, Stalinabad Diushambe (its original name) and, most traumatic of all, Stalingrad Volgograd. A Soviet quip of the moment had it that the dead leader sent a telegram to the delegates of the XXII Congress pledging unswerving fidelity to all its decisions, and signed it "Joseph Vissarionovich Volgin."

Some future historian may decide that the further "de-Stalinization" proceeded in the USSR, the more closely Khrushchëv approached the extent of power Stalin held. However, the evidence so far is not conclusive. Though Khrushchëv's enemies of 1957 were removed from high office after the XXII Congress, they were not yet brought to trial. The only change in the Presidium from the Congress to date (October 1963) has been the naming of L. N. Efremov as a new candidate member in November 1962. On the same day four new members of the Secretariat were designated: I. V. Andropov, V. I. Poliakov, A. P. Rudakov, and V. N. Titov. In April 1963 Kozlov, whom Khrushchëv had earlier indicated to be his probable successor, fell ill, but no other heir was designated in his place. The fact is that Khrushchëv, in addition to being given a great deal of attention by mass media as the chief Soviet leader, is the only man who is a member of all four of the following organs: of the Party, the Presidium, Secretariat, and Party Bureau of the RSFSR (to which Khrushchëv has apparently attached increasing significance since its creation in 1956); of the government, the Council of Ministers. His power apparently rests on firm organizational foundations.

In March 1963 he continued his sequence of rapid-fire, sweeping, and contradictory changes in the economy by scrapping the four-year-old Seven-Year Plan in favor of a new plan for the last years of the original period ending in 1965, and by proposing a new Five-Year Plan for 1966–1970. At the same time a new Supreme Economic Council (or Supreme Sovnarkhoz) was set up, with D. F. Ustinov as chairman. This body was to coordinate the USSR State Planning Commission (Gosplan), the USSR State Construction Commission (Gosstroi), and the USSR Eco-

• [8] He was dismissed in May 1962.

nomic Council, which had only been created in November 1962. In November the 17 "major economic regions" (themselves only created in April 1961) had been abolished, the number of local *sovnarkhozy* (1957) reduced by more than half, and the Party itself was decreed split into two complete vertical hierarchies, one for industry and one for agriculture. To be a Party official or an economic manager under Khrushchëv is assuredly to be required to adjust to change.

THE CUBAN CRISIS

In 1963 Khrushchëv's foreign policy had acquired considerable momentum in the direction of "peaceful co-existence," this policy being defined as before as the co-existence of different social systems, *not* of different ideologies. In other words, non-Communist systems were still slated for burial, but preferably by "peaceful" means. The nonexclusion of weapons and their use from this perspective was, however, indicated by several developments. In Laos in 1960–1961 the local Communists, apparently with both Soviet and Chinese Communist backing, made such gains in civil war that the United States had to decide whether to intervene with massive force or to accept a face-saving arrangement that would abdicate any serious hope of preserving Laos from Communist domination. It did the latter by sanctioning the establishment of a "coalition" regime in Laos. (The Soviets implied disapproval, however, of the Chinese offensive against India begun in October 1962. Evidently the Laotian guerrilla offensive was "peaceful," but the Indian one, conducted by regular troops, was not.) It was surmised that Khrushchëv at that point decided that the United States was not going to fight, for he made remarks to several foreign visitors to that effect.

He then proceeded to go rather far in testing his hypothesis by placing Soviet missiles and troops in Cuba, while offering bland assurances that he was not doing so—assurances that the Soviets must have been aware that the Americans knew to be lies. He was apparently surprised when President Kennedy, in October 1962, responded by a virtual ultimatum, to which he yielded by withdrawing (as far as is known) the missiles. He had certainly been placing great reliance on missiles and other new military devices. Since Major Gagarin orbited the earth in April 1961, while Colonel Glenn did not match (and go on to surpass) this feat until February 1962, there was evidence that the Soviets were advancing very satisfactorily in space technology. However, Khrushchëv showed in the Cuban crisis that his plans were, just as before, not primarily dependent on weapons, and viewed in terms of the larger perspectives in which he was operating, the crisis was a resounding victory for him. He had, by bringing the United States to accept limitation of its objective to the withdrawal of missiles, compelled it to scrap the Monroe Doctrine. A Soviet-controlled Cuba remained, at least for the time being, free from the threat of invasion and intact as a base for further subversion throughout the Western Hemisphere. Missiles, of course, might one day be brought back, if not to Cuba, perhaps to British Guiana (where a Marxist-Leninist, Cheddi Jagan, was prime minister), Brazil, Venezuela, or some other Latin American country. But power might be taken in any one or several of them without the use of missiles, and without fear of American intervention unless the Cuban precedent was overturned.

Khrushchëv chose to try to convert even the withdrawal of the missiles, his only loss in the Cuban crisis, into a victory for his policy of "peaceful co-existence." Boasting that Soviet policy had preserved the peace, he was able to gain sufficient international acceptance of that interpretation of the crisis to proceed to attempt to decrease "tensions" further. The first success achieved in this respect was the signing in August 1963 of a treaty among the USSR, Great Britain, and the U.S.A. (to which a great many other countries subsequently added their signatures), banning further nuclear tests except under ground. The danger of nuclear war, however real it had been, was apparently for the moment reduced. The danger of further Communist subversion of non-Communist governments, by guerilla warfare or political action or both, had not diminished; in the Western Hemisphere, at least, it may have increased.

Soviet relations with Communist China worsened as a result of the Cuban crisis and its aftermath. Peking was restrained enough in comments made during the crisis, but afterward charged that the withdrawal of missiles constituted a "Munich" for international Communism and said much about giving in to the "imperialists." In July 1963 talks between Chinese and Soviet Communist Party delegates were held in Moscow; though purportedly designed to resolve differences, they in fact served chiefly as an occasion for full publication of charges and countercharges by both sides. When the United Nations General Assembly opened in the fall, it was for the first time Albania and not the USSR which presented the perennial demand for the seating of Communist China in the place of the Nationalist Government.

THE KHRUSHCHËV ERA

In 1963 the USSR had enjoyed a decade marked by at least one clear blessing—the absence of Joseph Stalin—and for the rest a history of developments in all fields of life which was no longer almost exclusively the story of the whims of one man. In the words of a Russian who spent many years in a concentration camp under both Stalin and Khrushchëv, "Despite communism, Russia as a country has surged forward with gigantic strides. It is not the regime that has effected this progress: it is the people who have pushed it into being. . . . The old people have given up; they have bowed their heads and they haul their burdens. But the young people care about everything. They are on fire with the best aspirations. They fight against drunkenness, against crime. They practice cleanliness and hygiene. They read, read, read. They attend scientific lectures. The Russian youth of the Soviet Union are growing great wings."[9]

Although Khrushchëv inveighed against "spontaneity" as contrasted with "consciousness" (as Lenin had done in the context of the struggle with the Mensheviks), in his style of dictatorship there was some effort to take account of the spontaneous strivings of the Soviet peoples and especially of the youth, an attempt to harness and channel them where they could be of use to the regime, an endeavor to limit and frustrate them in the myriad areas where they could not. Since 1956 the USSR has engaged in cultural exchange programs with a number of countries and accepted large numbers of foreign tourists, a minority of whom were well enough prepared to interpret what they saw and to understand what kind of behavior was possible and desirable in the circumstances. The total impact of greater foreign contacts on Soviet society, or at any rate on Soviet youth, was noticeable, if difficult to measure. Concentration camps still existed, but their inmates were greatly reduced in number. Executions occurred for various "crimes," some of them highly dubious by the standards of Western jurisprudence, but the totals of the culprits were not to be compared with those of Stalin's victims. If consumer's goods were so scarce as to make Taipei an emporium of luxury in comparison with Moscow, and in fact the proportion of total production accounted for by consumer's goods had been slightly declining for decades (contrary to some foreign notions),[10] the proportion was very nearly holding steady. As a result, a steadily increasing gross national product was yielding more dividends to the ordinary man trying to live a decent life. If Party officials might be dismissed or transferred as suddenly as in Stalin's time, they might lose their jobs without losing their lives or being imprisoned. If

• [9] N. N. Krasnov, Jr., *The Hidden Russia: My Ten Years as a Slave Laborer* (New York: Henry Holt, 1960), p. 290.

• [10] See table on p. 47 of the May–June 1960 issue of *Problems of Communism,* giving figures from 1928 to 1960.

official propaganda still insisted that imperialists were aching to destroy not only the Soviet system but the Soviet people, they also declared that it was a common interest of the imperialists and the Communist-ruled countries to avoid nuclear war, and the very idea of a common interest between the two was in the eyes of some a startling innovation.

Khrushchëv had had, in the course of his rise to power, to make a number of concessions to various groups in the Party and to the people. This left him in a difficult position. The concessions, in the nature of things, might gain momentum, and if there were occasional and severe punishments for the people who crossed the uncertain and slightly shifting line of the permissible, there were many who seemed willing to take great risks to follow their notions of what either Communist imperatives or merely human dignity demanded. Khrushchëv faced the dilemma of permitting "spontaneity" to develop further at the expense of "consciousness" and running the risk of substantial unrest, or of reimposing the full vigor of Stalin's kind of controls, which might impair the ability of the world Communist movement to win support in its drive for a fully Communist world, and possibly cause dissension in the highest ranks of the Party. His preferred technique seemed to be alternately to make gestures in both directions. When he pursued a "soft" line, he encouraged those well-intentioned men the world over who preferred the vision of a brighter future to the sight of an unpleasant present. When he followed a "hard" one, he sought to inhibit those among Soviet youth who wanted to change the system by which the totalitarian party's leadership retained the prerogative and the power to dictate behavior in all realms of life and to punish the disobedient in the manner it saw fit, without effective restraint from any body of doctrine, law, or human institution outside of itself.

The structure of Soviet totalitarianism remained, but the ancient search for freedom of the peoples of Russia was not yet at an end. The minorities' republics were the scene of constant turnover of party leadership, and there were also many demotions and transfers in the RSFSR. To accept unquestioningly the values of the regime was still impossible for the collective peasant who was being forced into a state farm, the worker who was being urged on to higher levels of output, the artist or writer who was striving for "honesty," the ordinary man in every walk of life who tried to keep out of trouble by doing what he was told, but was not certain whether Stalin, or Stalin plus Molotov, Kaganovich, and Voroshilov, or all four of those gentlemen plus Khrushchëv himself, were responsible for the past misdeeds that accounted for some of his present miseries, and did not know whether the living men in question might cause him further pain in the future. Many were still waiting, as the poet Pushkin had done, for the time, near or distant, when

> The heavy-hanging chains will fall,
> The walls will crumble at a word;
> And Freedom greet you in the light,
> And brothers give you back the sword.[11]

• [11] Alexander Pushkin, "Message to Siberia," in Max Eastman, *Poems of Five Decades* (New York: Harper, 1954), p. 82.

A Selection of Materials for Further Reading

The books listed below are chosen for the general reader, teacher, or student who wishes to investigate further some of the topics discussed in this volume. Unfortunately there does not exist, to the author's knowledge, any comprehensive bibliography of the subject which lists works in all languages or which covers the whole period. It happens that much of the best work has been written in English, but in any case an effort is made to include volumes in English when material in several languages is available. In certain instances, when material in English is lacking, works in Russian and other European languages are mentioned. Although books on twentieth-century Russia, especially on the USSR, are very numerous, certain important topics have not yet received satisfactory treatment in any language, and where appropriate this is noted.

The materials are arranged in an order paralleling the sequence of topics discussed in the book, with repetition of author and title only when necessary. Authors' names are given as they appear in the books in question; thus one author's name may be spelled several ways.

Introduction: From Absolutism to Totalitarianism

On the geography of the USSR, three books are perhaps most useful. On the natural environment, see L. S. Berg, *Natural Regions of the USSR,* ACLS Translation Project (New York: The Macmillan Co., 1950); on institutional geography, Theodore Shabad, *Geography of the USSR: a Regional Survey* (New York: Columbia University Press, 1951); on economic geography, S. S. Balzak, V. F. Vasyutin, Ya. G. Feigin, *Economic Geography of the USSR,* ACLS Translation Project (New York: The Macmillan Co., 1949). Important statistical information long unavailable has been published by the Soviet government since 1956 in yearbook form. See Naum Jasny, "The Soviet Statistical Yearbooks for 1955 through 1960," *Slavic Review,* XXI (March 1962), 121–156.

Recent discussion of the character of Russian absolutism in modern times has been scanty, since few historians of Russia have been interested in comparative institutional analysis, while social scientists have seldom ventured to write on problems of the past. A challenging hypothesis is set forth by Karl A. Wittfogel in *Oriental Despotism* (Reprint; New

Haven: Yale University Press, 1963); he contends that a form of Oriental despotism was introduced into Russia by the Mongols and took root there. Two recent studies have attempted to explain changes within Russian absolutism in the nineteenth and twentieth centuries up to the Revolution: Victor Leontovitsch's excellent though misleadingly titled book, *Geschichte des Liberalismus in Russland* (Frankfurt am Main: Vittorio Klostermann, 1957), and Jacob Walkin, *The Rise of Democracy in Pre-Revolutionary Russia* (New York: Frederick A. Praeger, Inc., 1962). On totalitarianism, see Carl J. Friedrich and Zbigniew K. Brzezinski, *Totalitarian Dictatorship and Autocracy* (Cambridge: Harvard University Press, 1956, and Praeger Paperback); Jules Monnerot, *Sociology and Psychology of Communism* (Boston: Beacon Paperback, 1960), and my review article, "Toward Understanding Totalitarianism," in *Problems of Communism,* VI, No. 5 (September–October 1957), 37–43.

1. The Russian People

The most recent, detailed, and authoritative history of Russia (although its treatment of the pre-Petrine period is relatively brief) is Michael T. Florinsky, *Russia: a History and an Interpretation* (2 vols.; New York: The Macmillan Co., 1953). A shorter and more analytical account (though to be used with caution on the Soviet period) is B. H. Sumner, *Survey of Russian History* (2nd rev. ed.; London: Gerald Duckworth & Co., Ltd., 1947); the American edition, entitled *A Short History of Russia,* omits the excellent reference notes. A compendium reflecting the recent work of Soviet historians is the multivolume *Ocherki istorii SSSR* (eight volumes thus far published, 1953–1958, covering the period up to the end of the eighteenth century). An important work especially useful on the history of the Russian peasantry is Jerome Blum, *Lord and Peasant in Russia from the Ninth to the Nineteenth Century* (Princeton: Princeton University Press, 1961). The standard work from the pen of a non-Communist Russian historian, which emphasizes social and economic development and takes the story only to the early nineteenth century, is V. Kliuchevsky, *Kurs russkoi istorii* (reprint; 5 vols.; Ann Arbor, 1948, and as the first five volumes of the author's *Sochineniia,* Moscow, 1956–1958); there is a rather unsatisfactory English translation by C. J. Hogarth entitled *A History of Russia,* also in five volumes (New York: E. P. Dutton & Co., Inc., 1911–1931). A brilliant analysis of modern Russia is Paul Milyoukov, *Russia and Its Crisis* (Chicago: University of Chicago Press, 1906, and Collier paperback with author's name spelled "Miliukov"). On foreign policy, see the volume by many hands edited by Ivo J. Lederer, *Russian Foreign Policy: Essays in Historical Perspective* (New Haven: Yale University Press, 1962). On the cultural relationships discussed, see Wladimir Weidlé, *Russia: Absent and Present,* trans. A. Gordon Smith (New York: The John Day Co., Inc., 1952, and Vintage Paperback), and Georgii Florovsky, *Puti russkago bogosloviia* (Paris, 1937). Michael T. Florinsky, ed., *McGraw-Hill Encyclopedia of Russia and the Soviet Union* (New York: McGraw-Hill, 1961) provides authoritative articles on all aspects of the history of Russia, past and present.

On population, see Frank Lorimer, *The Population of the Soviet Union: History and Prospects* (Geneva: League of Nations, 1946). On migration and agricultural change, see Donald W. Treadgold, *The Great Siberian Migration* (Princeton: Princeton University Press, 1957). On the characteristics of the Russian people, see Sir Donald MacKenzie Wallace, *Russia* (rev. and enlarged ed.; London: Cassell and Co., Ltd., 1912, and Vintage Paperback); Stepniak (pseud. of S. M. Kravchinsky), *The Russian Peasantry* (New York: Harper and Brothers, 1888); and Sir John Maynard, *Russia in Flux: Before October* (London: Macmillan & Co., Ltd., 1946). This book is reprinted together with the "main substance" of *The Russian Peasant and Other Studies* under the title *Russia in Flux* (New York: The Macmillan Co., 1948).

A good treatment of the period indicated is Sergei Pushkarev, *The Emergence of Modern Russia, 1801–1917* (New York: Holt, Rinehart and Winston, 1963). Post-Emancipation Russia is surveyed in Hugh Seton-Watson, *The Decline of Imperial Russia, 1855–1914* (New York: Frederick A. Praeger, Inc., 1952) and discussed by various authors in Cyril E. Black, ed., *The Transformation of Russian Society: Aspects of Social Change Since 1861* (Cambridge: Harvard University Press, 1960). The standard works on post-Emancipation agriculture are George Pavlovsky, *Agricultural Russia on the Eve of the Revolution* (London: George Routledge & Co., Ltd., 1930); Geroid Tanquary Robinson, *Rural Russia Under the Old Regime* (New York: Longmans, Green & Co., 1949); and Alexis N. Antsiferov, Alexander D. Bilimovich, and others, *Russian Agriculture During the War* (New Haven: Yale University Press, 1930).

On religion, see Walter Kolarz, *Religion in the Soviet Union* (New York: St. Martin's Press, 1961). Nicolas Zernov in his fine book, *Eastern Christendom* (New York: G. P. Putnam's Sons, 1961), examines Russian Orthodoxy along with the other churches of Eastern Europe and the Near East. On relations between the Orthodox Church and the state, see John Shelton Curtiss, *Church and State in Russia: The Last Years of the Empire, 1900–1917* (New York: Columbia University Press, 1940).

Paul Miliukov deals with both the Russian Orthodox Church and Christian dissenters in *Outlines of Russian Culture,* Part I: *Religion and the Church,* trans. V. Ughet and E. Davis, ed. Michael Karpovich (Philadelphia: University of Pennsylvania Press, 1943). On Christian groups outside the Orthodox Church, see Serge Bolshakoff, *Russian Nonconformity* (Philadelphia: Westminster Press, 1950).

2. The State and the Intelligentsia

On the Imperial central government, no one work gives a satisfactory treatment. G. B. Sliozberg, *Dorevoliutsionnyi stroi Rossii* (Paris, 1933), surveys it along with other topics. V. I. Gurko, *Features and Figures of the Past,* ed. J. E. Wallace Sterling, Xenia Joukoff Eudin, H. H. Fisher, trans. Laura Matveev (Stanford: Stanford University Press, 1939), though in form only the memoirs of a second-rank bureaucrat, gives much insight into the workings of the central government, and the ample notes provide helpful reference material on many of its aspects and the personalities in it. N. I. Astrov and P. P. Gronsky, *The War and the Russian Government* (New Haven: Yale University Press, 1929), is useful, as is another volume in the Carnegie Endowment for International Peace's Russian Series of the Economic and Social History of the World War, on local government: T. I. Polner, *Russian Local Government During the War and the Union of Zemstvos* (New Haven: Yale University Press, 1930). Richard Hare in *Portraits of Russian Personalities Between Reform and Revolution* (New York: Oxford University Press, 1959) includes sketches of Pobedonostsev, Witte, and Stolypin.

On the intelligentsia, see the compendium edited by Richard Pipes, *The Russian Intelligentsia* (New York: Columbia University Press, 1960), which contains essays on both pre-Revolutionary and post-Revolutionary periods. On the development of political and social philosophy, see Thomas Garrigue Masaryk, *The Spirit of Russia,* trans. Eden and Cedar Paul (2nd ed.; 2 vols.; New York: The Macmillan Co., 1955), and V. V. Zenkovsky, *A History of Russian Philosophy,* trans. George L. Kline (2 vols.; New York: Columbia University Press, 1953). There is no adequate full survey of the revolutionary movement. Masaryk in the work mentioned deals with much of it in the latter portion of Volume II. Avrahm Yarmolinsky, *Road to Revolution* (New York: The Macmillan Co., 1959) is a lively account from Radishchev to 1891–1892. Populism is exhaustively dealt with in Franco Venturi, *Roots of Revolution: a History of the Populist and Socialist Movements in Nineteenth Century Russia* (New York: Alfred A. Knopf, Inc., 1960). On the terrorists of the People's Will group, see David Footman, *Red Prelude* (London: Cresset Press, Ltd., 1944). The emergence of socialism in Russia is dealt with by two excellent monographs: Martin Malia, *Alexander Herzen and the Birth of Russian Socialism, 1812–1855* (Cambridge: Harvard University Press, 1961), and James H. Billington, *Mikhailovsky and Russian Populism* (Oxford: Clarendon Press, 1958).

3. Marxism Comes to Russia

On Plekhanov see Samuel H. Baron, *Plekhanov: the Father of Russian Marxism* (Stanford: Stanford University Press, 1963); on his conversion to Marxism, see Leopold H. Haimson, *The Russian Marxists and the Origins of Bolshevism* (Cambridge: Harvard University Press, 1955). For a minority view of the rise of Russian Marxism, see Nicolas Berdyaev, *The Origins of Russian Communism,* trans. R. M. French (London: Geoffrey Bles, Ltd., 1948).

The standard full biography of Marx is Franz Mehring, *Karl Marx,* trans. Edward Fitzgerald (London: George Allen & Unwin, Ltd., 1948); a brilliant smaller work is Isaiah Berlin, *Karl Marx, His Life and Environment* (2nd ed.; London: Oxford University Press, 1948). Discussions of his thought are legion. A justly popular essay is Edmund Wilson, *To the Finland Station* (Garden City: Doubleday and Co., Inc., 1947). Thoughtful evaluations include M. M. Bober, *Karl Marx's Interpretation of History* (2nd rev. ed.; Cambridge: Harvard University Press, 1948); George Lichtheim, *Marxism: an Historical and Critical Study* (New York: Frederick A. Praeger, Inc., 1961); and Adam B. Ulam, *The Unfinished Revolution: An Essay on the Sources of Influence of Marxism and Communism* (New York: Random House, 1960). A short, well-written analysis for students is Sidney Hook, *Marx and the Marxists* (Princeton: D. Van Nostrand Co., Inc., 1955). On the early Marxist parties, see G. D. H. Cole, *A History of Socialist Thought,* Volumes III and IV, *The Second International, 1889–1914* (London: Macmillan & Co., Ltd., 1956), and James Joll, *The Second International, 1889–1914* (London: George Weidenfeld and Nicolson, Ltd., 1955).

4. Lenin's and Other Opposition Parties

On the relations and differences among the liberal, Socialist Revolutionary, and Marxist organizations see Donald W. Treadgold, *Lenin and His Rivals* (New York: Frederick A. Praeger, Inc., 1955). The liberals are dealt with by George Fischer, *Russian Liberalism* (Cambridge: Harvard University Press, 1958); the Socialist Revolutionaries, by Oliver H. Radkey, *Agrarian Foes of Bolshevism: Promise and Default of the Russian Socialist Revolutionaries, March to October, 1917* (New York: Columbia University Press, 1958). The beginnings of Russian Marxism are investigated by Leopold H. Haimson, *The Russian Marxists and the Origins of Bolshevism*, and Bertram D. Wolfe, *Three Who Made a Revolution* (New York: Dial Press, Inc., 1948). The decade of the 1890's has been studied by Richard Pipes, *Social Democracy and the St. Petersburg Labor Movement, 1885–1897* (Cambridge: Harvard University Press, 1963); Arthur P. Mendel, *Dilemmas of Progress in Tsarist Russia: Legal Marxism and Legal Populism* (Cambridge: Harvard University Press, 1961); and Richard Kindersley, *The First Russian Revisionists: a Study of "Legal Marxism" in Russia* (New York: Oxford University Press, 1962). An excellent history of the Russian Social Democrats from the beginning to the present is Leonard Schapiro, *The Communist Party of the Soviet Union* (New York: Random House, 1959); see also John S. Reshetar, Jr., *A Concise History of the Communist Party of the Soviet Union* (New York: Frederick A. Praeger, Inc., 1960), and Robert V. Daniels, ed., *A Documentary History of Communism* (New York: Random House, 1960). Alfred G. Meyer's *Leninism* (Cambridge: Harvard University Press, 1957) gives a careful analysis of Lenin's ideas. The biographies of Lenin are not wholly satisfactory; one of the better ones is David Shub, *Lenin* (Garden City: Doubleday and Co., Inc., 1949; the Mentor Books paperback is an abridged version). A selection of Lenin's works in English has been published in two volumes by Lawrence and Wishart (London, 1947) and in 12 volumes by International Publishers (New York, 1943); a complete edition of 40 volumes (translated from the fourth Russian edition) is being issued by the Foreign Languages Publishing House (Moscow, 1960–   ).

5. The Russo-Japanese War and the Revolution of 1905

The reign of Nicholas II is surveyed by Richard Charques in *The Twilight of Imperial Russia* (Fair Lawn, N.J.: Essential Books, 1958); other aspects of the period are illuminated by Henri Troyat, *Daily Life in Russia Under the Last Tsar* (New York: The Macmillan Co., 1962). On Russian imperialism in Asia, see David J. Dallin, *The Rise of Russia in Asia* (New Haven: Yale University Press, 1949); Victor A. Yakhontoff, *Russia and the Soviet Union in the Far East* (London: George Allen & Unwin, Ltd., 1932); Edward H. Zabriskie, *American-Russian Rivalry in the Far East: a Study in Diplomacy and Power Politics, 1894–1914*

(Philadelphia: University of Pennsylvania Press, 1946); B. A. Romanov, *Russia in Manchuria, 1892–1906,* trans. Susan W. Jones (Ann Arbor: J. W. Edwards, 1952); Richard A. Pierce, *Russian Central Asia, 1867–1917* (Berkeley: University of California Press, 1960); and Andrew Malozemoff, *Russian Far Eastern Policy, 1881–1904* (Berkeley: University of California Press, 1958).

There is no study in English of the Revolution of 1905 as such. See Treadgold, *Lenin and His Rivals;* James Mavor, *An Economic History of Russia* (2 vols.; New York: E. P. Dutton & Co., 1914), Volume II; M. N. Pokrovsky, *Brief History of Russia,* trans. D. S. Mirsky (2 vols.; London: Lawrence and Wishart, 1933), Volume II. On the First Duma, see V. A. Maklakov, *Pervaia gosudarstvennaia Duma* (Paris, 1939).

6. The "Silver Age" of the Arts

See Paul Miliukov's *Outlines of Russian Culture,* of which Part II treats *Literature* and Part III *Architecture, Painting, and Music* (Philadelphia: University of Pennsylvania Press, 1943); both are short essays which stop about 1930. Surveys of the development of individual arts include the masterpiece of D. S. Mirsky, *A History of Russian Literature,* ed. and abridged Francis J. Whitfield (New York: Alfred A. Knopf, Inc., 1949, and Vintage Paperback), which ranges from the beginnings of Russian literature to the Revolution, and Marc Slonim, *Modern Russian Literature: from Chekhov to the Present* (New York: Oxford University Press, 1953), which begins with the reign of Alexander II; George H. Hamilton, *The Art and Architecture of Russia* (Baltimore: Penguin Books, Inc., 1954); Tamara Talbot Rice, *Russian Art* (West Drayton, Eng.: Penguin Books Ltd., 1949); Cyril G. E. Bunt, *Russian Art from Scyths to Soviets* (New York: Studio-Crowell, 1946); Arthur Voyce, *Russian Architecture* (New York: Philosophical Library, 1948); Richard A. Leonard, *A History of Russian Music* (New York: The Macmillan Co., 1956); Michel Calvocoressi, *A Survey of Russian Music* (New York: Penguin Books, Inc., 1944); Nikolai A. Gorchakov, *The Theater in Soviet Russia* (New York: Columbia University Press, 1957), which begins with the pre-Revolutionary theater; Marc Slonim, *Russian Theater: from the Empire to the Soviets* (Cleveland: World Publishing Co., 1961); and Jay Leyda, *Kino: a History of the Russian and Soviet Film* (New York: The Macmillan Co., 1960). Wladimir Weidlé's *Russia: Absent and Present* treats broader problems of Russian culture with acute insight.

Special studies dealing partly or wholly with the Silver Age include the following. On literature, Renato Poggioli, *The Poets of Russia, 1890–1930*

(Cambridge: Harvard University Press, 1960); Oleg Maslenikov, *The Frenzied Poets: Andrey Biely and the Russian Symbolists* (Berkeley: University of California Press, 1952); Leonid I. Strakhovsky, *Craftsmen of the Word* (Cambridge: Harvard University Press, 1949), dealing with the Acmeists; Ernest J. Simmons, *Chekhov: a Biography* (Boston: Little, Brown & Co., 1952). On painting, see Camilla Grey, *The Great Experiment: Russian Art, 1863–1922* (New York: Harry N. Abrams, Inc., 1962).

On Russian education before 1917, see Nicholas A. Hans, *History of Russian Educational Policy, 1701–1917* (New York: Alfred H. King, Inc., 1931), and William H. E. Johnson, *Russia's Educational Heritage* (Pittsburgh: Carnegie Press, 1950).

7. Growth of the Russian Economy

On the general problems of Russian economic development, a theoretically distorted but factually valuable account is P. I. Lyashchenko, *History of the National Economy of Russia to the 1917 Revolution,* ACLS Translation Project (New York: The Macmillan Co., 1949). For the early twentieth century, see M. S. Miller, *The Economic Development of Russia, 1905–1914* (London: P. S. King & Son, Ltd., 1926). On trade-unionism, there is a rather unsatisfactory account by S. P. Turin, *From Peter the Great to Lenin: the History of the Russian Labour Movement with Special Reference to Trade Unionism* (London: P. S. King & Son, Ltd., 1935). Michael Karpovich's chapters (14, 29, and 38) on Russia in Witt Bowden, Michael Karpovich, and Abbott Payson Usher, *An Economic History of Europe since 1750* (New York: American Book Co., 1937), constitute the best survey of twentieth-century Russian economic history available in English.

8. The Last Years of Tsarism

On the government from 1906 to 1917, see Alfred Levin, *The Second Duma* (New Haven: Yale University Press, 1940); V. N. Kokovtsov, *Out of My Past: the Memoirs of Count Kokovtsov, Russian Minister of Finance, 1904–1914, Chairman of the Council of Ministers, 1911–1914,* ed. H. H. Fisher, trans. Laura Matveev (Stanford: Stanford University Press, 1935). On Rasputin, see M. V. Rodzianko, *The Reign of Rasputin: an Empire's Collapse; Memoirs* (London: Philpot, 1927).

On the coming of World War I, a standard work is Sidney Bradshaw Fay, *The Origins of the World War* (2 vols.; New York: The Macmillan

Co., 1929); an authoritative recent treatment is Luigi Albertini, *The Origins of the War of 1914,* trans. and ed. Isabella M. Massey (3 vols.; New York: Oxford University Press, 1952–1957). Hans Kohn sketches the role of pan-Slavism in *Pan-Slavism: its History and Ideology* (Notre Dame: University of Notre Dame Press, 1953). Russian foreign policy during the war is analyzed in C. Jay Smith, Jr., *The Russian Struggle for Power, 1914–1917* (New York: Philosophical Library, 1956). For the debate within the Second International, see Merle Fainsod, *International Socialism and the World War* (Cambridge: Harvard University Press, 1935). Winston S. Churchill deals with the military events in *The Unknown War: the Eastern Front* (New York: Charles Scribner's Sons, 1931). Two volumes of the Carnegie Series are especially concerned with Russia's actual participation in the war: N. N. Golovine, *The Russian Army in the World War* (New Haven: Yale University Press, 1931), and B. E. Nolde, *Russia in the Economic War* (New Haven: Yale University Press, 1928); perhaps the best of the series, which traces the background of the Revolution, is M. T. Florinsky, *The End of the Russian Empire* (New Haven: Yale University Press, 1931). Of the many journalistic and diplomatic accounts of value, perhaps the most interesting is M. Paléologue, *An Ambassador's Memoirs,* trans. F. A. Holt (3 vols.; London: Hutchinson & Co., Ltd., 1923–1925). The background of the February Revolution is treated in Bernard Pares, *The Fall of the Russian Monarchy* (New York: Alfred A. Knopf, Inc., 1939). Many sources are available in Frank Alfred Golder, ed., *Documents of Russian History, 1914–1917,* trans. Emanuel Aronsberg (New York: The Century Co., 1927); and Z. A. B. Zeman, ed., *Germany and the Revolution in Russia, 1915–1918: Documents from the Archives of the German Foreign Ministry* (New York: Oxford University Press, 1958).

9. The February Revolution

The standard treatment of the whole revolutionary period to the end of the Civil War remains William Henry Chamberlin, *The Russian Revolution, 1917–1921* (2 vols.; reissue; New York: The Macmillan Co., 1952). Four valuable works by participants are Leon Trotsky, *The History of the Russian Revolution,* trans. Max Eastman (3 vols.; New York: Simon & Schuster, Inc., 1932); V. M. Chernov, *The Great Russian Revolution,* trans. and abridged Philip E. Mosely (New Haven: Yale University Press, 1936); N. N. Sukhanov (pseud. of N. N. Himmer), *The Russian Revolution 1917; a Personal Record,* ed., abridged, and trans. Joel Carmichael from *Zapiski o revoliutsii* (New York: Oxford University Press,

1955); and W. S. Woytinsky, *Stormy Passage: a Personal History Through Two Russian Revolutions to Democracy and Freedom, 1905–1960* (New York: The Vanguard Press, 1961). Kerensky's version is in Alexander F. Kerensky, *The Catastrophe: Kerensky's Own Story of the Russian Revolution* (New York: Appleton-Century-Crofts, Inc., 1927). Edward Hallett Carr's *A History of Soviet Russia: The Bolshevik Revolution, 1917–1923* (3 vols.; London: Macmillan and Co., Ltd., 1950–1953), is actually somewhat misnamed, but is useful for those topics which it does treat. See also Oliver H. Radkey, *Agrarian Foes of Bolshevism.*

A useful collection of documentary materials is Robert Paul Browder and Alexander F. Kerensky, eds., *The Russian Provisional Government, 1917* (3 vols.; Stanford: Stanford University Press, 1961). The USSR Academy of Sciences has published a six-volume collection entitled *Velikaia Oktiabrskaia sotsialisticheskaia revoliutsiia: dokumenty i materialy* Moscow, 1957–1959).

On events in the borderlands, see Richard Pipes, *The Formation of the Soviet Union: Communism and Nationalism, 1917–1923* (Cambridge: Harvard University Press, 1954); Firuz Kazemzadeh, *The Struggle for Transcaucasia, 1917–1921* (New York: Philosophical Library, 1951); and John S. Reshetar, Jr., *The Ukrainian Revolution, 1917–1920* (Princeton: Princeton University Press, 1952).

10. The October Revolution

A classic work by an American Communist is John Reed, *Ten Days that Shook the World* (New York: International Publishers, 1919). A useful documentary collection is John Bunyan and H. H. Fisher, eds., *The Bolshevik Revolution, 1917–1918; Documents and Materials* (Stanford: Stanford University Press, 1934). Bolshevik treatment of opposition is analyzed in Leonard Schapiro, *The Origin of the Communist Autocracy, 1917–1922* (Cambridge: Harvard University Press, 1955). International relations are deftly explored by George F. Kennan, *Soviet-American Relations, 1917–1920:* Volume I, *Russia Leaves the War* (Princeton: Princeton University Press, 1956), and Volume II, *The Decision to Intervene* (1958); Richard H. Ullman, *Anglo-Soviet Relations, 1917–1921,* Volume I, *Intervention and the War* (Princeton: Princeton University Press, 1961); and J. W. Wheeler-Bennett, *The Forgotten Peace: Brest Litovsk, March 1918* (New York: The Macmillan Co., 1939); see also Robert D. Warth, *The Allies and the Russian Revolution: from the Fall of the Monarchy to the Peace of Brest-Litovsk* (Durham: Duke University Press,

1954). An admirable short monograph is Oliver Henry Radkey, *The Election to the Russian Constituent Assembly of 1917* (Cambridge: Harvard University Press, 1950). Radkey's sequel to *Agrarian Foes of Bolshevism* is *The Sickle Under the Hammer: The Russian Socialist Revolutionaries in the Early Months of Soviet Rule* (New York: Columbia University Press, 1963).

11. The Civil War: The White Challenge (1917–1919)

A reasonably satisfactory picture of the Civil War may be gained by combining Volume II of W. H. Chamberlin's *The Russian Revolution,* which concentrates on the Slavic areas, with Richard Pipes' *The Formation of the Soviet Union.* David Footman's *Civil War in Russia* (New York: Frederick A. Praeger, Inc., 1962) is a series of essays throwing light on certain problems and personalities of the struggle. A documentary sequel to Bunyan and Fisher's compilation on 1917–1918 is John Bunyan, ed., *Intervention, Civil War and Communism in Russia; April-December 1918 Documents and Materials* (Baltimore: Johns Hopkins Press, 1936). See also the documentary work edited by Elena Varneck and H. H. Fisher, *The Testimony of Kolchak and Other Siberian Materials* (Stanford: Stanford University Press, 1935). The Whites receive less than satisfactory treatment in George Stewart, *The White Armies of Russia* (New York: The Macmillan Co., 1933). Allied intervention has been the subject of a number of works: Leonid I. Strakhovsky's two books, *The Origins of American Intervention in North Russia* (Princeton: Princeton University Press, 1937), and *Intervention at Archangel* (Princeton: Princeton University Press, 1944); John A. White, *The Siberian Intervention* (Princeton: Princeton University Press, 1950); Betty M. Unterberger, *America's Siberian Expedition, 1918–1920* (Durham: Duke University Press, 1956); James William Morley, *The Japanese Thrust into Siberia, 1918* (New York: Columbia University Press, 1957).

12. The Civil War: The Red Victory (1919–1921)

Of the three chief White leaders, Kolchak was executed before he could write his memoirs, but he gave an account of part of his activity which is published in Varneck and Fisher, eds., *The Testimony of Kolchak and Other Siberian Materials.* Portions of the memoirs of the other two are translated: Anton Denikin, *The Russian Turmoil* (London: Hutchinson & Co., Ltd., 1922), covering the period prior to the October Revolution, and *The White Army* (London: Jonathan Cape, Ltd., 1930); and Piotr N. Wrangel, *The Memoirs of General Wrangel* (London: Williams and Norgate, Ltd., 1929). On the Russo-Polish war, see James T. Shotwell and Max M. Laserson, *Poland and Russia, 1919–1945* (New York: Carnegie Endowment for International Peace, 1945). There is a treatment of *The Far Eastern Republic of Siberia* by H. K. Norton (London: George Allen & Unwin, Ltd., 1923). On the Moslem minorities, see Serge A. Zenkovsky, *Pan-Turkism and Islam in Russia* (Cambridge: Harvard University Press, 1960), more than half of which deals with the Revolution and Civil War.

13. Lenin and the New Economic Policy (1921–1924)

On the chief Soviet leaders after 1914 (the earlier period is best covered by Bertram D. Wolfe's *Three Who Made a Revolution*), see David Shub, *Lenin;* Isaac Deutscher, *Stalin: a Political Biography* (New York: Oxford University Press, 1949), and *The Prophet Armed: Trotsky, 1879–1921* and *The Prophet Unarmed: Trotsky, 1921–1929* (New York: Oxford University Press, 1954, 1959); and Leon Trotsky, *My Life* (London: Thornton Butterworth Ltd., 1930).

On the NEP, see E. H. Carr's volumes in his *A History of Soviet Russia: The Bolshevik Revolution,* Volume II; *The Interregnum;* and *Socialism in One Country, 1924–1926* (2 vols.) (London: Macmillan and Co., Ltd., 1954, 1958, and 1959). On economic aspects of the period, see H. H. Fisher, *The Famine in Soviet Russia, 1919–1923: the Operations of the American Relief Administration* (New York: The Macmillan Co., 1927), and Alexander Erlich, *The Soviet Industrialization Debate, 1924–1928* (Cambridge: Harvard University Press, 1960), which focuses on the dispute between Bukharin and Preobrazhensky.

Good introductions to the problems of the Soviet economy in general are Robert W. Campbell, *Soviet Economic Power* (Cambridge: Houghton Mifflin Co., 1960), and Alec Nove, *The Soviet Economy: an Introduction* (New York: Frederick A. Praeger, Inc., 1961). Other standard works are Harry Schwartz, *Russia's Soviet Economy* (2nd ed.; New York: Prentice-Hall, Inc., 1954); Alexander Baykov, *The Development of the Soviet Economic System* (Cambridge, Eng.: Cambridge University Press, 1946), and Maurice Dobb (an able pro-Soviet economist), *Soviet Economic Development Since 1917* (London: George Routledge & Sons, Ltd., 1948).

The best account of the successive Soviet constitutions, as well as the best over-all analysis of Soviet government, is in Merle Fainsod, *How Russia Is Ruled* (rev. ed.; Cambridge: Harvard University Press, 1963). See also Barrington Moore, Jr., *Soviet Politics: the Dilemma of Power* (Cambridge: Harvard University Press, 1950); Julian Towster, *Political Power in the USSR, 1917–1947* (New York: Oxford University Press, 1948); Michael T. Florinsky, *Towards an Understanding of the USSR* (rev. ed.; New York: The Macmillan Co., 1951); Samuel N. Harper and Ronald Thompson, *The Government of the Soviet Union* (2nd ed.; New York: D. Van Nostrand Co., Inc., 1949). Especially useful for constitutional changes in the 1920's is Walter Batsell, *Soviet Rule in Russia* (New York: The Macmillan Co., 1929). The beginnings of the Soviet legal system are treated in John N. Hazard, *Settling Disputes in Soviet Society* (New York: Columbia University Press, 1960).

14. Stalin, Trotsky, and Bukharin (1924–1927)

The intra-Party struggle is studied by Robert V. Daniels, *The Conscience of the Revolution: Communist Opposition in Soviet Russia* (Cambridge: Harvard University Press, 1960). Some valuable material on the same subject is found in William Reswick, *I Dreamt Revolution* (Chicago: Henry Regnery Co., 1952). Well-known journalistic accounts including this period, favorable to the Soviets, are Maurice Hindus, *Humanity Uprooted* (London: Jonathan Cape, Ltd., 1931), and Walter Duranty, *I Write as I Please* (London: Hamish Hamilton, Ltd., 1937); an unfavorable account is Eugene Lyons, *Assignment in Utopia* (London: George G. Harrap & Co., Ltd., 1938). Trotsky's own *The Real Situation in Russia* (New York: Harcourt, Brace and Co., Inc., 1928) and *The Revolution Betrayed* (Garden City: Doubleday, Doran & Co., Inc., 1937), both translated by Max Eastman, are useful; see also N. Popov's *Outline History of the Communist Party of the Soviet Union* (2 parts; Moscow-Leningrad: Cooperative Publishing Society of Foreign Workers in the USSR, 1934), a Stalinist work yet later discarded by Stalin; Part II covers 1917–1931.

15. Finding a Soviet Foreign Policy (1917–1927)

George F. Kennan provides a readable introduction to Soviet foreign policy in *Russia and the West under Lenin and Stalin* (Boston: Little, Brown and Co., 1961). Standard detailed treatments of the period before World War II are Louis Fischer, *The Soviets in World Affairs, 1917–*

1929 (2 vols.; 2nd ed.; Princeton: Princeton University Press, 1951); Max Beloff, *The Foreign Policy of Soviet Russia,* Volume I, *1929–1936* (New York: Oxford University Press, 1947), Volume II, *1936–1941* (1949); and David J. Dallin, *Soviet Russia's Foreign Policy, 1939–1942* (New Haven: Yale University Press, 1942).

Material on Comintern activity before 1934 is contained in Franz Borkenau, *World Communism: a History of the Communist International* (New York: W. W. Norton & Co., Inc., 1939), and G. D. H. Cole, *Communism and Social Democracy, 1914–1931* (2 vols.; New York: St. Martin's Press, 1958), the two parts of which constitute Volume IV of *A History of Socialist Thought.* The entire history of world Communism is carefully surveyed in Hugh Seton-Watson, *From Lenin to Khrushchev* (New York: Frederick A. Praeger, Inc., 1960). There is an excellent study by Theodore Draper of *American Communism and Soviet Russia* (New York: Viking Press, Inc., 1960).

Useful documentary works include Alvin Z. Rubinstein, ed., *The Foreign Policy of the Soviet Union* (New York: Random House, 1960); Jane Degras, *Calendar of Soviet Documents on Foreign Policy, 1917–1941* (New York: Royal Institute of International Affairs, 1948), and under her editorship, *Soviet Documents on Foreign Policy* (3 vols.; New York: Oxford University Press, 1951–1953), of which Volume I covers 1917–1924, Volume II, 1924–1932, Volume III, 1933–1941, and *The Communist International, 1919–1943: Documents* (New York: Oxford University Press), of which Volume I (1956) covers 1919–1922 and Volume II (1960) 1923–1928. For the period before 1927, there are the two volumes edited by Xenia J. Eudin and Robert C. North, *Soviet Russia and the East, 1920–1927: a Documentary Survey,* and *Soviet Russia and the West, 1920–1927: a Documentary Survey* (Stanford: Stanford University Press, 1957). The materials seized in the Peking raid of 1927 are edited by C. Martin Wilbur and Julie How as *Documents on Communism, Nationalism, and Soviet Advisers in China, 1918–1927* (New York: Columbia University Press, 1956).

On Soviet and Communist activity in the Far East, see David J. Dallin, *The Rise of Russia in Asia* (1949), which covers the period from the middle of the nineteenth century to 1931, and *Soviet Russia and the Far East* (1948), which treats the subsequent years (New Haven: Yale University Press); and Peter S. H. Tang, *Russian and Soviet Policy in Manchuria and Outer Mongolia, 1911–1931* (Durham: Duke University Press, 1959). Franz H. Michael and George E. Taylor, *The Far East in the Modern World* (New York: Henry Holt & Co., 1956), in general the safest guide to the whole subject thus far published, contains much good analysis of Tsarist, Soviet, and Communist activity in all parts of the Far East.

On the attempts at Communist revolution in Germany, see Ruth Fischer, *Stalin and German Communism* (Cambridge: Harvard University Press, 1948), which covers the period from World War I to 1929; it is a detailed account by a then prominent KAPD leader who has since renounced Communism. On early German-Soviet relations, see Lionel Kochan, *Russia and the Weimar Republic* (Cambridge, Eng.: Bowes and Bowes, Ltd., 1954); and E. H. Carr, *German-Soviet Relations between the Two World Wars, 1919–1939* (Baltimore: Johns Hopkins Press, 1951). On the events in China, see Allen S. Whiting, *Soviet Policies in China, 1917–1924* (New York: Columbia University Press, 1954); Conrad Brandt, *Stalin's Failure in China* (Cambridge: Harvard University Press, 1959); Harold R. Isaacs, *The Tragedy of the Chinese Revolution* (2nd rev. ed.; Stanford: Stanford University Press, 1961); Robert C. North, *Moscow and the Chinese Communists* (Stanford: Stanford University Press, 1953); Benjamin I. Schwartz, *Chinese Communism and the Rise of Mao* (Cambridge: Harvard University Press, 1951); Conrad Brandt, Benjamin I. Schwartz, and John K. Fairbank, eds., *A Documentary History of Chinese Communism* (Cambridge: Harvard University Press, 1952); and Shao Chuan Leng and Norman D. Palmer, *Sun Yat-sen and Communism* (New York: Frederick A. Praeger, Inc., 1961).

16. The Revolution, the Arts, and the Church (1917–1927)

(See also suggested readings for Chapter 6.)

Gleb Struve, *Soviet Russian Literature, 1917–50* (Norman: University of Oklahoma Press, 1951), is authoritative. Kurt London, *The Seven Soviet Arts* (New Haven: Yale University Press, 1938) gives a survey of all the arts. Literature in the early Soviet period is studied in Helen Muchnic, *From Gorky to Pasternak* (New York: Random House, 1961); Richard Hare, *Maxim Gorky: Romantic Realist and Conservative Revolutionary* (New York: Oxford University Press, 1962); Vyacheslav Zavalishin, *Early Soviet Writers* (New York: Frederick A. Praeger, Inc., 1958). Leon Trotsky, *Literature and Revolution,* trans. R. Strunsky (London: International Publishers, 1925), is of unusual interest, and a revealing treatment is Max Eastman, *Artists in Uniform: a Study of Literature and Bureaucracy* (London: George Allen & Unwin, Ltd., 1934).

On religion, see Kolarz, *Religion in the Soviet Union;* John Shelton Curtiss, *The Russian Church and the Soviet State, 1917–1950* (Boston: Little, Brown and Co., 1953); Matthew Spinka, *The Church in Soviet Russia* (New York: Oxford University Press, 1956); and N. S. Timasheff,

Religion in Soviet Russia, 1917–1942 (New York: Sheed & Ward, Inc., 1942). An account sympathetic to the Bolsheviks is Julius Hecker, *Religion under the Soviets* (New York: Vanguard Press, 1927). Paul Miliukov, *Outlines of Russian Culture:* Part I, *Religion and the Church,* has a concluding chapter on post-revolutionary developments.

17. Stalin and the First Five-Year Plan (1928–1932)

Industrial development is studied in Naum Jasny, *Soviet Industrialization, 1928–1952* (Chicago: University of Chicago Press, 1961). Somewhat different assessments of growth are given in Abram Bergson, *The Real National Income of Soviet Russia Since 1928* (Cambridge: Harvard University Press, 1961); and G. Warren Nutter, *The Growth of Industrial Production in the Soviet Union* (Princeton: Princeton University Press, 1962). Useful eyewitness accounts of industrialization include W. H. Chamberlin, *Russia's Iron Age* (London: Gerald Duckworth & Co., Ltd., 1935); and John Scott, *Behind the Urals* (Boston: Houghton Mifflin Co., 1942). The Soviet factory system is treated by Joseph S. Berliner, *Factory and Manager in the USSR* (Cambridge: Harvard University Press, 1957); a comparison with U.S. management is made in David Granick's *The Red Executive* (New York: Doubleday, 1959). On the Cheka and its successors, see Simon Wolin and Robert M. Slusser, eds., *The Soviet Secret Police* (New York: Frederick A. Praeger, Inc., 1957). On the trade-unions, see Solomon M. Schwartz, *Labor in the Soviet Union* (New York: Frederick A. Praeger, Inc., 1952), and Isaac Deutscher, *Soviet Trade Unions: their Place in Soviet Labor Policy* (New York: Royal Institute of International Affairs, 1950). On the army, see John Erickson, *The Soviet High Command: a Military-Political History, 1918–1941* (New York: St. Martin's Press, 1962); D. Fedotoff White, *The Growth of the Red Army* (Princeton: Princeton University Press, 1944); and E. Wollenberg, *The Red Army,* trans. C. W. Sykes (2nd ed.; London: Martin Secker & Warburg, Ltd., 1940).

Informed discussions of collectivization are Naum Jasny, *The Socialized Agriculture of the USSR* (Stanford: Stanford University Press, 1949); Lazar Volin, *A Survey of Soviet Russian Agriculture* (Washington: U. S. Government Printing Office, 1951); and Roy D. Laird, *Collective Farming in Russia: a Political Study of Soviet Kolkhozy* (Lawrence: University of Kansas Publications, 1958). A remarkable personal account is Fedor Belov, *A History of a Soviet Collective Farm* (New York: Frederick A. Praeger, Inc., 1955).

The tax structure receives careful treatment in Franklyn D. Holzman, *Soviet Taxation* (Cambridge: Harvard University Press, 1955).

18. The Consolidation of Totalitarianism (1933–1941)

A judicious study is John A. Armstrong, *The Politics of Totalitarianism: The Communist Party of the Soviet Union from 1934 to the Present* (New York: Random House, 1961). On the Komsomol, see Ralph T. Fisher, Jr., *Pattern for Soviet Youth* (New York: Columbia University Press, 1959). Abdurrakhman Avtorkhanov, *Stalin and the Soviet Communist Party* (New York: Frederick A. Praeger, Inc., 1959) is an account by a former Soviet official. A unique work, based on captured archival material, is Merle Fainsod, *Smolensk Under Soviet Rule* (Cambridge: Harvard University Press, 1958). Two books based on interviews of refugees conducted by the Harvard Project on the Soviet Social System are Raymond A. Bauer, Alex Inkeles, and Clyde Kluckhohn, *How the Soviet System Works* (Cambridge: Harvard University Press, 1956, and Vintage Paperback) and Inkeles and Bauer, *The Soviet Citizen: Daily Life in a Totalitarian Society* (Cambridge: Harvard University Press, 1960). Useful accounts by former Communists include Victor Serge (pseud. of V. L. Kibalchich), *Destiny of a Revolution,* trans. Max Schachtman (London: Martin Secker & Warburg, Ltd., 1937), and *From Lenin to Stalin,* trans. R. Manheim (London: Jarrolds, Publishers, Ltd., 1937); A. Ciliga, *The Russian Enigma,* trans. F. G. Renier and A. Cliff (London: George Routledge & Sons, Ltd., 1940); and Boris Souvarine, *Stalin: a Critical Survey of Bolshevism* (New York: Alliance Book Co., 1939). On the concentration camps, see David J. Dallin and Boris I. Nicolaevsky, *Forced Labor in Soviet Russia* (New Haven: Yale University Press, 1947). On the Great Purges, see Alex Weissberg, *The Accused,* trans. Edward Fitzgerald (New York: Simon & Schuster, Inc., 1951); F. Beck and W. Godin, *Russian Purge and the Extraction of Confession* (New York: Viking Press, Inc., 1951); Nathan Leites and Elsa Bernaut, *Ritual of Liquidation: The Case of the Moscow Trials* (Glencoe, Ill.: The Free Press, 1954); Commission of Inquiry into the Charges Made Against Leon Trotsky in the Moscow Trials, *Not Guilty* (New York: Harper & Brothers, 1938); and Zbigniew K. Brzezinski, *The Permanent Purge* (Cambridge: Harvard University Press, 1956). Justly famed novelistic treatments of the Great Purges are Arthur Koestler, *Darkness at Noon* (Signet Paperback) and Victor Serge, *The Case of Comrade Tulayev* (Anchor Paperback); of Soviet totalitarianism in general, Eugene

Zamiatin, *We* (Dutton Paperback), and George Orwell, *1984* (Signet Paperback).

On the "new Soviet man," see Raymond A. Bauer, *The New Man in Soviet Psychology* (Cambridge: Harvard University Press, 1952).

19. Stalin and the Borderlands

Soviet treatment of minority nationalities is surveyed by Walter Kolarz in *Russia and Her Colonies* (London: George Philip & Son, Ltd., 1952); the same author has also treated *The Peoples of the Soviet Far East* (New York: Frederick A. Praeger, Inc., 1954). Some general issues are treated in Frederick C. Barghoorn, *Soviet Russian Nationalism* (New York: Oxford University Press, 1956). Stalin's wartime genocide is studied in Robert Conquest, *The Soviet Deportation of Nationalities* (New York: St. Martin's Press, 1960).

On the Ukraine, see Robert S. Sullivant, *Soviet Politics and the Ukraine, 1917–1957* (New York: Columbia University Press, 1962); Basil Dmytryshyn, *Moscow and the Ukraine, 1918–1953* (New York: Bookman Associates, Inc., 1956); Clarence A. Manning, *Ukraine Under the Soviets* (New York: Bookman Associates, Inc., 1953); Hryhory Kostiuk, *Stalinist Rule in the Ukraine: a Study of the Decade of Mass Terror, 1929–1939* (Munich: Institute for the Study of the USSR, 1960); and John A. Armstrong, *Ukrainian Nationalism, 1939–1945* (New York: Columbia University Press, 1955). On Belorussia, see Nicholas Vakar, *Belorussia* (Cambridge: Harvard University Press, 1956). On the Baltic states, see Albert N. Tarulis, *Soviet Policy Toward the Baltic States, 1918–1940* (Notre Dame: University of Notre Dame Press, 1959), and Adolfs Silde, *The Profits of Slavery: Baltic Forced Laborers and Deportees Under Stalin and Khrushchev* (Stockholm: Latvian National Foundation in Scandinavia, 1958). On the Caucasus, see David Marshall Lang, *A Modern History of Soviet Georgia* (New York: Grove Press, 1962), and Mary Kilbourne Matossian, *The Impact of Soviet Policies on Armenia* (Leiden: E. J. Brill, 1962). Central Asia is discussed by Olaf Caroe, *Soviet Empire: the Turks of Central Asia and Stalinism* (London: Macmillan and Co., Ltd., 1953); Alexander Park, *Bolshevism in Turkestan, 1917–1927* (New York: Columbia University Press, 1957); and Charles Warren Hostler, *Turkism and the Soviets* (New York: Frederick A. Praeger, Inc., 1957). The Jews are studied by Solomon M. Schwartz, *The Jews in the Soviet Union* (Syracuse: Syracuse University Press, 1951), and B. Z. Goldberg, *The Jewish Problem in the Soviet Union* (New York: Crown Publishers, 1961).

20. Stalinist Diplomacy and World Communism (1927–1935)
and
21. Stalinist Diplomacy and World Communism (1936–1941)

On the role of Communism in the rise of Hitler, R. T. Clark, *The Fall of the German Republic* (London: George Allen & Unwin, Ltd., 1935), is of some use. Charles B. McLane, *Soviet Policy and the Chinese Communists, 1931–1946* (New York: Columbia University Press, 1959), is especially useful on the Kiangsi period, 1931–1934; see also Tso-liang Hsiao, *Power Relations Within the Chinese Communist Movement, 1930–1934: a Study of Documents* (Seattle: University of Washington Press, 1961). On American recognition of the USSR, see Robert P. Browder, *The Origins of Soviet-American Diplomacy* (Princeton: Princeton University Press, 1953). For the period 1934 to 1949 in Communist activity in Europe, see Franz Borkenau, *European Communism* (London: Faber & Faber, Ltd., 1953). On the Popular Front in Chile, see John Reese Stevenson, *The Chilean Popular Front* (Philadelphia: University of Pennsylvania Press, 1942). On the Spanish Civil War, a fine study is Hugh Thomas, *The Spanish Civil War* (New York: Harper and Brothers, 1961); Franz Borkenau, *The Spanish Cockpit* (London: Faber & Faber, Ltd., 1937), and Herbert Feis, *The Spanish Story: Franco and the Nations at War* (New York: Alfred A. Knopf, Inc., 1948). David T. Cattell has studied the Communist role in two recent books, *Communism and the Spanish Civil War* (Berkeley: University of California Press, 1955), and *Soviet Diplomacy and the Spanish Civil War* (Berkeley: University of California Press, 1957). On the Nazi-Soviet Pact, see A. Rossi (pseud.), *The Russo-German Alliance, August 1939–June 1941* (Boston: Beacon Press, Inc., 1951); Gerhard L. Weinberg, *Germany and the Soviet Union, 1939–1941* (Leiden: E. J. Brill, 1954); Gustav Hilger and Alfred G. Meyer, *The Incompatible Allies: a Memoir-History of German-Soviet Relations, 1918–1941* (New York: The Macmillan Co., 1953). The authoritative Soviet work is V. P. Potëmkin, ed., *Istoriia diplomatii* (3 vols.; Moscow-Leningrad, 1941–1945). The Western role in the prewar negotiations is treated by J. W. Wheeler-Bennett, *Munich: Prologue to Tragedy* (New York: Duell, Sloan & Pearce, Inc., 1948), and L. B. Namier, *Diplomatic Prelude, 1938–1949* (London: Macmillan and Co., Ltd., 1948). For documents, see Raymond James Sontag and James Stuart Beddie, eds., *Nazi-Soviet Relations, 1938–1941: Documents from the Archives of the German Foreign Office* (Washington: Department of State, 1948). On the Finnish events, see Max Jakobson, *The Diplomacy of the Winter War: An Account of the Russo-Finnish War, 1939–1940* (Cambridge: Harvard University Press, 1961).

22 Stalin's Cultural Policy (1927–1945)

For the RAPP period of Soviet literary policy, there is a special study, Edward J. Brown, *The Proletarian Episode in Russian Literature, 1928–1932* (New York: Columbia University Press, 1953). A longer period in a single republic is treated in George S. N. Luckyj, *Literary Politics in the Soviet Ukraine, 1917–1934* (New York: Columbia University Press, 1956). On genuine "Formalism" as distinguished from the Soviet epithet, see Victor Erlich, *Russian Formalism: History—Doctrine* (The Hague: Mouton & Co., 1955). Three writers of talent are studied in Ernest J. Simmons, *Russian Fiction and Soviet Ideology: an Introduction to Fedin, Leonov, and Sholokhov* (New York: Columbia University Press, 1958).

On Soviet education, the most comprehensive study is Nicholas DeWitt, *Educational and Professional Employment in the USSR* (Washington: National Science Foundation, 1961). An excellent analysis is George S. Counts, *The Challenge of Soviet Education* (New York: McGraw-Hill Book Co., Inc., 1957). See also Alexander Korol, *Soviet Education for Science and Technology* (New York: John Wiley & Sons, Inc., 1957); George Kline, ed. *Soviet Education* (New York: Columbia University Press, 1957), a collection of reports by former teachers and students in the USSR; and Maurice J. Shore, *Soviet Education: its Psychology and Philosophy* (New York: Philosophical Library, 1947).

On Soviet philosophy, the best works are Gustav Wetter, *Dialectical Materialism,* trans. Peter Heath (New York: Frderick A. Praeger, Inc., 1958); I. M. Bocheński, *Der sowjetrussische dialektische Materialismus* (2nd ed.; Bern, 1956); and Henri Chambre, *Le Marxisme en Union Soviétique* (Paris, 1957). See also John Plamenatz, *German Marxism and Russian Communism* (New York: Longmans, Green & Co., 1954); Herbert A. Marcuse, *Soviet Marxism: a Critical Analysis* (New York: Columbia University Press, 1957); R. N. Carew Hunt, *The Theory and Practice of Communism* (New York: The Macmillan Co., 1951), and, by the same author, *Marxism; Past and Present* (New York: The Macmillan Co., 1955). (See suggested readings for Chapters 3 and 4 for materials on Marx and Lenin and their tnought.)

23. The USSR in World War II: The Military Crisis (1941–1943)

A convenient account of the military events of the war is Major General J. F. C. Fuller, *The Second World War, 1939–1945* (New York: Duell,

Sloan & Pearce, Inc., 1949). Especially useful on the Nazi-Soviet front are General Wladyslaw Anders, *Hitler's Defeat in Russia* (Chicago: Henry Regnery Co., 1953), General A. Guillaume, *La guerre germano-soviétique, 1941–1945* (Paris, 1949), and Kurt von Tippelskirch, *Geschichte des zweiten Weltkriegs* (Bonn, 1951). The current official Soviet version is presented in *Istoriia Velikoi Otechestvennoi Voiny Sovetskogo Soiuza, 1941–1945* (4 vols.; Moscow, 1960–1962). On Allied diplomacy vis-à-vis the Soviets, see Winston S. Churchill, *The Second World War* (6 vols.; Boston: Houghton Mifflin Co., 1948–1953), and Robert E. Sherwood, *Roosevelt and Hopkins* (New York: Harper and Brothers, 1948). Military and diplomatic developments are skillfully analyzed in their interrelations by Chester Wilmot, *The Struggle for Europe* (New York: Harper and Brothers, 1952). The memoirs of the two chief Allied commanders are Dwight D. Eisenhower, *Crusade in Europe* (New York: Doubleday & Co., Inc., 1948), and Field Marshal the First Viscount Montgomery of Alamein, *Normandy to the Baltic* (Boston: Houghton Mifflin Co., 1948).

On Nazi occupation of Soviet territory, see the fine study of Alexander Dallin, *German Rule in Russia, 1941–1945* (London: Macmillan and Co., Ltd., 1957); John A. Armstrong, *Ukrainian Nationalism, 1939–1945;* and Ihor Kamenetsky, *Hitler's Occupation of the Ukraine, 1941–1944* (Milwaukee: Marquette University Press, 1956). Careful examinations of the ordeals of the two great cities have been made by Leon Gouré and Herbert S. Dinerstein in *Moscow in Crisis* (Glencoe, Ill.: The Free Press, 1955) and by Gouré alone in *The Siege of Leningrad* (Stanford: Stanford University Press, 1962). The Vlasov movement is treated by George Fischer, *Soviet Opposition to Stalin* (Cambridge: Harvard University Press, 1952). Much useful information on the Soviet side in the war may be found in B. H. Liddell Hart, ed., *The Soviet Army* (London: George Weidenfeld & Nicolson, Ltd., 1956), and Robert A. Kilmarx, *A History of Soviet Air Power* (New York: Frederick A. Praeger, Inc., 1962). Edgar M. Howell's Department of the Army pamphlet, *The Soviet Partisan Movement* (Washington, 1956), is an uneven treatment. The Katyn murders are examined in J. K. Zawodny, *Death in the Forest* (Notre Dame: University of Notre Dame Press, 1962).

24. The USSR in World War II: Political Successes (1943–1945)

On Soviet relations with the Poles, see Stanisław Mikołajczyk, *The Rape of Poland* (New York: Whittlesey House, 1948) and Edward J.

Rozek, *Allied Wartime Diplomacy: A Pattern in Poland* (New York: John Wiley & Sons, 1951). Two books which attempt, with varying degrees of success, evaluations of the Yalta conference are R. F. Fenno, Jr., ed., *The Yalta Conference* (Boston: D. C. Heath & Co., 1955), and John L. Snell, ed., *The Meaning of Yalta* (Baton Rouge: Louisiana State University Press, 1956). Accounts of the conference at Yalta are given in Edward R. Stettinius, *Roosevelt and the Russians* (Garden City: Doubleday and Co., Inc., 1949), and James F. Byrnes, *Speaking Frankly* (New York: Harper and Brothers, 1947); Byrnes's book also treats Potsdam. The Big Three relationships in the making of war and peace are discussed by Herbert Feis in two books: *Churchill—Roosevelt—Stalin* and *Between War and Peace: The Potsdam Conference* (Princeton: Princeton University Press, 1957 and 1960).

25. Communist Expansion in Europe (1945–1953)

J. M. Mackintosh gives detailed examination to the period from 1944 to 1962 in *Strategy and Tactics of Soviet Foreign Policy* (New York: Oxford University Press, 1962). The best study of the Communist role in Eastern Europe is Hugh Seton-Watson, *The East European Revolution* (3rd ed.; New York: Frederick A. Praeger, Inc., 1956), which covers the period from 1939 to 1955 with a sure touch. Robert Lee Wolff in *The Balkans in Our Time* (Cambridge: Harvard University Press, 1956) treats Yugoslavia, Rumania, Bulgaria, and Albania, devoting roughly half his space to the period following Communist take-over. The series published by Praeger entitled "East-Central Europe Under the Communists" is useful for reference; it includes Stavro Skendi, ed., *Albania* (1956); L. A. D. Dellin, ed., *Bulgaria* (1957); Vratislav Brusek and Nicholas Spulber, eds., *Czechoslovakia* (1957); Oscar Halecki, ed., *Poland* (1957); Ernest C. Helmreich, ed., *Hungary* (1957); Stephen Fischer-Galati, ed., *Romania* (1957); and Robert F. Byrnes, ed., *Yugoslavia* (1957). On Communist take-over in Czechoslovakia, see Joseph Korbel, *The Communist Subversion of Czechoslovakia, 1938–1948* (Princeton: Princeton University Press, 1959), and Edward Taborsky, *Communism in Czechoslovakia, 1948–1960* (Princeton: Princeton University Press, 1961); in Poland, see M. K. Dziewanowski, *The Communist Party of Poland* (Cambridge: Harvard University Press, 1959), and Richard F. Staar, *Poland, 1944–1962: the Sovietization of a Captive People* (Baton Rouge: Louisiana State University Press, 1962). The beginnings of Bulgarian Communism are studied by Joseph Rothschild, *The Communist Party of Bulgaria, Origins and Development 1883–1936* (New

York: Columbia University Press, 1959). Eastern Germany is treated by J. P. Nettl, *The Eastern Zone and Soviet Policy in Germany, 1945–1950* (New York: Oxford University Press, 1951). A good survey is Nicholas Spulber, *The Economics of Communist Eastern Europe* (New York: Technology Press of Massachusetts Institute of Technology and John Wiley & Sons, Inc., 1957). For Western Europe, see Mario Einaudi, ed., *Communism in Western Europe* (Ithaca: Cornell University Press, 1951), and Alfred J. Rieber, *Stalin and the French Communist Party, 1941–1947* (New York: Columbia University Press, 1962). A superb analysis of the Cold War is Hugh Seton-Watson, *Neither War Nor Peace: The Struggle for Power in the Postwar World* (New York: Frederick A. Praeger, Inc., 1960). A lengthy work sympathetic to the Soviets is D. F. Fleming, *The Cold War and Its Origins, 1917–1960* (2 vols.; Garden City: Doubleday & Co., Inc., 1961). An interesting account of the intellectual's place under Communism, reflecting the experience of Poland, is Czeslaw Milosz, *The Captive Mind* (New York: Alfred A. Knopf, Inc., 1953).

Tito's excommunication is analyzed by Adam B. Ulam, *Titoism and the Cominform* (Cambridge: Harvard University Press, 1952). The course of Yugoslav developments after the break with Stalin is discussed by Charles P. McVicker, *Titoism* (New York: St. Martin's Press, Inc., 1957), Fred Warner Neal, *Titoism in Action* (Berkeley and Los Angeles: University of California Press, 1958); and Ernst Halperin, *The Triumphant Heretic* (London: William Heinemann, Ltd., 1958). Ample documentation is assembled in Robert Bass and Elizabeth Marbury, eds., *The Soviet-Yugoslav Controversy, 1948–1958* (New York: Prospect Books, 1959). Milovan Djilas, who supported Tito in the break and then later broke with him, examines Communism from the standpoint of his experience in Yugoslavia in *The New Class* (New York: Frederick A. Praeger, Inc., 1957).

26. Communist Expansion in Asia (1945–1958)

(See also suggested readings for Chapter 15.)

Postwar events in China are analyzed fairly by Herbert Feis in *The China Tangle* (Princeton: Princeton University Press, 1953). See also F. F. Liu, *A Military History of Modern China, 1924–1929* (Princeton: Princeton University Press, 1956), and the State Department White Paper, *United States Relations with China* (Washington, 1949), which concentrates on the period 1944–1949. The Chinese Communists in power are ably treated by Richard L. Walker, *China Under Communism: the*

First Five Years (New Haven: Yale University Press, 1955). Peter S. H. Tang carries the story up to 1961 in *Communist China Today* (2nd ed. rev. and enlarged; 2 vols.; Washington: Research Institute on the Sino-Soviet Bloc, 1961). See also Ygael Gluckstein, *Mao's China: Economic and Political Survey* (Boston: Beacon Press, 1957). On the "hundred flowers," see Roderick MacFarquhar, *The Hundred Flowers Campaign and the Chinese Intellectuals* (New York: Frederick A. Praeger, Inc., 1960). On foreign policy, see A. Doak Barnett, *Communist China and Asia: Challenge to American Policy* (New York: Harper and Brothers, 1960), and R. G. Boyd, *Communist China's Foreign Policy* (New York: Frederick A. Praeger, Inc., 1962). Communism in certain Asian countries is discussed in Rodger Swearingen and Paul Langer, *Red Flag in Japan* (Cambridge: Harvard University Press, 1952); Frank N. Trager, *Marxism in Southeast Asia: a Study of Four Countries* (Stanford: Stanford University Press, 1959), on Burma, Thailand, Vietnam, and Indonesia; John H. Kautsky, *Moscow and the Communist Party of India* (New York: John Wiley & Sons, Inc., 1956); Gene D. Overstreet and Marshall Windmiller, *Communism in India* (Berkeley: University of California Press, 1959); David N. Druhe, *Soviet Russia and Indian Communism, 1917–1947* (New York: Bookman Associates, 1959); Walter Z. Laqueur, *Communism and Nationalism in the Middle East* (New York: Frederick A. Praeger, Inc., 1956) and *The Soviet Union and the Middle East* (New York: Frederick A. Praeger, Inc., 1959); and Arnold C. Brackman, *Indonesian Communism: A History* (New York: Frederick A. Praeger, Inc., 1963). On the Moscow-Peking relationship, see the exhaustive study of Donald S. Zagoria, *The Sino-Soviet Conflict, 1955–1961* (Princeton: Princeton University Press, 1962); see also G. F. Hudson, Richard Lowenthal, and Roderick MacFarquhar, *The Sino-Soviet Dispute* (New York: Frederick A. Praeger, Inc., 1962), and Kurt London, ed., *Unity and Contradiction: Major Aspects of Sino-Soviet Relations* (New York: Frederick A. Praeger, Inc., 1962).

27. Stalin's Retrenchment (1945–1953)

Forced repatriation is discussed briefly by Eugene Lyons, *Our Secret Allies* (New York: Duell, Sloan & Pearce, Inc., 1953), and Boris Shub, *The Choice* (New York: Duell, Sloan & Pearce, Inc., 1950). The spy network, especially in Europe, before, during, and after World War II, is examined in David J. Dallin, *Soviet Espionage* (New Haven: Yale University Press, 1955), and Otto Heilbrunn, *The Soviet Secret Services* (New York: Frederick A. Praeger, Inc., 1956). The *Zhdanovshchina* and related developments are the subject of the useful and balanced work of George S. Counts and Nucia Lodge, *The Country of the Blind* (Boston: Houghton Mifflin Co., 1949), and a portion of Bertram D. Wolfe, *Communist Totalitarianism* (Boston: Beacon Press, Inc., 1961). On the change of line in history writing, see C. E. Black, ed., *Rewriting Russian History* (New York: Frederick A. Praeger, Inc., 1956). The XIX Party Congress and attendant developments are analyzed in Boris Meissner, *The Communist Party of the Soviet Union,* ed. and with a chapter on the XX Party Congress by John S. Reshetar, Jr. (New York: Frederick A. Praeger, Inc., 1956). See also Leo Gruliow, ed., *Current Soviet Policies I: the Documentary Record of the Nineteenth Communist Party Congress and the Reorganization After Stalin's Death* (New York: Frederick A. Praeger, Inc., 1953). Continuity between Stalin's last years and the post-Stalin period is emphasized in Marshall D. Shulman, *Stalin's Foreign Policy Reappraised* (Cambridge: Harvard University Press, 1963). An interesting study of the period from 1949 to 1960 is Robert Conquest, *Power and Policy in the USSR* (New York: St. Martin's Press, 1961).

28. The Rise of Khrushchëv (1953–1957)

The best attempt at a biography of Khrushchëv is Lazar Pistrak, *The Grand Tactician: Khrushchev's Rise to Power* (New York: Frederick A. Praeger, Inc., 1961). The period from 1952 to 1960 is ably analyzed by Wolfgang Leonhard in *The Kremlin Since Stalin,* trans. Elizabeth Wiskemann and Marian Jackson (New York: Frederick A. Praeger, Inc., 1962). The Berlin revolt is discussed by Rainer Hildebrandt, *The Explosion,* trans. E. B. Ashton (New York: Duell, Sloan & Pearce, Inc., 1955), and Stefan Brant, *The East German Rising* (New York: Frederick A. Praeger, Inc., 1957); the Vorkuta concentration camp revolt in Joseph Scholmer, *Vorkuta* (New York: Henry Holt & Co., Inc., 1955). On Bandung, see George M. Kahin, *The Asian-African Conference* (Ithaca: Cornell University Press, 1956).

On the XX Party Congress, see Leo Gruliow, ed., *Current Soviet Policies II: the Documentary Record of the 20th Communist Party Congress and its Aftermath* (New York: Frederick A. Praeger, Inc., 1957). The implications of Khrushchëv's "secret speech" are analyzed in Bertram D. Wolfe, *Khrushchëv and Stalin's Ghost* (New York: Frederick A. Praeger, Inc., 1957), and the *New Leader* edition of the speech, "The Crimes of the Stalin Era," with notes by Boris I. Nicolaevsky, which appeared as Section Two of the July 16, 1956, number. Important documents of the period of repercussions in other Communist parties and especially in

Eastern Europe are assembled in two Columbia University publications (both New York, 1956): *The Anti-Stalin Campaign and International Communism* and *National Communism and Popular Revolt.* On the Polish and Hungarian events, see Konrad Syrop, *Spring in October: the Polish Revolution of 1956* (New York: Frederick A. Praeger, Inc., 1958); Paul E. Zinner, *Revolution in Hungary* (New York: Columbia University Press, 1962), perhaps the best study to date; Ferenc A. Vali, *Rift and Revolt in Hungary* (Cambridge: Harvard University Press, 1961); Tibor Meray, *Thirteen Days that Shook the Kremlin* (New York: Frederick A. Praeger, Inc., 1959); and Paul Kecskemeti, *The Unexpected Revolution: Social Forces in the Hungarian Uprising* (Stanford: Stanford University Press, 1961). On literature, see Harold Swayze, *Political Control of Literature in the USSR, 1946–1959* (Cambridge: Harvard University Press, 1962), and George Gibian, *Interval of Freedom: Soviet Literature During the Thaw, 1954–1957* (Minneapolis: University of Minnesota Press, 1960). On foreign policy, see David J. Dallin, *Soviet Foreign Policy After Stalin* (Philadelphia: J. B. Lippincott Co., 1961).

29. Khrushchëv in Power (1957–1963)

On the XXI and XXII congresses, see Leo Gruliow, ed., *Current Soviet Policies III: The Documentary Record of the 21st Extraordinary Communist Party Congress* (New York: Columbia University Press, 1960); Charlotte Saikowski and Leo Gruliow, eds., *Current Soviet Policies IV: the Documentary Record of the 22nd Congress of the Communist Party of the Soviet Union* (New York: Columbia University Press, 1962); and Harry Schwartz, *Russia Enters the 1960's: a Documentary Report on the 22nd Congress of the Communist Party of the Soviet Union* (Philadelphia: J. B. Lippincott Co., 1962). On the Program adopted by the XXII Congress, see Leonard Schapiro, ed., *The USSR and the Future: An Analysis of the New Program of the CPSU* (New York: Frederick A. Praeger, Inc., 1963), and Herbert Ritvo, *The New Soviet Society: Final Text of the Program of the Communist Party of the Soviet Union* (New Leader Paperback, 1962).

Problems of the Communist orbit are examined in Zbigniew K. Brzezinski, *The Soviet Bloc: Unity and Conflict* (Cambridge: Harvard University Press, 1960). Important sources are given in Alexander Dallin, ed., *Diversity in International Communism: A Documentary Record, 1961–1963* (New York: Columbia University Press, 1963). On economic aid, see Joseph S. Berliner, *Soviet Economic Aid* (New York: Frederick A. Praeger, Inc., 1958). On problems of military strategy and nuclear weapons, see Raymond L. Garthoff, *Soviet Strategy in the Nuclear Age* (New York: Frederick A. Praeger, Inc., 1958); Herbert S. Dinerstein, *War and the Soviet Union* (New York: Frederick A. Praeger, Inc., 1959); Joseph L. Nogee, *Soviet Policy Toward International Control of Atomic Energy* (Notre Dame: University of Notre Dame Press, 1961); Arnold Kramish, *Atomic Energy in the Soviet Union* (Stanford: Stanford University Press, 1959); Albert Parry, *Russia's Rockets and Missiles* (Garden City: Doubleday & Co., Inc., 1960). On the reception of *Doctor Zhivago,* see Robert Conquest, *The Pasternak Affair: Courage of Genius* (Philadelphia: J. B. Lippincott Co., 1962); the work of an important dissenting writer is published as Aleksandr Sergeyevich Yesenin-Volpin, *A Leaf of Spring* (New York: Frederick A. Praeger, Inc., 1961). The Cuban events are scrupulously examined by Theodore Draper, *Castro's Revolution: Myths and Realities* (New York: Frederick A. Praeger, Inc., 1962). The miscarried "summit" is studied by David Wise and Thomas B. Ross, *The U-2 Affair* (New York: Random House, 1962). Two excellent recent journalistic accounts are Princess Zinaida Schakovskoy, *The Privilege Was Mine* (New York: G. P. Putnam's Sons, Inc., 1959), and Klaus Mehnert, *Soviet Man and His World* (New York: Frederick A. Praeger, Inc., 1962).

Russian Rulers Since Ivan III

TSARDOM OF MUSCOVY

House of Riurik

Ivan III	1462–1505	Fëdor I	1584–1598
Basil III	1505–1533	Boris Godunov	1598–1605
Ivan IV	1533–1584	"The Time of Troubles"	1604–1613

House of Romanov

Michael	1613–1645	Ivan V	1682–1696 (co-Tsar)
Alexis	1645–1676		
Fëdor II	1676–1682	Peter I	1682–1725

RUSSIAN EMPIRE

House of Romanov

Peter I	1682–1725 (after 1721 Emperor)	Peter III	1761–1762
		Catherine II	1762–1796
Catherine I	1725–1727	Paul	1796–1801
Peter II	1727–1730	Alexander I	1801–1825
Anna	1730–1740	Nicholas I	1825–1855
Ivan VI	1740–1741	Alexander II	1855–1881
Elizabeth	1741–1761	Alexander III	1881–1894
Nicholas II	1894–1917		

PROVISIONAL GOVERNMENT

Prime Ministers

G. E. Lvov	Mar.–July 1917	A. F. Kerensky	July–Nov. 1917

RSFSR, LATER USSR

Chairmen of the Council of People's Commissars, after 1946 Prime Ministers

V. I. Lenin	1917–1924	J. V. Stalin	1941–1953
A. I. Rykov	1924–1930	G. M. Malenkov	1953–1955
V. M. Molotov	1930–1941	N. A. Bulganin	1955–1958
N. S. Khrushchëv	1958–		

Congresses of the Russian Social Democratic Labor Party, later Bolshevik, later Communist, later All-Union Communist Party

R.S.D.L.P.	I *Congress*	MINSK	March 1–3, 1898 (Old Style)
"	II *Congress*	BRUSSELS & LONDON	July 17–Aug. 10, 1903
" (Bolsheviks only)	III *Congress*	LONDON	April 12–27, 1905
" ("Unification Congress")	IV *Congress*	STOCKHOLM	April 10–25, 1906
"	V *Congress*	LONDON	April 30–May 19, 1907
R.S.D.L.P.(B.)	VI *Congress*	PETROGRAD	July 26–Aug. 3, 1917
R.C.P.(B.)	VII *Congress*	PETROGRAD	March 6–8, 1918 (New Style)
"	VIII *Congress*	MOSCOW	March 18–23, 1919
"	IX *Congress*	"	March 29–April 5, 1920
"	X *Congress*	"	March 8–16, 1921
"	XI *Congress*	"	March 27–April 2, 1922
"	XII *Congress*	"	April 17–25, 1923
"	XIII *Congress*	"	May 23–31, 1924
ALL-UNION C.P.(B.)	XIV *Congress*	"	December 18–31, 1925
"	XV *Congress*	"	December 2–19, 1927
"	XVI *Congress*	"	June 26–July 13, 1930
"	XVII *Congress*	"	January 26–February 10, 1934
"	XVIII *Congress*	"	March 10–21, 1939
ALL-UNION C.P.	XIX *Congress*	"	October 5–15, 1952
"	XX *Congress*	"	February 14–25, 1956
"	XXI *Congress*	"	January 27–February 5, 1959
"	XXII *Congress*	"	October 17–31, 1961

Full Members of Politburo, After XIX Congress Presidium, of Russian, Later All-Union Communist Party

Lenin, V. I. 1917–1924
Zinoviev, G. E.[1] 1917–1926
Kamenev, L. B.[1] 1917–1925
Trotsky, L. D.[3] 1917–1926
Stalin, J. V. 1917–1953
Sokolnikov, G. Ia.[1] 1917–1919
Bubnov, A. S.[1] 1917–1919
Krestinsky, N. N.[1] 1919–1921
Rykov, A. I.[1] 1922–1930
Tomsky, M. P.[1] 1922–1930
Bukharin, N. I.[1] 1924–1929
Molotov, V. M. 1925–1957
Voroshilov, K. E. 1925–1960
Kalinin, M. I. 1925–1946
Rudzutak, Ia. E.[1] 1926–1932
Kuibyshev, V. V.[2] 1927–1935
Kaganovich, L. M. 1930–1957
Kirov, S. M.[2] 1930–1934
Kosior, S. V.[1] 1930–1938
Ordzhonikidze, G. K.[2] . . 1930–1937
Andreyev, A. A. 1932–1952
Chubar, V. Ia.[1] 1935–1938
Mikoyan, A. I. 1935–
Zhdanov, A. A.[2] 1939–1948
Khrushchëv, N. S.. . 1939–
Beria, L. P.[1] . . . 1946–1953
Malenkov, G. M. . . 1946–1957
Voznesensky, N. A.[1] 1947–1949
Bulganin, N. A. . . 1948–1958
Kosygin, A. N.
. . . . . .1949–1952, 1960–
Saburov, M. Z. . . . 1953–1957
Pervukhin, M. G. . 1953–1957
Kirichenko, A. I. . . 1955–1960
Suslov, M. A. . . . 1955–
Brezhnev, L. I. . . . 1957–
Zhukov, G. K. . . 1957 (July–Oct.)
Furtseva, E. A. . . . 1957–1961
Shvernik, N. M. . . 1957–
Aristov, A. B. . . . 1957–1960
Beliaev, N. I. . . . 1957–1960
Ignatov, N. G. . . . 1957–1961
Kozlov, F. R. . . . 1957–
Kuusinen, O. V. . . 1957–
Mukhitdinov, N. A. 1957–1961
Podgorny, N. V. . . 1960–
Poliansky, D. S. . . 1960–
Voronov, G. I. . . . 1961–
Kirilenko, A. P. . . 1962–

- [1] known to have been purged by Stalin or successors or committed suicide while under arrest.
- [2] died under circumstances strongly suggesting culpability of Stalin in death.
- [3] assassinated abroad, presumably on Stalin's orders.

Area and Population of the Union Republics

(January 1962. Source: *Narodnoe khoziaistvo SSSR*, Moscow, 1962)

		Area in 1000 sq. km.	Pop. in 1000's	Capital	Pop. in 1000's
1	RUSSIAN SFSR	17,075.4	122,084	Moscow	6,296
2	UKRAINIAN SSR	601	43,527	Kiev	1,208
3	BELORUSSIAN SSR	207.6	8,316	Minsk	599
4	UZBEK SSR	468.7	8,986	Tashkent	1,002
5	KAZAKH SSR	2,756	10,934	Alma-Ata	534
6	GEORGIAN SSR	69.7	4,271	Tbilisi	743
7	AZERBAIJANI SSR	86.6	4,117	Baku	1,067
8	LITHUANIAN SSR	65.2	2,852	Vilnius	264
9	MOLDAVIAN SSR	33.7	3,106	Kishinëv	244
10	LATVIAN SSR	63.7	2,170	Riga	620
11	KIRGHIZ SSR	198.5	2,318	Frunze	312
12	TADZHIK SSR	143.1	2,188	Diushambe	260
13	ARMENIAN SSR	29.8	1,958	Erevan	583
14	TURKMEN SSR	488.1	1,683	Ashkhabad	197
15	ESTONIAN SSR	45.1	1,235	Tallinn	305
	USSR	22,402.2	219,745	Moscow	

Largest Cities of the USSR

(January 1962. Source: *Narodnoe khoziaistvo SSSR v 1961 godu*)

1 MOSCOW	6,296,000	11 DONETSK	760,000
2 LENINGRAD	3,498,000	12 CHELIABINSK	751,000
3 KIEV	1,208,000	13 TBILISI	743,000
4 BAKU	1,067,000	14 DNEPROPETROVSK	722,000
5 GORKY	1,025,000	15 KAZAN	711,000
6 TASHKENT	1,002,000	16 ODESSA	704,000
7 KHARKOV	990,000	17 PERM	701,000
8 NOVOSIBIRSK	985,000	18 ROSTOV-ON-DON	661,000
9 KUIBYSHEV	881,000	19 OMSK	650,000
10 SVERDLOVSK	853,000	20 VOLGOGRAD	649,000

APPENDIX VI

Soviet Production of Selected Industrial Items

(Source: *Narodnoe khoziaistvo SSSR v 1961 godu*)

	1913	1940	1958	1961	
Pig iron	4.2	14.9	39.6	50.9	*million tons*
Steel	4.3	18.3	54.9	70.8	" "
Coal	29.2	165.9	496.1	510.5	" "
Petroleum	10.3	31.1	113.2	166.1	" "
Electric Power	2.0	48.3	235.4	327.6	*billion kwh*
Automobiles	(not known)	145,500	511,100	555,300	*vehicles*

INDEX

Dates of reigns are given for monarchs; for others dates of birth and death. The abbreviation *"bibl."* indicates that a work (or works) written by the author cited is listed in the bibliography.

A

B

D

E

F

G

H

I

J

K

O

P

Q

R

S

T

V

W

X

Y

Z

PRINTED IN U.S.A.